GNOMON

OF

THE NEW TESTAMENT

BY

JOHN ALBERT BENGEL.

ACCORDING TO THE EDITION ORIGINALLY BROUGHT OUT BY HIS SON,

M. ERNEST BENGEL;

AND SUBSEQUENTLY COMPLETED BY

J. C. F. STEUDEL.

WITH CORRECTIONS AND ADDITIONS FROM THE ED. SECUNDA OF 1759.

VOLUME III.

CONTAINING THE COMMENTARY ON THE ROMANS,
I. CORINTHIANS, AND II. CORINTHIANS, TRANSLATED BY

REV. JAMES BRYCE, LLD.

SEVENTH EDITION.

Wipf & Stock
PUBLISHERS
Eugene, Oregon

Wipf and Stock Publishers
199 W 8th Ave, Suite 3
Eugene, OR 97401

Gnomon of the New Testament, Volume 3
By Bengel, John A.
ISBN 13: 978-1-4982-9356-3
Publication date 3/1/2016
Previously published by T&T Clark, 1877

Five volume set ISBN: 978-1-59244-593-6

ANNOTATIONS

ON

PAUL'S EPISTLE TO THE ROMANS.

CHAPTER I.

1. Παῦλος, PAUL. The beginning of the Epistle, the inscription.[1] The Scriptures of the New Testament, as compared with the books of the Old Testament, have the epistolary form; and in those, not merely what has been written by Paul, Peter, James, and Jude, but also both the treatises of Luke, and all the writings of John. Nay, it is of more consequence, that the Lord Jesus Christ Himself wrote seven letters in His own name, by the hand of John (Rev. ii. and iii.); and the whole Apocalypse is equivalent to an epistle written by Himself. Epistles were usually sent, not to slaves, but to free men, and to those especially who had been emancipated; and the epistolary style of writing is better suited, than any other, for extending, as widely as possible, the kingdom of God, and for the most abundant edification of the souls of men. Moreover, Paul alone laboured in this field more than all the other apostles put together; for

[1] [*The Address*, or *Heading*.—ED.] The ancient Greeks and Romans used to put, at the beginning of their letters, those things which now, according to our mode of Subscription, come under the name of the Address and previous Salutation, and this generally very brief, as if it were to be said: *Paul wishes health (sends compliments) to the Christians at Rome.* But the apostle expresses those things, from a very large measure of spiritual feeling, in great exuberance of style, while he chiefly preaches Jesus Christ and His gospel, and forcibly declares his evangelical office of Apostle.—V. G.

fourteen of his epistles are extant, of which various is the arrangement, various the division. He wrote one to the Hebrews, without prefixing his name to it; he added his name to the rest; and these were partly addressed to churches, partly to individuals; and in the present day they are arranged in volumes,[1] in such a way as that the one with the greatest number of verses is put first. But the chronological order is much more worthy of consideration, of which we have treated in the *Ordo temporum*, cap. 6.[2] When that matter is settled, both the apostolic history, and these very epistles, shed a mutual light on one another; and we perceive a correspondence of thoughts, and modes of expression, in epistles written at one and the same time, and concerning the same state of affairs [as the apostolic history—the Acts—describes]; and we also become acquainted with the spiritual growth of the apostle. There is one division, which, we think, ought to be particularly mentioned in this place. Paul wrote in one way to churches, which had been planted by his own exertions, but in a different way to those churches, to which he was not known by face. The former class of epistles may be compared to the discourses, which pastors deliver in the course of their ordinary ministrations; the latter class, to the discourses, which strangers deliver. The former are replete with the kindness, or else the severity, of an intimate friend, according as the state of the respective churches was more or less consistent with the Gospel; the latter present the truths of the Gospel as it were more unmixed, in general statements, and in the abstract; the former are more for domestic and daily use, the latter are adapted to holidays and solemn festivals,—comp. notes on ch. xv. 30. This epistle to the Romans is mostly of this latter description.— δοῦλος Ἰησοῦ Χριστοῦ, *servant of Jesus Christ*) This commencement and the conclusion correspond (xv. 15, etc.) Χριστοῦ— Θεοῦ, *of Christ—of God*) Everywhere in the epistles of Paul, and throughout the New Testament, the contemplation *of God and of Christ* is very closely connected; for example, Gal. ii. 19, etc. [*And it is also our privilege to have the same access to God in Christ.*—V. g.]—κλητὸς ἀπόστολος, *a called apostle*), [*called to be an apostle.*—Eng. vers.] Supply, *of Jesus Christ;*

---

[1] *i.e.*, in the collected form.—Ed. [2] See Life of Bengel, sec. 22

for the preceding clause, *a servant of Jesus Christ,* is now more particularly explained. It is the duty of an *apostle,* and *of a called apostle,* to write also to the *Romans.* [*The whole world is certainly under obligation to such a servant as this.*—V. g.] The other apostles, indeed, had been trained by long intercourse with Jesus, and at first had been called to be followers and disciples, and had been afterwards advanced to the apostleship. Paul, who had been formerly a persecutor, by a call became suddenly [without the preparatory stage of discipleship] an apostle. So the Jews were saints [set apart to the Lord] in consequence of the promise; the Greeks became *saints,* merely from their *being called,* ver. 6, etc. There was therefore a special resemblance and connection between one *called to be an apostle,* and those whom he addressed, *called to be saints.* Paul applies both to himself and to the Corinthians a similar title (1 Cor. i. 1, 2); and that similarity in the designation of both reminds us of the ὑποτύπωσιν, *pattern,* or living exhibition [of Christ's grace in Paul himself, as a sample of what others, who should believe, might expect], which is spoken of in 1 Tim. i. 16. While Christ is calling a man, He makes him what He calls him to be,—comp. ch. iv. 17; and that, too, quickly, Acts ix. 3–15.—ἀφωρισμένος, *separated*) The root, or origin of the term Pharisee, was the same as that of this word; but, in this passage Paul intimates, that he was *separated by God* not only from men, from the Jews, and from the disciples, but also from teachers. There was a *separation* in one sense before (Gal. i. 15), and another after his call (Acts xiii. 2); and he refers to this very separation in the passage before us.—εἰς εὐαγγέλιον, *to the Gospel*) The conjugate verb follows ver. 2, προεπηγγείλατο, *He had promised before.* The promise was the Gospel proclaimed [announced beforehand], the Gospel is the promise fulfilled, Acts xiii. 32. *God promised the Gospel,* that is, He comprehended it in the promise. The promise was not merely a promise of the Gospel, but was the Gospel itself.[1]

2. "Ο, *which*). The copiousness of Paul's style shows itself in the very inscriptions: and we must, therefore, watchfully observe the thread of the parentheses. [*God promised that He would not only display His grace in the Son, but also that He*

---

[1] *i.e.,* in germ.—Ed.

would publish that very fact to the whole world. Listen to it with the most profound attention.—V. g.]—προεπηγγείλατο, *promised afore*) formerly, often, and solemnly. The truth of the promise, and the truth of its fulfilment, mutually confirm each other.— διὰ τῶν προφητῶν αὐτοῦ, *by His prophets*) That which the prophets of God have spoken, God has spoken, Luke i. 70; Acts iii. 24.—γραφαῖς, *in the Scriptures*) ch. xvi. 26. The prophets made use of the voice, as well as of writing, in the publication of their message; and the voice was likely to have greater weight in the case of a single people [the Jews], than among the countries of the whole globe : therefore, the greater weight in delivering the message, would give an advantage *to the voice* over *writing*: notwithstanding, as much respect is paid to *writing*, with a view to posterity, as if there had been no voice. To such an extent does Scripture prevail over tradition. [*The believing Romans were, in part, originally Jews,* and, *in part,* originally Gentiles (*exjudaei*, Ex-Gentiles), *and Paul particularly has regard to the latter*, ver. 13.—V. g.]

3. Περὶ, *concerning*) The sum and substance of *the Gospel is, concerning the Son of God, Jesus Christ our Lord.* An explanation is introduced in this passage, as to what this appellation, *the Son of God,* denotes, ver. 3, 4.[1]—τοῦ γενομένου), *who was* [*made* Engl. Vers.] *born.* So Gal. iv. 4.—κατὰ, *according to*) The determinative particle, ver. 4; ix. 5.

4. Τοῦ ὁρισθέντος υἱοῦ Θεοῦ, *who was definitively marked as* [*declared to be,* Engl. Vers.] *the Son of God*) He uses τοῦ again, not καὶ or δὲ. When the article is repeated, it forms an

---

[1] JESUS CHRIST IS THE SON OF GOD. This is the foundation of all rightful access, on the part of Jesus Christ, to His Father and His God; and, in like manner, of our approach by Him, as *our Lord,* to His Father and our Father, to His God and our God, who has delivered us to Him as His peculiar property. Even before His humiliation, He was indeed the Son of God; but this Sonship was in occultation by His humiliation, and was at length fully disclosed to us after His resurrection. His justification depends on these facts, 1 Tim. iii. 16; 1 John ii 1; and that is the foundation of our justification, Rom. iv. 25. Hence, in His passion, He placed all His confidence in the Father, not on account of His works (for not even did the Son give first to the Father any thing, which the Father was bound to pay back to Him), but for this reason, because He was the Son; and thus He went before us in the way, as the leader and finisher of our faith. Heb. xii. 2.—V. g.

epıtasis. [See Append.] In many passages, where both natures of the Saviour are mentioned, the human nature is put first, because the divine was most distinctly proved to all, only after His resurrection from the dead. [*Hence it is, that it is frequently repeated*, He, and not any other. Acts ix. 20, 22, etc.—V. g.] The participle ὁρισθέντος expresses much more than ἀφωρισμένος in ver. 1; for one, ἀφορίζεται, out of a number of other persons, but a person, ὁρίζεται, as the one and only person, Acts x. 42. In that well-known passage, Ps. ii. 7, חק [the decree] is the same as ὁρισμὸς ; [the decree implying] that the Father has *most determinately* said, *Thou art My Son*. The ἀπόδειξις, the *approving* of the Son, in regard to men, follows in the train of this ὁρισμόν.—Acts ii. 22. Paul particularly extols the glory *of the Son of God*, when writing to those to whom he had been unable to preach it face to face. Comp. Heb. x. 8, etc., note. —ἐν δυνάμει, *in* (or *with*) *power*), most powerfully, most fully; as when the sun shines in δυνάμει, *in his strength*.—Rev. i. 16.—κατὰ πνεῦμα ἁγιωσύνης, *according to the spirit of holiness*) The word קדוש ἅγιος, *holy*, when the subject under discussion refers to God, not only denotes that blameless rectitude in acting, which distinguishes Him, but the Godhead itself, or, to speak with greater propriety, the *divinity*, or the excellence of the Divine nature. Hence ἁγιωσύνη has a kind of middle sense between ἁγιότητα and ἁγιασμόν.— Comp. Heb. xii. 10, 14. [" *His holiness*," ἁγιότης; " without ἁγιασμός *sanctification*, no man shall see the Lord."] So that there are, as it were, three degrees, *sanctification* (sanctificatio), *sanctity* (or *sanctimony*, " sanctimonia,") *holiness* (sanctitas) *Holiness* itself (sanctitas) is ascribed *to God the Father,* and *to the Son*, and *to the Holy Ghost*. And since the *Holy Spirit* is not mentioned in this passage, but *the Spirit of holiness (sanctity,* sanctimoniæ), we must inquire farther, what that expression, which is evidently a singular one, denotes. The name *Spirit* is expressly, and that too, very often, given to the *Holy Spirit;* but *God* is also said to be a *Spirit;* and the *Lord,* Jesus Christ, is called *Spirit*, in antithesis indeed to the *letter*, 2 Cor. iii. 17. But in the strict sense, it is of use to compare with the idea here the fact, that the antithesis *flesh* and *spirit* occurs, as in this passage, so rather frequently, in passages speaking of Christ, 1 Tim.

iii. 16, 1 Pet. iii. 18. And in these passages that is called *Spirit*, whatever belongs to Christ, independently of the flesh [*assumed through His descent from David*, Luke, i. 35.—V. g.], although that flesh was pure and holy; also whatever superior to flesh belongs to Him, owing to His generation by the Father, who *has sanctified* Him, John x. 36; in short, the *Godhead* itself. For, as in this passage, *flesh* and *spirit*, so at chap. ix. 5, *flesh* and *Godhead* stand in contradistinction to each other. This spirit is not called *the spirit of holiness* (sanctitatis ἁγιότητος), which is the peculiar and solemn appellation of the *Holy Spirit*, with whom, however, Jesus was most abundantly filled and anointed, Luke i. 35, iv. 1, 18; John iii. 34; Acts x. 38; but in this one passage alone, the expression used is *the spirit of sanctity* (sanctimoniæ ἁγιωσύνης), in order that there may be at once implied the efficacy of that *holiness* (sanctitatis ἁγιότητος) or divinity, of which the resurrection of the Saviour was both a necessary consequence, and which it most powerfully illustrates; and so, that *spiritual* and *holy*, or divine power of Jesus Christ glorified, who, however, has still retained the *spiritual* body. Before the resurrection, the Spirit was concealed under the flesh; after the resurrection the *Spirit of sanctity* [sanctimoniæ] entirely concealed the flesh, although He did not lay aside *the flesh*; but all that is carnal (which was also without sin), Luke xxiv. 39. In respect of the former [His state before the resurrection], He once used frequently to call Himself the *Son of Man*; in respect of the latter [His state after the resurrection; and the *spirit of sanctity*, by which He rose again], He is celebrated as the *Son of God*. His [*manifested* or] *conspicuous* state [*as presented to men's view before His resurrection*] was modified in various ways. At the day of judgment, His glory *as the Son of God* shall appear, as also His body in the highest degree glorified. See also John vi. 63, note.—ἐξ ἀναστάσεως νεκρῶν, *by means of the resurrection of the dead*) 'Εκ not only denotes time, but the connection of things (for *the resurrection* of Jesus Christ is at once the source and the object of our faith, Acts xvii. 31). The verb ἀνίστημι is also used without a preposition, as in Herodotus, ἀναστάντες τῶν βαθρῶν: therefore, ἀνάστασις νεκρῶν might be taken in this passage for *the resurrection from the dead*. But it is in reality taken in a more pregnant sense; for it is intimated, that the resurrection of all is intimately connected with the resurrection of Christ. Comp. Acts iv. 2, xxiii. 6, xxvi. 23. Artemonius conjectures that the reading should be ἐξ ἀναστάσεως ἐκ νεκρῶν, Part I., cap. 41, p. 214, etc., and this is his construction of the passage: περὶ [ver. 3] ἐξαναστάσεως ἐκ νεκρῶν τοῦ υἱοῦ αὐτοῦ κ.τ.λ. *concerning the resurrection of His Son from the dead*, etc. But, I. There is a manifest Apposition, *concerning His Son, Jesus Christ*; therefore, the words, which come between parenthetically, are all construed in an unbroken connection with one another. II. There is an obvious antithesis: ΤΟΥ γενομένου ΕΚ ΚΑΤΑ : ΤΟΥ ὁρισθέντος— ΚΑΤΑ—ΕΞ.—III. ἀνάστασις, not ἐξανάστασις, if we are to have regard to Paul's style, is properly applied to Christ; but ἐξανάστασις to Christians; Comp. ἤγειρε, ἐξεγερεῖ, 1 Cor. vi. 14. Artemonius objects that Christ was even previously the Son of God, Luke iii. 22; John x. 36; Acts ii. 22, x. 38. We answer, Paul does not infer the Sonship itself, but the ὁρισμὸν, *the [declaration] definitive marking* of the Sonship by the resurrection. And in support of this point, Chrysostom compares with this the following passages: John ii. 19, viii. 28; Matt. xii. 39; and the preaching of the apostles follows close upon this ὁρισμόν, Luke xxiv. 47. Therefore, this mode of mentioning the resurrection is exceedingly well adapted to this introduction, as Gal. i. 1.

5. Δἰ οὗ, *by whom*), by Jesus Christ our Lord.—ἐλάβομεν, *we have received*), we, the other *apostles* and I.—χάριν καὶ ἀποστολὴν, *grace and the apostolic mission*) These two things are quite distinct, but very closely connected. *Grace*, nay, a singular measure of grace, fell to the lot of the *apostles*, and from it, not only their whole mission, Eph. iii. 2, but also all their actions proceeded, Rom. xii. 3, xv. 15, 16, 18. The word ἀποστολή occurs in this sense in Acts i. 25. With the LXX. it signifies, *sending away, a gift sent*, etc. *Obedience to the faith* corresponds to *grace and apostleship*.—εἰς ὑπακοὴν πίστεως, *for obedience to the faith*), that all nations may become and continue *submissively obedient to the word* of faith and doctrine concerning Jesus (Acts vi. 7), and may therefore render the *obedience*, which consists in *faith* itself. From its relation to the *Gospel*, the nature of this *obedience* is evident, ch. x. 16, xvi. 26; 1 Peter i. 2 : and ὑπακοὴ, obedience, is ἀκοὴ μεθ᾽ ὑποταγῆς, *hearing with submission*, ch. x. 3, at the close of

the verse. So, Mary *believing* said, *Behold, the handmaid of the Lord,* Luke i. 38, 45—ἐν πᾶσι τοῖς ἔθνεσιν, *among all nations*) As *all nations* outwardly obey the authority of the Romans, so all nations, and so the Romans themselves also ought, with their whole heart, *to be obedient to the faith*—ὑπὲρ τοῦ ὀνόματος αὐτοῦ), *for the name of Him, even Jesus Christ our Lord.* By Him *grace* has come, John i. 17; for Him, His ambassador's act; 2 Cor. v. 20; by Him *faith* is directed towards God, 1 Peter i. 21.

6. 'Ἐν οἷς), *among which* nations, *that have been* brought *to the obedience of the faith* by the *calling of Jesus Christ*—καὶ ὑμεῖς, *ye also*) Paul ascribes no particular superiority to the Romans. —Comp. 1 Cor. xiv. 36. He, however, touches upon the reason for his writing to the Romans. Presently, in the following verse, he directly addresses them—κλητοί, *called*), ver. 7.

V. 7. Πᾶσι τοῖς οὖσιν ἐν 'Ρώμῃ, *to all that be in Rome*) Most of these were of the Gentiles, ver. 13, with whom, however, Jews were mixed. They had been either born and educated at Rome, or, at least, were residing there at that time. They were dwelling scattered throughout a very large city, and had not hitherto been brought into the form of a regularly constituted *church.* Only *some* of them were in the habit of assembling in the house of Priscilla and Aquila, Rom. xvi. 5. What follows, *beloved,* etc., agrees with the word *all;* for he does not address the idolaters at Rome—ἀγαπητοῖς Θεοῦ, κλητοῖς ἁγίοις) These two clauses want the copulative conjunction, and are parallel; for he, who belongs to God, is holy [set apart]. Comp. Heb. iii. 1. The expression, *the beloved of God,* he particularly applies to the believing Israelites, ch. xi. 28; *called to be saints,* to believers of the Gentiles. The Israelites are holy by descent from their fathers, Acts xx. 32, note. Comp. with annot. on ver. 1 of this chapter; but believers of the Gentiles are said to be *sanctified* or *called saints,* holy by calling, as Paul interprets it ['sanctified'], 1 Cor. i. 2. We have here a double title, and I have referred the first part to the Israelites, the second to the Gentiles. Comp. ver. 5, 6, and add the passages, which have just now been quoted. The celebrated Baumgarten, in his German exposition of this Epistle, to which we shall often have occasion to refer, writes thus:. " *Hiedurch würde der gottesdienstliche Unterschied der Gläubigen und eingebildete Vorzug der* Israëliten *zu sehr bestätiget worden seyn, den* Paulus *vielmehr bestreitet und abgeschaffet oder aufgehoben zu seyn versichert.*"[1] We answer: The privilege of the Israelite (although he *who is called holy*, is as highly blessed, as he *who is the beloved of God*) is as appropriate to be mentioned in Paul's introduction, as the πρῶτον, ch. i. 16 [to the Jew *first*], is appropriate in the Statement of his subject[2] there; which [the statement of the priority of the Jew, at ver. 16] Baumgarten defends enough and more than enough.—χάρις, *grace*, etc. This form of expression is the customary one in the writings of Paul. See the beginnings of his epistles, and also Eph. vi. 23.—ὑμῖν, *to you*) Supply, *may there fall to your lot*.—εἰρήνη, *peace*) שלום, *peace*: a form of salutation in common use among the Hebrews, before which is placed χάρις, *grace*, a term altogether consonant to the New Testament, and to the preaching of the apostles. *Grace* comes from God; then, in consequence, man is in a state of *peace*, ch. v. 2, note.—ἀπὸ Θεοῦ πατρὸς ἡμῶν καὶ Κυρίου Ἰησοῦ Χριστοῦ, *from God our Father and the Lord Jesus Christ*) The solemn form of appellation used by the apostles, *God and the Father, God our Father*; and, when they speak to one another, they do not often say Κύριος, *Lord*, inasmuch as by it the proper name of GOD with four letters [יהוה were the four letters, *tetragrammaton*] is intended; but, in the Old Testament, they had said, *Jehovah our God*. The reason of the difference is: in the Old Testament they were, so to speak, slaves; in the New Testament they are sons; but sons so know their father, as to render it unnecessary to call him often by his proper name. Comp. Heb. viii. 11. Farther, when Polytheism was rooted out, it was not so necessary, that the true God should be distinguished from false gods, by His proper name. Κυρίου is construed, not with ἡμῶν; for *God* is declared to be *the Father of Jesus Christ, and our Father*, not, *our Father, and the Father of Jesus Christ*; but [Κυρίου is construed] with ἀπὸ, as is evident from 2 Tim. i. 2. There is one and the same grace, one and the same peace, from

---

[1] Here lay the difference in divine services among believers, and the imaginary superiority of the Israelites would have been too strongly confirmed, which Paul, to make quite sure of it, would much rather have disputed and cancelled or abolished.

[2] 'Propositioni' in the Latin: Cic. Inv. ii. 18, defines it as "per quem locus is breviter exponitur, ex quo vis omnis oportet emanet ratiocinationis."

God and Christ. Our confidence and prayers are directed to God, inasmuch as He is the Father of our Lord; and to Jesus Christ, inasmuch as He makes us, through Himself, stand in the presence of the Father.

8. Πρῶτον, *first*) A *next* does not always follow; and in this passage, the affectionate feeling and emotion of the writer have absorbed it.—μὲν) The corresponding δέ follows at ver. 13. You are, says he, already *indeed* in the faith; *but* yet I am desirous to contribute something to your improvement.—εὐχαριστῶ, *I give thanks*) Even at the beginning alone [besides similar beginnings in other epistles] of this epistle, there are traces of *all* the spiritual emotions. Among these, *thanksgiving* takes the pre-eminence: and with it almost all the epistles commence. The categorical idea of the sentence is: You have found faith. Thanksgiving, which is an accessory idea, renders the discourse modal (*i.e.*, shows the manner in which the subject and predicate, in the categorical sentence, are connected),—comp. note to ch. vi. 17. Paul rejoices that, what he considered should be effected by him elsewhere, as a debtor to all, was already effected at Rome.—τῷ Θεῷ μου, *my God*) This phrase, *my God*, expresses *faith, love, hope*, and, therefore, the whole of true religion, Ps. cxliv. 15; Hab. i. 12. *My God is the God whom I serve;* see next verse.—διά, *through*) The gifts of God come to us *through* Christ, our thanksgivings go to God through Christ.—ἡ πίστις, *faith*) In congratulations of this kind, Paul describes either the whole of Christianity, Col. i. 3, etc., or some part of it, 1 Cor. i. 5. He therefore mentions *faith* in this passage, as suited to the object, which he has in view, ver. 12, 17.—καταγγέλλεται, *is spoken of*) An abbreviated mode of expression for, You have obtained faith; I hear of it, for it is everywhere openly declared; so, 1 Thess. i. 8, he says, that the faith of the Thessalonians is spread abroad *in every place*.—ἐν ὅλῳ τῷ κόσμῳ, *throughout the whole world*) The Divine goodness and wisdom established the faith in the principal cities, especially in Jerusalem and Rome, from which it might be disseminated throughout the whole world.

9. Μάρτυς, *witness*) A pious asseveration respecting a matter necessary [Paul's secret prayer for them], and hidden from men, especially from those, who were remote and unknown,—2 Cor.

xi. 31.—λατρεύω, *I serve*), as an apostle, ch. xv. 16. The witness of God resounds [is often appealed to] in *spiritual service*; and he who serves God, desires and rejoices, that as many as possible should serve God, 2 Tim. i. 3.—μνείαν ὑμῶν, *mention of you*) Paul was wont to make distinct and explicit mention of the churches, and of the souls of their members.

10. Ἔιπως ἤδη ποτέ, The accumulation of the particles intimates the strength of the desire.

11. Μεταδῶ, *I may impart*), in your presence, by the preaching of the Gospel, ver. 15, by profitable discourses, by prayers, etc. Paul was not satisfied with writing an epistle in the meantime, but retained this purpose, ch. xv. 24. There is much greater advantage in being present, than in sending letters, when the former falls out so [when one can be present in person].—χάρισμα πνευματικὸν, *spiritual gift*) In these gifts, the Corinthians abounded, inasmuch as they had been favoured with the presence of Paul, 1 Cor. i. 7, xii. 1, xiv. 1; in like manner the Galatians, Gal. iii. 5. And those churches, which were gladdened by the *presence of the apostles*, had evidently distinguished privileges of this kind; for example, from the imposition of the apostles' hands, Acts xix. 2, 6, viii. 17, 18; and 2 Tim. i. 6. But hitherto, at least, the Romans were much inferior in this respect; wherefore also the enumeration of gifts at ch. xii. 6, 7, is extremely brief. He is, therefore, desirous to go to their assistance, that *they may be established*, for *the testimony of Christ was confirmed* by means of the gifts.—1 Cor. i. 6. Peter had not, any more than Paul, visited Rome, before this epistle was written, as we learn from this passage, and indeed from the whole tenor of the epistle; since Peter, had he been at Rome, would have imparted, what Paul was desirous to impart, to the Romans. Furthermore, Baronius thinks that this epistle was written A.D. 58; whereas the martyrdom of Peter took place A.D. 67; therefore, if he was at Rome at all, he could not have remained long at Rome.—στηριχθῆναι, *to be established*) He speaks modestly; *It is the province* of *God to establish*, ch. xvi. 25. Paul intimates, that he is only the instrument.

12. Τοῦτο δέ ἐστι, *Moreover, that is*) He explains the words, *to see you*, etc. He does not say, *Moreover, that is,* that I may bring you into the form of a regularly constituted *church*. Pre-

caution was taken [by Divine foresight] lest *the Church* of Rome should be the occasion of any mischief, which nevertheless arose in after-times.—ὑμῶν τε καὶ ἐμοῦ, *both of you and me*) He not only associates with himself the Romans, *together with whom he longs to be comforted* [or *stirred up together with whom*], but he even puts them first in the order of words, before himself. The style of the apostle is widely different from that of the Papal court at Rome.

13. 'Οὐ—ἀγνοεῖν, *not—to be ignorant*) A form of expression usual with Paul, which shows the candour of his mind.—ἀδελφοί, *brethren*) An address, frequent, holy, adapted to all, simple, agreeable, magnificent. It is profitable, in this place, to consider the titles, which the apostles use in their addresses. They rather seldom introduce proper names, such as *Corinthians, Timothy*, etc. Paul most frequently calls them *brethren;* sometimes, when he is exhorting them, *beloved*, or *my beloved brethren*. James says, *brethren, my brethren, my beloved brethren;* Peter and Jude always use the word *beloved;* John often, *beloved; once, brethren;* more than once, *little,* or *my little children,* as Paul, *my son Timothy.*—καρπὸν σχῶ, *I might have fruit) Have,* a word elegantly placed midway between *receive* and *give*. What is profitable to others is a delight to Paul himself. He esteems that as the *fruit [of his labour]* (Phil. i. 22). In every place, he wishes to have something [a gift] put out at interest. He somewhat modifies [qualifies] this desire of gain [spiritual gain], when he speaks of himself in the following verse as a *debtor*. He both *demands* and *owes*, ver. 12, 11. By the cords of these two forces, the 15th verse is steadied and strengthened.—καθὼς, *even as*) Good extends itself among as many as possible.

14. 'Ἕλλησί τε καὶ βαρβάροις, *alike to the Greeks and to the barbarians*). He reckons those among the Greeks, to whom he is writing in the Greek language. This division into Greeks and barbarians comprehends the entire *Gentile* world. There follows another division, *alike to the wise and to the unwise;* for there were fools even among the Greeks, and also wise men even among the Barbarians. To all, he says, I am *debtor*, by virtue of my divine commission to all, as being the servant of all (2 Cor. iv. 5.) Though men excel in wisdom or in power, the Gospel is still necessary to them; others [beside the wise and powerful] are not excluded.—(Col. i. 28, note.)

15. Οὕτω, *so*), therefore. It is a sort of epiphonema [exclamation, which follows a train of reasoning], and a conclusion drawn from the whole to an important part.—τὸ κατ' ἐμέ), that is, *so far as depends on me*, or *I for my part*, so far as I am not prevented; so Ezra vi. 11, καὶ ὁ οἶκος αὐτοῦ τὸ κατ' ἐμὲ ποιηθήσεται, and his house, so far as it depends upon me, shall be made [a dunghill].
—πρόθυμον, *ready*) supply *there is* [readiness in me; *I am ready*]. 3 Mac. v. 23, (26.)—τὸ πρόθυμον τοῦ βασιλέως ἐν ἑτοίμῳ κεῖσθαι, [*the readiness of the king to continue in a state of preparation*]—ἐν 'Ρώμῃ, *at Rome*), *to the wise*.—Comp. the preceding verse; *to the powerful*.—Comp. the following verse and 1 Cor. i. 24; therefore the following expression, *at Rome*, is emphatically repeated.—(See ver. 7.) Rome, the capital and theatre of the whole world—εὐαγγελίσασθαι, *to preach the Gospel*) The Statement of the Subject of the epistle is secretly implied here; I will *write*, what I would wish to have spoken in your presence concerning *the Gospel*.

16. Οὐ γὰρ ἐπαισχύνομαι, *for I am not ashamed*) He speaks somewhat less forcibly, as in the introduction; afterwards he says, *I have whereof I may glory* (ch. xv. 17). To the world, the Gospel is *folly* and *weakness* (1 Cor. i. 18); wherefore, in the opinion of the world, a man should be ashamed of it, especially at Rome; but Paul is not ashamed (2 Tim. i. 8; 2 Cor. iv. 2). τοῦ χριστοῦ, *of Christ*) Baumgarten gives good reasons, why Paul did not call it in this passage the Gospel of GOD, or of the SON OF GOD; but the reasons, which he alleges, are as strong for reading the words τοῦ Χριστοῦ, as for omitting them. Arguments are easily found out for both sides; but testimony ought to have the chief weight; and in reference to this passage, the testimony for the omission is sufficient.—(See App. Crit., edit. ii., on this verse.[1])—δύναμις Θεοῦ, *the power of God*), great and glorious (2 Cor. x. 4.)—εἰς σωτηρίαν, *unto salvation*) As Paul sums up the Gospel in this epistle, so he sums up the epistle in this and the following verse. This then is the proper place for presenting a connected view of the epistles. We have in it —

I. THE INTRODUCTION, i. 1–15.

[1] ABCD* omit the words; also, ΛG, *fg.*, Vulg. Orig. and Hilary. But Text has them.—ED.

II. THE SUBJECT STATED [Propositio], with a Summary of its Proof.
  1. Concerning Faith and Righteousness.
  2. Concerning Salvation, or, in other words, Life.
  3. Concerning "Every one that believeth," Jew and Greek, 16, 17.
    To these three divisions, of which the first is discussed from ch. i. 18 to ch. iv., the second from v. to viii. the third from ix. to xi., not only this Discussion itself, but also the Exhortation derived from it, correspond respectively and in the same order.

III. THE DISCUSSION.
  1. On Justification, which results,
    I. Not through works: for alike under sin are
      The Gentiles, 18.
      The Jews, ii. 1.
      Both together, 11, 14, 17; iii. 1, 9.
    II. But through faith, 21, 27, 29, 31.
    III. As is evident from the instance of Abraham, and the testimony of David, iv. 1, 6, 9, 13, 18, 22.
  2. On Salvation, v. 1, 12; vi. 1; vii. 1, 7, 14; viii. 1, 14, 24, 31.
  3. On "Every one that believeth," ix. 1, 6, 14, 24, 30; x. 1, 11; xi. 1, 7, 11, 25, 33.

IV. THE EXHORTATION, xii. 1, 2.
  1. Concerning FAITH, and (because the law is established through faith, ch. iii. 31) concerning love, which faith produces, and concerning righteousness towards men, 3.—xiii. 10. FAITH is expressly named, ch. xii. 3, 6. LOVE, xii. 9, and ch. xiii. 8. The definition of RIGHTEOUSNESS is given, xiii. 7, at the beginning of the verse.
  2. Concerning SALVATION, xiii. 11-14. SALVATION is expressly named, ch. xiii. 11.
  3. Concerning the joint union of JEWS and GENTILES, xiv. 1, 10, 13, 19; xv. 1, 7-13. Express mention of both, xv. 8, 9.

V. THE CONCLUSION, xv. 14; xvi. 1, 3, 17, 21, 25.

Ἰουδαίῳ, *to the Jew*) After the Babylonish captivity, all the Israelites, as Josephus informs us, were called Jews; hence the Jew is opposed to the Greek. For a different reason, the Greek is opposed to the Barbarian; ver 14.—πρῶτον) concerning this particle, see App. Crit. Ed. ii.,[1]) on this verse. The apostle, as I have shown, treats *of faith*, ch. i. to iv.; of *salvation*, ch. v. to viii.; of the Jew and the Greek, ch. ix. to xi. The knowledge of this division is very useful for the right understanding of the epistle. The third part of the discussion, that concerning the Jew and the Greek, neither weakens nor strengthens the genuineness of the particle πρῶτον. Paul uses it rather for the purpose of convicting [confuting their notion of their own peculiar justification by the mere possession of the law] the Jews, ii. 9, 10; but the Gospel is the power of GOD unto salvation, not more to the believing Jew, than to the Greek.

17. Δικαιοσύνη Θεοῦ, *the righteousness of God*) *The righteousness of God* is frequently mentioned in the New Testament, often in the books of Isaiah and Daniel, most often in the Psalms. It sometimes signifies that *righteousness*, by which *God* Himself is righteous, acts righteously, and is acknowledged to be righteous, ch. iii. 5; and also that righteousness, as it is termed in the case of [when applied to] men, either particular or universal, in which grace, and mercy also, are included, and which is shown principally in the condemnation of sin, and in the justification of the sinner; and thus, in this view, the essential *righteousness of God* is evidently not to be excluded from the business of justification, ch. iii. 25, etc. Hence it sometimes signifies this latter *righteousness*, by which a man (in consequence of the gift of *God*, Matt. vi. 33) becomes righteous, and is righteous; and that, too, either by laying hold of the righteousness of Jesus Christ through faith, ch. iii. 21, 22, or by imitating that [the former spoken of] righteousness of God, in

---

[1] *The margin of the* second edition considered the reading πρῶτον less firmly established, while the larger edition had left it to the decision of the reader. The German version gives no decisive opinion.—E.B. [ACD support πρῶτον; also, Λƒ Vulg. and Origen. BG*g*, omit πρῶτον.—ED.]

the practice of virtue, and in the performance of good works, James i. 20. That righteousness of faith is called *the righteousness of God* by Paul, when he is speaking of justification; because God has originated and prepared it, reveals and bestows it, approves and crowns it with completion (comp. 2 Pet. i. 1), to which, therefore, men's *own* righteousness is opposed, Rom. x. 3; with which comp. Phil. iii. 9. Moreover, we ourselves are also called *the righteousness of God*, 2 Cor. v. 21. In this passage, as well as in the statement of the subject [Proposition], the *righteousness of God* denotes the entire scheme of beneficence of God in Jesus Christ, for the salvation of the sinner.—ἀποκαλύπτεται, *is revealed*) Hence the necessity of *the Gospel* is manifest, without which neither righteousness nor salvation is capable of being known. The *showing forth* ['*declare.*'—Engl. vers.] of the righteousness of God was made in the death of Christ, ch. iii. 25, etc. [ἔνδειξιν τ. δικαιοσύνης]; the manifestation and revelation of that righteousness of God, which is through faith, are made in the Gospel: ch. iii. 21, and in this passage. Thus there is here a double *revelation* made; (comp. ver. 18 with this verse) namely, of wrath and of righteousness. The former by the law, which is but little known to nature; the latter, by the Gospel, which is altogether unknown to nature. The former precedes and prepares the way; the latter follows after. Each is *a matter of revelation* (ἀποκαλύπτεται), the word being expressed in the present tense, in opposition to the times of ignorance, Acts xvii. 30.—ἐκ πίστεως εἰς πίστιν, *from faith to faith*) Construe the *righteousness which is of* or *from faith*, as we have presently after *the just from faith* [*i.e.* he who is justified,—whose righteousness is, of faith]. The phrase, *from faith to faith*, expresses pure faith; for righteousness *of*, or *from* faith, subsists in faith, without works. Εἰς denotes the destination, the boundary, and limit; see ch. xii. 3, and notes on Chrysostom's work, De Sacerd, p. 415. So 1 Chron. xvii. 5. *I have gone* [lit. in the Heb. *I was* or *have been*] מאהל אל אהל *from tent to tent*, where one and another tent [different tents] are not intended; but a tent [the tabernacle] as distinguished from [or independently of] a house or temple. Faith, says Paul, continues to be faith; faith is all in all [lit. *the prow* and *stern*] in the case of Jews and Gentiles; in the case of Paul also, even up to its very final consummation, Phil. iii. 7–12. Thus εἰς sounds with a beautiful effect after ἐκ, as ἀπὸ and εἰς, 2 Cor. iii. 18, concerning the purest glory. It is to avoid what might be disagreeable to his readers, that Paul does not yet expressly exclude works, of which, however, in this Statement of Subject [Proposition], an exclusion of some kind should otherwise have appeared. Furthermore, the nature of a proposition, thus set forth, bears, that many other things may be inferred from this; for inasmuch as it is not said, ἐκ τῆς πίστεως εἰς τὴν πίστιν, *from the faith to the faith*, but indefinitely ἐκ πίστεως εἰς πίστιν *from faith to faith*, so we shall say [we may say by inference] *from one faith to another*, from the faith of God, who makes the offer, to the faith of men, who receive it, ch. iii. 2, etc.; from the faith of the Old Testament, and of the Jews, to the faith of the New Testament, and of the Gentiles also, ch. iii. 30; from the faith of Paul to the faith of the Romans, ch. i. 12; from one degree of faith to still higher degrees, 1 John v. 13; from the faith of the strong to the faith of the weak, ch. xiv. 1, etc.; from our faith, which is that of expectation, to the faith, which is to be divinely made good to us, by the gift of *life* [" The just shall *live* by faith"].—καθὼς, *as*) Paul has just laid down three principles: I. Righteousness is [of, or] from faith, ver. 17 : II. Salvation is by righteousness, ver. 16 : III. *To the Jew and to the Greek*, ver. 16. What follows confirms the whole, viz., the clause, *the just by faith, shall live*, which is found in the prophetical record, Hab. ii. 4; see notes on Heb. x. 36, etc. It is the same Spirit, who spoke by the prophets the Words, that were to be quoted by Paul; and under whose guidance Paul made such apposite and suitable quotations, especially in this epistle.—ζήσεται, *shall live*) some of the Latins, in former times, wrote *the present* 'lives' *for the future* " shall live" (*vivit* for *vivet*) ;[1] an obvious mistake in one small letter, and not worthy of notice or refutation. *Baumgarten*, following *Whitby*, refutes it, and observes, that I have omitted to notice it.

18. Ἀποκαλύπτεται, *is revealed*) See verse 17, note.—γὰρ, *for*) The particle begins the discussion; the Statement of Subject [Proposition] being now concluded, ch. vi. 19; Matt. i. 18; Acts ii. 15; 1 Cor. xv. 3. The Latins generally omit it.[2] This

[1] 'Vivit' *fg* Vulg. and Iren. But ABCΛG have ζήσεται.—ED.
[2] But the Vulg. has it "Revelatur *enim*."—ED.

is Paul's first argument: All are under sin; and that the law shows; therefore, no one is justified by the works of the law. The discussion of this point continues to the third chapter, ver. 20. From this he draws the inference, therefore [justification must be] by faith, ch. iii. 21, etc.—ὀργὴ Θεοῦ, *wrath of God*) [not as Engl. Vers. "*the* wrath"] Ὀργή without the article, in this passage [is denounced against all *unrighteousness*]; but ἡ ὀργή is denounced against those [*the persons*; not as ὀργή, against *the sin*], who disregard righteousness. Wrath is, as it were, different, when directed against the Gentiles, and when against the Jews. The righteousness and the wrath of God form, in some measure, an antithesis. The righteousness of the world crushes the guilty individual; the righteousness of God crushes beneath it the sin, and restores the sinner. Hence there is frequent mention of *wrath*, especially in this epistle, ch. ii. 5, 8, iii. 5, iv. 15, v. 9, ix. 22, and besides, ch. xii. 19, xiii. 4, 5.—ἀπ' οὐρανοῦ, *from heaven*) This significantly implies the majesty of an angry God, and His all-seeing eye, and the wide extent of His wrath : whatever is under heaven, and yet not under the Gospel, is under this wrath,—Ps. xiv. 2.—ἐπὶ πᾶσαν, *upon all*) Paul, in vividly presenting to view the *wrath* of God, speaks in the abstract, concerning sin : in presenting to view *salvation* [ver. 16, he speaks] in the concrete, concerning believers; he now, therefore, intimates enigmatically [by implication], that grace has been procured for *sinners*.—ἀσέβειαν καὶ ἀδικίαν, *ungodliness and unrighteousness*) These two points are discussed at the twenty-third and following verses. [*Paul often mentions* unrighteousness, ver. 29, *as directly opposed* to righteousness.—V. g.]—ανθρώπων τῶν) A periphrasis for the Gentiles.— τὴν ἀλήθειαν, *the truth*) to which belongs, whatever of really sound morality the heathen writings possess.—ἐν ἀδικίᾳ, *in unrighteousness*) The term is taken now in a larger sense, than just before, where it formed an antithesis to ἀσέβειαν, viz., in the sense of ἀνομία, ch. vi. 19.—κατεχόντων, *holding back*) [*holding*, Engl. Vers. less correctly] Truth in the understanding, makes great efforts, and is urgent; but man impedes its effect.

19. Τὸ γνωστόν) the fact that God is known : that principle, that God makes Himself known; that is to say, the existence of *an acquaintance with, or knowledge of, God* [the fact of *God*

being known; the objective knowledge of God], not merely that He can be known. For, at ver. 21, he says, γνόντες, of the Gentiles [asserting thus, that they *did know* God].—Plato b. 5. Polit. uses γνωστόν in the same way; τὸ μὲν παντελῶς ὂν, παντελῶς γνωστόν· μὴ ὂν δὲ μηδαμῆ, πάντη ἄγνωστον, whatsoever indeed has a positive existence, is positively *known*: but a thing, which has no existence at all, is utterly *unknown*.—ἐφανέρωσε) Paul used this word with great propriety, as well as ἀποκαλύπτω above.[1]

20. Ἀόρατα καθορᾶται, *the invisible things are seen*) An incomparable oxymoron[2] (a happy union of things opposite, as here *invisible*, yet *seen*). The invisible things of God, if ever at any time, would certainly have become visible at the creation; but even then they began to be seen, not otherwise, save by the understanding.—ἀπὸ κτίσεως, *from the creation*) Ἀπὸ here denotes either a *proof*, as ἀπὸ, in Matt. xxiv. 32, so that the understanding [comp. ver. 20, "*understood*"] of the fathers [respecting God, as He, whose being and attributes are proved] from the creation of the world, may refute the apostasy of the Gentiles; or rather, ἀπό denotes *time*, so that it corresponds to the Hebrew preposition מ, and means, *ever since the foundation of the world*, and beyond it, reckoning backward; and thus the ἀΐδιος, *eternal*, presently after, agrees with it. In the former mode of interpretation, ἀπὸ is connected with καθορᾶται, *are seen from*; in the second mode, with ἀόρατα, *unseen ever since*.—ποιήμασι) [the things made], *the works* that have been produced by κτίσιν, *creation*. There are *works*; therefore there is *a creation*; therefore there is *a Creator*.—νοούμενα) Those alone, who use their understanding, νῷ, καθορῶσι, look closely into a subject.—καθορᾶται, *are seen*) for the works [which proceed from the invisible attributes of God] are discerned. The antithesis is, ἐσκοτίσθη [ver. 21], *was darkened*.—ἥτε—καὶ) These words stand in apposition with ἀόρατα.—ἀΐδιος κ.τ.λ., *eternal*, etc.) The highest attribute of God, worthy of God—perfection in being and acting; in one word θειότης, which signifies *divinity* [not "Godhead," as Engl. Vers.], as θεότης, *Godhead*.—δύναμις, *power*) of all the attributes of God, this is the one, which was first revealed.

[1] Implying it is by *revelation* and *manifestation*, not by man's mere reasonings, *the knowledge of God* comes.—ED.
[2] See App. for the meaning of this figure.

His works, in a peculiar manner correspond to His several attributes [Isa. xl. 26]—εἰς τὸ) Paul not only speaks of some result ensuing, but directly takes away all excuse; and this clause, εἰς τo,—is equivalent to a proposition, in relation to [to be handled more fully in] the following verses. Construe it with φανερόν ἐστιν [ver. 19. The fact of their knowing God, is manifest in, or among them].—ἀναπολογήτους, *without excuse*). So also in regard to the Jews, ch. ii. 1.

21. Διότι. This διότι is resumed from ver. 19. They did not sin in ignorance, but knowingly.—Θεὸν ὡς Θεὸν, *God as God*). This is ἡ ἀλήθεια, *the truth* [of God, ver. 25], the perfection of conformity with nature,[1] where worship corresponds to the divine nature. Comp. in contrast with this, Gal. iv. 8 [when ye knew not God, ye did service unto them which] *by nature are no Gods*.—Θεὸν, *God*). [They glorified Him not as the God] eternal, almighty, and to be continually honoured by showing forth His glory, and by thanksgiving.—ἐδόξασαν ἢ εὐχαρίστησαν, *they glorified or were thankful*) We ought *to render thanks* for benefits; and *to glorify* Him on account of the divine perfections themselves, contrary to the opinion of Hobbes. If it were possible for a mind to exist extraneous to God, and not created by God, still that mind would be bound to praise God.—ἢ), *or*, at least.—ἐματαιώθησαν) This verb and ἐσκοτίσθη have a reciprocal force. הבל, μάταια, ματαιοῦσθαι are frequently applied to idols, and to their worship and worshippers, 2 Kings xvii. 15; Jer. ii. 5; for the mind is conformed [becomes and is assimilated] to its object [of worship], Ps. cxv. 8. Ματαιότης is opposed to τῷ δοξάζειν; ἀσύνετος καρδία to τῷ εὐχαριστεῖν.—διαλογισμοῖς [" imaginations," Eng. vers.], *thoughts*) Variable, uncertain, and foolish.

22. φάσκοντες, *professing*.—ἐμωράνθησαν) The LXX., Jer. x. 14, etc., ἐμωράνθη πᾶς ἄνθρωπος ἀπὸ γνώσεως—ψευδῆ ἐχώνευσαν—μάταιά ἐστιν, ἔργα ἐμπεπαιγμένα, (every man is a fool in his knowledge.— Their molten images are falsehoods, they are vain and deceitful works). Throughout this epistle Paul alludes to the last chapters of *Isaiah*, and to the first of *Jeremiah*, from which it appears, that this holy man of God was at that time fresh from the reading of them.

---

[1] Convenientia=the Stoic ὁμολογία Cic. de fin. 3. 6. 21—ED.

23. Ἤλλαξαν, *they changed*), with the utmost folly, Ps. cvi. 20; Jer. ii. 11. The impiety being one and the same, and the punishment one and the same, have three successive stages. In the first, these words are the emphatic ones, viz., καρδία, in ver. 21; καρδιῶν, in ver. 24; ἐδόξασαν, and δόξαν, and ἀτιμάζεσθαι τὰ σώματα, in ver. 21, 23, 24. In the second stage, μετήλλαξαν is emphatic, and the repetition of this verb, not, however, without a difference between the simple and compound forms [ἤλλαξαν τ. δόξαν, ver. 23; μετήλλαξαν τ. φυσικὴν χρῆσιν, ver. 26, the corresponding sin and punishment], gives the meaning of like for like [*talionis*, their punishment being *like* their sin], ver. 25, 26; as παρὰ changes its meaning, when repeated in the same place [παρὰ τ. κτίσαντα, ver. 25; παρὰ φύσιν, ver. 26]. In the third, οὐκ ἐδοκίμασαν, and ἀδόκιμον, ver. 28, are emphatic. In the several cases, the word παρέδωκε expresses the punishment. If a man worships not God as God, he is so far left to himself, that he casts away his manhood, and departs as far as possible from God, after whose image he was made.—τὴν δόξαν τοῦ ἀφθάρτου, *the glory of the incorruptible*) The perfections of God are expressed either in positive or negative terms. The Hebrew language abounds in positive terms, and generally renders negatives by a periphrasis.—ἐν), Hebrew ב, [So, after the verb to change *with*, or *for*] the Latin *pro, cum;* so, ἐν, ver. 25 [changed the truth of God into a lie].—ἀνθρώπου—ἑρπετῶν, *like to man—to creeping things*) A descending climax; *corruptible* is to be construed also with *birds*, etc. They often mixed together the form of man, bird, quadruped, and serpent.—ὁμοιώματι εἰκόνος, *in the likeness of an image*) *Image* is the concrete; *likeness* the abstract, opposed to δόξῃ, the *glory;* the greater the resemblance of the image to the creature, the more manifest is the aberration from the truth.

24. Διό, *wherefore*) One punishment of sin arises from its physical consequences, ver. 27, note, [that recompense of their error, which] *was meet;* another, moreover, from retributive justice, as in this passage.—ἐν ταῖς ἐπιθυμίαις, *in the lusts*) ἐν, not εἰς. Αἱ ἐπιθυμίαι, *the lusts*, were already present there. The men themselves were such as were the gods that they framed.—ἀκαθαρσίαν, *uncleanness*) Impiety and impurity are frequently joined together, 1 Thess. iv. 5; as are also the knowledge of God and purity of mind, Matt. v. 8; 1 John iii. 2, etc.—

ἀτιμάζεσθαι, to dishonour) Honour is its opposite, 1 Thess. iv. 4. Man ought not to debase himself, 1 Cor. vi. 13, etc.—ἐν ἑαυτοῖς,[1] among their ownselves), by fornication, effeminacy, and other vices. They themselves furnish the materials of their own punishment, and are at the cost of it. *How justly!* they, who dishonour God, inflict punishment on their ownselves. -Joh. Cluverus.

25. Τὴν ἀλήθειαν, the truth) which commands us to worship God AS God.—ἐν τῷ ψεύδει [into a lie—Engl. vers.] (exchanged) *for a lie*) the price paid for [mythology] idol worship; ἐν, the Lat. *cum*. —ἐσεβάσθησαν, they worshipped) implying internal worship.— ἐλάτρευσαν, they served) implying external worship.—παρὰ) *in preference to*, more than, ch. xiv. 5 [ἡμέραν παρ᾽ ἡμέραν].

26. Πάθη ἀτιμίας, lusts of dishonour) [vile affections—Engl. vers.] See *Gerberi* lib. unerkannte sünden (unknown sins), T. i., cap. 92; Von der geheimen Unzucht (on secret vices). The writings of the heathen are full of such things.—ἀτιμίας, dishonour). Honour is its opposite, 1 Thess. iv. 4.—θήλειαι women) In stigmatizing sins, we must often call a spade a spade. Those generally demand from others a preposterous modesty [in speech], who are without chastity [in acts]. Paul, at the beginning of this epistle, thus writes more plainly to Rome, which he had not yet visited, than on any former occasion anywhere. The dignity and earnestness of the judicial style [which he employs], from the propriety of its language, does not offend modesty.—χρῆσιν, use) supply *of themselves;* but it is elliptical; the reason is found, 1 Cor. xi. 9; *we must use,* not enjoy. Herein is seen the gravity of style in the sacred writings.

27. Ἐξεκαύθησαν, were all in a flame) [burned] with an abominable fire (πυρώσει, viz., of lust.)—τὴν ἀσχημοσύνην, *that which is unseemly*) against which the conformation of the body and its members reclaims.—ἣν ἔδει) which it was meet [or *proper*], by a natural consequence.—τῆς πλάνης, of their error) by which they wandered away from God.—ἀπολαμβάνοντες), the antithetic word used to express the punishment of the Gentiles; as ἀποδώσει, that of the Jews, ii. 6. In both words, ἀπό has the same force.

---

[1] So, late corrections in D; G Orig. 1, 260, *e.*—Vulg. and Rec. Text. But ABCΛ and Memph. Version read αὐτοῖς.—ED.

28. Ἔχειν *to have*) [or *retain*] the antithesis is παρέδωκεν, [God] *gave them over*: ἔχειν ἐν ἐπιγνώσει, *to have* [or *retain*] *in knowledge*, denotes more than ἐπιγινώσκειν, *to know*) [*to be acquainted with*]. *Knowledge* was not altogether wanting to them; but they did not so far profit in the possession of it, as to have [or *retain*] God, ver. 32.—ἀδόκιμον) As ἀδύνατος, ἄπιστος, and such like, have both an active and passive signification, so also ἀδόκιμος. In this passage, there is denoted [or *stigmatized*], in an active sense, the mind, which *approves* of things, which ought by no means to be approved of; to this state of mind they are consigned, who have *disapproved* of, what was most worthy of approbation. In this sense, the word ἀδόκιμον is treated of at ver. 32; συνευδοκοῦσι: and the words ποιεῖν τὰ μὴ καθήκοντα, at ver. 29–31.—τὰ μὴ καθήκοντα), an example of the figure Meiosis [by which less is said, than the writer wishes to be understood].

29. Πεπληρωμένους) a word of large meaning; μεστούς follows presently after.—ἀδικίᾳ, *with unrighteousness*) This word, the opposite of *righteousness*, is put in the first place; *unmerciful* is put in the last [ver. 31]. *Righteousness* has [as its necessary fruit], *life*; *unrighteousness*, *death*, ver. 32. The whole enumeration shows a wise arrangement, as follows: nine members of it respecting the affections; two in reference to men's conversation; three respecting God, a man's own self, and his neighbour; two regarding a man's management of affairs; and six respecting relative ties. Comp. as regards the things contrary to these, ch. xii. 9, etc.—πορνείᾳ) I have now, for a long time, acknowledged that this word should be retained.[1] It does not appear certain, that it was not read by Clemens Romanus.—πονηρίᾳ—κακίᾳ)[2] πονηρία is the *perverse wickedness* of a man, who delights in injuring another, without any advantage to himself: κακία is the

---

[1] *Although the* margin of the larger edition (A. 1734), *contains the opinion, that it should be omitted*. The 2d ed. *corresponds with the* Gnomon and the German Version.—E.B. [AC, and apparently B, Memph. Version, omit πορνείᾳ. But ΛGfg Vulg. insert it.—ED.]

[2] πονηρία Th. ὁ παρέχων πόνους, "one who puts others to trouble," aptness in mischief. κακία is the *evil habit* of mind; πονηρία, the *outcoming of it*: Opp. to χρηστός; as κακός to ἀγαθός. Κακοήθεια, as distinct from these, is not, as Engl. Vers. 'malignity,' but *taking everything in the evil part;* Arist. Rhet. ii. 13; arising from a baseness or evil ἦθος in the man himself.—See Trench's Gr. Test. Syn.—ED.

vicious disposition, which prevents a man from conferring any good on another.—πλεονεξία denotes *avarice*, properly so called, as we often find it in the writings of Paul: otherwise [were πλεονεξία not taken in the sense *avarice*] this sin would be blamed by him rather rarely. But he usually joins it with impurity; for man [in his natural state] seeks his food for enjoyment, outside of God, in the material creature, either in the way of pleasure, or else avarice; he tries to appropriate the good that belongs to another.—κακοηθείας), κακοήθεια, κακία κεκρυμμένη. Ammonius explains this as "wickedly inveighing against all that belongs to others; exhibiting himself troublesome to another."

30. Ψιθυριστάς, *whisperers*), who defame secretly.—καταλάλους, *back-biters*), who defame openly.—θεοςτυγεῖς) men who show themselves to be *haters of God*—ὑβριστὰς) those who *insolently drive away* from *themselves* all that is good and salutary.—ὑπερηφάνους) those who exalt themselves above *others*. On this vice, and others which are here noticed, see 2 Tim. iii. 2, etc.—ἀλαζόνας) ['*boasters*,' Engl. vers.], *assuming*, in reference to things great and good.[1]—ἐφευρετὰς κακῶν, *inventors of evil things*) of new pleasures, of new methods of acquiring wealth, of new modes of injuring others, for example in war, 2 Macc. vii. 31. Antiochus is said to have been πάσης κακίας εὑρετής [an inventor of every kind of evil] against the Hebrews.

30. 31. Γονεῦσιν ἀπειθεῖς, ἀσυνέτους, ἀσυνθέτους, ἀστόργους, ἀσπόνδους, ἀνελεήμονας, *disobedient to parents, without understanding, refractory,* [But *covenant-breakers*—Eng. vers.], *without natural affection, implacable, unmerciful*) Two triplets [groups consisting of three each], the former referring to one's conduct to superiors, the latter to inferiors.

31. Ἀσυνθέτους). The LXX. translate the Hebrew words בגד, to act with *perfidy*, מעל, to *prevaricate*, by ἀσυνθετεῖν.[2]

32. Δικαίωμα, [*judgment*.—Eng. ver.], the royal, divine, *principle of justice*, that God approves of virtues, hates vices, visits the wicked with the punishment of death, and justly and deservedly so, in order that He may show that He is not unjust.

---

[1] ἀλαζών, boastful in *words*; ὑπερήφανος, proud in *thoughts*; ὑβριστής, insolent in *acts*.—See Trench Syn.—Ed.

[2] The Vulg. translates ἀσυνθέτους 'incompositos.'—Ed.

For whilst He punishes the guilty with death, He Himself is justified [is manifested as just]. This Royal rule is acknowledged even among the Gentiles.—ὅτι) viz. that.—πράσσοντες· πράσσουσι) [those that *commit* or *practise.*] This verb, which is repeated after the interposition of ποιοῦσίν [*do*], accurately expresses the wantonness of profligate men, which is altogether opposed to divine justice. ποιοῦσιν)—*they do such things*, even with the affections, and with the reason. The same distinction between these two verbs occurs,[1] ch. ii. 3.—θανάτου, *of death*) Lev. xviii. 24, etc.; Acts xxviii. 4. From time to time every extremely wicked generation of men is extirpated, and posterity is entirely propagated from those, whose conduct has not been so immoral.—ἀλλὰ καὶ, *but also.*) It is a worse thing, συνευδοκεῖν, *to approve* [of the evil]; for he, who perpetrates what is evil, is led away by his own desire, not without an argument of condemnation against himself, or even against others,—(Comp. *thou that judgest*, ii. 1), and at the same time shows his approbation of the law.—Comp. with this, ch. vii. 16; but he who, συνευδοκεῖ, or *approves*, with the heart and with the tongue [that which is evil], has as the fruit of wickedness, wickedness itself; he feeds upon it; he adds to the heap of his own guilt the guilt of others, and inflames others to the commission of sin. He is a worse man, who destroys both himself and others, than he who destroys himself alone. This is truly a reprobate mind.—ἀδόκιμον and συνευδοκοῦσι are conjugate forms.—See ver. 28, note. The *judging*, in ch. ii. 1, is the antithesis to the *approving* here. The Gentiles not only do these things, but also approve of them. The Jew judges indeed, thereby expressing disapproval; but yet he does them.—τοῖς πράσσουσι, *them that do them*) themselves, and others. —Comp. Is. iii. 9.

[1] ποιέω to *do* or *make*. πράσσω, to *commit* or *practise.*—ED.

CHAPTER II.

1. Διό, *wherefore*). Paul passes from the Gentiles to the **Jews**, as the whole of the following discourse clearly shows; and yet he does not use the transitive, but the illative particle, of which two the latter, as being the more powerful, absorbs the former. The Gentile does evil; the Jew does evil. Then in the 6th and following verses, he comprehends both, Jews and Gentiles.—ἀναπολόγητος, *inexcusable*.) Man seeks to defend himself.—ἄνθρωπε, *O man*) In ch. i. he spoke of the Gentiles in the third person, but he deals with the Jew in the second person singular; even as the law itself deals with the Jew, not in the second, but in the third person singular; because it had no concern with any one but the Jew.—Comp. ch. iii. 19. But the apostle, who directs his discourse to Gentiles and Jews, addresses the *Jew* indeed in the second person singular, but calls him by the name [O *man*] common to all.—comp. ch. i. 18; nor does he acknowledge the *Jew*, as such, ver. 17, 28. The same difference between the third and second persons occurs again, ver. 14, 17. It is a not dissimilar circumstance, that the Gentiles are put off [as to their condemnation] till the final judgment, ver. 16; but the Jews are threatened by the law with a present judgment also [besides the final one ver. 2.]—ὁ κρίνων, *thou that judgest*) being removed [*i.e.* wherein thou art distinguished] from those that *have pleasure in* evil-doers, i. 32. Paul uses a weighty expression. The Jew esteems himself superior to the Greek, ver. 19, etc. Paul now calls that *an act of judging*, and by it opens up a way for himself, with a view to show the judgment of God. It is mere self-love in a man, that, in proportion as he thinks others worse than himself, he thinks the better of himself, Gal. vi. 4. The figure paregmenon[1] occurs here; for κατακρίνεις follows.—Comp. ch. xiv. 22, 23; 1 Cor. iv. 3, etc., xi. 29, etc.; James ii. 4.—ἕτερον, *another*) who is of no concern to thee; whose more open unrighteousness profits thee nothing; a heathen.

---

[1] A joining together of conjugate forms, or of simples and compounds, ex. gr. here, κρίνεις, κατακρίνεις.—ED.

2. Οἴδαμεν) *we know;* without thy teaching, O man, that judgest [we know].—τὸ κρίμα τοῦ Θεοῦ, *the judgment of God);* not thine, thou that exceptest thyself.—κατὰ ἀλήθειαν) *according to the truth* of the highest *kind,* without distinction; just as His judgment is called δίκαιον, *righteous,* at ver. 5, 6, 11; not merely having respect to external acts, but also to internal thoughts ver. 16 [the secrets of men].

3. σύ, *thou)* as distinguished from the Gentile; every one, even without a cause, makes his own self an exception [as regards condemnation]; and flatters himself, although he knows not himself, on what grounds.—ἐκφεύξῃ, *shalt thou escape?)* through the loopholes, which thou seekest. Every one, that is arraigned, φεύγει, *tries to escape* [ὁ φεύγων is the technical term for *a defendant;* ὁ διώκων, the *accuser*]; he who is acquitted, ἐκφεύγει, *escapes.*

4. Ἤ, *or).* Men easily become *despisers* of goodness, while they are not sensible of the judgment of God. The particle ἤ, *or,* properly acts as a disjunctive between the vain thought [on their part] of *escape,* and the palpable *treasuring up of wrath* in consequence of their abuse of goodness itself.—χρηστότητος, ἀνοχῆς, μακροθυμίας, *goodness, forbearance, long-suffering)* since thou hast both sinned, and art now sinning, and wilt sin. [*By goodness,* GOD *restrains His* wrath, ver. 5 : *by forbearance, He as it were, keeps Himself unknown, until* He is revealed, ver. 5 : *by long-suffering He delays His* righteous judgment, *ibid.*— V. g.] Presently after, τὸ χρηστὸν, *the goodness* of God, implies all these three. Even those, who shall be condemned hereafter, had the power, and it was their duty, to have repented.— ἀγνοῶν, *ignorant).* Paul wonders at this ignorance.—ἄγει) *leads* pleasantly; does not compel by necessity.

5. Δὲ, *but)* The antithesis is between the despising *of the riches of His goodness,* and *the treasuring up of wrath.*—σκληρότητα, *hardness)* Its antithesis is χρηστόν.—ἀμετανόητον καρδίαν) The antithesis is μετάνοιαν. He meant to say ἀμετανοησίαν : to which word, later writers show no aversion; but Paul avoided an unusual term.—θησαυρίζεις, *thou treasurest* up), although thou, O man, thinkest, that thou art treasuring up all kinds of blessedness. O what a treasure may a man lay up, during so many hours of his life, on either side! [either for heaven, or else hell],

Matt. xviii. 24; 1 Tim. vi. 18.—σεαυτῷ) *for thyself*, not for the other, whom thou judgest.—ὀργὴν—ὀργῆς, *wrath—of wrath*) The idea of Δεινότης [vehemence] of language is here conveyed with great force. Why is it, that many have no sense of wrath? [Because] The *day of wrath* is not yet; but it shall be.—ἐν ἡμέρᾳ).[1] When ἐν refers to time, it denotes the present; εἰς, the future.[2] That day is present to God [therefore ἐν ἡμέρᾳ, present, is used]. But this expression may also be construed with ὀργήν. [Beng. seems to have construed ἐν ἡμέρᾳ with θησαυρίζεις].—ἀποκαλύψεως, *of the revelation*) When God shall be revealed, the secrets of man shall be revealed, ver. 16.—καὶ δικαιοκρίσιας). By far the greatest weight of testimony, and the unquestionable antithesis between ἀνοχῆς and ἀποκαλύψεως, which is most worthy of the apostle (such as there is also between ἀνοχὴν and ἔνδειξιν, ch. iii. 26; Ps. l. 21), confirm the reading of the particle καί, ver. 4, τῆς χρηστότητος, καὶ τῆς ἀνοχῆς, καὶ τῆς μακροθυμίας· ver. 5, ὀργῆς καὶ ἀποκαλύψεως, καὶ δικαιοκρισίας.[3] Ἀνοχὴ and ἀποκάλυψις have respect to God, and are compared together, as ἀνοχὴ and ἔνδειξις are at ch. iii. 25 ; μακροθυμία and δικαιοκρισία refer to the sinner, χρηστότης and ὀργὴ are put generally. Wherefore the particle καί should not have been admitted, as it is by some ; it is supported also by Origen, in his work against Celsus, in the MS. at Bâle, as Sam. Battier informs us in his Biblioth. Brem., Class vi., p. 98. Instead of ἀποκαλύψεως the Alex. MS. has ἀνταποδόσεως. I formerly omitted to notice this various reading, which arose from its having the same letters at the beginning as the verb ἀποδώσει, and is quite out of place here ; nor do I use it now to defend that καί which follows immediately after. Erasmus observes, that δικαιοκρισίας, was a word newly coined to express a thing not formerly known among [acknowledged on the part of] men.

6. Ὃς ἀποδώσει ἑκάστῳ κατὰ τὰ ἔργα αὐτοῦ). So the LXX. expressly in Prov. xxiv. 12, and Ps. lxii. 13, σὺ ἀποδώσεις κτλ.

---

[1] Wrath to be revealed *in* the day of wrath.—ED.
[2] εἰς τὴν ἡμέραν would be *against* the coming day.—ED.
[3] The later Syr. Version, and Origen in three passages, also the Λ MS., read the καί before δικαιοκρ. But ABG Vulg. Syr. Memph. *fg*. Origen in three other passages, and Lucifer, agree with Rec. Text, in omitting καί.—ED.

This saying, and especially that below, ver. 11, is often quoted. —ἀποδώσει, *will render*) not only *will give*, but *will repay*. [*See that you make this the rule of your plans.*—V. g.]—κατὰ, *according to*) Paul describes those, who shall obtain either life or death, generally, and according to the condition [or else *in a way suited to the apprehension*] of those, with whom he is concerned in this place, cutting them off still from all special ground of obtaining or losing salvation. Therefore, this passage is of no advantage to the argument for the merit of good works.

7, 8. Τοῖς μὲν—τοῖς δέ, *to these on the one hand—but to them on the other*) a more important distinction, than many now think.

7. Τοῖς) sc. οὖσι; comp. the following verse; for κατὰ (see Acts xxv. 23,) is employed here nearly in the same sense as ἐξ, next verse; save that ἐξ implies a something natural to the sinner; κατὰ, a something supervenient [not natural, but *superinduced*]. You will see the difference, if you interchange the particles with one another: ἐξ ὑπομονῆς κτλ. In this view, τοῖς and ζητοῦσι stand in apposition, the conjunction being omitted by the figure asyndeton.[1]—ὑπομονὴν ἔργου, *patience in work*) so *the patience of hope*, 1 Thess. i. 3; ὑπομονὴ, *patience*, includes, in this passage, obedience, steadiness, and that, too, with submission.—ἔργου, *in work*. There is great force in the singular number here (*well-doing.*—Engl. Vers.; *the good work* is referred to, of which), Phil. i. 6; Rev. xxii. 12.—δόξαν, *glory*) The construction is, τοῖς δόξαν κτλ ζητοῦσιν (ἀποδώσει) ζωήν, *to those who seek for glory, etc.* (*he will render*) *life*. Pure love does not exclude faith, hope, desire, 1 Cor. xv. 58.—ζητοῦσι, *to them that seek*) Whereas thou, O Jew, thinkest, that thou hast no need of any seeking [*Industry is requisite.*—V. g.]

8. Τοῖς δὲ ἐξ ἐριθείας, *but unto them* that are [influenced by contention] *contentious*. Paul shrunk from saying directly: *God will render to them*, that are *contentious*, *death or everlasting destruction*. He therefore leaves that matter to be supplied, by the conscience of the sinner, from the preceding antithesis; *He will render*, not certainly eternal life; and he turns the discourse to those things, which follow. Τοῖς here, has therefore the force

---

[1] Beng. construes it " to them who are *animated by* (κατά) *patient* continuance in well-doing, even those who seek glory, etc.—Ed.]

of ᾿ prefixed, and signifies *as concerns.* Comp. ch. iv. 12, notes. Accordingly there follows, with great propriety, ἐπὶ πᾶσαν; for we have also, Ex. xx. 5, ἐπὶ τέκνα, ἐπὶ τρίτην καὶ τετάρτην γενεὰν, τοῖς μισοῦσί με, *upon the children, upon the third and fourth generation, as concerns them that hate me.* Furthermore, ἐξ, *from* or *of*, as in ver. 27, and often elsewhere, denotes a party or sect; in reference to those, who are of a contentious party or nation, like thee, O Jew, setting themselves in resistance to God. The character of false Judaism is disobedience, contumacy, impatience. —τῇ ἀληθείᾳ, τῃ ἀδικίᾳ, *truth, unrighteousness*) These two are often opposed to each other, 1 Cor. xiii. 6; 2 Thess. ii. 10, 12; *truth* includes *righteousness*, and *unrighteousness* implies at the same time *falsehood*.—θυμὸς καὶ ὀργή) LXX., Ps. lxxviii. (lxxvii.) 49, θυμὸν καὶ ὀργὴν καὶ θλίψιν; θυμὸς inflicts punishment; ὀργή follows up an offence. The propriety respectively of these words is seen in Eph. iv. 31, 32, where τὸ χαρίζεσθαι is opposed to τῇ ὀργῇ, and εὔσπλαγχνον to θυμὸς. θυμὸς is defined by the Stoics to be ὀργὴ ἀρχομένη, *the beginning of anger*. Nor should we despise the explanation of Ammonius, θυμὸς μὲν ἐστι πρόσκαιρος, ὀργὴ δὲ πολυχρόνιος μνησικακία; θυμὸς is only temporary; ὀργὴ is the lasting remembrance of injuries.[1]

9. Θλίψις καὶ στενοχωρία, *affliction and anxiety* [*tribulation and anguish*]. θλίψις, *affliction* or *tribulation* for the present; στενοχωρία, *anxiety* or *anguish*, in regard to things future; θλίψις, *affliction*, or *tribulation*, presses down; στενοχωρία, frets and harasses [œstuat et urget], Job xv. 20, etc. In these words we have a proof of the avenging justice of God; for the anger of God has for its object, to teach the sinful creature, who is experiencing wrath and every species of adversity, to hate himself, because in his whole conduct, he has set himself in opposition to God; and so long as the creature shrinks from this most just hatred of himself, he continues under punishment.—πᾶσαν ψυχὴν, *every soul*) This term adds to the universal character of the discourse, ch. xiii. 1.—πρῶτον, *first*). So Ps. xciv. 10: *He that chastiseth the nations, shall he not correct* (you among the people?). The Greek is a partaker [in the judgment] along with the Jew.

10. Δόξα δὲ καὶ τιμὴ, *but glory and honour*. *Glory*, originating

---

[1] θυμὸς Th. θύω, boiling *indignation*; ὀργή, abiding *wrath*, with a settled purpose of revenge, ἐπιθυμία τιμωρίας.—ED.

in the Divine good pleasure; *honour,* originating in the reward bestowed by God; and *peace,* for the present and for ever. For the δὲ, *but,* expresses the opposition between *wrath,* and *glory; indignation,* and *honour; affliction* and *anxiety* [*tribulation* and *anguish*], and *peace.* Comp. ch. iii. 17, 16, of which catalogue the joys are viewed, as they proceed from God; the sorrows as they are felt by man; for the latter are put absolutely in the nominative, while the former, on the contrary, are put in the accusative in ver. 7, as being such things, as God bestows. But why are *honour* and *sorrow* set in opposition to each other, since disgrace is the converse of honour, sorrow of pleasure? Ans.: In this passage, we must carefully attend to the word εἰρήνη, *peace,* which is here opposed to *sorrow,* that is to say, to *tribulation* and *anguish.* But at Isaiah lxv. 13, *joy* (and honour) is opposed to *shame* (and grief), each of the two parts of the sentence being expressed in abbreviated form, and requiring to be supplied from its own opposite. Besides, in the classification of goods, honour is the highest good, and, in the classification of punishments, sorrow is the greatest punishment; and the highest degree on the one side, including all below it, is opposed to the highest degree on the other; so we have *glorying* and *woe,* 1 Cor. ix. 16.

9, 10. Κατεργαζομένου· ἐργαζομένῳ). The distinction between these words is more easily felt, than explained, more easily ridiculed, than refuted. There is another distinction: ἐπὶ ψυχήν is said of the punishment; for punishment *falls upon it,* and the soul will bear it unwillingly; παντὶ τῷ ἐργαζομένῳ, the dative of advantage, is said of the reward.

12. Ὅσοι γὰρ, *for as many*) the Gentiles: and *as many,* the Jews. —ἀνόμως) This word occurs twice by antanaclasis,[1] in the sense, *not in the law, not by the law,* (οὐκ ἐν νόμῳ, οὐ διὰ νόμου) as is evident from the antithesis.—ἥμαρτον) *sinned*: the past tense, [past] in reference to the time of judgment [shall *then* be found to have sinned].—καὶ ἀπολοῦνται, *they shall also perish*) the word, *also,* denotes the correspondence between the mode of sinning, and the mode of perishing; he says, they shall also *perish;* for it was not convenient to say, in this instance, ἀνόμως, *they shall be judged*

---

[1] See Appendix.

without law, as he presently after says aptly, *they shall be judged by law.*—ἐν νόμῳ) [*in,* or] *with the law,* not, [as the heathen], ἀνόμως, *without law, i.e.* since they had the law.—διὰ νόμου, *by the law*) ch. iii. 20.

13. Οὐ γαρ, *for not*) A Proposition [Statement of Subject] clearly standing forth, the words of which have respect also to the Gentiles, but are particularly adapted to the Jews; concerning the former, ver. 14, etc. treats; concerning the latter, ver. 17, etc.; wherefore, also, ver. 16 depends on ver. 15, not on ver. 12. They have caused much confusion, who enclosed within a parenthesis the passage beginning at the 14th, nay, rather at the 13th verse, and ending with the 15.—οἱ ἀκροαταί, *hearers*), inactive, however sedulous [in hearing] they may be.—παρὰ τῷ Θεῷ, *before* [with] *God*) ver. 2.—ποιηταί, *doers*) namely, *if* men have shown themselves to be *doers,* ch. x. 5. They may *do* things *pertaining to the law,* but they cannot prove [warrant] themselves to be the *doers of the whole law.*—δικαιωθήσονται, *shall be justified*) This verb, in contradistinction to the noun δίκαιοι, which denotes *men actually righteous,* involves a condition, which is to be performed, and *then* [the condition being fulfilled] the declaration of their being righteous, as about to follow [as the consequence] in the day of the divine judgment.

14. Ὅταν, *when*) After Paul has finished the refutation of the perverse judgment of the Jews against the Gentiles, he next proceeds to show the true judgment of God against the latter. He treats here of the Gentiles more directly, for the purpose of convicting them; and yet, what is granted to them in passing, is granted with this end in view, that the Jew may be dealt with the more heavily; but ver. 26 treats of the Gentiles quite incidentally, in order to convict the Jew. Wherefore, ὅταν, *when,* is used here [ver. 14]; ἐὰν, *if,* there [ver. 26].—γὰρ *for*) He gives the reason, why the Gentiles should also be required to be the *doers of the law;* for when they do ever so little of it, they recognise their obligations to obey it. And yet he shows, that they cannot be justified by the law of nature, or by their ownselves. There are four sentences beginning with the words: *when—these—who—the conscience bearing witness along with.* The second is explained by the third, the first by the fourth.—ἔθνη) Not, τὰ ἔθνη; some individuals of the Gentiles; and yet there

is no man, who does not fulfil some of the requirements of the law (ἐκ τῶν τοῦ νόμου). He did not choose to say ἐθνικοί, which is usually taken rather in a bad sense.—μὴ νόμον· νόμον μὴ,—*not the law: the law not*) Not even here is the change in the arrangement of the words without a reason; in the former place, the *not* is the emphatic word, so that greater force may be given to the, *have not;* in the latter place, the word νόμον, *the law*, contains the emphasis, thus forming an antithesis to the ἑαυτοῖς, *unto themselves.* So also, νόμος, *law*, has sometimes the article, and sometimes not, and not without a good reason in each instance, ver. 13, 23, 27, iii. 19–21, vii. 1., etc.—φύσει, *by nature*) The construction is, μὴ νόμον ἔχοντα φύσει, *not having the law by nature.*[1] [But Engl. vers. joins *nature* with *do*, not with *having*] precisely as in ver. 27, ἡ ἐκ φύσεως ἀκροβυστία, *the uncircumcision by nature*, contrary to the Syriac version of ver. 27, which connects the word *nature* with *doing*, "*doing by nature the law.*" The Gentiles are *by nature* (that is, when left to themselves, as they are born, not as individuals, but as nations), destitute of the (written) law; the Jews are *by nature* Jews, Gal. ii. 15, and therefore have *by nature* the (written) law, ch. xi. 24, the end of the verse. Nor yet, however, is there any danger, that the force of the construction, which most follow, *do by nature those things, which are of* [contained in] *the law*, should be lost; for what the Gentiles, who have not the law, do, they in reality do by *nature*. The term *law*, in the writings of the apostle, does not occur in the philosophical, but in the Hebrew use; therefore, the phrase, *natural law*, is not found in sacred Scripture; ver. 12 shows, that the thing itself is true.—ποιῇ *do*), not only in actual performance, but also in their inmost thoughts, ver. 15, at the end.—οὗτοι, *these*) This little word turns the collective noun ἔθνη, *Gentiles*, to a distributive sense [so far *to wit* as *they really do it.*—V. g.]—νόμος, *a law*) What the law is to the Jews, that the Gentiles are to their ownselves.

15. Ἐνδείκνυνται, *they show*) [demonstrate] to themselves, to others, and, in some respects, to God Himself.—τὸ ἔργον τοῦ νόμου,

---

[1] It may be thought by this interpretation, *that* the clause *which precedes the words*, von Natur, in the German version *should be omitted to avoid the* ambiguity, *although, perhaps*, the Author *knowingly and willingly made use* of the ambiguous [equivocal] punctuation.—E. B.

the work of the law), the law itself, with its practical [active] operation. It is opposed to the letter, which is but an accident [not its essence].—γραπτὸν, *written*), a noun, not a participle, much less an infinitive [*to be written*]. Paul, by way of contrast, alludes to the tables of Moses. This *writing* is antecedent to the *doing* of those things, *which are contained in the law;* but afterwards, when any one has done, or (has not done) the things commanded, [*the demonstration, or*] *the showing* [of the work of the law] follows, and that permanent writing [viz., that on the heart] becomes more clearly apparent.—συμμαρτυρούσης, *simultaneously bearing witness*) An allegory; the prosecution, the criminal, the witnesses are in court; conscience is a witness; the thoughts accuse, or also defend. Nature, and sin itself, *bear witness:* conscience *bears witness along with them.*—αὐτῶν) *of themselves*, or *their own.*—τῆς συνειδήσεως, *the conscience*) The soul has none of its faculties less under its own control, than conscience. So συνείδησις and λογισμός are joined, Wisd. xvii. 11, 12.—μεταξὺ αλλήλων, *between one another*) as prosecutor and criminal. This expression is put at the beginning of the clause for the sake of emphasis, inasmuch as *thoughts* implicated in the trial *with thoughts*, are opposed to *conscience* referred *to the law.* —τῶν λογισμῶν κατηγορούντων, *their thoughts accusing*) Some explain [analyse] the words thus: *the thoughts, which accuse, testifying simultaneously* [taken from συμμαρτυρούσης] ; but *thoughts accusing* [τῶν λογισμῶν κατηγορούντων] is an expression, which stands by itself.—ἢ καὶ, *or even*) The concessive particle, *even*, shows that the thoughts have far more to accuse, than defend, and the defence itself (comp. 2 Cor. vii. 11, *defending* or *clearing of yourselves*) does not extend to the whole, but only to a part of the conduct, and this very part in turn proves us to be debtors as to the whole, i. 20.—ἀπολογουμένων, [excusing] *defending*). We have an example at Gen. xx. 4.

16. Ἐν ἡμέρᾳ, *in the day*) It is construed with *show*, for the present tense is no objection; ver. 5 employs the present in the same general way. And Paul often says, *in the day of the Lord*, which implies more than *against* [or *unto the day*] 1 Cor. v. 5— comp. *before*, or *in the presence of* 1 Tim. v. 21, note. Such as each thing *was*, such it shall then be seen, be determined, and remain. In that day, that writing of the law on the hearts of

men will be manifest, having also joined with it some defence of upright acts, although the man be condemned [fall] in the *judgment*, himself being his own accuser, on account of other offences. And that circumstance implies, as a consequence, [infers] (reasoning, from the greater to the less, *i.e.*, from the final judgment, to the judgments of conscience in the present life); accusation, or even defence, exercised in this life also, as often as either the future judgment itself is vividly presented before a man, or its anticipations, without the man's own privity (consciousness), are at work in the conscience.—Comp. 1 John iv. 17. And Scripture often speaks so of the future, especially of the last things, as that it presupposes those which precede them. The Jews at ver. 5, as the Gentiles in this passage, are threatened with the future judgment.—τὰ κρυπτὰ, *the secrets*) *the conscience*, and *the thoughts*.—Comp. 1 Cor. iv. 5. This confirms the connection of this verse with the preceding. The true quality of actions, generally unknown even to the agents themselves, depends on the secrets.—See ver. 29. Men judge by outward manifestations, even concerning themselves. Outward manifestations of good or evil will also be judged, but not then for the first time; for they are judged, even from the time in which they are wrought; deeds, that are secret, are then at length brought to judgment.—τῶν ἀνθρώπων, of *men*) even of the Gentiles.—κατὰ, *according to*) *i.e.* as my Gospel teaches. Paul adds this short clause, because he is here dealing with a man, who does not yet know Jesus Christ. The Gospel is the whole preaching as to Christ; and Christ will be the Judge; and the judgment in regard to the Gentiles, is not so expressly declared in the Old, as in the New Testament. And it is called the Gospel of Paul, as it was preached by Paul, even to the Gentiles.—Acts xvii. 31. All the articles of evangelical doctrine, and the article concerning the final judgment, greatly illustrate one another; and moreover, this very article, even in respect of believers, is altogether evangelical.—Acts x. 42; 1 Pet. iv. 5.

17. Εἰ δὲ, *but if*) *If*—comp. *when*, ver. 14—has some resemblance to an Anaphora,[1] with the exception that ὅταν, *when*, having reference to the Gentiles, asserts more; εἰ, *if*, used with

---

[1] See Appendix.

respect to the Jews, concedes less. After *if*, οὖν, *therefore* [ver. 21], follows, like ἀλλά, but, (ch. vi. 5)[1] and δέ, *truly* Acts xi. 17.[2]— Comp. Matt. xxv. 27. Moreover, the οὖν, *therefore*, in a subsequent verse (ver. 21), brings to a conclusion the somewhat long protasis, which begins with εἰ, *if*.—Ἰουδαῖος, *a Jew*) This, the highest point of Jewish boasting (a farther description of it being interposed at ver. 17–20, and its refutation being added, ver. 21–24), is itself refuted at the 25th and following verses. Moreover, the description of his boasting consists of twice five clauses, of which the first five, from *thou restest* (ver. 17), to, *out of the law* (ver. 18), show what the Jew assumes to himself; the rest, as many in number as the former, *thou art confident* (ver. 19), to, *in the law* (ver. 20), show, what more the Jew, from this circumstance, arrogates to himself, in reference to others. On both sides [in both series], the first clause of one corresponds to the first of the other, the second to the second, and so on in succession; and as the fifth clause in the former series, *instructed*, ver. 18, so the fifth in the latter, *having*, ver. 20 [the form of knowledge] denotes a cause : *because thou art instructed*, [answering to] *because thou hast*.—ἐπονομάζῃ) in the middle voice : *thou callest thyself by this name, and delightest to be so called*.—ἐπαναπαύῃ) *thou restest* in that, which threatens to put thee in a strait; thou hast in the law a schoolmaster, instead of a father [as you fancy the law to be].—Τῷ νόμῳ, *in the law*) Paul purposely [knowingly] makes frequent use of this name.—ἐν Θεῷ, *in God*), as though He were One, who is peculiarly thy God.

18. Τὸ θέλημα) *the will*, that is, whatever has been ratified by the law; so, *the will*, absolutely, Matt. xviii. 14 ; 1 Cor. xvi. 12. But this *will* is nothing else, than the will of God; but a strong feeling of piety [εὐλάβεια, pious caution] prevented Paul from adding, *of God*.—δοκιμάζεις) *provest*, approvest.

19. Ἐν σκότει, *in the darkness* of congenital ignorance [ignorance, accompanying the heathen from birth].

20. μόρφωσιν) The word is taken here in a good sense, in reference to the Jew, who is boasting : the *form*, or *correct out-*

---

[1] ABCΛ read ἀλλά there. G*fg* Vulg. read ἅμα, simul.
[2] EG*e* Rec. Text, Theb. Vers. read δέ, *who truly was I*, etc. ABC*d* Vulg. omit δέ.—ED.

line.—τῆς γνώσεως καὶ τῆς ἀληθείας, *of knowledge and of the truth*) a Hendiadys; *the truth* in this passage expresses accuracy in established doctrine, in our days called *orthodoxy.*

21. Οὐ διδάσκεις, *dost thou not teach*) a Metonymy for the consequent (that is, substituting the antecedent for the consequent), he, who doth not practise, doth not teach his own self.—κηρύσσων, *preaching*) loudly, clearly.

21, 22. Κλέπτεις, μοιχεύεις, ἱεροσυλεῖς, *dost thou commit theft, adultery, sacrilege?*) Thou sinnest most heinously against thy neighbour, against thyself, and against God. Paul had shown to the Gentiles, that their sins were first against God, secondly against themselves, and thirdly against others; he now inverts the order; for sins against God are very openly practised among the Gentiles; not so, in the case of the Jew.—ὁ βδελυσσόμενος, *thou that abhorrest*) even in speaking.—τὰ εἴδωλα, *idols*) The Jews, from the Babylonish captivity even to the present day, abhor idolatry, to which they had been formerly addicted: nevertheless they even put Christ to death, and [still] oppose tʰ· Gospel and the glory of God.—ἱεροσυλεῖς, *dost thou commit sacrilege?*) because thou dost not give God the glory, which peculiarly belongs to God.

24. Τὸ γὰρ ὄνομα) Is. lii. 5, in the LXX., δι' ὑμᾶς διὰ παντὸς τὸ ὄνομά μου βλασφημεῖται ἐν τοῖς ἔθνεσι, *through you My name is continually blasphemed among the Gentiles.*—Comp. Ezek. xxxvi. 20, etc.—καθὼς γέγραπται, *as it is written*) This short clause is fittingly placed at the end, as it refers to a thing evident of itself, but it is set down for the sake of the Jews, ch. iii. 19.

25. Ὠφελεῖ, *profiteth*) He does not say *justifieth*; the *profit* is described chap. iii. and iv. Circumcision was still practised among the (believing) Jews.—ἐὰν, *if*) Paul not only speaks, using the *ad hominem* argument [argument on his adversary's own principles to confute him], but also speaks according to his own sentiments, and shows, that they are deceiving themselves, who are trusting to circumcision, though they have violated the law.—παραβάτης, a *transgressor*) A word abhorred by a Jew, ver. 27.

26. Ἡ ἀκροβυστία, *uncircumcision*) that is, a person uncircumcised, for to this the αὐτοῦ, *his,* is referred.—λογισθήσεται) The future; *shall be counted*, by a righteous judgment. In ver. 25, γέγονεν, the preterite, implies, *is now made.*

27. Κρινεῖ, *shall judge*) Those, whom thou now judgest, will in their turn judge thee at the day of judgment, ver. 16. Matt. xii. 41; 1 Cor. vi. 2, 3.—τελοῦσα, *keeping* (if it fulfil): a word of large meaning. Therefore ἐὰν, *if*, ver. 26, has a conditional meaning, and does not positively assert.—σὲ, *thee*), who art its judge [the self-constituted judge of the uncircumcised].—τὸν) the article does not properly belong to παραβάτην, but τὸν διὰ is used as ἡ ἐκ.—διὰ [*by,* or] *with*) Thou hast the letter, but thou even abusest it; there is an antithesis between *by nature*, and *with the letter;* then follows a Hendiadys, *by the letter and circumcision*. Concerning the letter and spirit, see ch. vii. 6.

28. Ὁ ἐν), a periphrasis for the adjective.—ἐν σαρκί, *in the flesh*) opposed to [that] *of the heart*, ver. 29.

29. Οὗ, *whose*), who seeks praise and has it, not from men, etc.—ἔπαινος, *praise*) The allusion is to the name *Jew* [*Judah*], יְהוּדָה, *they shall praise thee*, Gen. xlix. 8. He therefore adds, οὗ, not ἧς [περιτομῆς]. This is the solution: *The Jew who is one inwardly, he is the Jew, who has praise;* as much as to say, this is true *Judaism*. It is opposed to the *judging* [ver. 3].—οὐκ ἐξ ἀνθρώπων, *not of men*), who, when they praise themselves, *boast*, ver. 17.—Θεοῦ, *of God*), who sees the *heart*.

CHAPTER III.

1. Τί, *what*). Paul's usual form of bringing in an objection. —οὖν) *then*. Since circumcision is unprofitable without observing the law, and since being a Jew outwardly is of no avail, what advantage does the latter possess, and of what profit is the former? It therefore must follow, that the Jews have no peculiar privileges whatever. Paul denies this conclusion. There are innumerable exceptions taken against the doctrine set forth in this epistle, by the perverseness of the Jews, and of mankind at large; but Paul sweeps them all away.—τὸ περισσὸν, *peculiar advantage*), יְתֵר, over [as compared with] the Gentiles. This

point is taken up at ver. 2.—ὠφέλεια τῆς περιτομῆς, the *profit of circumcision*) See on this subject ch. ii. 25.

2. Πολύ, *much*) In the neuter gender; supply περισσόν. It rather refers to the concrete, concerning the Jew, than to the abstract, concerning circumcision, ver. 1; this will be treated of at ch. iv. 1, 9, etc. So, ch. ii. 29, οὗ, viz. Ἰουδαίου, *the Jew* [instead of ἧς, though περιτομή had preceded].—πρῶτον) *i.e. first*, and therefore chiefly; the word signifying *in the next place*, does not always follow [after πρῶτον]. One privilege of the Jews, admirably adapted to Paul's object, is set forth in this passage (the others will follow, ch. ix. 4, 5); and by this very one, he is about, by and by, after he has ended this prefatory address of conciliation, so much the more to convict them.[1]—ἐπιστεύθησαν, *they were intrusted with*) He, to whom a treasure is intrusted, may manage it either faithfully and skilfully, or otherwise; and the Jews treated the Old Testament Scriptures in very different ways. But Paul says, that the *oracles* of God were intrusted to the Jews in such a manner [under this condition], that the *good about to come*, ver. 8, which they [the oracles] described, would belong to the Jews, if they would receive it by faith;—ideas extremely suggestive: God is true, faithful, intrusting His revelation to men, righteous; man is mendacious, perfidious, distrustful, unrighteous.—λόγια), a diminutive. The Divine answers were often brief, as in the Urim and Thummim: λόγιον is also [God's] *saying* [ver. 4], concerning circumcision, and the other privileges of the Israelites.

3. Τί γὰρ, *for what?*), viz. *shall we say*, ver. 5, where likewise μὴ, interrogative, follows; so, τί γάρ, LXX., Job xxi. 4.—εἰ, *if*) Thus might the Gentile rival easily object.—ἠπίστησαν) The words derived from a common root are, ἐπιστεύθησαν, ἠπίστησαν, ἀπιστία, πίστιν.—τινὲς, *some*) [for *many*, *most* of the Jews], a form of expression to avoid what is disagreeable [euphemy]. Moreover, unbelievers, though numerous, are considered as *some* indefinitely, because they do not very much come under enumeration, ch. xi. 17; 1 Cor. x. 7; 1 Tim. iv. 1.—πίστιν), the *faithfulness*, by which promises will be performed, and *good will come* [ver. 8]. This *faithfulness* remains, though all men should be *unfaithful*

---

[1] On the προθεραπεία, *i.e.*, precautionary address to disarm prejudices, when about to speak unwelcome truths. See Appendix.—ED.

[*unbelieving*]; it remains, chiefly in respect of *believers*. They who deny universal grace, have but little [*perception* or] knowledge of *the faithfulness* of God in respect to *unbelievers*. With respect even to the reprobate, the antecedent will of God ought, indeed, to be held as of great account; for what they have not, they, nevertheless, might have had; and this very circumstance confers upon them an altogether great privilege; and even though they do not perceive it to be so [or *uphold* it], still this *peculiar advantage* [ver. 1, τὸ περισσόν] remains, that the glory of God, and the glory of the *faithfulness* of God, are illustrated in them. Comp. the expression, *hath abounded*, ver. 7. This, the *peculiar advantage*, is not to be held as of no account. The apostle, when he would vindicate our faith, with great propriety praises the faithfulness of God. Comp. 2 Tim. ii. 13.—καταργήσει; *shall it make of no effect?*) The future, employed with great force in a negative address. The faithfulness of God is unchangeable.

4. Μὴ γένοιτο) Paul alone uses this form of expression, and only in his epistles to the Romans and the Galatians.—γινέσθω, *let him be made*) in judgment.—ὁ Θεὸς ἀληθής, *God true*) See Ps. cxvi. 12, where God's most faithful retribution is set in opposition to man's perfidy. This fact, and the term *lying*, are referred to again, in verse 7.—πᾶς ἄνθρωπος, *every man*), not even excepting David. Ps. cxvi. 11, the LXX. have πᾶς ἄνθρωπος ψεύστης, *every man a liar*. Hence David, 1 Sam. xxiv. 9, speaks of *man's words*, that is, falsehood.—ὅπως—κρίνεσθαί σε) So the LXX., Ps. li. 6 [4]. Those things are also [besides their application at David's time] prophetical, which David prayed in the agony [conflict] of his repentance.—ἄν), *if* only it [God's faithfulness] were to be had recourse to, and if man would dare to put it to the test.—δικαιωθῇς—νικήσῃς, *thou mayest be justified—mayest overcome*), in the name of faithfulness and truth. The human judge judges so, as that the offence of the guilty is the only consideration weighed [regarded] by him, nor is he otherwise concerned as regards [vindicating] his own righteousness; but God exercises judgment so, as that the unrighteousness of men is not more demonstrated thereby, than His own *righteousness:* νικᾶν is generally said of a *victory* after the hazard of war, or of a lawsuit for money, or of a contest in the public games.

In this passage, it is said of a judicial victory, which cannot but come to God [*i.e.* God is sure to be the victor].—ἐν τοῖς λόγοις σου) Hebr. בדברך, in which one passage דבר occurs in Kal, without the participle, that is, *when thou beginnest to speak*, and judicially to answer man, who accuses thee, or to proceed against him. [*In a general way, indeed, men acknowledge that* GOD *is just, but when the question refers to special cases, then they are wont* [*they love*] *to defend their own cause,* V. g.]—ἐν τῷ κρίνεσθαί σε) Hebr. בשפטך God at once both Κρίνει and Κρίνεται. Κρίνεται [*implead in judgment*] has the meaning of the middle voice, such as verbs of *contending* usually have: κρίνοντας applies to those who dispute in a court of law. LXX., Is. xliii. 26 ; Judg. iv. 5 ; Jer. xxv. 31. An instance in illustration is to be found in Micah vi. 2, etc.; also in 1 Sam. xii. 7. It is inexpressible loving-kindness in God to come down [condescend to stoop] to man for the purpose of pleading with him.

5. Εἰ δὲ, *but if*) This new argument, urged through a Jewish person, is elicited from the verb *thou mayest be justified*, in the preceding verse.—ἡ ἀδικία, *unrighteousness*) of which a man is guilty through *unbelief*.—τί ἐροῦμεν, *what shall we say*) Paul shows that this, their *peculiar advantage* [ver. i.], does not prevent the Jews from being under sin.—ὁ ἐπιφέρων) *the inflicter* of wrath [taketh vengeance] upon the *unbelieving* Jews. The article has a particular force. The allusion is to Ps. vii. 11, ὁ Θεὸς κριτὴς δίκαιος, καὶ μὴ (אל for אַל; the LXX. from the similarity of letters, mistaking God for *not*], ἐπάγων ὀργὴν καθ᾿ ἑκάστην ἡμέραν : *God is a just judge*, and (*not* being substituted for *God*) a God *inflicting wrath.*—κατὰ ἄνθρωπον, *as a man*) Man, according to the principles of human nature, might reason thus: My wickedness is subservient to the Divine glory, and makes it the more conspicuous, as darkness doth the light; therefore, I should not be punished.

6. Ἐπεί, *otherwise*) The consequence is drawn [bound, connected] from the less to the greater, as it ought to be in the case of *negatives*. If God were to act unrighteously, in taking vengeance on the Jew who acts unrighteously, a thing too absurd to be mentioned, He certainly could not judge the whole world. *Affirmatively*, the process of reasoning would take this form: He who (justly) judges the whole world, will doubtless also judge

justly in this one particular case. [Vice versa] The conclusion is, in its turn, drawn from the greater to the less at 1 Cor. vi. 2.—*τὸν κόσμον, the world*) For even the *unrighteousness* of the whole world (which is put in opposition to the Jews, at ch. xi. 12), *commends the righteousness of God;* and yet God pronounces, and with justice, the whole world to be unrighteous, Gen. xviii. 25. Nay, in the very judgment, the unrighteousness of man will greatly illustrate the righteousness of God. The Jew acknowledges the righteousness of the Divine judgment regarding the world; but Paul shows that there is the same ground for judgment regarding the unbelieving Jews.

7. Εἰ γὰρ, *for if*) An Ætiologia[1] [a sentiment, with the grounds on which it rests subjoined] set forth in the form of a dialogue, for the purpose of strengthening the objection which was introduced at the beginning of ver. 5. ψεύσματι, *through my lie*) The things which God says are true, and he who does not believe these, makes God a liar, being in reality himself the liar.—τί) that is, *why* do I even still excuse myself, as if I had some reason to fear? Comp. τί ἔτι, ch. ix. 19; Gal. v. 11.—κἀγὼ) *I also*, to whom the truth of God has been revealed; not merely the heathen.—κρίνομαι) corresponds to κρίνεσθαι, ver. 4, 6, lxx.; Job xxxix. 35 (xl. 4) τί ἔτι ἐγὼ κρίνομαι;

8. Καὶ μὴ, *and not*) supply, *act so, as* [and why should I not act so, as, etc.]; but a change of number or person is introduced, such as in ch. iv. 17.—καθὼς, *as*) Some were in the habit of calumniating Paul; others were of this way of thinking, and said that their opinions were approved by Paul.—φασί τινες, *some say*) who make our support the pretext to cover over [justify] their own perverseness. This epistle was principally written for the purpose of Paul's confuting such as these.—ἡμᾶς, *that we*) who maintain the righteousness of God.—ὅτι) This depends strictly [absolutely] on λέγειν.—ποιήσωμεν, *let us do*) without fear. τὰ κακὰ, *evil*) sins.—ἔλθῃ, τὰ ἀγαθὰ, *good may come*) The same phrase occurs with the lxx. int. Jer. xvii. 6. Those calumniators mean to say this: Good is at hand, ready to come; but evil should prepare the way for it.—τὰ ἀγαθὰ, *good*) the glory of God.—ὧν, *of whom*) that is of those who do evil, or even say

---

[1] See Appendix.

that we ought to do evil, in order that good may come.—τὸ κρίμα) *the judgment*, which these unprincipled men endeavour to escape by a subterfuge, as *unjust* [unrighteous], will peculiarly [in an especial degree] overtake them—ἔνδικον, *just*) Thus Paul removes to as great a distance as possible that conclusion, and abruptly repels such disputers.

9. Τί οὖν; *what then?*) He resumes the question with which he began at ver. 1.—προεχόμεθα;) *have we* any advantage *as compared with* the Gentiles?—οὐ πάντως [1]) the Jew would say πάντως: but Paul contradicts him. In the beginning of this passage, he speaks gently (for, in other places, where μηδαμῶς is used, οὐ πάντως cannot be substituted for it; and in this passage the expression, *by no means* [μηδαμῶς, had it been used], would take away the concession which he made to them at ver. 2); but he afterwards speaks with greater severity.—προῃτιασάμεθα) *we have proved, before* that I had mentioned the peculiar privilege of the Jews. Paul deals, in Chapters i. and ii., as a stern Administrator [Procurator] of divine justice; but yet he was unwilling to use the singular number. By the plural number, he expresses the assent of his believing readers: πάντας, *all* the Jews [as well as] *all* the Greeks.—ὑφ ἁμαρτίαν) ὑπό denotes subjection, as if *under* the tyranny of *sin*.

10. Καθὼς, *as*) That all men are under sin, is very clearly proved from the vices which always, and everywhere, have been prevalent [have stalked abroad] among mankind; just as, also, the internal holiness of Christ is displayed in [pourtrayed by means of] the innocency of His words and actions. Paul therefore quotes, with propriety, David and Isaiah, although it is concerning the people of their own times that they complain, and that accompanied with an exception in favour of the godly [some of whom are always to be found], Ps. xiv. 4, etc. For that complaint describes men such as God looking down from heaven finds them to be, not such as He makes them by His grace.

10. Ὅτι οὐκ ἔστι δίκαιος οὐδὲ εἷς κτλ.) Ps. xiv. 2, etc. The LXX., οὐκ ἔστι ποιῶν χρηστότητα, οὐκ ἔστιν ἕως ἑνός.—εἰ ἔστι συνιῶν ἢ ἐκζητῶν τὸν Θεόν.—ἑνός, The general phrase is, *there is none*

---

[1] Beng. seems to translate "not altogether;" quite different from "in no wise."—ED.

righteous; the parts follow: the dispositions and pursuits, ver. 11, 12; the conversation, ver. 13, 14; the actions, ver. 15, 16, 17; the general demeanour, (gestus et nutus), ver. 18.—δίκαιος, *righteous*) a suitable word in a discourse on *righteousness*.—οὐδὲ εἷς, *not even one*) who can except any one here? ver. 23, not so much as one *under heaven*. The exception, even of one, or at least of a few, might procure [conciliate] favour to all; as it is, wrath is on that account the greater.

11. οὐκ ἔστιν ὁ συνιῶν, *there is none that understandeth*) They are without understanding in relation to what is good.—οὐκ ἔστιν ὁ ἐκζητῶν, *there is none that seeketh after*) They are without the will to do good. To *seek after*, implies that God is מסתתר *hidden*, Is. xlv. 15.

12. Ἐξέκλιναν, *they have turned aside*) they have gone out of the way. Declension supposes, that all had formerly been in the right path.—ἅμα, *together*) at the same time.—ἠχρειώθησαν. *They have become unprofitable*) They have not the power of returning to do good. And on the contrary, in all these particulars they cling to what is evil, either secretly, or even openly. They have become *unfit for any useful purpose* (ἀχρεῖοι). The conjugate word χρηστότης presently after follows.

13. Τάφος—ἰὸς—αὐτῶν) so the LXX., Ps. v. 10, cxl. 4.—ἀνεῳγμένος) a *sepulchre* lately *opened*, and therefore very fetid.—ὁ λάρυγξ, *their throat*) Observe the course of the conversation, as it flows from the heart, by the avenue of *their throat, their tongues, and their lips*—the whole is comprised in the *mouth*; a great part of sin consists in words.—ὑπὸ τὰ χείλη) *under their lips;* for *on* their lips is the sweetness of honey.

14. ὧν τὸ στόμα ἀρᾶς καὶ πικρίας γέμει) Ps. x. 7, LXX., οὗ ἀρᾶς τὸ στόμα αὐτοῦ γέμει καὶ πικρίας καὶ δόλου.—τὸ στόμα, *the mouth*) In this and the following verse violence is described, as, in ver. 13, deceit.—ἀρᾶς, *cursing*) directed against God.—πικρίας, *bitterness*) against their neighbour.

15–18. Ὀξεῖς—οὐκ ἔγνωσαν) Is. lix. 7, 8, LXX., οἱ δὲ πόδες αὐτῶν—ταχινοὶ ἐκχέαι αἷμα—σύντριμμα οὐκ οἴδασι. So of the feet, Prov. i. 16.

16. Σύντριμμα καὶ ταλαιπωρία), שבר ושר, *wasting* and *destruction*.

17. Οὐκ ἔγνωσαν, *they have not known*) they neither know, nor wish to know.

18. Οὐκ αὐτῶν) so the LXX., Ps. xxxvi. 2, οὐκ—αὐτοῦς—φόβος, *fear*), not to say *love*, of which man in his natural state knows much less. Of several passages, in which human depravity is expressed, either in the complaint of God and of the saints, or else in the confessions of the penitent, Paul has written out a part of the words, and intimates that all the *rest* are to be sought for out of the same places.—ὀφθαλμῶν, *their eyes*) The seat of reverential awe is in the eyes.

19. Ὅσα) *whatsoever*. He has just now accumulated many testimonies from the law.—νόμος, *the law*) Therefore the testimony, ver. 10, etc., brought forward from the Psalms, arraigns [strikes] the Jews; nor ought they to think, that the accusations therein contained are against the Gentiles. Paul has brought no declaration of Scripture against the Gentiles, but has dealt with them by arguments drawn from the light of nature.— νόμος—νόμῳ) An instance of Διότης,[1] [impressive vehemence in words]—ἵνα, *that*) He presses this home to the Jews.— στόμα) *mouth*, bitter, ver. 14, and yet given to boasting, ver. 27. The Jews are chiefly intended here, as the Gentiles by the term *world*.—γένηται, *may be made*) [become] The world is always *guilty*, but *it is made* guilty, when the law accuses and condemns it.—πᾶς, *all*) not even excepting the Jews. *The guilt of the Gentiles*, as being manifest, is presupposed; *the Jews* are prosecuted to condemnation by arguments out of *the law*. These are guilty; and their condemnation completes the condemnation of the whole *world* as guilty.

20. Διότι) *for this reason*, *because*) [Beng. connects this verse with ver. 19. But Eng. vers. '*therefore*').—νόμου, *of the law*) indefinitely put, but chiefly referring to the moral law, ver. xix. 9, ch. ii. 21-26; which [the moral law] alone is not *made void*; ver. 31; for it was the works of it that Abraham was possessed of before he received circumcision. Paul, in affirming that we are not justified by the works of the law, as opposed to faith, not to any particular law, means the whole law, of which the parts, rather than the species, were the ceremonial and the moral; and of these the former, as being even then abrogated, was not so much taken into account; the latter does not bind

---

[1] See Appendix.

us [is not obligatory] on the same principle [grounds] as it was [when] given by Moses. In the New Testament we have absolutely no works of the law without [independently of] grace; for the law confers no strength. It is not without good reason, that Paul, when he mentions *works*, so often adds, *of the law;* for it was on these that his opponents were relying: and were ignorant of those better works, which flow as results from faith and justification.—οὐ δικαιωθήσεται, *shall not be justified*) on the signification of this word, see Luke vii. 35. In the writings of Paul at least, the judicial meaning is quite manifest, ver. 19, 24, etc., ch. iv. 5, taken in connection with the context. Concerning the future tense, comp. v. 30, note.—πᾶσα σὰρξ, *all flesh*) synonymous with the *world*, ver. 19, but with the accompanying notion implied of the cause: the world with its righteousness is flesh; therefore it is not justified [by works flowing] out of itself.—ἐνώπιον αὐτοῦ, *in His sight*) ch. iv. 2, ii. 29.—νόμου, *law*) which was given for that very purpose.—ἐπι, νωσις), *the knowledge* of sins does not justify by itself, but it feels and confesses the want of righteousness.—ἀμαρτίας, *of sin*) *Sin* and *righteousness* are directly and commensurately opposed to each other [adequate; so that one on its side is exactly commensurate with the other on its side]; but *sin* implies both guilt and depravity; therefore *righteousness* denotes the reverse of both. *Righteousness* is more abundant, ch. v. 15, 17. Apol. A. C. says well, *Good works in the saints are the fruits of* [appertain to] *righteousness, and are pleasing on account of faith; on this account they are the fulfilling of the law.* Hence δικαιοῦν is to make a man righteous, or in other words, to justify; a notion quite in accordance with the form of the verb in οω: nor is there any difficulty in the derivative verb, but in δίκαιος. He then, who is justified, is brought over [translated] from sin to righteousness, that is, from guilt or criminality to a state of innocence, and from depravity and corruption to spiritual health. Nor is there a homonymy,[1] or twofold idea, [when by analogy things different by nature are expressed by one word], but a signification at once simple, and pregnant in the terms *sin* and *righteousness*, the same as also everywhere prevails in the term ἄφεσις, *forgiveness*,

---

[1] See Appendix.

[remission], and in the words, by which it is implied, ἁγιάζω, to sanctify, ἀπολούω, to wash away, καθαρίζω, to purify, etc., 1 Cor. vi. 11, notes; Ps. ciii. 3; Mic. vii. 18, etc. And this pregnant [suggestive] signification itself of the verb *to justify*, implying the whole of the divine benefit, by which we are brought from sin to righteousness, occurs also, for example, in Tit. iii. 7; with which comp. 2 Cor. v. 21; Rom. viii. 4; with which comp. ch. v. 16. But elsewhere, according as the subject under discussion demands, it is restricted to some particular part, and especially to deliverance from sin, so far as guilt is regarded in it: and Paul always uses it so, when, according to his design, he is treating of God justifying the sinner by faith.

21. Νυνί) *now* [as it is] forms the antithesis, including the idea of time, ver. 26.—χωρὶς νόμου—ὑπὸ τοῦ νόμου καὶ τῶν προφητῶν, *without the law—by the law and the prophets*) A sweet antithesis. *The law* is taken both in a limited and extended sense [*David, for instance, must be reckoned among the prophets*, ch. iv. 6.— V. g.].—πεφανέρωται, *has been manifested*) by the Gospel of Jesus Christ.—μαρτυρουμένη, *being witnessed by, having the testimony of*) according to [by] promise.

22. Δὲ [*even*] *but*) An explanation is here given of the righteousness of God, ver. 21.—διὰ πίστεως Ἰησοῦ Χριστοῦ, *by faith of Jesus Christ*) *by faith* in Jesus.—See Gal. ii. 16, notes.—εἰς, *unto*) To. be connected with the *righteousness*, ver. 21.—εἰς πάντας, *unto all*) the Jews, who are, as it were, a peculiar vessel. —ἐπὶ πάντας, *upon all*) the Gentiles, who are as a soil which receives an exceedingly abundant rain of grace, comp. ver. 30. —οὐ γάρ ἐστι διαστολή, *for there is no difference*) Jews and Gentiles are both accused and justified in the same way. The same phrase occurs in ch. x. 12.

23. Ἥμαρτον, *have sinned*) that is, they have contracted the guilt of sin. Both the original act of sin in paradise is denoted, and the sinful disposition, as also the acts of transgression flowing from it. The past tenses often have an inchoative meaning along with the idea of continued action; such as ἐπίστευσα, ἤλπικα, ἠγάπηκα, ὑπήκουσα, ἕστηκα, *I have believed, and still continue to believe; I have hoped, and still continue to hope; I have loved, and still continue to love; I have obeyed, and still continue to obey; I have established myself, and still establish myself.*—καὶ ὑστεροῦνται,

and come short) From the past tense, *have sinned*, flows this present, *come short*, and by this word the whole *peculiar advantage* [ver. 1] of the Jews, and all the boasting of all flesh, are taken away; the former is a thing done [past], and the latter is a thing now established; each of them [ἥμαρτον and ὑστεροῦνται] denotes deficiency; *they do not attain*, ch. ix. 31.—τῆς δόξης τοῦ Θεοῦ, *of the glory of God*) The glory of the living God Himself is signified, which bestows *life*, ch. vi. 4; and to this, access was open to man if he had not sinned; but, as a sinner, he fell short of this end of his being; nor does he now attain to it, nor is he able, by any means, to endure that glory which would have [but for sin] shone forth in him, Heb. xii. 20, etc.; Ps. lxviii. 2. Hence he has become subject to *death;* for glory and immortality are synonymous terms, and so, also, are death and corruption; but Paul does not more expressly mention *death* itself, until after the process of justification, and its going forth even to [its issue in] *life*, have been consummated; he then looks at *death* as it were from behind, ch. v. 12. Therefore, the whole state of sin is most exquisitely pourtrayed thus, in this masterly passage: *They come short of*, or *are far from the glory of God;* that is, they have missed [aberrarunt a: *erred from*] the chief end of man; and in this very fact is implied [included], at the same time, every lesser aberration. But those who are justified recover the hope of that glory, along with most immediately realized glorying [viz., in Christ] in the meanwhile (of which [*i.e.* of *boasting*] in themselves, they had been deprived, ver. 27), and [recover] the kingdom in *life*. See, by all means, ch. v. 2, 11, 17, viii. 30, at the end of the verse. Wherefore, the antithetic idea to *they have sinned*, is explained at ver. 24, and the following verses; and ch. iv. throughout, on justification; the antithetic idea to *they have come short*, is set forth in ch. v., with which, comp. ch. viii. 17, and the following verses.

24. Δικαιούμενοι, *Those who are justified*) Suddenly, a more pleasant scene is thus spread before us.—τῇ αὐτοῦ χάριτι) *by His own grace*, not inherent in us, but as it were inclining of its own accord towards us; which is evident from the conjugate verbs χαρίζομαι and χαριτόω. Melancthon, instead of *grace*, often uses the expression *favour* and *mercy*. *His own* is emphatic. Comp. the following verse.—ἀπολυτρώσεως)—ἀπολύτρωσις,

redemption from sin and misery. *Atonement* [expiation] or *propitiation* (ἱλασμὸς) and ἀπολύτρωσις, *redemption*, are fundamentally one single benefit and no more, namely, *the restoration of the lost sinner*. This is an exceedingly commensurate and pure idea, and adequately corresponds to the name JESUS. *Redemption* has regard to *enemies* (and on this point the positive theology of *Koenig* distinctly treats in the passage where he discusses *Redemption*), and *reconciliation* refers to *God*; and here, again, there is a difference between the words ἱλασμὸς and καταλλαγή. Ἱλασμὸς, *propitiation* takes away the offence against *God*: καταλλαγή may be viewed from two sides; it removes (α) *God's* indignation against *us*, 2 Cor. v. 19; (β) *and our* alienation from *God*, 2 Cor. v. 20.—ἐν Χριστῷ Ἰησοῦ, *in Christ Jesus*) It is not without good reason that the name *Christ* is sometimes put before *Jesus*. According to the Old Testament [From Old Testament point of view], progress is made from the knowledge of Christ to the knowledge of Jesus; in the experience of present faith [From the New Testament point of view, the progress is] from the knowledge of Jesus to the knowledge of Christ. Comp. 1 Tim. i. 15, notes.

25. Προέθετο) *hath set forth before* the eyes of all. Luke ii. 31. The πρὸ in προέθετο does not carry with it the idea of time, but is much the same as the Latin *proponere*, to *set forth.*—ἱλαστήριον, *a propitiatory* [Eng. vers. not so strictly, "*propitiation*"]) The allusion is to the *mercy-seat* [propitiatory] of the Old Testament, Heb. ix. 5; and it is by this Greek term that the LXX generally express the Hebrew כפרת, Ex. xxv. 17–22. Propitiation goes on the supposition of a previous offence, which opposes the opinion of the Socinians.—ἐν τῷ αὐτοῦ αἵματι, *in His own blood*) This blood is truly propitiatory. Comp. Lev. xvi. 2, 13, etc.— εἰς ἔνδειξιν τῆς δικαιοσύνης αὐτοῦ, *to the declaration of* [for the demonstration of] *His righteousness*) This is repeated in the following verse, as if it were after a parenthesis, for the purpose of continuing the train of thought; only that instead of εἰς, Latin *in*, there is used in the following verse πρὸς, *ad*, which implies a something more immediate,[1] ch. xv. 2. Eph. iv. 12.—ἔνδειξιν

---

[1] εἰς, *towards, with a view to*; πρός, *for, with the effect of.*—ED.

[demonstration], *declaration*) Comp. notes at ch. i. 17.—διὰ τὴν πάρεσιν, *for* [Engl. Vers.] *the pretermission* [*passing by*]) Paul, in the Acts, and epistles to Ephesians, Colossians, and Hebrews, along with the other apostles, often uses ἄφεσιν, *remission:* None but he alone, and in this single passage, uses πάρεσιν, *pretermission;* and certainly not without some good reason. There was *remission* even before the advent and death of Christ, ch. iv. 7, 3; Matt. ix. 2, in so far as it implies the application of grace to individuals; but pretermission in the Old Testament had respect to transgressions, until (ἀπολύτρωσις) *redemption* of [or *from*] them was accomplished in the death of Christ, Heb. ix. 15; which *redemption,* ἀπολύτρωσις, itself is, however, sometimes also called ἄφεσις, Eph. i. 7. Παριέναι is nearly of the same import as ὑπεριδεῖν, Acts xvii. 30. Hence, in Sir. xxiii. 3 (2) μὴ φείδεσθαι and μὴ παριέναι are parallel; for both imply the *punishment of sin.* Ed. Hoeschel, p. 65, 376. πάρεσις, pretermission [*the passing over* or *by* sins] is not an imperfect ἄφεσις, *remission;* but the distinction is of quite a different sort; *abolition* or *entire putting away* is opposed to the former (as to this *abolition,* ἀθέτησις, see Heb. ix. 26), *retaining* to the latter, John xx. 23. Paul, at the same time, praises God's *forbearance*. The object of *pretermission* are sins; the object of *forbearance* are sinners, against whom God did not prosecute His claim. So long as the one and other of these existed, the justice [righteousness] of God was not so apparent; for He did not seem to be so exceedingly angry with sin as He really is, but appeared to leave the sinner to himself, ἀμελεῖν, *to regard not*. Heb. viii. 9 [ἠμέλησα, "I regarded them not"]; but in the blood and atoning death of Christ, God's justice [righteousness] was exhibited, accompanied with His vengeance against sin itself, that *He might be Himself just,* and at the same time accompanied with zeal for the deliverance of the sinner, *that He might be Himself* [at the same time also] *the justifier;* and therefore very frequent mention of this vengeance and of this zeal is made by the prophets, and especially by Isaiah, for example, ix. 6, and lxi. 2. And διὰ, *on account of* [not *for*, as Eng. vers.] that *pretermission in the forbearance of God,* it was necessary that at some time there should be made *a demonstration* [a showing forth, ἔνδειξιν] *of His*

ROMANS III. 26, 27.

justice [righteousness].—προγεγονότων) of sins which had been *committed, before* atonement was made for them by the blood of Christ. Comp. again Heb. ix. 15.

26. [ver. 25, Engl. Vers.] Ἐν, in marks *the time of forbearance* [but Engl. Vers., *through*]. The antithesis [to that, *the time of forbearance*] is, *in the present time* [ἐν τῷ νῦν καιρῷ] where also the νῦν, *present*, corresponds to the προ, *before*, in προγεγονότων—εἰς τὸ εἶναι αὐτὸν δίκαιον καὶ δικαιοῦντα, *that He might be just and the justifier*) The justice of God not merely appeared, but really exercised itself in the blood-shedding of Christ. Comp. the notes on the preceding verse, αὐτὸν, *He Himself*, in antithesis to the *person to be justified*. We have here the greatest paradox, which the Gospel presents; for, in the law, God is seen as *just* and *condemning;* in the Gospel, He is seen as being *just* Himself, and, at the same time, *justifying* the sinner.—τὸν ἐκ πίστεως) *him* who is *of faith* [*who believeth*, Engl. Vers.] comp. the ἐκ, ch. ii. 8, [ἐξ ἐριθείας, *influenced by* contention].

27. Ποῦ, *where*) A particle showing the argument to be complete and unanswerable. 1 Cor. i. 20, xv. 55; comp. 2 Pet. iii. 4.—ἡ καύχησις, *boasting*) of the Jew, over the Gentiles, towards God, ch. ii. 17, etc., iv. 2. He may boast, who can say, I am such as [all that] I ought to be, having fully attained to righteousness and life. The Jews sought for that ground for boasting in themselves.—διὰ ποίου νόμου) *by what law*, supply ἐξεκλείσθη ἡ καύχησις, *is boasting excluded;* or rather, *by what law is the thing* [justification] accomplished? A similar ellipsis is found at ch. iv. 16, [διὰ τοῦτο ἐκ πίστεως, *therefore it is accomplished of* or *by* faith].—οὐχί, *nay*) Although a man, according to the law, might have [*i.e.*, supposing he might have] righteousness and a reward, yet he could not boast before God; comp. Luke xvii. 10; now as it is, seeing that there is no righteousness to be had by the law, there remains much less room for boasting; and boasting is much more excluded by the law of faith, than by the law of works.—νόμου πίστεως, *the law of faith*) An appropriate catachresis [change[1] in the application] of the word *law*. This [justification by faith] is also a *law*, inasmuch as being of Divine appointment, to which *subjection* [submission]

---

[1] See Appendix.

is due, ch. x. 3. [They have not *submitted themselves to* the righteousness of God].

28. Λογιζόμεθα γάρ) γάρ for οὖν, in this sense: So far as regards these things; *for* we wished to set it forth as fully proved, that it is *by faith*, etc. Most copies read οὖν,[1] but it seems to have been repeated from ver. 27, and γάρ serves the purpose of the argument against boasting, which is now deduced from justification through faith, ver. 22.—πίστει, *by faith*) Luther, *allein durch den glauben; by faith alone*, or rather *only by faith*, as he himself explains, T. V. Jen. f. 141. Arithmetically expressed the demonstration stands thus:—

The matter in dispute involves two elements,
    Faith and Works, . . 2
    Works are excluded, . . 1
    ―――
    Faith alone remains, . . 1

If one be subtracted from two, one remains [comp. ch. xi. 6]. So the μόνον, *only*, is expressed at ver. 29; and so the LXX. added μόνον, *only* in Deut. vi. 13, in accordance with [to complete] the Sense: with which comp. Matt. iv. 10. The Vulgate has *solum, only*, Job xvii. 1, etc., πίστει μόνῃ, *by faith alone*, Basil., hom. 22, On Humility. In short, James, in discussing this very subject, and refuting the abuse of the doctrine of Paul, adds μόνον, *only*, ch. ii. 24. [*And, in fact*, volumes *are on sale, abounding with testimonies of persons who used the word allein*, only, *before the time of Luther.*—V. g.] Justification takes place through faith itself, not in so far as it is faith [not in the fact of its being faith; as if there were merit in itself] or a work of the law, but, in so far as it is faith of Christ, laying hold of Christ; that is, in so far as it has in it something apart from the works of the Law. Gal. iii. 12. [*Take care, however, lest this point should be misunderstood. Faith alone justifies; but it neither is, nor does it remain alone; it is constantly working inwardly and outwardly.*—V. g.]—ἄνθρωπον) שיא, *any man whatever*, Jew and Greek, with which comp. the following verse. So ἄνθρωπος, *a man*, 1 Cor. iv. 1.

―――
[1] BC and both Syr. Versions with Rec. Text οὖν. But AΛG*fg* Vulg. and Memph. Vers. read γάρ.—ED.

29. Ναὶ καὶ ἐθνῶν, *yea also of the Gentiles* [*although they are without the law.*—V. g.], as nature teaches, and the Old Testament prophecies.

30. Ἐπείπερ,[1] *seeing that indeed*) The inference is: if justification be by the law, then the Gentiles, who are without the law, cannot be justified; and yet they also rejoice in God, as a justifier, ch. iv. 16.—εἷς) εἷς, ὁ Θεὸς, *one*, namely *God;* the relative *who* depends on *one*, as its antecedent.—δικαιώσει, *shall justify*) The future, as we find it in many other passages, ch. i. 17, iii. 20, v. 19, 27; 2 Cor. iii. 8, therefore, we have in express terms, μέλλοντος, *that was to come*, ch. v. 14; μέλλει, *will be*, ch. iv. 24. Paul speaks as if he were looking forward out of the Old Testament [from the Old Testament stand-point] into the New. It is to this that those expressions refer, *ex. gr., foreseeing,* Gal. iii. 8; *the promise, ib.* 14; *the hope, ib.* v. 5. So John is said *to be about to come*, Matt. xi. 14, xvii. 11; *the wrath to come,* Matt. iii. 7, where we have the discourse of the forerunner, which presupposes the threatenings.[2]—ἐκ διὰ, *of* or *out of* [*by*, Engl. Vers.]—*through*) The Jews had been long ago in the faith; the Gentiles had lately obtained faith from them. So *through* is used, ver. 22; Eph. ii. 8; *of* or *out of* [*by*, ἐκ] in a number of passages. It is well [right] by all means to compare the same difference in the particles in ch. ii. 27; and difference in the thing signified [*i.e.*, the different footing of the Jew and Gentile] ch. xi. 17, etc.—διὰ τῆς) He does not say, διὰ τὴν πίστιν, *on account of faith*, but *through faith*.

31. Νόμον, *the law*) This declaration is similar to the declaration of our Lord, Matt. v. 17.—ἱστῶμεν, *we establish*) while we defend [uphold] that which the law witnesseth to, ver. 20, 21, and while we show, how satisfaction is truly made to the law through Christ.

---

[1] So AG; "quoniam quidem unus," *fg* Vulg. Iren. 186, 259. But ABC Orig. 4,228*a*, read εἴπερ εἷς; "si quidem unus," in *g*.—ED.

[2] *i.e.*, the wrath to come is taken for granted from the Old Testament; John's part is to warn them to flee from it.—ED.

CHAPTER IV.

1. Τί 'οὖν, *what then*) He proves from the example of Abraham; 1, That justification is of grace [gratuitous]; 2, That it has been provided for the Gentiles also, ver. 9.—τὸν πατέρα ἡμῶν, *our father*) [This, viz., his being *our father*, constitutes] the foundation of the consequence derived from Abraham to us.—εὑρηκέναι, *hath found*) It is applied to something new Heb. ix. 12 [Engl. Vers., *having obtained;* but εὑράμενος, *having found*]; and Paul intimates, that the way of faith is older than Abraham; and that Abraham, in whom the separation from the Gentiles by circumcision took place, was the first from whom, if from any one, an example seemed capable of being adduced in favour of works; and yet he, at the same time shows, that this very example [instance] is much more decisive in favour of faith; and so he finally confirms by examples, what he had already established by arguments.—κατὰ σάρκα, *according* [*as pertaining*, Engl. Vers.] *to the flesh*. Abraham is nowhere called *our father according to the flesh*. Therefore, it [the clause, *according to the flesh*] is not construed with *father;* for the expression *according to the flesh*, is added in mentioning the fathers, only when the apostle is speaking of Christ, ch. ix. 5; and Abraham by and by, at ver. 11, is shown to be the father of believers, even of those of whom he is not the father according to the flesh. The construction then is, *hath found according to* [*as pertaining to*] *the flesh*. In the question itself, Paul inserts something which has the effect of an answer, in order that he may not leave even the smallest countenance for [or, *a moment of time to*] the maintaining of Jewish righteousness, and for their boasting before God.

2. Εἰ, *if*) A particle implying reluctant concession [for argument's sake].—γὰρ, *for*) [The γάρ expresses] the cause after the proposition, and the reason why, in ver. 1, he added the limitation, *hath found as pertaining to the flesh*.[1]—πρὸς) *to*, or *before*.

[1] Ἐξ ἔργων, *from works*) Abraham was before the law, hence Paul introduces no mention of the law, ver. 1-12.—V. g.

He was not *justified by works before God,* and therefore, *he has no ground of boasting before God;* but both [hold good of him] *according to the flesh.*

3. Γὰρ, *for*) This word is to be referred to *but not.*—ἡ γραφή, *the Scripture*) The word *Scripture* is elegantly used. *Moses* does not speak in this passage, comp. ch. x. 5.—ἐπίστευσε δὲ Ἀβραάμ, κ.τ.λ.), Gen. xv. 6, lxx., καὶ ἐπίστευσεν Ἀβραμ, κ.τ.λ. *believed* in the promise of a numerous seed, and especially of the seed Christ, the seed of the woman, in whom all the promises are yea and amen, and on whose account a numerous seed had been desired.—ἐλογίσθη) λογίζεσθαι, to number, to estimate, to consider, to reckon, signifies here the act of a gracious will. It is repeated in this passage with great effect : ἐλογίσθη, the passive, as λογίζεται, ver. 4, 5, *is reckoned.* Heb. ; *He reckoned it to him,* namely, the *fact* [of his believing] or his *faith ;* for this is to be supplied from the verb immediately preceding, *believed.*—εἰς) So ch. ii. 26 [counted *for*]; Acts xix. 27, notes.

4. Δὲ) *but* [now]. Paul takes what is contrary [the case of *him that worketh*] out of the way, so as to enable him, in the following verse, to draw his conclusion regarding the man who does not trust to works, and to evince that Abraham was not such a one as he describes, by the words *him that worketh.*—ἐργαζομένῳ, *to him that worketh*) if there were, indeed, any such [which there is not]. We must take both expressions, *him that worketh* and *him that worketh not,* in a reduplicative sense : *to work,* and *wages,* are conjugates in the Heb. בעל. [*The man that worketh, in this passage, applies to him who, by his works,* performs (makes good) *all that the law requires.*—V. g.].—μισθὸς, *reward*), the antithesis to *faith.*—ὀφείλημα, a *debt,* by virtue of a contract between the parties. *Merit* in its strictest sense so called, and *debt,* are correlatives.

5. Τὸν ἀσεβῆ, *the ungodly*) This points out the excellence of faith, which hath established it *so* as that the ungodly are justified, ch. v. 6. Compare and consider the end of ver. 17 of this chapter. Translate τὸν ἀσεβῆ, *him who is ungodly.* Justification belongs to individuals. This word is a most conclusive proof that Paul is speaking, even most especially, of the moral law, by the works of which no one can be justified.—κατὰ τὴν πρόθεσιν τῆς χάριτος τοῦ Θεοῦ, *according to the purpose of the grace of God*) A

very ancient translator[1] of the Scriptures into Latin has this clause; following him, Hilarius, the deacon; then the scholiast on Jerome, etc. Beza acknowledges that it is exceedingly suitable; for there is a manifest antithesis between, *not according to grace, but according to debt* [ver. 4] etc., *according to the purpose of the grace of God.* The Greek transcribers might easily jump from κατὰ to καθάπερ [omitting κατὰ τ. πρόθεσιν, etc.] During the time that intervened between the publication of the Apparatus and the Gnomon, I have advanced on without inconsistency to the embracing of this clause, to which Beza is not opposed. Baumgarten has put in his negative. I have stated my reasons; he has given his; let those judge who are able. Paul sets in opposition to each other, *works* and πρόθεσιν, *the purpose;* and at the very time too, when he is speaking definitely of certain believers, the subjects of that purpose, as in this passage, of Abraham.

6. Καὶ, *even*) after the law was given by Moses.—Δαυίδ, *David*) David is very appositely introduced after Abraham, because both, being among the progenitors of the Messiah, received and propagated the promise. No direct promise regarding the Messiah was given to Moses, because the latter (Christ) is placed in opposition to the former, and was not descended from the stem of Moses.—λέγει τὸν μακαρισμὸν) he [*describes*] *declares the blessedness of the man,* μακαρίζω, *I pronounce him blessed.* The words are to be thus construed: λέγει, *declares without any reference to works;* that is, David, in recounting the ground of bestowing salvation on man, makes no mention at all of works. The argument derived from the silence of Scripture is often quite conclusive. But David, it may be said, immediately adds, *and in his spirit there is no guile,* which is all the same as an allegation of works. Ans. It is not all the same. This addition has no part in the definition of the subject, but forms a part of the predicate, although not even then would the merit of works be established; for the thief who confesses his crime, and does not guilefully deny it, does not merit pardon for his offence by that confession of his. But this is the meaning: *blessed is the man to whom the*

---

[1] Some old copies of the Vulg. have the words. But the Cod. Amiatinus, the oldest MS. of the Vulg., omit them.—ED.

Lord hath not imputed sin: blessed is he, and *in his spirit there is no guile;* that is, he is sure of his condition, of the forgiveness of his sins; he may have good confidence; *his spirit,* his heart does not deceive him, so as to become, as it were, a קשת רמיה, *a deceitful bow,* Ps. lxxviii. 57. The act of Phinehas was also imputed to him for righteousness, Ps. cvi. 31; not, indeed, in viewing it as a work: but it was, as it were, unmixed [mera] faith. He seemed neither to see nor hear anything else, by reason of his unmixed zeal, that he might maintain the honour of his God.

7. Ἀφέθησαν κτλ) So the LXX., Ps. xxxii. 1. The synonymous words are, ἀφιέναι, ἐπικαλύπτειν, οὐ λογίζεσθαι, that sin committed may be accounted as not committed.

8. ᾯ, *to whom*) Greater force is given to the sense, by the transition from the plural in the preceding, to the singular in this verse; as also the more express mention of the *man* and of the *Lord* lends additional force.

9. Ὁ) Paul comprehends in this what he lately said respecting Abraham and David.—περιτομήν) *Does it come on the circumcision* only, by itself, to the exclusion of others? or *upon the circumcision also?*—λέγομεν, *we say,* ver. 3.

10. Πῶς, *how*) This word implies more than *when.*—οὐκ ἐν περιτομῇ, *not in circumcision*) For justification is described, Gen. xv.; circumcision, Gen. xvii.

11. Σημεῖον, *a sign*) Circumcision itself was a sign, a mark, namely, imprinted on the body, and the expression, *the sign of circumcision,* is used just as *taking of rest in sleep* [κοίμησις τ. ὕπνου], John xi. 13; and *the virtue of piety,* that is, piety a virtue.—ἔλαβε, *received*) obediently.—τῆς ἐν τῇ) τῆς is to be construed with πίστεως; with which compare the next verse.—δι ἀκροβυστίας) διά, *with;* as in ch. ii. 27 [not as Eng. vers. "*by* the letter, and circumcision;" but '*with,*' or '*in.*' Eng. vers. here, Rom. iv. 11, renders διὰ ἀκροβ, *though they be not circumcised*]. 11, 12. Πατέρα) the construction is, *that he might be the father of all who believe with* [*i.e.* being in] *uncircumcision*—and *the father of the circumcision. Father* and *seed* are correlatives.

12. Περιτομῆς, of *circumcision*) The Abstract for the concrete, *of the circumcised nation.*—τοῖς) Heb. ל: see *Nold.* on this

particle, n. 30, 10, 15, 19, 22. Generally, it implies *as to* [as regards, in relation to]; so τοῖς, 1 John v. 16; Luke i. 50, 55. LXX. 1 Chron. xiii. 1 : μετὰ τῶν ἀρχόντων κτλ. παντὶ ἡγουμένῳ, add to these passages 2 Chron. xxxi. 2, 16; Num. xxix. 4.—οὐκ —μόνον) Abraham, therefore, is not the father of *circumcision* to such as are merely of the circumcision, and do not also follow the faith of Abraham.—ἐκ περιτομῆς, *of the circumcision*) ἐκ, *of*, means something more weighty than ἐν, *in*. *Circumcision* was at least a sign, *uncircumcision* was not even a sign.[1]—ἀλλὰ καὶ τοῖς) so in ver. 16.—ἴχνεσι, *in the traces* [*steps*]) The *traces* of faith are opposed to the *traces* of outward circumcision; the path is not trodden by many, but there are foot-traces found in it; it is, however, an open way.

13. Οὐ γὰρ διὰ νόμου ἡ ἐπαγγελία, *for the promise was not through the law*) This is evident in the very terms; and the promise was given before the law. *Through the law*, that is, *through the righteousness of the law*, but Paul did not wish in his statement to connect righteousness and the law.—ἢ τῷ σπέρματι, *or to his seed*) This constitutes the foundation of the consequence derived from Abraham to all believers.—τοῦ κόσμου, *of the world*) and therefore *of all persons and things*. Comp. 1 Cor. iii. 21. *Heir of the world*, is the same as *father of all the nations*, who accept the blessing. The whole *world* was promised to Abraham and to his seed conjointly throughout the whole world. The land of Canaan fell to the lot of Abraham, and so one part was allotted to one, and another to another. So also corporeal things are a specimen of things spiritual. Christ is heir of the world, and of all things, Heb. i. 2, ii. 5, x. 5; Rev. xi. 15; and so also are they who believe in Him according to the example of Abraham, Matt. v. 5, notes.

14. Εἰ, *if*) The promise and faith complete the whole : and we ought not to add the law, as if it were something homogeneous. —οἱ ἐκ νόμου, *those who are of the law*) This phrase recurs in a milder sense in ver. 16.—κεκένωται—κατήργηται—*made void— and of no effect*), words synonymous but not interchangeable. Comp. Gal. iii. 17, 15; the word antithetic to these is *sure* [βεβαίαν], ver. 16. Faith *receives* [ver. 11] blessings in all their

---

[1] Therefore ἐκ is used with περιτομῆς, ἐν with ἀκροβυστία.—ED.

fulness, it is therefore said, on the opposite side, to be made *void*, to be *of no effect*.—πίστις—ἐπαγγελία, *faith—the promise*) words correlative : and they are appropriately put in retrograde order [comp. ver. 13] in an argument like the present, wherein is shown the absurdity which would flow from the opposite theory [by the *reductio*, or *argumentum ad absurdum*].

15. Νόμος, *the law*) It occurs twice in this verse; first, with the article, definitely; next, indefinitely.—ὀργὴν, *wrath*) not *grace*, see the next verse. Hence the *law* is not of *promise* and of *faith*.—οὐδὲ παράβασις, *there is not even transgression*) He does not say, *not even sin*, comp. ch. v. 13, ii. 12; *offence*, ch. v. 20, and *transgression* have a more express reference to the law which is violated. Transgression rouses wrath.

16. Ἐκ πίστεως, *of faith*) So ἐκ, ch. iii. 30, v. 1. Supply *heirship* (the *heirship* is of faith) comp. ver. 14.—ἐκ τοῦ νόμου, *of the law*) so *of the circumcision*, ver. 12, where the *not only* belongs to *of the circumcision*, but in this verse, *not only* refers to the expression, *to that seed which*.

17.[1] Ὅτι—τέθεικά σε) so the LXX., Gen. xvii. 5. The construction, τέθεικά σε, κατέναντι—Θεοῦ, is like the following, ἵνα εἰδῆτε, ἄρον, Matt. ix. 6. Comp. Rom. xv. 3; Acts i. 4.— κατέναντι—Θεοῦ, *before God*) since those nations did not yet exist *before* men.—οὗ), that is, κατέναντι Θεοῦ, ᾧ ἐπίστευσε, *before God, in whom he believed*.—ζωοποιοῦντος, *quickening*) Heb. xi. 19, notes. The dead are not dead to God, and things which be not, are to God.—καλοῦντος, *calling*) The seed of Abraham did not yet exist, nevertheless God said, So shall thy seed be. The multiplication of the seed presupposes the previous existence of the seed. For example, the centurion says to his servant, who was living and moving in the natural course of the world, Do this; but God says to the light, whilst it is not in existence, just as if it were, Come forth, γενοῦ, come into existence. Think of that often recurring and wonderful יהי, Gen. i., it expresses the transition from *non-existence* to *existence*, which is produced by God *calling*, Ezek. xxxvi. 29.

---

[1] πατὴρ πάντων ἡμῶν, *father of us all*). Hence it is, that although Christ is said to be the *Son of David*, yet believers are not called the sons of David, but of Abraham.—V. g.

18–21. Ὅς, *who*) Paul shows, that the faith, to which justification is ascribed, is no frail thing, but an extraordinary power.

18. Παρ' ἐλπίδα ἐπ' ἐλπίδι ἐπίστευσεν, *past [against] hope believed in hope*) We lay hold of one and the same object both by *faith* and *by hope; by faith*, as a thing, which is truthfully enunciated [proclaimed]; *by hope*, as an object of joy, which for certain both can and will be realized. *He believed in the hope* of the promise, *past [beyond,* 'præter'] *the hope* of reason, [which reason would have suggested]. παρά and ἐπί, *past* [*against*] and *in*, the particles opposed to each other, produce a striking oxymoron.[1]—οὕτως, *so*) as the stars, Gen. xv. 5. LXX. also, οὕτως.—σου. Comp. Gal. iii. 8, notes.

19. Μὴ ἀσθενήσας, *being not weak*) Reason [had he hearkened to it] might have afforded causes of weakness.—ἑαυτοῦ—Σάῤῥας, *his own—of Sarah's*) The old age of both the husband and wife, and the previous barrenness of the latter, increase the difficulty, and prove the birth of Isaac to have been miraculous. The course of the history shows, that Sarah gave birth to Isaac only [*not save,* 'nonnisi'] in conjunction with Abraham. The renewed vigour of his body remained even in his marriage with Keturah.—ἑκατονταέτης που, *when he was about a hundred years old*) After Shem, we read of no one begetting children, who was a hundred years of age, Gen. xi.

20. Εἰς, *at*) The promise was the foundation of his confidence.—οὐ διεκρίθη, *did not [stagger or] doubt*) It is clear, what *doubt* is, from its opposite *was strong*. We should observe, that it is the reverse of doubting.—δούς, *giving*) These things, *giving glory to God*, and *being fully persuaded*, are very closely connected.—δόξαν) *the glory* of truth (its opposite is stigmatized in 1 John v. 10, in the case of him, who does not believe) and of power.

22. διὸ, *therefore*) namely, because he gave glory to GOD.—V. g.

23. Δι' αὐτὸν, *for his sake*) who was dead long before.—ὅτι, *that*.

Δι' ἡμᾶς, *for us*) who ought to be stirred up by the example of Abraham.—V. g.

---
[1] See Appendix.

24. Ἐγείραντα, *Him, who raised up*) Comp. v. 17, *quickening the dead.* The faith of Abraham was directed to that, which was about to be, and which could come to pass, ours to that which has actually taken place; the faith of both, is directed to the Quickener [Him, who makes alive].
Παρεδόθη, *was delivered*) so the LXX. Is. liii. 12, καὶ διὰ τὰς ἀνομίας αὐτῶν παρεδόθη, *and for their iniquities He was delivered up.* God is not said to have inflicted death upon Christ; although He inflicted on Him [put Him to] *griefs;* but [God is said] to *have delivered up* Christ, or else Christ is said to *have died*, ch. viii. 34. I do not deny the fact itself, see Zech. xiii. 7; but the phrases are moulded in such a way that they rather express that the *passion* was enjoined upon Christ by the Father, as also that the *death* was obediently endured by Christ to the utmost ['*exantlata;*' the cup of suffering to death drained to the dregs].—δικαίωσιν, *justification*) a verbal noun, differing from δικαιοσύνη, *righteousness.* Faith flows from the resurrection of Christ, and so also does justification, Col. ii. 12; 1 Pet. i. 21. The ground on which our belief in God rests, is, that He has raised Jesus Christ from the dead. Yet this ground of belief does not impair the truth, that the obedience of Jesus Christ, and His own blood, is the source of our justification. See ch. iii. 25, v. 19.

CHAPTER V.

1. Δικαιωθέντες οὖν ἐκ πίστεως, *therefore being justified by faith*) This clause is a *recapitulation of the preceding reasonings;* comp. *justification*, ch. iv. 25.—εἰρήνην, *peace*) we are no longer *enemies*, ver. 10, nor do we fear *wrath*, ver. 9, *we have peace and we glory*, which is the principal topic of Chapters, v. vi. vii. viii. [*Hence Paul so often puts* peace *by the side of* grace.—V. g.]—πρὸς, *to*) *towards, in relation to;* God embraces us in the arms of peace.—τοῦ) Paul gives the full title, *our Lord Jesus Christ*, especially at the beginning or end of any discussion, ver. 11, 21, vi. 11, 23,

which last verse, however [vi. 23] is more closely connected with those that go before, than with those that follow, at the beginning of which, the word *brethren* is placed [ch. vii. 1].

2. Προσαγωγὴν, *access*) Eph. ii. 18, iii. 12.—ἐσχήκαμεν, *we have had*) the preterite antithetic to the present, *we have*, ver. 1. Justification is *access unto grace; peace* is the state of permanent remaining in grace, which removes the enmity. So, accordingly, Paul in his salutations usually joins them together, *grace to you and peace;* comp. Num. vi. 25, 26. It comprehends both the *past* and *present;* and, presently after, speaking of hope, the *future;* wherefore construe the words in this connection, *we have peace and* we [rejoice] *glory.*—ἐν ᾗ, *in which*) Grace always remains *grace;* it never becomes *debt.*—ἐστήκαμεν, *we have stood*) we have obtained a standing-place.—καυχώμεθα, [rejoice] *we glory*) in a manner new and true ; comp. ch. iii. 27. —ἐπ ἐλπίδι τῆς δόξης τοῦ Θεοῦ, *in* [*over, concerning,* 'super'] *hope of the glory of God*) comp. ch. iii. 23, viii. 30 ; Jude, ver. 24. Christ in us, *the hope of glory*, Col. i. 27 ; John xvii. 22. Therefore, *glory* is not *glorying itself,* but is its surest object, as regards the future.

3. Καυχώμεθα, *we* [rejoice] *glory*) Construe with ver. 11, see notes there.—ἐν ταῖς θλίψεσιν, in *tribulations*) Tribulations during the whole of this life seem to deliver us up to *death*, [ver. 12], not to *glory*, and yet not only are they not unfavourable to hope, but even afford it assistance.—ὑπομονὴν κατεργάζεται, *worketh patience* [patient perseverance]) namely in the case of believers ; for in the case of unbelievers the result is rather impatience and apostacy. *Patience* is not learned without adversity ; it [patience] is the characteristic of a mind not only ready [prompt in resolution], but also of one courageous [hardy] in endurance.

4. Ἡ δὲ ὑπομονὴ δοκιμήν) Again, conversely, τὸ δοκίμιον τῆς πίστεως, ὑπομονήν. [*The trying of your faith*, or *experience*, worketh *patience*] James i. 3. It will be difficult to find an instance of any one having used δοκιμὴ before Paul : δοκιμὴ is the quality of that man, who is δόκιμος.—[—*who has been* proved *through various casualties and trying circumstances of peril.*—V. g.]—δοκιμὴ ἐλπίδα, *experience, hope*) Heb. vi. 9, 10, 11 ; where ver. 10 illustrates δοκιμὴ, *experience* ; ver. 9, 11, illustrate *hope*. Comp.

Rev. iii. 10.—ἐλπίδα, *hope*) to which our attention is directed at the end of ver. 2. The discourse returns in a circle [reverting to *hope*, from which he started in ver. 2]; and it is to this whole [*i.e.*, from *rejoice*, in ver. 2, to *maketh not ashamed*, ver. 5] that the Aetiology[1] [reason assigned by the] *because*, at ver. 5, refers.

5. Οὐ καταισχύνει, *does not make ashamed*) We have here an instance of the figure Ταπείνωσις, [by which less is said than the writer wishes to be understood]; that is, *hope* affords us grounds for the highest *glorying*, and will not prove fallacious; hope will be a reality.—ὅτι, *because*) The [believer's] present state is described, ver. 5–8. From this, hope as to the future is inferred, ver. 9–11.—ἡ ἀγάπη) [not *our love to God*, but] the *love* [of God] εἰς ἡμᾶς, *toward us*; [as proved by] ver. 8; from which we derive our hope; for it [God's love] is an eternal love —ἐκκέχυται, *is shed abroad*) most abundantly; whence we have this very feeling αἴσθησις [Sense, perception of His love]—ἐν ταῖς καρδίαις, *in our hearts*) not *into our hearts*. This form of expression indicates, that the Holy Spirit Himself is in the heart of the believer—διὰ, *through* [*by*]) We have the reason assigned for the whole of our present condition, in which the Holy Spirit is the earnest of the future. [The Holy Spirit *is here mentioned for the first time in this discussion. When a man is really brought to this point, he at length perceives distinctly* (in a marked manner) *the operation of the Holy Spirit.*—V. g.]—δοθέντος) *given*, through faith. Acts xv. 8; Gal. iii. 2, 14.

6. Ἔτι, *as yet*) This is to be construed with ὄντων, *when we were*.—γὰρ, *for*) The marvellous love of God is set forth.— ἀσθενῶν, *powerless* [*without strength*]) Ἀσθένεια is that [*want of strength*] *powerlessness* which characterises a mind when made ashamed (comp. the beginning of ver. 5) which [*powerlessness*] is opposed to *glorying* [ver. 2, 3] (comp. notes on 2 Cor xi. 30); we have the antithetic word at ver. 11, [*we glory* (joy) *in God*] where this paragraph also, which begins with the words, *being without strength*, returns in a circle to the point, from which it started. There was powerlessness, and that a deadly powerlessness (comp. 1 Cor. xv. 43), on the part of—

[1] See Appendix.

The ungodly,		(Good men.
Sinners,	the opposite of whom, re-	The righteous.
Enemies,	spectively, are	The reconciled.

See on the powerlessness and on the strength of glorying [*i.e.*, the *powerlessness* of the ungodly, and *the strength of glorying* of the righteous] Ps. lxviii. 2, and the following verses; [lxxi. 16, civ. 35] Is. xxxiii. 24, ch. xlv. 24; 1 Cor. i. 31; Heb. ii. 15. Add the verbal parallelism, 2' Cor. xi. 21.—κατὰ καιρὸν ἀπέθανε, *in due time died*) בְּעִתָּהּ, κατὰ καιρὸν, Is. lx. 22. When our powerlessness had reached its highest point, then Christ died, at the time which God had previously determined, and in such a manner, that He died neither too soon nor too late (comp. the expression *in the time that now is* [*at this time*] ch. vii. 26), and was not held too long [longer than was needful] under the power of death. Paul fixes the limits [of *the due time*] and he cannot speak in this passage of the death of Christ, without, at the same time, thinking of the counsel of GOD, and of the resurrection of Christ, ver. 10, ch. iv. 25, viii. 34. The question, why Christ did not come sooner, is not an idle question; see Heb. ix. 26; Gal. iv. 4; Eph. i. 10; Mark i. 15, xii. 6, just as also the question, why the law was not given sooner, is no idle question, ver. 14.

7. Δικαίου. τοῦ ἀγαθοῦ) Masculines; with which comp. ver. 6, 8, as *Th. Gataker* rightly shows, Book 2, Misc. c. 9, but in such a way, that he thinks them to be merely synonymous. When there is any doubt respecting the peculiar force of an expression, and a difference between words, it will be of much advantage if you either suppose something in the meanwhile, or transpose the words. Accordingly, by transposing the words in this passage, we shall read: μόλις γὰρ ὑπὲρ ἀγαθοῦ τις ἀποθανεῖται, ὑπὲρ γὰρ δικαίου τάχα τὶς καὶ τολμᾷ ἀποθανεῖν, *for scarcely for a good man will one die, for peradventure for a righteous man, some one would even dare to die*) suppose, to wit, also, that ἀγαθοῦ is put without the article. You will immediately perceive the disadvantage to the sense, with which this change would be attended, and it will appear evident, that there is both some difference between δίκαιον and ἀγαθὸν, and a great one between δίκαιον and τὸν ἀγαθὸν, wheresoever that difference in the consecutive words may be found hereafter. In fact, the

article so placed, makes a climax. Every good man is righteous; but every righteous man is not good. *Gregory Thaumaturgus*; περὶ πολλοῦ καὶ ΤΟΥ παντός. Chrysostom; μικρὰ ταῦτα καὶ ΤΟ μηδὲν, *those things of little importance, and that which is of no importance whatever.* The Hebrews call a man צדיק, who performs his lawful duties; חסיד, who performs acts of kindness. The Greeks call the former δίκαιος; the latter, ὅσιος; comp. צדק and ענוה, Zeph. ii. 3, but in this passage we have not ὁσίου, but τοῦ ἀγαθοῦ. Wherefore the distinction between the Hebrew words does not determine the point. But this much is certain, that just as ὅσιος, so also ἀγαθὸς expresses more than δίκαιος. (See Matt. v. 45, and lest they should be thought there also to be merely synonymous, try that same transposition, and it will be seen, that to make mention of the *genial* sun in connection with the *just*, and the *useful* rain in connection with *the good*, is not so suitable [as the converse order of the original], likewise Luke xxiii. 50.) And so Paul, in this passage, judges τὸν ἀγαθὸν, *the good man* to be more worthy, that one should die for him, than δίκαιον, *a righteous man*. Ἀσεβεῖς [ver. 6] and ὁ ἀγαθὸς, *the ungodly* and *the good man*, also δίκαιος and ἁμαρτωλοὶ [ver. 8], *a righteous man* and *sinners*, are respectively opposed to each other. What, then, is the result? δίκαιος, indefinitely, implies *a harmless* [guiltless] *man*; ὁ ἀγαθὸς, *one perfect in all that piety* [duty towards God and man] *demands*, excellent, bounteous, princely, blessed, for example, the father of his country.—ὑπὲρ γὰρ) here γὰρ has a disjunctive force, of which we have many examples.—τάχα, τὶς, καὶ, τόλμᾷ, *peradventure, one, even, dares*) These several words amplify that which is stated in ver. 8; τάχα (instead of τάχιστα) diminishes the force of the affirmation; τὶς, *one*, is evidently put indefinitely; nor is it regarded [nor does it enter into the consideration], whether the person, who may die for a just or for the good man, is in a state of wrath or of grace; καὶ, *even*, concessive, shows, why it is not said simply, *dies*, as if it were a daily occurrence; but that the writer should rather say, *dares to die*, inasmuch as it is something great and unusual. τολμᾷ, *dares*, as though it were an auxiliary verb, corresponds to the future, *will one die*; *dares* [endures to], ventures.—ἀποθανεῖν, *to die*) Dost thou wish to have the steadiest friends? be *a good man*.

8. Συνίστησι) *commends;* a most elegant expression. Persons are usually [commended] recommended to us, who were previously unknown to us or were aliens [strangers]. Comp. *He descended into the midst* [He stooped down to *interpose between us and Himself*] (ἐμεσίτευσε) Heb. vi. 17.—δὲ, *but*) This comparison presupposes that God's love toward Christ, is as great as God's love toward Himself. Therefore the Son is equal to God.—ἁμαρτωλῶν, *sinners*) We were not only not *good*, but not even *righteous*.

9. Δικαιωθέντες, *Being justified*) The antithesis *to sinners*, ver. 8.—νῦν, *now*) The remembrance of Jesus Christ's death was at that time *fresh* among believers.—ἀπὸ τῆς ὀργῆς, *from wrath*) which otherwise does not cease : wrath abides upon those who do not attain to grace.

10. Εἰ, [since] *if*) Often εἰ, *if*, especially in this and the eighth chapter of this epistle, does not so much denote the condition as strengthen the conclusion.

11. Καυχώμεθα, *we glory (joy)*) The whole discourse from ver. 3 to 11 is comprehended in one construction, thus : οὐ μόνον δὲ, ἀλλὰ καὶ καυχώμεθα ἐν ταῖς θλίψεσιν (εἰδότες ver. 3—ἐν τῇ ζωῇ αὐτοῦ —ver. 10) οὐ μόνον δὲ, ἀλλὰ καὶ καυχώμεθα ἐν τῷ Θεῷ κ.τ.λ. So the edition of *Colinaeus, Barb.* 4, cod. MS. in colleg. prædicatorum apud *Basileam*, Bodl. 5. *Cov.* 2. *L. Pet.* 1. *Steph. ια. Aeth. Arab. Vulg.* make the words οὐ μόνον δε, ἀλλὰ καὶ καυχώμεθα be repeated after a long intervening parenthesis [*by epanalepsis*,[1] Not. crit.], and the sense, suspended by it, be most elegantly and most sweetly completed, according to the following arrangement of the apostle, although it was only lately that we discovered it, *We have peace, and we glory not only in the* HOPE *of the glory of God; but, even in the midst of tribulations, we glory*, I say, *in God Himself, through our Lord Jesus Christ, by whom we have* NOW [opp. to HOPE above] *received the atonement* [*reconciliation*]. Most of the more recent copies have made it καυχώμενοι, as if the construction were, *being reconciled, we shall be saved and glorying;* according to the reading, which is more generally received.[2]—ἐν τῷ Θεῷ, *in God*) not *before God*, ch. iv. 2.—τὴν καταλλαγὴν) the

---

[1] See Appendix.
[2] BCΛ, the weightiest authorities, read καυχώμενοι. *Gfg* Vulg. read καύχωμεν, *gloriamur.* Others, καυχώμεθα.—ED.

reconciliation. Glorying as to love, which means something more [than merely *reconciliation*] follows upon *the reconciliation* and deliverance from wrath.[1]

12. Διὰ τοῦτο, *wherefore*) This has regard to the whole of the preceding discussion, from which the apostle draws these conclusions concerning sin and righteousness, herein making not so much a digression as a regression. In imitation of Paul's method, we must treat, in the first place, of actual sin, according to the first and following chapters, and then go back to the source in which sin originated. Paul does not speak altogether expressly of that which theologians call original sin ; but, in truth the sin of Adam is sufficient to demonstrate man's guilt; the very many, and most mournful fruits resulting from it, are sufficient for the demonstration of man's habitual corruption. And man, in consequence of justification, at length looks back upon, and apprehends the doctrine concerning the origin of evil, and the other things connected with it. This second part, however, is in special connection with the first part of this chapter ; comp. the *much more*, which reigns [ver. 17] on both sides [*i.e.* grace reigning and triumphing abundantly over *both original sin* and *habitual corruption*] ; ver. 9, etc., 15, etc., for the very glorying of believers is exhibited; comp. ver. 11 [*we glory*, or Engl. vers. *we joy*] with ver. 21. The equality, too, of Jews and Gentiles, and consequently of all men, is herein included.—ὥσπερ, *as*) The Protasis, which the words *and so* continue ; for it is not *so also* that follows [which would follow, if the apodosis began here]. The apodosis, from a change in the train of thoughts and words, is concealed in what follows.—ἀνθρώπου, *man*) Why is nothing said of the woman ? Ans. 1. Adam had received the commandment. 2. He was not only the Head of his race, but also of Eve. 3. If Adam had not listened to the voice of his wife, not more than one would have sinned. Moreover, why is nothing said of Satan, who is the primary cause of sin ? Ans. 1. Satan is opposed to God ; Adam to Christ ; moreover, here the economy of grace is described as it belongs to Christ, rather than as it belongs to God : therefore, God is once mentioned, ver. 15 ; Satan

---

[1] *The atonement*, Engl. Vers. But τὴν implies "*the* reconciliation," already spoken of ver. 10, *reconciled*.—ED.

is never mentioned. 2. What has Satan to do with the grace of Christ?—ἡ ἁμαρτία—ὁ θάνατος, *sin—death*) These are two distinct evils, which Paul discusses successively at very great length.—εἰς τὸν κόσμον) *into* this *world*, which denotes the human race—εἰσῆλθε, *entered*) began to exist in the world; for it had not previously existed outside of the world.—καὶ διὰ, *and by*) Therefore, death could not have entered before sin.—καὶ οὕτως) *and so*, namely, by one man.—εἰς) *unto* [or *upon*] all, wholly.—διῆλθεν, *passed*) when sin once entered, which had not been in the world from the beginning.—ἐφ' ᾧ) 'Εφ' ᾧ with the verb ἥμαρτον has the same signification, as διὰ with the genitive, τῆς ἁμαρτίας. The meaning is, *through the fact that*, or in other words, *inasmuch as all have sinned*, comp. the ἐφ' ᾧ, 2 Cor. v. 4, and presently after, the other ἐπὶ, occurring in ver. 14.—πάντες) *all* without exception. The question is not about the particular sin of individuals; but in the sin of Adam all have sinned, as all died in the death of Christ for their salvation, 2 Cor. v. 15. The Targum on Ruth, ch. iv., at the end: על *On account of the counsel, which the serpent gave to Eve, all the inhabitants of the earth became subject to death*, אתחייבו מותא, Targum on Eccl. ch. vii., at the end. *The serpent and Eve made the day of death rush suddenly upon man and upon all the inhabitants of the earth.* Sin precedes *death;* but the *universality of death* becomes known earlier than the *universality of sin*. This plan of arrangement is adopted with respect to the four clauses in this verse.

13. Ἄχρι, *until*) Sin was in the world, not only after the law was given by Moses, but also during the whole period before the law from Adam down to Moses, during which latter period sinners *sinned without the law*, ch. ii. 12, for the condition of all before Moses, and of the Gentiles subsequently [after Moses' time], was equal; but this sin was not, properly speaking, the cause of death: because there is no imputation of sin without the law, and consequently there is no death; comp. ver. 20. The sin committed by Adam, entailing evil on all, is called *the sin* (ἡ ἁμαρτία) twice in the preceding verse; now, in this verse, sin in general is called ἁμαρτία without the article.—οὐκ ἐλλογεῖται, *is not imputed*) The apostle is not speaking here of men's negligence, which disregards sin in the absence of a law, but of the Divine judgment, because sin is not usually taken into any

account, not even into the Divine account, in the absence of the law.—Comp. ἰλλόγει, *impute*, or *put it to my account*, Philem. v. 18, note. *Sin* therefore does not denote notorious crimes, such as those, for which the inhabitants of Sodom were punished before the time of Moses, but the common evil. Chrysostom on this passage shows exceedingly well, what Paul intended to prove by this argument, ὅτι οὐκ αὐτὴ ἡ ἁμαρτία τῆς τοῦ νόμου παραβάσεως, ἀλλ' ἐκείνη ἡ τῆς τοῦ Ἀδὰμ παρακοῆς, αὐτὴ ἦν ἡ πάντα λυμαινομένη, καὶ τίς ἡ τούτου ἀπόδειξις; τὸ καὶ πρὸ τοῦ νόμου πάντας ἀποθνήσκειν, "that it was not the very [actual] sin of transgressing the law, but that of the disobedience of Adam—this was the sin that brought universal destruction, and what is the proof of this? The fact that all died before the giving of the law."

14. Ἐβασίλευσε, *reigned*) Chrysostom says, πῶς ἐβασίλευσεν; ἐν τῷ ὁμοιώματι τῆς παραβάσεως Ἀδάμ. "How did it reign? in the likeness of Adam's transgression." He therefore construed *in the likeness* with *reigned*; and no doubt [*death*] *reigned, I say,* may be supplied [before the words *in the likeness of Adam's transgression*]; comp. vi. 5. A *reign* is ascribed to death, as well as *power*, Heb. ii. 14. Scarcely indeed has any sovereign so many subjects, as are the many even kings whom death has taken away. It is an immense kingdom. This is no Hebraism; sin rules; righteousness rules.—ἀπὸ—μέχρι, *from—until*) The dispensation respecting the whole human race is threefold. 1. Before the law. 2. Under the law. 3. Under grace. Men severally experience the power of that dispensation, chap. vii.— καὶ, *even*) The particle indicates a species of persons subject to death, whom death might have seemed likely to spare in preference to all others; and so therefore it establishes the universality of death. [*Not only against those,* he says, *who committed many sins after the age of Moses, which were to be reckoned to them according to the law, but even against those, long before, who did not commit such sins*—V. g.].—ἐπὶ, *over*) This is a paradox; *death reigned over those who had not sinned*. Paul shows an inclination to use such paradoxes in speaking of this mystery, comp. v. 19; 2 Cor. v. 21; Rom. iv. 5.—τοὺς μὴ ἁμαρτήσαντας, *those who had not sinned*) All indeed from Adam to Moses have committed sins, although some were virtuous, others profligate; but because they sinned without law, without which sin is not

reckoned, they are spoken of as *those, who had not sinned:* but Adam is spoken of as *the one who sinned,* ver. 16. Observe, if these seven precepts of Noah, were what they are said to be, Paul would have described *those who had not sinned,* from Adam to Noah, not to Moses.—ὁμοιώματι, *in the likeness*) As Adam, when *he transgressed* the law, died, *in like manner* also they died, *who did not transgress,* or rather, who *did not sin;* for Paul varies the words in speaking of Adam, and of all others. This is the conclusion; That men died before the law, is a thing which befell them *on account of the similitude of Adam's transgression;* that is, Because the ground on which they stood, and on which Adam stood, [their footing and that of Adam] was one and the same:—they died on account of another guilt, not on account of that, which they themselves had contracted, namely, the guilt which had been contracted by Adam. In fact, the death of many is ascribed directly to the fall of the one, ver. 15. Thus it is not denied, that death is the wages of any sin whatever; but it is proved, that the primary cause of death was the first sin. It is this fact, which has brought us to destruction, just as the robber, who has plundered his victim, after having murdered him, is punished for the murder, and yet he did not commit the robbery with impunity, since the punishment of the robbery merged in the punishment of the murder; but, as compared with the greater punishment of murder, it was scarcely taken into account.—Ἀδάμ, *of Adam*) In this one verse we have the name of the individual Ἀδάμ, in all the others, the appellative noun, *man.* But, while the name of Adam is consigned to oblivion, the name of Jesus Christ is distinctly preached [proclaimed] ver. 15, 17.—ὅς ἐστι τύπος τοῦ μέλλοντος) ὅς for ὁ, *which thing,* agrees in gender with τύπος: *that which was to come,* τὸ μέλλον, is in the neuter gender [But Eng. vers., " of Him, that was to come."] Hence what is said respecting the future, ver. 17, 19. This paragraph from ver. 12 by implication contains the whole comparison of the first and second Adam, so far as they correspond to each other; for what follows refers to the differences between them, and the apodosis should be inferred from the protasis in this manner at ver. 12 : [*As by one man sin entered—and death,* etc.], so in like manner *by one man* righteousness *entered into the world and by* righteousness life; *and so* life *passed upon all men, because all* are justified. And at ver. 14, All shall reign in life, *after the similitude of Christ*, who has rendered all obedience; *although* those who thus reign have not by themselves fulfilled all righteousness [answering to the words " *even* over them,"etc., and ' nevertheless' in ver. 14.] Again Chrysostom says, πῶς τύπος; φησιν. ὅτι ὥσπερ ἐκεῖνος τοῖς ἐξ αὐτοῦ, καίτοιγε μὴ φαγοῦσιν ἀπὸ τοῦ ξύλου, γέγονεν αἴτιος θανάτου τοῦ διὰ τὴν βρῶσιν εἰσαχθέντος. οὕτω καὶ ὁ Χριστὸς τοῖς ἐξ αὐτοῦ, καίτοιγε οὐ δικαιοπραγήσασι, γέγονε πρόξενος δικαιοσύνης, ἣν διὰ τοῦ σταυροῦ πᾶσιν ἡμῖν ἐχαρίσατο· διὰ τοῦτο ἄνω καὶ κάτω τοῦ ἑνὸς ἔχεται, καὶ συνεχῶς τοῦτο εἰς μέσον φέρει. " How is he a type or figure? because just as that man [Adam] has become the source of death, which was brought in by the eating of the forbidden fruit, to those descended from him, although they had not eaten of the fruit of that tree, so also Christ has become the provider of righteousness to those belonging to Him, although they have not performed what is righteous; and this righteousness He has freely bestowed upon us all by the cross; therefore IN EVERY DIRECTION AND ON ALL OCCASIONS he maintains this One thing, and perpetually brings it into view." We may farther add; as the sin of Adam, independently of the sins, which we afterwards committed, brought death upon us, so the righteousness of Christ, independently of good works, which are afterwards performed by us, procures for us life; nevertheless, as every sin receives its appropriate punishment, so every good action receives a suitable reward.

15. Ἀλλ' οὐχ, *but not*) Adam and Christ, according to contrary aspects [regarded from contrary points of view], agree in the positive [absolutely], differ in the comparative [in the degree]. Paul first intimates their agreement, ver. 12–14, expressing the protasis, whilst leaving the apodosis, meanwhile, to be understood. Then next, he much more directly and expressly describes the difference: moreover, *the offence and the gift* differ; 1. In extent, ver. 15; 2. That self-same man from whom sin was derived, and this self-same Person, from whom the gift was derived, differ in power, ver. 16; and these two members are connected by anaphora [*i.e.*, repeating at the beginning, the same words] *not as*, [at the beginning of both] ver. 15 and 16, and the aetiology in ver. 17 [cause assigned; on aetiology, and anaphora, see Appendix] comprehends both. Finally, when

he has previously stated this difference, in the way of προθεραπεία [see Appendix; *Anticipatory, precaution* against misunderstanding], he introduces and follows up by protasis and apodosis the comparison itself, viewed in the relation of effect, ver. 18, and in the relation of cause, ver. 19.—τὸ παράπτωμα—τὸ χάρισμα, *the offence—the gift*) The antitheses in this passage are to be observed with the utmost care, from which the proper signification of the words of the apostle is best gathered. Presently after, in this verse, and then in ver. 17, the gift is expressed by synonymous terms.—οἱ πολλοί, the *many*) this includes in its signification *all*, for the article has a meaning relative to *all*, ver. 12, comp. 1 Cor. x. 17.—ἡ χάρις, *grace*) Grace and the *gift* differ, ver. 17; Eph. iii. 7. Grace is opposed to the *offence;* the *gift* is opposed to the words, *they are dead,* and it is the *gift of life.* The Papists hold that as grace, which is a gift, and what follows grace, as they define it, they do not consider as a gift, but as merit. But all is without money or price of ours [the whole, from first to last, is of grace, not of debt or merit of ours].—ἐν χάριτι Χριστοῦ, *in the grace of Christ*) see Matt. iii. 17; Luke ii. 14, 40, 52; John i. 14, 16, 17; Gal. i. 6; Eph. i. 5, 6, 7. The grace of God is the grace of Christ, conferred by the Father upon Christ, that it may flow from Him to us.—τῇ τοῦ) Articles most forcible, Col. i. 19: τῇ especially, is very providently [to guard against mistake] added; for if it were wanting, any one, in my opinion, might suppose that the words *of one,* depended on the word *gift,* rather than on *grace.* As it is, [the τῇ being used] it is evident that the grace of God, and the grace of Jesus Christ, are the things predicated; comp. similarly, viii. 35, 39, concerning love [the attribution of it, both to God and to Christ, as here].—ἑνὸς ἀνθρώπου, *of one man*) Paul (more than the other apostles, who had seen Him before His passion) gladly and purposely calls Jesus *man,* in this His work, as man for man, 1 Cor. xv. 21; 1 Tim. ii. 5. Can the human nature of Christ be excluded from the office of Mediator? When Paul in this verse calls Christ *man,* he does not give that appellation to Adam; and ver. 19, where he gives it to Adam, he does not bestow it upon Christ (comp. Heb. xii. 18, note). The reason is, doubtless, this, both Adam and Christ do not sustain *our manhood* at the same time; and either Adam rendered himself unworthy of the name of man; or the name of man is scarcely sufficiently worthy of Christ. Moreover, Christ is generally denominated from His human nature, when the question is about bringing men to God, Heb. ii. 6, etc.: from His Divine nature, when the subject under discussion is the coming of the Saviour to us, and the protection which He affords us, against our enemies, Tit. ii. 13. No mention is here made of the Mother of God; and if her conception was necessarily immaculate, she must have had no father, but only a mother, like Him, to whom she gave birth. [Cohel. or Eccles. vii. 29.]

16. Καὶ, *and*) The meaning is to this effect: *and not, as by one that sinned* (is the judgment) (so by one, the author of righteousness is) *the gift* [Engl. Vers. is different]; that is to say; And [moreover] the proportion [the *ratio*] on both sides, is not the same.—κρίμα, the *judgment*) namely, *is*.—ἐξ ἑνὸς, *from one*) namely, *offence*, [Engl. Vers. differs]; for the antithesis, *of many offences*, follows. The one offence was of the one man; the many offences are of many men.[1]

17. Τοῦ ἑνὸς—διὰ τοῦ ἑνὸς, *of the one man, by the one*) A very significant repetition; lest the sins committed by individuals should seem rather [than the offence of the one man] to have produced death.—ἐβασίλευσε, *reigned*) The word in the preterite tense looks back from the economy of grace to the economy of sin; as presently after the expression *shall reign*, in the future, looks forward from the economy of sin, to the economy of grace and eternal life; so ver. 19.—τὴν περισσείαν) Πλεονάζειν, and περισσεύειν differ, as *much* in the positive, and *more* in the comparative,

---

[1] *I frankly confess, that I do not clearly understand how this plural proves, that* Paul is not treating here of original sin, as if it ever exists without the accompaniment of other sins, *which is the assumption of some one of the more recent commentators. Doubtless the Apostle distinctly shows,* that the gift in Christ *is the cure* both for original sin, and for the actual offences of individuals BESIDES. *There are, certainly,* many actual sins, *which are not to be considered* as the necessary consequence *of the first sin (otherwise all the morality of our actions would now cease.); but there is* no *sin, whether it be called original or actual, the pardon and removal of which, ought not to be considered* as the mere effect *of the gift,* χαρίσματος. *Therefore the power of the gift,* τοῦ χαρίσματος, *is greater than that of the judgment,* τοῦ κρίματος.—E. B.

ver. 20. *Abundance* of grace, is put in opposition to the one offence.—λαμβάνοντες, *receiving*) Λαμβάνειν may be rendered either as a neuter-passive verb, *empfangen, erlangen, kriegen* to receive, to acquire, to get; or actively, *annehmen*, to take. The former is the better sense; still the relation to δωρεὰν *a gift*, is more suitable to the act of *taking*. In justification, man does something; but the act of taking, so far as it is an act, does not justify, but that which is taken or laid hold of. *The gift* and *taking*, are correlatives. Furthermore, this verb is not used, when we are speaking of sin; and it is for the same reason, owing to which it happens that we are not said to *reign* in death, but death *reigned;* but life reigns in us, 2 Cor. iv. 12, and we in life. Christ, in this passage, is King of them that reign. *Life* and *reigning* are mentioned in connection also, in Rev. xx. 4. The term *life* is repeated from ch. i. 17, and often recurs, presently after, in ver. 18, 21, and in the following chapters.

18. Ἄρα οὖν) ἄρα draws the inference, syllogistically: οὖν concludes, almost rhetorically: for this subject is not farther discussed than in this and the following verse.—ἑνὸς—ἑνὸς, *of one* —*of one*) In the masculine; as is manifest from the antithesis, *all*. The word *one*, generally put without the addition, *man*, designates with the greatest force, *one*, either of the two.— δικαιώματος—δικαίωσιν) Δικαίωμα is, so to speak, the material substratum, the foundation for δικαιώσει, *justification;* obedience, righteousness fulfilled. It may be called *justificament (justificamentum)* The ground and material of justification, as ἑδραίωμα denotes a firmament [or means of making firm]; ἔνδυμα, vestment; ἐπίβλημα, additament [or the thing wherewith addition is made]; μίασμα, defilement; ὀχύρωμα, muniment; περικάθαρμα, the means of purgation; περίψημα, the thing scraped of; σκέπασμα, a tegument or the thing wherewith a covering is made; στερέωμα, firmament; ὑπόδημα, a thing wherewith the foot is covered, a shoe; φρόνημα, *sentiment* [the material of φρόνησις] French *sentiment*. Aristot. Eth. Book v. c. 10, has put ἀδίκημα and δικαίωμα in opposition to each other, and defines the latter to be the correction of injustice [τὸ ἐπανόρθωμα τοῦ ἀδικήματος] the putting right what is wrong; which is tantamount to *satisfaction* [or *atonement*], a term undeservedly hateful to the Socinians.

The following scheme exhibits the exquisite propriety of the terms:—

	A.	B.	C.	D.
Ver. 16.	κρίμα, judgment.	κατάκριμα· condemnation.	χάρισμα, free gift.	δικαίωμα, righteousness.
	A.	B.		C.
Ver. 18.	παράπτωμα, offence.	κατάκριμα· condemnation.		δικαίωμα, righteousness.
			D. δικαίωσις ζωῆς, justification of life.	

In both verses A and B are of the same class, συστοιχεῖ, [are co-ordinate] and likewise C and D; but A and C correspond in the opposite classes, ἀντιστοιχεῖ; so also B and D. In ver. 16 the transaction on the part of God is described; in ver. 18 on the part of Adam and of Christ; and that, with less variety of words in the case of the economy of sin, than in the case of the economy of grace. Δικαίωσις ζωῆς, *justification of life*, is that Divine declaration, by which the sinner, subject to death, has life awarded to him, and that too, with justice on his side.

19. Παρακοῆς) παρὰ in παρακοή very appositely points out the principle of the initial step, which ended in Adam's fall. The question is asked, how could the understanding or the will of an upright man have been capable of receiving injury, or of committing an offence? Ans. The understanding and the will simultaneously gave way [tottered] through carelessness, ἀμέλεια, nor can we conceive of any thing else previous to carelessness, ἀμέλεια, in this case, as the initial step towards a city being taken is remissness on the part of the guards on watch. Adam was seduced through carelessness and *indolence of mind*, διὰ ῥᾳθυμίαν; as *Chrysostom* says, Homil. xxvii. on Gen., and at full length in Homil. lx. on Matt., " whence did man wish to disobey God? from *weakness and indolence of mind*," πόθεν ἠθέλησεν ὁ ἄνθρωπος παρακοῦσαι Θεοῦ ; ἀπὸ ῥᾳθυμίας, κ.τ.λ.—παρακοή, *disobedience*, implies this carelessness or weakness. The opposite in this passage is ὑπακοή, *obedience*, from which is derived an excellent argument regarding active obedience, without which the

atonement of Christ could not have been called *obedience;* it is for this reason He is so often praised as, ἄμωμος, *blameless*.— κατασταθήσονται, *shall be constituted) It is one thing* for a man to be constituted righteous, *even where imputation is spoken of, it is another thing* to *be justified, since the former exists as the basis and foundation of justification, and necessarily precedes true justification, under which it is laid as the substratum* [on which it rests] ; *for a man must of necessity stand forth as righteous, before he can be truly justified. But we have both the one and the other from Christ, for both the merit of Christ's satisfaction for sin, imputed to a man in himself unrighteous, already constitutes that same person righteous, inasmuch as it procures for him the righteousness, by which he is righteous; and by virtue of this righteousness, which is obtained by that merit, he is necessarily justified whereinsoever that justification be needed; that is, he is justly acquitted by merit, who in this way stands forth righteous,* Thom. Gataker. Diss. de novi instr. stylo, cap. 8. This is quite right. Nevertheless the apostle, as at the end of the period, seems to set forth such a *constituting* of men as righteous, as [which] may follow upon the act of justification, and which is included in the expression *being found,* Phil. iii. 9; comp. with Gal. ii. 17.— οἱ πολλοί, *the many) all men,* ver. 18, 15.

20. Νόμος, *law)* the omission of the article tends to increase the sublimity [elevation of tone].—παρεισῆλθε) *came in stealthily* by Moses, ver. 14. The Antithetic word is, *entered,* ver. 12 ; Sin therefore is more ancient than the law.—πλεονάσῃ, *might abound)* ch. vii. 7, etc. Sin is not reckoned in the absence of the law; but when the law came in stealthily, sin appeared as *abounding;* but, before the law, the fall of Adam should be held as the cause of death.—τὸ παράπτωμα, *the offence)* supply καὶ ἡ ἁμαρτία *and sin.* All the sins of mankind, compared with the sin of Adam, are as it were offshoots; it is the root. Ἁμαρτία, *sin,* in the singular number, is considered as a plague most widely spread; and it also comprehends all actual παραπτώματα, *offences,* ver. 16.—ἡ ἁμαρτία [*the*] *sin)* or in other words, *the offence and sin;* for there is a difference between them;[1] see notes on ver. 14; *the sin,* in the singular number, John i. 29.—ὑπερεπερίσ-

---

[1] The latter being the result of the former.—ED.

σευσε, *superabounded* [*did much more abound*] A third party conquering the conqueror of the conquered is superior to both : sin conquered man : grace conquers sin ; therefore the power of grace is greatest.

21. 'Εν τῷ θανατῳ—εἰς ζωήν, *in death—unto life*) The difference is here exemplified between the particles ἐν and εἰς. [Death has its limits and boundary, whereas life is everlasting, and [by divine power] divinely extended. Death is not said to be eternal ; whereas life is said to be eternal, ch. vi. 21, etc.—ἡ χάρις βασιλεύσῃ, *that grace might reign*) Grace therefore has had, as it were, no reign, that is, it has had a most brief reign before the fall. We may believe, that Adam sinned not long after that he was created.—'Ιησοῦ, *Jesus*) Now no longer is Adam even mentioned : the mention of Christ alone prevails.

CHAPTER VI.

1. 'Επιμενοῦμεν ; *shall we continue ?*) Hitherto he treated of the past and the present : now he proceeds to treat of the future ; and the forms of expression are suited to those, which immediately precede, whilst he speaks respecting the ' abounding' of grace. In this passage the *continuing* in sin is set before us ; in the 15th verse, the *going back* to sin, which had been overcome. The man, who has obtained grace, may turn himself hither or thither. Paul in this discussion turns his back on sin.

2. 'Απεθάνομεν, *we are dead*) in baptism and justification.

3. "H) *Or?* [' an,' Latin. The second part of] a disjunctive interrogation.—ἀγνοεῖτε, *know ye not?*) The doctrine concerning baptism was known to all. The same form of expression occurs again ch. vii. 1. to which the phrase, *know ye not?* corresponds, ver. 16, xi. 2 [Wot ye not ?] and 1 Cor. throughout. *Ignorance is a great obstruction ; knowlege is not sufficient.*[1]—ὅσοι, *whoso-*

---

[1] The point in this sentence is putting *officit* in antithesis to *sufficit*, but

ever) [as many soever]. No one of the Christians was by that time unbaptized.—ἐβαπτίσθημεν, *were baptized*) The mentioning of *Baptism* is extremely well suited to this place; for the adult, being a worthy candidate for Baptism, must have passed through the experience of these things, which the apostle has hitherto been describing. Paul in his more solemn epistles, sent to the churches (Rom. Cor. Gal. Eph. Col.), at the beginning of which he calls himself an apostle, mentions *Baptism* expressly; in the more familiar (Phil. Thess.) he presupposes it.—εἰς) *into*. The ground on which we are baptized.—Χριστὸν Ἰησοῦν, *Christ Jesus*) The name Christ is here put first, because it is more regarded here, ver. 4, Gal. iii. 27.—εἰς τὸν θάνατον αὐτοῦ, *into His death*) He who is baptized puts on *Christ*, the second Adam; he is baptized, I say, into a whole Christ, and so also into His death, and it is the same thing as if, at that moment, Christ suffered, died, and was buried for such a man, and as if such a man suffered, died, was buried with Christ.

4. Συνετάφημεν, *we were buried with Him*) The fruits of the burial of Christ. Immersion in baptism, or at least the sprinkling of water upon the person, represents burial, burial is a confirmation of [facit ratam] death.—εἰς, *into*) Construed with *baptism*, with which comp. ver. 3.—ὥσπερ—οὕτω, *as—so*) An abbreviated expression for,[1] *As Christ was raised from the dead by the glory of the Father*, so we should also rise, and as Christ reigns for ever in the glory of the Father, and in that life to which He has risen, *so we also should walk in newness of life*.— διὰ, *by*) *By* concerning the Father is also found at 1 Cor. i. 9.— τῆς δόξης, *the glory*) Δόξα is the *glory* of the divine life, *of incorruptibility*, ch. i. 23, of the power and virtue, by which both Christ was raised, and we are restored to a new life, and are conformed to God, Eph. i. 19, etc.—ἐν καινότητι, *in newness*) Ch. vii. 6; 2 Cor. v. 15, etc. This newness consists in life.

5. Σύμφυτοι) LXX. βουνὸς σύμφυτος, δρυμὸς σύμφυτος, *a planted hill*, a *planted forest*, Amos ix. 13; Zech. xi. 2, and on this account ὁμοιώματι here may be taken in the ablative. But it cannot be imitated in English—it might be, *ignorance* is exceedingly *officient*, knowledge is not *sufficient*, were *officient* an English word, which it is not.—Tr.

[1] See App., under the title *Concisa Locutio*.

Hesychius has σύμφυτον, συμπορευόμενον, συνόν, and so σύμφυτοι with the dative is a word very significant; comp. ver. 4, 6. Cluverus translates it, engendered together [connaturati, *endowed with the same nature together*] *grown together*[1].) All spiritually quickening power is in Christ, and that power has been conferred upon [brought together into] baptism; σὺν is used [in the compound σύμφυτοι], as in the opposite word συνεσταυρώθη; and the simple [root] word φύομαι refers to θάνατον, and ἀνάστασιν.—ἀλλὰ, *but*) The contrast is between death and the resurrection.—τῆς) that is, τῷ ὁμοιώματι τῆς ἀναστάσεως, *in the likeness of His resurrection*.—ἐσόμεθα) scil. σύμφυτοι, *we shall be*, viz. planted in a new life. The future, see ch. v. 19.

6. "Ἄνθρωπος, *man*) The abstract for the concrete, as in ch. vii. 22, and in many other places.—ἵνα—τοῦ μηκέτι) The particles should be carefully noticed; as also the three synonymous nouns, and the verbs added to them.—καταργηθῇ, *may be destroyed*) may be stripped of its *dominion* [ver. 14].—τὸ σῶμα τῆς ἁμαρτίας, *the body of sin*) the mortal body, abounding in sin and lusts, etc., ver. 12, *so the body of death*, ch. vii. 24, note.

7. Ἀποθανὼν, *dead*) *to sin*, ver. 2.—δεδικαίωται, [*is freed from sin*] *is justified*) Sin has now no longer any claim against him in law; with which comp. ver. 6, 9, so that he is no longer *a debtor*, ch. viii. 12. In respect of the past, he is justified [just] from the guilt of sin; in respect of the future, from its dominion, ver. 14.

8. Ἐι, *if*) The Apodosis falls principally on the verb, *we shall live with*.

9. Εἰδότες, *knowing*) This word depends on, *we believe*.—θάνατος, *death*) without the article, *any kind of death*.—οὐκ ἔτι, *no more*) *Death* never *had dominion over Christ*, but yet it had assailed Him, Acts ii. 24; and if it had held Him, it might have been said to have had dominion over Him; which God forbid. Paul was unwilling to say here, βασιλεύει, *reigneth*.

10. ὅ, *in that*) This has more force than ὅτι, *that*.—τῇ ἁμαρτίᾳ, *to sin*) The dative of disadvantage, as in ver. 11. Sin had been cast upon Christ, but Christ abolished it by His death for us; He truly *died*.—ἐφάπαξ) This has a stronger meaning in this

---

[1] *Concreti.*

passage than ἅπαξ. So Heb. vii. 27, and ἅπαξ, 1 Pet. iii. 18.—
ζῇ τῷ Θεῷ) *He lives to God*, a glorious life derived from God, ver. 4 [raised up—by the *glory* of the Father] full of divine vigour, lasting for ever. For God is the God of the living.

11. Λογίζεσθε, *you reckon*) The indicative; for the imperative begins in the following verse. So λογιζόμεθα, iii. 28 [we *conclude* that a man is justified by faith, etc.] Whatever is the standing in which every one is, in and according to that standing he ought to account himself.[1]—εἶναι) is omitted by a few copies, but they are ancient. Baumgarten adopts this reading—I consider it doubtful.[2]—ἐν, *in*) It is construed with *alive*, nay even with *dead* too: So ver. 8, only that the prepositions *with* [σὺν, ver. 8] and *by*, ch. vii. 4 [διὰ, *by* the body of Christ] are rather used in that connection.—τῷ κυρίῳ ἡμῶν) See App. crit. Ed. II. on this passage.[3]

12. Μή, *not*) Refer the ἀλλὰ *but* [yield yourselves unto God, ver. 13] to μή, *not* [here]: and refer καὶ τὰ μέλη, *and your members*, etc., to μηδὲ, *neither* [both in ver. 13] [*There is a remarkable force in this dehortation on the one hand and exhortation on the other*, V. g.]—μὴ οὖν βασιλευέτω, *let not sin therefore reign*) The same verb occurs in ch. v. 21. A synonymous term in ver. 9. It is a correlative of *serve*, ver. 6.—θνητῷ, *mortal*) For you, who are now alive, are become alienated from your body, ch. viii. 10.—αὐτῇ ἐν) This savours somewhat of a paraphrase. *Baumgarten* and I, as usual, hold each his own opinion, as to the mode of interpreting this passage.—ἐν ταῖς ἐπιθυμίαις αὐτοῦ, *in its lusts*) viz. σώματος, *of the body*. The bodily appetites are the fuel; sin is the fire.

13. Μηδὲ παριστάνετε) *neither yield ye*. The first aor. παραστήσατε, which occurs presently, has greater force than this present.—τὰ μέλη ὑμῶν· ἑαυτοὺς καὶ τὰ μέλη, *your members; yourselves and your members*) First, the character of the Christian is brought under consideration; secondly, His actions and

---

[1] So also the Christian, whose standing is, that of being dead to sin with Christ, and raised with Him in newness of life.—ED.

[2] AD(Λ)G Memph. Vers. Hilary, omit the εἶναι. But BC Vulg. *fg* and Rec. Text retain it.—ED.

[3] ABD(Λ)G*fg* Vulg. Hilary, reject τῷ κυρίῳ ἡμῶν. But C Memph. and Syr. Versions retain the words.—ED.

duties. Man, who is dead in sin, could not, with propriety, be said to *yield* HIMSELF [Sistere seipsum, *to present himself*] *to sin:* but the man, who is alive, may yield [present] himself to God.—ὅπλα, *arms*) [*instruments*] a figurative expression, derived from war, as *wages*, ver. 23.—ἀδικίας, *of unrighteousness*) which is opposed to the righteous will of God.—τῇ ἁμαρτίᾳ, *to sin*) Sin is here considered as a tyrant.—παραστήσατε [*yield*] *present*) as to a king.—ἐκ νεκρῶν, *from the dead*) The Christian is *alive from the dead.* He had been dead, he is now alive. Comp. Eph. v. 14, *note*, Rev. iii. 1–3. Sleep, too, in these passages, is the image of *death.*—δικαιοσύνης, *of righteousness*) The antithetic word is ἀδικίας, *of unrighteousness.*

14. Οὐ κυριεύσει, *Shall not have dominion*) Sin has neither the right nor the power; it will not force men to become slaves to it against their will.—ὑπὸ νόμον, *under the law*) Sin has dominion over him, who is under the law.

15. Ὑπὸ, *under*) ch. vii. 2, 14.

16. Δούλους, *servants*) *Servitude* is here denoted, from which *obedience* follows as a consequence.—δοῦλοι, *servants*) The state of *servitude*, which follows as the consequence of *obedience*, is signified, 2 Pet. ii. 19.—εἰς, *unto*) εἰς, *unto*, occurs twice in this verse, and in both cases it depends on *servants.*—ὑπακοῆς, *or obedience*) *Obedience*, used absolutely, is taken in a good sense. Righteousness, too, promptly claims as her own, those who act obediently to her.—εἰς δικαιοσύνην, *unto righteousness*) Supply, *and of righteousness unto life:* as appears from the antithesis [*death*], with which comp. the similar antithesis, ver. 20 and 22, iii. 20, *note.*

17. Χάρις δὲ τῷ Θεῷ, *but God be thanked*) This is an idiom peculiar to Paul, who usually expresses categorical propositions, not categorically and nakedly, but, as it were, with some modifying qualification, *i.e.*, with an intimation of affection, thanksgiving, prayerful wish for them, etc.—1 Cor. xiv. 18; 2 Tim. ii. 7, *note.* The enthymeme[1] of this passage stands thus: *you were the servants of sin; but now you have become obedient to righteousness:* but there is added the moral mode[2] or moral

---

[1] The simple enunciation. See Appendix.
[2] See Appendix, under the title, Modalis Sermo A proposition not

sentiment, *God be thanked, that though ye were the servants of sin, ye have now obeyed righteousness.* This mode, however, in this place, implies this also, that this is the blessed state of the Romans, which they ought by all means to maintain. This observation will clearly bring out the meaning of the apostle's language in many passages, and will show the ardour that was within his breast.—ὅτι, *that*) so *that*, with *indeed*, to be understood, John iii. 19.¹—δοῦλοι, *servants*) especially in heathenism. —ἐκ καρδίας, *from the heart*) The truth and efficacy of the Christian religion [lies in its having its root *in the heart.*] Wicked men cannot be altogether wicked with their whole heart, but even unconsciously and continually repent of their past conduct, and of their slavery to sin; but good men are good from the heart, and without constraint. [*It is not any doctrine of men, but the doctrine of God alone, which takes by storm* (takes complete possession of) *the human heart.*—V. g.]— εἰς ὅν) This is the explanation ὑπηκούσατε εἰς τύπον διδαχῆς ᾧ or εἰς ὅν παρεδόθητε, comp. εἰς, Gal. i. 6; *you were obedient to* [with respect to, towards] *the form of doctrine* (*comp.* εἰς πάντα ὑπήκοοι, *obedient in all things*, 2 Cor. ii. 9) *unto which you were delivered* (*which was delivered to you*). The case of the relative, expressed in abbreviated form,² depends on the word preceding, ch. iv. 17, or following ch. x. 14.—παρεδόθητε, *you were delivered*) Elsewhere the *doctrine* is said to be *delivered*. That phrase is here elegantly inverted, and is a very graceful expression respecting those who, when freed from sin, devote and yield [present] themselves, ver. 16, with a great change of masters, to the honourable service of righteousness.—τύπον, *form*) a very beautiful term, Ex. xxv. 40. The form meant is the 'form' of Christ, Gal. iv. 19.— διδαχῆς, *of doctrine*) That rule and standard, to which the servant conforms himself, is merely shown to him *by the doctrine;* he does not need to be urged by constraint.

---

stated nakedly, but with intimation of feeling accompanying it. Instead of the naked statement, "Ye were servants of sin," Paul says, in the *moral mode,* "Thanks be to God, that, though ye were servants of sin, ye have now obeyed," etc.

¹ Light *is* (*indeed*) come into the world, and (*yet*) men loved darkness, etc. So here, = *though ye were,—yet now,* etc.—ED.

² See App., tit. "Concisa Locutio."

ROMANS VI. 18.

18. 'Ἐλευθερωθέντες, *being made free*) It will be of use to have this connected view of the plan of the apostle, up to the point which it has now reached:—

I. *Sin,*	. . . .	Ch. iii. 9.
II. The perception [the coming to "the knowledge"] of sin from the law; the sense of *wrath;* internal [spiritual] *death,*	. . . .	iii. 20.
III. The revelation of the righteousness of God in Christ, by the Gospel, directed against sin, and yet in behalf of the sinner,	. . . .	iii. 21.
IV. The centre of Paul's system, FAITH; embracing that revelation without reservation, and striving after, and succeeding in its effort to reach righteousness itself,	. . .	iii. 22.
V. The remission of sins, and justification, by which God the judge, views sin committed by man, as if it had not been committed, and righteousness lost, as if had been preserved [retained],	. . . .	iii. 24.
VI. The gift of the Holy Spirit; *love* Divine shed abroad in the heart; the inner new *life,*	. . .	v. 5, vi. 4.
VII. The free service of *righteousness* in good works,	. . .	vi. 12.

From this view, it is evident why Paul, in proving justification by faith alone, against those who are in doubt or error, makes frequent mention of the gift of the Holy Spirit, and of the other things, which follow as the consequences of justification. As righteousness flows from faith; adoption [sonship] accompanies righteousness; the gift of the Holy Spirit, with the cry, *Abba, Father,* and with newness of life, follows upon adoption; but faith and righteousness are not in themselves clearly perceived by sense; whereas the gift of the Holy Ghost produces very conspicuous and prominent [standing out palpable] effects; comp. [God] *bare them witness* [giving them *the Holy Ghost*] Acts xv. 8. Farther, the surpassing excellence of these fruits, most effectually proves the worthlessness of men's works.

19. Ἀνθρώπινον, *after the manner of men*) Language after the manner of men, is frequent, and in some measure always occurring, whereby Scripture condescends to suit itself to our capacity. Too plain language is not always better [the best] adapted to the subject in hand. The accusative is used for the adverb. [*According to our mode of speaking, it may be translated,* Ich muss es euch mir massiv sagen, *I must speak to you with great plainness and simplicity.*—V. g.]—διὰ, *because of*) Slowness of understanding arises from weakness of the flesh, *i.e.,* of a nature merely human, comp. 1 Cor. iii. 3. Ἀσθένειαν, *weakness*) Those who desire discourse to be continuously in all respects quite plain, should perceive in this a mark of their own weakness, and should not take amiss [take offence at] a more profound expression of the truth, but they should consider it with gratitude, as an ample benefit, if in one way or the other, they have had the good fortune to understand the subject: at first, the mode of expressing the truth is more sublime, then afterwards it is more plain, as in the case of Nicodemus.—John iii. 3, 15. That which pleases most [the greatest number] is not always the best.—V. g.—τῇ ἀνομίᾳ εἰς τὴν ἀνομίαν, *to iniquity unto iniquity*) A ploce[1] not observed by the Syriac version. The word [to] *iniquity* [ἀνομίᾳ] (before which *uncleanness* is put, as a part before a whole) is opposed to *righteousness;* the word [unto] *iniquity* [ἀνομίαν] is opposed to *holiness* [end of verse] *Righteousness* corresponds to the Divine will, *holiness* as it were, to the whole of the Divine nature. Those who are the servants of righteousness, make progress [*i.e.,* advance from *righteousness* to *holiness,* whereby they partake of the Divine nature]; ἄνομοι, workers of iniquity are workers of iniquity, nothing more.

20. Τῆς ἁμαρτίας, *of sin*) This case contains the emphasis of the sentence; *sin* had taken possession of you.—τῇ δικαιοσύνῃ, *to* [towards] *righteousness*) that is in respect of righteousness.

---

[1] See App., tit. *Ploce.* A word twice put, once in the simple sense, and once again to express some attribute of the word.

21. Τίνα οὖν καρπὸν εἴχετε τότε, ἐφ' οἷς νῦν ἐπαισχύνεσθε) This whole period has the force of a negative interrogation. He says, that the righteous have their *fruit* unto holiness; but he does not consider those things which are 'unfruitful' [ἄκαρπα] worthy of the name of *fruit*.—Eph. v. 11. He says, therefore, those things which now cause you to feel ashamed, were, indeed, formerly not *fruits*. Others put the mark of interrogation after τότε, *then*, so that ἐφ' οἷς may be the answer to the interrogation; but then the apostle should have said ἐφ' ᾧ, sc. καρπῷ [Sanctification is the *reverse of this shame*, ver. 22, *evidently just as in* 1 Cor. i. 28, 30, that which is base ("base things") *and* sanctification, *are in antithesis; but the multitude of Christians are now* ashamed *of* sanctification, *which is esteemed as something* base. *What a fearful death hangs over such persons! O the degeneracy of the times and the manners* (principles of men)!—V. g.]—νῦν, *now*) when you have been brought to repentance.—γὰρ, *for*) instead of *moreover* [autem]; but it has a greater power of separation, comp. ver. 22 at the end, δὲ, *and moreover* [autem]; so γὰρ, *for*, ch. v. 7.—ἐκείνων, *of those things*) He does not say, *of these* things; he looks on those things as the remote past.—θάνατος, *death*) The epithet *eternal* (αἰώνιος) ver. 23, is never added to this noun, not only in relation to those, in the case of whom, death yields to life, but not even in relation to those who shall go away into *everlasting fire, torment, and destruction*. If any one can think, that it is by mere chance, and not design, that Scripture, when *eternal life* is expressly mentioned, never names its opposite, *eternal death*, but everywhere speaks of it in a different manner, and that, too, in so many places, I, for my part, leave to him the equivalence of the phrases, *eternal destruction*, etc.[1] The reason of the difference, however, is this: Scripture often describes *death*, by personification, as an enemy, and an enemy, too, to be destroyed; but it does not so describe *torment*.

22. Νυνὶ δὲ, *but now*) Paul has used νυνὶ very often, and always with δὲ, *but*.—ἔχετε, *you have; or, have ye*, with which comp. ver. 19.—εἰς ἁγιασμὸν, *unto sanctification* [*holiness*], an antithesis to; ἐφ' οἷς ἐπαισχύνεσθε, *of which you are ashamed*, ver. 21. Ye are a holy priesthood of God. The reference seems to be to

[1] I leave him to his own foolish notion, that the phrases *eternal destruction*, etc., are equivalent to *eternal death*.—ED.

Amos ii. 11, לִנְזִרִים, LXX, εἰς ἁγιασμόν; Engl. Vers. has *Nazarites*.

23. Τὰ, τὸ) The mark of the subject.—ὀψώνια—χάρισμα, *wages*—*gift*) Bad works earn their own proper pay; not so, good works; for the former obtain wages, the latter a gift: ὀψώνια, *wages*, in the plural: χάρισμα, *a gift*, in the singular, with a stronger force.

CHAPTER VII.

1. ῏Η) The disjunctive interrogation. There is a close connection here with ch. vi., the words of which, at ver. 6, 14, 21, καταργεῖσθαι, κυριεύειν, καρπὸς, θάνατος κ.τ.λ. again occur prominently in this chapter. The comparison of the Old and New state is continued.—γινώσκουσι, *to them that know*) the Jews; although it is the duty of all Christians to know the law.—ὁ νόμος, *the law*) for example, of marriage. The whole *law*, in consonance with the opening of this portion, is put by synecdoche,[1] for the *law of marriage*.—τοῦ ἀνθρώπου, *over a man*) i.e., over a woman, ver. 2, comp. 1 Pet. iii. 4, where the *inner* ["the hidden man"] presupposes the outer man, and the parallelism consists in this, that *man* is predicated also separately of *the woman*, not merely of Adam, the husband ['viro,' *the man*, in the restricted sense of the term.] *Man* here is used generically; but in the second verse, Paul applies it in a special and subordinate sense to the woman, as falling under the generic term.—ἐφ' ὅσον, *as long as*) neither any longer nor any shorter.—ζῇ, *lives*) the Law [lives. But Engl. Vers. "As long as *he*—the husband—liveth."] A personification. In the apodosis, life and death are ascribed, not to the law, but to us; whereas, here we have the protasis, in which, according to the meaning of the apostle, life or death is ascribed to the [marriage] law itself, and to the husband. What

---

[1] See Appendix.

is here said, depends on the nature of the things related, which are the law and man. When either party dies, the other is considered to be dead. Thus the protasis and apodosis cohere.

2. Ὕπανδρος) So the LXX.—δέδεται, *is bound*) It may be construed with *to her husband*, and with *by* [*to*] *the law*.—τοῦ νόμου τοῦ ἀνδρὸς) It would not be an unsuitable apposition, were we to say, *from the law* [that is, *from*] *her husband*.

3. Χρηματίσει) viz. ἑαυτὴν, *she will come under the appellation of an adulteress*, and that too by the power of the law. *She shall bring upon herself the name of an* adulteress.—ἐὰν γένηται ἀνδρὶ ἑτέρῳ, LXX. Deut. xxiv. 2.

4. Ὥστε) This word has a stronger meaning than if οὕτως had been used.—ἐθανατώθητε, *ye have become dead*) which denotes more than *ye are dead*. The comparison is thus summed up: the husband or wife, by the death of either, is restored to liberty; for in the protasis, the party dying is the husband; in the apodosis, the party dying is that, which corresponds to the wife.—διὰ τοῦ σώματος, *by the body*) A great mystery. In the expiation [atonement] for sin, why is it that mention generally is made of the body, rather than of the soul of Christ? Ans. The theatre and workshop of sin is our flesh; and for this, it is the holy flesh of the Son of God, which is the remedy.—ἐγερθέντι, *who is raised*) and so is alive [which the law no longer is to the believer].—καρποφορήσωμεν, *we should bring forth fruit*) He comes from the second person to the first; *fruit* corresponds to offspring; for the simile is derived from marriage.

5. Ἦμεν ἐν τῇ σαρκὶ, *we were in the flesh*) that is [we were] carnal. See the opposite ver. 6, at the end.—διὰ, *by*) ver. 8.—τῷ θανάτῳ, *to that death*) of which ver. 13, ch. viii. 6, speak.

6. Ἀποθανόντες, *being dead*) So ver. 4, *ye became dead*, said of that party, which corresponds to the wife: comp. Gal. ii. 19. I have shown *in der Antwort wegen des N. T. p.* 55. A. 1745, that Chrysostom also read ἀποθανόντες, not ἀποθανόντος.[1]—ᾧ) A plain construction in this sense: we have been set free by death from the law, which held us fast.—κατειχόμεθα) an expres-

---

[1] So also A (B?) C, both Syr. Versions, Memph. The first correction of the Amiatine MS. of Vulg. read ἀποθάνοντες. D (Λ) G *fg* Vulg. read τοῦ θανάτου [The law of death]. Rec. Text (and B?) ἀποθάνοντος.—ED.

sive term; comp. συνέκλεισε, ch. xi. 32, ἐφρουρούμεθα, Gal. iii. 23.—ἐν καινότητι πνεύματος, καὶ οὐ παλαιότητι γράμματος, *in newness of spirit, and not in the oldness of the letter*) We have the same antithesis, ch. ii. 29; 2 Cor. iii. 6. *The letter* is not the law considered in itself, inasmuch as, thus considered, it is spiritual and living [instinct with life] ver. 14; Acts vii. 38 [the *lively* oracles], but in respect of the sinner, to whom it cannot give spirit and life, but leaves him to death, nay even it to a more profound extent hands him over to its power: although he may in the mean time aim at the performance of what the letter and its mere sound command to be done; so that the appearance and the name may still remain, just as a dead hand is still a hand. But the Spirit is given by the Gospel and by faith, and bestows life and newness, 2 Cor. iii. 6; comp. John vi. 63. The words *oldness* and *newness* are used here by Paul in relation to the two testaments or covenants, although believers have now for a long time enjoyed the first fruits of the New Testament; and at the present day unbelievers retain the remnants, nay rather the whole substance, of the Old Testament. Observe too, the ἐν, *in*, is put once, not twice [The Engl. Vers. wrongly supplies *in* before *the oldness*. But Beng. That we should not *serve the oldness*, etc.] We have served *oldness* not God: comp. Gal. iv. 9, οἷς, *to which* [The beggarly elements, *whereunto* ye desire again *to be in bondage*]; now we serve not *newness*, but [we serve] God *in newness*, ch. vi. 22.

7. ὁ νόμος ἁμαρτία; *is the law sin?*) He, who has heard the same things predicated of the law and of sin, will perhaps make this objection: is, then, the law sin, or the sinful cause of sin? comp. ver. 13, note.—τὴν ἁμαρτίαν, *sin*) We must again observe the propriety of the terms, and the distinction between them:

    ὁ νόμος· τὸ λέγειν τοῦ νόμου.
    the law; the fact of the law *saying* [Taken out of,
               " Except the *law* had *said*"].
    ἡ ἁμαρτία· ἡ ἐπιθυμία.
     sin;   lust.

οὐκ ἔγνων, (from γινώσκω·) οὐκ ᾔδειν, (from οἶδα.) ἔγνων is the greater, οἶδα the less. Hence the latter, since even the less degree is denied, is expressive of increase.[1] Ἁμαρτία, *sin*, is as it were sinful matter, from which *all* manner of [The *all* taken from πᾶσαν ἐπιθυμίαν, ver. 8] disease and paroxysm *of concupiscence* [ver. 8] originates.—οὐκ ἔγνων, *I had not known*) Paul often sets forth his discourse indefinitely in the first person, not only for the sake of perspicuity, but from the constant application of what is said to himself; see 1 Cor. v. 12, vi. 12. And so also in this passage.—τήν τε γὰρ ἐπιθυμίαν, *for even lust*) Ἡ ἁμαρτία, *sin*, is more deeply seated [inward] and recondite: ἡ ἐπιθυμία, *lust*, rather assails [rushes into] the sense, and at the same time betrays [the inwardly seated] *sin*, as smoke does fire. The particles τὲ γὰρ, *for even* indicate this διορισμός, this contra-distinction; and *sin*, that one indwelling evil, works out [produces] a variety of *lust* [all manner of concupiscence]: see what follows; and again lust brings forth sin consummated [*finished*], James i. 15. [*Sin lies concealed in man, as heat in drink, which, if we were to judge by mere sensation, may possibly at the time be very cold*, V. g.]—οὐκ ᾔδειν, *I had not known*) lust to be an evil; or rather, I had not known [even the existence of] lust itself; its motion at length [when the *law* came, then and not till then] met the eye.—ἔλεγεν, *said*) Moreover it said so, [first] by itself; then, [also] in my mind: comp. *when the law came*, ver. 9.

8. Διὰ τῆς ἐντολῆς, *by the commandment*) The construction is with the following verb [κατειργάσατο, *wrought concupiscence by the commandment*. Not as Engl. V., *Taking occasion by the commandment*, here and at ver. 11]; as in ver. 11 twice.—χωρὶς—νεκρὰ, *without—dead*) A self-evident principle.—νεκρὰ, *dead*) viz. *was*: it did not so much rage through concupiscence: or the word to be supplied may be, *is*.

9. Ἔζων, *I was alive*) ζῆν here does not merely signify *to pass one's life*, but it is put in direct antithesis to *death*. This is the pharisaic tone, comp. the following verse. [*I seemed to myself indeed* to be *extremely* well, V. g.]—χωρὶς νόμου, *without the law*) the law being taken out of the way, being kept at a distance, as if it did not exist.—ἐλθούσης) The antithesis to χωρὶς.—ἐντολῆς, *the commandment*) ἐντολὴ, *a commandment* is part of the law, with the addition of a more express idea in it of

---

[1] The increase in force is this; I had not *full* knowledge (ἔγνων) of sin, nay I had not even been *at all sensible* (ᾔδειν) of lust.—ED.

compulsory power, which restrains, enjoins, urges, prohibits, threatens.—ἀνέζησεν, *revived*) just as [even as] it had been alive, when it had entered into the world by Adam.

10. Ἀπέθανον, *I died*) I lost that life, which I [fancied that I] had.—εὑρέθη, *was found*) So εὑρίσκω, *I find*, ver. 21.—εἰς ζωὴν, *to life*) on the ground of the original intention of God, and in another point of view, on the ground of my own opinion, which I held, *when I was living without the law*. *Life* pointedly indicates both joy and activity; while *death* implies the opposite.— αὐτὴ, *itself*) the same [the very same commandment]. It is commonly written αὕτη, but *Baumgarten* has αὐτὴ, which is correct.[1] Comp. Acts viii. 26, note.

11. Ἐξηπάτησε, *deceived*) led me into by-paths, as the robber leads the traveller; and while I supposed that I was going onward to life, I fell into [upon] death.—ἀπέκτεινεν, *slew me*) This is the termination of the economy of sin, and is on the confines of that of grace.

12. Ἅγιος, *holy*) supply from what follows, *and just and good;* although it was necessary to accumulate these synonymous terms chiefly in defence of the *commandment*, with its stinging power [rather than of *the law*]: *holy, just, good*, in relation respectively to its efficient cause, its form, and its end; (as we find *in the MS. notes of Dorscheus*) or *holy* in respect of my duties to God; *just*, in respect of my neighbour; *good* in respect of my own nature;[2] with which whatever is commanded is in harmony, for life is promised, ver. 10. The third of these three epithets is taken up with very great propriety in the following verse.

13. Τὸ) *therefore what is good.*—The power of the article is to be noticed.—θάνατος, *death*) the greatest *evil*, and the cause of

---

[1] Lachmann and Tischendorf, the two ablest exponents of modern textual criticism, prefer αὕτη.—ED.

[2] Δίκαιος Th. δίκη, is that which is precisely what it should be, without regard to the question whether good or evil flow from it, *just, right*. But ἀγαθός, what is *profitable and of benefit* to men. The commandment is δίκαια, for it teaches nothing but what is *just;* ἀγαθή, for it regards the *happiness* of those, to whom it is given. It is also ἅγια, not because it makes holy, but because it is *holy in itself, sacred to God*, and therefore to be held inviolate.—See Tittmann *Syn. Gr. Text.*—ED.

death, the grestest evil: κατεργαζομένη, *working* [*death in me*].—
ἀλλὰ ἡ ἁμαρτία, *but sin*) namely, *was made death to me;* for the
participle κατεργαζομένη, *working*, without the substantive verb,
does not constitute the predicate.—ἵνα φανῇ ἁμαρτία, *that it might
appear sin*) Ploce[1] : sin, [which, as opposed to the law, which is
good, is] by no means *good*. This agrees with what goes before.—
διὰ τοῦ ἀγαθοῦ—θάνατον, *by that which is good—death*) A paradox;
and the adjective *good* is used with great force for the substantive
[of which it is the epithet] the *law*.—κατεργαζομένη, *working*) A
participle, which must be explained thus: sin was made death
to me, *inasmuch as being that which* accomplished my death even
by that which is good. It is no tautology; for that expression,
by that which is good, superadds strength to the second part of
this sentence.—ἵνα γένηται, *that it might become*) This phrase is
dependent on *working*. So ἵνα, *that*, repeated twice, forms a
gradation. If any one should rather choose to make it an
anaphora,[2] the second part of the sentence will thus also explain
the first.—καθ᾽ ὑπερβολὴν ἁμαρτωλὸς) Castellio translates it, *as
sinful as possible:* because, namely, [sin,] by *that which was* [*is*]
good, *i.e.* by the commandment, works in me that which is *evil*,
i.e. death.—διὰ, *by*) It is construed with *might become* [that sin
might by the commandment become exceeding sinful].

14. Πνευματικός ἐστι, *is spiritual*) it requires, that every feeling
of man should correspond to the feeling [*i.e.* the will] of God;
but God is a Spirit.—σαρκικὸς, *carnal*) ver. 18.—εἰμί, *I am*) Paul,
after he had compared together the twofold state of believers,
the former in the flesh, ver 5, and the present in the Spirit,
ver. 6, proceeds in the next place from the description of the
first to the description of the second, and does so with a view
both to answer two objections, which, in consequence of that
comparison might be framed in these words: *therefore the law is
sin*, ver. 7, and, *therefore the law is death*, ver. 13; and to inter-
weave in the solution of those objections the whole process of a
man, in his transition from his state under the law to his state
under grace, thinking, sighing, striving, and struggling forth,

[1] See Appendix. The same term twice used, once expressing the idea
of the word itself, and once again expressing an attribute of it.

[2] See Appendix. The frequent repetition of the same word in the beginnings of sections or sentences.

and to show the function of the law in this matter : this, I say, he does, ver. 7–25, until at ch. viii. 1, he proceeds to the topics, which are ulterior to these. Therefore in this 14th verse the particle *for* does not permit any leap at all, much less does the subject itself allow so great a leap to be made from the one state into the other; for Paul diametrically opposes to each other the carnal state in this verse, and the spiritual state, ch. viii. 4, as also slavery in this ["*sold* under sin"] and the 23d ["bringing me into *captivity*"] verse, and liberty, viii. 2, ["*free* from the law]. Moreover he uses, before the 14th verse, verbs in the preterite tense ; then, for the sake of more ready expression [more vivid realization of a thing as present], verbs in the present tense, which are to be resolved into the preterite, just as he is accustomed to exchange cases, moods, etc., for the sake of imparting ease to his language; and as an example in ch. viii. 2, 4, he passes from the singular to the plural number, and in the same chapter ver. 9, from the first to the second person. Also the discourse is the more conveniently turned from the past to the present time, inasmuch as a man can then, and then only, understand really the nature of that [his former] state under the law, as soon as he has come under grace ; and from the present he can form a clearer judgment of the past. Finally, that state and process, though being but one and the same, has yet various degrees, which should be expressed either more or less in the preterite tense, and it is step by step that he sighs, strives eagerly, and struggles forth to liberty : The language of the apostle becomes by degrees more serene, as we shall see. *Hence it is less to be wondered at, that interpreters take so widely different views.* They seek the chief force [the sinews] of their arguments, some from the former, others from the latter part of this passage, and yet they endeavour to explain the whole section as referring to one simple condition, either that under sin, or that under grace. [*We must observe in general, that Paul, as somewhat often elsewhere, so also in this verse, all along from ver.* 7, *is not speaking of his own character, but under the figure of a man, who is engaged in this contest. That contest is described here at great length, but the business itself, so far as concerns what may be considered the decisive point, is in many cases quickly accomplished ; although believers must contend with* the enemy, even till their deliverance is fully accomplished, ver. 24, ch. viii. 23, V. g.]—πεπραμένος, *sold*) A man, sold to be a slave, is more wretched, than he who was born in that condition, and he is said to be a man sold, because he was not originally a slave. The same word occurs in Judg. iii. 8, 1 Kings xxi. 25. *Sold: Captive*, ver. 23.

15. Ὁ γὰρ, *for that which*) He describes slavery in such a way as not to excuse himself, but to accuse the tyranny of sin, and to deplore his own misery, ver. 17, 20. Γὰρ, *for*, tends to strengthen the word *sold*. The slave serves an unworthy master, first, with joy, then afterwards, with grief, lastly, he shakes off the yoke.—οὐ γινώσκω, *I do not acknowledge* [*allow*]) as good; ([γινώσκω] the same as *to consent to it, that it is good*, ver. 16, which forms the antithesis); its opposite is *I hate*.—θέλω, I *would*, [*wish*]) he does not say, *I love*, which would imply more, but *I would*, intending to oppose this [I would] to, *I hate*, following immediately after.—πράσσω—ποιῶ) There is a distinction between πράσσω and ποιῶ commonly acknowledged among the Greeks;[1] —the former implies something weightier than the latter. The former is put twice in the present tense, first in a negative assertion, and then in an affirmative assertion, οὐ πράσσω *I practise not*, the thing is not put in practice; ποιῶ *I do*, refers to action both internal and external. These words are interchanged, ver. 19, xiii. 3, 4; and this interchange is not only not contrary to the nature of the discourse which is gradually rising to a climax, but it even supports and strengthens it; for at ver. 15, the sense of the evil is not yet so bitter, and therefore he does not so much as name it, but by the time he reaches ver. 19, he is now become very impatient [takes it exceedingly ill] that he should thus impose evil on himself. The farther the soul is from *evil*, the greater is its distress [torture], to touch even the smallest particle of evil with so much as one finger.

16. Σύμφημι, *I consent*) Συνήδομαι, *I delight* is a stronger expression, ver. 22, note. The assent of a man, given to the law against himself, is an illustrative trait of true religion, a powerful testimony for God.—καλὸς, *beautiful*) The law, even apart from

---

[1] See my previous note. Πράσσω is *ago*. Ποιέω, *facio*. Ἐργάζομαι, *operor*.—Ed.

its legality, is beautiful: καλὸς, *beautiful*, suggests holiness, justice, and goodness, ver. 12.

17. Οὐκ ἔτι, *no longer*) These words are repeated, ver 20.—οἰκοῦσα, *dwelling*) ver. 18, 20. This word is afterwards used concerning the Spirit, ch. viii. 9.

18. Οἶδα, *I know*) This very knowledge is a part of this state, which is here described.—τουτέστιν, *that is*) It is a limitation of the sense; *in me* is more than *in my flesh*, and yet the flesh is not called sin itself[1] (we must make this observation contrary to the opinion of Flacius); but what Paul says, is: sin dwells in the flesh. And already this state, of which Paul is treating, carries along with it some element of good.—θέλειν *to will*) The Accusative, *good*, is not added after *to will;* and the delicacy [minute accuracy] of this language expresses the delicacy [minute accuracy] in the use of the expression, *to will*.—παράκειται) [*is present*] *lies in view*, without [my being able to gain] the victory. The antithesis, concerning the performance of good works, is the *not* [I find *not*] which occurs presently after. My mind, though seeking [that, which is good], does not in reality find it.

20. Οὐκ ἔτι) *no longer*,[2] namely, as I formerly used to perpetrate it [taken from κατεργάζομαι]. Some degree of serenity and deliverance gradually arises. *I* is emphatic, in antithesis to *sin*. He who says with emphasis, it is not *I that will* it [non *volo ego*], instead of the former, *I would not* [*non volo* (without *ego*) I do not will] (ver. 15) is already farther removed from sin.

21. Εὑρίσκω) In this distressing conflict *I find* the law, [But Engl. Vers. " *a* law"] without which I formerly lived. This is all [I merely find the law]. That proposition, which occurs at ver. 14, is repeated.—τὸν νόμον) *the law* itself, which is in itself holy.—τῷ θέλοντι, [*for,* or *to me*] *willing*) The Dative of advantage: I find the law, which is not sinful or deadly [*for,* or] to me [so far as I am concerned; in my experience]. The first principles of harmony, friendship, and agreement between the law and man, are expressed with admirable nicety of language. The participle is purposely put first, τῷ θέλοντι ἐμοί, *for,* or *to the*

---

[1] It is only called *sinful*.—ED.
[2] *Not now, as in former times,* when I was *wholly dead* in sin.—ED.

person willing, viz. *me*,[1] in antithesis to the second [*with*] *me*, which presently after occurs absolutely. With the words, *for*, or *to me willing*, comp. Phil. ii. 13.—ὅτι, *because*) [But Engl. Vers. I find *a* law, *that, when I would* do good, evil is present with me]. —παράκειται, *lies near*, [*is present with me*]) Here the balance is changed; for at ver. 18, the good will *lies near* [*is present;*] the same word, παράκειται] as the lighter part [side of the scale]; whereas by this time, now the evil, though not the evil will, *lies near* [*is present*], as the lighter part [side of the scale].

22. Συνήδομαι, *I delight*) This too is already a further step in advance than σύμφημι, *I consent*, ver. 16.—τὸν ἔσω, *the inward*) He already upholds the name and character of the inward, but not yet however of the *new* man; so also in ver. 25 he says, "with my *mind*," not, with my *spirit*.

23. Βλέπω) *I see*, from the higher department of the soul, as from a watch-tower, [the department, or region of the soul] which is called νοῦς, *the mind*, and is itself the repository of conscience.—ἕτερον, *another* [law] and one alien [to the law of my mind].—μέλεσι, *in the members*) The soul is, as it were, the king; the members are as the citizens; sin is, as an enemy, admitted through the fault of the king, who is doomed to be punished by the oppression of the citizens.—τῷ νόμῳ τοῦ νοός μου) *the dictate* [*law*] *of my mind, which delights in* the Divine law.— αἰχμαλωτίζοντά με, *bringing me into captivity*) by any actual victory which it pleases.[2] The apostle again uses rather a harsh term, arising from holy impatience:[3] the allegory is taken from war, comp. the similar term, *warring*.

24. Ταλαίπωρος ἐγὼ ἄνθρωπος) [" *O wretched man that I am!*" Engl. Vers. But Beng.] *wretched me, who am* [inasmuch as I am] *a man!* Man, if he were without sin, is noble as well as blessed; with sin, he rather wishes not to be a man at all, than to be such a man as man actually is: *The man* [whom Paul personifies] speaks of the state of *man* in itself, as it is by nature. This cry for help is the last thing in the struggle, and,

---

[1] The participle cannot be placed first in English Tr. What he means is; the *law is found* by *him who wills to do good*, which is now the case *with me*.—ED.

[2] *i.e.* leading me at will to do whatever it pleases.—ED

[3] To express his holy impatience to be rid of the tyrant.—ED.

after that henceforth convinced, that he has no help in himself, he begins, so to speak, unknowingly to pray, *who shall deliver me?* and he seeks deliverance and waits, until God shows Himself openly in Christ, in answer to that *who.* This marks *the very moment of mystical death.*[1] Believers to a certain extent continue to carry with them something of this feeling even to the day of their death,[2] viii. 23.—ῥύσεται, *shall deliver*) Force is necessary. The verb is properly used; for ῥύεσθαι, is, ἐκ ΘΑΝΑΤΟΥ ἕλκειν (to drag from DEATH), Ammonius from Aristoxenus.—ἐκ) *from.*—τοῦ σώματος, *from the body of death*) the body being dead on account of sin, ch. viii. 10. The death of the body is the full carrying into execution of that death, of which ver. 13 treats, and yet in death there is to be deliverance. —τούτου) σῶμα θανάτου τούτου is said for σῶμα θανάτου τοῦτο, *the body of this death,* for, *this body of death.*—Comp. Acts v. 20, note.

25. Εὐχαριστῶ, *I give thanks*) This is unexpectedly, though most pleasantly, mentioned, and is now at length rightly acknowledged, as the one and only refuge. The sentence is categorical : God *will deliver* me by Christ; the thing is not in my own power: and that sentence indicates the whole matter: but the moral mode [*modus moralis.* See Append.] (of which, see on ch. vi. 17), *I give thanks,* is added. (As in 1 Cor. xv. 57 : the sentiment is : God giveth us the victory; but there is added the ηθος, or moral mode, *Thanks be to God.*) And the phrase, I *give thanks,* as a joyful hymn, stands in opposition to the miserable complaint, which is found in the preceding verse, *wretched that I am.*—οὖν, *then*) He concludes those topics, on which he had entered at ver. 7.—αὐτὸς ἐγὼ) *I myself.*—νόμῳ Θεοῦ—νόμῳ ἁμαρτίας, *the law of God—the law of sin*) νόμῳ is the Dative, not the Ablative, ver. 23. Man [*the* man, whom Paul personifies] is now equally balanced between slavery and liberty, and yet at the same time, panting after liberty, he acknowledges that the law is holy and free from all blame. The balance is rarely even. Here the inclination to good has by this time attained the greater weight of the two.

[1] The becoming figuratively *dead* in a spiritual sense *to the law and to sin,* ver. 4.—ED.

[2] This longing for deliverance from the body of this death.—ED.

CHAPTER VIII.

1. Οὐδέν ἄρα νῦν κατάκριμα, *There is therefore now no condemnation*) The apostle comes now to deliverance and liberty. Moreover he does not employ the adversative δέ, *but;* he uses the conclusive ἄρα, *therefore*, comp. on ch. ii. 1 ; because at the end of ch. vii. he had already reached the confines of this condition. He also now evidently returns from his admirable digression to the path, which is pursued [he had entered on] at ch. vii. 6. And, as a proof of this, the particle *now*, which denotes present time (like the German *würklich*, actually, truly) was used there, and is resumed here. *Condemned* ["God c. sin"] in ver. 3, refers to *condemnation* here.

1, 2. Περιπατοῦσιν· ὁ γὰρ νόμος, *to them that walk: for the law*) the aetiology [assigning of the reason, see Append.] by a parenthesis suspends the train of thought (*for the law of death* (ver. 2) : *in us who walk* [resuming the *same word* and train of thought as ver. 1], ver. 4); and as this parenthesis is terminated by epanalepsis,[1] the expression *but according to the spirit* completes the period, in which the *but* is opposed rather to the *not* in ver. 1, than to the *not* in ver. 4. The phrase, *but after the spirit* (ἀλλὰ κατὰ πνεῦμα) is omitted in the first verse on the most respectable testimony.[2] Baumgarten retains it. But Paul immediately treats of that expression μὴ κατὰ σάρκα, *not according to* or *after the flesh ;*[3] then as he advances,[4] he adds,

---

[1] See Appendix. When the same word or words are in the beginning of the preceding member and in the end of the following member : as here μὴ κατὰ σάρκα περιπατοῦσιν, *before*, and *at the close* of the parenthesis.

[2] A and the later corrector of D Vulg. Syr. add with Rec. Text. the words μὴ κατὰ σάρκα περιπατοῦσιν. But they omit ἀλλὰ κατὰ πνεῦμα. BCD (Λ) G*gf*, Memph. and Theb. Versions omit the whole μὴ κατα—πνεῦμα. Rec. Text has, of ancient authorities, only *ff*, one or two later uncial MSS. and Theodoret.—ED.

[3] Which makes it likely, that not κατὰ πνεῦμα, but κατὰ σάρκα was what went immediately before.—ED.

[4] And not till then.—ED.

ἀλλὰ κατὰ πνεῦμα, *but according to* or *after the spirit,* ver. 4, note.

2. Νόμος τοῦ πνεύματος) *the law of the spirit,* the Gospel inscribed on the heart; comp. ch. iii. 27; 2 Cor. iii. 8. *The spirit makes alive, and this life* invigorates [vegetat] the Christian.—ἠλευθέρωσέ με, *hath made me free*) a mild term, and in the preterite tense; he had formerly put the weightier verb ῥύσεται in the future. Grace renders that most easy, which seems difficult to man under the law, or rather does it itself. Both are opposed to the phrase, *bringing me into captivity,* ch. vii. 23.—τῆς ἁμαρτίας καὶ τοῦ θανάτου, *of sin and death*) He has respect to those things which he said in behalf of the law of God, ch. vii. 7 and 13. Observe that *and* is put here, and is not put at the beginning of the verse in the antithesis, πνεύματος τῆς ζωῆς, *of the spirit of life,* where either the conjunctive particle is wanting, *of spirit,* [and] *of life,* or it must be explained thus, τὸ Πνεῦμα τῆς ζωῆς, the Spirit of life.

3. Τὸ) This word has the force of an adjective [or *epithet*], to be simply explained thus: God has accomplished the condemnation of sin, which was beyond the power of the law; God condemned sin in the flesh (*a thing which the law could not do,* namely, condemn sin, while the sinner is saved). Τὸ ἀδύνατον, *what was impossible,* has an active signification in this passage; and the paraphrase of Luther is according to the meaning of the apostle.—See Wolfii Cur. on this place.—τοῦ νόμου) *of the law,* not only ceremonial, but also moral; for if the moral law were without this *impossible* [impossibility of condemning sin, yet saving the sinner], there would have been no need that the Son of God should have been sent. Furthermore, the word *impossible,* a privation [of something once held], supposes that the thing was previously possessed: formerly the law was able to afford righteousness and life, ch. vii. 10. Hence it is that man so willingly follows the traces of that first path even after the fall.—ἑαυτοῦ) ἴδιον, ver. 32. *His own,* over whom sin and death had no power.—πέμψας, *sending*) This word denotes a sort of separation, as it were, or estrangement of the Son from the Father, that He might be the Mediator.—ἐν ὁμοιώματι σαρκὸς ἁμαρτίας, *in the likeness of the flesh of sin* [*sinful flesh*]) The construction is with κατέκρινε, *condemned* [not as Engl. Vers.

His own *Son in the likeness* of sinful flesh]. We, along with our flesh, utterly tainted as it was with sin, ought to have been consigned to death; but *God, in the likeness* of that *flesh* (for justice required the likeness), that is, in the flesh of His own Son, which was real and at the same time holy, and (that too) *for sin, condemned* that *sin* (which was) in (our) flesh,[1] that we might be made free; ἐν [before ὁμοιώματι] is construed with *condemned*, compare *by*, ch. vii. 4 [Dead *by* (διὰ) the body of Christ].—περὶ ἁμαρτίας τὴν ἁμαρτίαν, *for sin, sin*) The substantive is here repeated, as in Luke xi. 17, note, *when the house is divided, the house falls*. But the figure ploce[2] is here added, as is indicated by the use of the article only in the latter place [on the second employment of the word ἁμαρτία]. These two terms mutually refer to one another, as do the words *the likeness of flesh* and *flesh*, περὶ, *for* : περὶ ἁμαρτίας is equivalent to a noun, as in Ps. xl. (xxxix.) 6 ; Heb. x. 6, 8. But here, in the epistle to the Romans, I explain it thus: *God condemned sin on this account, because it is sin.* Sin was condemned *as sin*. So sin is put twice in the same signification (not in a double signification as happens in an antanaclasis), but the article τὴν adds an epitasis.[3]—κατέκρινε, *condemned*) took away, finished, put an end to, destroyed all its strength, *deprived sin of its power* (compare the word *impossible* above [What the law was *powerless* to do, God had *power* to do, and *deprived* the law and sin of *their power*]—sin which was laid on the Son of God. For the execution of the sentence also follows the *condemnation* of sin. It is the opposite of the expression *to justify*, ver. 1 ; ch. v. 18, and 2 Cor. iii. 9.

4. Τὸ δικαίωμα, *the law's just commandment* [*jus.* Engl. Vers. '*righteousness*']) an antithesis to *condemnation*, ver. 1.—πληρωθῇ, *might be fulfilled*) That *fulfilment* is presently after described, ver. 5–11; thence it is that we have the *for*, ver. 5. *Works of justice* [*righteousness*] follow *him that is justified* [*i.e.* follow as the con-

---

[1] God condemned that sin, which was in our flesh, in the likeness of that sinful flesh, [*i.e.* in His incarnate Son,] and that too, for sin.

[2] See Appendix. The same word repeated, once expressing the simple idea of the word, next expressing an attribute of it.

[3] See Appendix. Epitasis, when to a word, which has been previously used, there is added, on its being used again, some word augmenting its force.

sequent fruits of his justification] : sin is condemned, he who had been a sinner, now acts rightly, and the law does not prosecute its claims against him.—ἐν ἡμῖν) *in us*.—μὴ κατὰ σαρκὰ, *not after the flesh*) an antithesis to, *in the flesh*, ver. 3. Now at length Paul has come to the open distinction between *flesh* and *spirit*.[1] The spirit denotes either the Spirit of God, or the spirit of believers, ver. 16. The latter is a new power produced and maintained in us by Him; and it is to this that the reference is, wherever *flesh* stands in opposition.

5. Οἱ γὰρ, *for they that*) From this passage and onward Paul primarily describes the condition of believers ; and secondarily, for the purpose of illustrating it, what is contrary to that state. —ὄντες, *who are*) This refers to a state, or condition.—φρονοῦσι [*mind*] *have a feeling for*) A feeling which flows from the condition.

6. φρόνημα, [*minding*] *feeling for*, or *of*) Fr. *sentiment*. Corresponds to the verb, *have a feeling for* [*mind*] (φρὸνουσι, ver. 5).—θάνατος—ζωή, *death,—life*) in this present life with its continuation in another, comp. ch. vi. 23.—ζωὴ καὶ εἰρήνη, *life and peace*) By the addition of the word *peace*, he prepares the way for himself for the transition to the following verse, where *enmity* is described.

7. οὐδὲ—δύναται, *neither can he*) Hence the pretext of impossibility, under which they are anxious to excuse themselves, who are reproved in this very passage, as carnal.—V. g.

8. Δὲ) is ἐπιτατικόν, [employed to give epitasis (See Appendix): *i.e.* where to an enunciation already stated, there is added some word to give increased emphasis, or an explanation].—ἀρέσαι) ἀρέσκω here, as elsewhere, signifies not only *I please*, but *I am desirous* to please, 1 Cor. x. 33; Gal. i. 10; it is akin to the phrase, *to be subject*, in the preceding verse.

9. Πνεῦμα Θεοῦ, πνεῦμα Χριστοῦ, *the Spirit of God, the Spirit of Christ*) A remarkable testimony to the doctrine of the Holy Trinity, and its economy in the hearts of believers, comp. ch. v. 8, 5, xiv. 17, 18, xv. 16, 30; Mark xii. 36; John xv. 26; Gal. iv. 6; Eph. i. 17, ii. 18, 22; 1 Pet. i. 2; Acts ii. 33; Heb. ii. 3, 4; 1 Cor. vi. 11, 13, etc.; 2 Cor. iii. 3, 4. We are to refer ver. 11 [*The Spirit of Him that raised Jesus*] to "the Spirit

---

[1] A proof against the words ἀλλὰ κατὰ πνεῦμα, ver. 1, which would be too premature a distinguishing of πνεῦμα and σὰρξ.—ED.

of God" in this verse, and *Christ in you*—[*the Spirit is life*] ver. 10, to "the Spirit *of Christ*" in this verse. For the distinctive marks [*Gnorismata* of the Christian] proceed in this order: He who has the Spirit, has Christ; he who has Christ, has God.— Comp. respecting such an order as this, 1 Cor. xii. 4, etc; Eph. iv. 4, etc.—ἐν ὑμῖν, *in you*) *In*, a particle very carefully to be attended to in this chapter, ver. 1–4, 8–11, 15, concerning the carnal and spiritual state. We in God, God in us.—οὗτος) *this man* in particular does not belong to Christ; and therefore this whole discourse has no reference to Him.—αὐτοῦ, *His*) Christ's; he is a Christian, who belongs to Christ.

10. Εἰ δὲ Χριστὸς, *And truly if Christ*) Where the Spirit of Christ is, there Christ is, comp. the preceding verse.—σῶμα) *the body*, sinful, for here it is opposed to the Spirit, not to the soul. —νεκρὸν) The concrete [not the abstract *death*; as the antithetic ζωή *life* in the abstract]: he says *dead*, instead of, *about to die*, with great force; [already] adjudged, and delivered over to death. This is the view and feeling of those, who have experienced in themselves [in whom there succeeds] the separation of soul and spirit, or of nature and grace.—δὲ, *but*) Implying, that the opposition is immediate [and direct between *the body* and *the spirit*], which excludes Purgatory, [a notion] suited neither to *body* nor *spirit*, and not consonant to the remaining economy of this very full epistle, ver. 30, 34, 38, ch. vi. 22, 23.—ζωὴ, *life*) The abstract.—διὰ *on account of*) Righteousness brings forth life, as sin brings forth death; life does not bring forth righteousness, [justification] contrary to the opinion of the Papists.—δικαιοσύνην, *justice* [*righteousness*]) *The just—shall live* [Rom. i. 17].

11. Ἰησοῦν, *Jesus*) Afterwards in Apodosis, *Christ*. The name *Jesus* has respect to Himself; the name *Christ* has reference to us. The former appellation, as a proper name, belongs to the person; the latter, as an appellative, belongs to the office.— ζωοποιήσει, *shall quicken* [make alive]) comp. *life*, ver. 6. This life knows no condemnation, ver. 1.—διὰ *on account of* [or *by means of*]) 2 Cor. i. 22. He is one and the same Spirit, who is the Spirit of Christ, and who is in believers; therefore as Christ lives, so believers shall live: See App. Crit. Ed. ii. on this passage.[1]

---

[1] ABC and acc. to Dial. c. Maced. "Several old MSS.," Memph. and

12. Ἐσμέν) *we are*, we acknowledge and consider ourselves to be. A kind of teaching, which borders on exhortation; (so, *we are*, is also used in Gal. iv. 31) and which presupposes men already of their own accord well inclined. *A feeling of delight* [see ch. vii. 22] mitigates the sense of *debt*. [But what is the condition of carnal men? These are really debtors, and confess themselves to be debtors, as often as they declare that it is not in their power to live spiritually.—V. g.].—οὐ τῇ σαρκί, *not to the flesh*) add, *but to the spirit;* but this is elegantly left to be understood. —κατὰ σάρκα, *after the flesh*) which endeavours to recall us to bondage.

13.[1] Τοῦ σώματος) Others read, τῆς σαρκός. Baumgarten defends the former, I leave it undetermined.[2]—ζήσεσθε, *ye shall live*) He does not say, μέλλετε ζῆν, *you are about* (thereby) *to obtain life*, but ζήσεσθε, *you will remain in life*. In the repentance of those, over whom the flesh had dominion, and in the temptations of those, over whom the spirit reigns, the flesh and the spirit are, so to speak, evenly balanced; grace preventing [*i.e.* in the old English sense of *prevent: going before, so as to give a good will to*] the former, sin, preventing [going before, so as to get the advantage over] the latter; to whichsoever side a man turns himself, from it he receives his denomination. Beginning with this passage, Paul entirely dismisses the carnal state, and now that he has finished that part, which he had begun at ch. vi. 1, he describes the pure and living state, which is the inheritance of believers.

14. Ἄγονται) In the middle voice: *are led* willingly [This is the sum *of the antecedents* (the preceding statements); υἱοὶ Θεοῦ εἰσιν, the sum of *the consequents* (the statements that follow) is, υἱοὶ Θεοῦ εἰσιν.—V. g.]—εἰσὶν υἱοὶ Θεοῦ) Others read υἱοὶ Θεοῦ εἰσιν later Syr. Versions read διὰ τοῦ ἐνοικοῦντος—πνεύματος. But D(Λ)Gfg Vulg. Syr. Theb. Versions, Orig. 2, 534a, and 3, 618c, 812d, Iren. 304, Hil. 803, read διὰ τὸ ἐνοικοῦν—πνεῦμα. With the accus. the meaning will be *on account of* the Spirit, etc. with the genit. *by* or *through*. Beng. translates it 'propter.'—ED.

[1] γάρ, *for*) the flesh repays with the worst retribution [or is a very bad paymaster]: and is there a man, who would wish to owe anything to it?— V. g.

[2] ABC Orig. 1, 616a; 721b; 732b; 3, 591b read τοῦ σώματος. But (Δ) DGfg Vulg. Orig. 2, 26b; 3, 170b Iren. and Cypr. read τῆς σαρκός.—ED.

or *υἱοί εἰσι Θεοῦ*. There are thus three readings, of which Baumgarten defends the first, I the second, which is supported by the third, inasmuch as the word *υἱοί* is placed first for the sake of emphasis; and it was the emphasis that induced me to touch upon this variety in the readings.[1]—*υἱοὶ sons*) The Spirit is given to sons, Gal. iv. 6. At this passage Paul enters upon the discussion of those topics, which he afterwards comprehends under the expression, *He glorified*, ver. 30, but he does not describe unmixed glory, but only such glory, as that, the taste of which is still diluted with the cross. Therefore the sum of what he says is: through sufferings [we must pass] to glory; patient endurance [or else, *support*] is interwoven with sufferings. Hence the whole connection of the discourse will be obvious.

15. Γὰρ, *for*) This word has reference to *sons* in the preceding verse.—*πνεῦμα δουλείας, the spirit of bondage*) The Holy Spirit was not even in the Old Testament a Spirit of bondage; but He so unfolded His power in the case of those believers, in whom He then dwelt, that there however was lurking, beneath, a feeling and sense, which carried with it something of bondage, inasmuch as being in the case of those who [under the law] were still but *children*, Gal. iv. 1.—*πάλιν, again*) as formerly [under the law]. The Romans in their state as Gentiles had had groundless [vain] fear; but not the spirit of fear, as those had had, into whose place the Gentiles had come. The Church of all ages is, as it were, one individual, moral person; so the word, *again*, Gal. iv. 9, v. 1.—*εἰς φόβον, to fear*) See Heb. ii. 15, note.—*υἱοθεσίας, of adoption*) See Gal. iv. 1, etc.—*κράζομεν, we cry*) one and all. *Cry* is a word implying vehemence, accompanied with desire, confidence, a just claim, perseverance. And the Holy Spirit himself *cries: Abba, Father*, Gal. iv. 6, note. [*If, while you are alive, you have not attained to this experience, it ought to be the subject of lamentation to you, and you ought eagerly to seek it; but if you have attained it, see that you joyfully continue in it.*—V. g.]

16. Τῷ) Our spirit *testifies*: the Spirit of God Himself *testifies along with* our spirit. [Our *spirit is human*, 1 Cor. ii. 11;

---

[1] Υἱοὶ εἰσιν Θεοῦ is read by BG*g* Vulg. (Amiat. MS.) Orig. 1, 574*c* Hilary. But (Δ)DAC Fuld. MS. of Vulg. *f*, Orig. 1, 685*c* Cypr. have *υἱοὶ Θεοῦ εἰσιν*. Rec. Text with Iren. has *εἰσιν υἱοὶ Θεοῦ*.—ED.

and therefore its testimony is in itself not infallible, Mal. ii. 16.—
V. g.] Blessed are they, who distinctly perceive this testimony.—
αὐτὸ τὸ has reference to ver. 14.

17. Συγκληρονόμοι, *joint-heirs*) that we may know, that it is a very great inheritance, which God gives to us: for He has assuredly given a great inheritance to His Son.—εἴπερ, *if indeed*) This short clause is a new proposition, which has respect to those things, which follow.—συμπάσχομεν, *we suffer with*) To this word refer *sufferings* in the following verse, and in like manner, *we may be glorified together* in this verse refers to *the glory* in the following verse.

18. Γὰρ, *for*) The reason assigned,[1] why he just now made mention of suffering, and of glorification.—τοῦ νῦν καιροῦ, *of the present time*) The cross [laid on the children of God], in the New Testament is greater than it formerly was, but it is of short continuance. καιρὸς, a short *time*; the present and future are opposed to each other.—πρὸς, *to be compared with*) that is, if they be compared together.—εἰς ἡμᾶς, *with respect to* [towards] *us;* comp. 2 Cor. v. 2.

18, 19. Ἀποκαλυφθῆναι—ἀποκάλυψιν) The glory is *revealed*, and then also the sons of God *are revealed*.

19. Ἀποκαραδοκία. This term denotes the hope of the coming event, and the effort of the mind, which is eagerly panting for [gaping for] it. *The expectation of the creature*, that is, the creature waiting, or expecting. Luther on this passage in Post. eccl. calls it, *das endliche Harren, final waiting.*—τῆς κτίσεως, *of the creature*) *The creature* here does not denote angels, who are free from *vanity* [weakness]; nor men of every kind, provided only they are men, although not even the weakest men [those most under bondage to vanity] are excluded, who, although in the bustle of life they consider vanity as if it were liberty, and partly stifle, partly conceal their groaning, yet in times of sobriety, quietness, sleeplessness and calamity, they have many sighs, which are heard by God alone; nor are the virtuous Gentiles excluded; but believers are expressly opposed to the *creature.* As to the rest, all the visible creation [the whole aggregate of creatures: " creaturarum universitatem"] without

---

[1] Aetiologia. See Appendix.

exception is intended (as κτίσμα in *Macarius* everywhere denotes the visible creation [creaturam], Homil. vi. § 5, etc.), and every kind of creature according to its condition (captu) [ver. 39, i. 25]. As every creature stands in its relation to the sons of God, so, in this passage, the things predicated of the former stand in relation to the things predicated of the latter. The wicked neither desire, nor will obtain liberty. Disadvantages have redounded to the creature in consequence of [from] sin; reparation will accrue to the creature in consequence of [from] the glory of the sons of God.—υἱῶν) τέκνων, ver. 21.—ἀπεκδέχεται) Ἀπὸ in this compound verb signifies the waiting for a thing *hoped for* in consequence of the promise. The same word is in ver. 23 and in like manner ἀποκαραδοκία above.

20. Ματαιότητι, *to vanity*) whence the first of believers, whom the Scriptures commend, was called הבל, *Abel* [*vanity*]. *Glory* is opposed both to *vanity and corruption;* and the greatest *vanity* is idolatry, ch. i. 21, 23. *Vanity* is abuse and waste; even the malignant spirits themselves have dominion over the creature. —ὑπετάγη, *was made subject*) In the passive voice, with a middle signification, though it has however in it somewhat of the figure, personification.—οὐχ᾿ ἑκοῦσα, *not willingly*) For in the beginning it was otherwise: thence it is that the creature would rather be *made subject to Christ* [" Thou hast put all things in *subjection* under His feet"], Heb. ii. 7, 8.—διὰ τὸν ὑποτάξαντα, *on account of* [propter: *owing to*] *Him who hath subjected*) that is on account of [by reason of] God, Gen. iii. 17, v. 29. Adam rendered the creature obnoxious [liable] to vanity, but he did not *subject it.*

21. Ἐπ᾿ ἐλπίδι [*super spe:* resting on hope], *in hope*) It is construed with, *was made subject,* so, *in hope* [super spe], is put absolutely, Acts ii. 26; and comp. *by hope* [spe], ver. 24.—αὐτὴ ἡ κτίσις) *itself*, to wit, *the creature.*—ἐλευθερωθήσεται, *shall be delivered* [*set free*]) Deliverance is not accomplished by means of complete destruction; otherwise quadrupeds, when they are butchered, would fall with pleasure.[1]—ἀπὸ τῆς δουλείας τῆς φθορᾶς εἰς τὴν ἐλευθερίαν τῆς δόξης, *from the bondage of corruption into the glorious*

[1] *i.e.*, were death and annihilation a deliverance. Therefore the coming restoration of the creature and its deliverance will not consist in their destruction and annihilation.—E.n

liberty) Ἀπὸ, *from,* and εἰς, *into,* are opposed to each other. *From* denotes the point, from which we set out; *into,* the point at which we arrive. *Bondage* and *liberty* belong to the creature; *corruption* and *glory* to men, even believers [the latter, *glory* to believers alone: the former, *corruption,* to men in general]. *Vanity,* ver. 20, is something more subtle than φθορὰ, *corruption.* Not only *deliverance,* but also *liberty,* is that goal, to which the creature in its own way is directing its course.—εἰς τὴν ἐλευθερίαν, *into the liberty*) In order that they may in freedom be subservient to the glory of the sons [of God].—Cluverus.

22. Γὰρ, *for*) This aetiology[1] [assigning of a reason] supposes, that the groaning of the creature is not in vain, but that it is heard by God.—πᾶσα) *all* [*the whole*]. It is considered as one whole, comp. ver. 28, 32, 39.—συστενάζει, *groaneth together*) with united groanings [sighings]. Dio Cassius, book 39, gives a singular example of this in the *wailing* of the elephants, which Pompey devoted to the public shows contrary to an express pledge [promise given], as men at the time interpreted it; and the people themselves were so affected by it, that they imprecated curses on the head of the commander.—ἄχρι, *until*) He insinuates, that there will be an end of pains and groans, the pains and groans of the creature.

23. Οὐ μόνον δὲ, *but* [and] *not only*) The conclusion is drawn from the strong groaning [of the creature] to that which is much stronger [that of ourselves].—αὐτοὶ—καὶ ἡμεῖς αὐτοί, *ourselves—even we ourselves*) The former αὐτοί, ourselves, is to be referred [has reference] by antithesis to *the creature* [the whole *creation groaneth*] ver. 22: the latter refers to ver. 26, concerning the *Spirit* [maketh intercession for us with *groanings*]; and yet one and the same subject is denoted [the two αὐτοί belong to ἡμεῖς]; otherwise, the apostle would have said, αὐτοὶ οἱ τὴν ἀπαρχὴν κ.τ.λ. [the article οἱ would have followed the first αὐτοί, had it referred to a different subject from the second αὐτοί].— τὴν ἀπαρχὴν τοῦ πνεύματος, *the first fruits of the Spirit*) that is the *Spirit,* who is the *first fruits;* see 2 Cor. i. 22, note. *We are a kind of first fruits of God's creatures,* James i. 18; and we have the *first fruits of the Spirit;* and the same Spirit enters

---

[1] See Appendix.

into all *creatures*, Ps. cxxxix. 7, a passage, from which the groaning of the creature is distinctly explained. The sons of God are said to have the *first fruits*, so long as they are in the way [whilst as yet they have not reached the end, when they shall have full fruition]. They who possess the *first fruits*, and the good, which attends the first fruits, are the same.—ἔχοντες, *having*) This word involves the idea of cause; *because we have.* —ἐν ἑαυτοῖς, *in ourselves*) It implies, that the groaning of believers is widely different from the groaning of the creature.—στενάζομεν) Στενάζω here, and in ver. 22, signifies *to desire* [yearn after] *with groaning*; comp. 2 Cor. v. 4.—τὴν) This article shows by the apposition, that this sentiment, if it be resolved [analyzed], is contained in it, *the redemption of our body is what constitutes the adoption.*—τὴν ἀπολύτρωσιν [*redemption*] *deliverance*) This will be at the last day, which already at that time they were setting before themselves as being at hand; ἐλευθερία, *liberty* [ver. 21], is a kindred expression to this ἀπολύτρωσις.—Comp. Luke xx. 36. [*That* liberty *is not intended here, by which we are delivered from the body, but that, by which the body is delivered from death.*— V. g.]

24. Ἐλπίδι) the dative, not of the means, but of the manner; *we are so saved*, that there may even yet remain something, for which we may hope,—both salvation and glory. He limits the present salvation, but, while he limits, he by that very circumstance takes it for granted.—τί καὶ) *why yet* does he hope for it? Where there is vision, there is no need of hope. The blessed will be sure of the eternity of their blessedness, because they shall have no need of hope; and therefore they will be established in it.

25. Εἰ δὲ, *but if*) The patient waiting of believers is deduced from the nature of hope.

26. Καὶ, *even*) Not only the whole creation (every creature) groans, but the Holy Spirit Himself affords assistance; comp. ver. 23, note 2. On both sides, believers have such as groan with them, and make common cause with them;—on the one side, they have the whole *creation* [*creature*], on the other, what is of still more importance, they have the *Spirit*. In as far as the Spirit groans, it respects *us*: in as far as He *also* affords assistance ['helps,'] it respects *the creature* [*creation*].—συναντι-

λαμβάνεται) σὺν has the same force in this compound as in συμμαρτυρεῖ, ver. 16, [*i.e.*, *along with* us].—ταῖς ἀσθενείαις) *infirmities*, which exist in our knowledge and in our prayers ; the abstract for the concrete, *infirmities*, that is *our prayers*, which are in themselves infirm.—γὰρ, *for*) Paul explains what the *infirmities* are.—τί—καθὸ, *what—as*) comp. *how or what*, Matt. x. 19.— ὑπερεντυγχάνει) ὑπὲρ, *abundantly* [over and above] as in ver. 37, ὑπερνικῶμεν, and ὑπερεπερίσσευσεν, ch. v. 20. Both ὑπερεντυγχάνει in this verse, and ἐντυγχάνει, ver. 27, are the predicates of the same subject, viz. the Holy Spirit. It is the general practice, first to put the compound verb with its proper emphasis, and then afterwards merely to repeat, in its stead, the simple form. Thus in Rom. xv. 4 we have first προεγράφη, and subsequently in the second place, ἐγράφη follows, which is the genuine reading.— στεναγμοῖς, *with groans*) Every groan (the theme or root of the word being στενός, *strait*) proceeds from the pressure of great straits : therefore the matter [the component material] of our groaning is from ourselves ; but the Holy Spirit puts upon that matter its form [puts it into shape], whence it is that the groanings of believers, whether they proceed from joy or sorrow, cannot be uttered.

27. Δὲ) [Not *and*, as Engl. Vers., *but*] refers to *a* privative in ἀλαλήτοις [Though they can *not* be uttered, *yet*, etc.]—τὰς καρδίας, *the hearts*) The Spirit dwells in the hearts [of believers], and *makes intercession*. Christ is in heaven. *He who searches the hearts* is the Father, to whom especially that act is attributed in Scripture.—τὸ φρόνημα τοῦ πνεύματος, *the mind of the Spirit*).—Comp. φρόνημα, ver. 6, *Sensum*,[1] the nominative : from the plural *sensa*, *sensorum*.—τοῦ πνεύματος, *of the Spirit*) the Holy Spirit, as in the preceding verse.—κατὰ) *according to* [*ad*], κατὰ Θεὸν, *according to God*, not κατὰ ἄνθρωπον, *according to man* (comp. 1 John iii. 20) [after the manner of God, not man], as is worthy of God, and in a manner acceptable and manifest to Him. The Holy Spirit understands the style of the court of heaven, which is acceptable to the Father. Κατὰ is the emphatic word of the sentence, inasmuch as it is placed at the

---

[1] Beng. uses *sensum* here to express φρόνημα, not the accus. of *sensus*, but an old disused nominative singular, the plural of which is often found *sensa sensorum*.—ED.

beginning of the clause.—ὑπὲρ ἁγίων, *for saints*) The article is not added; they are *saints*, who are both near *to God*, and are deemed worthy of assistance, being those for whom [the Spirit] *makes intercession*.

28. Οἴδαμεν δὲ, *Moreover we know*) An antithesis to, *we know not*, ver. 26.—τοῖς ἀγαπῶσι, *to them that love*) The subject is here described from the fruit of those things, which have been hitherto mentioned,—namely, love to God; and this *love* also makes believers [by a happy art] dexterously to take in good part *all things* which God sends upon them, and perseveringly to overcome all difficulties and temptations, [James i. 12. *Paul is an example*, 2 Cor. i. 3–11.—V. g.] Presently after, in the case of *the called*, the reason is given, why a predicate so excellent is attributed to this subject [why such blessed things are predicated of *them who love God*].—πάντα συνεργεῖ) *all things work together*, by means of groanings, and in other ways. So 1 Macc. xii. 1, ὁ καιρὸς αὐτῷ συνεργεῖ, *time works with* (*serves*) *him*.—εἰς ἀγαθὸν, *for good*) even as far as to [up to] their glorification, ver. 30, at the end.—τοῖς κατὰ πρόθεσιν κλητοῖς οὖσιν, *to those who are the called according to His purpose*) This is a new proposition in reference to what follows. The apostle designs to give a recapitulation of all the advantages involved in justification and glorification, ver. 30, and accordingly returns now first of all to its deepest [most remote] roots, which only can be known from these their sweetest fruits themselves:[1] he at the same time hereby prepares us for the ninth chapter [which treats chiefly of *God's election and calling*]: πρόθεσις is *the purpose*, which God determined to carry into effect concerning the salvation of His own people. κλητοῖς, *the called*, is a noun, not a participle; inasmuch as οὖσιν is added [which it would not be, if κλητοῖς were a participial adjective], who *are* the called:—the *purpose* is unfolded, ver. 29, the *called*, ver. 30.

29. Προέγνω) *He foreknew*. Hafenreffer translates it—*He formerly acknowledged*. πρόθεσις, the *purpose*, comprehends πρόγνωσιν, *foreknowledge*, and προορισμὸν, *predestination*, for *calling* is annexed both to the former (πρόθεσις) and to the two latter

[1] i.e. the root, *God's calling* and everlasting election, is known from the blessed fruits (*all things working for their good*) which it bears to *the called*.—ED.

(πρόγνωσις and προορισμός), ver. 28–30; Eph. i. 9, where however θέλημα, *His will*, is in a more extensive sense, than *predestination*, and assuredly *predestination* accompanies *foreknowledge*, for *foreknowledge* takes away *rejection* or *reprobation* [*casting away*]: ch. xi. 2. Moreover *reprobation* [*casting away*] and *predestination* are opposed to each other.—προώρισε, συμμόρφους, *predestined*, (to be) *conformed*) He declares, who they are, whom *He foreknew*, namely, those who are *conformed*. This is the *character* of those [impress of God's *seal* on those: referring to *seal*, 2 Tim. ii. 19], who were foreknown and are to be glorified, 2 Tim. ii. 19; Phil. iii. 10, 21.—τῆς εἰκόνος, *to the image*) construed with συμμόρφους, although σύμμορφον, Phil. iii. 10, governs the dative. Here it has more the power of a substantive with [followed by] the genitive. This likeness [conformity to His Son's likeness] constitutes the very *adoption of sons* itself, not the cross or glory; for this [the glory] follows only after [not till after] *justification;* concerning which, see ver. 30: but they who are the *sons* of God are the *brethren* of Christ [at an earlier stage in the successive links, viz. ver. 29]. *Conformity* to His cross or His glory is the consequence that follows in the train of *conformity* to the Son of God, Gal. iv. 19. So Eph. i. 5, *predestinating us unto the adoption of sons (children)*.—εἰς τὸ) The cause, why *predestination* is conjoined with *foreknowledge*, namely, Christ ought to have many brethren; but this multitude of brethren would fail, or at least would be diminished, if there were *foreknowledge* without *predestination*. *Predestination* overcomes everything that obstructs the salvation of believers, and changes adversity into prosperity.—εἶναι) *that He might be*, and might be seen to be.—πρωτότοκον, *the first-born*) The glorious resurrection of Christ, and of believers, is itself a kind of generation [*the regeneration*], Matt. xix. 28.

30. Τούτους καὶ ἐδικαίωσεν, *them He also justified*) Paul does not fix the number of those, who are called, justified, glorified, to be absolutely equal; he does not affirm that the believer may not fail between the special call, and final glory, ch. xi. 22; nor does he deny that there are also persons called, who may not be justified; but he shows, that God, so far as He Himself is concerned, conducts His people from step to step.—ἐδόξασε, *He glorified*) ver. 17–24. He speaks in the preterite, as if he were looking back

from the goal to the race of faith, and from eternal glory, as it were, backward to the eternity itself, in which God decreed the glorifying of His people.—[*Comp. Ps.* xvi. 3.]

31. Πρὸς ταῦτα) *to* [as regards] *these things*, which have been spoken of in chapters iii. v. viii. : that is to say, we cannot go, we cannot think, we cannot wish for anything farther. And if any one, by reason of his unbelief, should feel inclined to bring forward anything in opposition to these things (comp. Luke xiv. 6, *to*=*in opposition to* these things) he cannot do it. [*It may be justly said, that the gate of heaven is thrown open in this passage,* ver. 31–39.—V. g.]—εἰ) *if.* The conditional used instead of the causal, renders the conclusion the stronger. Many are of opinion, that there are three sections [*periochæ*, complete portions of the discourse] in this passage, every one of which begins by an interrogation with τίς, *who?* with an anaphora,[1] and has its answer immediately following, which is called anthypophora.[2] But the apostle contemplated a different analysis. There are four sections beginning with this verse; one, a general section; and three special ones: every one of them has glorying concerning Grace in the first instance; and then presently after a suitable question, challenging all opposition, to which the expression, *I am persuaded,* is an answer. The first, a general section, is this: *If God be for us,* WHO *can be against us?* The first special section is this, which concerns the past: *He who did not even spare His own Son, but delivered Him up for us all; How shall He not also with Him forgive* [But Engl. Vers. *freely give*] *us all things?* WHO *shall lay anything to the charge of God's elect?* (Where in the question, the logical consequence is from [is drawn from] glorying concerning the past: for the nature of the subject did not admit of the section being only expressed by *preterite tenses.* Accordingly there is [besides the Preterites] also a double *future* in, *shall He forgive, shall lay to the charge;* but it has a manifest reference to *past events.* God will forgive all the sins, that have been committed [by believers]. No one can now accuse God's

---

[1] The frequent repetition of the same word in the beginnings of sections. —See Appendix.

[2] See Appendix. The answer to a foreseen objection of an adversary, by anticipation, or an answer to an objection actually made, by the statement of an opposite sentiment or fact.

elect on account of those sins committed by them. And the *how* and *who* are thus combined in one and the same section, but there is also a double relation, 1.) *God did not spare His own Son.* Therefore, *He will also forgive us with Him all things.* 2.) *He delivered Him up for us all.* Therefore, *no one shall lay anything to the charge of God's elect.*) The second section has respect to the present; *It is God that justifieth*, WHO *is he that condemneth;* comp. by all means, Isa. l. 8, 9. The third section is concerning the future; *It is Christ* [that died], etc. WHO *shall separate us?* For it is a future non-separation which is implied in the *shall separate*, as appears by comparing this with the end of ver. 38. The Past and Present are the foundation of the Future, and often the love of Christ is inferred from His death, ch. v. 5, etc.; Gal. ii. 20; Rev. i. 5. An interrogative apodosis such as this is frequent, and is admirably suited to a spirited discourse.—Acts viii. 33; Num. xxiv. 9; Job ix. 12, xxxiv. 29; Ps. xxvii. 1; Isa. xiv. 27, xliii. 13; Lam. ii. 13, at the end of verse; Amos iii. 8.

32. Ὅσγε, *who*) This first special section has four sentences: the third has respect to the first, the fourth to the second. He did not spare His own Son: therefore there is nothing, which He will not forgive. He delivered up His Son for us: therefore no one shall accuse us on account of our sins, ch. iv. 25. *He was delivered* [for our offences]. Nor does the clause, *who shall lay anything to the charge*, so closely cohere with that which follows, as with that which goes before; for the delivering up of Christ for us forbids all *laying ought to our charge*: whereas *our justification* [ver. 33, it is God that *justifieth*] does not forbid *the laying things to our charge*, but overcomes it. Γὲ has a sweetness full of exultation, as the καὶ, *even—also*, ver. 34, repeated: ὅς, *who*, has its apodosis, *he*, implied in the following words.—οὐκ ἐφείσατο, *did not spare*) LXX. οὐκ ἐφείσω τοῦ υἱοῦ σου κ.τ.λ., Gen. xxii. 16, concerning Abraham and Isaac, and Paul seems to have had that passage in his mind. God, so to speak, offered violence to His love as a Father.—ἡμῶν πάντων, *us all*) In other places it is generally said, *all we*, *of all* of us; but here *us* is put first with greater force and emphasis. The perception of grace in respect to *ourselves* is prior to our perception of *universal* grace [grace in respect to *the world at large*]. Many examples of its application

are found without any mention of its universality, for instance, 1 Tim. i. 15, 16: whereas its universality is subsequently commended for the purpose of stimulating to the farther discharge of duties, ib. ii. 1, etc.—παρέδωκεν) *delivered up.* So LXX., Isa. liii. 6.—καὶ σὺν αὐτῷ, *with Himself also*) καὶ *also* adds an epitasis[1] to the reasoning from the greater to the less. It was more [a greater stretch of love] *not to spare His Son;* now, *with the Son*, that is, when we have the Son already sacrificed, at all costs, to us [by the Father], He will certainly forgive us [give us freely] *all things*.—πάντα) *all things*, that are for our salvation.—χαρίσεται, *will freely give* [*and forgive*]) The antithesis to *He did not spare.* The things which are the consequence of redemption, are themselves also *of grace* [*freely* given: χαρίσεται, χάρις].

33. Ἐκλεκτῶν Θεοῦ, *of God's elect*) ver. 29.—δικαιῶν, *that justifieth*) *To justify* and *condemn* are the words in antithesis to each other, ver. 3, note. In Isa. l. 8, 9, a passage, which we have previously quoted, there similarly comes first an hypothesis in each of the consecutive sections, and there follows the Answer subjoined by the speaker, in each case respectively, expressed in the form of a question; for example,

A. *He is near, who justifies me:*[2]
B. 1. *Who will contend with me? we shall (let us) stand together.*
   2. *Who is the lord of my cause? let him draw near to me.*
C. *Behold the Lord God will help me:*
D. *Who is he that shall condemn me?*

Here the apostle seems to have assumed A, and on the contrary to have omitted B, and likewise to have omitted C, and on the contrary to have quoted D

34. Ὁ ἀποθανών, μᾶλλον δὲ—ὃς καί—ὃς καί, *that died, yea rather —who even—who also*) The order of the enumeration of the

---

[1] See Appendix. Some word added to give increased emphasis or clearness to a previous enunciation.

[2] This expression, that He is *near*, seems to be in the meanwhile said in the Old Testament sense, whereas, on the contrary, He is said in the Romans to be *the God that justifieth*, without any restriction.

things contrary, ver. 35, 38, 39, corresponds to these four weighty turning points of his argument. In ver. 35, the former are lighter and less considerable [than in ver. 38], and may be all referred to [reduced to the one head, viz.] *death*, ver. 38, inasmuch as they are, as it were, previous tendencies towards *death*. The contraries in the way of the elect, enumerated in ver. 38, 39, are more weighty ones. That topic will be by and by brought out more fully.—μᾶλλον, *rather*) ch. v. 10. Our faith ought to lean on the death of Christ, but it ought *rather* also to make such progress, as to lean on His resurrection, kingly dominion, and second coming.—ἔστιν ἐν δεξιᾷ τοῦ Θεοῦ, *is at the right hand of God*) He is able to save; He Himself and the Father. The ascension is not previously mentioned, nor does the mention of His glorious coming follow: for the former is the act of sitting at the right hand of God, the latter entirely takes away all, that threatens separation from the love of God, and brings in the state of glory, of which ver. 30 treats.—ἐντυγχάνει, *intercedes*) He is willing to save: He Himself and the Father.

35. Τίς ἡμᾶς χωρίσει, *who shall separate us*) The perpetuity of the union, for the time to come, with *the love* of Christ and of God, is deduced from the *death* of Christ, from His *resurrection*, His *sitting at the right hand of God* and His *intercession*, comp. ch. v. 5, 6, 9, 10; Heb. vii. 25. But the *who* is presently after explained by the enumeration [shall tribulation or distress, etc.], without an aetiology following after: from which again it is evident, that the aetiology, [assigning of the reason] must be sought for before the words, *who shall separate us*, in ver. 34: and he says *who*, not *what*, although he subjoins [shall] *affliction*, etc., because personal enemies lurk under these adverse things.— τῆς ἀγαπῆς, *from the love*) towards us, ver. 37, 39. The foundation of the impossibility of being separated from the love of Christ is love; the foundation of this confidence is love clearly perceived.—τοῦ Χριστοῦ, *of Christ*) The love of God is one with the love of Christ, ver. 39.—γυμνότης) *nakedness, the want of clothing*, the extreme of poverty, 1 Cor. iv. 11; 2 Cor. xi. 27. The enumeration for the most part goes on in pairs, *hunger and nakedness*, etc.—κίνδυνος, *peril*) Hypocrites often sink under mere dangers.—ἢ μάχαιρα, *or sword*) an instrument of *slaughter*. Paul mentions the kind of death, with which he himself had been

sometimes threatened, ch. xvi. 4; Phil. ii. 17, note. Many martyrs, who survived other tortures, *were despatched* with the sword, ἐτελειώθησαν [consummati sunt].

36. Καθὼς, *as*) He gives the reason, why he enumerates in the preceding verse so many trials.—ὅτι—σφαγῆς) So the LXX., Ps. xliv. 23. Both the church of the Old Testament, and much more that of the New Testament, might have so spoken; and the latter may still so speak.—ἕνεκα σοῦ, *for thy sake*) It is a good thing thus [*i.e.* for Christ's sake] to suffer: the sorrows, in which the world abounds, and which are braved for other reasons, are vain.—θανατούμεθα, *we are killed*) The first class of the blessed [departed saints] is for the most part filled up with those, who met a violent death, Matt. xxiii. 34, 35; Heb. xi. 37; Rev. vi. 11, xx. 4.—ὅλην τὴν ἡμέραν) *all the day*. So the LXX., in many passages, כל היום, a proverbial expression; *the whole day, all the day*: Matt. xx. 6. Ps. quoted above, ver. 16, 9.—ἐλογίσθημεν, *we are accounted*) by our enemies, as also by ourselves.

37. Ὑπερνικῶμεν, *we are more than conquerors*) We have strength not only equal and sufficient, but far more than sufficient for overcoming the preceding catalogue of evils: and not even shall the catalogue of evils, which follows, injure us, because Christ, because God is greater than all. In this section there is designated that (as it were) highest mark which the Christian can attain, before his departure to the abodes of the blessed.— διὰ τοῦ ἀγαπήσαντος) The Aorist: *through Him, who hath with His love embraced* us in Christ, and for that very reason proves us by trials and adversity.

38. Πέπεισμαι, *I am persuaded*) all doubt being overcome.— γὰρ) Things of less weight do not hurt us: *for* even things of greater weight shall not hurt us.—οὔτε θάνατος, κ.τ.λ., *neither death*, etc.) This is introduced from ver. 34, in an admirable order:

Neither death shall hurt us,	for *Christ hath died:*
nor *life*: comp. ch. xiv. 9.	*He rose again:*
nor *angels*, nor *principalities*, nor *things present*, nor *things to come*: comp. Eph. i. 20, 21.	*Christ is at the right hand of God.*
nor *power*, nor *height*, nor *depth*, nor any other creature.	*He makes intercession.*

Hence we have an illustration of the order of the words. For the enumeration moves in pairs; *neither death nor life; nor things present, nor things to come.* The other two pairs are subjoined by chiasmus;[1] *nor power* [1], *nor height* [2], *nor depth* [3], *nor any other* [4] *creature;* [the *first* referring to the *fourth,* the *second* to the *third*]; in such a way, however, that in some sense, also *power* and *height, depth* and *any creature* may be respectively joined together. A similar chiasmus occurs at Matt. xii. 22, *so that the blind and dumb both spake and saw,* [*blind* referring to *saw; dumb* to *spake*]. But if any one should prefer the more commonly received reading of the order of enumeration, he may read as follows :—

Neither death, nor life :
nor angels, nor principalities, nor powers :
nor things present, nor things to come :
nor height, nor depth, nor any other creature,

so that there may be four pairs of species, and the second and fourth pairs may have the genus added in the first or last place. But testimony of higher antiquity maintains the former order of enumeration to be superior.[2] See App. Crit. Ed. ii., p. 329, etc. I acknowledge for my own part that the generally received order of the words is more easy, and the reader is free to choose either. At all events the relation of this enumeration to ver. 34, which was demonstrated above, is so evident, and so full of the doctrine of salvation, that it cannot be admitted to be an *arbitrary* interpretation. Now, we shall look at the same clauses one by one.—θάνατος, *death*) *Death* is considered as a thing most terrible and here it is put first, with which comp. ver. 34, and the order of its series, and ver. 36. Therefore the death also, which is inflicted by men, is indicated : burning alive, strangulation, casting to wild beasts, etc.[3]—ζωή, *life*) and in it θλίψις,

---

[1] See Appendix. From the Greek X. When the component parts of two pairs of words or propositions have a mutual relation, inverse or direct.

[2] ABCD(Λ)G*fg*. Memph. later Syr. Versions, Orig. Hilary 291, Vulg. put the δυνάμεις before ὄυτε ὕψωμα. Rec. Text has no *very* ancient authority but Syr. Vers. for putting δυνάμεις before ὄυτε ἐνεστῶτα.—ED.

[3] The author *in his* Germ. Vers. expresses the suspicion, that the state of

affliction, etc., ver. 35 : likewise length of life, tranquillity, and all living *men* [as opposed to *angels*]. None of these things shall be hurtful, comp. 1 Cor. iii. 22 [in ver. 21 *men* are included].—ἄγγελοι, *angels*) The mention of *angels* is made, after the implied mention of men, in the way of gradation; 1 Cor. xv. 24, note. In this passage the statement may be understood as referring to good angels (conditionally, as Gal. i. 8), and of wicked angels (categorically): (for it will be found that the latter are also called *angels* absolutely, not merely *angels of the devil;* Matt. xxv. 41); 1 Cor. iv. 9, vi. 3, xi. 10; 1 Tim. iii. 16, 1 Pet. iii. 22; 2 Pet. ii. 4; Jude, ver. 6; Rev. ix. 11, etc., Ps. lxxviii. 49.—ἀρχαὶ, *principalities*) These are also comprehended under the general name angels, as well as other orders, Heb. i. 4, 14; but those seem to be specially denominated *angels*, who are more frequently sent than the rest of the heavenly orders. They are thus called *principalities*, and also *thrones,* Col. i. 16; but not *kingdoms*, for the *kingdom* belongs to the Son of God, 1 Cor. xv. 24, 25.—οὔτε ἐνεστῶτα οὔτε μέλλοντα, *nor things present nor things to come*) Things *past* are not mentioned, not even sins; for they have all passed away. *Present things* are the events, that happen to us during our earthly pilgrimage, or which befall the whole world, until it come to an end. For the saints are viewed either individually, or as a united body. *Things future* refer to whatever will occur to us either after our time in the world, or after that of the whole world has terminated, as the last judgment, the conflagration of the world, eternal punishment; or those things, which, though they now exist, will yet become known to us at length by name in the world to come, and not till then.—οὔτε δύναμις,[1] *nor power*) [2] Δύναμις often corresponds to the Hebrew word צבא, and signifies *forces, hosts.*

39. Οὔτε ὕψωμα, οὔτε βάθος, *nor height nor depth*) Things *past* and *future* point to differences of times, *height and depth* to

---

the dead *is here indicated rather than* actual slaughter; from the consideration, *that already in* ver 35, *every kind of death may be comprehended under the term* sword. —E. B.

[1] *fg* Vulg. Ambrose and Augustine support the singular δύναμις. But all the other authorities quoted in my last note support δυνάμεις.—ED.

[2] D corrected by a later hand, *d*.

differences of places. We do not know, the number, magnitude, and variety of things, comprehended in these words, and yet we do not fear them. *Height* here, in sublime style, is used for heaven; *depth* for the abyss; with which comp. ch. x. 6, 7; Eph. iv. 8, 9, 10, that is, neither the arduous and high ascents, nor the precipitous and deep descents, I shall not say, of the feelings, of the affections, of fame, and of pecuniary resources, Phil. iv. 12, nor shall I say [the arduous ascents, etc.], of walls, of mountains, and of waters, but even of heaven and of the abyss itself, of which even a careless consideration has power sufficient to make the human mind beside itself [to fill it with strange awe], produce in us no terror. Furthermore, Paul does not say in Greek, ὕψος, βάθος, as he does elsewhere in another sense; nor ὕψωμα, βάθυσμα (as Plutarch says, ὑψώματα τῶν ἀστέρων, *the heights of the stars*, and Theophrastus, βαθύσματα τῆς λίμνης, *the depths of the lake*) but ὕψωμα, βάθος; using purposely, as it were, the derivative and primitive, which strike the ear with variety in sound. Ὕψος, the primitive noun, signifies *height* absolutely; ὕψωμα, a sort of verbal noun, is not so much height, as something that has been elevated, or made high; ὕψος belongs to God, and the third heaven, from whence we receive nothing hurtful; ὕψωμα has perhaps some likeness in sound [resemblance by alliteration] to the word στερέωμα, *firmament*, which is frequently used by the LXX. interpreters; and in this passage certainly points to those regions, to which it is difficult to ascend, and where the powers of darkness range, *exalting* themselves awfully against us [2 Thess. ii. 4, *exalteth* himself, Ephes. ii. 2, vi. 12] : βάθος, how far soever it descends, does no injury to us.—κτίσις, *creature*) whatever things exist outside of God, and of what kind soever they are. He does not so much as condescend to mention visible enemies.—δυνήσεται, *shall be able*) although they should make many attempts.—χωρίσαι, *to separate*) neither by violence, ver. 35, nor in the way of law [just right], ver. 33, 34.

CHAPTER IX.

1. Ἀλήθειαν, *truth*) Concerning the connexion, see on ch. i. 16, note. The article is not added here; comp. 2 Cor. vii. 14, xi. 10, because his reference is not to the whole truth, but to something true in particular [a particular truth], and in this sense also ἀλήθειαι in the plural is used in Ps. xii. 2, LXX.; 2 Macc. vii. 6. This asseveration chiefly relates to ver. 3, where *for* is put as in Matt. i. 18. Therefore in ver. 2 ὅτι denotes *because* [not as Engl. Vers. *that*], and indicates the cause of the prayer. For verse 2 was likely to obtain belief of itself without so great an asseveration [being needed; therefore ὅτι is not = *that* in ver. 2.]—λέγω, *I speak*) The apostle speaks deliberately.—ἐν Χριστῷ) ב, *ἐν*, has sometimes the same force as an oath.—οὐ ψεύδομαι, *I lie not*) This is equivalent to that clause, *I speak the truth*. Its own confirmation is added to each [both to, *I lie not*, and to, *I speak the truth*]. This chapter throughout in its phrases and figures comes near to the Hebrew idiom.—συνειδήσεως, *conscience*) The criterion of truth lies in the conscience and in the *heart*, which the internal testimony of the Holy Spirit enlightens and confirms.

2. Λύπη, *grief*, [*heaviness*]) In spiritual things grief and (see the end of the eighth chapter) joy in the highest degree may exist together. Paul was sensible, from how great benefits, already enumerated, the Jews excluded themselves, and at the same time he declares [makes it evident], that he does not say those things, which he has to say, in an unfriendly spirit towards his persecutors.—μοι—τῇ καρδίᾳ μου, *to me—in my heart*) These are equivalent in each half of the verse.

3. Ηὐχόμην, *I could wish*) A verb in the imperfect tense, involving in it a potential or conditional signification, involving the condition, *if Christ would permit*. *His grief* was *unceasing* [continual], but this *prayer* does not seem here to be asserted as unceasing, or absolute. Human words are not fully adequate to include in them [to express fully] the emotions of holy souls; nor are those emotions always the same; nor is it in the power

of those souls always to elicit from themselves such a prayer as this. If the soul be not far advanced, it is incapable of [cannot comprehend] this. It is not easy to estimate the measure of love, in a Moses and a Paul. For the narrow boundary of our reasoning powers does not comprehend it; as the little child is unable to comprehend the courage of warlike heroes. In the case of those two men [duumvirs] themselves, the intervals in their lives, which may be in a good sense called extatic, were something sudden and extraordinary. It was not even in their own power to elicit from themselves such acts as these at any time they chose. *Grief* [heaviness] and *sorrow* for the danger and distress of the people; shame for their fault; zeal for their salvation, for the safety of so great a multitude, and for still farther promoting the glory of God through the preservation of such a people, so carried them away, as to make them for a time forget themselves, Exod. xxxii. 32. I am inclined to give this paraphrase of that passage: *Pardon them; if thou dost not pardon them*, turn upon me the punishment destined for them, that is, as Moses elsewhere says, *kill me*, Num. xi. 15. It is therefore the book of temporal life, as distinguished from that of eternal life, according to the point of view, economy, and style of the Old Testament; comp. Ex. xxxiii. 3, 5. The book of temporal life is intended in Ps. cxxxix. 16.—αὐτὸς ἐγὼ, *I myself*) construe these words with *to be* [*were*].—ἀνάθεμα εἶναι, *to be accursed*) It will be enough to compare this passage with Gal. iii. 13, where Christ is said *to have been made a curse for us*. The meaning is, I could have wished to bring the misery of the Jews on my own head, and to be in their place. The Jews, rejecting the faith, were accursed from Christ; comp. Gal. i. 8, 9, v. 4. Whether he would have wished only the deprivation of all good, and his own destruction, and annihilation, or the suffering also of every evil, and that too both in body and in soul, and for ever, or whether, in the very excitement [paroxysm] of that prayer, he had the matter fully present before his understanding, who knows whether Paul himself, had he been questioned, would have been able exactly to define? At least that word [*Ego*] *I* [all thought of *self*] was entirely suppressed in him; he was looking only to others, for the sake of the Divine glory; comp. 2 Cor. xii. 15. From the loftiest pinnacle of faith (chap. viii.) he now shows the highest degree of love, which was kindled by the Divine love. The thing, which he had wished, could not have been done, but his prayer was pious and solid, although under the tacit condition, *if it were possible to be done;* comp. Rom. viii. 38, I *am persuaded;* Ex. xxxii. 33.—ἀπὸ τοῦ Χριστοῦ, *from Christ*) So ἀπὸ *from* 1 Cor. i. 30 ; or, as Christ, being made *a curse,* was abandoned *by the Father;* so Paul, filled with Christ, wished in place of the Jews to be forsaken *by Christ,* as if he had been accursed. He is not speaking of excommunication from the everlasting society of the church. There is a difference between these two things, for κατάρα קללה, *curse,* has the greater force of the two, and implies something more absolute : חרם, *anathema,* something relative, Gal. i. 8, 9, 1 Cor. xvi. 22, the former is rather more severe, the latter milder ; the former expresses the power of reconciliation by the cross of Christ ; the latter is more suitable to [more applicable as regards] Paul ; nor can the one be substituted for the other, either here, or in the passages quoted.— Τῶν) The apostle is speaking of the whole multitude, not of individuals.—ἀδελφῶν μου, *for my brethren*) This expresses the cause of his so great love toward them.—συγγενῶν μου κατὰ σάρκα, *my kinsmen according to the flesh*) This expresses the cause of his prayer, showing why the prayer, other things being supposed to be equal [*cæteris paribus,* supposing there were no objection on other grounds], was right ; and by adding *kinsmen,* he shows that the word *brethren* is not to be understood, as it usually is, of Christians, but of the Jews. Christ was made a *curse* for us, because we were his *kinsmen.*

4. οἵτινες, *inasmuch as being those who*) He now explains the cause of his sorrow and grief : viz. the fact that Israel does not enjoy so great benefits. He uses great 'euphemia' [softening of an unwelcome truth. Append.] in words.—ὧν ἡ υἱοθεσία—ἐπαγγε- λίαι, *whose is the adoption of* [*as*] *sons—the promises*) Six privileges are enumerated by three pairs of correlatives ; and in the first pair, regard is had to *God the Father;* in the second, to *Christ;* in the third, to *the Holy Spirit:* with which comp. Eph. iii. 6, note.—ἡ υἱοθεσία καὶ ἡ δόξα, *the adoption of sons and the glory*) i.e. that Israel is the first-born son of God, and the God of glory is their God, Deut. iv. 7, 33, 34 ; Ps. cvi. 20,

(xlvii. 5); but by the force of the correlatives, God is at the same time the Father of Israel, and Israel is the people of God. In like manner this relation is expressed in abbreviated form (the two respective correlatives being left to be supplied. See Append. on *locutio concisa*) in Rev. xxi. 7; comp. Rom. viii. 18, 19. Some understand δόξαν, *the glory*, of the ark of the covenant; but Paul is not speaking here of anything corporeal. God Himself is called the *Glory* of His people Israel, by the same metonymy, as He is called the *Fear*, instead of the God [the Object of fear], of Isaac, Gen. xxxi. 42, 54.—καὶ αἱ διαθῆκαι, καὶ ἡ νομοθεσία, *and the covenants and the giving of the law*) comp. Heb. viii. 6. The reason why the *covenants* are put before the *giving of the law*, is evident from Gal. iii. 17. Διαθῆκαι is plural, because the *testament*, or covenant, both was frequently repeated, Lev. xxvi. 42, 45; Eph. ii. 12; and was given in various modes [πολυτρόπως], dispositions [one, the law received by the *disposition* of angels, the other the Gospel covenant under Jesus], Heb. i. 1; and because there were two administrations of it, Gal. iv. 24, the one promising, the other promised [the subject of the promise].—καὶ ἡ λατρεία καὶ αἱ ἐπαγγελίαι, *and the service of God and the promises*) Acts xxvi. 6, 7; Eph. i. 13; Heb. viii. 5, 6. Here *the giving of the law and the service of God, the covenants and the promises* correspond by chiasmus.[1] For *the promises* flow from *the covenants;* and *the service of God* was instituted by *the giving of the law*. [*It was the promises that procured (gained) for the service of God its peculiar dignity. Moreover, the Holy Spirit was promised*, Gal. iii. 14.—V. g.]

5. Ὧν οἱ πατέρες, κ.τ.λ.) *whose are the fathers*, etc. Baumgarten has both written a *dissertation* on this passage, and has added it to his Exposition of this Epistle. All, that is of importance to me in it, I have explained *im Zeugniss*, p. 157, etc. (ed. 1748), [c. 11, 28].—καὶ ἐξ ὧν, *and of whom*, i.e. of the Israelites, Acts iii. 22. To the six privileges of the Israelites lately mentioned are added the seventh and eighth, respecting the fathers, and respecting the Messiah Himself. *Israel is a noble and a holy people*.—ὁ ὤν) i.e. ὅς ἐστι, but the participle has a more narrow meaning. Artemonius with great propriety proves

---

[1] See Appendix.

from the grief of Paul, that there is no doxology in this passage: Part I. cap. 42: but at the same time he along with his associates contends, that Paul wrote ὧν ὁ ἐπὶ πάντων, Θεός, κ.τ.λ. So that there may be denoted in the passage this privilege of the Israelites, that the Lord is their God; and he interprets the clause, ὁ ἐπὶ πάντων, thus: that this privilege is the greatest of all the honours conferred upon Israel. But such an interpretation of the ὁ ἐπὶ πάντων, with which comp. Eph. iv. 6 (that we may remove this out of our way in the first place), implies a meaning, which owes its birth merely to the support of an hypothesis, and which requires to be expressed rather by a phrase of this sort; τὸ δὴ πάντων μεῖζον. The conjecture itself, ὧν ὁ, carries with it an open violation of the text. For I. it dissevers τὸ κατὰ σάρκα from the antithetic member of the sentence, κατὰ πνεῦμα,[1] which is usually everywhere mentioned [expressed]. II. It at the same time divides the last member of the enumeration [of the catalogue of privileges], before which καὶ, *and*, is suitably placed, καὶ ἐξ ὧν, κ.τ.λ. into two members, and in the second of these the conjunction is by it harshly suppressed.

Artemonius objects: I. Christ is nowhere in the sacred Scriptures expressly called God. *Ans.* Nowhere? Doubtless because Artemonius endeavours to get rid of all those passages either by proposing a different reading, or by a different mode of interpretation. He himself admits, that too many proofs of one thing ought not to be demanded, page 225. In regard to the rest, see note on John i. 1. He objects, II. If Paul wrote ὁ ὤν, he omitted the principal privilege of the Israelites, that God, who is the Best and Greatest of all, was their God. *Ans.* The *adoption* and the *glory* had consisted in that very circumstance; therefore he did not omit it; nor is that idea, *the Lord is the God of Israel*, ever expressed in these words, *Thine, O Israel, is God blessed for ever*. He urges further; Christ is included even in the *covenants*, and yet Paul presently after makes mention of *Christ;* how much more would he be likely to make mention of God the Father Himself? *Ans.* The reason in the case of Christ for His being mentioned does not equally hold good in the case of God. Paul

---

[1] *i.e., according to His divine nature.* The words ὁ ἐπὶ πάντων Θεός are equivalent to κατὰ πνεῦμα, and form a plain antithesis to τὸ κατὰ σάρκα = *His human nature.*—ED.

mentions in the order of time all the privileges of Israel (the fathers being by the way [incidentally] joined with Christ). He therefore mentions Christ, as He was manifested [last in order of time]; but it was not necessary that that should be in like manner mentioned of God. Moreover, Christ was in singularly near relationship to the Israelites; but God was also the God of the Gentiles, ch. iii. 29: and it was not God, but Christ, whom the Jews rejected more openly. What? In the very root of the name *Israel*, and therefore of the *Israelites*, to which the apostle refers, ver. 4, 6, the name *El*, *God*, is found. He objects, III. The style of the Fathers disagrees with this opinion: nay, the false Ignatius [pseudoignatius] reckons among the ministers of Satan those, who said, that Jesus Himself is God over all. Ans. By this phrase, he has somewhat incautiously described the Sabellians, and next to them he immediately places the Artemonites in the same class. In other respects the fathers often apply the phraseology of Paul respecting Christ to the Father, and by that very circumstance prove the true force of that phraseology [as expressing Divinity]; and yet the apostle is superior to [should have more weight than] the fathers. Wolfius refutes Artemonius at great length in vol. ii. Curar. ad N. T., p. 802, etc.—ἐπὶ πάντων, *over all*) The Father is certainly excepted, 1 Cor. xv. 27. *Christ is of the fathers, according to the flesh; and at the same time was, is, and shall be over all, inasmuch as He is God blessed for ever. Amen!* The same praise is ascribed to the Father and the Son, 2 Cor. xi. 31. *Over all*, which is antithetic to, *of whom*, shows both the pre-existence (προΰπαρξιν) of Christ before the fathers, in opposition to His descent from the fathers according to the flesh, and His infinite majesty and dominion full of grace over Jews and Gentiles; comp. as to the phrase, Eph. iv. 6; as to the fact itself, John viii. 58; Matt. xxii. 45. They are quite wrong, who fix the full stop *either* here [after πάντων], (for the comma may be placed with due respect to religion); for in that case the expression should have been, εὐλογητὸς ὁ θεός [not ὁ—θεὸς εὐλογητός], if only there had been here any peculiar occasion for such a doxology; *or* [who fix a full stop] after σάρκα; for in this case τὸ κατὰ σάρκα would be without its proper antithesis [which is, " who in His divine nature is God over all"].—Θεός, *God*) We should greatly rejoice, that in this solemn description Christ is so plainly called God. The apostles, who wrote before John, take for granted the deity of Christ, as a thing acknowledged; whence it is that they do not directly treat of it, but yet when it comes in their way, they mark it in a most glorious manner. Paul, ch. v. 15, had called Jesus Christ *man;* but he now calls Him God; so also 1 Tim. ii. 5, iii. 16. The one appellation supports the other.—εὐλογητὸς, *blessed*) הַקָּבְּה. By this epithet we unite in giving all praise to God, 2 Cor. xi. 31.—εἰς τοὺς αἰῶνας, *for ever*) [He] *Who is above all—for ever*, is the *first and the last*, Rev. i. 17.

6. Οὐχ᾽ οἷον,) *This is not of that kind* [*not as though*] The Jews were of opinion, that, if all the Jews were not saved, the word of God becomes of none effect. Paul refutes this opinion, and at the same time intimates, that the apostacy of the Jews had been foretold, rather than otherwise, by the word of God.— δὲ) *but*; namely, although I profess great sorrow for Israel, who continue without Christ.—ἐκπέπτωκεν, *hath taken none effect*) A suitable expression, 1 Cor. xiii. 8, note. If all Israel had failed, the word of God would have failed; but the latter cannot occur, so neither can the former: for even now there are some, [Israelites believers], and in future times there will be all. For this sentence comprehends all the statements in Chapters ix. x. xi., and is most aptly expressed. It is closely connected with what goes before in ver. 2, and yet in respect of what follows, where *the word* λόγος occurs again, there is a studied gentleness of expression and anticipatory caution[1] that whatever is said of a disagreeable description may be softened before it is expressed; as in 1 Cor. x. 13.—ὁ λόγος, *the word*) of promise, which had been given to Israel.—οὐ γὰρ πάντες, *for not all*) γὰρ, *for* begins the discussion, *not all*, is mildly said instead of, *there are not many*. This was what the Jews held: *We all and we alone are the people of God.* Wherefore the *all* is refuted here; and the *alone* at ver. 24, etc. The Jews were Particularists ('Particularistæ'); therefore Paul directly refutes them. His whole discussion will not only be considered as tolerable, but will even be much admired by those, and those alone, who have gone

---

[1] See on 'Euphemia' and προθεραπεία the Appendix.

through the former chapters in faith and repentance; for in this the prior regard is had to *faith* [rather than to repentance]. The sum of this discussion, in the opinion of those who deny universal grace, is as follows. GOD *gives* FAITH *to whom He will; He does not give it, to whom He will not;* according to the mind of Paul, it is this: *God gives* RIGHTEOUSNESS *to them that believe, He does not give it to them that work; and that is by no means contrary to His word.* Nay, He himself has declared by types and testimonies, that those, the *sons of the promise* are received; that these, the *children of the flesh* are rejected. This decree of God is certain, irrefragable, just; as any man or people listens to this decree or strives against it, so that man or that people is either accepted in mercy or rejected in wrath. The analysis of *Arminius*, which has been gleaned from *Calovius* Theol. Apost. Rom. Oraculo lxviii., and adopted Oraculo lxix., comes back to this [amounts to this at last]. Compare by all means i. 16, note. In the meantime Paul, in regard to those, whom he refutes, does not make any very wide separation between the former chapter [or *head*] concerning faith and the latter concerning righteousness; nor indeed was it necessary.—'Ισραήλ, 'Ισραήλ, *Israël, Israël*) Ploce.[1]

7. Ὅτι) *because;* this particle makes an epitasis[2] in respect of the preceding sentence.—Ἀβραάμ, *of Abraham*) That, which happened to the children of the Fathers in the most ancient times, may much more happen to their later descendants.—ἀλλ' ἐν Ἰσαάκ, κ.τ.λ., *but in Isaac,* etc.) This clause is put as a "Suppositio Materialis" [See Append.]; for we supply, *it was written, and it is being fulfilled,* LXX., Gen. xxi. 12: ὅτι ἐν σπέρμα. Here we even find a suitableness in the origin of the name Isaac; for they are the seed, who embrace the *covenant* of grace with a pure and noble-minded *joy,* Gen. xvii. 19 [*Isaac* Heb. = *laughter, joy*].

8. Τουτέστιν) The apostle, using boldness in speaking, puts *that is* for *therefore.*—ταῦτα) דן, that is, *are.* The substantive pronoun for the substantive verb; so οὗτοι, *these,* ver. 6: and

---

[1] See Appendix. A word twice put, once in the simple sense, once to express an attribute of it.

[2] Appendix. An addition made to a previous enunciation, to explain, or give emphasis.

frequently οὗτος *this*, ver. 9. The mode of expression in this chapter becomingly assumes the Hebrew idiom, so ver. 28, etc.

9. Ἐπαγγελίας, *of promise*) It corresponds to the expression, *of the promise*, ver. 8.—οὗτος, *this*) viz., *is*.—κατὰ τὸν καιρὸν τοῦτον ἐλεύσομαι, καὶ ἔσται τῇ Σάῤῥᾳ υἱός) *At this time will I come, and Sarah shall have a son*. LXX., Gen. xviii. 10 : ἰδοὺ ἐπαναστρέφων ἥξω πρός σε κατὰ τὸν καιρὸν τοῦτον εἰς ὥρας, καὶ ἕξει υἱὸν Σάῤῥα ἡ γυνή σου; comp. Gen. xvii. 21.

10. Οὐ μόνον δέ, *and not only so*) That is : it is wonderful, what I have said; what follows is still more wonderful. Ishmael under Abraham, Esau under Isaac, and those, who resembled Ishmael and Esau under Israel, rebelled.—Ῥεβέκκα, *Rebecca*) viz., ἐστίν, *is, i.e.* occurs in this place. She, the mother, and presently after Isaac the father, are named.—ἐξ ἑνὸς, *by one*) Isaac was now separated from Ishmael, and yet under Isaac himself, in whom Abraham's seed is called, Esau also is separated from Jacob. Ishmael and Isaac were born not of the same mother, nor at the same time,—and Ishmael was the son too of a bondmaid, Isaac of a free woman. Jacob and Esau were born both of the same mother, and she a free woman, and at the same time.—κοίτην) so LXX. for שכבה; it often occurs, *e.g.* Lev. xviii. 20, οὐ δώσεις κοίτην σπέρματος, said of the man, which is opposed to the phrase ἔχειν κοίτην, of the woman in this passage.

11. Μήπω γεννηθέντων, *when they were not yet born*) Carnal descent profiteth nothing, John i. 13.—μηδὲ πραξάντων, *and when they had done nothing*) This is added, because some one might think as to Ishmael, that he was driven out, not so much because he was the son of a bondmaid, as because he was a mocker; although this slave-like scurrility afterwards shows itself in [lays hold of] the son of the bondmaid, so that he [מצחק, and κακόζηλος τοῦ יצחק] *laughs and mocks at Isaac*, whom he envies and insults. —κατ᾽ ἐκλογὴν) The *purpose*, which is quite free, has its reason founded on election alone ; comp. κατὰ ch. xvi. 25; Tit. i. 9. It might be said, in Latin, *propositum Dei electivum, the elective purpose of God*.—μένῃ, *might stand* [*remain*]) incapable of being set aside. It is presupposed that the πρόθεσιν, *the purpose*, is prior to the, *might stand*.—οὐκ ἐξ ἔργων, *not of works*) not even of works foreseen. Observe, it is not faith, which is opposed to *election*, but works.—ἐκ τοῦ καλοῦντος, *of Him that calleth*) even *Him, who*

called Jacob to be the superior, Esau to be the servant: comp. ver. 25.

12. Αὐτῇ, *to her*) It was often foretold to mothers before conception or birth, what would happen to their sons.—ὅτι ὁ—ἐλάσσονι) Gen. xxv. 23, LXX., καὶ ὁ—ἐλάσσονι.—ὁ μείζων) *the elder*, who, it might be reasonably thought, should command, as the younger should obey.—δουλεύσει, *shall serve*) and yet not so for ever, Gen. xxvii. 40.

13. Καθὼς, *as*) The word spoken by Malachi, at a period so long subsequent, agrees with that spoken in Genesis.—τὸν 'Ιακὼβ ἠγάπησα κ.τ.λ.) Mal. i. 2, LXX., ἠγάπησα τὸν 'Ιακὼβ κ.τ.λ.—ἠγάπησα —ἐμίσησα, *I have loved—I have hated*) The reference is not to the spiritual state of each of the two brothers : but the external condition of Jacob and Esau, in like manner as the corporeal birth of Isaac is a type of spiritual things, ver. 9. All Israelites are not saved, and all Edomites are not damned. But Paul intimates, that as there was a difference between the sons of Abraham and Isaac, so there was a difference among the posterity of Israel. So far has he demonstrated what he purposed; he in the next place introduces an objection, and refutes it; μισεῖν properly signifies *to hate*, nay, *to hate greatly*. See Mal. i. 4, at the end.

14. Τί οὖν, *what then ?*) *Can we then* on this ground be accused of charging God with unrighteousness and iniquity by this assertion ? By no means; for what we assert is the irrefragable assertion of God ; see the following verse.—Μὴ γένοιτο, *God forbid*) The Jews thought, that they could by no means be rejected by God ; that the Gentiles could by no means be received. As therefore an honest man acts even with greater severity [ἀποτομίᾳ] towards those who are harshly and spitefully importunate, than he really feels (that he may defend his own rights, and those of his patron, and may not at an unseasonable time betray and cast away his character for liberality) so Paul defends the power and justice of God against the Israelites, who trusted to their mere name and their own merits ; and on this subject, he sometimes uses those appropriate phrases, to which he seems to have been accustomed in former times in the school of the Pharisees. This is his language : *No man can prescribe anything to the Lord God, nor demand and somewhat insolently extort anything from Him as*

a debt, nor can he interdict *Him* in anything [which He pleases to do] or require a reason, why He shows Himself kind also to *others* [as well as to himself]. Therefore Paul somewhat abruptly checks by a rather severe answer the peevish and spiteful objectors. Luke xix. 22, 23, is a similar case. For no man is allowed to deal with God as if by virtue of a bond of agreement, [as if he were His creditor], but even if there were such a bond, God even deals more strictly with man [*i.e.* with a man of such a *hireling* spirit]; let the parable, Matt. xx. 13–15, which is quite parallel, be compared: *I do thee no wrong*, etc. There is therefore one meaning of Paul's language, by which he gives an answer to those who contend for good works: another, of a milder description, in behalf of believers, lies hid under the veil of the words. In the Sacred Scriptures too, especially when we have come from the thesis [the proposition] to the hypothesis [that on which the proposition rests], the *manners*, τὰ ἤθη, as well as the *reasonings*, οἱ λόγοι, ought to be considered; and yet there can be no commentary so plain, which he, who contends for justification by good works, may more easily understand than the text of Paul.

15. Τῷ γὰρ Μωσῇ, *for to Moses*) Many are of opinion, that the objection extends from this verse to ver. 18; in which view the *for*, is used, as in ch. iii. 7, and thus *thou wilt say then*, ver. 19, concludes the objection, which was begun at ver. 14. And indeed by this introduction of a person speaking there would be a fitting expression of that ἀνταπόκρισις (*rejoinder of the opponent*), which is censured at ver. 20, and is subsequently refuted by taking up the words themselves or their synonyms. In the meantime Paul so expresses himself, as to make ὁ ἀνταποκρινόμενος, the objector whilst replying at the same time answer himself; and therefore the words in this verse may be also taken, without injury to the sense, as spoken in the person of the apostle, as we shall now endeavour to show. Moses, Exod. xxxiii., had prayed for himself and the people by חן, *the grace* of the Lord, ver. 12, 13, 16, 17, and had concluded with, *show me thy glory*. The Lord answered: *I will make all My goodness pass in the presence of thy face, and I will proclaim the name of the Lord before thy face*. וחנתי את־אשר אחן ורחמתי את־אשר ארחם, *And will be gracious, to whom I will be gracious, and will show mercy, to whom I will show*

mercy, ver. 19. The Lord did not disclose even to Moses without some time intervening, to whom He would show grace and mercy, although the question was respecting Moses and the people of Israel alone, not respecting the Gentiles. To this Moses, then, not merely to others by Moses (Μωσῆ, says Paul, as presently after, τῷ Φαραὼ) the Lord spoke thus: *By My proclamation, and by My most abundant working, subsequently, I will designate* [mark out] *him, as the object of grace and mercy, whosoever he be, whom I make the object of grace and mercy.* By these words He intimated, that He would make proclamation [would reveal His own character] as regards grace and mercy; and He shortly after accordingly made proclamation, Ex. xxxiv. 5, רחום וחנון [ΟΙΚΤΙΡΜΩΝ καὶ ΕΛΕΗΜΩΝ κ.τ.λ. εἰς χιλιάδας], *merciful and gracious*, etc., *to thousands;* and added [καὶ τὸν ἔνοχον οὐ καθαριεῖ, ἐπάγων ἁμαρτίας πατέρων, κ.τ.λ.], *and He will not clear the guilty*, etc. Therefore according to the subsequent proclamation itself, the following meaning of the previous promise comes clearly out: *I will show thee the most abundant grace, even to that degree that thou mayest see concerning Me* [see centred in Me] *all whatsoever thou dost both desire and canst receive* [comprehend] *in order that thou mayest furthermore understand, that it is* [all of] *grace; and for this reason inasmuch as I have once for all embraced thee in grace, which thou acknowledgest to be grace; and as to the rest of the people, I will show them the most abundant mercy, in not visiting them with immediate destruction for their idolatry, that they may further understand it to be mercy; and for this reason inasmuch as I have once for all embraced them in mercy, which thou in their behalf acknowledgest to be mercy.* The LXX. Int. and Paul have expressed the meaning of this sentence by the difference between the present and future tense: ἐλεήσω ὃν ἂν ἐλεῶ, καὶ οἰκτειρήσω ὃν ἂν οἰκτείρω, *I will have mercy on whom I have mercy, and I will have compassion on whom I have compassion.* And there is the figure Ploce [see Appen.], which nearly signifies the same as below, ch. xiii. 7, and here it expresses the liberty of the Agent, of whom the apostle is speaking, as in Ex. xvi. 23. Moreover, each of the two verbs, placed in the two clauses [*i.e.* repeated twice], contains the emphasis in the former clause; [*i.e.* the emphasis is on the verb in each of the two clauses on its *first* mention, not on it *when repeated;* I *will have mercy*, on whom I have mercy, etc.]: although generally in other passages the emphasis is on the verb in the latter clause [*i.e.* on its repetition] Gen. xxvii. 33, xliii. 14; 2 Kings vii. 4. That the acknowledgment of grace and mercy, on the part of Moses, and the true Israelites, is entwined together, is evident from this, that Paul, ver. 16, speaks, on the opposite side, of the man *that willeth* and *that runneth*, to whom grace is not grace, and mercy is not mercy. אשר את ὅν ἄν is put twice, and intimates in the former passage that Moses (to whom the word חן, *grace*, is repeated in reply, taken from his own very prayers from Ex. xxxiii. ver. 13: where there occurs the same Ploce), and that in the latter passage, the others, were εἰς χιλιάδας *among the thousands* [as to whom God said of Himself, *keeping mercy for thousands*], to whom sinners, their children, grandchildren, etc., are opposed, Ex. xxxiv. 7. And thus, this testimony is extremely well fitted to prove, that there is no unrighteousness with God. This sentiment is manifest to believers. But in regard to those, who maintain the efficacy of good works, it sounds too abrupt: the reason why God should be merciful, is none other than His own mercy, for no other is mentioned in the writings of Moses, concerning Moses and Israel. *I will have mercy, i.e. no one can extort anything by force; all things are in My hand, under My authority, and dependent on My will, if I act otherwise, no one can charge Me with injustice.* This answer is sufficient to give to the defender of good works; and if any farther answer is given to him, it is superfluous.

16. Ἄρα οὖν, *therefore*) so also ver. 18. The inference of Paul here is not drawn from the particle ὃν ἄν, *whomsoever*, but from the words ἐλεῶ and οἰκτείρω, *I have mercy*, and *I have compassion.* —οὐ τοῦ) *not of the man that willeth, nor of him that runneth*, supply *it is*, the *business*, or, *will, course* [the *race* is not of him that runneth, etc.]; not that it is in vain to will rightly, and, what is of greater importance, to run, or strive rightly, 1 Cor. ix. 26; Phil. iii. 14: but because to will and to run produce none of the things aimed at by those, who trust to their works. The human will is opposed to divine grace, and the course [the *run*] of human conduct to divine operation.—Comp. ver. 30, 31.

17. Λέγει) *saith, i.e.* exhibits God speaking in this manner, comp. ch. x. 20, *saith*.—γάρ, *for*) He proves, that it is *of Him*

who shows mercy, even *God*.—τῷ Φαραὼ, to *the Pharaoh*) who lived in the time of *Moses*.—ὅτι εἰς αὐτὸ τοῦτο ἐξήγειρά σε, ὅπως ἐνδείξωμαι ἐν σοὶ τὴν δύναμίν μου κ.τ.λ.) *Even for this same purpose have I raised thee up that I might show my power in thee.* The LXX, Ex. ix. 16, καὶ ἕνεκεν τούτου διετηρήθης ἕως τοῦ νῦν, ἵνα ἐνδείξωμαι ἐν σοὶ τὴν ἰσχύν μου κ.τ.λ. *For this cause, thou hast been preserved until now, that I might show my power*, etc.—ἐξήγειρά σε) העמדתיך LXX. Int. διετηρήθης (as Exod. xxi. 21, עמד, διαβιοῦν, to *pass one's life*), but Paul according to his custom says more significantly, ἐξήγειρά σε : but it should be carefully observed, that by ἐξεγείρω here the meaning of the word הקים is not expressed, as it is used in Zech. xi. 16, but העמיד, which in all cases presupposes the subject previously produced. See the difference of these two Hebrew verbs in 1 Kings xv. 4. The meaning then is this: I have raised thee up to be a king very powerful (in whom I might show My power) and illustrious (by means of whom [owing to whom] My name might be proclaimed throughout all the earth). Therefore this ἐξέγερσις, *raising up*, includes the διατηρεῖν, *preserving*, as the LXX. render it, using the milder term : and also includes the ἐνεγκεῖν, which in ver. 22, is introduced from this very passage of Moses. The predecessor [the former Pharaoh] had previously begun rather to oppress Israel; Exod. ii. 23 : nor yet did the successor repent. The *Ordo Temporum*, p. 161 [Ed. II. 142], determines his reign to have been very short, and therefore his whole administration was an experiencing of the Divine power. It must be added, that this was told to Pharaoh not at first, but after he had been frequently guilty of excessive obstinacy, and it was not even then intended to discourage him from acknowledging Jehovah and from letting the people go, but to bring about his reformation.—δύναμιν, *power*) by which Pharaoh with all his forces was drowned.—διαγγελῇ, *might be declared*) This is being done even to the present day.

18. Ὃν θέλει) *whom He will.* Moreover, as regards the question, to whom God wills to show mercy, and whom He wills to harden; Paul shows that in other passages.—ἐλεεῖ, *has mercy*) as for example on Moses.—σκληρύνει, *hardens*) as He did Pharaoh. He uses, *hardens*, for, *has not mercy*, by metonymy of [substituting, for the antecedent,] the consequent, although *not to have mercy* has a somewhat harsher meaning: so, *is sanctified*, for,

is not unclean, 1 Cor. vii. 14; and, *you rescued from*, [ἐῤῥύσασθε |, instead of *you did not deliver up*. Jos. xxii. 31.

19. Ἔτι, *as yet*) even still. This particle well expresses the peevish outcry. To the objection here put, Paul answers in two ways. I. The power of God over men is greater than the power of the potter over the clay, ver. 20, 21. Then II. He answers more mildly: God has not exercised His power, not even over the vessels of wrath, ver. 22.—αὐτοῦ, *His*) It is put for, *of God*, and expresses the feeling, by which objectors of this description show their aversion from God.

20.[1] Ἄνθρωπε, *O man*) weak, ignorant of righteousness [*i.e.* the true way of justification].—μὴ ἐρεῖ, κ.τ.λ.) Isa. xxix. 16. Οὐχ ὡς πηλὸς τοῦ κεραμέως λογισθήσεσθε ; μὴ ἐρεῖ τὸ πλάσμα τῷ πλάσαντι αὐτό, οὐ σύ με ἔπλασας. The same prophet, ch. xlv. 9, μὴ ἐρεῖ ὁ πηλὸς τῷ κεραμεῖ: τί ποιεῖς, ὅτι οὐκ ἐργάζῃ, οὐδὲ ἔχεις χεῖρας. μὴ ἀποκριθήσεται τὸ πλάσμα πρὸς τὸν πλάσαντα αὐτό; *Shall ye not be reckoned as the potter's clay? Shall the thing formed say to Him that formed it, Thou hast not formed me?* Is. xlv. 9, *Shall the clay say to the potter, what art thou doing, that thou dost not work, thou hast no hands? Shall the thing formed answer Him that formed it?*—(Vers. LXX.)

21. Ἤ) particle of interrogation [*an*?].—ἐξουσίαν, *power*) construed with, *over the clay*. The potter does not make the clay but digs it out; God makes man, therefore He has greater power [over man], than the potter [over the clay]. But absolute power and liberty do not imply, that the will and decree are absolute. If God had left the whole human race under the power of sin and death, He would not have done unjustly, but He did not exercise that right. [*Man is struck with the vivid exhibition of Divine power, so that he ever after unlearns all the outrageous* (unreasonable) *suspicions of his thoughts, against the justice* [*righteousness*] *of God*, Matt. xx. 15; Ex. xx. 20; Job xlii. 2, 6.—V. g.].—φυράματος) *lump*, which has been prepared from clay and softened by steeping, and has its

---

[1] Μενοῦνγε, *but truly*) This answer savours of a severe and somewhat vehement nature. Men of fierce dispositions must certainly be restrained; but the sweetest foundation of the whole argument is subsequently disclosed to them that are called, ver. 24. In this discussion, he who merely cuts off a portion of it from the rest, must be perplexed and stick at trifles; but he proceeds easily, who thoroughly weighs the whole connection of chapters ix., x., xi.—V. g.

parts now more homogeneous.—*εἰς ἀτιμίαν, to dishonour*) Paul speaks circumspectly, he does not yet say, *to wrath: vessel* must be construed with these words [To make one, a vessel unto honour, etc.]

22. Εἰ δὲ, *but if*) This particle has this as its apodosis to be supplied at the end of ver. 23 from ver. 20: God has much greater cause to complain concerning man, and man has less cause to expostulate with God [than the potter concerning the clay, and the clay with the potter]. Comp. ἐὰν, John vi. 62, where also the apodosis is to be supplied. It is a question, but one implied, not expressed, with an ellipsis, *What reply hast thou to make* [if God willing to show, etc., endured, etc.].—θέλων, *willing*) Corresponds to the, *His will*, ver. 19, and to, *He will*, ver. 18. Paul speaks κατ' ἄνθρωπον, [" after the manner of man :" or, *taking advantage of his opponent's unavoidable admission*] in the words of his opponent; and so εἰ signifies *whereas*, [since, as you must grant]. At the same time, we must observe that what he says of the vessels of wrath is more scanty, and of the vessels of mercy more copious; *willing to show*, he says, not, [willing, putting forth His will] *that he might show*, comp. next verse [where in the case of the vessels *of mercy*, he says, ἵνα γνωρίσῃ, though here ver. 22 in the case of the vessels *of wrath*, he says, γνωρίσαι], and Eph. ii. 7.— ἐνδείξασθαι—τὸ δυνατὸν αὐτοῦ, *to show His power*) These words are repeated from ver. 17.—τὴν ὀργὴν, *wrath*) He does not say, the *riches of his wrath*; comp. ver. 23.—τὸ δυνατὸν) This signifies, what He can do (*potentiam* 'might') not what He *may do* (*potestatem* 'right' [ἐξουσία]).—ἤνεγκεν, *endured*) as He endured Pharaoh. — ἐν πολλῇ μακροθυμίᾳ, *with much long-suffering*) viz: in order that it might allure the wicked [the reprobate] from their state of alienation from Him to repentance, ch. ii. 4 ; 2 Pet. iii. 9. God endures many bad men, in the enjoyment of great and long continued good fortune in this life, when He might at the very first have consigned them to death. The gate of mercy and grace is still open to them. This long-suffering, humanly speaking, precedes His " will to show His wrath," nor does it merely follow it. His *enduring* is not wont to be exercised until He is about *to show His wrath*] : wherefore ἤνεγκεν should be translated, *had endured* [previous to His will to show His wrath.] By

this very circumstance the question, *who hath resisted?* ver. 19, is most powerfully refuted.—ὀργῆς) *of wrath*, which is not indeed without cause, but presupposes sins ; he does not say, *of disgrace,* nor *unto wrath,* but *of wrath,* [*i.e.* the fault is *in themselves.*]—κατηρτισμένα, *fitted*) It denotes the disposition [fitness] internal and full, but now no longer free [no longer now liable to change], not the destination ; he does not say, *which He* προκατήρτισε, *previously fitted,* although he says in the next verse, *which he prepared,* comp. ver. 19, ch. xi. 22, note ; Matt. xxv. 34, with ver. 41, and Acts xiii. 46, with ver. 48. This is distinct from the efficient cause ; what is said merely refers to the state in which God finds the reprobate, when He brings upon them His wrath.—εἰς ἀπώλειαν, *to destruction*) The antithesis is, ver. 23, *unto glory*.

23. Ἵνα, *that*) Denotes more distinctly the end and aim, without excluding means.—γνωρίσῃ, *might make known*) This verb is applied to things not formerly known ; it is therefore put both here and in the preceding verse, but ἐνδείκνυσθαι, *to show,* is only used in verse 22 concerning wrath ; of which even the Gentiles have some knowledge.—ἐπί, *upon*) The sentence is thus quite consistent. *But if God that He might make known the riches of His glory,* supply, *did this,* or, in other words, *made known the riches* [of His glory] *on the vessels of mercy* ; respecting the apodosis, see the beginning of the note, ver. 22.—τῆς δόξης) *of His glory* : of His goodness, grace, mercy, wisdom, omnipotence, Eph. i. 6.—ἐλέους) *of mercy,* ver. 15, 16, 18, 25, which presupposes the former misery of those, styled vessels.—προητοίμασεν, *previously prepared*) antecedently to works, ver. 11, by the arrangement of all the external and internal circumstances, which he, *who is called,* finds tending to his salvation, at the first moment of *his call*. This is implied by the preposition in προητοίμασεν. So *a vessel unto honour, prepared,* 2 Tim. ii. 21.

24. Οὓς καί, *whom also*) καί, *also,* in chap. viii. 30, Cluverus : *whom (having been previously prepared for glory) He hath also called.*—ἐκάλεσεν, *called*) in some respects an antithesis to, *He endured,* ver. 22. Again, *I will call,* occurs in the next verse.— ἡμᾶς, *us*) This gnome[1] leads Paul to come to the proposition

[1] 'Noëma,' a gnome or religious and moral sentiment appertaining to human life and action.—See Appendix.

respecting grace, which it laid open to Jews and Gentiles; and he proceeds to refute the Jewish Particularism, and to defend the universality of grace.—οὐ μόνον ἐξ, not only from) The believing Jew is not called on the very ground that he is a Jew, but he is called *from* the Jews. This is the root of the word ἐκκλησία. [*The epistle to the Ephesians most especially corresponds to this whole section, as well as to the exhortation,* chapters xiv. xv., *deduced from it.*—V. g.]—ἐξ 'Ιουδαίων, *from the Jews*) He treats of this at ver. 27.—ἐξ ἐθνῶν, *from the Gentiles*) He treats of this, ver. 25, etc.

25. Λέγει, *saith*) God. Paul asserted the prior right of God in calling the Gentiles, and their actual calling, and now at last that the event is shown, he brings in one testimony from the Old Testament, and ch. xv. 9, etc., a number more in succession, by a method worthy of notice. The predictions, though numerous and quite clear from their fulfilment, yet in the first instance do not easily obtain belief. The strength of the following quotation is not in the verb καλέσω *I will call* [*name*], but in the other part of the expression: ἐκάλεσεν, He called, is used as in viii. 30. Nevertheless *naming* immediately accompanies *calling,* and in a manner precedes it.—καλέσω τὸν οὐ λαόν μου, λαόν μου. καὶ τὴν οὐκ ἠγαπημένην, ἠγαπημένην) *I will call them my people, who were not my people, and her beloved who was not beloved,* Hos. ii. 25. The LXX. have, *And I will have mercy on her, on whom I have not had mercy, and I will say to them who are not my people, thou art my people.*—[καὶ ἐλεήσω τὴν οὐκ ἠλεημένην. καὶ ἐρῶ τῷ οὐ λαῷ μου, λαός μου εἶ σύ.]—ἠγαπημένην *loved*) as one betrothed, as a bride.

26. καὶ—ἐκεῖ κληθήσονται—(ζῶντος) Hos. ii. 1, LXX. καὶ—κληθήσονται καὶ αὐτοὶ—ζῶντος.—ἐκεῖ) *there*: So it is not necessary for them to change their country and betake themselves to Judaea, comp. Zeph. ii. 11.

27. Κράζει) *crieth.* See Isa. x. 22, where the accents also may be compared. Israel utters an opposing reclamation [*cries against*]: Isaiah with a still louder exclamation [*cry*] declares, a remnant shall be saved.—ὑπὲρ) *for* Israel, Fr. *en faveur*, in behalf of.— ἐὰν ᾖ ὁ ἀριθμὸς τῶν υἱῶν 'Ισραὴλ—κατάλειμμα—ποιήσει Κύριος ἐπὶ τῆς γῆς) Isa. x. 22, 23, LXX., καὶ ἐὰν γένηται ὁ λαὸς 'Ισραὴλ—κατάλειμμα αὐτῶν—Κύριος ποιήσει ἐν τῇ οἰκουμένῃ ὅλῃ. In the last clause Sym-

machus and Theodotion have ἐν μέσῳ πάσης τῆς γῆς. The word ἀριθμὸς Paul introduced from Hos. ii. 1 [i. 10]. If Israel shall have been [or *have been*] as numerous as the sand, a remnant [only] shall be saved, namely, from the misery of the Babylonish captivity and from spiritual misery. That a remnant should remain in the multitude of the remnant [*i.e.* in a case where the body from which the remnant is taken is a multitude] is less wonderful. The *Many* are hardened; but *the seed* implies a small number, ver. 29, note. When the rebellion of Israel reaches its height, at that point salvation begins.

28. Λόγον) a thing *heard*, and therefore *spoken*, Isa. xxviii. 22.—συντελῶν και συντέμνων) supply, as is often necessary in Hebrew, the word *is*, comp. Acts xxiv. 5; 2 Pet. i. 17; Heb. כלה ונחרצה and כליון הרוץ. The Lord συντελεῖ, will consummate His λόγον *word* [decree] concerning Israel, in respect to the appointed [fixed] punishment (so that it becomes כלה, *consummated, completed*); and at the same time συντέμνει λόγον, *cuts short* His word, in respect to the termination [will make a speedy termination] of the punishment (so that נחרצה becomes כלה, this *decree* becomes *consummated*). The word *Lord* is to be supplied from the following clause ; and the word συντελῶν may be taken either as the subject, or rather, since the article is wanting, as a part of the predicate [the Lord *is about to consummate*, etc.]—ἐν δικαιοσύνῃ, שוטף צדקה. Is. x. 22.

29. Εἰ μὴ—ὠμοιώθημεν) Is. i. 9, LXX., καὶ εἰ μὴ ὠμοιώθημεν.— προείρηκεν, *said before*) *Before* the event, or before the prophecy quoted at ver. 28.—σαβαὼθ) In 1 Samuel and in Isaiah, σαβαὼθ is put for the Heb. word צבאות; in all the other books it is translated παντοκράτωρ, *Ruler over all*. From this circumstance there is strong ground for conjecturing, that one or perhaps several persons were employed to translate those two books, and that different persons translated the rest. And in the same first book of Sam. Scripture begins to give this title to God, although others had been formerly used as it were in its place.—Exod. xxxiv. 23.—σπέρμα, *a seed*) There is denoted 1) a small number at the present time, 2) the propagation of a multitude after deliverance from captivity.—ὡς Σόδομα, *as Sodom*) where not a single citizen escaped ; no *seed* was left.

30. Τί, *what*) He returns from the digression, which he had

commenced at the middle of ver. 24, and takes in summarily the whole subject, ver. 30-32. There is a mitigation of the severity of the discussion continued from ver. 6 to ver. 23; but it will only be comprehended by him, who is acquainted with the way of faith. In short, by this tone of feeling the foregoing remarks are judged of.—κατέλαβε) *have attained* [Luke xiii. 29, 24.]—πίστεως, *by faith*), ver. 33, at its close.

31. Νόμον δικαιοσύνης εἰς νόμον δικαιοσύνης, *the law of righteousness to the law of righteousness*) He did not use the word *law*, in the preceding verse, concerning the Gentiles; but now uses it in speaking of the Jews; and there is a ploce or repetition of the words in a different sense; concerning legal and also concerning evangelical righteousness. While Israel is following the one law, he does not attain to the other. The apostle appropriately uses the expression, *the law of righteousness*, for, *the righteousness of the law*. The Jews rather looked to the law, than to righteousness: νόμος, *doctrine*, תורה.—οὐκ ἔφθασε) *did not attain*.

32. Ὅτι *because*) viz. *they sought after it* [*followed after it*].— οὐκ—ἀλλ᾽ ὡς) The Basle Lexicon says: ὡς *in comparing things dissimilar is doubled, and the one ὡς is elegantly understood in the former member, and ὡς is only joined to* [expressed in] *the latter part*. Examples are there subjoined from Aristotle; we may compare John vii. 10; 2 Cor. xi. 17; likewise Acts xxviii. 19; Philem. v. 14`; Phil. ii. 12.

33. Ἰδοὺ τίθημι ἐν Σιὼν λίθον προσκόμματος, καὶ πέτραν σκανδάλου· καὶ πᾶς ὁ πιστεύων ἐπ᾽ αὐτῷ οὐ καταισχυνθήσεται) LXX., Is. xxviii. 16, ἰδοὺ ἐγὼ ἐμβαλῶ εἰς τὰ θεμέλια Σιὼν λίθον πολυτελῆ, ἐκλεκτὸν, ἀκρογωνιαῖον, ἔντιμον εἰς τὰ θεμέλια αὐτῶν, καὶ ὁ πιστεύων ἐπ᾽ αὐτῷ οὐ καταισχυνθῇ, Is. viii. 14. καὶ οὐχ ὡς λίθου προσκόμματι συναντήσεσθε, οὐδὲ ὡς πέτρας πτώματι. Such a one will not be made ashamed, and so will obtain glory; comp. ch. v. 2, 5. This denotes *eternal life*, Is. xlv. 17.

CHAPTER X.

1. Ἀδελφοί, *brethren*) Now that he has got over, so to speak, the severity of the preceding discussion, he kindly addresses them as *brethren.*—μὲν, *indeed*) δὲ usually follows this particle, but δὲ, ver. 2, is absorbed in ἀλλὰ, *but.*—εὐδοκία, *well-wishing, desire*) I would *most gladly* hear of the salvation of Israel.— δέησις, *prayer*) Paul would not have prayed, if they had been utterly reprobates [cast away.]

2. [1]Ζῆλου Θεοῦ, *a zeal of God*) Acts xxii. 3, note. *Zeal of God*, if it is not against *Christ*, is good.—οὐ κατ᾽ ἐπίγνωσιν, *not according to knowledge*) An example of Litotes [expressing in less strong terms a strong truth] *i.e.* with great blindness; it agrees with the word, *ignorant*, in the next verse. Flacius says: *The Jews had and now have a zeal without knowledge; we on the contrary, alas! to our shame, have knowledge without zeal.* Zeal and ignorance are referred to at ver. 19.

3. Ζητοῦντες, *seeking*) by all means.—οὐχ ὑπετάγησαν, *have not been subject*) and have not *obeyed*," (ὑπήκουσαν) ver. 16. Ὑποταγή, *submits itself to the Divine will*, τῷ θέλειν, *the will of* GOD.

4. Τέλος, *the end*) bestowing righteousness and life, which the law points out, but cannot give. Τέλος, *the end*, and πλήρωμα, *the fulfilment*, are synonymous; comp. 1 Tim. i. 5, with Rom. xiii. 10, therefore comp. with this passage Matt. v. 17. The law presses upon a man, till he flies to Christ; then even the law itself says, *thou hast found a refuge. I cease to persecute thee, thou art wise, thou art safe.*—Χριστὸς, *Christ*) the subject is, *the end of the law.* [Not as Engl. Vers. "Christ is the end of the law"]. The predicate is, *Christ* (viz. ὢν, who is) *in* [every one that believeth; not as Engl. Vers., "the end of the law *to* every one"] etc. [ver. 6, 7, 9.]—παντὶ τῷ πιστεύοντι, *in every one that believeth*) The words, *in the believer*, are treated at ver. 5, etc.: and the words, *every one*, at ver. 11, etc. παντὶ, *in every one*, namely, of the Jews and Gentiles. The ix. chap. must not be

---

[1] Γὰρ, *for.*) Therefore even in those, who are not in a state of grace, something at least may be found which may induce those, who rejoice in the Divine favour, to intercede for them.—V. g.

shut within narrower limits than Paul permits in this x. chap., which is more cheerful and more expanded; and in it the word *all* occupies a very prominent place, ver. 11, etc.

5. Γράφει, *writes of*), [thus exhibiting the truth that] " the letter killeth." It is antithetic to ver. 6, 8 : [the righteousness by faith] *speaks*, with the living voice [not *writes*, as Moses]. There is also another similar antithesis : *Moses* in the concrete; *the righteousness which is of faith* in the abstract.—ὅτι ὁ ποιήσας, κ.τ.λ.) Lev. xviii. 5, LXX.,ποιήσετε αὐτὰ ἃ ποιήσας, κ.τ.λ.

6. Ἡ ἐκ πίστεως δικαιοσύνη, *the righteousness which is of faith*) A very sweet Metonymy, *i.e.* a man seeking righteousness by faith.—λέγει, *speaks*) *with himself.*—μὴ εἴπῃς, *say not*) for he, who says so, does not find in the law what he seeks; and he does not seek, what he might find in the Gospel: viz. righteousness and salvation, which are in Christ and are ready for believers in the Gospel. And yet, whoever only hears and heeds that from Moses, *The man that doeth shall live*, considers it necessary, thus to say [who shall ascend into heaven, etc.]—καρδίᾳ, *in the heart*) The *mouth* [ver. 9] is also attributed to faith; for faith speaks; but *unbelief* generally mutters.—τίς, κ.τ.λ.) Deut. xxx. 11-14, LXX., ὅτι ἐντολὴ αὕτη, ἣν ἐγὼ ἐντέλλομαι σοι σήμερον οὐχ᾽ ὑπέρογκός ἐστιν, οὐδὲ μακρὰν ἀπὸ σοῦ ἐστιν. οὐκ ἐν τῷ οὐρανῷ ἐστι, λέγων· τίς ἀναβήσεται ἡμῶν εἰς τὸν οὐρανὸν, καὶ λήψεται ἡμῖν αὐτήν; καὶ ἀκούσαντες αὐτὴν ποιήσομεν. οὐδὲ πέραν τῆς θαλάσσης ἐστί, λέγων· τίς διαπεράσεται ἡμῖν εἰς τὸ πέραν τῆς θαλάσσης καὶ λήψεται ἡμῖν αὐτήν. καὶ ἀκούσαντες αὐτὴν ποιήσομεν. ἐγγύς σου ἐστὶ τὸ ῥῆμα σφόδρα: ἐν στόματί σου καὶ ἐν τῇ καρδίᾳ σου, καὶ ἐν ταῖς χερσί σου, ποιεῖν αὐτὸ. "For this commandment which I command thee this day is not overwhelmingly great ; nor is it far from thee ; it is not in heaven, that thou shouldst say, who amongst us shall go up to heaven and obtain it for us, that we may hear it and do it? nor is it across the sea, that thou shouldst say, who shall cross the sea and bring it to us, that we may hear it and do it? The word is very near to thee, in thy mouth and in thy heart and in thy hands to do it." This paraphrase, so to speak, very sweetly alludes to this passage, without expressly quoting it. Moses speaks of heaven, as well as Paul, but the former afterwards says, *across the sea*, instead of which Paul most dexterously turns his discourse to *the abyss*, that he may

on the contrary [in antithesis to their question as to the abyss] make mention of the resurrection of Christ from the dead. The abyss is a huge cavity in the terraqueous globe, at once under the sea and the land. Compare, as to many things connected with this subject, Job xxviii. 14, 22 ; Phil. ii. 10, note.—τίς ἀναβήσεται ; *who shall ascend?*) He, who thus speaks, shows his willingness, but declares his inability to ascend and descend, so as to fetch righteousness and salvation from afar.—τοῦτ' ἔστι, *that is*) Their perverseness is reproved, who say, *Who shall ascend into heaven?* for they speak just as if the word concerning the *Lord of heaven* were not at hand, whom the mouth of the believer confesses to be Lord, ver. 9, and they who wish to bring salvation down from heaven, wish to bring Christ (as being the One, without whom there is no salvation) down from heaven, whence He has already descended : but as the latter cannot take place, so neither can the former. The words, *That is*, in the present is thrice used, with great force.

7. Τοῦτ' ἔστι), *that is*. *That* is construed with *to say*, as substantive and adjective. Moreover, they are again reproved for perverseness, who say, *who shall descend into the deep?* for they speak just as if the word *concerning the resurrection of Christ from the dead* were not nigh at hand, and the heart of the believer acknowledges, that He has risen, in the same ver. 9 : and they who wish to fetch salvation from the *depths of the earth*, wish to bring Christ (since there is no salvation without Him) from the deep, which He left once for all at His resurrection ; but as the latter cannot happen, so neither can the former. Therefore the believer, so far as this is concerned, regards not either heaven or the deep, since he has the thing which he desires, as near to him, as he is to himself. But unbelief is always fluctuating ; it is always wishing, and knows not what it wishes ; it is always seeking, and finds nothing. Hence it looks down at the deep with giddiness, nor can it look up to the heaven with joy.—Χριστὸν, *Christ*) The unbeliever does not fetch Christ in His own name, that is in the name of Christ [in His peculiar attributes as anointed Saviour] either from heaven or from the deep : but the righteousness by faith, speaking here, suggests to the ignorant unbeliever to call upon the name of Christ, as much as to say, that which thou art seeking, O unbeliever [O

unbelief], whilst thou art moving heaven and the deep, and art taking refuge in heaven or the deep, (as we find in Virgil, *I will move hell*[1] [*Acheronta movebo*], know that it can neither be thought of by me, nor be found by thee, without [outside of] Christ, ver. 4. The expression is hypothetical. That, which cannot be done,—to fetch *righteousness from afar* [opposed to, *is nigh thee*], from heaven or out of the deep; Paul sets this aside: and so leaves one only refuge, the word of Christ, which is *very near*.

8. Ἀλλὰ, *but*) The particle here either has an *augmentative* [ἐπιτατικήν: See Append. on *Epitasis*] meaning as in Matt. xi. 8, 9, or falls upon ἐγγὺς, *nigh* thee.—ἐγγὺς, *nigh*) We ought not to seek Christ at a distance, but within us. For while *faith* is beginning to believe, Christ dwells in the heart. This seeking for Christ [*at a distance*, instead of *within one's own heart*] is found not only in those who are merely beginning, but even in those who are making progress in faith, Song of Sol. iii. 1; Ps. cv. 3, 4. For he is here speaking, as if the righteousness of faith were itself conversing with itself.—ἐν τῷ στόματί σου καὶ ἐν τῇ καρδίᾳ σου) so it is in the Hebrew, but the LXX. add καὶ ἐν ταῖς χερσί σου τοῦτ᾽ ἔστι) *The word, that is, the word of faith is nigh thee.*

9. Ἐὰν) *if* only—ὁμολογήσῃς, *thou shalt confess*) Confession in itself does not save; otherwise infants would not be saved: but only in as far as it includes faith.—Κύριον, *the Lord*) The summary of faith and salvation is found in this appellation. He who confesses that Jesus is *Lord*, does not now any longer [now for the first time ceases to] endeavour to bring Him down *from heaven*.—ἤγειρεν ἐκ νεκρῶν, *hath raised Him from the dead*) The special object of faith. He who believes the *resurrection* of Jesus does not now any longer endeavour to bring Him from the dead, ver. 7.

10. Καρδίᾳ, *with the heart*) From the mentioning of the 'heart' and 'mouth' by Moses [in Deut. xxx. 14, quoted here at ver. 8], the consequence is [here by Paul referred, or] proved in reference to 'faith,' and 'confession;' namely, because the 'heart' is the proper subject of 'faith' and the 'mouth,' of 'confession;' there-

---

[1] Aen. vii. 312.

fore Paul here in this verse begins his sentences, by saying, *with the heart,* and *with the mouth.*

11. Λέγει, *saith*) ix. 33, note.¹

12. Οὐ γὰρ ἔστι διαστολὴ, *for there is no difference*) ch. iii. 22 Here the words *first to the Jews,* are not added, as at the beginning, ch. i. 16.—ὁ γὰρ αὐτὸς, *for the same*) ch. iii. 29, 30.—Κύριος, *Lord*), ver. 9.—πλουτῶν) *rich* and liberal, whom no multitude of believers, how great soever it may be, can exhaust; who never finds it necessary to deal more sparingly.

13. Πᾶς ὅς ἄν, *whosoever,* Acts ii. 21, note. This monosyllable, πᾶς (*all*), more precious than the whole world, set forth [as a theme] ver. 12, is so repeated, ver. 12 and 13, and farther confirmed, ver. 14, 15, as not only to signify that whosoever shall call upon the name of the Lord, shall be saved, but that God wills that He should be called upon by all, for their salvation.

14, 15. Πῶς, *how*) A descending climax; by which Paul argues from each higher to the next lower degree, and infers the necessity of the latter, as also from that necessity [infers] its very existence. He who wills the end, wills also the means. God wills that men should call upon Him for their salvation; therefore He wills that they should believe; therefore He wills that they should hear; therefore He wills that they should have preachers. Wherefore He sent preachers. He has done all that the matter [the object aimed at, viz., man's salvation] required. His antecedent will is universal and efficacious.

14. Οὗ οὐκ ἤκουσαν) *whom,* namely, when speaking in the Gospel, ver. 15, or offering Himself, *they have not heard.*

15. Πῶς δὲ κηρύξουσιν, *but how* [how then] *shall they preach*) viz., οἱ κηρύσσοντες, *those preaching.* This word, as well as those going before, is put in the future tense, in imitation of Joel, in whose writings this expression, *shall call,* is found, ver. 13, by that [manner, which Paul has at times, of] looking from the Old Testament [standing-point] to the New.—καθὼς, *as*) *i.e.* messengers [of the good tidings] were not wanting. Isaiah in spirit saw their eager steps.—ὡς—εἰρήνην, τῶν εὐαγγελιζομένων τὰ ἀγαθά) Is. lii. 7. LXX ὡς—ἀκοὴν εἰρήνης ὃς εὐαγγελιζόμενος ἀγαθά.

¹ Οὐ καταισχυνθήσεται, *shall not be ashamed*) Unrighteousness and destruction lead to shame: righteousness and salvation to glory.—V. g.

·—ὡραῖοι) it is properly said of what is beautiful and pleasant in nature.—οἱ πόδες, *the feet*) at a distance, how much more their countenances [or else *mouths*, as preachers] close at hand.—τῶν εὐαγγελιζομένων, *of them that bring glad tidings*) for while they speak, the Lord Himself speaks, Is. lii. 7, with which comp. ver. 6.

16. 'Αλλ᾽, *but*) Here the fault is at last pointed out.—οὐ πάντες, *not all*) An antithesis to *every one, whosoever,* ver. 11, etc. The fault lies with men, especially with the Jews : *not all, i.e.* almost nobody, comp. the *who?* which immediately follows.—ὑπήκουσαν) comp. ὑπὸ in ὑπετάγησαν, ver. 3. Those, too, should and might have obeyed, who have not become obedient.—λέγει) *says,* presently after the words quoted from him in ver. 15, [by Paul]. See John xii. 38, note.

17.[1] "Αρα, *then*) From the complaint of the prophet respecting the unbelief of his hearers, he infers, that the word of God and preaching, the proper source and handle of faith, were not wanting.—ἐξ ἀκοῆς) ἀκοή, *hearing,* and hence [the thing heard] *speech, word, preaching.*

18. Μὴ οὐκ ἤκουσαν, *Have they not heard?* [μή Interrog. implies a negative answer is expected : so Latin *num; you cannot say they have not heard, can you?*]) *You cannot say, can you,* that the faculty of hearing was wanting in them, since faith comes only by hearing?—εἰς πᾶσαν—ῥήματα αὐτῶν) So the LXX., Ps. xix. 5. In that Psalm, there is a comparison drawn, and the protasis is accordingly, ver. 2–7, and the apodosis, ver. 8, etc. Hence we clearly perceive the same reason for the Proclamation made by the heavens, and the Gospel,[2] which penetrates into all things [So the proclamation of the heavens, " There is no speech," etc., " where their voice is not heard," etc.] The Comparison rests mainly on the quotation of the apostle, and offers no violence to the text.—ὁ φθόγγος, the sound, Ps. xix. 5, קו. Aquila had at a former period translated that word κανών, *rule.*—Comp. by all means, 2 Cor. x. 13. Every apostle had his own region and province, as it were, defined, to which his voice was to come, but a *rule* only refers to single individuals, a *sound* or *word* extends to the whole earth.

---

[1] Ἡμῶν, [the report] of *us*) thy ambassadors, he means.—V. g.

[2] "The heavens *declare* the glory of God," etc.: κηρύσσειν *to preach,* is properly to *proclaim as a herald.*—ED.

ROMANS X. 19–21.

19. Μὴ οὐκ ἔγνω Ἰσραήλ; *Did not Israel know?*) The meaning is, that Israel could and should have known the righteousness of God, but did not wish to know it, ver. 3, and that is now shown from Moses and Isaiah. Paul in ch. ix.–xi. frequently calls the people, *Israel*, not *Jews*.—πρῶτος Μωϋσῆς, *first Moses*) Moses, under whom Israel took the form of a people or nation, has already at that early time said.—ἐγὼ—ὑμᾶς—ὑμᾶς) Deut. xxxii. 21. LXX., κᾀγὼ—αὐτούς—αὐτούς—οὐκ ἔθνει) This may be expressed in Latin by *ne-gente*, a not-nation. As the people followed gods, that were no gods, so God avenges the perfidy of the people, and took up a people that was no people, a people, who had not God as their God, a people quite unlike to Israel. So the term *people* does not recur ver. 20, [of the Gentiles] but ver. 21 [of Israel].—ἀσυνέτῳ, *foolish*) Wisdom makes a people, Job xii. 2. Therefore a foolish people is *not a nation*; [a not-nation] a people that knows not God is foolish. גוי is a middle term, by which even Israel is denoted [μέσον; applicable to the *people* Israel, and the *not-people*, the Gentiles]. The epithet נבל denotes other nations.

20. Ἀποτολμᾷ) What Moses had merely hinted at, Isaiah boldly and openly proclaims.—εὑρέθην, *I was found*) I was ready at hand for, Isa. lxv. i., LXX., ἐμφανὴς ἐγενήθην τοῖς ἐμὲ μὴ ζητοῦσιν, εὑρέθην τοῖς ἐμὲ μὴ ἐπερωτῶσιν, *I was made manifest to them that sought Me not, I was found by them who asked not after Me*.

21. Ὅλην, *whole*) Isa. *ibid.* ver. 2, LXX., ἐξεπέτασα τὰς χεῖράς μου ὅλην τὴν ἡμέραν πρὸς κ.τ.λ., comp. *the whole day*, [all the day long] ch. viii. 36, see the remarkable dissertation of *J. C. Pfaffius*, on the continued grace of God.—ἐξεπέτασα, *I extended*) A metonymy [see Appen.] of the antecedent [for the consequent]. *They permit Me to extend My hands, nor do they come.* Even by this one word alone the doctrine of the double will of God, viz., a mere good-will [which is towards *all* men], and a will of sealing [*certain* persons as His *elect*; beneplaciti et signi; εὐδοκία, Luke ii. 14, *good will*; but σφραγίς, *sealing as the Lord's own*, 2 Tim. ii. 19, or else the "voluntas beneplaciti" is God's *effectual* good will towards the elect, Eph. i. 5, εὐδοκία τοῦ θελήματος αὐτοῦ; the "voluntas signi," His mere *figurative* and ostensible good will, whereby it is said in accommodation to human modes of thought "God willeth all men to be saved."

Comp. Calvin Instit. B. iii. c. 20 and c. 24, sect. 17], is shown to be absurd.—ἀπειθοῦντα, *not believing*) with the 'heart.'— ἀντιλέγοντα, *gainsaying*) with the 'mouth;' comp. ver. 8, etc.

CHAPTER XI.

1. Μὴ ἀπώσατο) *hath He cast away* entirely? So Gideon, expostulating in faith, says νῦν ἀπώσατο ἡμᾶς, *now He has forsaken us* (*cast us away,* Judg. vi. 13). But οὐκ ἀπώσεται Κύριος τὸν λαὸν αὐτοῦ, *but the Lord will not cast away His people,* Ps. xciv. (xciii.) 14. Has He cast them away, says Paul, so that they are no longer the people of God? In ch. x. after he so impressively exhibited the grace [which God exercised] towards the Gentiles, and the rebellion of the Jews, this objection might be made. He therefore answers, far be it from us to say, that God has rejected His people, when the very appellation, *His people* contains a reason for denying it. The negative assertion, *far be it,* [God forbid], is made distinctly, (1.) concerning the present time of the offending people; both that there are now some, [believers among them]; comp. Acts xxi. 20, note; and that in the successively increasing admission of Gentiles, there will be very many of Israel, who shall believe. These are called the *remnant* and the *election* ver. 5, 7. (2.) As to the future; that the people themselves, will at last be converted ver. 24, note.—ἐγὼ, *I*) Paul would rather draw a favourable conclusion from the individual [believing Israelites, as himself] to the genus, [the whole nation,] than one, on the unfavourable side, from the genus [the unbelieving nation] to the species [the individual];—I, formerly a persecutor, deserved to be cast away. The genus is the whole Jewish people: the species is believers among the Jews (of whom Paul was one as an individual) or such of that people as should hereafter believe.

2. Προέγνω) *foreknew,* as a people peculiar to Himself, ver. 29. —ἐν Ἠλίᾳ, *in Elias*) in the history of Elias, who was in the greatest straits, and thought himself to be alone; when Israel had become fewer than at any time before or since, [1 Kings xx. 15].—ἐντυγχάνει, Hesychius, ἐντυγχάνει, προσέρχεται; comp. Acts xxv. 24; 1 Macc. viii. 32.

3. Κύριε, τοὺς προφήτας σου—τὴν ψυχήν μου) 1 Kings xix. 14, LXX., ἐγκατέλιπον τὴν διαθήκην σου οἱ υἱοὶ Ἰσραὴλ, τὰ θυσιαστήριά σου καθεῖλον, καὶ τοὺς προφήτας σου ἀπέκτειναν ἐν ῥομφαίᾳ, καὶ ὑπολέλειμμαι ἐγὼ μονώτατος, καὶ ζητοῦσι τὴν ψυχήν μου λαβεῖν αὐτήν. *The children of Israel have forsaken Thy covenant, thrown down Thine altars, and slain Thy prophets with the sword, and I, even I only, am left, and they seek my life to take it away.* The nicety of the apostle's style is remarkable; the LXX. in this passage use μονώτατος, as they often do; Paul μόνος.

4. Κατέλιπον, *I have left* [Engl. Vers. not so well, *reserved*]) who were not to be slain by Hazael, Jehu, or Elisha. The LXX., 1 Kings xix. 18, have καὶ καταλείψω ἐν Ἰσραὴλ ἑπτὰ χιλιάδας ἀνδρῶν πάντα γόνατα, ἃ οὐκ ὤκλασαν γόνυ τῷ Βάαλ. *And I will have in Israel seven thousand men, all the knees, which have not bowed to Baal.* From the verb λείπω [in κατέλιπον, I have *left*] we derive λεῖμμα *a remnant* [a portion *left*]; see what follows.—ἐμαυτῷ, *to myself*) Paul adds this for the sake of emphasis, in antithesis to the complaint of Elias about his being *left alone*. The Lord knows His own people.—ἑπτακισχιλίους, *seven thousand*) among a people, who had become reduced to a wonderfully small number, the number is not small, nay it was itself the whole people, 1 Kings xx. 15. From these the whole posterity of the ten tribes at least were descended. Heb. בָּל, *i.e. purely such as these*, without any admixture of the worshippers of Baal. I do not say, that they were the same individuals, who are mentioned in 1 Kings xx. 15, and xix. 18; but the number is equal, viz., seven thousand, in ch. xx. 15, and about seventy years afterwards, in ch. xix. 18, after the time of Hazael, Jehu and Elisha, comp. 2 Kings xiii. 7, 14.—ἄνδρας, *men*) Men were chiefly taken into account in reckoning, and were present at public worship; therefore their wives and children also are to be added to the seven thousand.—Τῇ Βάαλ) In the feminine gender, supplying εἰκόνι, the *image* of Baal, used by way of contempt, and antithetic to *men*. So the LXX. also Judg. ii. 11, etc. Under the assertion of guiltlessness as to the worship of Baal, guiltlessness as to the worship of the golden calves[1] is included.

5. Οὖν, *then*) The conclusion drawn from the Old to the New Testament.

---

[1] Set up by Jeroboam in Dan and Bethel, 1 Kings xii. 29.—ED

ROMANS XI. 6–8.

6. Χάριτι, *by grace*) The meaning of the dative is one, and that of the particle ἐκ with the genitive is another [is different]. The former rather indicates the vehicle or instrument, as a canal, in the pure and simple sense ; the latter, more properly the material cause, the principle [first origin], the source.—οὐκ ἔτι, *now no longer* [*no more*]) This phrase used four times shows the strength of the conclusion. This decree, which God has decreed, is absolute : *I will make men righteous only by faith, no man by works.* This decree no one shall break through.—γίνεται—ἐστίν, [becomes] *is made*—*is*) This is a nice and just distinction between these words [lost sight of in the Engl. Vers.]. Nature asks for works; faith acknowledges supervenient grace, γενομένην [grace coming into exercise]. So, ἐγένετο [came into exercise] John i. 17. φερομένην χάριν, 1 Pet. i. 13.—εἰ δὲ ἐξ ἔργων, οὐκ ἔτι ἐστὶ χάρις· ἐπεὶ τὸ ἔργον οὐκ ἔτι ἐστί ἔργον. *But if it is of works, then is it no more grace, otherwise work is no more work*) From this short clause, *it is no more of works*, this inference is drawn, *Israel has not obtained* : and from that short clause, *it is no more grace*, the inference is, *the election has obtained.* The first part of this verse excludes works, the second establishes grace ; with this comp. ver. 5. The first part forms the protasis, the last, the apodosis, which is always the more necessary part, and is improperly omitted by some in this passage, comp. by all means ch. iv. 4, 5 ; Eph. ii. 8, 9. *Grace* and *work* are opposed to each other, הַפְעֻלָּה, LXX. for the most part interpret it ἔργον, *work*, for example Ps. cix. 20.

7. Ἡ ἐκλογὴ, *the election*) chiefly of the Israelites, *the election,* that is, the elected, inasmuch as being elected, obtain.

8. Ἔδωκεν αὐτοῖς ὁ Θεὸς πνεῦμα κατανύξεως, ὀφθαλμοὺς τοῦ μὴ βλέπειν καὶ ὦτα τοῦ μὴ ἀκούειν) Deut. xxix. 4, *yet the Lord God hath not given you a heart to perceive, and eyes to see, and ears to hear, unto this day.* Is. xxix. 10, LXX., πεπότικεν ὑμᾶς Κύριος, πνεύματι κατανύξεως, καὶ καμμύσει τοὺς ὀφθαλμοὺς αὐτῶν κ.τ.λ. *The Lord hath made you drunk with the spirit of slumber,* and *He will shut their eyes,* etc. Add Matt. xiii. [12,] 14, note. Ἔδωκεν, *hath given,* by a most righteous judgment, and hath said to them, have.¹—κατανύξεως) Κατάνυξις in this passage

¹ According as you have *chosen*. The *have*, refers to spiritual goods. "From him who hath not (his spiritual privileges to any good purpose)

denotes suffering from frequent pricking, which terminates in stupor. It is taken in a good sense, Acts ii. 37, and very often among ascetic writers. The Latins use similarly *compunctio, compunction.*—ἕως, *even unto*) A tacit limitation, 2 Cor. iii. 14.

9. Γενηθήτω—αὐτῶν εἰς παγίδα καὶ εἰς θήραν καὶ εἰς σκάνδαλον καὶ εἰς ἀνταπόδομα αὐτοῖς—σύγκαμψον) Ps. lxix. 22, 23, LXX., γενηθήτω—αὐτῶν ἐνώπιον αὐτῶν εἰς παγίδα καὶ εἰς ἀνταπόδοσιν καὶ εἰς σκάνδαλον. *Let their—be made before their eyes into a snare,* and *for a recompence, and for an offence.*—σύγκαμψον.—τράπεζα, *a table*) שׁלחן, Ps. lxix. 22, where, on comparing with it the preceding verse, there is an allegory, *i.e.*, while they are carelessly taking their food, let them be taken themselves.—σκάνδαλον, *stumbling-block*) It is taken in the more literal sense in this passage, to correspond with the synonyms, *noose* and *instrument of capture* (*laqueus* and *captio*); for σκάνδαλον is the moveable stick in a trap. It corresponds to מוקשׁ in the above psalm. There is a gradation: the noose (laqueus) catches a part, for example, the foot; the *instrument of capture* (*captio,* θήρα, *trap*) holds the whole; the *stumbling-block* (scandalum) not only catches, but also hurts.—ἀνταπόδομα, *recompence*) Their fault, therefore, not the absolute decree of God, was the mediating cause of their rejection.

10. Σκοτισθήτωσαν.—σύγκαμψον) They, who have their eyes darkened, and their back bent, are sure to *stumble,* ver. 11, and rush into a snare.

11. Ἔπταισαν) πταίω is properly used for the stumbling *of the feet.*—Comp. James iii. 2, note. The physical propriety of the word πταίω, both respecting the foot and the tongue, is contrasted with its moral signification.—ἵνα πέσωσι) *that they should fall* entirely, all of them, and that too without any hope of being lifted up again. A proverbial expression: they *have fallen* in some measure, ver. 22, but not utterly.—τοῖς ἔθνεσιν, *to the Gentiles*) We have here the article itself of the thing performed [ἡ σωτ.—τοῖς ἐθν. By their fall has come *the* salvation which *the* Gentiles now enjoy], Acts xiii. 46, *lo!* [and, *Behold,* ver. 22].

shall be taken away even that *he hath.*" God *gives* to men, that which they choose for themselves. *You fancy you have, I give you accordingly.*—ED.

—εἰς τὸ παραζηλῶσαι αὐτούς, *that they might be provoked to jealousy*) That the Israelites might be provoked to believe, ver. 14. [*Reader, see that you also be provoked, by every means whatever, to jealousy; you will thus in no ordinary degree be strong in grace.*—V. g.] This word occurs elsewhere, ch. x. 19.

12. Εἰ δέ, *Now if*) This verse has two parts, the first is treated of, ver. 13, etc.: the latter, *how much more*, etc., ver. 23, 24.—κόσμου—ἐθνῶν, *of the world—of the Gentiles*) *The world* denotes quality [in reference to the] παράπτωμα, the original *fall* [*i.e.*, the fall of man in Adam]; the *Gentiles*, quantity, or, in other words, multitude, to which *fewness* [*diminishing*, Engl. Vers.], ἥττημα, is opposed; whence τὸ πλήρωμα [*the fulness*] signifies, presently after, the *large numbers* of Israel abounding in grace. —ἥττημα) *the fewness*, in opposition to πλήρωμα, *fulness* [abundance]. Is. xxxi. 8, ἔσονται εἰς ἥττημα, [His young men shall become a mere handful; lit. *a fewness*].—πόσῳ μᾶλλον, *how much more*) for where there are many seeds, their increase is the greater.—τὸ πλήρωμα αὐτῶν, *their fulness*, [abundance]; supply, *will be the riches of the Gentiles*. Therefore, even if the Jews had believed from the very first, the Gentiles would not have been excluded. The same word occurs in ver. 25.

13. Ὑμῖν) *to you*, not that you may be elated, but that the Jews may be invited.—διακονίαν, *ministry*) apostleship among the Gentiles.—δοξάζω, *magnify*) To wit, Paul enhances the grace given to the Gentiles and its fulness, as about to be reciprocated upon [towards] the Israelites themselves [intended to have a reflex influence on Israel]; and here he gives a reason for his so enhancing that grace.

14. Τὴν σάρκα, *the flesh*) *i.e.*, brethren. Is. lviii. 7.

15. Γάρ, *for*) The particle connecting the discussion with the proposition.—ἀποβολή, *the casting away*) an antithesis to *receiving*, but in this sense, that God is said to *receive* by grace, men *to be cast away* [to suffer casting away] by their own fault. Upon the casting away of the Jews, the Gentiles *were received*, and obtained grace, ver. 30.—πρόσληψις) αὐτῶν, Hesychius : πρόσληψις, γνῶσις, comp. προσελάβετο, ch. xiv. 3. Τίς, concludes from the less to the greater : ἀποβολή, *casting away*, and πρόσληψις, *receiving*, are contrary to each other; therefore, καταλλαγή, *reconciliation* [*of the world*, in the former clause], precedes τῇ ζωῇ

ἐκ νεκρῶν, [*of the Israelites*, in the latter clause] *life from the dead, which implies much more* [than καταλλαγή].—ζωὴ, *life*) *of the world*, ver. 12.—ζωὴ ἐκ νεκρῶν, *life from the dead*) a thing much greater, and more desirable. The meaning is: *the life of those who had been dead,* Ez. xxxvii. 3, etc., so ἐκ, *from*, ch. vi. 13; 2 Cor. iv. 6. He is speaking of bringing the whole to life, that there may be no dead mass remaining. The conversion of the whole human race or the world will accompany the conversion of Israel.

16. Ἡ ἀπαρχὴ, *the first fruits*) The patriarchs.—ἁγία, *holy*) appropriated and acceptable to God.—Comp. ver. 15, with 1 Tim. iv. 4, 5.—φύραμα, *a lump*) Num. xv. 20, 21, ἀπαρχὴ φυράματος.—ἡ ῥίζα, *the root*) the patriarchal stock, considered naturally, as also being regarded as in possession of circumcision and of the promise. In the opinion of *Weller*, after Origen, Christ is the *root*, the patriarchs also are the *branches*, from whom the *first fruits* were derived.

17. Σὺ, *Thou*) O Roman, who art a Gentile.—ἀγριέλαιος, *a wild olive*) the graft of *the wild olive;* a singularly expressive [δεινή. See Append. δεινότης] Synecdoche. [*Sad experience even in our age proclaims this fact. A promiscuous multitude, unwilling to bear true Christianity, labour under the wildest ignorance; nor do we even except those, who boast no ordinary attainments in virtue and knowledge.*—V. g.]—ἐν αὐτοῖς) *among them:* The word, *them*, is not to be referred to the word, *some*, but to the branches generally.—συγκοινωνὸς) Paul often uses σὺν concerning the Gentiles, Eph. ii. 19, 22, iii. 6; comp. μετὰ, Rom. xv. 10.

18. Μὴ κατακαυχῶ, *Boast not against*) Let them, who deny the [possibility of the] conversion of the Jews, take care, that *they boast not against them.*—οὐ σὺ, it is *not thou* that) supply *know or remember that; know, or remember that it is not thou that bearest the root,* but, etc.

19. Ἵνα, *in order that*) This particle expresses the chief force of the *boasting* [of the Gentiles]; but in opposition to this *boasting* compare the, *for your sakes*, ver. 28, and τῷ, ver. 31 [sc. ὑμετέρῳ ἐλέει, they disobeyed to the end that through *the* mercy showed *to you* they might obtain mercy.]

20. Τῇ ἀπιστίᾳ—τῇ πίστει, *by* [because of] *unbelief—by faith*) Neither of the two events (says Paul) [was ordered] absolutely.

for if it were absolutely, there would be room for boasting, which is here shown to be out of place : *faith*, the gift of God, making men humble [could not be such as to give room to *boasting*].—ἕστηκας) thou hast obtained and still holdest this standing, contrasted with the words, *them, who fell*, ver. 22.—μὴ ὑψηλοφρόνει, ἀλλὰ φοβοῦ) *be not high-minded, but fear;* Prov. iii. 7, μὴ ἴσθι φρόνιμος παρὰ σεαυτῷ, φοβοῦ δὲ τὸν θεόν, Be not wise in thine own eyes ; but fear God.—φοβοῦ, *fear*) Fear is opposed not to confidence, but to superciliousness, and security.

21. Μήπως) Repeat, φοβοῦ.—φείσεται) The Indicative, the particle μήπως being here in a manner disregarded, [by the Indic. instead of the subjunctive, the regular mood after μή] has a more categorical [positive, unconditional] force. *Baumgarten* would rather read φείσηται with μήπως. But *Mart. Crusius* shows, that ἵνα, ὡς, ὅπως, μή, are sometimes joined with the future indicative, Gram. Gr. Part II. page 867, and beside other examples, he specifies that passage of Demosthenes, ὅπως τὰ παρόντα ἐπανορθωθήσεται. *Blackwall* has collected other examples in the Sacred Classics, p. 432, ed. Woll., where he praises this very passage of Paul on account of its elegance. Certainly language, framed, as this is, rather categorically, tends to excite fear [more than conditional or potential language, as φείσηται would be.]

22. Χρηστότητα καὶ ἀποτομίαν, *goodness and severity*) An important disjunction.—ἐπιμείνῃς, *thou shalt have continued*) To continue is in respect to what is good, in this verse ; in respect to what is evil in the next [ἐπιμείνωσιν, abide in unbelief]. The one is described on the part of God, the other on the part of man · comp. ver. 28, 30, etc. The Roman [Church] has not remained in goodness, since the righteousness of works has been introduced.—ἐπεί, *otherwise*) Believers may utterly fall away.—ἐκκοπήσῃ, *thou shalt be cut off*) by the sword ; not merely, *shalt be broken off* [ἐκκλασθήσῃ], as they were, by the hand. ברת, LXX., ἐκκόπτω, *I cut off*, Jer. xliv. 8, not however generally in that sense, in which, *I utterly destroy*, (ἐξολοθρεύω), is used.

23. Ἐὰν μή, *if not*) Therefore their conversion will not be [the effect of] irresistible [grace].—δυνατός, [able] *powerful*) it might be a principal objection : how will the Jews be converted, who for so many ages act so as to withdraw themselves from the

faith, separate [draw aside] the Old Testament revelations from the true Messiah, and snatch them out of the hands of believers? Paul answers, God has *power:* comp. the, *powerful* [able], ch. xiv. 4 : and He will show the glory of this power, against which no one in the Gentile world can strive. There will then be a great work !—πάλιν, *again*) not only in [with] a smaller [comparatively small] number, as now, but in [with] a greater number, as formerly, when they were the people of God.

24. Ἀγριελαίου, *of the wild olive tree*) There is as great a distinction between those, who either have not, or have the revealed word, as there is between the wild and cultivated olive-tree.—παρὰ φύσιν) quite *contrary to nature,* for in the art of gardening, the process of engrafting, which unites two trees of a different nature, commits the soft graft, which is followed by the fruit, to the woody stem : but Paul says, that the graft of the wild olive is inserted into the good olive-tree, in order that it may follow [in consequence partake of] the fatness of the good olive.—πόσῳ μᾶλλον, *how much more*) He gradually comes from that which *can* be, to that which actually *is.* The discourse in fact assumes an augmentation of force ; formerly Paul demonstrated from the prophets, that in Israel there were more wicked than good men, he now demonstrates in like manner from the prophets, that there will be hereafter more good than wicked men ; and while he is drawing forth this statement, he calls it a *mystery,* fitted to check the pride of the Gentiles, lest they should think that the part assigned to the Jews was to be always inferior.

25. Μυστήριον, *a mystery*) Paul does not always apply the term, *mysteries,* to those doctrines, which from the very first are necessary to be known by believers, but to the secrets, which were unknown even to many believers, until, as the case required, for the sake of faith or love they were opened up to them from the Scriptures, heretofore in this respect sealed. Comp. 1 Cor. xv. 51, and on a similar occasion Eph. iii. 3. The calling of the Gentiles had been a *mystery,* ch. xvi. 25. But now the conversion of Israel is likewise a *mystery.* [*Therefore something different is intimated from such conversions, as were exhibited day by day in the times of Paul.*—V. g.] Each of these

forms a great part of that *mystery*, which is confirmed in Rev. x. 7. Furthermore, since it is a mystery, they ought to be treated with patient forbearance who do not recognise it so quickly, and we should hope for the time, when it will be recognised by all.—[1]φρόνιμοι, *wise*) *dreaming, that the church at Rome cannot fail.* Cluverus. The very term, *mystery*, checks the reader's pride. Hence the admonition is repeated at. ch. xii. 16, which is already to be found at ver. 20, note.—ἀπὸ μέρους, *in part*) He speaks in a way softening the unwelcome truth; for οἱ πωρωθέντες, *those, who were hardened*, were as "the sand of the sea," ver. 7; comp. with ch. ix. 27. Therefore, in the following verse, the conversion, which will not be *in part* [as their hardening was, which yet comprised as many as the sand], but will include *all Israel* (see foll. verse), will be by far the most abundant. And in the mean time also, there are always some being converted, and for this desirable object it becomes believers to be always on the watch.—πλήρωμα, *fulness*) *a most abundant supply;* the antithesis is *in part.* No nation shall remain, to which the Gospel shall not have been preached in the whole world; although a great part of mankind will still continue to be wicked.—εἰσέλθη, *shall come in*) John x. 9, 16. For many ages, now, many obstacles retard [put a drag on the wheels of] this coming in, obstacles which will be broken through at the proper time, so that the fulness of the Gentiles, who have been long since called, may entirely come in; and then the *hardening* of Israel will terminate, Ps. cxxvi. 2, 3. Paul *provokes* the Israelites to Christian *jealousy;* and this presupposes the conversion of the Gentiles before that of Israel, and yet the remaining abundance of the Gentiles may afterwards be gained by the full conversion of Israel, ver. 11, 12, 15, 31; Ez. xxxix. 7, 21–27.

26. καὶ οὕτω, *and so*) he does not say *and then*, but with greater force, *and so*, in which very expression the *then* is included; to wit, the blindness of Israel will be terminated by the very coming in of the Gentiles.—πᾶς ᾿Ισραήλ, *all Israel*) Israel contradistinguished from the Gentiles, of which ver. 25 treats. The words, שארית, *a remnant*, and פליטה, *deliverance*, are

---

[1] We should never consider a mystery for the sake of curiosity: we should always seek to be humbled before it.—V. g.

used in respect of those that perished; but *the Remnant* itself, numerous in itself, will be wholly converted, Mic. ii. 12.—σωθήσεται) *shall be saved:* The Latin Vulgate has expressed this by, *salvus fieret;* and not inappropriately.[1] It contains this sentiment, *the fulness of the Gentiles shall be brought in and so all Israel shall be made safe;* but ἄχρις οὗ, *until,* has changed the former verb εἰσελεύσεται [Indic.] into εἰσέλθῃ [Subj.], the second verb, σωθήσεται, remaining [Indicative].—See similar instances noticed at Mark iii. 27. The Latin Vulg. has expressed the meaning.—ἥξει ἐκ Σιὼν—διαθήκη, ὅταν ἀφέλωμαι τὰς ἁμαρτίας αὐτῶν) *shall come out of Zion—the covenant, when I shall take away their sins.* Is. lix. 20, 21, LXX., καὶ ἥξει ἕνεκα Σιὼν—διαθήκη, εἶπε Κύριος, κ.τ.λ., *and shall come for the sake of Zion—the covenant, saith the Lord,* etc. Is. xxvii. 9, LXX., καὶ τοῦτό ἐστιν ἡ εὐλογία αὐτοῦ, ὅταν ἀφέλωμαι τὴν ἁμαρτίαν αὐτοῦ, κ.τ.λ., *and this is His blessing, when I shall take away his sin.* Heb. בָאוּ לְצִיּוֹן, *and there shall come to Zion* (and for its benefit) *the Redeemer, and to those turning from transgression in* Jacob. Paul, ch. iii., in describing sin had quoted Ps. xiv., and chiefly ch. lix. of Isaiah: now in describing salvation, he joins together the same texts. He says, ἐκ Σιὼν, *out of Sion,* as the LXX., Ps. xiv. 7. The Deliverer or Redeemer comes (ἐκ) out of Sion and (ὃ, ἕνεκα) for good to Sion. His coming has been already accomplished, and the fruit will arrive at perfection at the proper time. *Sion* is a whole, in a good sense, *Jacob* here is a whole, in a less favourable sense; those *returning* are a part.

27. Αὕτη, *this*) of which see in the preceding verse.—παρ' ἐμοῦ, *from me*) He himself will do it.—διαθήκη, *testament* [*covenant*])—namely, it shall then be and shall be unfolded.—τὰς ἁμαρτίας) *sins,* and the miseries arising from them.

28. Ἐχθροί) *enemies.* Therefore the obstinacy of the Jews ought not to be alleged to the prejudice of their conversion. Moreover, they are called *enemies,* in an active sense; presently [by and by] they shall be called *beloved* in a passive sense (both in respect of God, not merely, of Paul); the evil is to be imputed to man; the good proceeds from God. So also mercy

---

[1] Thus the Vulg. makes σωθήσεται depend on ἄχρις οὗ, *donec,* "until the fulness of the Gentiles shall come in, and until all Israel shall thus be saved."—ED.

and unbelief are opposed to each other, ver. 30, etc.— δι' ὑμᾶς, *for your sakes*, ver. 31, 12, 15.

29. 'Αμεταμέλητα, *without repentance*) Truly an apostolic axiom. Something absolute is signified; for God will not give way to the unbelief of His own people [so as to suffer it to continue] for ever. Repentance is hid from the eyes of the Lord [*i.e.* change of His purpose, as to raising Israel from its present spiritual ' death,' is impossible with God], Hos. xiii. 14.—χαρίσματα, *gifts*) towards the Jews.—κλῆσις, *calling*) towards the Gentiles.

30. καὶ) [1]I formerly admitted this particle marked with an obelus, thus †, and am now glad that Baumgarten agrees with me.—ἠπείθησατε, *ye have not believed*) unbelief falls upon [applies to] even those, who themselves have not heard the word of God, because they had however received it primitively in the persons of the patriarchs Adam and Noah. [The Gentiles are accountable for not having retained the revelation received from Adam, Noah, etc.]

31. 'Ηπείθησαν, *they have disbelieved*) They have been left to their unbelief.—τῷ ὑμετέρῳ, *your* [of you]) the Genitive of the object, [your mercy, *i.e.* the mercy, of which *you* are the *objects*,] as τὰ ἐλέη Δαυίδ, *the mercies of David*, 2 Chron. vi. 42, רצון עמך, *the favour directed to thy people*, Ps. cvi. 4.—ἐλέει, *through mercy*) construed with ἐλεηθῶσι, *might obtain mercy;* for ἵνα, *that,* is often transposed; and in verse 30, the *disbelief* of the Jews precedes the *mercy* of the Gentiles; wherefore in verse 31 the *mercy* of the Gentiles does not [is not to be supposed to] precede the same *disbelief* of the Jews [as would be the case, if ἐλέει, *owing to your partaking of mercy*, were taken with ἠπείθησαν]. See App. crit. Ed. ii. on this passage.—ἐλεηθῶσι, *might obtain mercy*) that mercy, which goes before faith, and which is only acknowledged and received through faith, by which ἀπείθεια, *disbelief* is retracted.

32. Συνέκλεισε, *hath concluded together*), Jews and Gentiles, comp. Gal. iii. 22, note. The phraseology of the LXX. Int., Ps. lxxviii. 50, is εἰς θάνατον συνέκλεισε, *He shut up to death*, he

---

[1] The German version agrees in this.—E. B.

ABCD (later correction), G*fg*, omit καί, before ὑμεῖς. But Vulg. and Rec. Text. have it.—ED.

gave over.—εἰς ἀπείθειαν, *in* [*unto*] *disbelief*) Eph. ii. 2. Those who have experienced the power *of disbelief*, at length betake themselves with the greater sincerity and simplicity to faith.— ἵνα) *that*. The thing itself will be accomplished.—τοὺς πάντας) *them all without exception*, [less accurately, *all*, in Engl. Vers.] all together; comp. ver. 30, 31.—ἐλεήσῃ, *might have mercy*) His mercy being acknowledged by them, ver. 6, when faith is given to them by Himself.

33. ῏Ω βάθος, *O the depth*) Paul in ch. ix. had been sailing, as it were, on a narrow sea; he is now embarked on the ocean. *The depth of the riches* is described in ver. 35, and has respect to ch. ix. 23, x. 12. (wherefore it (*of the riches*) ought not to be resolved into a mere epithet); *the depth of wisdom* is described in ver. 34; *the depth of the knowledge*, in ver. 34. Comp. concerning riches and wisdom, Eph. iii. 8, note, and Rev. v. 12. The different meanings of biblical terms are worthy of being well noticed and collected. *Wisdom* directs all things to the best end; *knowledge* knows that end and issue.—ὡς, *how*) No one examines, no one searches out, but He Himself. Here and in ver. 34, there is a Chiasmus;[1] as is seen by comparing the antecedents and consequents together. *The depth* is described in the second part of ver. 33 [How *unsearchable*, etc., answering to the *depth*]. *Knowledge* itself, as we have said, is described in ver. 34, *for who* [hath *known*, etc.]—*wisdom* itself is described in the words *or who* [hath been His *counsellor*] : *riches* themselves, in ver. 35 [who hath first given to Him, etc.]—τὰ κρίματα, *His judgments*) respecting unbelievers.—αἱ ὁδοί, *His ways*) respecting believers. A gradation. His ways are as it were on the surface, His judgments more profound; we do not even search out His ways [much less His judgments].

34. Τίς γὰρ—ἐγένετο) Isa. xl. 13, LXX., τίς ἔγνω—καὶ τίς αὐτοῦ σύμβουλος. *Who?* i.e. none: but He Himself.—γάρ, *for*. The more express quotation of Scripture follows. In proving doctrines the phrase is used, *it is written*, in other places, it is often omitted, ch. xii. 20.—νοῦν Κυρίου, *the mind of the Lord*) Isaiah has את רוח יהוה, *the Spirit of Jehovah*. Paul uses the version of the LXX. Otherwise רוח and νοῦς are not synonymous; but the conclusion arrived at is very good; no one apprehends

[1] See Appendix.

the Spirit, therefore no one apprehends the mind or sense of the Lord. Reference to the Holy Trinity is implied, comp. on the words, εἰς αὐτὸν, *to Him*, ver. 36, Isa. xxxiv. 16, at the end of the verse.—σύμβουλος Paul says, not only that no one has been σύμβουλος, but not even now can be so: σύμβουλος is either a *partner in counsels*, or, one at least *privy to them*; for he had said just now, *for who hath known the mind of the Lord?* And yet many in their discussions, for example, on the origin of evil, which touch upon the recesses of the Divine economy much more deeply than this, which is from religious reverence broken off by the apostle between ver. 32, 33 (for there is a great difference between the fall of many angels and of the whole human race on the one hand, and, on the other, the fall of the Israelites [the latter is a much less profound mystery than the former]) many such, I say, boast, as if they were not only the Lord's counsellors, but also His inquisitors, His patrons, or His judges. Scripture everywhere stops short at this point, that the Lord hath willed, and hath said, and hath done it: It does not unfold the reasons of things universal or particular; respecting those things that are beyond our present state of infancy, it refers believers to eternity, 1 Cor. xiii. 9, etc. The thirst of knowing will torture and burn others, who unreasonably pry into mysteries, throughout eternity.

35. ῍Η τίς, κ.τ.λ) Some adopt these words in the LXX., Isa. xl. 14: others do not; but Job xli. 2, Hebr. and Vulg. have it thus: *Who hath previously given to Me, that I may render to Him again? All things which are under heaven are Mine.*

36. Ἐξ αὐτοῦ καὶ δἰ αὐτοῦ καὶ εἰς αὐτὸν, *of Him, and through Him, and to Him*) The Origin, Course, and End of [The Source from whom come, the Agent through whom is maintained the continuance of, the End for whom are] all things, is here denoted, comp. 1 Cor. viii. 6. [*Furthermore*, ἐξ αὐτοῦ, *refers to riches; δἰ αὐτοῦ, to wisdom;* εἰς αὐτὸν, *to knowledge.*—V. g.]—ἡ δόξα, *the glory*) of the Riches, Wisdom, Knowledge. [*Along with this doxology to* Omnipotence, *is included the praise of Divine* Wisdom *and* Love, *from which the creatures derive* their strength, understanding, *and* blessedness.—V. g.]—ἀμήν. The final word, with which the feeling of the apostle, when he has said all, makes a termination.

CHAPTER XII.

1. Παρακαλῶ, *I exhort*) Moses commands: the apostle exhorts. Paul commonly gives exhortations consonant to the doctrines, which had been previously discussed, Eph. iv. with which comp. ch. iii. So in this passage the general application drawn from the whole discussion is contained in ver. 1, 2, as the allegations which immediately follow prove. We have shown at i. 16 the special applications from ver. 3 up to the conclusion of the epistle.—διὰ τῶν οἰκτιρμῶν, *by the mercies*) The whole sentiment is derived from Chapters i.–v.; the word has its origin in the antithesis to *wrath*, ch. i. 18: for the whole economy of grace or mercy, exempting us from wrath, and rousing the *Gentiles* especially to the discharge of duty, is indicated in this passage, ch. xv. 9. He who is rightly affected by *the mercy* of God, enters into the whole *will* of God. [*But the soul exposed to wrath scarcely derives any benefit from exhortations. You are "pouring oil on a stone."*—V. g.]—παραστῆσαι, *that ye present*) In so large a list of duties, Paul has none of those things, which in the present day among the followers of the Church of Rome, generally make up both sides of the account. παραστῆσαι is repeated from ch. vi. 13, 16, 19, *to yield, to present*. The oblation *is presented alive*, not sacrificed.—σώματα, *bodies*) antithetic to the abominable abuse of their bodies among the Gentiles, ch. i. 24. For more antitheses presently follow in respect of this same topic. The body is generally an impediment to the soul: present the body to God, and the soul will not be wanting, ch. vi. 12. See also ch. vii. 4; Heb. x. 5. *Vice versa*, the *soul*, when subject to the magistrate, will be obedient with the body also, ch. xiii. 1.— σώματα, λατρείαν, *bodies*, [*worship*] *service*) We have here the apposition of these two words by metonymy,[1] indicating body and soul.—θυσίαν, *sacrifice*) Sin having become dead: comp. on this sacrifice, ch. xv. 16.—ζῶσαν, *living*) That life, which is men-

---

[1] Antecedent for consequent, or vice versa, as here: *service*, for, the *soul* which serves.—Appendix.

tioned in ch. i. 17, vi. 4, etc. It is an abomination to offer a dead carcase.—ἁγίαν, *holy*) such as the holy *law* demands, ch. vii. 12.—εὐάρεστον, *acceptable, well-pleasing*) ch. viii. especially ver. 8.—τῷ Θεῷ, *to God*) construed with παραστῆσαι, *to present.* —λογικήν, *reasonable*) sincere (1 Pet. ii. 2) in respect of understanding and will : the verb δοκιμάζειν, ver. 2, is in consonance with this ; and φρονεῖν, κ.τ.λ., ver. 3. The *service* [worship], λατρεία, of the Gentiles is *unreasonable*, ἄλογος, ch. i. 18–25, the confidence of the Jews is *unreasonable*, ἄλογος, ii. 3, but the Christian considers all things rightly, and collects [infers] his duty from the kindness of a merciful God. The epithet λογικήν now corresponds to that verb, λογίζεσθαι, which is often used, ch. iii. 28, vi. 11, viii. 18. λογικὸν γάλα, 1 Pet. ii. 2, is a periphrasis for the *Word* itself,—*the Milk of the word;* but here λογική, *reasonable*, is an epithet of λατρεία, *service* [worship]. Peter uses the word, "Αδολον. The *Word* is sincere, and *the Service* [*worship*] in accordance with [resulting from] the word is sincere.

2. Μὴ συσχηματίζεσθε—ἀλλὰ μεταμορφοῦσθε) μορφή, *form, conformation*, denotes something more inward and thoroughly finished, than σχῆμα, *fashion* or *external appearance* [habitus].—Comp. Phil. ii. 6, 8, iii. 21. The external *appearance* of the saints should not be inconsistent with the internal form [conformation]. —αἰῶνι, *to the world*) which neglects the *will of God*, and is entirely devoted to selfish pursuits.—δοκιμάζειν, *to prove* [approve by testing]) This also refers to that new μορφήν, *form*. The antithesis is in ch. i. 28. [*While a man's mind continues in its original condition* (the old man), *how sagacious soever he may be, he cannot prove the will of God. He will endeavour to defend at one time this, and at another that* (objectionable thing), *thinking that God is such a one as himself.*—V. g.]—[1] καὶ τέλειον, *and perfect*) He, who presents [his body] an oblation, *living, holy, acceptable*, knows the will of God as *good*, requiring what is living and holy, *acceptable*, and, with the progress of believers [in course of time, as believers make progress] *perfect*. [*They*

[1] Τὸ θέλημα, *the will*) For special reasons very many questions occasionally arise, whether it would be right to do this or that, or not. They can easily decide, who make the *will* of GOD their great concern and chief delight. But they require experience [to prove and test things] and intelligence. Eph. v. 17.—V. g.

ROMANS XII. 3–6.

by unworthy means shun this perfect *will, who are continually seeking after such things as they are at liberty still to engage in without sin (as they think). The conduct of such men as these resembles that of the traveller, who takes a delight in walking, not in the safe path, but without necessity on the extreme verge of the bank.*—V. g.]

3. Λέγω) Flacius explains; *I distinctly declare* [edico]. This word adds the meaning of an imperative, to the subsequent affectionate [moratæ, *i.e.*, having ἦθος. See Append.] exhortation.—γὰρ, *for*) He shows what the will of God intends.—διὰ τῆς χάριτος, *through the grace*) Paul himself affords an example, σωφροσύνης, *of the sobriety*, which he commends; lest, by this form of expression, λέγω, *I distinctly declare* [*ordain*], which Christ alone could have used absolutely, he should seem rashly to prescribe things so difficult to others, comp. ver. 6.—ὄντι) to each one, *who is among you*, of your rank, a believer.—ἐν ὑμῖν, *among you*) there were many reasons, why the Romans might think that they might exalt themselves, and they afterwards did so.—δεῖ) *ought*, according to truth and duty.—φρονεῖν) *to think*, and thence, *to act.*—εἰς) the particle limits.[1]—ἑκάστῳ, *to every man*) No man ought to hold himself up as the only rule, according to which he tries others, and he ought not to think that others should be entirely such as he is, and should do the same things and in the same way as he does.—ὡς) *as*, and not more, ver. 5; but yet not less, ver. 6, 7; therefore δὲ, *but* [*and on the other hand:* not *then*, as Engl. Vers.] is used, ver. 6.—μέτρον, *measure*) Both faith and the measure [proportion given] of faith is the gift of God.—πίστεως, *of faith*) *from which the rest of the gifts flow* (Cluverus); and that, too, those gifts that sanctify and do service [even sanctifying and administrative gifts flow from faith]. Faith is the source of them all, and the rule to regulate us in their very use. *Of faith*, which has been treated of ch. i., and following chap. [Love *follows*, ver. 9.—V. g.]

5. Ὁ δὲ καθεὶς) see Mark xiv. 19, note.—μέλη, *members*, Eph. iv. 25.

6. Ἔχοντες, *having*) This word also depends on ἐσμέν [ver. 5]:

---

[1] Σωφρονεῖν, *to use moderation*) σωφροσύνη, an excellent virtue among those that are spiritual.—V. g.

for there is an apodosis at the end of ver. 4; but ἐσμὲν denotes *we are*, and at the same time inclines to [borders on] a gentle exhortation [*let us be*, by implication], as Gal. iv. 28, note. Hence in the several parts of this enumeration, the imperative ought to be understood, comp. ver. 14; but it is Paul's characteristic ἦθος, not to express the imperative often, after it has been once put at the beginning, as in ver. 3.—χαρίσματα, *gifts*) these are of *different kinds*, χάρις, *grace* is one.—προφητείαν, *prophecy*) This stands first among the gifts. Acts ii. 17, 18, xi. 27, xiii. 1, xv. 32, xix. 6, xxi. 9, 10; 1 Cor. xi. 4, etc., 12, etc.; Eph. ii. 20, iii. 5, iv. 11; 1 Thess. v. 20; 1 Tim. i. 18, iv. 14; Rev. i. 3, etc. When these passages are compared together, it is evident, that prophecy is the gift, by which the heavenly mysteries, sometimes also future events, are brought under the notice of men, especially believers, with an explanation of Scripture prophecies, which could not be elicited by the ordinary rules of interpretation. But the other gifts, which we find in the first epistle to the Corinthians, are not added in this epistle, which is otherwise so copious. See ch. i. 11; 1 Cor. ix. 2, notes.—κατὰ, *according to*) Repeat, *we having*, viz., *the gift, prophecy*, and so in succession. So just before, *according to the grace*, [as here, "*according to* the proportion of faith"]. As it is given to a man, so ought a man to be of service to others.—τὴν ἀναλογίαν τῆς πίστεως, *the proportion* [*analogy of faith*]) *i.e.*, as God distributes (to every prophet) *the measure of faith*, ver. 3: for there already Paul slightly touched upon this point, and he now returns to it, after some other topics had been introduced in the intervening verses. *Prophecy* and *faith* are closely connected, 1 Cor. xii. 9, 10, xiii. 2. Peter treating of the same subject, first epistle iv. 11, says, Ὡς λόγια Θεοῦ, *as the oracles of God.* It is much the same as if Paul were to say, whether it be *prophecy*, [let it be restricted *within the limits of*, or] *in prophecy;* with which compare what follows: let it not be carried outside of and beyond the bounds of faith; nor let any one prophesy from the promptings of his own heart, beyond what he has seen; and again, on the other hand, let him not conceal or bury the truth; let him only speak so far as he has seen, and knows, and believes,[1]

[1] The construction is, *whether it be prophecy, we are* [*i.e.* we ought to be as Christians] *persons who have it according to the proportion of faith.*—Ed.

see Col. ii. 18; Rev. i. 2. Paul himself affords an example of such a proportion [analogy], 1 Cor. vii. 25. Erasmus says, *The phrase,* ACCORDING TO THE PROPORTION, *gives one to understand, that the gifts are the greater* [are bestowed in the greater number], *in proportion as one's faith shall have* [hath] *been the more perfect;* so also, Corn. a Lapide, Piscator, Peter Martyr. Basilius M. on the Holy Spirit, *He fills all things with His powerful working, and they, who are worthy, can alone receive Him, nor is He merely received in one,* μέτρῳ, *measure, but,* κατὰ ἀναλογίαν τῆς πίστεως, *according to the proportion of faith, He distributes his operations,* c. 9. Chrysostom: *for although it is grace, yet it is not poured out uniformly, but taking the several measures* [the various proportions in which it is poured out] *from the* [several states] *of those who receive it, it flows* in proportionally *to what it has found* the size of *the vessel of* faith *presented to it.* Lichtscheid discusses this point at great length in Tr. Germ. *vom ewigen evangelio* (*of the everlasting Gospel*), p. 60, etc. As with Paul here, so with Mark the Hermit, the *measure,* μέτρον, and *the proportion,* ἀναλογία, are one and the same thing: see his book, περὶ τῶν οἰομένων ἐξ ἔργων δικαιωθῆναι (*concerning those who think that they are justified by works*), a little past the middle. *The knowledge of a man's affairs* (*business, conduct*) *depends on the proportion in which he puts in practice the precepts of the law, but the knowledge of the truth* (of the doctrine of salvation) *depends on the measure of faith in Christ;* and this same writer often uses the word, ἀναλογίαν, in this sense. In the writings of Paul, however, the word μέτρον is used in the sense of limiting, in reference to moderation or the avoiding of excess; whereas ἀναλογία has a fuller meaning (if we compare it with what follows) in reference to the avoiding of deficiency [the *full* proportion]. In what theologians call the creed, all the heads agree together in an admirable analogy [completeness of proportion], and each article, respecting which a question occurs, should be decided according to the articles already certainly known, the interpretation of the rest should be adjusted according to the declaration [the dictum] of Scripture clearly explained; and this is the analogy of Scripture itself, and of the articles of faith, which form the creed. But every man does not know all things; and, of what he does know, he does not know all with equal certainty; and yet he holds the things, which he certainly knows, by that very faith, by which the creed is formed; wherefore both he himself, in prophesying, should determine all things according to the analogy of the faith by which he believes, and others, in hearing [also ought to determine all points] according to the analogy of the faith, whereby they believe [and form their creed]. 1 Cor. xiv. 29, 37; Heb. xiii. 8, 9; 1 John ii. 20, and the following verses.

7. Εἴτε, *or*) This word is thrice repeated by the figure Ploce [See Append.] *Do*, what thou *art doing*, in earnest, in order that the reality may correspond to [keep] its own name [that what you do, may correspond to what you profess to do], Eccles. ix. 10. The principle of the subsequent sentiments is the same.[1]

8. Μεταδιδούς) διδόναι signifies *to give; μεταδιδόναι to impart*, [*to give a share,*] so that, he who gives, may not strip himself of all, that he has.—*ἐν ἀπλότητι*) as God gives, James i. 5, ' *liberally*,' abundantly, 2 Cor. viii. 2, [*neither prevented by the desire of private advantage, nor by anxious deliberation, whether or not another may be worthy of the favour given, and whether proper moderation be observed in giving.*—V. g.]—ὁ προϊστάμενος) one *who has the care of* [*rules*, Engl. V.] others, and has them under his patronage.—*ἐν σπουδῇ, with diligence*) The force of this word is very extensive; ver. 11; 2 Cor. vii. 11, note.

9. Ἡ ἀγάπη, *love*) He treated of faith from ver. 3; he is now to treat of love. Verses 9, 10, 11 have respect to ch. vii.; ver. 12 to ch. viii.; ver. 13 to ch. ix. and the following chapters, concerning the communion of believers whether Jews or Greeks. The third clause of the sixteenth verse is repeated from ch. xi. 25.—ἀποστυγοῦντες—κολλώμενοι, *abhorring—cleaving*) both in the mind and in the outward manifestation of it, even when at the risk of incurring danger and ill-will. The ἀνυπόκριτος, *the man without dissimulation*, is shown in Prov. viii. 7, *Let my lips* HATE *wickedness; wickedness is an* ABOMINATION *to my lips*. This is rightly connected with *love*, 1 Cor. xiii. 6. Very emphatic words. He, who is without hatred of evil, does

---

[1] Ἐν τῇ διακονίᾳ, *on the ministry*) Let not the minister assume too much to himself and after all not fully discharge his duty.—V. g.

not really love good. From this passage, the discourse moves forward in pairs of sentences. [*There are men* 1) *who patronise evil and assail good :* 2) *who love good, but do not abhor evil with that indignation which it deserves :* 3) *who disdain evil, but cherish good more coldly than is proper :* 4) *who so abhor evil and cleave to good, as that in their case no one can be ignorant of it.*—V. g.]

10. Φιλόστοργοι, *kindly affectioned*) στοργὴ, the spiritual *love of brethren.*—προηγούμενοι, [Engl. V. *preferring*] *anticipating,* or *leading the way* in doing honour to one another) if not always in gesture and actions, at least always in the judgment of the mind. That will be so, if we rather consider the good qualities of others and our own faults. These are the social virtues of the saints [homileticæ. Or perhaps, "their virtues are a kind of *living sermon* to the world."] The Talmudists say: *whosoever knows, that his neighbour has been in the habit of saluting him, should anticipate him by saluting him first.*

11. Τῇ σπουδῇ—τῷ πνεύματι, *in diligence* [*business*, Engl. Vers.]—*in spirit*) The external or active, and the internal or contemplative life is thus set in due order.—τῷ Κυρίῳ δουλεύοντες, *serving the Lord*) We ought to serve Christ and God, ver. 1, ch. vii. 6, xiv. 18, xvi. 18 ; Acts xx. 19 ; Phil. iii. 3 ; Ps. ii. 11, where *serving* and *rejoicing* are parallel, as in this passage. [*See App. Crit. Ed. II. on this passage, which shows that the reading* καιρῷ[1] *is quite unsupported and unworthy of the apostle.* Not. crit.]

12. Ἐλπίδι, *in hope*) So far respecting faith and love, now also concerning hope, comp. ch. v. and viii. Then concerning our duties to others, to the saints, ver. 13, to persecutors, ver. 14, to friends, strangers, enemies, ver. 15, etc.—χαίροντες, *rejoicing*) True joy is not only an emotion of the mind and a benefit [privilege], but also a Christian duty, ver. 15. It is the highest complaisance in God. He wishes us to rejoice and to spend our spiritual life joyously.

13. Ταῖς χρείαις) τῇ θλίψει, Phil. iv. 14. There was much occasion for this especially at Rome. It is particularly remarkable, that Paul, when he is expressly treating of duties arising

---

[1] AB and prob. all Gr. MSS. of Jerome, Vulg. and most Versions read Κυρίῳ. But D(Λ) corrected later, and G*fg* read καιρῷ.—ED.

from the communion of saints, nowhere gives any charge concerning the dead.—διώκοντες, *following after*) so that you not only are to receive to your house strangers, but are to seek them out.

14. Διώκοντας, *persecuting*) for the sake of Christ.—καὶ μὴ καταρᾶσθε, *curse not*) not even in thought.

15. Χαίρειν, *rejoice*) the infinitive for the imperative, a thing not unfrequent among the Greeks, and here a gentle mode of expression [*moratus*, indicative of ἦθος, a feeling, viz. here the avoidance of the *authoritative* Imperative]. I *exhort* is understood, taken from ver. 1. *Laughter* is properly opposed to *weeping*, but in this passage as in 1 Cor. vii. 30, *joy* is used, not *laughter*, which is less suitable to Christians in the world.

16. Τοῖς ταπεινοῖς, *to lowly things* [Engl. V. " to men of low estate"]) Neuter, for the phrase *high things* precedes.—συναπαγόμενοι, *being* [suffering yourselves to be] *carried along with*) the verb has the force of the middle voice, by which *voluntary* συγκατάβασις, *condescension*, is denoted. The proud think, that he, who is humble, is led away, but it is a good thing to be led away in this manner; so it was with David.—μὴ γίνεσθε φρόνιμοι παρ' ἑαυτοῖς) Prov. iii. 7, LXX, μὴ ἴσθι φρόνιμος παρὰ σεαυτῷ [comp. Rom. xi. 25.]

17. Προνοούμενοι καλὰ ἐνώπιον πάντων ἀνθρώπων) *Providing things honest in the sight of all men.* Prov. iii. 4, LXX., προνοοῦ καλὰ ἐνώπιον Κυρίου καὶ ἀνθρώπων.—καλὰ, *becoming*) A precious stone should not merely be a precious stone, but it should also be properly set in a ring, so that its splendour may meet [attract] the eye.—πάντων, *of all*) For many are suspicious and unjust. See the following verse.

18. Ἐι, *if*) *if possible.* He makes it conditional, and this clause may be construed with the 17th verse, inasmuch as good actions, especially if circumspection be wanting, may often appear to some not so good as they really are.—τὸ ἐξ ὑμῶν, *so far as it lieth in you*) This is a limitation, for it is not always *possible* owing to *others*.—μετὰ πάντων ἀνθρώπων, *with all men*) of whom there was a very great conflux at Rome. No man is so savage, as not to have the feelings of humanity towards some individuals, but we ought to be peaceful, gentle, meek towards all, Phil. iv. 5; 2 Tim. ii. 24; Tit. iii. 2. [*Once and again at*

some time or other in the whole course of our life, we have to transact business with some individual, and according as we behave to him, so he ever after forms his estimate of our character and general conduct.—V. g.]—*εἰρηνεύοντες, being at peace*) xiv. 17, 19.

19. Ἀγαπητοί, *beloved*) By this appellation he soothes those who might feel angry; and he often uses it in the exhortations, that flow from a sense of the Divine grace which had been exercised towards the exhorter and those to be exhorted: comp. ver. 1.—δότε τόπον, *give place*) He who avenges himself, flies upon [seizes unwarrantably] all that appertains to the wrath of God.— τῇ ὀργῇ) that *wrath*, of which so many things are said in Scripture; that is: the wrath of God, which alone is just and alone deserves to be called wrath [Not as Engl. V. seems to imply, *Yield to the wrath of your enemy*]. This is an ellipsis, due to a feeling of religious reverence, 2 Chron. xxiv. 18.—ἐμοί, *to me*) supply, *let it be* [left to Me, as My Divine prerogative], Deut. xxxii. 35, ἡμέρᾳ ἐκδικήσεως ἀνταποδώσω, *I will repay in the day of vengeance*.—ἐκδίκησις, *vengeance*) Hence Paul inferred—*not avenging yourselves*, ἐκδικεῖν, to exact by law, to prosecute a law-suit to the utmost.—ἐγὼ ἀνταποδώσω, *I will repay*) i.e. leave this to me. [*This consideration easily suppresses all* desire of vengeance. Suppose, that your adversary is not better, and that you are not worse than you think of yourself and him: he will either obtain at length the Divine grace, or he will not. If he shall obtain it, he will also acknowledge no doubt the injury, which he did to you, even though you should not be alive; and in this case you will not desire, I hope, in consequence of any grudge of yours, to debar him from access to GOD, but rather would feel delight in assisting him in every way with your prayers. If he shall not obtain it, GOD at least in His own behoof as supreme Judge, will by no means fail to punish him severely for the fault, for which you have granted him pardon.—V. g.]—λέγει Κύριος, *saith the Lord*) A form of expression used by the prophets, which the apostles did not use, but when they quoted the prophets; because, the prophets had one mode [ratio] of inspiration and the apostles another.

20. Ἐὰν οὖν πεινᾷ—ψώμιζε—αὐτοῦ) LXX. Prov. xxv. 21, 22, ἐὰν πεινᾷ—τρέφε [ψώμιζε in LXX. ed. by Holmes and Bos] αὐτοῦ, ὁ δὲ Κύριος ΑΝΤΑΠΟΔΩΣΕΙ σοι ἀγαθά. *If he hunger, feed him* [*his*

head], *and the Lord will repay thy good deeds.* The apostles applied the phrase, *it is written* more to doctrines, than to morals.—ἐχθρὸς, *an enemy*) This especially holds good of a bitter and violent enemy. —ψώμιζε, *feed*) with thy hand. So LXX., 2 Sam. xiii. 5. Thus will even thy iron-hearted enemy be softened.—ἄνθρακας πυρὸς, *coals of fire*) The end of all vengeance is that an enemy may be brought to repent, and that an enemy may deliver himself into the hands of the avenger. A man will very easily attain both objects, if he treat his enemy with kindness. Both are described in this remarkable phrase; for it is such a repentance as that, which in the greatest degree *burns;* 4 Esd. xvi. 53, and an enemy becomes willingly the property of his avenger; you will then have him entirely in your power [ready at your nod to obey].—ἐπὶ τὴν κεφαλὴν αὐτοῦ, *upon his head*) *i.e.* upon himself, upon him wholly, in that part too where he will feel it most.

21. Μὴ νικῶ, *be not overcome*) νικῶ in the middle voice. They, whom the world consider to be conquerors, are in reality conquered.—κακοῦ) by the *evil,* of your enemy, and of your own nature.—νίκα, *overcome*) He is a brave man, who can endure.— ἐν τῷ ἀγαθῷ τὸ κακὸν, *evil with good*) So also ch. xiii. 3, 4, with which there is a charming connection.

CHAPTER XIII.

1. Πᾶσα, *every*) The apostle writes at very great length to the Romans, whose city was the seat of empire, on the subject of the magistracy, and this circumstance has all the force of a public apology for the Christian religion. This, too, may have been the reason why Paul, in this long epistle, used only once, and that too not until after this apology, the phrase, *the kingdom of God,* on other occasions so customary with him; xiv. 17, for, instead of *the kingdom,* he calls it *the glory;* comp., however, Acts xxviii. 31, note. Every individual should be under the authority of the magistrate, and be liable to suffer punishment, if he has done evil, ver. 4.—ψυχὴ, *soul*) He had said that their bodies ought to be presented to God, ch. xii. 1, presupposing

ROMANS XIII. 2, 3.   109

that the souls would be; now he wishes *souls* to be subject to the magistrate. It is *the soul*, which does either good or evil, ch. ii. 9, and those in authority are a terror to the evil work, *i.e.* to the evil doer.—A man's high rank does not exempt him from obedience.—ἐξουσίαις ὑπερεχούσαις) ἐξουσία from εἰμί, ὑπερέχω from ἔχω; *being* is before *having*: ὑπερεχούσαις contains the aetiology [See Append. Be subject to the powers *because* they are ὑπερέχουσαι: the cause or reason], 1 Pet. ii. 13, Fr. *Souverain, Sovereign.*—ὑποτασσέσθω) The antithesis to this is ἀντιτασσόμενος, ver. 2. The Conjugates are τεταγμένοι, διαταγή. *Let him be subject*, an admonition especially necessary to the Jews.—ἐξουσία, *power*) ἐξουσία denotes the office of the magistrate in the abstract; αἱ δὲ ἐξουσίαι, ver. 2, *those in authority* in the concrete, therefore δὲ is interposed, ἐπιτατικὸν [forming an *Epitasis, i.e.* an emphatic addition to explain or augment the force of the previous enunciation.—Appen.]. The former is more readily acknowledged to be from God than the latter. The apostle makes an affirmation respecting both. All are from God, who has instituted all powers in general, and has constituted each in particular, by His providence,—εἰ μὴ ἀπὸ) See App. crit. Ed. ii. ad h. v.[1]

2. Διαταγῇ, the *ordinance*) the abstract, in which the concrete is implied. So 1 Pet. ii. 13, κτίσις, *creature*, in the abstract [but Engl. Vers. *the ordinance*]; it at the same time includes, for example, *the king*, in the concrete.—ἀνθέστηκεν) The Preterite, *i.e.* by that very act resists.—κρίμα) Divine *judgment*, through the magistrate.—λήψονται, *they shall bring on themselves*) While they *take* to themselves another's power, they shall by their own spontaneous act *take* [bring] on themselves, receive judgment. We have here the figure [2] Mimesis [an allusion to the words of another with a view to refute him].

3. [3] Οὐκ—ἀγαθῶν) *not—of good works.* This is immediately

---

[1] G Orig. D corrected later, read ἀπό. But AB read ὑπό. Vulg. *fg* and Iren. have the transl. Lat. *a*.—ED.

Jerome omits from αἱ δὲ to εἰσίν. But ABD(Λ)G Vulg. Memph. *fg* Versions, Iren. 280, 321, retain the clause, omitting, however, ἐξουσίαι: which word is retained by Orig. and both the Syr. Versions and Rec Text.—ED.

[2] See Appendix.

[3] The margin of the 2d Ed. prefers the reading, τῷ ἀγαθῷ ἔργῳ, ἀλλὰ τῷ

discussed, *Wilt thou—as to good.*—κακῶν, *of evil*) This is treated of at ver. 4, *if* [thou do that which is evil]—*upon him that doeth* [evil]. They especially do evil who are also rebellious. *For* at the beginning of the verse thus retains its own proper force. —θέλεις, *wilt thou*) All in some degree *will*, but they do not in an equal degree so act.—μὴ φοβεῖσθαι, *not be afraid*) One kind of fear precedes bad actions, and deters men from committing them; this fear continues, ver. 7: another kind follows bad actions, and from this fear, they are free, who do well.—ἔπαινον, *praise*) 1 Pet. ii. 14, along with a reward; comp. 1 Cor. iv. 5.

4. Θεοῦ γὰρ, *for of God*) There is here an Anaphora or repetition of the same word at the beginning of different clauses. There is a trace of Divine providence in this, that even wicked men, appointed to the magistracy, give their support to what is good, and visit evil with punishment.[1]—σοι, *to thee*) This *to thee* is used with great elegance respecting him, that doeth well, but τῷ is used indefinitely respecting the evil-doer.—εἰς) *so far as concerns* what is good, what is for your advantage.—τὸ κακὸν, *evil*) Good is marked as in direct antithesis to this *evil* in ver. 3, not in ver. 4.—φορεῖ, *wieldeth* [*beareth*]), not merely φέρει, *carries*: [*gestat*, not *gerit*; *wields*] according to Divine appointment.

5. Ἀνάγκη) *Baumgarten* remarks that this word is wanting in *some MSS.* It is only wanting in the Graeco-Latin, which are unworthy of the name of MSS. where they have no Greek copies agreeing with them (as also happens, ch. i. 19). I do not mention this for the sake of contention, but because I am well assured of the advantage conferred on the Greek New Testament by him, who lessens the authority of the bilingual copies in any passage.—διὰ τὴν ὀργὴν, *for* [on account of, through fear of] *wrath*) which hangs over the evil-doer, ver. 4. Hence we have another manifest connection of this with the preceding chapter, in which see ver. 19, [give place] *unto wrath.*—διὰ τὴν

κακῷ. So also the German version.—E. B. So the oldest authorities ABD corr. later, G, Vulg. *fg* Iren. Memph. But both Syr. Versions have τῶν ἀγαθῶν ἔργων—κακῶν.—ED.

[1] Διάκονός ἐστιν, *He is the minister*) Paul uses the same words concerning the magistracy, as he uses to express on other occasions the ministry of the Gospel. So also ver. 6.—V. g.

συνείδησιν, *for conscience' sake*) which expects the praise of a good action from the minister of God, ver. 3.

6. Λειτουργοί, *ministers*) The *ministry* and *the magistracy* are adorned with the same titles. So ver. 4, διάκονος, comp. Is. xliv. 28; Jer. xxv. 9.—προσκαρτεροῦντες, [attending continually] *persevering*) O that all men would do so rightly.

7. 'Οφειλὰς), *debts*.—τῷ, an abbreviated mode of expression,[1] as in 2 Cor. viii. 15, note.—φόρον, τέλος) with respect to the thing itself; φόρος is the genus, τέλος the species.—φόβον, τιμὴν, *fear, honour*) with the mind, and words and gestures. φόβος, *respect*, a higher degree of *honour*.

8. Μηδενί, *to no man*) From our duties to magistrates, he proceeds to general duties, *such as we owe to one another*.—ὀφείλετε, *owe*) a new part of the exhortation begins here.—ἀγαπᾷν, to *love*) a never-ending debt. Song of Sol. viii. 7, at end of ver. If you will continue to love, you will owe nothing, for love is the fulfilling of the law. To love is liberty.

9. Οὐ μοιχεύσεις, *thou shalt not commit adultery*) Paul goes over the commandments without binding himself down to their order.—οὐ ψευδομαρτυρήσεις, *thou shalt not bear false witness*) I did not think that this came from Paul's pen, but Baumgarten thinks so, as he writes, that *Whitby should be* consulted. See App. crit. Ed. ii. on this passage.[2]—εἴ τις ἑτέρα, *if there be any other*) for example, *honour thy father*.—ἐντολὴ) ἐντολὴ, *a commandment*, a part; νόμος, *the law*, the whole.—λόγῳ, *in the saying*) a short, easy one.—ἀνακεφαλαιοῦται) *it is briefly comprehended*, so that although particular precepts may not be thought of, yet no offence can be committed against any one of them by the man, who is endued with love; comp. *is fulfilled* [in one word] Gal. v. 14, likewise, *hang* [all the law and the prophets] Matt. xxii. 40.—ὡς σεαυτόν) So *Seidelianus* along with some; others read ὡς ἑαυτόν, which Baumgarten approves. I was of opinion that one sigma had been written instead of two, and those, who are

---

[1] See Appendix. Concisa Locutio.

[2] The German Version has the clause, rather, I should think, from a slip of memory, than from change of opinion.—E. B.

ABD(Λ)G*fg* Origen, the best MSS. of Vulg. omit οὐ ψευδομαρτυρήσεις. Rec. Text keep the words, with which a few MSS. of the Memph. Vers. agree. —ED.

acquainted with the habits of the transcribers, will readily agree with me. Examples will be found in App. crit., p. 383.[1]

10. Κακὸν οὐκ, *no evil*) Moreover, most duties are of a negative character; or at least, where there is no one injured, positive duties are pleasantly and spontaneously performed. Where there is true love, there a man is not guilty of adultery, theft, lying, covetousness, ver. 9.[2]

11. Καὶ τοῦτο, *and this*) supply *do*, those things, which are laid down from ch. xii. 1, 2, and especially from xiii. 8.—καιρὸν) the *time* [opportunity, season] abounding in grace, ch. v. 6., iii. 26; 2 Cor. vi. 2.—ὥρα, *the hour*) viz. *it is*. This word marks a short period of time. We take account of the *hour* for [with a view to] rising.—ἤδη, *already*) without delay; presently after there occurs νῦν, *at the present time* [now].—ἐξ ὕπνου, *out of sleep*) The morning dawns, when man receives faith, and then sleep is shaken off. He must therefore rise, walk and do his work, lest sleep should again steal over him. The exhortations of the Gospel always aim at HIGHER AND HIGHER DEGREES of perfection, [something farther beyond], and presuppose the oldness of the condition in which we now are, compared with those newer things, which ought to follow, and which correspond to the nearness of salvation.—ἡμῶν) construed with ἐγγὺς, which is included in ἐγγύτερον, rather than with σωτηρία; for in other passages it is always called either the *salvation of God*, or *salvation* absolutely, not *our salvation*, [which Engl. Vers. wrongly gives]; comp. on this *nearness of salvation*, Gal. iii. 3, v. 7. In both places the apostle supposes, that the course of the Christian, once begun, thereupon proceeds onward continually, and comes nearer and nearer to the goal. Paul had long ago written both his epistles to the Thessalonians; therefore when he wrote of the nearness of salvation, he wrote considerately [for he here, after having had such a time meanwhile to consider, repeats his statement], comp. 1 Thess. iv. 15, note. Observe also: he says elsewhere, that we are near to salvation, Heb. vi. 9: but here,

---

[1] ABD(Λ) Vulg. Orig. have σεαυτόν. But G and Rec. Text ἑαυτόν.—ED.

[2] Οὖν, *then*) Love is not extinguished of itself; for well-doing, unless it meets with some obstruction from some evil, goes on without interruption: hence it is that from the avoiding of evil the fulfilment of the law, which also includes good, is derived [is made to flow].—V. g.

that salvation, as if it were a day, is near to us. He who has begun well ought not to flag, when he is near the goal, but to make progress [deficere, proficere: not to *recede*, but *proceed*]. —ἡ σωτηρία) *Salvation* to be consummated at the coming of Christ, which is the goal of hope, ch. viii. 24, and the end of faith, i. Pet. i, 9. The making mention of *salvation* is repeated from ch. v. and viii. [*Moreover from that whole discussion, this exhortation is deduced, which is the shorter, in proportion as that was the longer.*—V. g.]—ἢ ὅτε ἐπιστεύσαμεν) *than at the time, when we began to believe* at the first, and entered upon the path described, ch. i.—iv.; so, πιστεύειν, *to take up faith*, [to accept it, to become believers] Acts iv. 4, 32, and in many other places. [*He, who has once begun well, from time to time approaches either nearer to salvation, or salvation, as it is said here, comes nearer to him. He has no need to feel great anxiety, excepting the eagerness of expectation.*—V. g.]

12. 'Η νύξ) *the night* of this dark life, προέκοψεν, *has come to its height; the day* of complete salvation has drawn nigh,—the day of Christ, the last day, Heb. x. 25, the dawn of which is this whole time, which intervenes between the first and second coming of our Lord. Paul speaks as if to persons awaking out of sleep, who do not immediately comprehend that it is bordering between night and day. He who has been long awake, knows the hour; but he to whom it needs now at last to be said, it is no longer night, the day has drawn near, is understood to be regarded as one, who is now, and not till now, fully awake.— ἔργα, *the works*) which they, whilst even still lying [and not yet awake] perform: comp. Gal. v. 19, note; works, which are unworthy of the name of *arms*. Farther, *works* come from internal feelings: *arms* are supplied from a different quarter; during the night men are without even their clothes; during the day, they have also arms.—ὅπλα, *arms*) this word is repeated from ch. vi. [13, Neither yield your members as *instruments* of unrighteousness]: such *arms* as became those, who are light-armed [ready for action], as the breastplate and the helmet, 1 Thess. v. 8.

13.¹ Εὐσχημόνως) with *good clothing* (*honestly*, Engl. Vers., in

¹ 'Ως ἐν ἡμέρᾳ, *as in the day*) See that you bear yourself so now, as you would desire to be seen to be at the last day.—V. g.

the archaic sense, = *becomingly*; in becoming attire).—κώμοις καὶ μέθαις, not in *riotings and drunkenness*) as to ourselves. κῶμος, *feasting*, a lascivious banquet, with dancing and various disorderly acts.—Wisd. xiv. 23; 2 Macc. vi. 4.—κοίταις καὶ ἀσελγείαις, in *chamberings and wantonness*) accompanied with others. —ἔριδι καὶ ζήλῳ, in *strife and envying*) directed against others. In ver. 13, 14, there is a chiasmus:[1] α. *not in rioting*—β. *not in strife* and *envying*: γ. *but put on*, in love [opposed to strife, and inseparable from Christ], *the Lord Jesus Christ*—δ. *and—not—for the lusts*. β and γ correspond, α and δ.

14. Τὸν) Here is summarily contained *all the light and power of the New Testament, as it is the whole of salvation [everything that is wrong being excluded.*—V. g.] 1 Cor. vi. 11.—Ἰησοῦν Χριστὸν, *Jesus Christ*) ch. vi. 3, 4.—σαρκὸς, *of the flesh*) This has respect to ch. vii. and viii.—πρόνοιαν, *care*) *The care of the flesh is neither forbidden in this passage as bad, nor praised as good, but it is reduced to order and fortified against the dangers to which it is liable, as something of a middle character [between bad and good], and yet in some respects the object of suspicion.* Πρόνοια, *previous* [anticipatory] *care* of the flesh is opposed to holy *hope*.—ἐπιθυμίας, *lusts*) of pleasure and passion: with this comp. ver. 13 [and ch. vi. 7.]

CHAPTER XIV.

1. Ἀσθενοῦντα) The participle is milder than the adjective ἀσθενῆ, *weak*.—πίστει, *in faith*) Even still the apostle refers all things to *faith*.—προσλαμβάνεσθε, *receive ye*) We have the same word, ver. 3, ch. xi. 15, xv. 7; Philem. ver. 17. [*Salvation has come to both Jews and Gentiles by faith; therefore neither party should impede the other, but both should afford mutual assistance.* —V. g.]—μὴ εἰς, *not into*) He who urges another to do, what he himself is doing, appears to receive him, but then he receives him so, that his *thoughts*, διαλογισμοὶ, are driven into [to enter-

[1] See Appendix.

tain] doubts, διακρίσεις, so that he cannot in his own feeling on the particular point, be borne along with full satisfaction, πληροφορεῖσθαι [be fully persuaded, ver. 5], the word ἀδιαφορεῖν is the antithesis to the word διακρίνειν. He calls them *doubts in the thoughts,* for *those in doubt think* more than they *speak*.

2. Πιστεύει, *believes*) This word has a more direct sense in the predicate; the participle ἀσθενῶν conceals, as it were, the weakness of him who eats herbs.—λάχανα, *herbs*) vegetable food (in preference to meats, ver. 21), which we have the most undoubted liberty to eat, Gen. ix. 3.

3. αὐτὸν, *him*) *who eats* in faith.—προσελάβετο, *hath received*) [taken to Himself] for example, from among the Gentiles.

4. Σὺ) *thou*, O weak man.—τίς εἶ) *who art thou*, who takest so much upon thyself.—ἀλλότριον οἰκέτην, *another man's servant*) He calls him in another respect *thy brother*, as it suits his purpose, ver. 10.—Κυρίῳ, [Master] *Lord*) Christ, ver. 6, 7, 9, 10, 14, 15, 18.—στήκει, *he stands*) although thou, O weak man, dost not think so.—σταθήσεται δὲ, *yea, and he shall be holden up*) if he shall fall; *he will be upheld* by sure knowledge.—δυνατὸς γὰρ, *for He is able*) In the works of Divine grace, the conclusion is often valid, when drawn from what is possible (*posse*) to what actually is (*esse*) : against those especially, who judge otherwise; and in behalf of those who are weak.

5. Πᾶσαν ἡμέραν) πᾶσαν ἡμέραν κρίνει ἡμέραν, *another judges every day a day*. He judges that he should equally do good at all times.—ἰδίῳ νοΐ, *in his own mind*) his own, not another's. νοῦς does not signify the opinion of the mind, but the *mind* itself.—πληροφορεῖσθαι, *to be borne along with full satisfaction* [lit. *course*]) *i.e.*, *let each one act, and let another permit him to act* (this is the force of the Imperative, as at ver. 16) *according to his own judgment*, without anxious disputation, and with cheerful obedience, comp. v. 6. He is not speaking positively [precisely] of the understanding; for these two things are contradictory : *you may eat, you may not eat*, and therefore cannot at the same time be true; and yet a man, who has determined either on the one or the other, may *be fully persuaded* (lit. *be carried, full course*) *in his own mind*, as a boat may hold on its course uninjured either in a narrow canal or in a spacious lake.

6. Εὐχαριστεῖ γὰρ—καὶ εὐχαριστεῖ, *for he gives thanks—and*

gives thanks) Thanksgiving sanctifies all actions, however outwardly different, which do not weaken it, 1 Cor. x. 30; Col. ii. 7, iii. 17; 1 Tim. iv. 4. The, *For*, however, has greater force than *and*, as thanksgiving is more connected with eating, than with abstinence from eating; and in him, who *eats*, there are both the fruits and the criterion, and in some respects the ground of faith, even of that faith, of which we have an account at ver. 22, and of an assured conscience; with respect to him who does *not eat*, that faith, of which we read at ver. 22, is no doubt defective as to its fruits, criterion, and the ground on which it rests, but yet the man retains all the three as regards a conscience void of offence [not violated].—καὶ εὐχαριστεῖ, *and gives thanks*) for herbs, ver. 2.

7. Ἡμῶν, *of us*) believers; for all others live and die to themselves.—ἑαυτῷ, *to himself*) Wellerus says: *No man ought to live to himself, neither formally* [formaliter], *so that, as one at his own disposal, he should regulate his life according to his own desires; nor materially* [materialiter], *because, satisfied with himself, he may wish to give way to self-indulgence; nor* [finaliter] *with this end in view, that he may make the scope of his life the enjoyment of pleasures.*—ζῇ, ἀποθνήσκει, *lives, dies*) the art of dying is the same as that of living.

8. Τῷ Κυρίῳ, *to the Lord*) implying the Divine majesty and power of Christ.—ἐσμέν) *we are*, not merely we begin to be.

9, Καὶ ἀπέθανε καὶ ἔζησεν, *both died and revived*) This agrees with what goes before and with what follows. Baumgarten reads καὶ ἀνέστη, and alleges the probability of omission on the part of the transcribers, but gives no reason for this probability. I think the addition probably is due to this, that the transcribers very easily laid hold of a very well-known expression concerning Christ, ἀπέθανε καὶ ἀνέστη, 1 Thess. iv. 14; and when this was done, some omitted καὶ ἔζησεν, others, however, also retained it, and moreover placed it either first, as in *Iren.* l. iii. c. 20; or in the middle, as in the Syriac version; or third in order, as in Chrysostom, who, however, in his exposition, passes over the καὶ ἀνέστη. Whitby, who, according to Baumgarten, ought to be consulted, refutes himself; for he says, that ἀπέθανεν and νεκρῶν, ἔζησεν and ζώντων correspond to each other (as also Origen observes, c. Cels., p. 103, ed. Hoesch.) ἀνέστη finds nothing to which it corresponds. I have cleared away the objection from the testimonies of the fathers, adduced by him, in the *Apparatus*. The reading ἔζησεν is well supported; ἀνέζησεν rests on much weaker authority.[1]—νεκρῶν, *of the dead*) The dying and the dead rejoice in the Lord Jesus, who has died and abolished death and vanquished the devil, Heb. ii. 14.—ζώντων, *of the living*) The living and those, who are made alive again, triumph with their living Redeemer, their Kinsman (Heb. *Goel.*) The living God is the God of the living, Matt. xxii. 32. Christ, who lives again, is Lord of those who are brought to life again. Paul places here, ver. 7, 8, this *life* before *death*, and, in ver. 9, by gradation, after *death*, that *life*, as ch. viii. 38, with which comp. ver. 34. *Christ*, says he, *died, that he might have dominion over the dying, Christ revived, that He might have dominion over the living*. Christ has *died,* therefore *death* (the act or rather the passive suffering of dying and the state of death) will not separate us from Him. Christ has *risen again*, therefore *the life* (of the world to come) will not separate us from Him; hence the notion of [2] *the insensibility of the soul during the whole night*, whilst the body is in the grave, is set aside by the dominion of Christ over the dead; and against this doctrine solid arguments are derived from the appearance of Moses and Elias, Matt. xvii. 3, as also from the resurrection of the saints, Matt. xxvii. 52, 53; and from the hope of Paul, etc., Phil. i. 23; 2 Cor. v. 8; Heb. xii. 23. To these we may add "the fifth seal," Rev. vi. 9, note, and the ὄχλοι, multitudes of the blessed, Rev. vii. and xiv., etc. The apostles themselves declined, 1 Cor. v. 12, to judge "those that are without." The state of deserving [the state in which men are capable of deserts] (taking the word in a large sense on both sides [in a good and a bad sense]) is doubtless not extended beyond this present life. The condition of man for all eternity depends on [his state at] the moment of death, although without man's co-operation, different degrees may exist. Comp. Luke xvi. 9, 22, 25; John ix. 4 (comp. Ecc. ix. 10); Gal. vi. 10; 2 Tim.

[1] ABC Memph. Syr. later, read ἀπέθανεν καὶ ἔζησεν. But G*g*, Vulg. and Origen, ἀπέθανεν καὶ ἀνέστη; for which last Fulgentius and the Fuld. MS. of Vulg. corrected by Victor, have ἀνέζησεν. D(Λ)*f* Iren. have ἔζησεν καὶ ἀπέθανεν καὶ ἀνέστη. Rec. Text, ἀπέθ. κ. ἀνέστη. ν ἀνέζησεν.—ED.

[2] ψυχοπαννυχίαν.

iv. 6, 8; Tit. ii. 12; Heb. iii. 13, vi. 11, ix. 27; Rev. ii. 10; Rom. viii. 23, etc.

10. Σὺ δὲ, *But thou*) thou, who art the weaker; it was with him the apostle has hitherto been dealing: he now addresses the stronger, *or* [dost] *thou also*.—κρίνεις, *judgest*) He, who judges, demands, that the knees should be in fact bent to Him.[1]— ἐξουθενεῖς, *dost thou set at nought?*) in thy mind and by thy conduct.

11. Γέγραπται, *it is written*) Christ is God; for He is called *Lord* and *God*: It is He Himself to whom we live and die. He swears by Himself.—ζῶ ἐγὼ, λέγει Κύριος· ὅτι—καὶ πᾶσα γλῶσσα ἐξομολογήσεται τῷ Θεῷ) Is. xlv. 22, 23, LXX., ἐγὼ εἰμι ὁ Θεὸς καὶ οὐκ ἔστιν ἄλλος—ὅτι—καὶ ὀμεῖται πᾶσα γλῶσσα τὸν Θεόν.[2] *I am God and there is none else, and every tongue shall swear by God.*

12.[3] Δώσει, *shall give*) A gentle exhortation: let no man fly upon [seize] the office of a judge.

13. Κρίνατε, *judge ye*) A beautiful Mimesis[4] in relation to that which precedes, [If we are to *judge*, be this our *judgment*] *let us no longer judge.* [*This matter requires diligent attention.*—V. g.] —πρόσκομμα, *a stumbling-block*) if a brother be compelled by one to do the same thing [as one's self], ver. 20.—σκάνδαλον, *an offence*) if he, the same, abhors you, for what you have done.

14. Ἐν Κυρίῳ Ἰησοῦ, *in the Lord Jesus*) All cases are best and most certainly resolved in the face of Christ; *I know and am persuaded*, a rare conjunction of words, but adapted to this place for confirmation against *ignorance* and *doubt*.

15. Δὲ, *but*) An antithesis. Not only faith, ver. 14, *but* also love ought to be present.—διὰ βρῶμα) μείωσις, [less is said than is intended]: comp. Heb. ix. 10: xii. 16: xiii. 9.—λυπεῖται, *is grieved*) The antithesis to this is the *joy* in ver. 17.—οὐκ ἔτι, *now no longer*) He places before his mind some one who stands stedfast in love, and intimates that he ought never lose sight of love. Love and joy, not love and grief, are connected together.—κατὰ ἀγάπην, *according to love, charitably*) Hence the connection of

---

[1] Τοῦ Χριστοῦ, *of Christ*) God will judge by Christ, ch. ii. 16.—V. g.

[2] Ἐξομολογήσεται, *shall confess*) seriously. The oath of believers corresponds to the oath of God, Is. xlv. 23.—V. g.

[3] Περὶ ἑαυτοῦ, *concerning himself*) not any other.—V. g.

[4] See Appendix. An allusion to some word or thing previous which had been the subject of refutation; as here, *judging*.

the first verse with the preceding chapter, ver. 8, is manifest.—τῷ βρώματί σου, *with thy food* [*meat*]) Do not value thy food more than Christ valued His life.—μὴ ἀπόλλυε, *do not destroy*) 1 Cor. viii. 11. Even the true brother may perish, for whom Christ most lovingly died.

16. Μὴ, *not*) Liberty is the good of [peculiar to] believers, 1 Cor. x. 29, 30, flowing from the privileges of the kingdom of God. Generous *service* in ver. 18, is opposed [antithetic] to the abuse of this liberty. In the writings of the fathers the Lord's Supper also is usually denominated τὸ ἀγαθὸν, *the good*, as Suicer shows, Observ. Sacr., p. 85, which is indeed not inconsistent with this very passage of Paul, who, writing on the same subject, 1 Cor. x. 16, takes his argument from the Lord's Supper. It is comprehended under the *good* of believers. But he speaks of τὸ ἀγαθὸν, *the good*, to show the unworthiness of *evil-speaking*, of which either the weak, who consider the liberty of the stronger, licentiousness, or even others might be guilty.

17. Ἡ βασιλεία τοῦ Θεοῦ, *the kingdom of God*) The kingdom of God is, when a man is under the power [influence] of God, so 1 Cor. iv. 20.—βρῶσις καὶ πόσις, *eating and drinking* [not *meat and drink*, which would be βρῶμα, etc.]) It does not consist in the bold and careless use of liberty, for example in relation to meat and drink.—δικαιοσύνη, *righteousness*) in respect of God. The three points of this definition relate to the sum of the whole epistle in their order. The one peculiar characteristic of faith and life [in the Christian], independently of the article of the sinner's justification [through faith] is *righteousness*.—εἰρήνη, *peace*) in respect of our neighbour; comp. ch. xv. 13.—χαρὰ, *joy*) in respect of ourselves: comp. ch. xv. 13.

18. Ἐν τούτοις, *in these things*) whether he eats or not; the *Alex.* and others, *Lat.* [Vulg.] have ἐν τούτῳ : τούτῳ in the singular has no antecedent, to which it can be made to refer. It may have arisen from its alliteration with τῷ, which follows.[1]— εὐάρεστος—δόκιμος, *acceptable—approved*) He does that, by which he pleases God and approves himself to, and ought to be ap-

---

[1] ABCD corrected later, G*fg* Memph. Theb. Versions, Origen, have ἐν τούτῳ. Rec. Text is supported by the two Syr. Versions alone of ancient authorities in reading ἐν τούτοις.—ED.

proved by, men: he is even approved by those, whom he has nc desire to please.

19. Εἰρήνης, οἰκοδομῆς, *of peace, of edification*) These two things are very closely connected. Theology is in itself a peace-maker and is designed for edification. Controversy is not so directly useful for *edification*, although it should sometimes be added.—. Comp. Nehem. iv. 17.

20. Μὴ κατάλυε, *do not destroy*) The effects of even one sin may be distressing and important moreover, ver. 15.—ἕνεκεν βρώματος, *on account of meat*) a very small matter.—τὸ ἔργον τοῦ Θεοῦ, *the work of God*) a very great matter: *the work*, which God accomplishes within in the soul, by *edification*, and in the church by *harmony* [*Faith is principally intended*, John vi. 29.— V. g.]—κακὸν, *evil*) the word *to eat* [is evil], is to be supplied from what follows: He does not say κακὰ, *evils*.—διὰ προσκόμματος, *with offence*) so that another may be offended by his eating.

21. Μηδὲ, ἐν ᾧ) *neither*, viz. to eat, drink, do anything, *in which*, etc.—προσκόπτει) *stumbleth*, and is wounded, induced rashly to imitate thee, with the loss of *righteousness*. As there is a difference between *righteousness* and *joy*, so there is a difference between the loss of each.—σκανδαλίζεται, *is offended*) is ensnared and impeded, feeling a repugnance to thy action [in eating, and yet doing it in imitation of thee], accompanied with the loss of *peace*.—ἀσθενεῖ) *is made weak*, or at least remains so, 1 Cor. viii. 9, 10; defective in mental strength, and hesitating between imitation and horror, with the loss of *joy*: comp. ver. 17. בשל, LXX., ἀσθενεῖν.

22. Πίστιν, *faith*) concerning the cleanness of meat [all meats alike].—σεαυτὸν,—Θεοῦ, *thyself—of God*) a double antithesis, in relation to our neighbour; as in ch. xv. 3.—ἔχε, *have*) The foundation of real prudence and judicious concealment [of our views on non-essentials, for the sake of our neighbour].—μακάριος, *happy*) These words down to the end of the chapter, contain the antithesis to ch. xv. 1, *but*.—κρίνων, *judging* [*condemning*]) [*Condemning*] *judging* and *approving* are the words in antithesis: by combining the two, the doubting conscience is exquisitely described, when a man approves a thing, and yet [condemns] judges his own action.

23. Ὁ δὲ) The reason, why the stronger ought not to induce the weak to eat.—ἐὰν φάγῃ, *if he eat*) This must be understood both of a single act and much more of frequent eating.—κατακέκριται, *is condemned*) Comp. Gal. ii. 11, note.—ἐκ πίστεως, *of faith*) of which ver. 2, 5 at the end, 14 at the beginning, 22. Therefore it is faith itself that is indicated, by which men are reckoned to be believers, informing and confirming, as it does, the conscience, and constituting partly the foundation and partly the standard of upright conduct.—ἁμαρτία, *sin*) and therefore obnoxious to *condemnation*.

CHAPTER XV.

1. [1] Δὲ, [*on the other hand*] *but*) [This is in antithesis to *Happy—Sin*, last ch. ver. 22, 23]. There is great danger, and we are only kept guarded by the power of God; *but* we ought [owe that debt to others] to watch over [pay attention to] one another.—ἡμεῖς) *we*. He counts himself also in common with others a debtor, as an apostle, and as an apostle of the Gentiles. —οἱ δυνατοί, *the strong*) comp. Gal. vi. 1, note.—βαστάζειν, *to bear*) It is indeed a burden.—ἀρέσκειν) Ἀρέσκω, *I am anxious to please*. He who is anxious to please himself, is indifferent about pleasing another, and pays little respect to his conscience. This is a Metonymy of the antecedent for the consequent [See Append.]

2. Εἰς τὸ ἀγαθὸν, πρός οἰκοδομὴν, *for good, to edification*) εἰς, *unto*, denotes the internal end, in respect of God; πρὸς, *to*, the external end, in respect of our neighbour. *Good*, the genus; *edification*, the species.

3. Ὁ Χριστὸς, *Christ*) who alone was truly δυνατὸς, *strong*, comp. ver. 1 with ch. v. and vi.: δυνατοὶ *strong*, ἀσθενεῖς *weak*.—οὐχ ἑαυτῷ, *not Himself*) Admirable συγκατάβασις, condescension! Not Himself but us, ver. 7, 8; Ps. lxix. 32: Christ procured ἀρέσκειαν, *what is well-pleasing* to God for those, who *see* and *are glad*

[1] Ὀφείλομεν, *we ought*) for Christ's sake, ver. 3.—V. g.

[Referring to Ps. lxix. 32, which see].—ἀλλὰ) *but*, viz., He took that upon Himself, which is written.—γέγραπται, *it is written*) Ps. lxix. 10, with which comp. ver. 11, 12, in the latter hemistich of either, it matters not which.—οἱ—ἐμὲ) So the LXX.—ἐπέπεσον, *fell on*) By right Christ might have borne Himself as God, and have enjoyed Divine honours, but He did not use His right, for our sakes, Phil. ii. 6. He indeed thoroughly felt the reproaches, which wicked men cast upon God, with that sorrow, which they ought to have felt, who gave utterance to them; and He Himself bore and expiated those reproaches as patiently, as if He Himself had been the guilty person. His whole sufferings are here intended; He at that time performed the *office of a minister* [a servant], Matt. xx. 28. [*At that time, He did not please Himself, but He interposed Himself, in order that in respect to* [in the case of] *all who had dishonoured* GOD, GOD *might receive what was well-pleasing* [" caperet beneplacitum."] Or rather, *that God might* by the atonement, *be enabled to exercise good-will* consistently with justice]. *It behoved Him to endure many things with patience*, ver. 1, 4.—V. g.]

4. Γὰρ, *for*) This assigns the reason for the quotation just made.—προεγράφη) *were written before* the time of the New Testament; as was that, which is quoted, ver. 3, as having been written concerning Christ.—ἡμετέραν) *our*, or of us believers in the New Testament, ch. iv. 24; 1 Cor. x. 11.—ὑπομονῆς, *patience*) of which Christ afforded an example, *not pleasing Himself*.—καὶ) a hendiadys [See Append.], the *comfort* [paraclesis] of the Scriptures leads us to *patience*. A summary of the ends [the main aim] of sacred Scripture.—παρακλήσεως, *comfort*) which holds the middle place between *patience* and *hope*; ch. v. 4. There is *comfort* [*paraclesis*, consolation], when the soul re-echoes the sentiment, *thou art* δόκιμος [Comp. the Gr. James i. 3, 12] *approved*. 2 Cor. i. 6.—τῶν γραφῶν, *of the Scriptures*) It is in the plural, and corresponds with *whatsoever*. [The Scriptures *testify of Christ, and teach us by His example, what we should do or what we should leave undone*.—V. g.]—τὴν ἐλπίδα, *the hope*) The article must not be overlooked, comp. on *patience* and *hope*, ch. v. 4, on *hope*, ver. 12, 13. For from this mention of *patience* and *comfort* the fifth verse is deduced, and from the mentioning of *hope* the thirteenth verse.—ἔχωμεν, *may have*) The former part

of this verse treats of the use of the whole Scripture, the latter principally of the use of the Saying quoted at ver. 3. Hence comes the twofold prayer, ver. 5, 13, suitable to the approaching conclusion.

5. Θεὸς τῆς ὑπομονῆς καὶ παρακλήσεως, *The God of patience and consolation*) So, the *God of hope*, ver. 13, *the God of peace*, ver. 33. Titles from the thing, which is treated of. Elsewhere, *the God of glory, the God of order, the God of the living, the God of heaven.*—τῆς παρακλήσεως—τὸ αὐτὸ φρονεῖν—κατὰ) So plainly, Phil. ii. 1, 2.

6.[1] ʽΟμοθυμαδὸν, *with one mind*) with one believing mind.—στόματι, *with the mouth*) confessing.—δοξάζητε, *ye may glorify*) Ye Jews and Gentiles, ver. 7, 9.—τὸν Θεὸν καὶ πατέρα τοῦ Κυρίου ἡμῶν ʼΙησοῦ Χριστοῦ, *the God and Father of our Lord Jesus Christ*) a frequent appellation, 2 Cor. i. 3, xi. 31; Eph. i. 3; Col. i. 3; 1 Pet. i. 3. It is to be resolved in this manner: *The God of our Lord*, etc., Eph. i. 17, and *the Father of our Lord*, etc., instead of what men of old said, *God the Creator and the Lord of heaven* and earth, Ps. cxxiv. 8, and *the God of Abraham and Isaac and Jacob*, thereby subscribing [signifying their assent] to the faith of these believers. So elsewhere *God and our Father*, Gal. i. 4. Christ has a double relationship to God and the Father, as compared with us; we also have a double relationship, through Christ, John xx. 17.

7. ὑμᾶς, *you*[2]) who were formerly weak, Jews and Greeks without distinction.—εἰς δόξαν Θεοῦ, *to the glory of God*) It is construed with *received*, comp. ver. 6, 8, 9.

8. Λέγω δὲ, *Now I say*) By this verse the preceding clause concerning Christ is explained.—Χριστὸν Ἰησοῦν.) Others say, Ἰησοῦν Χριστὸν.[3] Those, who have omitted the name Jesus in this passage, seem to have had respect to ver. 3 and 7. The nomen-

---
[1] Τὸ αὐτὸ φρονεῖν, *to think alike*) Patience and comfort promote harmony. He who disagrees with himself shews himself very morose to others. Harmony is founded in Christ Jesus, as full hope is subsequently founded in the Holy Spirit, ver. 13.—V. g.

[2] ACD corrected later, G*g* Vulg. read ὑμᾶς. Rec. Text reads ἡμᾶς with BD early corrected, *f.*—ED.

[3] ABC read Χριστὸν only. But D(Λ)G*fg* and both Syr. Versions and Rec. Text ʼΙησοῦν Χριστόν.—ED.

clature, *Jesus Christ*, and *Christ Jesus*, ought not to be considered as promiscuously used. *Jesus* is the name, *Christ* the surname. The former was first made known to the Jews, the latter to the Gentiles. Therefore he is called *Jesus Christ* according to the natural and common order of the words; but when He is called *Christ Jesus*, by inverting the order of the words, peculiar reference is made to the office of Christ, with somewhat of a more solemn design. And this is especially suitable to the present passage. Sometimes in one place, both arrangements of the words prevail, ver. 5, 6; Gal. ii. 16, note; 1 Tim. i. 15, 16, vi. 13, 14; 2 Tim. i. 9, 10. See also 1 Cor. iii. 11; with which comp. 1 Tim. ii. 5.—διάκονον, *a minister*) a suitable appellation; comp. ver. 3; Matt. xx. 28. [*Remarkable humiliation! Here indeed there was need* of patience, ver. 4, 5.— V. g.]—Moreover, Jesus Christ became the *minister* of the Father for the salvation of the circumcision. Christ was subservient to the will of the Father: the Father devoted Him for the salvation of many, whence the Genitive, *of circumcision*, has the same meaning as in Gal. ii. 7, 8. Presently after, *reigning* is ascribed to this minister, ver. 12. But this appellation (*minister*) is not repeated in the next verse, for the calling of the Gentiles coheres with His state of exaltation;—it is accordingly said there, *that they might glorify*, for greater thanksgiving is rendered by the Gentiles,[1] than by the circumcision.—περιτομῆς, *of the circumcision*) that is, of Israel.—πατέρων, *of the fathers*) The Genitive here contains the emphasis of the sentence, Matt. xv. 26.

9. Διὰ—ἔθνεσι—ψαλῶ) Ps. xviii. 50, LXX., διὰ—ἔθνεσι, Κύριε—ψαλῶ.—ἐξομολογήσομαι, *I will confess*) Paul says that the Gentiles do that, which Christ declares in the Psalm, that He will do; in fact, Christ is doing this among [or rather, *in the person of*] the Gentiles, Heb. ii. 12, where Paul quotes Ps. xxii., as here Ps. xviii. is quoted. In Ps. xxii. Christ announces the name of the Lord to His brethren; in Ps. xviii. He confesses to the Lord among [or *in the person of*] the Gentiles, and the Gentiles confess to Him in [the person of] Christ. Afterwards in Ps. cxvii.

---

[1] Naturally so: Because they have received grace extraordinarily, they being but as the *wild* olive graffed in on the *elect* stock, Israel.—ED.

the Jews invite all tribes and all nations; לאם signifies a multitude, and עם a political community.—ψαλῶ, *I will sing*) The Gentiles sing and praise, because they have obtained mercy, Heb. אזמרה, using the organ.

10. Λέγει) viz., ὁ λέγων.—εὐφράνθητε ἔθνη μετὰ τοῦ λαοῦ αὐτοῦ) So the LXX., Deut. xxxii. 43. Comp. Ps. lxvii. 5, *the nations in the earth*. The Imperative, put by apostrophe,[1] is equivalent to a categorical indicative, for the promise was not made to the Gentiles.—μετὰ, *with*) The Gentiles were not His people;—this is mercy [ver. 9], because they are admitted notwithstanding.

11. Αἰνεῖτε—καὶ ἐπαινέσατε) Ps. cxvii. 1, LXX., αἰνεῖτε—ἐπαινέσατε.

12.[1] Ἡσαΐας, *Isaiah*) Three sayings had been quoted without the name of Moses and David; he now mentions the name of Isaiah, of whose book the *Haphtara* (The portion publicly read in the synagogue) with this Saying, is read on the eighth day of the Passover, at that time of the year, at which this epistle seems to have been written.—ἔσται ἡ—καὶ ὁ—ἐπ' αὐτῷ—) Is. xi. 10, LXX. καὶ ἔσται ἐν τῇ ἡμέρᾳ ἐκείνῃ ἡ—ὁ—ἐπ' αὐτὸν.—ἡ ῥίζα, *the root*) Christ is elsewhere called the *root of David*, Rev. xxii. 16; but, if we compare this passage taken from the passage in Isaiah quoted above with ver. 1, He is called the *root of Jesse*. The descent of kings and of the Messiah from His house was divinely appointed to Jesse in His own name, before it was so in the name of David, and that descent might have been expected even from another son of Jesse, 1 Sam. xvi. 7. But David was king, not Jesse; and the kingdom of Christ was in some measure hereditary from David, Luke i. 32, in respect of the Jews, but not in respect of the Gentiles. He is therefore called here, not the *root of David*, but, that which was next to it, the *root of Jesse*. The Messiah, who was to descend from Jesse, had been promised neither entirely to him, nor to the Gentiles: and yet He was bestowed on both. Those things, however, which immediately precede, where He is called the *root of Jesse*, and the passage, 1 Sam. xvi. 7, where it is said of the first-born son of Jesse, *I*

---

[1] See Appendix. When the discourse is suddenly turned from what it began with and directed to some other person, present or absent.

[2] Αἰνεῖτε, *praise ye*) on account of grace and truth. For these things follow in the Psalm, where Israel cries aloud to the Gentiles.—V. g.

have refused him, testify that the Messiah was divinely appointed to Jesse.—ὁ ἀνιστάμενος) So the LXX. interpreted the word or Isaiah, נס, *a banner*: There is a pleasant antithesis: the root is in the lowest place; the banner rises on high [to the greatest height], so as to be seen even by the remotest nations.—ἐλπιοῦσιν, *shall hope*, [*trust*]) Divine worship is implied here as due to Christ even in His human nature. The Gentiles formerly had no 'hope,' Eph. ii. 12.

13. Ἐλπίδος, *of hope*] Comp. *they shall hope*, in the preceding verse and immediately after, *in hope*. *The God of hope*, a name glorious to God; a name heretofore unknown to the Gentiles. For Hope had been one of their false divinities, whose temple, Livy mentions in the 21st book of his history, was struck with lightning, and, again in the 24th book, was burnt with fire.— χαρᾶς καὶ εἰρήνης, *with joy and peace*) We may look back to ch. xiv. 17. Concerning *joy* comp. ver. 10, *Rejoice ye;* concerning *peace*, ibid. *with* [His people].—ἐν δυνάμει) construed with περισσεύειν.

14. Ἀδελφοί μου, *my brethren*) As one street often conducts men going out of a large city through several gates, so the conclusion of this epistle is manifold. The first begins with this verse; the second with ch. xvi. 1; the third with xvi. 17; the fourth with xvi. 21; and the fifth with xvi. 25.—καὶ αὐτὸς ἐγὼ, *I myself also*) not merely others, hold this opinion of you, ch. i. 8.—καὶ αὐτοί, *you yourselves* also) even without any admonition of mine.—δυνάμενοι, *who are able*) By this very declaration he exhorts them to exercise that ability.—καὶ ἀλλήλους, *also one another*) not merely that every one should be his own monitor; comp. 2 Tim. ii. 2.—νουθετεῖν, *to admonish*) He points to this ability, [viz. such as consists in this] that a man may be μεστὸς, *full of goodness*, *full* from the new creation itself; *filled* (πεπληρωμένος) *with all knowledge, filled*, viz. by daily exercise; in the understanding and the will. So, *goodness and knowledge* are joined, 1 Pet. iii. 6, 7, and the former is especially recommended to women, the latter to men. Γνῶσις, is properly *knowledge;* and such *knowledge*, as shows respect to the weaker vessel, obtains the name of *moderation*, yet it is in reality *knowledge*.

15. Τολμηρότερον, *more boldly*) That is, I have acted somewhat

boldly in writing to you, who are unknown to me, when I should rather have gone to you in person. He says, that the degree of *boldness* on his part consisted in the very fact of writing at all, not in the manner of writing. Διὰ, *because of*, depends on, *I have written.*—ἀπὸ μέρους, *in part*) [*in some sort*, Engl. V.] He uses this phrase from modesty, and does not assume to himself the whole office of teaching, but only one part of it, that of *admonition*, and that not entirely; for he subjoins ἐπαναμιμνήσκων with ὡς, *as*, before it; he does not say simply, ἀναμιμνήσκων, *putting you in mind*, but ἔπαν.

16. Λειτουργὸν, ἱερουργοῦντα, προσφορὰ) This is allegorical. Jesus is the priest; Paul the servant of the priest; the Gentiles themselves are the *oblation:* ch. xii. 1; Is. lx. 7, lxvi. 20: and that oblation is very *acceptable*, because it is *sanctified* (John xvii. 19), along with [as well as] its gifts [*i.e.* their contribution to the saints at Jerusalem is also *acceptable*, ver. 26], ver. 31.—ἐν πνεύματι ἁγίῳ, *in the Holy Spirit*) whom the Gentiles receive by the Gospel of God.

17. Καύχησιν, *glorying*) Paul had a large heart; so he says at ver. 15, *more boldly*, and ver. 20, " I have strived *ambitiously*," φιλοτιμούμενον.—ἐν Χριστῷ Ἰησοῦ, *in Christ Jesus*) This is explained in the following verse. My glorying with respect to those things, which pertain to God, has been made to rest [rests] in Christ Jesus.—τὰ πρὸς Θεὸν, *in those things, which* pertain *to God*) Paul makes this limitation; otherwise he was poor and an outcast in the world, 1 Cor. iv. 9, etc.

18. Οὐ γὰρ τολμήσω, *for I will not dare*) That is, my mind shrinks [from speaking of the things wrought by me] when unaccompanied with [except when accompanied with] Divine influence.—λαλεῖν τι, *to speak anything*) to mention anything, that I have accomplished, or rather, to preach the doctrine of the Gospel, for the expression is abbreviated, in this manner; I *will not dare to speak any* (or do any) of those things *which Christ* (would *not* speak, or) *do by me;* for, *by word and deed*, follows. The Inspiration [Theopneustia] of Paul is here marked: 2 Cor. xiii. 3.

19. Ἐν δυνάμει σημείων καὶ τεράτων, [Engl. V. *through mighty*] *in the power of signs and wonders*) This expression should be referred to, *by deed.*—ἐν δυνάμει πνεύματος Θεοῦ, [*by*] *in the power*

of the Spirit of God) This should be referred to, *by word*. We have here a gradation, [ascending climax]: for he attributes more to the Spirit of God, than to the signs.—ἀπὸ—μέχρι, *from— unto*) A large tract of country.—'Ιλλυρικοῦ, Illyricum) of which Dalmatia is a part; 2 Tim. iv. 10.—τὸ εὐαγγέλιον, *the Gospel*) the office of preaching the Gospel.

20. Δὲ, *moreover* [*yea,* Engl. V.]) He gives the reason for taking those regions under his own care.—φιλοτιμούμενον) The Accusative absolute, in the neuter gender,[1] the same as ἀρξά-μενον, Luke xxiv. 47.[2]—οὐχ ὅπου, *not where*) This is more emphatic, than if he had said, *where not;* for he intimates, that he had as it were avoided those places, where Christ had been already known. So Col. ii. 1; Gal. i. 22. Paul is said to have been 'unknown' to those, who had previously received the faith.—ἀλλότριον, *another man's*) Paul here does not term Christ Himself the foundation, but the work of others in preaching the Gospel of Christ.

21. Οἷς—συνήσουσι) Is. lii. 15. So plainly the LXX.

22. Πρὸς ὑμᾶς, *to you*) as persons, to whom the name of Christ was now no longer unknown.

23. Κλίμασι, *regions*) This term is applied in contradistinction to the political divisions of the world; for the Gospel does not usually follow such divisions; even the fruit of the Reformation at a very early period had an existence beyond Germany.— ἐπιποθίαν ἔχων) This signifies something more than ἐπιποθῶν.[3]

24. Ὡς ἐὰν) Ὡς is the principal particle; ἐὰν, *soever*,[4] παρέλκει, is redundant, *in whatsoever manner, at whatsoever time, and by whatsoever route.*—εἰς τὴν Σπανίαν, *into Spain*) where the Gospel was not yet preached.—διαπορευόμενος, *passing through on my journey*) because the foundation of the faith was already laid at Rome.—προπεμφθῆναι, *to be brought on my way*) The passive voice with a reciprocal signification, that is, to leave or commit himself to their care to be escorted by them on his journey; he

---

[1] *It being the object of my ambition.* But Engl. V. takes it mascul., *I have strived.*—ED.

[2] But the oldest authorities read ἀρξάμενοι.—ED.

[3] The former implies a *lasting state* of mind : the latter, *a feeling for the time being.*—ED.

[4] But the oldest MSS. have ἄν, viz. ABCD(Λ)G.—ED.

writes familiarly to the brethren whom he had not yet seen, as though by virtue of right [as if his claim on them were matter of right].—ὑμῶν, *you*) He speaks modestly. The Romans were rather likely to have reason to be *filled* (to be *fully gratified*) with Paul's company.—ἀπὸ μέρους, *in some measure*) He intimates to them, that he would not however be so long at Rome, as he wished; or else, that it is Christ, and not believers, with whom believers should be *perfectly* filled.

25. Διακονῶν, *ministering*) after the example of Christ, ver. 8.—τοῖς ἁγίοις, *to the saints*) See note at Acts xx. 32.

26. Μακεδονία καὶ Ἀχαΐα, *Macedonia and Achaia*) From this expression the time, at which the epistle was written, may be gathered, Acts xix. 21.—Κοινωνίαν, *an act of communion, or communication* [*a contribution*]) A term of description [applied to their gift of brotherly love] honourable and exceedingly just.—τῶν ἁγίων, *of the saints*) He does not say, *poor saints* (Gr. *the poor among the saints*). Therefore not all the *saints* were *poor*. Therefore the community of goods had now ceased at Jerusalem, after the death of Ananias and Sapphira, and after the persecution, Acts viii. 1.

27. Εὐδόκησαν γάρ, *for they have been pleased*) supply, *I say*, comp. the beginning of the preceding verse. *Pleased*, and *debt*, are twice mentioned.—καὶ, *and*) Liberty and necessity in good works are one and the same [found together].—εἰ γάρ, *for if*) This mode of reasoning applies also to the Romans; he therefore mildly invites and admonishes them, in this epilogue of the epistle, to contribute : comp. ch. xii. 13.—ὀφείλουσι, *they owe it*) by virtue of the debt of brotherly kindness, 2 Cor. ix. 7.—λειτουργῆσαι, *to minister*) The inferior *ministers* to the superior.

28. Ἐπιτελέσας καὶ σφραγισάμενος) Words nearly related to each other, 2 Kings xxii. 4, וְיַתֵּם אֶת־הַכֶּסֶף, LXX., καὶ σφράγισον τὸ ἀργύριον, *and seal the silver*. Paul finished this first; nothing interrupted him, how eager soever he might be as to other objects, Acts xix. 21. σφραγισάμενος, *as soon as I shall have sealed*, not only that they might perceive the good faith of him, who delivered it, but that they might also be confirmed in spiritual communion. ἀπελεύσομαι, *I will go away*) even though I may never be about to return from Spain. This is the force of the compound verb.—Σπανίαν, *Spain*) Paul does not seem to

have reached Spain. A holy purpose often exists in the minds of godly men, which, although it is not fulfilled, is nevertheless precious [in God's eyes], 2 Sam. vii. 2, 4.

29. Πληρώματι, *in the fulness*) comp. ver. 19. There is a real parallelism in the *fulness* of the Gospel, both intensive and extensive.[1]—εὐλογίας, *of the blessing*) which is conspicuous [such *fulness of blessing* as it is conspicuously seen to possess] both at Jerusalem and Rome.—τοῦ εὐαγγελίου) Some have omitted this word: The cause of the omission is easy to be perceived, viz. from the recurrence of τοῦ.[2]

30. Κυρίου, *Lord*) He exhorts them by the *name of the* Lord; comp. *by* [*for*] *the love*, immediately after.—ἀγάπης, *love*) The love of the Spirit is most widely extended; it brings home [it makes a matter of interest] to thee, even what might seem to belong to another.—συναγωνίζεσθαί μοι, *to strive with me*) He himself must pray, who wishes others to pray with him, Acts viii. 24, 22. Prayer is a *striving*, or *contest*, especially when men resist. Paul is the only one of the apostles, who asks for himself the prayers of believers. He does this moreover generally at the conclusion of his epistles, but not indiscriminately so in all. For he does not so write to those, whom he treats as sons, with the dignity of a father, or even with severity, for example, Timothy, Titus, the Corinthians, the Galatians, as he does to those, whom he treats as his equals with the deferential regard of a brother, for example, the Thessalonians, Ephesians, Colossians (with whom he had not been), and therefore so also the Romans and likewise the Hebrews. It [the request for their

---

[1] That is, the internal fulness, and the expansive capabilities of the Gospel externally, have a real correspondence.—ED.

[2] Either S. R. D. Foertschius in Progr. to this passage, or S. R. D. Ernesti in his review of the Program, affirms, that Bengel was satisfied with the omission of this word, see Bibl. th. T. V. p. 474, but this is a mistake. The margin of both editions (where the sign δ had marked an omission instead of a reading less certain) may be compared, s. pl., also the German Version which expresses the words *des Evangelii* without a parenthesis.— (E. B.)

The τοῦ alluded to by Beng. as *recurring* refers to Rec. Text τοῦ εὐαγγελίου τοῦ, which reading is supported by both Syr. Versions and Vulg. (later MSS.) But ABCD(Λ)G Cod. Amiat. (the oldest MS.) of Vulg. Memph. *fg* Versions omit the three words.—ED.

prayers] is introduced with great elegance at 2 Cor. i 11; Phil. i. 19; Philem. ver. 22.

31. Καὶ ἵνα, *and that*) This is also an important matter.—εὐπρόσδεκτος, *accepted*) that the Jews and Gentiles may be united in the closest bonds of love. The liberality of the Gentiles, which was shown for the sake of the name of Jesus, afforded to the Jews an argument for the truth and efficacy of the Christian faith, and for lawful communion with the Gentiles, 2 Cor. ix. 13.

32. Ἐν χαρᾷ ἔλθω, *that I may come to you with joy*) *I may come*, has respect to the former part of ver. 31, and, *with joy*, to the latter.

33. Ὁ Θεὸς τῆς εἰρήνης, *the God of peace*) A gradation in reference to ver. 5, 13: *The God of patience, hope;* so, *the God of love and peace,* 2 Cor. xiii. 11, *The God of peace,* ch. xvi. 20; 1 Cor. xiv. 33; Phil. iv. 9; 1 Thess. v. 23; Heb. xiii. 20.[1]

CHAPTER XVI.

1. Φοίβην, *Phœbe*) The Christians retained the names borrowed from the heathen gods, as a memorial of the heathenism, which they had abandoned.—οὖσαν διάκονον, who is *a [servant] minister*) without the office of teaching. She might have been considered as a *minister* in respect of this very errand, on which she was sent.—Κεγχρεαῖς, *at Cenchrea*) near Corinth.

2. Ἐν Κυρίῳ, *in the Lord*) There is very frequent mention *of the Lord, Christ,* in this chapter: *In the Lord:* at the present day we say, *in a Christian manner* [*as Christians*]. The phrase is peculiar to Paul, but often used.—καὶ γὰρ, *for even*) a strong argument, 1 Cor. xvi. 15, 16; Phil. ii. 29. There is an all-embracing [comprehensive] relationship among believers:

---

[1] Ἀμήν, the Greek transcribers loved to add the final *Amen* from its very frequent use, not to say, in doxologies only, which have *Amen* in Ps. xli. 14, lxxii. 19, etc., but in prayers and at the conclusions of books.—*Not. crit.*

AG*g* omit ἀμήν. B (judging from its silence), CD(Λ)*f* Vulg. have it. Tischend. therefore supports it. Lachm. brackets it.—ED.

Phœbe is recommended to the Romans for acts of kindness, which she had done far from Rome.—προστάτις, *a succourer*) We may believe, that Phœbe was wealthy, but she did not shrink by subterfuges from the duty of *ministering*, in the case of strangers, the needy, etc.; nor did she regard in the case of [on the part of] her fellow-citizens, who were wholly intent on self interest, the opinion entertained of her bad economy.—πολλῶν, *of many*) Believers ought to return a favour not only to him, who has been of service to themselves, but also to him, who has been of service to others.

3. Ἀσπάσασθε, *salute*) We should observe the politeness of the apostle in writing the salutations; the friendly feeling of believers in joining theirs with his, ver. 21, 22; again, the humility of the former in attending to them, and the love of the latter in the frequent use of them.—Πρίσκαν, *Prisca*) strong testimony sufficiently confirms this reading; Baumgarten prefers Πρίσκιλλαν, *Priscilla*.[1] A holy woman in Italy seems to have borne the Latin name Priscilla, which is a diminutive, Acts xviii. 2, but in the Church the name, *Prisca*, is more dignified. The name of the wife is put here before that of the husband, because she was the more distinguished of the two in the Church; Acts xviii. 18: or even because in this passage there had gone before the mention of a woman, Phœbe.—Ἀκύλαν, *Aquila*) The proper names of believers, Roman, Hebrew and Greek, set down promiscuously, show the *riches* of Grace in the New Testament *exceeding* all expectation [Eph. iii. 20].—συνεργούς, *fellow-workers*) in teaching, or else, protecting: See the following verse.

4. Οἵτινες, *who*) They are individually distinguished by their own respective graces, or duties; but Scripture never praises any one so as to give him any ground for extolling himself, but for praising God and rejoicing in Him.—ὑπέθηκαν) The force of the verb is not unsuitably explained by the noun ὑποθήκη, *a stake laid down*.—αἱ ἐκκλησίαι, *the churches*) even the Church at Rome, for the preservation of Paul, and we still are bound in some measure to give thanks to Aquila and Priscilla, or we shall do so hereafter.

[1] ABCD(Λ)G Vulg. *fg* support Πρίσκαν against Πρίσκιλλαν, of the Rec Text.—ED.

5. Κατ' οἶκον, *in the house*) When any Christian was the possessor of a spacious mansion, he gave it as a place for meeting together. Hitherto the believers at Rome had neither bishops nor ministers. Therefore they had nothing at that time resembling the papacy. It does not appear that there were more of these house-churches then at Rome; otherwise Paul would have mentioned them also [as he does those in this ch.] Aquila therefore was at Rome, what Gaius was at Corinth, ch. xvi. 23; although the persecution had particularly pressed upon him, Acts xviii. 2.—Ἐπαίνετον, *Epaenetus*) Paul had not hitherto been at Rome, and yet he had many intimate acquaintances there from Asia, or even from Greece, Palestine, Cilicia, Syria. There is no mention here of Linus or Clement, whence we may conclude, that they came to Rome afterwards.—ἀπαρχὴ, *first fruits*) This is evidently a title of approbation, 1 Cor. xvi. 15.—Ἀχαΐας) others have Ἀσίας,[1] and Grotius, along with the British writers quoted by Wolfius approves of it, with whom he says, how far he is correct I know not, that Whitby agrees. *D. Hauberus* in particular supports Ἀχαΐας, and somewhat too liberally ascribes to the transcribers the same skill in reasoning, for which he himself is remarkable. *Bibl. Betracht.*, Part 3, page 93. See App. crit. Ed. ii., on this passage.

7. Συγγενεῖς, *kinsmen*) So ver. 11, 21. They were Jews, ch. ix. 3.—ἀποστόλοις, *among the apostles*) They had seen the Lord, 1 Cor. xv. 6; hence they are called *apostles*, using the word in a wider meaning, although some of them perhaps after the ascension of the Lord turned to the faith by means of the first sermons of Peter. Others might be veterans, and I acknowledge as such the brethren, who numbered more than five hundred. The passage quoted from 1 Cor. implies, that there was a multitude of those, who had seen Christ and were from that fact capable of giving the apostolic testimony.—πρὸ ἐμοῦ, *before me*) Age makes men venerable, especially in Christ. Among the men of old, *it was a mark of veneration to have the prece-*

---

[1] Ἀσίας is the reading of ABCD (corrected later) G Vulg. Memph. *fg.* Versions. Ἀχαΐας is only supported by the two Syr. Versions, of very ancient authorities.—ED.

dence by four years.[1]—γεγόνασιν ἐν Χριστῷ,) they began to be in Christ.

8. Ἐν Κυρίῳ, *in the Lord*) Construed with *beloved*; for *greet* or *salute* at ver. 6 and throughout the chapter is employed absolutely [and it is not therefore to be connected with ἐν Κυρίῳ].

9. Ἡμῶν, *of us*. Comp. ver. 21.[2]

10. Τὸν δόκιμον, *approved*) an incomparable epithet [*This man was of tried excellence*.—V. g.]—τοὺς ἐκ τῶν) Perhaps *Aristobulus* was dead, and *Narcissus* too, ver. 11, and all in their respective families had not been converted. Some of them seem not to have been known by face to Paul, but by the report of their piety. Faith does not make men peevish, but affable. Not even the dignity of the apostolic office was any hindrance to Paul.

11. ὄντας, *who are*) Therefore a part of that family were heathens.

12. Τὰς κοπιώσας, *who laboured*) although they have their name [Τρύφαινα, Τρυφῶσα] from τρυφή, *a luxurious life;* as Näomi (*agreeable*). It is probable that these two were sisters according to the flesh.

13. Ἐκλεκτὸν, *chosen*) a remarkable title, 2 John, ver. 1, 13; 1 Tim. v. 21.

14. Ἀσύγκριτον, κ.τ.λ., *Asyncritus*, etc.) Paul joins those together, among whom there was a peculiar tie of relationship, neighbourhood, etc. The salutation offered by name to the more humble, who were perhaps not aware that they were so much as known to the apostle, could not but greatly cheer their hearts.

16. Ἀσπάσασθε ἀλλήλους, *salute ye one another*) supply: in *my name*.—ἐν φιλήματι ἁγίῳ, *with a holy kiss*) This was the flower of faith and love. *The kiss of love*, 1 Pet. v. 14. This was the practice after prayers. Paul mentions *the holy kiss* at the conclusion of the first epistle to the Thessalonians, of both his epistles to the Corinthians, and of this to the Romans. Paul wrote these epistles at the earliest period. Afterwards purity of

---

[1] A quotation from Juvenal Sat. xiii. 58—
"Tam venerabile erat præcedere quatuor annis."—ED.

[2] Where we find "*my* work-fellow:" but here "*our* helper," or *work-fellow*.—ED.

love was in some cases extinct or abuses arose, for in writing to the Ephesians, Philippians and Colossians, when he was in prison, he gave no charge concerning this kiss. The difference has regard to the time, not to the place, for the Philippians were in Macedonia, as well as the Thessalonians. I do not say however that the difference of time was altogether the only reason, why the holy kiss was commanded or not commanded. In the second Epistle to the Thessalonians there was no need to give directions about it so soon after the first had been received. The condition of the Galatians at that time rendered such directions unsuitable.—*αἱ ἐκκλησίαι*[1]) *the churches*) with whom I have been, ch. xv. 26. He had made known to them, that he was writing to Rome.

17. Ἀδελφοί, *brethren*) While he is embracing in his mind, in ver. 16, the churches of Christ, exhortation suggests itself incidentally; for when it is concluded in the form of a parenthesis, they, *who send salutations*, are added to those, *who receive them:* ver. 21.—*τοὺς τὰς*) There were therefore such men at Rome. The second epistle to the Thessalonians, which was written before this to the Romans, may be compared, ch. ii.—*τὰς διχοστασίας, divisions*) by which [what is even] good is not well defended.—*τὰ σκάνδαλα, offences*) by which [what is positively] evil gains admittance.—*ἐμάθετε, ye have learned*) To have once for all learned constitutes an obligation, 1 Cor. xv. 1; 2 Cor. xi. 4; Gal. i. 9; Phil. iv. 9; 2 Tim. iii. 14.—*ἐκκλίνατε*) comp. *στέλλεσθαι*, 2 Thess. iii. 6; *παραιτοῦ*, Tit. iii 10; comp. 1 Cor. v. 11; 2 John ver. 10. There was not yet the form of a church at Rome. The admonition therefore is rather framed so as to apply to *individuals*, than to the whole body of believers. There is however a testimony regarding the future in this epistle to the Romans, as the Song of Moses was a rule to be followed by Israel.

18. *οἱ τοιοῦτοι*) *such* as these. The substance with its quality is denoted.—*κοιλίᾳ*, the *belly*) Phil. iii. 19.—*χρηστολογίας*) as

---

[1] The Germ. Ver. has restored the reading of *πᾶσαι*, although it was declared on the margin of both Ed. as not quite so certain.—E. B.

DG*fg* omit *ἀσπαζ. ὑμ. αἱ ἐκκλ.* Πᾶσαι τ. Χριστοῦ, but add these words at the end of ver. 21. ABC Vulg. have all the words, including πᾶσαι, which Rec. Text omits without any good authority.—ED.

concerns themselves by promising.—εὐλογίας) as concerns you, by praising and flattering.—τῶν ἀκάκων) פה, a word of a middle signification, μέσον, for the sake of euphemy (See Append.), which the LXX. translate ἄκακος, and which occurs more than once in Proverbs. They are called ἄκακοι, who are merely free from badness, whereas they should also be strong in prudence, and be on their guard against the κακίαν, the badness of others.

19 'Υπακοή, *obedience*) which belongs to οἱ ἄκακοι, *the simple*. Their obedience itself, not merely its report, reached all, since by frequent intercourse believers from among the Romans came also to other places, and their obedience itself was observed face to face. It thus happens, that, as contagion is bad in the case of bad men, so it is good among the good, in a good sense.— πάντας, *all*) you, or others also.—ἀφίκετο) Hesychius explains ἀφίκετο by παρεγένετο.—τὸ ἐφ' ὑμῖν, *as far as you are concerned*) in opposition to those turbulent persons, who occasion him anxiety, not joy.—θέλω δὲ, *but I wish*) an antithesis : you are evidently not wanting in obedience and ἀκακία, simplicity; but you should add to them discretion.—σοφούς, *wise*) contrary to those, of whom Jeremiah speaks, iv. 22, σοφοί εἰσι τοῦ κακοποιῆσαι, τὸ δὲ καλῶς ποιῆσαι οὐκ ἐπέγνωσαν, *they are wise to do evil, but to do good they have no knowledge*.—ἀκεραίους) say, if any evil presents itself: I consider this a thing, which is alien to me; ἀκέραιος is taken here in a passive sense.[1]

20. Δὲ, *but*) [not *and*, as Engl. Ver. has it)] The power of God, not your prudence, will bring it to pass.—τῆς εἰρήνης, *of peace*) an antithesis to *seditious*, ver. 17, see 1 Cor. xiv. 33.— συντρίψει) the future, *shall bruise* Satan, when he shall bruise His apostles [viz. those breeders of *divisions*, ver. 17, 18.]—τὸν Σατανᾶν, *Satan*) the sower of strifes. Once in the course of this whole epistle he names the enemy, and nine times altogether in all his epistles, he calls him Satan; six times, the devil. Scripture indeed treats of God and Christ directly; of Satan and Antichrist indirectly.—ὑπό τοὺς πόδας, *under your feet*) Eph. vi. 15. Every victory achieved by faith is the cause of new grief to Satan.—ἐν τάχει) *speedily*, which refers to the beginnings of bruising [Satan, viz.] in the case of sudden danger [a sudden

---

[1] Unaffected by evil.—ED.

assault by him.]—ἀμήν) The transcribers very often added this word to prayers, although here almost all the copies are without it. *Baumgarten* however defends it.[1]

21. Συνεργός, *fellow-labourer*) He is placed here before the *kinsmen*. His name however is not found in ch. i. 1, because he had not been at Rome.

22. Ἀσπάζομαι, *I salute*) Tertius either by the advice or good-natured permission of Paul put in this salutation. Paul dictated, from which it is evident, how ready the apostles were in producing their books, without the trouble of premeditation.— Τέρτιος, *Tertius*) a Roman name. An amanuensis no doubt well known to the Romans.—ἐν, *in*) construed with *I who wrote;* an implied confession of faith.

23. Γάϊος, *Gaius*) a Corinthian, 1 Cor. i. 14.—ὅλης, *of the whole*) For very many used to resort to Paul.[2]—οἰκονόμος, *the chamberlain*) The faith of a man so very high in station could not but be a matter of joy to the Romans.—τῆς πόλεως, *of the city*) doubtless of Corinth.

24. Ἡ χάρις—ἡμῶν) The Alexandrians were without this reading.[3]—ἀμήν, we have lately spoken of this particle.

25. Τῷ δὲ, *now to Him*) As a doxology concludes the disquisition, ch. xi. 36, so it now concludes the whole epistle. So 2 Pet. iii. 18; Jude, ver. 25. The last words of this epistle plainly correspond to the first, ch. i. 1–5; especially in regard to " the Power of God," the ' Gospel,' ' Jesus Christ,' the ' Scriptures, the " obedience of faith," " all nations."—δυναμένῳ, *that is of power*—κατὰ τὸ εὐαγγελιόν μου, *according to my Gospel*) The power of God is certain, i. 16; Acts xx. 32, note.—ὑμᾶς, *you*) Jews and Gentiles.—στηρίξαι) we have the same word, i. 11.—ἀποκάλυψιν) This same word is found at i. 17.—κατὰ ἀποκάλυψιν must be construed with εὐαγγελιόν μου.—μυστηρίου, *of the mystery*) concerning the Gentiles being made *of the same body*, Eph. iii. 3, 6.—χρόνοις αἰωνίοις, *since the world began*)

---

[1] Rec. Text has it in opposition to ABCD(Λ)G Vulg. and almost all versions.—ED.

[2] Whom, as well as Paul, Gaius entertained.—ED.

[3] ABC Vulg. (Amiat. MS.) Memph. Versions omit it, whom Lachm. follows. But D(Λ)G*fg* have the words (except that G*g* omit Ἰησοῦ Χριστοῦ) and Tischend. accordingly reads them; as also the ἀμήν.—ED.

[during the eternal ages], from the time, when not only men, but even angels, were created, to both of whom the mystery had been at first unknown, Eph. iii. 9, 10. The *times* are denoted, which with their first commencement as it were touch upon the previous eternity, and are, so to speak, mixed with it; not eternity itself, of which times are only the streams; for the phrase, BEFORE *eternal* ages (Engl. Ver. *before the world began*) is used at 2 Tim. i. 9; Ps. lxxvii. (lxxvi.) 6, ἡμέρας ἀρχαίας καὶ ἔτη αἰώνια.—σεσιγημένου, *kept secret*) The Old Testament is like a clock in its silent course: the New Testament like the sound of brass, that is struck [viz. brazen cymbals, or drums]. In the Scriptures of the prophets, the calling of the Gentiles had been foretold; but the Jews did not understand it.

26. Φανερωθέντος, *made manifest*) Col. i. 26; 2 Tim. i. 10; Tit. i. 3.—ἐπιταγὴν, *commandment*) The foundation of his apostleship, 1 Tim. i. 1; Tit. i. 3.—τοῦ αἰωνίου Θεοῦ, *of the eternal God*) a very proper epithet, comp. the preceding verse, *during the eternal* ages, so Tit. i. 2. The silence on the part of God presupposes eternal knowledge, Acts xv. 18. The new Economy implies no change in God Himself; His own work is well known to Him from eternity. Comp. presently after, *to Him who is the only wise.*—ἔθνη, *nations*) not merely that they may know, but also that they may enjoy [the blessing so known].

27. Σοφῷ) *to the wise*) The wisdom of God is glorified by means of the Gospel in the Church, Eph. iii. 10; *who is of power* [able] ver. 25, and *to the wise* [both predicated of God], are joined together in this passage, as 1 Cor. i. 24, where Christ is said to be *the power of God and the wisdom of God.*—ᾧ, *to whom*) is put for αὐτῷ, *to Him.* So ὧν, ch. iii. 14; comp. 2 Tim. iii. 11; Acts xxvi. 7; 2 Cor. iv. 6, note, LXX., Is. v. 28. There would be a hiatus in the sentence without a pronoun.[1]—Ἀμήν, *amen*) and let every believing reader say, *Amen*.

---

[1] ACD(Λ) Hilary and Vulg. read ᾧ. B the oldest MS. omits it. Lachm. suggests we should adopt this omission and read with the Vulg. no τε between διὰ and γραφῶν and γνωρισθέντι, 'cognito,' for γνωρισθέντος. "To the only-wise God who is *made known through Jesus Christ.*" Else he *conjectures* that if we retain τε, ᾧ, and γνωρισθέντος, we must read χάρις after Θεῷ, "To the only-wise God be thanks through Jesus Christ. to whom be glory," etc.—ED.

ANNOTATIONS

ON

PAUL'S FIRST EPISTLE TO THE CORINTHIANS.

CHAPTER I.

1. Παῦλος, *Paul.* The epistle consists—

I. OF THE INSCRIPTION, ch. i. 1–3.

II. OF THE DISCUSSION; IN WHICH WE HAVE—
   I. An exhortation to concord, depressing the elated judgments of the flesh, ver. 4, iv. 21.
   II. A reproof,—
     1) For not putting away the wicked person, v. 1–13.
     2) For perverse lawsuits, vi. 1–11.
   III. An exhortation to avoid fornication, vi. 12–20.
   IV. His answer to them in regard to marriage, vii. 1, 10, 25, 36, 39.
   V. On things offered to idols, viii. 1, 2, 13—ix. 27—x. 1,—xi. 1.
   VI. On a woman being veiled, xi. 2.
   VII. On the Lord's Supper, xi. 17.
   VIII. On spiritual gifts, xii. xiii. xiv.
   IX. On the resurrection of the dead, xv. 1, 12, 29, 35.
   X. On the collection: on his own coming, and that of Timothy and Apollos; on the sum and substance of the whole subject, xvi. 1, 5, 10, 12, 13, 14.

III. OF THE CONCLUSION, xvi. 15, 17, 19, 20.

—ἀπόστολος Ἰησοῦ Χριστοῦ, *an apostle of Jesus Christ*) ver. 17.— διὰ θελήματος Θεοῦ, *by the will of God*) so 2 Cor. i. 1; Eph. i. 1; Col. i. 1; 2 Tim. i. 1. His apostleship is said to be " by the *commandment* of God," in 1 Tim. i. 1. This was the principle on which rested the apostolic authority in regard to the churches: and the principle of the zealous and humble mind which characterized Paul himself; comp. Rom. i. 1, note. For by the mention of *God*, human claim to wages (auctoramentum) is excluded, Gal. i. 1; by the mention of *the will of God*, merit on the part of Paul is excluded, ch. xv. 8, etc.: whence this apostle is in proportion the more grateful and zealous, 2 Cor. viii. 5, at the end of the verse. Had Paul been left to his own will, he would never have become an apostle.[1]—Σωσθένης, *Sosthenes*) a companion of Paul, a Corinthian. Apollos is not mentioned here, nor Aquila; for they do not appear to have been at that time with Paul, although they were in the same city, ch. xvi. 12, 19. In the second epistle, he joins Timothy to himself.

2. Τῇ ἐκκλησίᾳ τοῦ Θεοῦ, *To the Church of God*) Paul, writing somewhat familiarly to the Thessalonians, Corinthians, and Galatians, uses the term, *Church;* to the others he employs a more solemn periphrasis. The Church *of God in Corinth:* a great and joyful paradox.[2]—τῇ οὔσῃ, *which is*), [at Corinth and moreover] flourishing [there], ver. 5, 6. So, [the Church] *which was* [at Antioch], Acts xiii. 1.—ἡγιασμένοις, *to them that are sanctified*) them, who have been claimed for God [by being set apart as holy to Him]. Making a prelude already to the discussion, he reminds the Corinthians of their own dignity, lest they should suffer themselves to be enslaved by men. [*Then in the Introduction also*, ver. 4–9, *he highly praises the same persons, how near soever they may have come to undue elation of mind. The praise which is derived from Divine grace rather*

---

[1] It is of the greatest advantage to have the will of GOD for our guide. To attempt anything under the guidance of a man's own will is an undertaking full of hazard, under however specious a name it may be capable of being commended. In the world it readily produces embarrassments, troublesome and *very* difficult to be got rid of.—V. g.

[2] Religion and Corinth, a city notorious for debauchery, might have seemed terms utterly incapable of combination.—ED.

cherishes humility, besides being subservient to awakening.—
V. g.] The force of the participle is immediately explained, *called to be saints*, [said of the *Gentiles*, who are *saints by calling*, whilst the Israelites are so *by descent*]; comp. Rom. i. 7, note.—σὺν πᾶσι, *with all*) To be connected with, *sanctified*, and, *saints*, not with, *to the Church*; compare *ours*, at the end of the verse. Consequently the epistle refers also to the other believers in Achaia, 2 Cor. i. 1. The universal Church however is not shut up within the neighbourhood of *Corinth*. As Paul was thinking of the localities of the Corinthians and Ephesians, the whole Church came into his mind. The consideration of the Church universal sets the mind free from party bias, and turns it to obedience. It is therefore set forthwith before the Corinthians; comp. ch. iv. 17, vii. 17, xi. 16, xiv. 33, 36.— τοῖς ἐπικαλουμένοις) *that call upon*, so that they turn their eyes to Him in worship, and call themselves by His name; comp. ver. 10, on the authority of the name of Christ. [*This passage certainly prepares the way for that exhortation, which follows the verse now quoted* (ver. 10).—V. g.]—αὐτῶν [*theirs*], *of them*) near Corinth.—ἡμῶν [*ours*], *of us*) where Paul and Sosthenes were then staying.

5. Λόγῳ—γνώσει, *in word* (*utterance*)—*in knowledge*) The *word* (utterance) follows *knowledge*, in point of fact: and it is by the former that the latter is made known. He shows, that the Corinthians ought to be such in attainments, that it should be unnecessary to write to them. Moreover they were admirers of spiritual gifts; therefore by mentioning their gifts, he gains over to himself their affections, and makes a way for reproof.

6. Καθὼς, *even as*) That the Corinthians wanted nothing, he declares from this, that the testimony of Christ was confirmed in them. The particle is here demonstrative.—τοῦ Χριστοῦ, *of Christ*) Christ is not only the object, but the author of this testimony, Acts xviii. 8, note.—ἐβεβαιώθη, *was confirmed*) by Himself, and by the gifts and miracles, which accompanied it, xii. 3; 2 Cor. i. 21, 22; Gal. iii. 2, 5; Eph. iv. 7, 8; Heb. ii. 4.

7. Ὥστε ὑμᾶς μὴ ὑστερεῖσθαι, *So that ye are not behind*) This clause depends on *ye are enriched* by antithesis.—ἀπεκδεχομένους, *expecting*, [*waiting for*]) The character of the true or false Christian is either to expect or dread the revelation of Christ. [*Leaving*

to others their MEMENTO MORI, do thou urge this joyful expectation.—V. g.].

8. Ὅς, *who*) God, ver. 4 [not Jesus Christ, ver. 7] : comp. ver. 9.—ἕως τέλους, *even to the end*) an antithesis to the *beginning* implied in the phrase, *which was given*, ver. 4. This *end* is immediately described in this verse, comp. ch. xv. 24.—ἐν τῇ ἡμέρᾳ, *in the day*) construed with *unblamed* [*blameless*], 1 Thess. v. 23. After that day, there is no danger, Eph. iv. 30; Phil. i. 6. Now, there are our own days, in which we work, as also the days of our enemies, by whom we are tried; then there will be the day of Christ and of His glory in the saints.

9. Πιστὸς, *faithful*) God is said to be *faithful*, because He performs, what He has promised, and what believers promise to themselves from His goodness.—ἐκλήθητε, *ye were called*) Calling is a pledge of other benefits, [*to which the end, ver.* 8, *will correspond.*—V. g.]—Rom. viii. 30; [1 Thess. v. 24]; 1 Pet. v. 10.

10.[1] Δὲ, *Now*) The connection of the introduction and discussion: You have [already sure] the end and your hope, maintain also love. *Brethren*, is a title or address suitable to the discussion, on which he is now entering.—διὰ) *by*. This is equivalent to an adjuration.—τοῦ Κυρίου, *of the Lord*) Paul wishes that Christ alone should be *all things* to the Corinthians; and it is on this account, that he so often names Him in this chapter.—τὸ αὐτὸ λέγητε, *ye may speak the same thing*) In speaking they differed from one another; ver. 12.—σχίσματα, *divisions*) antithetic to κατηρτισμένοι, *joined together*: comp. Matt. iv. 21. Schism, a 'division' of minds [sentiments]: John vii. 43, ix. 16.—νοΐ, *in the mind*) within, as to things to be believed.—γνώμῃ, *judgment*) displayed, in things to be done. This corresponds to the words above, *that ye* [all] *speak* [*the same thing*].

11. Ἐδηλώθη, *it hath been declared*) an example of justifiable giving of information against others,—such information as ought not to be concealed without a reason, ch. xi. 18.—ὑπὸ τῶν Χλόης, *by those, who are of the house of Chloe*) These men seem to have obtained the special approbation both of Paul and of the Corinthians; as also the matron Chloe [sc. seems to have had

---

[1] Παρακαλῶ, *I exhort*) Though they required reproof, he employs a word, that takes the form *of exhortation*.—V. g.

their approbation], whose sons the Corinthians sent with letters to Paul, ch. vii. 1. They had sent Stephanas, Fortunatus and Achaicus, ch. xvi. 17, of whom the one or the other might even be a son of Chloe's, by Stephanas as the father, ver. 16, xvi. 15. —*ῥίδες, contentions*) He calls the thing by its own [right] name.

12. Λέγει, *says*) in a boasting manner; ver. 31, ch. iii. 21, 22.— Παύλου, *of Paul*) a gradation [ascending climax], in which Paul puts himself in the lowest place. Kephas, Paul and Apollos were genuine ministers and teachers of the truth, to boast of one of whom above the rest was in a greater degree unlawful, than if a believer of Corinth had said that he was a Christian belonging to Paul, with a view to distinguish himself from the followers of the false apostles.—Κηφᾶ, *of Kephas*) Peter does not seem to have been at Corinth, ch. iv. 6, and yet he was held there in high esteem, and that too justly; but some, however, abused it [this esteem for Peter into a party cry], and the apostle Paul detests this *Petrism*, which afterwards sprang up so much more rankly at Rome, just as much as he did *Paulism*. How much less should a man say, or boast, *I am of the Pope.*—ἐγώ—Χριστοῦ, *I—of Christ*) These spoke more correctly than the others, ver. 2, iii. 23, unless they despised their *ministers*, under this pretext, ch. iv. 8.

13. Μεμέρισται, *has* [Christ] *been divided?*) Are then all the members not now any longer under one Head? And yet, since He alone was crucified for you, is it not in the name of Him alone that ye have been baptized? The glory of Christ is not to be divided with His servants; nor is the unity of His body to be cut into pieces, as if Christ were to cease to be one.—μή) Lat. *num*:[1] it is often put in the second clause of an interrogation; ch. x. 22; 2 Cor. iii. 1.— ἐσταυρώθη—ἐβαπτίσθητε, *was crucified—ye were baptized*) The cross and baptism claim us for Christ. The correlatives are, redemption, and self-dedication.

14. Εὐχαριστῶ, *I give thanks*) The Providence of God reigns often in events, of which the reason is afterwards discovered. This is the language of a godly man, indicating the importance

---

[1] It expects a negative answer. "Was it Paul (*surely you will not say so*) that was crucified for you." This illustrates the *subjective* force of μή (*i.e.* referring to something in the *mind of the subject*); whilst οὐκ is objective.—ED.

of the subject, instead of the common phrase, *I rejoice.*—Κρίσπον καὶ Γάϊον, *Crispus and Gaius*) He brings forward his witnesses. Paul baptized with his own hand, the most respectable persons, not many others ; and not from ambition, but because they were among the first, who believed. The just estimation of his office is not pride, ch. xvi. 4. The administration of baptism was not so much the duty of the apostles, as of the deacons, Acts x. 48 ; nor did that circumstance diminish the dignity of this ordinance.

15. Ἵνα μὴ, *lest*) Paul obviates [guards beforehand against] the calumnies, which might otherwise have arisen, however unjust ; and takes them out of the way ; 2 Cor. viii. 20.—ἐμὸν, *my own*) as if I were collecting a company [of followers] for myself.

16.[1] Λοιπὸν, *for the rest* [as to what remains]) He is very anxious to be accurate in recording the facts as they occurred.—οὐκ οἶδα, *I do not know*) It does not occur to my memory without an effort.—εἴ τινα, *if any*) *i.e.* I have baptized no one else, or scarce any other ; comp. the following verse. He left it to the memory of the individuals [themselves to say], by whom they were baptized.

17. Ἀπέστειλε, *sent*) A man should attend wholly to that, for which he is sent.—βαπτίζειν, *to baptize*) [even] in His own name, much less in mine. The labour of baptism, frequently undertaken, would have been a hinderance to the preaching of the Gospel ; on other occasions [where not a hinderance to preaching] the apostles baptized ; Matt. xxviii. 19 ; especially [they administered that sacrament to] the first disciples.—εὐαγγελίζεσθαι, *to preach the Gospel*) This word, in respect of what goes before, is an accessory statement :[2] in respect of what follows, a Proposition. Paul uses this very [word as a] mode of transition, which is such that I know not, whether the rules of Corinthian eloquence would be in accordance with it. [*Therefore the Apostle*

---

[1] Καὶ τὸν Στεφανᾶ οἶκον, *the house of Stephanas also*) viz. the first fruits of Achaia, xvi. 15. The rest of the believers at Corinth may have been baptized by Silvanus, Timotheus, Crispus, Gaius, or at least by the members of the family of Stephanas.—V. g.

[2] The Latin, or rather the Greek word, is *syncategorema*. In logic categorematic words are those capable of being employed by themselves as the terms of a proposition. Syncategorematic words are merely accessory to the terms, such as adverbs, prepositions, nouns not in the nominative case, etc. —See Whateley's Logic, B. II., Ch. i. § 3.—T.

1 CORINTHIANS I. 18—20.

in this very passage furnishes a specimen, so to speak, of apostolic folly; *and yet there has been no want of the greatest wisdom throughout his whole arrangement.*—V. g.]—σοφία λόγου, *wisdom of words*) [*On account of which some individuals of you make me of greater or less importance than they do the rest.*—V. g.]—The nouns *wisdom* and *power* are frequently used here. In the opinion of the world, a *discourse* is considered *wise*, which treats of every topic rather than the cross; whereas a discourse on the cross admits of nothing heterogeneous being mixed up with it.—ὁ σταυρὸς τοῦ Χριστοῦ, *the cross of Christ*) ver. 24. Ignorance of the mystery of the cross is the foundation, for example, of the whole Koran. [*The sum and substance of the Gospel, as to its commencements, is implied,* ver. 18, 23, ii. 2. *He, who rejects* the cross, *continues in ignorance also of the rest of revealed truth; he, who receives it, becomes afterwards acquainted with its* power (or, *virtue,* 2 Pet. i. 5) *and* glory.—V. g.]

18. Μωρία, *folly*) and *offence*. See, immediately after, its antithesis, *power*. There are two steps in salvation, Wisdom and Power. In the case of them that perish, when the first step is taken away, the second [also] is taken away; in the case of the blessed, the second presupposes the first.—σωζομένοις, *to them, that are being saved*) The Present tense is used, as in the phrase, *to them that perish*. He, who has begun to hear the Gospel is considered neither as lost, nor as saved, but is at the point, where the two roads meet, and now he either is perishing, or is being saved.—δύναμις, *the power*) and *wisdom*, so also, ch. ii. 5.

19. Ἀπολῶ—ἀθετήσω) Isa. xxix. 14, LXX. καὶ ἀπολῶ—κρύψω; the intermediate words of them (LXX.) and of Paul are the same. —ἀπολῶ, *I will destroy*) hence *to bring to nought,* ver. 28, ch. ii. 6.

20. Ποῦ σοφός, ποῦ γραμματεύς; ποῦ συζητητὴς τοῦ αἰῶνος τούτου) Isa. xxxiii. 18, LXX., ποῦ εἰσι γραμματικοί; ποῦ εἰσιν οἱ συμβουλεύοντες; ποῦ ἐστιν ὁ ἀριθμῶν τοὺς συστρεφομένους. Hebr. איה ספר איה שקל את־המגדלים. The first half of the verse proposes two questions, of which the former is cleared up in the second half, and the latter in the verse following (We have also a similar figure in Isa. xxv. 6): *Where is the scribe? where is the weigher* (or, *receiver*)? *where is the scribe with the towers? where is the weigher* (or, *receiver*) *with a strong people, on whom thou canst not*

bear to look? For the expression appears to be proverbial, which the particle את, *with*, usually accompanies, and in this mode of speaking denotes universality, Deut. xxix. 18. That some charge of the towers was in the hands of the scribes, may be gathered from Ps. xlviii. 12, 13. The term, *weighers* (or *receivers*) is readily applicable to commanders of forces. Comp. Heinr. Scharbau Parerg. Phil. Theol. P. iv. p. 109, who has collected many facts with great erudition, and has furnished us with the handle for [the suggestion which originated] these reflections of ours. Paul brings forward both the passages in Isaiah against the Jews; but the second has the words so changed, as to apply more to recent times, and at the same time to the Gentiles, ver. 22. Some think that the three classes of learned men among the Jews, חכמים ספרים דרשים, are intended. We certainly find the first and second in Matt. xxiii. 34. There is moreover a threefold antithesis, and that too a very remarkable one, in Isa. xxxiii. 22, where the glorying of the saints in the Lord is represented. But this is what the apostle means to say: The wise men of the world not only do not approve and promote the Gospel, but they oppose it, and that too in vain.—τοῦ αἰῶνος τούτου) *of this world*, which is quite beyond the sphere of the " preaching of the cross" [ὁ λόγος ὁ τοῦ σταυροῦ, ver. 18].—ἐμώρανεν, *made foolish*) so that the world cannot understand the ground of the Divine counsel and good pleasure [εὐδόκησεν], ver. 21.—τὴν σοφίαν, *the wisdom*) *The wisdom of this world* [ver. 20], and *in the wisdom of God* [ver. 21], are antithetic.—κόσμου[1]) *of the world*, in which are the Jews and the Greeks.

21. Ἐν τῇ σοφίᾳ, *in the wisdom*) since [' because'] the wisdom of God is so great, ver. 25.—οὐκ ἔγνω, *knew not*) Before the preaching of the cross, although the creature proclaimed the Creator, although the most eloquent prophets had come, still the world knew not God. Those, who heard the prophets, despised them; those, who did not hear them, were of such a spirit, that they would have despised them.—διὰ τῆς σοφίας, *by*

---

[1] The margin of both editions defends the pronoun τούτου as the reading in this verse, although it is omitted in the Germ. Ver.—E. B.
ABC corrected later, and D corr. later, Orig. 3, 175c, omit τούτου. But Ggf Vulg. Orig. 3, 318e; Cypr. 324: Hilary 811, 822, have τούτου. —ED.

wisdom) viz., by the wisdom of *preaching*,[1] as is evident from the antithesis, by the *foolishness of preaching.*—εὐδόκησεν Θεὸς) *it pleased God*, in mercy and grace to us. Paul seems evidently to have imitated the words of the Lord, Luke x. 21.—διὰ τῆς μωρίας, *by the foolishness*) God deals with perverse man by contraries, so that man may deny himself, and render glory to God, through *belief in the cross.*—κηρύγματος, *of preaching*) inasmuch as it is concerning the cross.

22. [2] Αἰτοῦσι, *require*) from the apostles, as formerly from Christ.—σοφίαν, *wisdom*) [The Greeks require in] Christ the sublime philosopher, proceeding by demonstrative proofs.[3]

23. Ἡμεῖς, *we*) Paul, Apollos.—κηρύσσομεν, *we preach*) rather historically, than philosophically.—Χριστὸν ἐσταυρωμένον, *Christ crucified*) without the article. The cross is not mentioned in the following verse. The discourse begins with the cross of Christ, ii. 2; those who thus receive it are made acquainted with all connected with Christ and His glory, those who do not receive it, fall short of the whole, Act xxv. 19, xvii. 32.—σκάνδαλον, *a stumbling-block*) As *folly* and *wisdom*, so a *stumbling-block* and *a sign* are opposed to each other, for *a sign* is an attractive work of Omnipotence, as a *sign* and *power* are often synonymous, but *a stumbling-block*, properly applied to a snare or trap, is a very weak thing. [*So things extremely worthless in the present day come under the name* of trifles. *Germ.* Schwachherten.—V. g.] To such a degree do the Jews and Greeks[4] dread the cross of Christ, that along with it they reject even a sign and wisdom.

24. Αὐτοῖς) *to them*, construe with, *Jews*, and *Greeks.*—κλητοῖς,

[1] Not, "the world by *its* wisdom:" but, *notwithstanding the preaching of true wisdom by creation and by prophets of God, the world knew not God.*—ED.

[2] Σημεῖα, *signs*) powerful acts. We do not find any sign given by Paul at Corinth, Acts xviii.—V. g.

[3] They are not satisfied because Christ, instead of giving philosophic and *demonstrative* proofs, demands man's belief, on the ground of *His word*, and a reasonable amount of evidence.—ED.

[4] The Germ. Ver. prefers the reading of ἔθνεσι, equal, according to the margin of both editions, to "Ελλησι, which is doubtless more passable with German readers.—E. B.

ABC corrected later, D corr. 1. G*fg* Vulg. Orig. Cypr. Hilary have "ἔθνεσιν. Rec. Text, with Orig. 1, 331*e*, reads "Ἕλλησι.—ED.

who are called) Refer the calling, ver. 26, to this word.—Χριστὸν, *Christ*) with His cross, death, life, and kingdom. [*The surname* Crucified *is not added in this passage. When the offence of the cross is overcome, the whole mystery of Christ is laid open.*—V. g.]—δύναμιν—σοφίαν, *power—wisdom*) Power is first experienced, then wisdom.

25. Τοῦ Θεοῦ, *of God*) in Christ.—σοφώτερον—ἰσχυρότερον, *wiser—stronger*) ver. 30.—τῶν ἀνθρώπων, *than men*) The phraseology is abbreviated;[1] it means, wiser than the wisdom of men, stronger than the strength of men, although they may appear to themselves both wise and powerful, and may wish to define what it is to be wise and powerful.

26. Βλέπετε) *ye see*. *For* shows it to be the indicative mood.—τὴν κλῆσιν ὑμῶν, *your calling*) the state, in which the heavenly calling proves an offence to you; so, *calling*, vii. 20.—οὐ πολλοὶ, *not many*) Therefore, however, some supply, *have been called*. As a comparison has been made with the preachers, so also with the hearers of the Gospel. The ellipse contains a euphemism [see Append.[2]]—κατὰ σάρκα, *according to the flesh*) a phrase nearly related to the expression, *of the world*, which presently after occurs in ver. 27. The *world* judges according to the *flesh*.—εὐγενεῖς, *noble*) who are generally also wise and powerful. [*Can it be believed, that this is the distinctive characteristic of the society of those, who, in our vernacular tongue* (German) *are styled* Freymaurer, *Freemasons*.—V. g.]

27. Τὰ) The article has this force: *those things* in particular and especially, *which are foolish*, etc.—ἐξελέξατο, *hath chosen* [viz., *in great numbers*]) Acts xviii. 10—V. g.] ("I have *much people* in this city," *i.e.*, Corinth). This word is put thrice; election [*choosing*] and calling, ver. 26, are joined in one; Ez. xx. 5. The latter is a proof of the former. Election is the judgment of Divine grace exempting in Christ from the common destruction of men, those who accept their *calling* by faith. Every one who is *called*, is *elected* from the first moment of his faith; and so long as he continues in his *calling* and faith, he continues to be *elected;* if at any time he loses calling and faith, he ceases to be

---

[1] See App., under the title, Concisa Locutio.

[2] Σοφοὶ, *wise*) Hence such a small number of men were gained at Athens, which was the seat of Grecian wisdom.—V. g.

1 CORINTHIANS I. 28–30.

elected; when he brings forth fruit in faith, he confirms that *calling and election* in his own case: if he returns to faith, and believing falls asleep, he returns to his state of election, and as one *elected* falls asleep. And these κατ' ἐξοχήν, pre-eminently, are the men who are *elected* and *foreknown*. *Election* relates either to *peoples* or *individuals*. The question here and in Ez. xx. 5 : also Acts xviii. 10 ; 1 Thess. i. 4 : is concerning the election *of a people;* and this species of *election* in a greater degree falls under the distinct perceptions of men that are believers, than *the election of individuals;* for some individuals of the people may fall away, and yet the breadth of *calling* and *election* [*i.e.* the calling viewed in its comprehension of the whole people as such] may be equally preserved. The election of some outside of the church is a Thing Reserved for God Himself, and must not be tried by the rule of the preaching of the Gospel.[1]—τοὺς σοφοὺς, *the wise*) In the masculine to express a very beautiful idea ;[2] the rest are neuter, as all standing in opposition to τοὺς σοφοὺς, yea even *foolish things.*—καταισχύνῃ, *might put to shame* [*confound*]) This word is twice repeated ; we have afterwards, *might bring to nought* [ver. 28]. By both of these words *glorying* [ver. 29, 31] is taken away, whether the subject of boasting be more or less voluntary.

28. Τὰ μὴ ὄντα, *the things that are not*) A genus, under which are included things *base* and *despised*, as also things *foolish* and *weak*. There is therefore an apposition, to the whole of which is opposed this one phrase, *which are.*—τὰ ὄντα) *which are* something.

29. "Οπως μὴ, *that not*) The antithesis to, *that*, ver. 31.—πᾶσα σὰρξ, *all flesh*) a suitable appellation ; *flesh* is beautiful and yet frail, Is. xl. 6.—ἐνώπιον, *before*) We may not glory *before* Him, but *in* Him.

30. Ἐξ αὐτοῦ, *of Him*) Ye are *of God*, not now any longer *of the world*, Rom. xi. 36 ; Eph. ii. 8.—ὑμεῖς, *ye*) An antithesis to *many*, ver. 26. Those persons themselves, whom the apostle addresses, *ye*, were *not the many wise men according to the flesh*, etc.—ἐστὲ ἐν Χριστῷ Ἰησοῦ, *ye are in Christ Jesus*) ye are Chris-

---

[1] Which restricts salvation to them that believe.—ED.
[2] Viz., That even *things* (and, those too, foolish things) are chosen by God to confound *persons* (and, those too, persons who are wise).—ED.

tians, etc. The antithesis is between, *things which are not* [ver. 28], and, *ye are* [ver. 30]; likewise *flesh* [ver. 26, 29], and *Christ* [ver. 30].—ἐγενήθη ἡμῖν, *is made to us*) More is implied in these words, than if he had said; *we have become wise*, etc., He is made to us wisdom, etc., in respect of our knowledge, and, before that was attained, by Himself in His cross, death, resurrection. *To us* the dative of advantage.—σοφία, *wisdom*) whereas we were formerly *fools*. The variety of the Divine goodness in Christ presupposes that our misery is from ourselves.— δικαιοσύνη, *righteousness*) Whereas we were formerly *weak* (without strength) [Rom. v. 6], comp. Is. xlv. 24. *Jehovah, our righteousness*, Jer. xxiii. 6, where (comp. ver. 5) he is speaking of the Son: for the Father is not called *our righteousness.*—ἁγιασμὸς, *sanctification*) whereas we were formerly *base.*—ἀπολύτρωσις) *redemption*, even to the utmost; whereas we were formerly *despised*, ἐξουθενημένοι [ver. 28].

31. Ἵνα, *that*) viz. *it may be.*—ὁ καυχώμενος, *he who glories*) It is not the privilege of all to glory.—ἐν Κυρίῳ, *in the Lord*) not in himself, not in the flesh, not in the world.

CHAPTER II.

1. Κἀγω, *and I*) The apostle shows, that he was a suitable instrument in carrying out the counsel and election *of God.*— οὐ) This word is not construed with ἦλθον, but with the words that follow.—λόγου ἢ σοφίας, *of speech or of wisdom*) Speech follows *wisdom*, a sublime discourse [follows] a sublime subject.— καταγγέλλων ὑμῖν τὸ μαρτύριον, *declaring* [announcing] *unto you the testimony*) Holy men do not so much testify, as declare the testimony, which God gives.—τὸ μαρτύριον τοῦ Θεοῦ, *the testimony of God*) in itself most wise and powerful. The correlative is, *faith*, ver. 5.

2. Οὐ γὰρ ἔκρινα, *for I determined not*) Although I knew many other things, yet I so acted, as if I did not know them. If a minister of the Gospel however abstains from the things, in which he excels, in order that he may simply preach Christ, he

derives the highest benefit from them. The Christian doctrine ought not, for the sake of scoffers and sceptics, and those who admire them, to be sprinkled and seasoned with philosophical investigations, as if in sooth it were possible to convince them more easily by means of natural theology. They, who obstinately reject revelation, will not be gained by any reasonings from the light of nature, which only serves the purpose of instructing in the first rudiments of (theological) education.— ἔκρινα) This word with its compounds is often used by Paul in this epistle to the Corinthians, ver. 13, etc., iv. 3, etc., xi. 29, 31, 32, 34.—Ἰησοῦν Χριστὸν, *Jesus Christ*) Paul well knew, how little the world esteemed this name.[1]

3. Καὶ ἐγὼ, *and I*) The antithesis is, *my speech*, ver. 4; and, to *know*, ver. 2. For he describes the subject [ver. 2, *to know Christ crucified*], the preacher [ver. 3, *and I*], the mode of speaking [ver. 4, *my speech—not with enticing words*].—ἀσθενείᾳ, *in weakness*) It is opposed to, *power* [ver. 4]. We must not suppose that the apostle's state of mind was always pleasant and quite free from all perturbations, 2 Cor. vii. 5, xi. 30; Gal. iv. 13.—καὶ ἐν φόβῳ καὶ ἐν τρόμῳ πολλῷ, *and in fear and in much trembling*) This is a proverbial saying, and denotes the fear, which abounds to such a degree as even to fall upon the body and its gestures and movements, Mark v. 33; Eph. vi. 5; Phil. ii. 12; LXX., Deut. xi. 25. So Is. xix. 16, LXX., ἔσονται ἐν φόβῳ καὶ ἐν τρόμῳ, "*They shall be in fear and trembling.*"[2] The world admires any thing but this [the very contrary to all this].— ἐγενόμην,) *I began to be, with* you, towards you.

4. Λόγος, *speech*) in private.—κήρυγμα, *preaching*) in public.— πειθοῖς) *enticing*, a very appropriate term, to which the antithesis is *in demonstration*. Didymus quotes this passage, Lib. 2 de Spir. S. Jerome translates πειθοῖς λόγοις, *with persuasions*,[3] so that there should be an apposition, πειθοῖς λόγοις [πειθοῖς being regarded as a noun]. It comes in this view from πειθὼ, to which πειθή is a kindred form. Hesychius has πειθή, πεισμονὴ, πίστις.— σοφίας, *of wisdom*) He explains in the following verses, what the

---
[1] Εσταυρωμένον, *crucified*) An antithesis to "sublime wisdom," ver. 1.—V. g.
[2] An antithesis to "excellency of speech," ver. 1.—V. g.
[3] Cod. Amiat. of Vulg. reads "persuasione verbi." Other old MSS. "persuasibilibus verbis."—ED.

wisdom is, of which the speeches and arguments are to be set aside.

5. Σοφίᾳ, *in the wisdom*) and power.—δυνάμει, *in the power*) and wisdom.

6. Σοφίαν δὲ λαλοῦμεν, *but we speak wisdom*) He returns, as it were after a parenthesis, to what he had slightly mentioned at i. 23–25 : *we speak*, contains by implication an epanalepsis[1] of the words, *we preach* [ch. i. 23] ; but *we speak* refers to something secret, as appears from comparing ver. 7, 13 ; *we preach*, to something public ; for *wisdom* here denotes not the whole of the Christian doctrine, but its sublime and secret leading principles. There is also an antithesis of the past tense, ver. 1, etc. [*came—determined*, etc.], and of the present in this passage [we speak].—ἐν τοῖς τελείοις) *in the case* of [" *penes* perfectos ;" as far as concerns] *them that are perfect*, at Corinth or elsewhere. Construe with, *we speak*. The knowledge of God and Christ is the highest knowledge. Comp. ἐν, xiv. 11 [ὁ λαλῶν ἐν ἐμοὶ βάρβαρος,—a barbarian, *unto* me] Phil. i. 30.[2] Not only worldly and natural men are opposed to the *perfect*, even to the end of the chapter, but also *carnal men* and *babes*, ch. iii. at the beginning ; Heb. v. 14, 13.—οὐ—οὐδὲ, *not—nor*) *God* is opposed to the *world*, ver. 7 ; the *apostles, to the princes of the world*, ver. 8, etc.—ἀρχόντων, *of the princes*) i. 20. Paul uses a word of wide signification, in which he comprehends men of rank both among the Jews and Greeks.—τῶν καταργουμένων, *who come to nought*) i. 19, 28. This epithet applies to the princes of the world, and to the world itself ; whence it is evident, that the wisdom of the world is not true, because it does not lead men to immortality.

7. Ἐν μυστηρίῳ, τὴν ἀποκεκρυμμένην, *in a mystery*, [even] *the hidden* [wisdom]) It is concealed before it is brought forward, and when it is brought forward, it still remains hidden to many, namely to those that are imperfect.—προώρισεν, *ordained before*) The allusion is to *hath prepared*, ver. 9.—πρὸ, *before*) therefore *it does not come to nought*, ver. 6. This wisdom very far surpasses

---

[1] See App. Where the same word or words are in the beginning of a preceding member, and in the end of a following member ; thus marking a parenthesis ; as here, from c. i. 23–25, to c. ii. 6.

[2] "The same conflict which ye saw *in* me, and now hear to be *in* me," ἐν ἐμοί. So here, " we speak *in the case of* the perfect."—ED.

worldly wisdom in antiquity.—αἰώνων, *the ages* [of the world]) in the plural. The antithesis to it is, *of this world*, ver. 6.—εἰς, *unto*) that it may be our *glory;* comp. the following verse, and *glorying*, i. 31.—δόξαν) *glory*, from the Lord of glory; ver. 8, afterwards to be revealed, at the time when the princes of the world *shall come to nought*. It is an antithesis to, *mystery*.

8. "Ἡν, *which*) a reference to *wisdom*.—οὐδεὶς τῶν ἀρχόντων— ἔγνωκεν, *none of the princes—knew*) *none*, almost none, nay, none at all, as [quâ] *a prince*. The antithesis to this predicate is in the *but* ver. 9; to the subject, in the *but* ver. 10.—τὸν Κύριον, *the Lord*) who surpasses all *princes*.—ἐσταύρωσαν) *The cross*, the punishment of slaves. It was with this *the Lord* of glory was slain.

9. Ἀλλὰ, *but*) viz. *it has happened*, comp. Rom. xv. 3, 21, and 1 Cor. i. 31.—καθὼς, *as*) He shows that the princes of the world knew not wisdom.—ἃ ὀφθαλμὸς) Isa. lxiv. 4, in the LXX., ἀπὸ τοῦ αἰῶνος οὐκ ἠκούσαμεν, οὐδὲ οἱ ὀφθαλμοὶ ἡμῶν εἶδον Θεὸν πλὴν σοῦ, καὶ τὰ ἔργα σου, ἃ ποιήσεις τοῖς ὑπομενοῦσιν ἔλεος. " Since the beginning we have not heard, nor have our eyes seen any god besides Thee and Thy works, which Thou wilt do to them that wait for mercy."—ἃ, *which*) *what eye hath not seen* are those things, *which God hath prepared*.—ὀφθαλμὸς, οὖς, the *eye, the ear*) of man.—οὐκ ἀνέβη) *neither have ascended* [*entered*], that is, have not come into the mind.—ἡτοίμασεν, *prepared*) Hebr. יעשׂה, *he will do;* what was future in the time of Isaiah, had been actually accomplished in the time of Paul. Hence the one was speaking to *them that were waiting for Him* [Isa. lxiv. 4], the other to *men that love* [Him, who *has* appeared, 1 John iv. 19]: comp. *things that are freely given*, ver. 12, by the *grace* of the New Testament, the fruits of which are perfected in eternity.—[Rom. viii. 28; James ii. 5.]

10. Ἡμῖν) *to us*, apostles.—ἀπεκάλυψε, *hath revealed*) an antithesis to, *hidden* [*wisdom*, ver. 7]. Comp. Isa. xlv. 19, 15; Ps. li. 8, and again Luke x. 21.—πάντα, *all things*) ver. 9.—τὰ βάθη, *the deep things*) very much hidden, Ps. xcii. 6; not merely those things, which believers search out, ver. 9 [10] and 12, in both at the end. The deep things of God, even of His divine nature, as well as of His kingdom.

11. Τίς γὰρ οἶδεν ἀνθρώπων τὰ τοῦ ἀνθρώπου; *For who among men*

knoweth the things of a man?) The Alexandrian MS. and it alone omits 'Ανθρώπων, and yet Artem. Part I. cap. 47 desires it to be marked with a stroke as spurious.[1] But this variety of cases, viz. *among,* or *of men, of man, of a man,* is extremely appropriate to the purpose of the apostle here; for he notices the similarity of nature, which appears to give men the mutual knowledge of each other's feelings as men, and yet does not give it; how much less will any one know God without the Spirit of God?—τὰ τοῦ ἀνθρώπου, *the things of a man*), the things that are within him.— τὸ πνεῦμα τοῦ ἀνθρώπου, *the spirit of that man*). The Article τὸ evidently denotes the spirit peculiar to man, not that entering into him from any other quarter.—τὸ ἐν αὐτῷ, *which is in him*) The criterion of truth, the conscious nature in man (conscience). —οὐδεὶς) *not one,* of all outside of [excepting] God. Not even his fellow-man knows a man; God is One alone, [having no fellow] and known to Himself alone.—τὸ πνεῦμα, *the Spirit*) The Godhead cannot be separated from the Spirit of God, as manhood cannot be separated from the spirit of man.

12. Τὸ πνεῦμα τοῦ κόσμου, *the spirit of the world*) Eph. ii. 2.— ἐλάβομεν) The spirit of the world *is not received;* but they are always under its influence, who are of the world. *We have received* the Spirit of God.—ἐκ, *from* [God]) an antithesis to *in* [*him,* man], ver. 11.

13. Καὶ, *also*) Thus the phrases, *we might know* and *we speak* are joined.—διδακτοῖς, *taught*) consisting of doctrine and instruction. The word σοφίας with λόγοις is not to be resolved into an epithet; *wisdom* is the gushing fountain of *words.*—ἀλλ' ἐν, *but in*) an immediate antithesis; nor can it be said, that the apostles compared merely the natural power of speech, as distinguished on the one hand from art, and on the other, from the Spirit.— διδακτοῖς) διδαχῇ[2] *by the teaching,* which the Holy Spirit[3] fur-

---

[1] BCD (Λ) G*fg* Vulg. Orig. 1, 197*a*; 524*a*; 3, 571*b*; Hilary, read ἀνθρώπων. A and Orig. 2, 644*c*, omit it.—ED.

[2] The Germ. Ver. agrees to this reading, although the Greek editions have left the matter undecided.—E. B.

[3] The Germ. Vers., with the margin of Ed. 2, approves of the omission of the adjective, ἁγίου, more distinctly than the margin of the older edition. —E. B.

Διδακτοῖς is the reading of ABCD(Λ)G Orig. (B, according to Bartolocci,

nishes through us seems to be a better reading. That *doctrine* comprehends both wisdom and words.—πνευματικοῖς πνευματικὰ, *spiritual things to* [*with;* Engl. Vers. and Vulg.] *spiritual*) We interpret [But Engl. Vers. and Vulg. *comparing*) spiritual things and spiritual words in a manner suitable to spiritual men, ver. 6, 15, so that they may be willing and able to receive them; συγκρίνω, σύγκριμα, σύγκρισις, are frequently used by the LXX. for example, in respect to the interpretation of dreams, Gen xl. and xli.; Dan. ii. iv. v. vii.

14. Ψυχικὸς, *the natural* [animal] *man*) whatsoever and how great soever he may be, who is without the Spirit of God. Ephraim Syrus well remarks: "The apostle called men, who lived according to nature, *natural,* ψυχικοὺς; those who lived contrary to nature, *carnal,* σαρκικοὺς; but those are *spiritual,* πνευματικοί, who even change their nature into the spirit, *i.e.* conform their natural disposition to what is spiritual," [μεθαρμοζόμενοι τὴν φύσιν εἰς τὸ πνεῦμα], f. 92. So *flesh* and *blood*, Matt. xvi. 17, note. —οὐ δέχεται, *does not receive*) although they be offered, yet *he does not wish* to avail himself of the offer; comp. δέξασθε, *receive.* Here presently after there follows the corresponding phrase, *he cannot.* Comp. Rom. viii. 7. The reason is added to each [aetiology, see Appen.], by the words, *for,* and *because.* [*Each forms an antithesis to the mind of Paul expressed at* 1 Tim. i. 15, *faithful and worthy of all* ACCEPTATION, πιστὸς καὶ πάσης ἀποδοχῆς ἄξιος.—V. g.]—τὰ τοῦ πνεύματος,[1] *the things of the Spirit*) In like manner, *the things of God,* ver. 11.—μωρία, *folly*) Whereas he seeks wisdom, i. 22.—οὐ δύναται, *he cannot*) he has not the *spirit and the power.*—γνῶναι, *to know*) *the things of the Spirit of God.*—πνευματικῶς) only *spiritually.*

15. 'ο) There is great beauty here in the addition of the article [*the* spiritual man]; ψυχικὸς [*a* natural man] is without

reads διδακτῷ). But *fg*, Vulg. Syr. read διδαχῇ. Ἁγίου is placed before or after πνεύματος in the later Syr. and Rec. Text. But ABCD corrected later, G, Origen 1, 197*b*, Vulg. omit ἁγίου (Vulg. corrected by Victor has *Sancti*).—ED.

[1] The Germ. Vers. does not conceal that τοῦ Θεοῦ is added, although the omission on the margin of both editions is considered to be better established. —E. B.
ABCD(Λ)G*fg* Vulg. Orig. Hilary 64, read τοῦ Θεοῦ. But Syr. Version, Iren. and Hilary, 344, omit the words.—ED.

the article.—πάντα, *all things*) The neuter plural, as ver. 9–14, *all things* of all men, and therefore also [he judges] all men. The Masc. is comprehended in the Neut. as Matt. xi. 27.—αὐτὸς) *he himself.*—ὑπ' οὐδενὸς, *by no*) *natural man.*

16. Τίς, *who*) no one who is a mere man; comp. Jer. xxiii. 18; Isa. xl. 13; the LXX., τίς ἔγνω νοῦν Κυρίου—ὃς συμβιβάσει αὐτὸν. —ὅς, *who*) This is not the interrogative, but the relative, by which the force of the question, which is in the τίς, is extended [continued to the latter clause, ὅς συμβιβ. αὐτὸν], it means, *and therefore.*—νοῦν Χριστοῦ, *the mind of Christ*) The Spirit of the Father and of the Son is the same.—ἔχομεν, *we have*) That is both more and less than *to know*: he who has the mind of Christ, *judges* [judicially decides upon] all things, and *is judged* by no man.

CHAPTER III.

1. Καὶ ἐγὼ, *and I*) He spoke, ii. 1, of his first 'coming' among them: he now speaks of his progress.—ὡς σαρκικοῖς, *as to carnal*) This is a more gentle expression, than *natural*, especially with the additional mitigation, *as babes in Christ*, in regard to the degree of attainment, which immediately followed.

2. Γάλα, *milk*) He speaks in this way to bring the Corinthians to humility.—οὐ, *not*) supply, *I have fed*, or any other word, akin to, *I have given you drink*. An instructor does not necessarily teach what he himself knows, but what is suitable to his hearers. Scripture is perfect; for, as an example, to the Corinthians *milk* is supplied; to the Hebrews, *solid food*.

3. Ὅπου) *where.*—ζῆλος, *envying*) This refers to the state of feeling.—ἔρις, *strife*) to the words.—διχοστασίαι, *divisions*) to the actions. The style of writing increases in strength; he had used the word *contentions*, i. 11; he now multiplies the words; in like manner he uses the word *glorying*, iii. 21; afterwards, a severer expression, *to be puffed up*, iv. 6.—κατὰ ἄνθρωπον, *according to the ways of men*) not *according to the ways of God; after the manner of men.*

1 CORINTHIANS III. 4–9.

4. Οὐχί,[1] *are ye not*) For the Spirit does not endure party-spirit among men.

5. Τίς; *who?*) He returns to what he began with.—διάκονοι, *ministers*) a lowly expression and on that account appropriate here.—δι' ὧν, *by whom*), not in whom. Pelagius correctly observes on this passage, *If we, whom He himself has constituted ministers, are nothing, how much more those, who glory in carnal things?*—ἑκάστῳ, *to every man*) i.e. *every man as well as they*.—ὁ Κύριος, *the Lord*) The correlative is, διάκονοι, *ministers*.—ἔδωκεν, *has given*) in various ways and degrees; see the following verse.

6. Ἐφύτευσα—ἐπότισεν, *I planted—he watered*) Acts xviii. 1, xix. 1. Afterwards with the same view, he speaks of *the foundation* and *what is reared upon it*; of *a father, and instructors* [ch. iv. 15].—ηὔξανεν, *gave the increase*) ver. 10, at the beginning; Acts xviii. 27, at the end.

7. Ὁ φυτεύων, ὁ ποτίζων) *he that planteth, he that watereth*, as such; or the very act of *planting* and *watering*.—ὁ αὐξάνων, [God] *who gives the increase*) viz.: ἐστὶν τὶ, *something*; and therefore, because He alone is some thing, He is all things [all in all]. Without this increase, the grain from the first moment of sowing would be like a pebble; from the increase, when given, belief instantly springs up, ver. 5.

8. Ἕν) *one*; neither of them is so much as *anything*. As one star in the heavens shines high above another; but the unscientific man does not perceive the difference in the height; so the Apostle Paul shone far above Apollos; but the Corinthians did not understand this, and Paul in this passage does not instruct them much on that point; he merely asserts the eminent superiority of Christ.—ἴδιον—ἴδιον, *his own—his own*) an appropriate repetition, and an antithesis to *one*.—μισθὸν, *reward*) something beyond salvation, ver. 14, 15. The faithful steward will receive praise, the diligent workman a reward.—κόπον, *labour*) not merely *according to the work* [*done*], but according to each man's *labour*].

9. Θεοῦ, *of God*) This word is solemnly repeated immediately after,[2] and is emphatically put at the beginning thrice; as in

---

[1] Ὅταν γὰρ, *for when*) See how important a matter may be, which seems to be of no consequence.—V. g.

[2] By the figure anaphora, *i.e.*, the frequent repetition of words in the

ver. 10, *grace;* and in ver. 11, *foundation.*—συνεργοί, *labourers together with*) We are God's *labourers,* and in turn *labourers together with* Him.—γεώργιον, *husbandry*) This constitutes the sum of what goes before; γεώργιον, a word of wide and comprehensive meaning, comprising the field, the garden, and the vineyard.—οἰκοδομὴ, *building*) This constitutes the sum of what follows.

10. Χάριν, *grace*) By this word he takes anticipatory precaution [προθεραπείαν], not to appear arrogantly to pronounce himself *wise.*—δοθεῖσαν, *given*) it was therefore a something habitual in Paul.[1]—σοφὸς) [*wise*] *skilful.* The knowledge of Jesus Christ makes men so.—θεμέλιον, *foundation*) The foundation is the first beginning.—ἄλλος) *another,* whoever he is. He elegantly avoids mentioning the proper name. The predecessor does not see his successor, and Paul has regard to the dignity of Apollos; so immediately after, *every man;* for there were also others, iv. 15. —βλεπέτω, let him see [take heed]) I, says Paul, have done my part; let them see to theirs, who follow me in this work.—πῶς) *how,* how far *wisely,* how far in *builder*-like style.

11. Γὰρ, *for*) The reason, why he says so deliberately, *builds thereon.*—οὐδεὶς, *no man*) not even Apollos.—θεῖναι, *lay*) at Corinth, and wherever Christ was made known.—Ἰησοῦς Χριστὸς, *Jesus Christ*) each name here is properly placed.

12. Εἰ) *whether* [But Engl. Ver. *if*]. Comp. *of what sort,* ver. 13. There is an indirect question, which does not require the mark of interrogation. In ver. 13, there is the apodosis, whether εἰ be taken as an interrogative, or means *if.*—χρυσόν, *gold*) He enumerates three kinds of things, which bear fire; as many, which are consumed by it; the former denote men that are true believers; the latter, hypocrites: Moreover, the abstract is included in the concrete, so that on the one hand true and solid doctrines, or, on the other hand, false and worthless doctrines are denoted together; in both cases, doctrines either of greater or less importance. Even a grain of gold is gold: even the lightest straw feeds the fire.—λίθους τιμίους, *precious stones*) This does not apply to small *gems,* but to noble stones, as *marble,* etc.—ξύλα, *wood*) In the world, many buildings are fitly con-

beginnings of Sections, or in adorning and amplifying weighty arguments. —Append.—T.

[1] Which is the force of the article, τὴν χάριν τὴν δοθεῖσαν.—ED.

structed of wood; but not so in the building of God, comp. Rev. xxi. 18, 19.—καλάμην) *stubble.*
13. Ἔργον) the *work,* which any one has erected.—ἡ ἡμέρα, *the day*) of the Lord. So Heb. x. 25, comp. presently ch. iv. 3, 5, where, after an interval, as usual, he speaks more clearly. Previous days, which vividly realize to us the fire, for instance, in adversity and at death, are not altogether excluded.—δηλώσει, *shall declare*) to all.—[*Many things are also revealed sooner, at least to some, but Paul lays down the last and most certain day of fiery trial.*—V. g.]—ἐν πυρὶ ἀποκαλύπτεται) is revealed in fire, viz., the Lord, whose day that is; or, the work [so Engl. Vers.]; 2 Thess. i. 7, 8, *is revealed,* as present, because it is certain and near, Rev. xxii. 20.—τὸ πῦρ, *the fire*) a metaphor, as throughout this whole discourse. The fire of the last day and of the Divine judgment is intended, as is evident from the subsequent language, which peculiarly applies to the last judgment, iv. 5; 2 Cor. v. 10 [2 Thess. i. 8]; to which the visible fire on that day will correspond.—δοκιμάσει) *shall try,* not *shall purge.* This passage not only does not support [add fuel to] *the fire of purgatory,* but entirely extinguishes it; for it is at the last day, and not till then, that the *fire* shall finally try every man's work; therefore the fire of purgatory does not precede it. Nor on that very day, shall the work be *purged;* but it shall be tried, of what sort it *previously* was on either side [good or bad], when it shall either remain or be burnt up.
14. Εἴ τινος, *if any man's*) Hence Paul is accustomed to promise glory to himself from the constancy of his brethren [*hence also to derive exhortations*], 2 Cor. i. 14; Phil. ii. 16; 1 Thess. ii. 19.
15. Ζημιωθήσεται, *he shall suffer loss*) He shall fail in obtaining the reward, not in obtaining salvation.—αὐτὸς) he *himself.*— σωθήσεται, *shall be saved*) because he does not forsake *this* foundation, ver. 12.—ὡς, *as*) a particle of explanation and limitation; *as* one who should be obliged to go through *fire.*—διὰ, *through*) So διὰ, through [= *with*], Rom. ii. 27 : *not without fire,* comp. ver. 13. As the shipwrecked merchant, though he has lost his merchandise and his gain, is saved through the waves.[1]

---

[1] Is saved, though having to pass through the waves.—ED.

16. Ναὸς, *the temple*) The most noble kind of *building.*—ἐστὲ, *ye are*) the whole of you together.—τὸ πνεῦμα, *the Spirit*). The indwelling of the Holy Spirit, and that of God, are held in the same estimation [are equivalent]: therefore the high honour due to the Holy Spirit is the same as that due to God, vi. 19.

17. Φθείρει, *destroys*] by schisms according to the wisdom of the world.—φθερεῖ, *shall destroy*) by a most righteous retaliation in kind [φθερεῖ answering to φθείρει]. There are many punishments, which do not flow from sin by physical connection.—ἅγιος, *holy*) divine, inviolable.

18. Δοκεῖ) This word is frequently used, as well as λογίζομαι, in the epistles to the Corinthians; but δοκῶ more in the first; the other, with a milder signification in the second. The meaning here is, *if any man be wise, and think that he is so.* For often, in this epistle especially, δοκῶ has such a force as that the fact of the thing itself is not denied, but there is denoted along with the fact, the estimation, which the man, who has that thing [that subject of his self-esteem], entertains concerning himself, whether [that estimation] be just or inflated [exaggerated] vii. 40, viii. 2, x. 12, xi. 16, xiv. 37.—σοφὸς, *wise*) Hereby he entirely cuts off all wisdom, whether of this world or divine. [*It is indeed wretched wisdom* to deceive *one's own self.*—V. g.] For in whatever species of wisdom every man wishes to be distinguished, in the same kind of wisdom he ought first of all to deem himself a fool, that he may become wise.

19. Ὁ δρασσόμενος τοὺς σοφοὺς ἐν τῇ πανουργίᾳ αὐτῶν) Eliphaz in Job v. 13, in the LXX., says, ὁ καταλαμβάνων σοφοὺς ἐν τῇ φρονήσει. The apostles seem to have kept very much by the words of the LXX. Interpreters in passages very well known to the Hellenists [the Greek-speaking Jews], for example in the Parschijoth[1] and Haphtaroth, and likewise in the Psalms; but they have recourse to the Hebrew, in passages less generally used, such as this passage of Job. Paul has also in another place referred to Job. See Phil. i. 19, note.—ἐν, *in*) not only whilst they think that they are acting wisely, but in such a way, that their very wisdom is a snare to them.

---

[1] Parschijoth, sections of the Pentateuch; Haphtaroth, sections of the Prophets, read publicly.—T.

20. Σοφῶν, *of the wise*) LXX. have ἀνθρώπων, *of men*. The word, *thoughts*, not in itself, but with this addition, *of the wise*, corresponds to the Hebrew word מחשבות, Ps. xciv. 11, LXX.—εἰσὶ, *are*) *men*, namely with their thoughts; see Ps. now quoted in the Hebrew.

21. Ἐν ἀνθρώποις, *in men*) This appertains to [has the effect of] extenuation.[1]—πάντα, *all things*) not only *all men*.—ὑμῶν, *yours*) Those things are yours; not you theirs, i. 12; 2 Cor. iv. 5.

22. Παῦλος, *Paul*) Paul, as if a stranger to himself, comes forward in the third person and shows how it was the duty of the Corinthians to speak of him, and he places himself, as if he were lowest in rank,[2] first in the enumeration.—Κηφᾶς, *Cephas*) They were wont to glory also in Peter, which also was wrong. See note on i. 12.—κόσμος, *the world*) He by a sudden bound extends his remarks from Peter to the whole world, as if he were in some degree impatient of enumerating all the other things. Peter and every one else in the whole world, how distinguished soever he may be by his talents, gifts, or office whether ecclesiastical or political, all *are yours;* they are instrumental in promoting your interests, even though unwittingly: comp. respecting, *the world*, ver. 19, iv. 9, vi. 2, vii. 31; Rom. iv. 13; Gal. iv. 3.—εἴτε ζωὴ, εἴτε θάνατος, *whether life or death*) and so therefore *the living and the dead*. Comp. Rom. xiv. 8; Phil. i. 21.—ἐνεστῶτα, *things present*) on the earth.—μέλλοντα, *things to come*) in heaven.

23. Ὑμεῖς δὲ Χριστοῦ, *and ye are Christ's*) Immediately; not by the intervention of Peter.—Χριστοῦ—Θεοῦ, *of Christ—of God*) To this iv. 1 has respect.—Χριστὸς δὲ, Θεοῦ, *and Christ is God's*) xv. 28; Luke ix. 20.

[1] See App., under the tit. Litotes. Using a *weaker* expression, when a strong one is meant.—T.

[2] In Greek and Latin, a person speaking of himself along with another, puts himself first, in modern languages last. Christ says, more than once, *I and the Father:* so here, Paul is first as being of least importance.—T.

CHAPTER IV.

1. Οὕτως, *so*) is determinative, and resumes the subject from what precedes.—λογίζεσθω, *account*) without glorying, iii. 21.—ἄνθρωπος, *a man*) שׁיא, any *man*, one like ourselves, iii. 21.—ὑπηρέτας, *ministers*) Luke i. 2.—Χριστοῦ, *of Christ*) in His office [as the only Great Mediator]; not [ministers] of *men*.—οἰκονόμους μυστηρίων Θεοῦ, *stewards of the mysteries of God*) Paul, where he describes the ministers of the Gospel in the humblest language, still acknowledges them to *be stewards:* see Tit. i. 7, note; comp. *of Christ*, and, *of God*, with iii. 23. [Mysteries *are heavenly doctrines, of which men are ignorant without the revelation* of GOD.—V. g.]

2. "Ο δὲ) *Furthermore what* God *requires*, and men too, *in their stewards*, is, *that a man be found faithful*. Ver. 3 corresponds to this paraphrase.—ζητεῖται, *is inquired after* [*is required*]) by investigation, wnen the time comes. The correlative is, *may be found*.—πιστός, *faithful*) The Corinthians were not content with that.—εὑρεθῇ, *may be found*) Every man in the mean time wishes to be thought faithful.

3. Ἐμοὶ) *to me*, for my part.—δὲ) *but*, although I be capable of being found faithful.—εἰς, *unto*) a particle of mitigation. I do not despise your judgment in itself; but when I think of the judgment of God, then yours comes almost *to* nothing.—ἐλάχιστον, *a very little thing*) The judgment of God alone should be held of great account.—ὑφ᾽ ὑμῶν, *by you*) privately. An antithesis to *by human or man's day of judgment*, publicly. [*He limits what had been said* at iii. 21, " All things are yours."—V. g.]—ἀνακριθῶ, *I should be judged*) whether I am faithful, or not. The Corinthians certainly appeared not to be contented with faithfulness alone, but the apostle cuts the matter short [agit ἀποτόμως].—ἀνθρωπίνης, *human*) This word has the effect of diminishing. [*All days previous to the day of the Lord* are man's days.—V. g.].—ἡμέρας, *day*) So he calls it as an antithesis to the day of the Lord: ἡμέρα, *the day* appointed for the trial. It is here the abstract for the concrete; compare, *by you:*

it is likewise a hypothetical phrase; for none of the believers was likely to appoint a day for the trial of the apostle.—ἀνακρίνω, *I decide in judgment on*) for we ought not to *decide* in our own case, but to form a judgment of it. ἀνάκρισις, is the *decision in judgment* [dijudicatio] upon [of] one, in respect of others;—κρίσις, simple *judgment*. Here we have set forth the happy forgetfulness of all that is good in one's self. So the *decision in judgment* of the Corinthians respecting Paul is forcibly refuted.

4. Οὐδὲν) *nothing*, unfaithful: comp. *faithful*, ver. 2. So the LXX. οὐ γὰρ σύνοιδα ἐμαυτῷ ἄτοπα πράξας, Job xxvii. 6. He, whom conscience accuses, is held as deciding in judgment on himself.—οὐκ ἐν τούτῳ δεδικαίωμαι) *I am not justified in this*, if I decide in my own case. For the judgment remains. It is the Lord who will pronounce me justified, ver. 5. Paul may be regarded either as a judge, or a witness, in his own case. As a witness, he knows, that he is unconscious of any crime. As a judge, he dares not on that account decide in his own case, or pronounce himself to be justified.—ἀνακρίνων με) *He who decides in my case*, whose decision I do not decline, at His coming, ver. 5, and who declares me justified.[1]

5. Κρίνατε, *judge*) He does not say ἀνακρίνατε, *decide;* he more closely alludes to the judgment, which the Lord will give.—ὁ Κύριος, *the Lord*) Jesus whom we serve, ver. 1.—καί) *also:* He will not only judge, but will bring forth to light His judgment.—φωτίσει) φωτίζειν is *to throw light upon any object*, for example, φωτίζειν τὴν νύκτα, *to throw light upon the night*, Ex. xiv. 20, on the margin of the ed. Wech.: or *to bring a thing to light*, 2 Tim. i. 10. Both of these will be done at that time.—τὰ κρυπτὰ, *the hidden things*) The *heart* of man is truly a *hidden cavern* [crypt].—τοῦ σκότους, *of the darkness*) into which no human eye penetrates.—φανερώσει, *will make manifest*) so that you will then at length clearly know us.—τὰς βουλὰς, *the counsels*) showing, who hath been faithful or not.—τῶν καρδιῶν, *of the hearts*) according to the state of the *heart*, so the conduct is *just* [*justified*, ver. 4] and *praiseworthy* or the reverse.—τότε, *then*) Therefore wait.—ἔπαινος, *praise*) The world praises its

---

[1] Κύριός ἐστιν, *is the Lord*) Jesus Christ, v. 5. He is mentioned along with God, as in ver. 1.—V. g.

princes, warlike leaders, ambassadors, wise men, artists: God will hereafter praise His ministers.—ἑκάστῳ) *to every one*, who is a *praiseworthy*, faithful steward; you only praise one, for example, Paul. So *every one*, iii. 8. Concerning praise from God, see Matt. xxv. 21. Those too, who are not faithful, expect praise, but their praise will be reproach. Therefore the contrary is also included by implication in the word *praise*, which is a euphemism [the opposite of praise being not expressed, though implied]; so the euphemism in, *shall try* or *prove*, etc., c. iii. 13, viii. 8, 10, notes. So *blessing* also comprehends *cursing*, Gen. xlix. 28, 7. There is a similar passage, 1 Sam. xxvi. 23 (24).

6. Ταῦτα) *these things*, which are found from c. i. 10 and onward.—μετεσχημάτισα, *I have transferred*) Comp. 2 Sam. xiv. 20. *The figure* [Schema] consists in this, that Paul wrote those things with a view to admonish the Corinthians, not only in the second, but chiefly in the first person, ver. 3, 4: so that the reasons for moderate *sentiments* [φρονεῖν], by which Paul and Apollos were actuated, might also actuate the Corinthians, ver. 16, and the Corinthians might think of Paul, as Paul thought of himself.—μάθητε, *ye might learn*) By this word Paul calms the puffed-up Corinthians.—γέγραπται,[1] *is written*) Comp. בכתוב, 2 Chron. xxx. 5. *Written*, *i.e.* in the whole of Scripture, from which some quotations, iii. 19, 20, have just been made: for *we ought not* to entertain any sentiment (φρονεῖν) beside [*i.e.* in disagreement with] it, and beyond it, Rom. xii. 3, xv. 4. This is our rule in respect to all spiritual sentiments, and we are not allowed to depart from this rule, 2 Cor. x. 13. In Scripture, the archetype of which is in heaven, the general principle in relation to all believers is described, by which the Lord will judge each man, and by which every man ought to look up to Christ alone, and by which each ought to estimate himself, rather than by those gifts, wherein he excels, or thinks he

---

[1] The author has omitted in the Germ. Vers. the verb φρονεῖν after γέγραπται, everywhere met with, but left as it were undecided by the margin of both editions.—E. B.

ABD corrected later, G*fg* Vulg. omit φρονεῖν. Rec. Text reads it, in which it has the support only of C (as is probable, though not certain) of ancient authorities.—ED.

excels, others (Luke x. 20.) [*Add, that Scripture ascribes glory to* GOD *alone; to man no glory whatever,* i. 31: *and therefore human glorying is contrary to Scripture and its universal feeling* (sentiments), Luke xvi. 15–18, 29; Is. lxvi. 2.—V. g.] In accordance with this is the expression presently after, *one* [puffed up] *for one*. In this manner all *good* and *bad* men (Jude, ver. 4) have long ago been respectively distinguished in Scripture.—εἰς ὑπὲρ τοῦ ἑνὸς, *one for the one*) The definition of a sect, where individuals admire and follow individuals. The article τοῦ adds emphasis. A single minister is not the only one.—φυσιοῦσθε) The subjunctive, for φυσιῶσθε, as ζηλοῦτε for ζηλῶτε, Gal. iv. 17. But that is an irregular form of the subjunctive, which some call the indicative. The mode of contraction is singular. For it is not credible, that, in these verbs only, the indicative is put for the subjunctive.—ἑτέρου, *another*) for example against Apollos.

7. Τίς) *who?* not thou, not another man; but even supposing thou hast some excellent gift, it is God alone [who maketh thee to differ].—σὲ, *thee*) This word may be referred both to some one at Corinth and, by changing the *figure* of speech [σχῆμα referring to μετεσχημάτισα], to Paul: σὲ, *thee*, thyself, how great soever thou art: in antithesis to the gifts, which thou mayest or mayest not have received.—διακρίνει, *makes to differ*) or, peculiarly distinguishes by some difference.—τί δὲ ἔχεις, ὃ οὐκ ἔλαβες, *but what hast thou, which thou hast not received?*) The meaning is: *whatever thou hast, thou hast received it, not from thyself, but from God: or, there are many things, which thou hast not received, and therefore thou hast them not and canst not boast of them: either thou hast, or hast not received; if thou hast not received, thou hast them not: if thou hast received, thou hast nothing but what has been received, without any cause for glorying.* He, whom Paul here addresses, is a man; for example, Paul, whose way of thinking the Corinthians ought to take as a pattern. The latter sense renders the meaning of the καὶ, *even*, which immediately follows, more express, and shows the antanaclasis[1] in *thou hast not received:* [as if] *not receiving*.—ὡς μὴ λαβὼν, *as if thou hadst not received it*) as if thou hast it from thyself.

[1] See App. The same word in the same context twice, but in a different sense.

8. Ἤδη, *now*), in comparison with us. The words *without us*, which immediately after occur, agree with this.—κεκορεσμένοι, *full*) A gradation [ascending climax]: *full, rich, kings.* Its opposite is, *we hunger*, etc., ver. 11, 12. As the two epistles to the Corinthians exhibit great variety in mental feeling [ἦθος, Append.], incomparable urbanity [asteismus, Append.], and abundant and playful acuteness, so the passage before us is to such a degree remarkable for these qualities, that it should be understood, in respect either of the Corinthians or of the apostles, concerning their internal or external condition, concerning the facts themselves or concerning the puffed-up opinion of the Corinthians. The spiritual condition of the Corinthians was truly flourishing—flourishing also was that of the apostles. This was right: but troubles [the cross] from without galled the apostles and prevented them from pleasing themselves on that account: the Corinthians, inasmuch as being in a flourishing state even in things external, were pleased with and were applauding themselves, which was wrong. Therefore, the Corinthians were imitating the conduct of sons, who, after they have become illustrious, care little for their humble parents: in consequence of fulness, they were fastidious; of opulence, they were insolent; of kingly power, they were proud.—χωρὶς ἡμῶν, *without us*) A new and apt ambiguity; you have not us as your partners; consequently you have not had us as your assistants; you have forgotten us, as the saying expresses it, "many pupils become superior to their teachers," τολλοὶ μαθηταὶ κρείττονες διδασκάλων.—ἐβασιλεύσατε, *ye have reigned*) ye have come to your kingdom. In this is implied the majesty of Christians.—καὶ ὄφελόν γε, *and I wish*) i.e. I do not envy you, my only desire is, that it may really promote your best interests, 2 Cor. xii. 14, 15.—ἵνα καὶ ἡμεῖς, *that we also*) When you shall be perfected, the apostles will enjoy ease, and reach the end of all their troubles.—συμβασιλεύσωμεν, *we might reign together*) This is modestly said: *with you;* comp. ix. 23, iii. 22.

9. Δοκῶ, *I think*) A feeling of humility; a gentle mimesis.[1] The Corinthians *thought* [or, *seemed* to themselves, δοκεῖ, c. iii.

---

[1] See Appendix. A delicate allusion to the words of another whom we wish to set right: as the apostle's δοκῶ here refers to the Corinthians' δοκεῖ, chap. iii. 18.—ED.

1 CORINTHIANS IV. 10–12.

18] *that they excelled.*—τοὺς ἀποστόλους, ἐσχάτους, *the apostles, last*) ἔσχατος, *the most worthless,* ver. 10, 11. The antithetical words are put down in one and the same passage. The prophets also were afflicted, but the apostles much more; and the prophets were able to destroy their enemies, for example Elias [*and so greatly were they esteemed among men, that even the Nobles considered themselves bound to reverence them, and to follow or send for them with every mark of honour,* 2 Kings i. 10, v. 9, viii. 9, 12.—V. g.], but it was the lot of the apostles to suffer and endure to the end.—ἀπέδειξεν) In Latin, *munus ostendere, munus declarare,* are the idiomatic expressions applied to the public shows among the Romans.—ἐπιθανατίους) προσδοκωμένους ἀποθανεῖν, *expecting to be put to death.* See Hesychius.—τῷ κόσμῳ, *to the world*) which is immediately after divided into angels and men, without the repetition of the article.—καὶ ἀγγέλοις καὶ ἀνθρώποις, *to angels and men*) *i.e.* those that are good; but rather, those that are *bad.*

10. Μωροὶ, *fools*) i. 21.—διὰ Χριστὸν—ἐν Χριστῷ, *for Christ's sake—in Christ*) These words must be repeated in the two following clauses. Without any violation of the truth, different things may be predicated of one subject; or of different subjects, who are regarded as standing on the same footing; for example, of Paul and the Corinthians; according to the different point of view in which they are regarded, and which the words, *for the sake of,* and, *in,* here express; *for the sake of* is applied to slaves; *in,* to partners.—ἔνδοξοι) men in the highest estimation; but ἄτιμοι, applies to persons, who are deprived of even ordinary esteem.—ἡμεῖς δὲ, *but we*) Here the first person takes the second place, and so it goes on in the following verse.

11. Γυμνητεύομεν, *we are naked*) The highest degree of poverty, 2 Cor. xi. 27. [*So far were the heralds of the kingdom of Christ from being adorned with any splendour. We imagine ourselves to be quite the reverse of all this.*—V. g.]—κολαφιζόμεθα, *we are buffeted*) as slaves, therefore we are not *kings.*

12. Κοπιῶμεν, *we labour*) as if compelled by necessity. Few of the Corinthians did so.—εὐλογοῦμεν—ἀνεχόμεθα,—παρακαλοῦμεν, *we bless—we endure—we entreat*) *i.e.* we do not return reproaches, persecution, evil speaking, but we only bless; nothing else is lawful; the world thinks that despicable.

13. Περικαθάρματα περίψημα) both words are used for *filth*, by which not only men utterly outcast, but those devoted as an expiation for others, are denoted. כפר, περικάθαρμα δικαίου, ἄνομος, *the wicked shall be a ransom for the upright*, Prov. xxi. 18. τὸ ἀργύριον περίψημα τοῦ παιδίου ἡμῶν γένοιτο, *let money be as refuse in respect of our child*, Tob. v. (18) 26 : add Jer. xxii. 28, where עצב נבזה has been translated by some περίψημα φαῦλον, *vile offscourings*, Hesychius : περίψημα, περικατάμαγμα, ἀντίλυτρα, ἀντίψυχα, ἢ ὑπὸ τὰ ἴχνη πάντων. περίψημα in Eustathius is, σπόγγισμά τι, something wiped away with a sponge, and therefore more subtle [smaller and less perceptible] than λῦμα ; the latter word, λῦμα, is a less forcible term than κάθαρμα, the meaning of which the περί strengthens. Wherefore Paul calls himself and the apostles περικαθάρματα τοῦ κόσμου—περίψημα, the offscouring not only of a persecuting *world*, but of all men [Engl. Vers. " of all *things*"], although they do not persecute us ; *the world* hates us ; *all* men despise us.—ἕως ἄρτι, *until now*) an epanalepsis [a repetition of the same words in the beginning of a preceding member and in the end of the following member of a sentence. See Append.], comp. ver. 11, at the beginning.

14. Οὐκ ἐντρέπων, *not making ashamed*) An exquisite epitherapeia.[1] The dissimilarity between themselves and Paul, between the sons and the father, might have made the Corinthians *ashamed*. This Ἐντροπὴ, *putting them to shame*, in the mind of the apostle, was not an end, but a means, as he says also on another occasion, that he was unwilling to make them sad, though he had actually done so. The apostle often introduces a certain degree of refined pleasantry, without forgetting the apostolic gravity, for example, 2 Cor. xii. 13, note.—νουθετῶ, *I warn*) you as a father, Eph. vi. 4.

15. Παιδαγωγοὺς, *instructors*) however evangelical they are, being *in Christ*, not legal instructors. The antithetical terms respectively are, 'planting,' and 'watering ;' " laying the foundation," and " building upon it :" 'begetting' and 'instructing.'— οὐ πολλοὺς, *not many*) In like manner every regenerate man has not many fathers. Paul does not say, *one Father ;* for that ap-

---

[1] See App. An after addition to words, which might give offence, and a kind of softening of what went before by a declaration of friendly feeling towards the persons addressed.

plies to God alone; *not many*, is however sufficiently explained by the following word, *I*. Not only Apollos, his successor, is excluded, but also his companions Silas and Timotheus, Acts xviii. 5. Spiritual fatherhood has in it a peculiar tie of relationship and affection connected with it, above every other kind of propinquity.—ἐν γὰρ Χριστῷ Ἰησοῦ, *for in Christ Jesus*) This is more express than the phrase above, *in Christ*, where he is speaking of other instructors.

16. Παρακαλῶ, *I exhort*) A short exhortation after a long and true account of his own example is valuable.—μιμηταί μου, *imitators of me*) *as sons*. Having laid aside pride, cultivate that feeling even without the cross, which is fostered in us by means of the cross. He proposes the imitation of himself to those, with whom he had been, Gal. iv. 12; Phil. iii. 17.

17. Τιμόθεον, *Timotheus*) xvi. 10.—τέκνον μου, *my son*) and therefore *imitator*. Paul calls Timothy his brother; see 2 Cor. i. 1, note; but in this passage the affection of *the father* is uppermost in his thought.—ἀγαπητόν, *beloved*) to whom I have willingly committed the business.—πιστόν, *faithful*) to whom I could safely commit the business.—ἀναμνήσει, *will remind you*) He does not say *will teach*. The Corinthians had knowledge; they had need of admonition.—τὰς ὁδούς μου, *my ways*) in which I walked whilst with you.—καθὼς, *even as*) as διάκονος, *a minister*.—ἐκκλησίᾳ, *in the church*) emphatically in the singular number.

18. Ὡς, *as though*) Because I send Timothy, they think, that I will not come. This is the meaning of the particle δὲ, *but*.— ἐφυσιώθησάν τινες, *some were puffed up*) Paul wrote this under Divine illumination, laying bare and clearly showing their thoughts, which would rise in their minds at the very time, when they were reading these words. They were puffed up about various things; see next verse, and ch. v. 2. He says, I will restrain such persons, when I come. Perhaps also the apostle might have learned about this puffed up spirit of the Corinthians from the members *of the house of Chloe* (i. 11). But the Corinthians seem to have been puffed up about the delay of the coming of Paul, not until after he had sent Timothy, his second self, with this very epistle. Then indeed these puffed up thoughts suddenly arose in their minds; Paul himself, then,

will not come. *A puffed up spirit* was the frequent fault prevalent among the Corinthians.

19. Ἐλεύσομαι, *I will come*) Paul writes to the churches everywhere about his coming to them, and thus keeps them in the discharge of their duty.—ἐὰν ὁ Κύριος θελήσῃ, *if the Lord will*) He wisely adds this condition. Afterwards some things occurred to prevent his immediately going to them.—γνώσομαι, *will take cognizance*) A word used in courts of law. Here, and at ver. 21, the man, who was such an outcast abroad in the world, shows his paternal *authority*, see ver. 9, 10.—οὐ τὸν λόγον, *not the speech*) big, but empty.

20. Οὐ γὰρ, *for not*) An axiom.—ἐν δυνάμει, *in power*) The absence of the article gives force to the meaning, as in Eph. iv. 21. [*Weigh thoroughly that in which* the power *of thy Christianity consists.*—V.g.]

21. Τί θέλετε, *what will ye?*) Choose. [Comp. 2 Cor. xiii. 3. *So this phrase*, what wilt thou? *is still of importance both as to the principal point, and as to its various accessory cases; see that you make room* (that you choose rather to leave scope) for Love. —V.g.]—ἐν ῥάβδῳ, *with a rod*) wielded by a father's hand. Comp. Isa. xi. 4.—ἤ, *or*) Paul would prefer the latter.

CHAPTER V.

1. Ὅλως, *absolutely* [Engl. Vers., *commonly*]) Paul has nowhere else used this particle, but it is found thrice in this epistle (here, and in vi. 7, and xv. 29), as well fitted to express his thoughts, and in these and in all other places, the particle, ὅλως, *omnino*, is either put in a negative sentence, or it by implication contradicts a negative sentence : So Chrys. Homil. 5, c. Anom., *Nevertheless, although man differs little from an angel,* ἐπειδὴ ΟΛΩΣ ἐστί τι μέσον, *since nevertheless there is some difference between them, we do not accurately know, what angels are* : so in this passage, no fornication, ὅλως, *at all* should be reported among you ; nevertheless it is, ὅλως, *absolutely* reported. The same principle applies to the particle, τὴν ἀρχὴν, *absolutely*.—ἐν ὑμῖν, *concerning you* [Engl.

Vers. *among*]) in your name [case].—πορνεία, καὶ τοιαύτη πορνεία, *fornication* and such *fornication*) An important repetition; by which the Corinthians might be more affected.—οὐδὲ, *not even*) It was a crime not named even among the Gentiles, with the exception of a few monsters; ὥστε is the Protherapeia[1] of the following clause. The apostle shows, that such infamous conduct was held in abhorrence even by the Gentiles.—γυναῖκα, *wife*) She was no doubt a heathen; therefore he does not direct his rebuke against her, ver. 12, 13. *The father*, we may suppose, was dead. —ἔχειν, *should have*) by a single act, or by habitual intercourse, ver. 2, 3.

2. Καὶ ὑμεῖς, *and ye*) He presses their sin home to them.— πεφυσιωμένοι, *puffed up*) [*as if you were free from blame in the matter.*—V. g.]—The force of the word is evident from its antithesis, to *mourn*.—ἐστε, *ye are*) hitherto.—ἐπενθήσατε, *you have mourned*) Paul himself wrote these words mourning, nay weeping; 2 Cor. ii. 4; we should mourn over the transgressions of others; 2 Cor. xii. 21, and *repent* of our own; and we should do both as regards the first and original sin.—ἵνα, *that*) you have felt no grief, which might stir you up, *that*, etc.—ἀρθῇ, *he might be taken away*) Paul has already in his mind what he is about to write at ver. 13.—αἴρειν is a milder word here, than ἐξαίρειν afterwards.[2]

3. Ἐγὼ μὲν γὰρ, *I indeed for my part*) An antithesis between the lighter punishment, which would have been inflicted by the Corinthians, and the severer one, which is threatened by Paul: thence also we have in ver. 2, ποιήσας, *he that hath done*, a gentler expression; but in ver. 3 κατεργασάμενον, *he that hath perpetrated*, a much more severe expression. Afterwards the Corinthians did what they ought, 2 Cor. ii. 6. Therefore the severer punishment pronounced on the sinner (here in ver. 5) admitted of being superseded. Thence arose the joy of Paul, 2 Cor. i. 24, ii. 1, etc.—τῷ πνεύματι, *in spirit*) Col. ii. 5, 2 Kings v. 26.— ἤδη κέκρικα, *I have already judged*) A weighty effect is produced by the sense of the sentence continuing to be gravely suspended and poised [as it were a lance], till we come to ver. 5, where

---

[1] See App. Anticipatory mitigation of what follows.
[2] Τὸ ἔργον, *the daring deed*) It was a wicked action, without marriage —V. g.

the expression, *he who hath perpetrated* [κατεργασάμενον] is again taken up in the expression, *such a one* [τὸν τοιοῦτον].—ὡς παρὼν, *as though I were present*) It is construed with, *to deliver*, ver. 5.— τὸν οὕτω τοῦτο) A triple demonstrative.—οὕτω, *so*) very shamefully, *so*, while he was called a brother.

4. Ἐν τῷ ὀνόματι, *in the name*) It is construed with, *to deliver*.— τοῦ ἐμοῦ πνεύματος, *and my spirit*) ver. 3.—σὺν τῇ δυνάμει, *with the power*) The *spirit* and *power* are almost synonymous. Paul, speaking of himself, uses the word, *spirit*; of Christ, *power*, 2 Cor. xiii. 3; Matt. xxviii. 20, xviii. 20. A Hypotyposis,[1] *i.e.* so that the power of the Lord may immediately exert itself.

5. Παραδοῦναι, *to deliver*) This was the prerogative of the apostle, not of the Corinthians; comp. 2 Cor. xiii. 10, note, and 1 Tim. i. 20, note. This is a specimen of the highest degree of punishment in the Christian republic, adapted to those early times.—ὄλεθρον, *destruction*) death although not sudden. The Hebrew word כרת corresponds to it: comp. ch. xi, 30.— τῆς σαρκὸς, *of the flesh*) with which he had sinned. [1 Pet. iv. 6; *comp. as to* the Spirit, Rom. viii. 10.—V. g.]

6. Οὐ καλὸν, *not good*) The *not*, is directed against the careless indifference of the Corinthians.—τὸ καύχημα, *glorying*) This in itself is something good and becoming, xv. 31; but wherever it is not anxiously watched, it is at fault, and comes very near to a *puffing up* of the spirit, ver. 2.—μικρά—ζυμοῖ) an Iambic verse of six feet [Senarius], Gal. v. 9.—ζύμη, *leaven*) even one sin and one sinner.—φύραμα, *lump*) the assembly of Christians.— ζυμοῖ, *leavens*) with guilt and its example creeping on to a very wide extent. [*Alas! for how long a period of time, and in how great a degree, must the Christian world, if we except those portions of it which are renewed, be a lump, or collection of filth most thoroughly leavened!*—V. g.]

7. Τὴν παλαιὰν, *the old*) leaven of heathenism and natural corruption.—ἵνα ἦτε νέον φύραμα, *that you may be a new lump*) the whole of you, evil being taken away.—καθώς, *even as*) The third clause of this verse depends rather on the first, than on the second.—ἄζυμοι, *unleavened*) individuals among

---

[1] A vivid presenting of a thing in words, as if before one's very eyes. See Append.

you, in consequence of conversion, vi. 11.—τὸ πάσχα, *the passover*) The epistle was written about the time of the passover, xvi. 8.—ἡμῶν, [*our* or] *of us*) Christians. The Jewish passover was a type of the Christian and new passover.—ἐτύθη) *was sacrificed.* Paul speaks in the past time; he was much more likely to speak in the present, as his scope so required, if he had acknowledged the sacrifice of the Mass. Hesychius: ἐτύθη, ἐσφάγη.

8.'Εορτάζωμεν, *let us keep the feast*) The Vulgate has *epulemur,* " *let us feast :*" an apposite expression.—παλαιᾷ, *with the old*) of Judaism and heathenism. These constitute the genus.—κακίας καὶ πονηρίας) These constitute the species: κακία is vice, the reverse of virtue, and that too, virtue unmixed, or *in sincerity*, τῇ εἰλικρινείᾳ. πονηρία is in those, who strenuously retain and defend κακίαν, and is opposed, τῇ ἀληθείᾳ, to the truth. Ammonius writes thus: πονηρός, ὁ δραστικὸς κακοῦ, *he who is disposed* TO DO *evil ;*[1] comp. ver. 13. *Sincerity* takes care not to allow evil to be mixed up with good; *truth*, not to allow evil to be mistaken for good.

9. ῎Εγραψα, *I wrote*) A new part of the epistle, corresponding to the former part; comp. ver. 1.—ἐν τῇ ἐπιστολῇ, *in the epistle*) written before this one. The Corinthians had not sufficiently understood it; he now therefore explains it. There is no doubt, that Paul and Peter and the rest of the apostles wrote many things, which are not now extant; comp. xvi. 3; 2 Cor. x. 10.—μὴ συναναμίγνυσθαι, *not to be mixed together*) in the way of association; ver. 11 at the end.—πόρνοις, *with fornicators*) πόρνος, on other occasions signifies a male prostitute, but here it applies to every one, who commits fornication. Supply here also from ver. 11, *or covetous*, etc.

10. Καὶ) *and that.*—οὐ πάντως, *not altogether*) What is here said is not a universal, but a particular negative, Rom. iii. 9, note.—τοῦ κόσμου τούτου, *of this world*) [*there is no place wherein you may not fall in with the covetous and extortioners,* etc.—V. g.] In antithesis to *a brother*, ver. 11.[2]—ἅρπαξιν, *extortioners*) He

---

[1] Κακία is the evil habit of the mind : πονηρία, the outcoming of the same. Calvin defines κακία, "animi pravitas," *on Eph.* iv. 32. πονηρός is ὁ παρέχων πόνους. See Trench, Syr. Gr. Text.—ED.

[2] πλεονέκταις, *covetous*) Those greedy of gain for themselves.—V. g.

gives them this name rather than that of *thieves;* because their *theft* is not apparent. [*They are included by implication, who try to get the property of others, either by violence or injustice.—V. g.*]—He mentions three kinds of flagitious crimes, which are committed against the man himself, against his neighbour, and against God.—ἐπεὶ ὀφείλετε, *for then must ye needs*) Others have written ὠφείλετε¹ [Ye ought to have gone out, etc.], for ὀφείλετε, but the present is also used, vii. 14, ἐπεὶ ἄρα τὰ τέκνα ὑμῶν ἀκάθαρτά ἐστι. What is written without express limitation, should not be always taken absolutely, if there should follow from it any unsuitable consequence. In the present day there is room for this paraphrase; "otherwise you must needs go out of a land inhabited by Christians." They are therefore especially to be avoided, who among Christians wish to be considered virtuous above others, and yet are *fornicators*, etc.—ὀφείλετε) *you must needs.* For thus all intercourse as citizens would be done away with: That, which is evangelical perfection to monks, is absurd (ἄτοπον, out of place) and unsuitable in the eyes of Paul.—κόσμου, *of the world*)· which abounds in profligate men.

11. Ἀδελφὸς, *a brother*) an ordinary appellation.—ὀνομαζόμενος, *who is called*) A word in the middle voice [or rather, *used in a middle sense*, neither a favourable nor unfavourable sense].—πόρνος, *a fornicator*) the crimes are here enumerated, on account of which others are to be avoided; then in vi. 9, 10, more are added, on account of which every man should fear for himself.²—μηδὲ συνεσθίειν, *not so much as to eat*) not only not with such a man as a host, but not even *with* him at the house of a third person. The lowest degree of intercourse, which men have, *when mixed up in company with one another, is to eat together.* Even among the Jews, חרם, excommunication took away all intercourse in regard to eating together. We must not eat with the man, who shall be unfit *to eat along* with the saints in the kingdom of God, vi. 10. Let the Church of the present day take heed, in which the guests at the Lord's table are not like chil-

---

¹ So ACD(Λ)G Vulg. both Syr. and Memph. Versions. But B (judging from silence) favours Rec. Text's reading, ὀφείλετε.—ED.

² Μέθυσος, *a drunkard*) It indicates the man who drinks large quantities of wine, although he does not break out into unbridled revellings.—V. g.

dren in one family, but like a number of strangers of various kinds in a large inn.

12. Τί γάρ μοι καὶ τοὺς ἔξω κρίνειν; οὐχὶ τοὺς ἔσω ὑμεῖς κρίνετε;) Artemonius, p. 212, refers to the conjecture of Le Clerc, and after changing a few words presents it in this form: τί γάρ μοι καὶ τοῖς ἔξω; καὶ νῦν οὖν τοὺς ἔσω ὑμεῖς κρίνετε. There are here various changes of letters, by which the word κρίνειν, the most necessary of them all, is cancelled. If the meaning of Paul had been, *what have I to do with those that are without?* the Greek idiom would have required ἐμοί, not μοι. Τί γάρ μοι καὶ τοὺς ἔξω κρίνειν, viz. ἐστί; *for what have I to do to judge those that are without?* (Verbals [such as Bengel's " externos *judicatio*"] govern the case of the verb, *ex. gr.: Curatio hanc rem*, taking charge of this matter.) Expressions very similar occur, ἱνατί μοι ζῆν, Gen. xxvii. 46: οὐ σοί, 'Οζία, θυμιᾶσαι, 2 Chron. xxvi. 18: οὐκ ἔστι γὰρ χαίρειν, λέγει Κύριος, τοῖς ἀσεβέσιν, Is. xlviii. 22: ὅπως μὴ γένηται αὐτῷ χρονοτριβῆσαι, Acts xx. 16: πόθεν σοι ταῦτα εἰδέναι, *Hippolytus* de antichristo, chap. 32. These remarks apply to the whole sentence; we shall now consider the words one by one.—καὶ) *also,* which intimates, that those, *who are within,* give me enough to do.[1]—κρίνειν, *to judge*) He judges, *who is not mixed up with them, does not keep company with them.*— οὐχὶ, *do not ye?*) From what is wont to occur in the Church, you ought to have interpreted my admonition, alluded to in ver. 9, You judge your fellow-citizens, not strangers; how much more should I? *You judge,* will thus signify righteous judgment. But this may also be a previous [anticipatory], and, that too, a seasonable sting to the Corinthians, *who were judging* [bringing before heathen courts of justice] *them that were within,* while [though] they considered *the saints removed* [exempt] from judgments *concerning things pertaining to this life,* vi. 1, 2, 3.

13. Τοὺς δὲ ἔξω, *them that are without*) The knowledge concerning the destruction or salvation of the Gentiles is a matter reserved for God alone.—κρινεῖ, *shall judge*) Rom. ii. 16. Supply,

[1] This very particle καὶ, *also*, however, is considered of less importance in the 2d, than in the 1st Ed., and it is entirely omitted in the Germ. Vers.—E. B.
ABCG Vulg. Memph. *fg* (ante-Hieron. Lat.) Versions omit καὶ. D and later Syr. retain καὶ.—ED.

and this judgment we in all humility leave to God. Thus the *and*, that follows, more closely coheres with this clause.—καὶ, *and*) an Epiphonema¹ suited to both parts of this chapter. The particle καὶ with the whole sentence is quoted here, from the LXX., Deut. xvii. 7, xix. 19, xxiv. 7, καὶ, *and so*. But the phrase, *as it is written*, is not prefixed here, and this is the case either for the sake of *severity* [c. iv. 21], or because ἐξαρεῖτε, Heb. ובערת, is used by Moses for taking away a wicked man from among the people by capital punishment, by the apostle for taking away a wicked man from the Church by excommunication.—τὸν πονηρὸν, *the wicked person*) ver. 2, 9.—ὑμῶν αὐτῶν, *from among yourselves*) So it is found in the LXX. often. The antithesis in this passage is, *those that are without.*

CHAPTER VI.

1. Τολμᾷ, *dare*) Treason against Christians is denoted, by this high-sounding word.—τὶς, *any one*) even one single person.—κρίνεσθαι) in the middle voice, that is κρίμα ἔχειν, *obtain a judgment, go to law*, v. 7.—ἀδίκων, *before the unjust*) Every *unbeliever is unjust*; generally so, even as a citizen.—ἐπὶ τῶν ἁγίων, *before the saints*) Christians. The great privilege of believers was to settle even civil matters among themselves, and the magistrate ought not to interfere at all with private affairs, unless in the case of those who especially apply to him. The heathen magistrates were very indulgent to the Jews; and in this department no difference was hitherto made between the Jews and the Christians.

2. Οὐκ οἴδατε, *do you not know?*) This phrase is used with great force six times in this single chapter. The Corinthians knew, and rejoiced that they knew; but they were acting contrary to their knowledge.—οἱ ἅγιοι, *the saints*) being themselves first judged.—τὸν κόσμον, *the world*) all those who are not *saints*. The antithesis is to, *the smallest matters*; comp. iii. 22.—κρινοῦσι,

---

¹ An exclamation after a weighty demonstration or narration. Append.

they shall judge) The future, comp. ver. 3; Rev. xx. 4. The present, *is judged*, is interposed; comp. John xv. 8. The saints took possession of the civil authority also under Constantine the Great, which is the prelude of things to come. [*Scripture from time to time casts a ray of light on the most important affairs, as it were in passing. The proud despise such things; but the humble keep them laid up in their heart, with a truly sober mind. The majesty of the saints is hidden, but it will be revealed at its proper time.*—V. g.]—ἐν, *in*[1]) Comp. Acts xvii. 31.—ἀνάξιοί ἐστε, *are ye unworthy*) The figure Communicatio.[2]

3. Ἀγγέλους, *angels*) Those who are not *holy* [referring to *saints*], and so also wicked men. The article is not added; a gradation in respect of *the world* [*i.e.* an ascending climax, arguing *a fortiori*; if *angels*, much more *the world*].—βιωτικὰ, *things belonging to life*) worthless if they be compared with angels.

4. Τοὺς ἐξουθενημένους ἐν τῇ ἐκκλησίᾳ) *those who are even least esteemed in the church*, any persons whatever rather than the heathen. Every one, even the least, is capable of taking on him the decision of even the greatest interests in external affairs [*and therefore is able to come to a decision, not indeed according to the ancient laws* of the heathens, *but on the true principles* of equity.—V. g.]—Comp. i. 28, xi. 22, and therefore καθίζετε, *set ye*, is the imperative. [*It was not, however, to be thought of to give way at all in that matter to the jurisdiction of heathen judges.*—V. g.]

5. Πρὸς ἐντροπὴν, *to your shame*) The *puffed up* spirit [ch. v. 2] of the Corinthians is hereby checked: Comp. xv. 34.—σοφὸς, *a wise man*) They admired wisdom on other occasions, and wisdom produces the *ability* for *judging between* brethren in deciding causes.—οὐδὲ εἷς, *not even one*) Even the least among believers is a wiser and more desirable judge than an ungodly man.—δυνήσεται) the future; *shall be able* if he be applied to.—διακρῖναι) *to determine between* parties. It differs from κρῖναι, *to judge*.—ἀδελφοῦ, *a brother*) The singular for the plural, to denote how easy a matter it is; he wishes that the plaintiff and the defendant

---

[1] *In the person of; by.*—ED.
[2] See Append. An appeal to the reader's own candour to decide.

should settle the dispute between themselves, without any interference on the part of the judge.

6. Καὶ τοῦτο, *and that*) So also καὶ ταῦτα, v. 8; Heb. xi. 12.

7. Ὅλως) A particle implying a feeling; comp. ch. v. 1 [note]: it is opposed by implication to μηδόλως. You ought to have no cases ὅλως, *at all*, against one another, but you have ὅλως, *after all, notwithstanding*.—ἥττημα, [*a fault*] *defect*) even on the part of him, who has the juster cause, and thinks he *has the superior cause* [Matth. v. 39.] He does not say, *sin*, yet this readily is added in such cases, v. 8; *defect* [*fault*] and *praise* are in opposition; comp. xi. 17, note. *Praise* is not indeed expressly found in this passage. Some such antithetic word, however, is intended, because he does not expressly use the term, *sin*, either. The thing which is *praised*, is something as it were more blooming and uncommon than the mere action agreeable to the law. So in its opposite.—ὑμῖν, *to you*) There is a similar dative in xv. 32.[1]—μᾶλλον, *rather*) all men do not understand this word *rather*. Many desire neither to injure nor to be injured. They do not attempt to inflict an injury, which is a mere pretence to moderation in regard to justice.—ἀδικεῖσθε) *suffer wrong*, in the Middle voice; as ἀποστερεῖσθε.

8. Ὑμεῖς, *ye*) Emphatic. The Antithesis is to those, from whom they ought rather to suffer injury.—ἀδικεῖτε, *ye do injury*) by taking away.—ἀποστερεῖτε, *ye defraud*) by refusing [to give back a trust] and retaining.—ἀδελφούς, *brethren*) This increases the fault.

9. Ἤ) Latin *an* [*or;* the second part of a disjunctive interrogation].—ἄδικοι, *unrighteous*). Comp. v. 8.—βασιλείαν Θεοῦ, *the kingdom of God*) In this kingdom righteousness flourishes.—οὐ κληρονομήσουσι, *they shall not inherit*) because they are not the sons of God.—μὴ πλανᾶσθε, *be not deceived*) by yourselves and others.—πόρνοι—ἅρπαγες, *fornicators—extortioners*) Scandalous crimes common at Corinth, 2 Cor. xii. 20, 21; at Rome, Rom. xiii. 13; in Galatia, Gal. v. 19, 20: at Ephesus, 1 Tim. i. 9, 10: and in Crete, Tit. i. 12. This remark applies to the act of *fornication*, etc., and much more to the habit.—εἰδωλολάτραι, *idolaters*) Idolatry is placed between fornication and

---

[1] Κρίματα, *trials*) Although concerning a cause not unjust.—V. g.

adultery, for, it usually had these crimes joined to it.—μαλακοί, *effeminate*) Even the hand in the deepest solitude ought to be chaste, a necessary warning to youth.

11. Ταῦτα, *such*) The Nominative neuter for the masculine; or the accusative with κατα understood, as ἴσα, Phil. ii. 6 : Even the accusative as an adverb may be construed with the substantive verb *to be*.—ἀλλὰ ἀπελούσασθε, ἀλλὰ ἡγιάσθητε, ἀλλ᾿ ἐδικαιώθητε, *but ye have been washed, but ye have been sanctified, but ye have been justified*) you have been set entirely free from *fornication* and sins of impurity, in regard to yourselves; from *idolatry* and impiety against God; from *unrighteousness* against your neighbour, and that too, in relation both to the guilt and dominion of sin : chap. v. 7, 10.—ἡγιάσθητε, *you have been sanctified*) a man is called *holy* in respect to God.—ἐδικαιώθητε, *ye have been justified*) corresponds to, *the unrighteous*, ver. 9. I was formerly unwilling to commit to paper, what emphasis the apostrophe in ἀλλ᾿ adds to this verb more than to the two preceding (comp. 2 Cor. vii. 11), lest some one should hiss me. Consider however the antithesis, *the unrighteous*. Without an apostrophe, ἀλλὰ is emphatic, but when ἀλλ᾿ has the apostrophe, the accent and emphasis fall upon the verb, (which stands in opposition to that fault, which is reproved at ver. 7, etc.,) namely, on the word ἐδικαιώθητε, *ye are justified*, because the discourse here is directed against [injustice] *unrighteousness;* and so in 2 Cor. vii. 11. [ἀλλ᾿ is apostrophised before] ἐκδικησιν, *revenge*, for, this is a principal part of the *zeal*, previously spoken of, arising from holy sorrow; add Mark ii. 17.—ἐν τῷ ὀνόματι, *in the name*) From this name we have the forgiveness of sins.—ἐν τῷ Πνεύματι, *by the Spirit*) From this Spirit, the new life.—ἡμῶν, *of our*) For these reasons, he shows them, that there is now no longer any hinderance to their becoming heirs of the kingdom of God.

12. Πάντα, *all things*) The apostle takes care that no one should abuse those remarks of his, which he was soon about to make concerning meats and the belly; comp. x. 23. The expression, *all things*, is to be referred to what follows; not to fornication, although this is the principal subject of his argument; but to a subject accessory and incidental, in regard to the eating of meats, on which he treats also below, x. 29. On that same point it is repeated, that all things are lawful to me, which can

be lawful at all.—μοι, *to me*) Paul often speaks in the first person singular, which has the force of a gnome [or *moral maxim*], especially in this epistle, ver. 15, vii. 7, viii. 13, x. 23, 29, 30, xiv. 11. *To me, i.e.*, the Corinthians ought to think as *I do*.—συμφέρει, *are expedient*) We must above all consider, what may be expedient.—ἔξεστιν—ἐξουσιασθήσομαι) Conjugate words. He, who does not freely use his legitimate power and liberty, steps aside from his own power, and passes into the power of another, for example, into that *of a harlot*, ver. 15 ; comp. vii. 4. He would be a stupid traveller, who, though his road lay in the middle of the plain, would always walk on the bank of the river and at the very edge of the stream. And yet many so live, who pass even for godly men. The *Power* ought to be in the hands of the believer, not in the things, which he uses. [*Liberty good in itself is destroyed by its abuse*, Gal. v. 13; 1 Pet. ii. 16.—V. g.] The very expression *I will not* [οὐκ ἐγώ, *not I*] has *power*, with application to the individual himself. *Not I!* another may venture it, so far as I am concerned. The believer establishes this principle in respect of himself : he says in respect of his neighbour, *all things do not edify*, x. 23.—τινὸς) any thing Neuter, the same as πάντα.

13. Τὰ βρώματα, *meats*) viz. ἐστί. The conclusion drawn from the lawfulness of meats to that of lust has no weight.—καὶ ταύτην καὶ ταῦτα, *both it and them*) Demonstrative, twice used concerning the present time ; the *it* precedes, inasmuch as food is for [on account of] the belly.—καταργήσει) *shall destroy* ; and that too, not merely in the same way as *the body* is destroyed at death;[1] from the antithesis of the belly and the body, it may be inferred, that there will be a difference of sexes even in the state similar to that of the angels.[2] Those things which shall be destroyed, considered in themselves, have their use unrestricted [free], Col. ii. 20, etc., Mark vii. 18, [whatsoever thing from without entereth a man] *cannot* [defile him]. Now [δὲ, *whereas*] is here and in the following verse elegantly put instead of *for ;* for a severer denunciation [" God shall destroy both it," etc.] is subjoined to the concession ["meats for the belly," etc.]; a joyful declaration [God

---

[1] The destruction of meats and the belly will be a *permanent* destruction.—ED.

[2] For though the *belly* is to be for ever destroyed, not so *the body*.—ED.

1 CORINTHIANS VI. 14, 15.

will raise up us also, etc.], to the prohibition [the body is not for fornication]. *He will raise up*, directly corresponds from the antithetic side to, *He will destroy.*—τὸ δὲ σῶμα, *now* [but] *the body*) The body here is not opposed to the belly [alvo], but to meats.[1]—πορνείᾳ, *for fornication*) an abstract noun.—τῷ Κυρίῳ, *for the Lord*) Christ. The body is His due, for He Himself assumed the body, and hath thereby sanctified us; and we are joined to Him by the resurrection of the body.—τῷ σώματι, *for the body*) How great honour!

14. Ἤγειρε—ἐξεγερεῖ, *hath raised—and will raise*) [Paul introduces here in the way of prelude those topics, which he was to discuss more fully and distinctly in ch. xv.—V. g.] The simple verb is appropriately applied to [Christ] the first fruits, the compound, of rare occurrence, to the general mass of them that sleep. Ἐξ in composition often signifies consummation. The practical application from the resurrection of our flesh is, sin once committed in the flesh will never be undone.—διὰ, *by*) Paul would rather connect this with the mentioning of the resurrection, than with that of destruction.—δυνάμεως, *power*) who then can doubt? God is omnipotent.

15. Σώματα, *bodies*) whether regard is had to the whole or the parts.—ἄρας οὖν τὰ μέλη τοῦ Χριστοῦ ποιήσω πόρνης μέλη;) Some copies have ἄρα for ἄρας;[2] Paul often says ἄρα οὖν, but in such places where the conclusion is subjoined, after a somewhat long discourse. ἄρας is more suitable to this place, and they have it, whose testimony is of highest value, among whom is Irenæus: and there is the utmost ἐνάργεια, *graphic power*, in this participle, depicting as it were the baseness of the thing: *taking away*, spontaneously alienating the members of Christ, *shall I make them the members of a harlot?* So the participle φέρων is often redundant, of which I have spoken, on Chrysost. de Sacerdot. p. 394, at the passage, φέρων ἑαυτὸν κατεκρήμνισε, *he took and threw himself down.*—ποιήσω, *shall I make?*) For they cannot be at the same time the *members of a harlot* and *of Christ*.

---

[1] The Germ. Vers., however, thinks that the body is opposed to the belly [ventri], and it has on the margin these words: The body is much more noble than the belly.—E. B.

[2] So ABCD (Λ), Orig. 1, 520c: 'tollens' in *f*. Vulg. Iren. Lucif.: 'auferens' in Cypr.: "an tollens" in *g*. Ἡ ἄρα is read by G.—ED.

16. Ὁ κολλώμενος τῇ πόρνῃ, *he who is joined to a harlot*) A syllepsis,[1] *i.e.* [by this figure, there being *mentally* understood] *the harlot* and *he who is joined to her;* for so the predicate, *is one body*, appropriately is in accordance [with such a *double* subject]; and the expression, *these two* [οἱ δύο], agrees with this view.—ἔσονται, *they shall be*) This is said in the first instance of husbands and wives; and, by parity of reasoning, is applied to those, who become one flesh without a conjugal covenant. By covenant the woman becomes the *wife of the husband* before the husband *is joined* (carnally) to her; and the reason, why their union is indissoluble, chiefly rests on this circumstance; otherwise even the union of men with harlots would also be indissoluble.

17. Τῷ Κυρίῳ, *to the Lord*) Christ. It is the same syllepsis [the Lord and he who is joined to Him are, etc.]—ἓν πνεῦμα, *one spirit*) so closely, as husband and wife are one body. Make this your experience.

18. Φεύγετε τὴν πορνείαν, *flee fornication*) Severity with disgust; *flee*, for danger is near.—πᾶν ἁμάρτημα, *every sin*) even gluttony and drunkenness; comp. v. 13; even self-murder [*even idolatry, however much more grievous the sin may otherwise be.*—V. g.] It is a more serious matter to abuse the members of Christ, than food or wine, and the belly: and the body of a fornicator is more debased by the agency of a flagitious deed, than the carcase even of the man who has perished by his own hand. The comparison at Prov. vi. 30, etc., is not unlike this.—ἐκτὸς, *without*) a man indeed sins with the body and by the body, but not εἰς *against* the body; the sin is not terminated in his body; and he certainly injures, but does not alienate the body, he rather sins against the κοιλίαν, *belly*, than against the *body*, as the apostle makes the distinction. Such moral sentiments are not to be harshly pushed to extremes, nor in their utmost ἀκρίβειᾳ, *strictness*. The viscera, which stand in a peculiar relation to the animal economy, seem likely to be destroyed permanently, and not to be restored at the resurrection. The Scripture refers much to the bones, as to the solid parts, in respect of good and evil, of punishment and reward; whence it is no vain conjecture, that the most intense pain, and so also the most intense degree of joy and pleasure, will be in the bones.

[1] See Appendix.

19. *Ἢ) a particle denoting the second part of a disjunctive interrogation. The expression, *his own*, ver. 18, is in this ver. sweetly limited. Our body is so constituted, as that it may be the temple of God, *i.e.* His peculiar and perpetual habitation.— τοῦ ἐν ὑμῖν, *which is in you*) This expression assigns the reason [ætiology.—See Append.]. The Holy Spirit is in you; therefore you are His temple.—οὗ) *whom*, the Spirit.—καὶ οὐκ ἐστὲ ἑαυτῶν, *and ye are not your own*) This appropriately follows, but yet it is connected more closely with, *ye are bought*, and in its construction, it also depends on ὅτι, *because*.

20. Ἠγοράσθητε, *ye are bought*) You are entirely in the power of another. *To sell* is used for *to alienate; to buy* for *to claim for one's self*, and here too with propriety; for the mention of *a price* is added.—τιμῆς, *with a price*) This word has thus much greater force, than if an epithet were added. So also vii. 23.—δοξάσατε, *glorify*) An Epiphonema [an exclamation subjoined to a weighty argument.—Appen.] They are in error, who think that God should be only internally, or only externally worshipped.—ἐν τῷ σώματι ὑμῶν,[1] *in your body*) Rom. xii. i.; Phil. i. 20.

CHAPTER VII.

1. Περὶ δὲ ὧν ἐγράψατε, *Now concerning the things whereof ye wrote*) He sets before us his subject at the first with elegance, rather generally than particularly. The apostles in their epistles often treat of marriage; the apostle Paul alone, once and not of his own accord, but when he was asked, advises celibacy, and that

[1] The words which follow to the end of this clause, are declared by the margin of both Ed. as a reading not genuine; wherefore, also, in the German Vers., they are only within a parenthesis. Not. Crit. on this passage agrees to it: ὑμῶν, περὶ) a sure reading; the question here is about the use and abuse of the body.—E. B.

Rec. Text adds καὶ ἐν τῷ πνεύματι ὑμῶν ἅτινα ἐστὶν τοῦ Θεοῦ. Both Syr. Vers. alone of the oldest authorities support this reading. But ABC corrected later, D corr. lat., G Vulg. *fg* Iren. Cypr. Lucif. Memph. omit the words.—ED.

too very gently. [*So far is this from being a subject, which ought to be obtruded upon mankind by human precepts.*—V.g.]—καλὸν, *good*) This agrees with the feeling, which pervades the preceding chapter. Comp. below ver. 7, 8, 26, 34, in the middle of the verse, 35 at the end, 40. It is *good, i.e.* becoming, suitable, for the sake of liberty and exemption from *what is due* [by a husband to his wife], ver. 3, and for the sake of keeping one's 'power,' which he has over himself undiminished, ver. 4; though on the other hand *touching*, ver. 1, has always *modesty* as its accompaniment among them that are chaste.—ἀνθρώπῳ, *for a man*) in general, although he be not a Christian, ver. 7, 26.—γυναικὸς, *a woman*) and in like manner for the woman not to be touched. In what follows, the one relation involves the other.

2. Διὰ, *on account of*) comp. the *for*, ver. 5.—τὰς πορνείας, *fornications*) constantly practised at Corinth [*and not even considered to be sins by the heathens, and especially by the Greeks.*—V.g.], to which unmarried persons might be easily allured. The plural denotes irregular lusts, and is on that account more opposed to the unity of the marriage relation [wherein there is but *one* consort].—τὴν ἑαυτοῦ, *his own*) the same as ἴδιον, *her own*, which immediately after occurs. The same variation occurs in Eph. v. 22, 23. ἑαυτοῦ, *his own*, indicates the rights of the husband. Both words exclude all community, in which polygamy consists, comp. ver. 4. Now the reason, why a man should have a wife, is the same as that, for which he should retain her, namely, *to avoid fornication.* Hence also *concubinage* is refuted, for a concubine is either a wife or she is not; if she is not, there is sin, if she is, then she ought to continue, ver. 10, 11.

3. Ὀφειλὴν, *what is due* [*due benevolence*, Engl. Vers.]) This is explained in the next verse. Gataker shows, that the same duty was called by the Greeks χάριν, by the poets φιλότητα. The reading of this passage, *due benevolence*, ὀφειλομένην εὔνοιαν, is a spurious paraphrase.[1] [ὀφειλὴν *is the native* (genuine) *and simple reading.* —Not. crit.]

4. Ἰδίου, *of her own*) This word with the phrase, *she has not power*, makes an elegant paradox. The rights of both are equal.

[1] Ὀφειλὴν is the reading of ABCDG Vulg. *fg* Memph. Orig. Cypr. Ὀφειλομένην εὐνοίαν of Rec. Text is the reading of both the Syriac Versions, but of none other of the oldest authorities.—ED.

5. Μὴ ἀποστερεῖτε, *defraud not*) So the LXX., Exod. xxi. 10, *he shall not defraud her of her duty of marriage*, τὴν ὁμιλίαν αὐτῆς (עֹנָתָהּ) οὐκ ἀποστερήσει. This word agrees with the word *due*, ver. 3.—εἰ μή τι ἄν, *except it be*) It is very much limited. When these conditions occur, it is not privation, but abstinence.—ἵνα σχολά-ζητε, *that you may be at leisure*) The apostle speaks here of great leisure, σχολήν, and ease. Previous abstinence is subservient to prayer. [*Those who fasted among the Greeks added here* fasting.— Not. crit.[1]]. Abstinence may also have other motives originating it [besides the object of prayer], and those of a bad kind.—καὶ πάλιν, *and again*) Concerning such intervals, and their measure, see Selden on the Hebrew wife.—ἐπὶ τὸ αὐτὸ, *together*) This does not mean the very act of connubial intercourse, but is opposed to the previous separation.—πειράζῃ, *should tempt*) to fornication, etc., ver. 2.—ὁ Σατανᾶς, *Satan*) who amid the exercises of the sublimer virtues seeks an opportunity of doing the greatest injury. Temptation cannot be easily presupposed without Satan.— ἀκρασίαν, *incontinency*) ver. 9.

6. Τοῦτο, *this*) what has been mentioned all along from ver. 2.—κατὰ συγγνώμην οὐ κατ' ἐπιταγήν) See ver. 25, note.

7. Θέλω) *I would* for my part, ver. 32. Paul had tasted the sweetness of celibacy, and was desirous that others should have the same pleasure in it. The expression, *I would*, may be also taken absolutely for *it is to be wished*, comp. vi. 12, note: as he says on other occasions, οὐκ ἦν θέλημα, *there was no wish*.—γὰρ) *for*, used in its strict sense. The reference is to ver. 6.—ὡς καὶ ἐμαυτὸν, *as even myself*) unmarried. The Corinthians seem to have looked to the example of Paul, ver. 8.—χάρισμα, *gift*) That, which in the natural man is a natural habit, becomes in the saints *a gift*. The *gift* here is the entire habit [habitual bearing] of the mind and body in the Christian, in so far, for example, as marriage or celibacy is more suitable to him, along with the actions consonant to each state, being in accordance with the commandments of God. But in the case of godly men in an involuntary condition, the assistance of grace is more sure.

8. Λέγω δὲ, *but I say*) Comp. ver. 12, where the statement is

---

[1] Rec. Text inserts before τῇ προσευχῇ the words τῇ νηστείᾳ καὶ with both Syr. Versions. But ABCD(Λ)G *fg* Vulg. Orig. Cypr. omit the words. —ED.

more express.—τοῖς ἀγάμοις, *to the unmarried*) of both sexes, comp. ver. 10, 11.—χήραις, *to widows*) including widowers.—μείνωσιν, *let them remain*) at liberty.—ὡς κἀγώ, *even as I*) Paul was evidently without a wife at that time, comp. ix. 5; and although he speaks here also of widowers, yet he seems rather to have been a bachelor, than a widower; comp. Acts vii. 58, and what follows after

9. Κρεῖσσον, *better*) This comparative does not nullify the positive in ver. 38.—ἢ πυροῦσθαι, *than to be inflamed*) A very strong word. A man, who maintains continence, may have that, with which he has to struggle, although he may not be inflamed. Thomas Aquinas on this passage says, to be inflamed [to burn], *that is to be overcome by concupiscence; for concupiscence is a certain noxious heat. He, then, who is assailed by it, becomes warm indeed, but he does not burn, unless, overcome by concupiscence, he loses the dew of God's grace.* This *burning* thrusts men at last into hell-fire.

10.[1] Παραγγέλλω, οὐκ ἐγώ, *I command, yet not I*) a similar zeugma to, *I live, yet not I*, Gal. ii. 20. The force of the word, *I command*, is affirmatively connected with *the Lord.*—ὁ Κύριος, *the Lord*) Christ, who had given instructions on this subject, Matt. v. 32, xix. 4, 5; or even spoke to Paul respecting this matter; comp. ver. 12.—μὴ χωρισθῆναι, *not to be separated*) The less noble party, the wife is *separated*; the more noble, the husband, puts away; then in a converse point of view the believing wife also is said to *put away*, and the unbelieving husband to be *separated*, ver. 13, 15.

11. Ἐάν, *if*) This word also at the end of this verse is to be understood of the husband.—καὶ χωρισθῇ, *she even be separated* [*be put away*: not '*depart*,' as if of herself, Engl. Vers.]) contrary to the commandment.

12. Τοῖς δὲ λοιποῖς) *but to the rest*, who are living in marriage. —ἐγώ, *I*) see ver. 25, note.—λέγω, *I say*) he does not use the expression, *I command*, as in ver. 10. I say, viz. this, which is spoken of, ver. 12, 13, 15, 16, and mostly indeed at ver. 15, 16; for if ver. 12-14, be considered separately, they flow from

[1] Τοῖς—γεγαμηκόσι, *to the married*) when both husband and wife are among the number of believers. The antithesis is τοῖς λοιποῖς, ver. 12; when one or other of the parties is an unbeliever.—V. g.

ver. 10.—συνευδοκεῖ, *she be pleased*) There might be many, who either doubted or were not averse from the faith.—Μὴ ἀφιέτω, *let him not put away*) This rule was stricter in the Old Testament. That the difference between the Old and New Testament is here regarded, we gather from ver. 18, 15, note.

13. Γυνὴ, *the woman*) a sister.

14. Ἡγίασται) *has been sanctified*, so that the believing party may hold intercourse with the other in the exercise of holiness, and ought not to put him or her away: comp. 1 Tim. iv. 5. A very significant word is here used, because Scripture wishes to guarantee to us conscience being left everywhere unencumbered.—ἐν τῇ γυναικί) [*by the wife*] *in respect to the wife*, with whom he willingly remains; so ἐν, xiv. 11.—πιστῇ, *the believing*, is not added to γυναικί, in accommodation to human modes of thought [κατ᾽ ἄνθρωπον]: for an *unbelieving* husband does not know what *faith* is.—ἐπεὶ ἄρα, *otherwise*) For [otherwise] the children would follow the condition of the *unbelieving* parent. The marriage is Christian, and so also are the offspring.—τέκνα, *children*) who are born of a believing and an unbelieving parent. —ἀκάθαρτα, *unclean*) as those who are born of parents, who are both unbelievers, although they be not bastards.—ἁγιά ἐστιν, *they are holy*) ἡγίασται differs from this expression as, *to become holy*, from *to be holy*; but the holiness itself of the children and of the *unbelieving* parent is the same. He is speaking of a purity, which not only makes the children legitimate, not bastards, such as those also have, who are born from the marriage of two unbelievers; but which also imports a degree of nearer relationship with the Church, and a more open door to faith itself, just as if both parents were Christians. Comp. Rom. xi. 16. Timothy is an example, Acts xvi. 1, who was the bearer of this epistle, and there might have been many such among the children at Corinth. [*A husband is in other respects preferred; but the faith of the wife has more influence than the unbelief of the husband.*— V. g.]

15. Ὁ) ἢ ἡ ἄπιστος.—χωριζέσθω, *let—be separated*) Let him be divorced. A brother or a sister should be patient, and not think that that ought to be changed, which he or she cannot change. [*The believing party is not bound to renounce the faith for the sake of the unbelieving party.*—V. g.]—οὐ δεδούλωται, *is*

not under bondage) There was more decided liberty in the latter case on this account, that the believing party was not likely to obtain much assistance from the unbelieving magistrate; although, even in the present day, the same principle holds good for liberty and peace; but with that exception [proviso], *let her remain unmarried*, ver. 11.—ἐν δὲ εἰρήνῃ, *but in peace*) An axiomatic truth; one that proceeds from things internal to things external. There had been formerly *enmity*, Eph. ii. 15.

16. Τί γὰρ, *for what*) Therefore thou oughtest not to distress thyself too anxiously; but to preserve the tranquillity of thy mind, exertions must be made according to the measure of hope.—ἄνδρα—γυναῖκα, *husband, wife*) averse from thee, and therefore from the faith.—σώσεις, *thou shalt save*) The one consort ought to lead, as far as possible, the other consort to salvation.

17. Εἰ μή, *if not*) that is, *if this be not so*, or, *otherwise* [*but*]. There is a digression *from husbands and wives*, ver. 10, to any external condition of life.—ἑκάστῳ, *to each*) It may be thus resolved, *let every man walk, as God hath distributed to him*.—ἐμέρισεν, *hath distributed*) ver. 7.—ὡς κέκληκεν, *as He hath called*) The state in which the heavenly calling has found every one.—ὁ Κύριος, *the Lord*) Christ.—περιπατείτω, *let him walk*) This conclusion in which *permission* and *command* are blended together, is repeated and explained at ver. 20 and 24. Calling from above does not destroy our external conditions. Paul shows that what any one has done or would have done without it, is lawful to be done in it.—καὶ οὕτως, *and thus*) a universal doctrine, in which the Corinthians also may acquiesce.

18. Μὴ ἐπισπάσθω, *let him not draw*) [become uncircumcised]. Many, who had apostatized from the Jews to the Gentiles, recovered their uncircumcision to some extent by surgical skill, 1 Macc. i. 15. See *Reineccius* on this passage. It may be gathered from the admonition of Paul, that they were imitated by some, who from Jews had become Christians.

19. Οὐδέν ἐστι, *is nothing*) Comp. viii. 8. So also by parity of reasoning, *slavery* and *liberty; marriage* and *celibacy*, are nothing.—τήρησις, *keeping*) An axiom worthy of particular notice. —ἐντολῶν, *of the commandments*) Circumcision had been also commanded; but not for ever, as was the case with love.

20. Ἐν τῇ κλήσει, *in the calling*) The state in which the [heavenly] calling stumbles upon [finds] any one, is equivalent to a calling.

21. Μή σοι μελέτω, *care not for it*) Do not anxiously seek to be set free; so, *do not seek* [a wife], ver. 27.—μᾶλλον χρῆσαι, *use it rather*) *use the power of obtaining liberty*, or rather *use* [continue in] *slavery;* for he, who might become free, has a kind master, whom it is better to serve, than to follow any other course of life, 1 Tim. vi. 2; comp. the beginning of the next verse: therefore in ver. 23, he does not say, *be not*, but *do not become the servants of men*.

22. Ἀπελεύθερος, *freedman*) Ἐλεύθερος, one *free*, and who also was never a slave; ἀπελεύθερος, *a freedman*, who had been a slave.—Κυρίου, *of the Lord*) *Christ*, which presently after occurs.—ὁ ἐλεύθερος κληθείς, *he that being free is called*) At the beginning of the verse the word *called* is put before *a servant;* here *free* is placed before the word *called*, for the sake of emphasis, that he may be also included, who, in consequence of his calling, obtains the power of acquiring freedom. Comp. on the arrangement of the words, Gal. iv. 25, note.

23. Ἠγοράσθητε, *you have been bought*) by God [*as the servants of Christ*.—V. g.]—μὴ γίνεσθε, [not as Engl. Vers. "*be* not ye"] *do not become*) The internal and external state should, so far as it is attainable, agree together, and the latter should be subservient to the former. *To become* here, is properly applied to those, who are not slaves. [*Let not him who is free, cast away his liberty*. Not. crit.]

24. Παρὰ Θεῷ, *with God*) An antithesis to men, Rom. xiv. 22. Those who are always looking to God maintain a holy indifference about external things. By this principle [viz., regard to God], however, the rule laid down at ver. 20, is limited. For example, a man, from being a slave, may become free [and thus *not abide in the same calling*] without any change of his condition before God.

25. Παρθένων, *virgins*) of both sexes: See the following verses. So the word, *virgin*, Rev. xiv. 4.—οὐκ ἔχω, *I have not*) He does not say, *we have not*. The Corinthians expected a special commandment by revelation, which Paul was to receive.—γνώμην δὲ) A word used with deliberate choice here and at ver. 40, as pre-

sently νομίζω. *Aristotle*, carefully pointing out the propriety of Greek words, especially in his Ethics, makes the following observations : ἡ καλουμένη γνώμη ἡ τοῦ ἐπιεικοῦς ἐστὶ κρίσις ὀρθή, " that which is termed γνωμη, *opinion*, is the right judgment of the equitable man :" and again, ἡ δὲ συγγνώμη, γνώμη ἐστὶ κριτικὴ τοῦ ἐπιεικοῦς ὀρθή. ὀρθὴ δὲ ἡ τοῦ ἀληθοῦς, " and indulgence [concession] is the upright judicious opinion of what is equitable; and the indulgence of the truthful man is right," Lib. 6, Eth. Nic. c. 11.[1] There the discussion is more extended, and when we read it all, we shall more clearly understand, what γνώμη and συγγνώμη are. Ἐπιταγή implies command : γνώμη relates to opinion, and has συγγνώμη [a *common sentiment, fellow-feeling*, and so *indulgence*] closely connected with it, which is a γνώμη, accommodated to the state or mind of another, as in regard to a thing done, so also in case of a thing to be done. See ver. 6, and 2 Cor. viii. 10, 8, where both of these words, are opposed to τῇ ἐπιταγῇ. Each has regard to τὸ συμφέρον, the *profit* of him, whose advantage is consulted; in the same verse 10, and here 1 Cor. vii. 35. Such is the nature of those things which are treated of in this chapter, that they partly fall under ἐπιταγὴν, and partly under γνώμην and συγγνώμην. But it was becoming, that ἐπιταγὴ should be throughout written in the name of the Lord, γνώμη and συγγνώμη, in the name of the apostle. Therefore on that point, which falls under ἐπιταγὴν, the Lord had expressly suggested to the apostle what he should write, but on this point, which falls under γνώμην, it was not necessary to make any suggestion ; for, the apostles wrote nothing, which was not inspired, θεόπνευστον ; but they sometimes had a special revelation and command, xiv. 37 ; 1 Thess. iv. 15 : they derived the rest from the habitual faith, which had taken its rise within them from their experience of the Lord's mercy ; as in this verse ; and also from the treasury of the Spirit of God [which they possessed], ver. 40 : and consequently in cases like this, they might very freely apply various methods according to the variety of circumstances and persons, as their holy feelings [affections of mind] allowed,

---

[1] Taylor's translation of this passage is as follows : " What is called upright decision is the right judgment of the equitable man ; but pardon is an upright judiciary decision of the equitable man, and the decision is right which is made by a man observant of truth."

1 CORINTHIANS VII. 26—28.

and they might give up their own right, humble or reprove themselves, prefer others to themselves, beg, entreat, exhort (2 Cor. vi. 1, vii. 8, xi. 17, note), at one time treat with greater severity, at another with greater mildness; and hence Paul, for example, uses the softer word νομίζω, and not λέγω, ver. 26, 12. He therefore here also, though without ἐπιταγὴν, wrote those things, which nevertheless exactly agreed with the mind of the Lord, who willed it, that this γνώμη, *opinion*, alone should be given. But at the same time, the apostle faithfully informs us, according to what principle every thing was written (a modesty from which how far I would ask, has the style of the Pope departed?) and furnishes a proof, that those, who have already sufficient assistance [safeguard] from the word and Spirit of God, should not demand anything extraordinary.—ὡς ἠλεημένος, *as having obtained mercy*) The mercy of the Lord makes men faithful; faith makes a man a true casuist.—ὑπὸ Κυρίου, *from the Lord*) Christ.—πιστὸς, *faithful*) having faith in the Lord; evincing that faith both to Him and to men.

26. Διὰ τὴν ἐνεστῶσαν ἀνάγκην, *for the present distress*) The famine in the time of Claudius, Acts xi. 28. It was very long and severe, especially in Greece. Therefore this counsel of Paul was, partly at least, suited to the time.—ἀνθρώπῳ, *for a man*) This term is intended to apply to both sexes.— οὕτως, *so*) as he is [in the same state in which he is]: comp. ver. 27.

27. Δέδεσαι—λέλυσαι, *thou art bound—thou art loosed*) There is an argument in the very words. When *bound to a wife*, a man is often prevented, with or without any blame to him, from being able so munificently to practise liberality and the other virtues, as he might wish. In the verb λέλυσαι, *thou art loosed*, the participle is latently contained [thou art one *untied*], and it has the force of a noun, so that *loosed* denotes not only him, who is no longer bound to a wife, but also him, who never was so bound. We find a similar phrase in Job xxxix. 5.—μὴ, *not*) twice, *i.e.* thou art not forced to seek.

28. Τῇ σαρκὶ, *in the flesh*) Not in the *spirit*, to which the *trouble* is sin—but in this present case here there is no sin.— ἐγὼ δὲ, *but I*) He writes to them with the affection of a father, ver. 32.—φείδομαι, *I spare*) It is more difficult and requires

greater firmness to regulate well the state of marriage, than of celibacy.

29. Τοῦτο δέ φημι, *but this I say*) The same form of expression occurs xv. 50, for the purpose of explanation, in summing up the whole.—ἀδελφοί, *brethren*) Paul is wont, especially when writing about external circumstances, to introduce the most noble digressions, as the Holy Spirit is always calling him to the things that are most excellent.—ὁ καιρός) the present *time*, either of the world ver. 31, ch. x. 11, or of individuals, the time of weeping, rejoicing, etc.—συνεσταλμένος) *narrow, short*, the contrary of unencumbered liberty, ver. 26.—τὸ λοιπὸν, [*but*] *as to what remains*) The particle here is very suitable. [*He hints, that the consummation of the world is not far off.*—V. g.]—ἵνα, *that*) Time in short, is of such a nature, *that* they ought, etc. [*Some spend much of their time in seeking the superfluous conveniences of life, in wandering thoughts, in a too pertinacious pursuit of literature, in the length and frequency of their feasts and amusements: and it is a virtue in the opinion of worldly men, when any one knows how to spend with his boon companions in a manner not without its charm, half or even whole days and nights in empty conversation and pursuits. But if it should become necessary either to engage in prayer, or to watch over the education of his children, or to exemplify the duty of love to his neighbour, then truly the want of time is made an obstacle; nay, he has not even leisure to consider, how much guilt is contracted by such conduct.*—V. g.]— γυναῖκας, *wives*) and so, *children, friends, patrons*. We ought to consider nothing our own.—μή, *not*) Thus Christian self-denial is appropriately expressed. They, who have [earthly goods], as persons who have and are likely long to have, are void of Christian self-denial.]—ὦσι, *may be*) This word is supplied also in the following verses.

30. Οἱ χαίροντες, *they who rejoice*) he does not say, *they who laugh*. [Rom. xii. 15. The train of thought is *here* (in the words, " they that *rejoice*") *of* nuptial feasts; *as in the preceding words* (they that *weep*) *of the death of* a wife, etc.—V. g.] He speaks soberly as is suitable in the vale of tears.—ὡς μὴ κατέχοντες, *as though they possessed not*) *To possess*, after, *to buy*, makes an epitasis [an emphatic addition to the previous words. Append.]: as after *use, abuse* comes, in the next verse, from

which it is evident, that the figure Ploce [the same word twice, once simply, next expressing an attribute. Append.] occurs in the three preceding clauses; for as the Apostle Paul exhorts *the teacher to teach*, and every one employed in doing good to be active in doing it, Rom. xii. 7; so *they, that rejoice, rejoice in the world*, which same is the very thing that he forbids.

31. Οἱ χρώμενοι, *they that use*) Paul seems to have used this expression for, and *they that sell*, because according to the general practice of the world, *selling* in itself is most suitable to travellers. We must use, not enjoy.—ὡς μὴ καταχρώμενοι) *as not abusing*. The compound verb both in Greek and Latin denotes not only the *perversion* of the use, but also ['abundantiam,' *the abundant use*] an *over-much* using.—παράγει, *passeth away*, every moment, not merely *shall pass away*.—τὸ σχῆμα τοῦ κόσμου τούτου, *the fashion of this world*) the world itself and the *fashion* of it, which is to marry, to weep, to rejoice, to buy, etc., Heb. עֹלָם, Ps. xxxix. 7, lxxiii. 20. While a man, for example, is advancing from the twentieth to the fortieth year of his age, he has almost lost all his former relations and acquires new connexions.

32. Ἀμερίμνους, *without carefulness*) not only without affliction, ver. 28, but also without any care distracting the mind.— ὁ ἄγαμος, *he that is unmarried*) namely if he wishes to use wisely the condition in which he is placed.—τοῦ κυρίου, *of the Lord*) Christ. ἀρέσει, *may please*) by holiness of body and spirit.

33. Πῶς ἀρέσει) *how he may please*. The word *please* is repeated from the preceding verse, and comprehends here all the duties of a husband, which the wife may demand in everthing relating to the married state.

34. Μεμέρισται καὶ ἡ γυνὴ καὶ ἡ παρθένος) That is, *there is a difference also between a wife and a virgin*. Not only the unmarried and the married man have duties differing from each other; but also the duties of the wife, and virgin (of the female sex) differ as far as possible from each other. Some connect the word μεμέρισται, having the particle καὶ *also* before it,[1] by a different pointing, with the foregoing words, but Paul refers it to those

---

[1] Lachm. reads καὶ μεμέρισται καὶ with AB Vulg., and punctuates thus, γυναικί, καὶ μεμέρισται. καὶ ἡ γυνὴ, etc., G *fg* read μεμέρισται καί. Tischend. reads as Lachm., but puts the full stop at γυναικί.—ED.

which follow. *The difference*, namely between marriage and celibacy, each of which claims for itself a different class of duties, rather refers to women than to men; for the woman is the helper of the man;—the woman undergoes a greater change of her condition, than the man, in contracting marriage; comp. ver. 39, 40. Further, he is speaking here chiefly of virgins, ver. 25 : therefore the word μεμέρισται is particularly well adapted to this place ; and the *singular* number does not prevent it from being construed with *wife* and *virgin*. So 2 Kings x. 5, in the Hebrew, *He that was over the house, and he that was over the city, the elders also and the bringers up of the children* SENT" [singular verb] (Heb. שלח), so below, ix. 6, ἢ ΜΟΝΟΣ ἐγὼ καὶ Βαρνάβας, κ.τ.λ., " or I ONLY [instead of μονοί] and Barnabas."— ἵνα ἡ ἁγία, *that she may be holy*) She thus *pleases* the Lord, if she be holy, being wholly devoted to him. *Holiness* here implies something more than at ver. 14.

35. Αὐτῶν, *your own*.—βρόχον, *a snare*) *A snare*, the fear of committing sin, where there is no sin, or even forced service. Men are unwillingly drawn into a snare, Prov. vii. 21, LXX. That is readily considered as a snare, which is most conducive to *profit* [σύμφερον].—εὔσχημον) an antithesis to ἀσχημονεῖν, in the following verse.—εὐπάρεδρον) akin to this is the verb προσεδρεύειν, in ix. 13. An example is found in Luke x. 39.—τῷ Κυρίῳ, *to the Lord*) εὐπάρεδρον, as well as παρεδρεύω, governs the dative.— ἀπερισπάστως) This explains the word εὐπάρεδρον, for *assiduous attendance* upon the Lord, and *distraction*, are the reverse of each other. *Sitting* [involved in the εὐπάρεδρον] assists the devout mind. Comp. Luke x. 39, 40. Paul says something similar of the widow, 1 Tim. v. 5.

36. Τίς, *any man*) a parent.—ἀσχημονεῖν) viz. ἑαυτόν.—τὴν παρθένον αὐτοῦ) *a virgin*, *his* daughter.—νομίζει, *thinks*) Antithesis to, *I think* (*suppose*), ver. 26.—ἐὰν ᾖ ὑπέρακμος) if she pass, ἀκμὴν, *the flower*, of her age without marriage, as it were despised by suitors.—ὀφείλει, *it so ought to be* [*need so require*, Engl. V.] [*because he cannot see how better to consult the advantage of his daughter*.—V. g.], *having no necessity*, in the following verse is the antithesis.—οὐχ' ἁμαρτάνει, *he sinneth not*) The matter is sweetly expressed by short clauses.

37. Ἕστηκεν, *he who standeth stedfast*) There is in this passage

an admirable synonymy [accumulation of synonymous clauses] and description of liberty.—μὴ ἔχων ἀνάγκην, *having no necessity*) on account of which he should prefer celibacy to marriage, ver. 26, or marriage to celibacy.—ἐξουσίαν) *control* [*power*], without any interference.—ἔχει, *has*) for *having :* for *not* and *but* are in mutual relation to each other. There is the same enallage in Col. i. 6, note.—περὶ, *over*) For often the will is one thing, and the power an altogether different thing.—ἰδίου, *his own*) Liberty is elegantly denoted. [*Those who have now a regard to the Divine will, are often led to think, that they have been appointed to obtain only by one way, the things which correspond to the Divine will. Nevertheless, God grants to man full liberty regarding what is agreeable to His law*, Deut. xxxvi. 6.[1]— V. g.]—κέκρικεν) *has so judged* [*decreed*, has come to this as his decided opinion].—καλῶς ποιεῖ, *doeth well*) he not only does not sin ; he acts *very well* (καλῶς).

38. Ὥστε, *therefore*) We must observe, with how great earnestness, fidelity, and fulness, Paul dwells on this passage.—καὶ) *also*.

39. Ἐν Κυρίῳ, *in the Lord*) So that Christ is here also all things. Christians and unbelievers mixed in society and dwelt together. He therefore commands Christian men to marry Christian women.

40. Μακαριωτέρα, *happier*) ver. 1, 28, 34, 35 ; Luke xxiii. 29.—δοκῶ, *I think*) The Corinthians *thought* more of themselves than was right, and less of Paul. Paul with delicate pleasantry, ἀστείως, gives them back their own expression.—κἀγὼ) *I also*, no less certainly, than any of you [who may think he has the Spirit].—Πνεῦμα Θεοῦ, *the Spirit of* GOD) whose counsels are spiritual, divine.

---

[1] Rather Numb. xxxvi. 6. Let them marry *to whom they think best.*—ED.

CHAPTER VIII.

1. Περί—οἴδαμεν, *as touching—we know*) This topic is taken up again at ver. 4, when the parenthesis, which follows, has been concluded.—ὅτι) *that.* This explains the "*we know.*"—γνῶσιν, *knowledge*) The article is not added,[1]) that he may not concede too much.—ἔχομεν, *we have*) He speaks in the first person of himself and others, more established in the faith; when speaking more generally, he uses the third, ver. 7. Thus we easily reconcile the *all* [ver. 1] and *not in all* [ver. 7].—ἡ γνῶσις, *knowledge*) without love. [*Although the fundamental doctrines and those most necessary and difficult are spoken of.* V. g.]—φυσιοῖ, *puffeth up*) when a man pleases himself; comp. *thinks*, ver. 2.—ἡ δὲ ἀγάπη, *but love*) the right use of *knowledge*, love, towards God, ver. 3, and towards our neighbour.—οἰκοδομεῖ, *edifieth*) when a man pleases his neighbour. *Knowledge* only says, *all things are lawful for me*; love adds, *but all things do not edify.*

2. Εἰδέναι, *that he knows*) This has respect to the "*we know*," ver. 1; it differs from *to be acquainted with.*[2]—τι, *anything.* Paul makes some small concession here; comp. the following clause.—οὔπω, *not yet*) like a novice.—καθὼς, *as* [in the way that]) namely in the way of love, [taught] by God.

3. Τὸν Θεόν, *God*) The love of our neighbour follows the love of God.—οὗτος, *this same*) who loves.—ἔγνωσται) *is known.* Active follows passive knowledge, xiii. 12. In this expression we have an admirable metalepsis[3]—he was known, and therefore he hath

---
[1] Therefore, also, in the Germ. Vers., the article ought to be wanting in this passage.—E. B.

[2] The Latin synonyms are *scire* and *cognoscere*. *Scire*, to know, to be skilful in, chiefly applied to things; *cognoscere*, to know, to become acquainted with persons or things formerly unknown; however, ἐγνωκέναι is the reading of ABD (Δ) G *f* (cognovisse). Εἰδέναι of Rec. Text is supported by Vulg. (scire) Cypr. Hil.—ED.

[3] See Append. A twofold trope, or figurative use of the same word or phrase.

1 CORINTHIANS VIII. 4–7.

known, Gal. iv. 9, note. The knowledge is mutual.—ὑπ' αὐτοῦ) by Him.

4. Βρώσεως) He more closely limits the subject proposed at ver. 1: *as concerning, therefore, the eating,* etc.—οὐδὲν) *nothing,* is the predicate; *nothing,* the force of which is augmented by the antithetic words, *in the world,* יהוה, 1 Sam. xii. 21, LXX., οὐδεν; comp. ch. x. 19, note. [*A piece of wood or stone and* nothing *besides.*—V. g.]

5. Λεγόμενοι, *that are called*) God is said to be the supremely powerful One. Hence by homonymy [things or persons distinct in nature receiving by analogy the same name], angels who are powerful on account of their spiritual nature, and men who are powerful from being placed in authority, *are called gods.*— ἐν οὐρανῷ, *in heaven*)—ἐπὶ γῆς, *on earth*) The provinces of the gods among the Gentiles were divided into heaven, and earth, along with the sea; but each of these belongs to God.—θεοὶ πολλοὶ καὶ κύριοι πολλοί, *gods many and lords many*) Ps. cxxxvi. 2, 3.

6. Ἡμῖν) *to us,* believers.—ἐξ οὗ τὰ πάντα, *of whom are all things*) Therefore, we have one God.—τὰ πάντα, *all things*) by creation.—ἡμεῖς, *we*) believers.—εἰς αὐτὸν, *unto Him*) He is the end for whom believers live.—καὶ εἷς, *and one*) Christ, the object of divine and religious worship. The apostles also, for the purpose of avoiding the appearance of polytheism, more frequently called Christ Lord, than God, when they wrote to the Gentile churches.—Κύριος, *Lord*) This appellation comprehends in itself the notion of *the Son of God,* and therefore also *of God,* along with the idea of Redeemer.—δι' οὗ, *by whom*) The dominion of Christ is hereby proved; *by Him* all things are *of God.*—δι' αὐτοῦ, *by Him*) We come by Him, εἰς, *to* the Father. The plan of this sentence is as follows:—

Of whom are all things } by creation; } *to Him,*
by whom are all things } *and we*   } *by Him,* } by restitution.

7. Ἀλλ') We have γνῶσιν, *knowledge;* but others have it not in the same degree.—τινὲς, *some*) an antithesis to *all,* ver. 1. Some, viz. the Jews, holding the idol in abomination; the Greeks regarding it with reverence, x. 32.—τοῦ εἰδώλου, *of the idol*)

VOL. III. R

They had this feeling,[1] as if the idol were something; or at least as if the thing offered to the idol were polluted thereby.—ἕως ἄρτι, *until this hour*) when by this time they should have knowledge.—ὡς) *as:* on this depends the distinction.—μολύνεται, *is defiled*) a suitable expression, by a metaphor derived from flesh.—βρῶμα, *food*) used indefinitely, ver. 13.—ἡμᾶς, *us*) having or not having knowledge.—οὐ παρίστησι) neither as regards pleasing Him in the judgment, nor as regards displeasing Him, πρὸς τὸ ὑστερεῖσθαι [so as to be accounted the worse for it] ; συνίστημι, *I commend;* but the word παρίστημι occupies a middle place between a good and a bad sense, as is evident from the Ep. of Athanasius, πρὸς 'Αμοῦν, where he makes this periphrasis, φυσικὴ τις ἔκκρισις ἡμᾶς οὐ παραστήσει πρὸς τιμωρίαν.[2] So ver. 10, οἰκοδομηθήσεται is used as a word in a middle sense. This is the foundation of *lawful power* [*liberty*, ver. 9], ἐξουσίας ; comp. δὲ in the next verse.—οὔτε—περισσεύομεν οὔτε—ὑστερούμεθα, neither *are we the better:* nor—*are we the worse*) because in both cases thanksgiving is retained, Rom. xiv. 6.

9. Ἡ ἐξουσία, *lawful power* [liberty]) a word frequently used for *power* and *liberty* in this discussion, ix. 1, 4, etc.: comp. vi. 12.—ὑμῶν, *of yours*) which you so eagerly uphold, ver. 11.

10. Εἰδωλείῳ) A word fitted to deter. It is found in 1 Macc. i. (47), 50, x. 83 ; 3 Esdr. ii. 10.—οἰκοδομηθήσεται, *shall be built up in* [*emboldened to*]) An antiphrasis.[3] You ought to *have built up* your brother in doing good ; but you by your example impel him to do evil. [*The force of example is great.—*V. g.]—τὰ εἰδωλόθυτα ἐσθίειν, *to eat things offered to idols*) By these very words

---

[1] Ernesti says, Bibl. th. noviss. T. i., p. 511, that Bengel, along with Heumann, prefers the reading συνηθείᾳ in this verse to the common reading συνειδήσει, and approves of it, but without foundation. Certainly Bengel's older margin has marked συνηθείᾳ with γ, the later with δ; and the Germ. Vers. has expressly printed συνειδήσει.—E. B.

Tisch. prefers συνειδήσει with D (Λ) G Vulg. both Syr. Versions, and *fg*. Lachm. reads συνηθείᾳ with AB Memph.—ED.

[2] Any natural ejection in the animal functions will not bring us to punishment.

[3] See Appendix : When words are used to signify the contrary of what is expressed, as here, shall be *built up* (usually applied to what is good), meaning, shall be impelled to what is bad.—ED.

the horror of the weak man is expressed, who eats notwithstanding.

11. 'Ἀπολεῖται, *shall perish*) He will lose his faith, and, if he do not recover it, his salvation, Rom. xiv. 23. [*See, what important results a single action may produce, although externally considered it seemed to be of little consequence.*—V. g.]—δι' ὅν, *for* [on account of] *whom) For* rather than *instead of* suits the passage before us; that we may be taught, what we ought to do *for the sake* of our brethren.—ἀπέθανεν, *died*) prompted by the love, which thou so very little imitatest.

12. Τύπτοντες, *striking*) [Engl. V. not so well, *wounding*], as the weary cattle are urged on by the lash. *Striking* is elegantly used, not *wounding*, for a wound is seen, a stroke is not so discernible. You strike brethren, or make them strike themselves.—εἰς Χριστὸν, *against Christ*) to whom the brethren are united. The expression, *against Christ*, in the latter clause bears the chief emphasis; *when ye sin*, in the former.

13. Κρέα, *flesh*) In order to avoid with the greater certainty flesh sacrificed to an idol, I would abstain from all kinds of flesh.—σκανδαλίσω, *I should make to offend*) The person is changed: he just now said, *if meat offend*.

CHAPTER IX.

1. Οὐκ εἰμὶ ἐλεύθερος; οὐκ εἰμὶ ἀπόστολος;) *am I not free? am I not an apostle?*) There is a transposition of these two clauses in the present received reading:[1] but Paul first lays down the proposition, *I am free;* then, the reason of it [by aetiology. Append.], *I am an apostle;* and there is a hendiadys in this sense, *I am entitled not only to Christian, but also to apostolic liberty.* We have a chiasmus[2] in the discussion of the subject: for in it he first claims for himself the *apostleship*, ver. 1–3, then he asserts his *liberty*, and that too as an apostle, ver. 4, 5, 19,

---

[1] AB Vulg. Memph. Syr. Orig. 4,266 *b*, support the order as in Bengel D G *fg* later Syr. put ἀπόστολος before ἐλεύθερος, as in Rec. Reading.—ED.

[2] See Appendix.

[whereas in the statement of subject, ver. 1, '*free*' comes first, '*apostle*' next]. That, which *free* is in the adjective, ver. 1, ἐξουσία, *power*, is in the substantive, ver. 4; comp. viii. 9.—οὐχί—ἑώρακα, *have I—not seen?*) Observe the firmness of the apostle.—τὸ ἔργον μου, *my work*) A testimony derived from actual *facts*, which is the strongest.

2. Ὑμῖν, *to you*) to whom I came; who have received the Gospel; you cannot deny it: ὑμῖν, *as far as you are concerned*. Similar datives are found at ver. 21.—ἡ γὰρ σφραγίς, *for the seal*) From the Church of believers an argument may be derived for the truth of the Gospel, and of the Christian religion.—ἀποστολῆς, *of apostleship*) A person even, who was not an apostle, might bring men by means of the Gospel to the faith, as Philip, Epaphras, and others; but Paul calls the Corinthians the seal not of *calling* of whatsoever kind, but of *his apostolic calling*: because he had the signs of an apostle, 2 Cor. xii. 12; Rom. xv. 18, 19; nor did the Corinthians merely receive faith, but also a singular abundance of gifts, 1 Cor. i. 7.

3. Ἡ) This is an anaphora with[1] ἡ σφραγίς, ver. 2—ἀπολογία, *a defence* [or *answer*]) The Roman Pontiff, in his desire to be *irresponsible*, ἀνυπεύθυνος, assumes more to himself.—τοῖς ἐμὲ ἀνακρίνουσιν, *to those who debate my case* [*examine me*]) who have any doubt of my apostleship.

[2]4. Μὴ οὐκ ἔχομεν; *have we not?*) He comes from the singular to the plural, including his *colleagues* [in the apostleship].—φαγεῖν καὶ πιεῖν, *to eat and to drink*) without labouring with his hands.

5. Ἀδελφὴν γυναῖκα, *a sister, a wife*) Expressed in the nominative case this is the proposition implied, *this sister is my wife;* wherefore the name, *sister*, does not prevent marriage.—περιάγειν, *to lead about*) an abbreviated expression[3] for *to have and to lead about;* for he had no wife. Expense was laid upon the Churches, not from having, but from leading about a wife.—ὡς, *as well as*) this word also refers to ver. 4.—οἱ λοιποί, the *others*) The article shows that all the others had done so. We

---

[1] See Append. The frequent repetition of the same word in the beginnings of sections.

[2] Αὕτη ἐστί, *is this*) namely, that you are the seal of my office.—V.g.

[3] See Appendix, "locutio concisa."

may presume the same of John.—καὶ οἱ ἀδελφοὶ τοῦ Κυρίου, *and the brethren of the Lord*) Acts i. 14; Gal. i. 19.—καὶ Κηφᾶς, *and Cephas*) There is a gradation here; comp. iii. 22, note.

6. Τοῦ μὴ ἐργάζεσθαι), *to forbear working with the hand*.

7. Τίς, *who*) The minister of the Gospel is beautifully compared to a soldier, a vine-dresser, a shepherd. The apostle speaks of that which is a common occurrence; although, even then, there had been some, who were soldiers on their own charges—*volunteers*.—φυτεύει; *plants*) iii. 6.

8. Καὶ) *also*. Not only do I not speak this *as a man* [according to mere human modes of thought], but with the approbation of the law itself.

9. Οὐ φιμώσεις βοῦν ἁλοῶντα) So the LXX., Deut. xxv. 4.—ἁλοῶντα, *threshing*) Horses in the present day are employed in threshing corn in some parts of Germany.—μὴ τῶν βοῶν, *does God care for oxen*) It is not at all denied, that God cares for oxen, since the man, who would have muzzled the ox, threshing the corn, would have committed a sin against the law. But the conclusion proceeds from the less to the greater. [If God cares for mere oxen, much more for men]. This is a specimen of the right mode of handling the Mosaic laws, enacted regarding animals.

10. Πάντως, *altogether*) The word, 'saying,' is put into the question itself.—ὅτι) namely, *that*—ἐπ' ἐλπίδι), לבבה, which the LXX. always render ἐπ' ἐλπίδι : comp. Acts ii. 26.—ὀφείλει, *ought*) There is a change of person. *The obligation* [implied in ὀφείλει] is with them that remunerate, not with them that labour; otherwise the latter would commit sin by not receiving. So also regarding the precept, ver. 14 : comp. *I ought*, 2 Cor. xii. 11.—ὁ ἀροτριῶν, *that* [animal] *which ploweth* [or *he that ploweth*]) This also is the labour of oxen. It seems to be an adage, something like this; *hope supports the husbandman*.—τῆς ἐλπίδος αὐτοῦ,[1] *of*

---

[1] The margin of the 2d Ed. prefers the shorter reading, ἐπ' ἐλπίδι τοῦ μετέχειν, of which there is not a vestige, either in the older Ed., or in the Gnomon, or in the Germ. Vers.—E. B.

ἐπ' ἐλπίδι τοῦ μετέχειν is the reading of ABC both Syr. (Memph.) Theb. Vulg. (in spe fructus percipiendi) Orig. 1,170; 541 c. But D (Λ) corrected later, G fg read τῆς ἐλπίδος αὐτοῦ μετέχειν : to which Rec. Text adds ἐπ' ἐλπίδι.—ED.

his hope) The abstract for the concrete: *of the fruits, in the hope of which* he, who now threshes, *plowed,*—μετέχειν, *to become partaker*) viz. *ought.* *To become partaker of his hope* is a periphrasis for the verb *to thresh.* Namely, he who plows, plows *in the hope* of threshing and eating; he, who threshes, possesses that *hope*, which he had in plowing, and threshes in the *hope* of eating.

11. ʹΥμῖν, *unto you*) he does not say *yours*, as afterwards.—μέγα, *a great thing*) Comp. 2 Cor. xi. 15, 14, where it is explained as the same as " *a marvel.*"

12. "Ἄλλοι, *others*) true apostles, ver. 5: or false ones, 2 Cor. xi. 20.—ὑμῶν) *over you*.—μᾶλλον, *rather*) on account of our greater labour.— τῇ ἐξουσίᾳ ταύτῃ) The repetition gives force to the meaning; *this power* [such a power as this].—στέγομεν) στέγω signifies properly *to cover;* them to *protect, to defend;* likewise *to conceal, to bear* and *endure with a desire to conceal*, as here [1] and in xiii. 7. On the other hand, οὐ στέγειν, *not to forbear*, in a burst of strong feeling, 1 Thess. iii. 1, 5. [*The minister of the Gospel requires to put in practice this forbearance: For reproaches of this kind are cast upon him,* viz. *on the ground of arrogance or avarice, which among politicians* (or *men of the world*) *are considered virtues.*—V. g.]—ἵνα μὴ ἐγκοπήν τινα δῶμεν, *lest we should hinder*), *i.e.* that we should as far as possible forward the Gospel. Those, who are least encumbered, do more work and cause less expense; hence the celibacy of the priests among the Papists and of soldiers in the commonwealth.

13. Τὰ ἱερὰ) *sacred things.*—ἐκ τοῦ ἱεροῦ, *of the temple*)—θυσιαστηρίῳ, *at the altar*) If the Mass were a sacrifice, Paul would have undoubtedly accommodated to it the apodosis in the following verse.

14. Ὁ Κύριος, *the Lord*) Christ Matt. x. 10.

15. "Ἔγραψα, *I have written*) lately.—μᾶλλον, *rather*) construed with *die*. The reason of such a solemn affirmation is explained at 2 Cor. xi. 7, etc.—τίς, *any man*) who should either give me a livelihood by the Gospel, or should declare that I thus gained my living.

16. Γὰρ, *for*) He now states, in what this glorying consists.—

---

[1] "We suffer without speaking or complaining."—ED.

εὐαγγελίζωμαι [if], *I preach*) This must be taken in the exclusive sense; if I preach, and do so not gratuitously; if I do nothing besides.—ἀνάγκη, *necessity*) Owing [duty] takes away glorying.— οὐαί δὲ, *but* [yea] *woe*) *but* intensive; not only have I nothing, whereof I may glory, but even *woe* [to me, if I do not], Jon. i. 4; Ex. iv. 14; Jer. xx. 9.

17. Ἑκών, *willingly*) This is here used instead of *gratuitously*, whence *I have a reward* makes an oxymoron;[1] moreover he defines the *reward* and *gain* in the following verses. Paul often, when speaking of his own affairs, uses increase and diminution [αὔξησις and μείωσις], not unlike a catachresis, and suitable to express his self-abnegation. He might have *willingly* preached the Gospel, and yet have received a reward from the Corinthians; but if he should receive a reward, he considers that as equivalent to his preaching unwillingly; so in the following verse the use of his legitimate ʼ*power*ʼ might be without *abuse;* but he considers in his case the former in the light of the latter;[2] comp. Rom. xv. 15; 2 Cor. xi. 8, 9, i. 24, ii. 5, vii. 2, 3.—οἰκονομίαν πεπίστευμαι, *a dispensation of the Gospel is committed to me*) I cannot withdraw myself, although I should fail of my reward. Again, the language is exclusive, as in ver. 16.

18. Ἵνα, *that*) This is an answer to the question.—θήσω, future subjunctive.[3]—εἰς τὸ μὴ καταχρήσασθαι) *that I abuse not*, *i.e.* that I may withdraw myself as far as possible from any abuse.

19. Ἐκ πάντων, *from all men*) Masculine, as we have immediately after, *unto all;* comp. *the more.* I was free from all men, *i.e.* no one could have held me as subject to his power.— ἐδούλωσα, *I made myself a servant*) a servant suits himself entirely to another.—τοὺς πλείονας, *the more*) The article has a force relative to *all*, *i.e.* as many of them as possible.—κερδήσω, *I might gain*) This word agrees with the consideration of *a reward*.

20. Ὡς Ἰουδαῖος, *as a Jew*) in regard to those things which

---

[1] See Appendix. The pointed combination of contraries. "*Gratuitously*, yet I have a *reward.*"—ED.

[2] *i.e.* He would regard his using his *power* as if it were an *abuse*.—ED.

[3] Fut. subj. is an obsolete form seldom found, but legitimate. Indeed, the subjunctive itself is an old future.—See Donaldson's New Cratylus. —ED.

are not defined by the *law;* for *as under the law* follows, although even those, who observed the laws of Noah, might have been called men occupying a place midway between the Jews *under the law* and men *without the law.*—ὡς ὑπὸ νόμον) μὴ ὢν αὐτὸς ὑπὸ νόμον is subjoined in the oldest copies.¹ It was an omission easily made in others from the recurrence of the word νόμον.—τοὺς) The article seems to be put here not so much for the sake of emphasis as of necessity, as ὑπὸ *under* follows.

21. Ἀνόμους) This is here used in that sense, which the meaning of the primitive word precisely produces, as ἀνυπότακτον, Heb. ii. 8.—ὡς ἀνόμος, *as without law*), by omitting things that may be omitted in regard to things ceremonial.—μὴ ὢν ἄνομος, *who am not without the law*) Paul was not (*anomus*) *without the law,* much less was he (*antinomus*) *opposed to the law*.—μὴ ἄνομος, Θεῷ, ἀλλ' ἔννομος Χριστῷ) Χριστὸς, Θεοῦ ἐστι, iii. 23 : whence, he who is *without the law to God,* ἄνομος Θεῷ, is also *without the law to Christ*, ἄνομος Χριστῷ : he *who is under the law to Christ,* ἔννομος Χριστῶ, is *under the law to God,* ἔννομος Θεῷ. Concerning the law of Christ, comp. Gal. vi. 2, note. Ἔννομος has a milder meaning than ὑπὸ νόμον.

22. Τοὺς ἀσθενεῖς, *the weak*) The article is not added to Ἰουδαίους, nor to ἀνόμους. It is added to ἀσθενεῖς, because he is chiefly speaking of them, viii. 7 : and all these are easily gained, if they be rightly treated.—γέγονα, *I am become*) When the verb is thus put [in the Perf. middle, a tense almost *present* in meaning], the transition is easily made from the past ἐγενόμην to the present ποιῶ.

23. Ἵνα συγκοινωνὸς αὐτοῦ γένωμαι) The Σὺν and γίνομαι show great modesty. Those things which follow, are referred to this verse, as to the proposition [the theme to be handled].—αὐτοῦ, *of it*) of the Gospel and salvation ; comp. the words, *I might save,* ver. 22.

24. Οὐκ οἴδατε, *know ye not?*) The comparison is to a thing

---

¹ And, therefore, both in the margin of the 2d Ed. it is elevated from the mark γ to the mark β, and in the Germ. Vers. it is inserted in the context. —E. B.

These words, μὴ—νόμον, are read in ABCD (Λ) G *fg* Vulg. Theb. But Rec. Text omits the words with Memph. Syr. and Orig. 1,391 *c* ; 3,515 *f,* 4,166 *d*.—ED

very well known to the Corinthians.—[1]εἷς, *one*) Although we knew, that *one alone* would be saved, still it would be well worth our while to run. [*For what will become of those, who never cease to defend themselves by the inactivity of others.* Comp. x. 5.—V. g.]—οὕτω τρέχετε, ἵνα καταλάβητε, *so run that ye may obtain*) Paul speaks of himself to the end of the chapter; he does not yet exhort the Corinthians directly; therefore he seems here to introduce into his discourse by a third party[2] that sort of encouragement, which P. Faber, i. 2, Agonist. c. 32, shows that the judges of the combats, the instructors of the young in gymnastics and the spectators were accustomed to give;—also Chrysostom Hom. on the expression ἐὰν πεινᾷ; and Caesarius, quaest. 29; for the words, *he says, they say*,[3] are more than once omitted. See ch. v. 13, xv. 32, 33; Eph. vi. 2; Col. ii. 21; Ps. cxxxvii. 3; Jer. ii. 25, li. 9. Therefore this is the sense here; they say, *so run*, etc.; and this clause belongs to the protasis, which is continued at the beginning of the following verse, οὕτω, *so*, a particle expressive of praise as well as of exhortation, Phil. iv. 1.— τρέχετε, *run*) All are urged, as if each, not merely one, was to obtain the prize.—ἵνα, *that*) to the end that.

25. Πᾶς, *every man*) There were many sorts of contests.— δὲ, *but*) an emphatic addition (ἐπίτασις). The race was among those contests that were of a lighter description; wrestling, to which allusion is presently made, is among those that were more severe.—πάντα, *all things*) supply κατὰ, *as to, throughout.*— ἐγκρατεύεται, *is temperate*) Those, who were to strive for the mastery, were distinguished by their admirable mode of living. See the same Faber, and the same Chrysostom de Sacerd., l. 4, c. 2, at the end.—ἐκεῖνοι) *they*, who run and wrestle. Christians had abandoned the public games.—φθαρτὸν, *corruptible*) formed

---

[1] πάντες, *all*) Comp. x. 1.—V. g.

[2] See Appendix, under the title Sermocinatio. "So run that ye may obtain" is not Paul's direct exhortation to the Corinthians, but the language of the spectators of the games, etc., to the racers, quoted by Paul as applying to himself. Comp. v. 26. *Obliquely* reference was meant to the Corinthians.—ED.

[3] Beng. means that Paul's omitting, in the allusion or quotation, "As the saying is," does not militate against its being a quotation. For he elsewhere omits this express marking of quotations.—ED.

of the wild olive, of the apple tree, of parsley and of the fir tree. Not only the crown, but the remembrance of it perishes.

26. 'Εγὼ) *I for my part.*—οὕτως) *so*, as I said, ver. 23: comp. οὕτω, *so*, ver. 24.—οὐκ ἀδήλως, *not uncertainly*, I know what I aim at, and how to aim at it. He who runs with a clear aim looks straight forward to the goal, and makes it his only object, he casts away every encumbrance, and is indifferent to what the standers bye say, and sometimes even a fall serves only to rouse him the more.—πυκτεύω, *I fight*) Paul adds the pugilistic contest to the race, in preference to the other kinds of contest.—ὡς οὐκ ἀέρα δέρων, *not as one beating the air*) In the *Sciamachia* [sparring in the school for mere practice] which preceded the serious contest, they were accustomed to beat the air; comp. [ye shall speak to] *the air*, xiv. 9.

27. Ὑπωπιάζω) Eustathius says, ὑπώπια φασὶ τὰς περὶ τοὺς ὀφθαλμοὺς πληγάς· ἐξ ὧν ἐκ μέρους καιριωτάτου, καὶ τὸ ὑπωπιάζειν, καὶ σώματος ὑπωπιασμὸς μεταφορικῶς, ὁ κατὰ συντηξιν.[1] He at the same time shows, that πρόσκομμα, applies to the foot, as ὑπώπιον to the head; therefore compare πρόσκομμα and τύπτοντες with ὑπωπάζω, viii. 9, 12.—τὸ σῶμα, *the body*) A near antagonist, Rom. viii. 13; 1 Pet. ii. 11.—δουλαγωγῶ) I lay my hand upon my body, as on a *slave*, and *restrain* it; comp. respecting a slave, Sir. xxxiii. 25. ὑπωπιάζω, as a *pugilist*, δουλαγωγῶ, *as a runner*. The one word is put after the other; the one denotes rather the act, the other the state; the one is weightier than the other; for at first greater austerity is necessary, till the body is subdued.—κηρύξας) Κήρυκες were present at the games [*who placed the crowns on the brows of the conquerors announcing their names.*—V. g.]—ἀδόκιμος, *one rejected, cast away*) Unworthy of a prize, of a crown. It is a word which was used in the public games.

---

[1] Blows around the eyes are termed ὑπώπια; from which, on account of it being a most tender [susceptible] part, we have both ὑπωπιάζειν, and ὑπωπιασμὸς, applied to the severe disciplining of the body metaphorically, viz., that disciplining which is in the way of mortification.

CHAPTER X

1. Οὐ θέλω δὲ ὑμᾶς ἀγνοεῖν, *Moreover, I would not that you should be ignorant*) The phrase refers to the whole passage; for the Corinthians were acquainted with the history; comp. ix. 13. [1]The particle *moreover* transfers the discourse from the singular, ix. 26, to the plural.—οἱ πατέρες ἡμῶν, *our fathers*) even the fathers of the Corinthians; for the Gentiles succeeded to the place of the Jews. [*Our ancestors*, he says, *in respect of communion with God.*—V. g.]—πάντες, *all*) had gone out of Egypt—there was not so much as one of so great a multitude detained either by force or on account of disease, Ps. cv. 37. Five divine benefits are mentioned, 1–4, and as many sins committed by our fathers, 6–10.—ὑπὸ τὴν νεφέλην ἦσαν, *were under the cloud*) Ex. xiii. 21, 22.—διὰ τῆς θαλάσσης διῆλθον, *passed through the sea*) Ex. xiv. 29.

2. Καὶ πάντες εἰς τὸν Μωϋσῆν ἐβαπτίσαντο, *and all were baptized unto Moses*) καί, *and so*. He resumes what he slightly touched upon in the preceding verse about the cloud and the sea, and shows to what each refers. They were baptized in the cloud, so far as they were under it; and in the sea, so far as they passed through it. They were neither wet with the cloud nor with the sea, much less were they immersed in either (although some conjecture, that a miraculous rain fell from that cloud, from what is said in Ps. lxviii. 9, cv. 39), nor is the term baptism found in the writings of Moses. But Paul uses this term with great propriety, 1. Because the cloud and the sea are in their own nature water (wherefore also Paul is silent respecting the pillar of fire); 2. The cloud and the sea took the fathers out of sight and restored them again to view, and this is what the water does to those who are baptized. 3. They were initiated

---

[1] Preference, however, is given to the particle γὰρ, both in the margin of the first and second Ed., and in the Germ. Vers.—E. B.
ABCD(Λ)G*fg* Vulg. Orig. 4,143*e*; 144*a*, Iren. 264 Cypr. 157,277 have γαρ. Rec. Text δὲ with Orig. 1,541*e*, some MSS. of Vulg. and both Syr. Versions.—ED.

by the cloud and by the sea; and as initiation, at Col. ii. 11, is described by circumcision, so here by baptism, a metaphor common to the Old and New Testament; comp. ch. v. 7. But they were baptized unto Moses, as the servant of God, Ex. xiv 31, because they had begun to believe (in) him, and that they might afterwards believe (in) him; comp. εἰς, Rom. iv. 20.[1] ἐβαπτίσαντο, in the middle voice, *received baptism*. In the 1st verse it is hinted what God did for them; in ver. 2, what the fathers received. The sacraments of the Old Testament were more than two, if we take into account these extraordinary ones, at the time of their exodus out of the land of Egypt.—καὶ ἐν τῇ θαλάσσῃ, *and in the sea*) *In* repeated indicates a new step in their progress and privileges.

3. Καὶ πάντες, *and all*) The three former particularly refer to baptism; this and the following, to the Lord's Supper. If there were more sacraments of the New Testament, Paul would have laid down something that bore likewise a resemblance to the others.—τὸ αὐτὸ) *the same*, in respect of the fathers that fell, or did not fall; not in respect of them and us; for in the New Testament there is none of the Mosaic manna; comp. *of one* [partakers *of* that *one* bread], ver. 17.—βρῶμα, *meat*) Ex. xvi. 14.— πνευματικὸν, *spiritual*) Manna was spiritual food, not in itself, John vi. 32; nor merely in the way of prefiguration; but because there was given *from Christ* to the Israelites, along with food for the body, food for the soul, the manna, which is far more noble than external food: comp. the next verse; and in this better sense, the denomination is given; comp. Ps. lxxviii. 24, 25: and there was spiritual food not only to believers, but also, on the part of God [as far as God's part is concerned], to the others.

4. Πόμα, *drink*) This relates rather to Ex. xvii. 6, than to Numb. xx. 8, where mention is made also of cattle.—γὰρ, *for*) Such as is the rock, such is the water.—ἐκ πνευματικῆς ἀκολουθούσης πέτρας, *from the spiritual rock, that followed them*) The article τῆς is not added. The people did not know, what the rock was; therefore Paul long after adds, *but the rock was Christ*. This spiritual

---

[1] [He staggered not] *at* [*in reference to*], the promise of God: so here, baptized unto Moses, viz., in relation to him as their divinely appointed leader.—ED.

rock is spoken of as *following them*, not on account of its following the people; for it rather went before them; but because, although at that time it was really present with them, ver. 9, yet it was only in after ages that at length it was made known to them; comp. on the word ἀκολουθεῖν, to follow, 1 Tim. v. 24; on the order of natural and spiritual things, 1 Cor. xv. 46.

5. Ἀλλ, *but*) although they had so many signs of the Divine presence.—οὐκ ἐν τοῖς πλείοσιν αὐτῶν, *not with the most of them*) The position of the particle *not* should be noticed. Reason might suggest, that God certainly *was well pleased* ἐν τοῖς πλείοσιν, *with the most of them*. This the apostle denies. He not only points out those, who are particularly described presently afterwards, but at the same time many others.—ὁ Θεὸς, *God*) whose judgment alone is valid.—κατεστρώθησαν, *were overthrown*) in great heaps, and with great force. The LXX. have used this word in Numb. xiv. 16.—γὰρ, *for*) The event showed, that they had not pleased God.—ἐν τῇ ἐρήμῳ, *in the wilderness*) far from the land of promise.

6. Ταῦτα, *these*) benefits, which the people received, and the sins which they at the same time committed.—τύποι, *examples*) by which we may be instructed, from which we may learn, what punishments, we must expect, if, receiving such benefits, we should sin in a similar manner.—εἰς τὸ μὴ, *that not*) The benefits are put down in the order, in which they are arranged by Moses, in the different chapters of Exodus; the offences, with their punishments, in a different order. The fundamental principle, from which the offences proceed, is concupiscence: afterwards, the mention of idolatry most of all serves his purpose, ver. 7, 4: fornication was usually joined with idolatry, ver. 8: temptation with murmuring; see the following verses. Those offences are chiefly mentioned, which relate to the admonition of the Corinthians.—ἐπιθυμητὰς) The LXX. have this verbal noun.—κακῶν, *after evil things*) Rom. xiv. 20.—ἐπεθύμησαν, *lusted*) Numb. xi. 4.

7. Γίνεσθε, *be ye*) In this ver., and ver. 10, the matter is set before them in the second person; for Paul was beyond the danger of idolatry, nay, he was even the object of their *murmuring*; the other things are put in the first person—both becomingly so. So 1 Pet. iv. 1, 3, in the second person.—τινὲς αὐτῶν, *some of them*) We should mark *some*; where *some* begin,

the majority of the multitude easily follow, rushing both into sin and to punishment.—ἐκάθισεν, κ.τ.λ.) So the LXX., Exod. xxxii. 6.—φαγεῖν καὶ πιεῖν, *to eat and drink*) This quotation is much to the purpose; comp. ver. 21.—παίζειν, *to play*) A joyful festival is here indicated (*celebrated with lascivious dancing around the calf.*—V. g.), and at the same time the vanity of the festival on account of the idol is implied.

8. Ἐπόρνευσαν, *committed fornication*) Num. xxv. 1.—εἴκοσι τρεῖς χιλιάδες, *twenty-three thousand*) They are said to have been *twenty-four thousand*, Num. xxv. 9. A stroke from God swept them away; but besides, the princes ["the heads of the people," Num. xxv. 4] were hanged, and the judges were commanded to put to death *their men*, over whom they presided, who had been joined to Baal-peor. Moses as well as Paul gives the number of them, whom *the plague itself of that day* destroyed. Why then does Paul subtract a thousand? The precise number of the dead, we may suppose, was between the round numbers, 23,000, and 24,000, say 23,600, and had been known by tradition. We do not follow the subtilties of other interpreters.

9. Μηδὲ ἐκπειράζωμεν) The compound verb, as in Matt. iv. 7. The simple verb follows immediately after.—τὸν Χριστὸν, *Christ*) Paul mentions five benefits, ver. 1–4, of which the fourth and fifth were closely connected; and five crimes, of which the fourth and fifth were in like manner closely connected. In speaking of the fifth benefit, he expressly mentions Christ; and in speaking of the fourth crime, he shows that it was committed against Christ. [*See App.*, P. II., *on this passage, where the reading* Χριστὸν *is defended against Artemonius*, Not. Crit.[1]].—ἐπείρασαν, *tempted*) Num. xxi. 5. *Christ is therefore God.* Comp. Ex. xvii. 2. Often those things which are declared concerning the Lord in Old Testament, are spoken of Christ in New Testament, Rom. xiv. 10, 11; and that *temptation*, by which the people sinned, was an offence peculiarly against Christ, Ex. xxiii. 20, xxxii. 34; Is. lxiii. 9; for when they had drunk from that Rock,

---

[1] Lachm. reads Κύριον with BC, and some MSS. of Memph. Vers. But Tischend., with D(Λ)Gfg Vulg., both Syr. Versions, Memph., Theb., and Marcion, according to Epiphanius (ὁ δὲ Μαρκίων ἀντὶ τοῦ Κύριον Χριστὸν ἐποίησεν), Iren. 264, Χριστόν. This last is the better attested reading therefore. A has Θεόν.—ED.

which was Christ, ver. 4, tney yet complained for want of water, Num. xxi. 5. Therefore they were also preserved from the fiery serpents, by raising a serpent on a pole, a type of *Christ*. As Abraham " saw Christ's day" [John viii. 56], as Moses embraced " the reproach of Christ" [Heb. xi. 26], so the Israelites tempted Christ : and yet the Corinthians could more directly tempt Christ.

10. Μηδὲ γογγύζετε, *do not murmur*) comp. ver. 22. Moses and Aaron were the *secondary* objects of murmuring in the Old Testament.—ἐγόγγυσαν, *murmured*) Num. xvi. 41. With Moses, *murmuring* preceded the *temptation;* but Paul places *murmuring* after the *temptation* in the last place, as being most like to that sin, into which the Corinthians were liable to fall. He who is weaker [than the Lord], ought not to murmur; comp. ver. 22 ; Ex. xvi. 8, 10, at the end of the ver.—ἀπώλοντο, *perished*) ibid. ver. 49.—ὀλοθρευτοῦ, *destroyer*) Comp. Wisd. xviii. 22, 25 ; Heb. xi. 28, note.

11. πάντα, *all things*) He resumes what he said, ver. 6, and in this recapitulation adds, *all things*, which stands in apposition with *ensamples*.—[1] τύποι) *ensamples*.—ἐκείνοις, *to them*) construed with *happened*.—ἐγράφη, *were written*) The use of the Old Testament Scripture is in the fullest force in the New Testament. It was not written out *in the beginning* [but subsequently : for the edification of us in the *ends* of the world].—τὰ τέλη τῶν αἰώνων, *the ends of the ages*) οἱ αἰῶνες, all things, even former ages ; τὰ τέλη, in the New Testament, comp. Rom. x. 4. The plural has great force. All things meet together, and are coming to their height : benefits and dangers, punishments and rewards ; comp. the following verse. All that now remains is that Christ should come, as the avenger and judge ; and until that happens, these ends, being many, include various periods succeeding each other.— κατήντησεν, *have come upon*) as it were unexpectedly. He does not say, *we, who have come upon the ends*. The same word occurs, xiv. 36.

---

[1] The Germ. Ver. shows on the margin of the 2d Ed. the reading τυπικῶς; raised from the mark ε to the mark γ.—E. B.

Lachm. reads τυπικῶς, with ABC Orig. 1, 170 ; 536*f* ; 4, 8*e* ; *fg* Vulg. Iren. (" in figura "), Hilary (in præformationem). Tisch. reads τύποι, with D(Λ)G Memph., Theb., later Syr. (Syr. has *in exemplum nostrum*).—ED.

12. Ὁ δοκῶν) *he, who* stands, and *thinks* that he stands.—ἱστάναι, *that he stands*) *well-pleasing to God*, ver. 5.—μὴ πέσῃ, *lest he fall*) ver. 8, 5.

13. Πειρασμὸς, *temptation*) It is mere human temptation, such as may be overcome by a man, when the man has to do either with himself, or with others like himself; to this is opposed *the temptation of demons*; comp. ver. 20, 14. Paul had greater experience; the Corinthians were inexperienced, and therefore more free from concern.—οὐκ εἴληφεν, *has not taken*) he says οὐκ, not οὐκέτι. He is, therefore, speaking of some temptation, with which they are at present struggling; comp. with εἴληφεν, *hath taken*, Luke v. 5, 26; 2 Cor. xii. 16.—πιστὸς δὲ, but *faithful*) An abbreviated expression, of which the one member must be supplied from the other. Hitherto you have not been severely tempted; you owe that not to your own care, but to the protection of God; but now a greater temptation hangs over you; in it God also will be your defence, but be ye watchful. Thus δὲ, *but*, extends its meaning to ver. 14. God is *faithful* in affording the assistance which both His word and His former works promise.—πειρασθῆναι, *to be tempted*) by men or demons.—δύνασθε, *you are able*) viz., *to bear*, from the end of the verse.—σὺν, *with*) God permits us to be moderately tempted; and at the same time provides a way of escape.—καὶ, *also*) the connection being unbroken.—ἐκβασιν) *a way of escape*, which takes place gradually, even while some things remain to be *borne*. The same word is found, Wisd. ii. 17, viii. 8, xi. (14), 15.

14. Ἀπὸ τῆς εἰδωλολατρείας, *from idolatry*) The consequent [idolatry] is put for the antecedent [things offered to idols], with a view the more to deter the Corinthians from indulging in this sin: *i.e.* avoid things offered to idols, and the religious use of them, in so far as they are things offered to idols. Having premised this caution in the 23d ver., he shows that the use of those things in a civil point of view is indeed lawful, but still they ought to be used with great caution.

15. Φρονίμοις, *to the wise*) to whom a few words are sufficient to enable them to form their *judgment* concerning this mystery.

16. Τὸ ποτήριον, *the cup*) The cup is put before the bread; because according to his design [to reprove the eating of *meats* sacrificed to idols, answering to the *bread* of the Lord's Supper],

he dwells more on the consideration of *the meat*, ver. 21; mention is however made of the cup, because it is inseparable from the other element. The interchange of the order here is a proof, that the body of Christ is received separately, not inasmuch as it has the blood accompanying it. In mentioning food more respect is paid to meat, than drink; but in the mystery of redemption the blood is oftener named, than the body of Christ. Hence Paul's promiscuous arrangement [sometimes *the bread*, at other times *the wine* coming first].—τῆς εὐλογίας, *of blessing*) on that account it is distinguished from a common cup, Matt. xxvi. 27.—ὁ εὐλογοῦμεν, *which we bless*) plural as in *we break*, supply, *we*, ministers and believers, each for his own part: comp. ch. v. 4. All, who bless and break together, enter the more closely into communion.—κοινωνία, *communion*) This predicate used in the abstract shows that the subject should likewise be taken in the abstract. *The cup, which we use*, i.e. *the use of the cup* (comp. Mark vii. 30, note). He who drinks of this cup, is a partaker of the blood of Christ; so ver. 18, *they who eat*. The highest degree of reality is implied: comp. ver. 19, note.—τοῦ αἵματος, *of the blood*) that was shed. Now, he who is a partaker of the blood and body of Christ, is also a partaker of the sacrifice, that was offered on the cross: comp. ver. 18; a partaker in short of Christ himself; comp. what is put in antithesis to this, ver. 20, at the end.—τὸν ἄρτον) There is a construction similar to this, vii. 17: and in the LXX., Num. xxxii. 4. Τῆς εὐλογίας is here again to be supplied; the bread *of blessing*.—τοῦ σώματος τοῦ Χριστοῦ, *of the body of Christ*) *of the body* delivered up to death for us; comp. the opposite [the antithesis] to this, ver. 20, at the beginning. The body of Christ is also the Church, as in the following verse; but here the very body of Christ is intended, from which *the blood* is contradistinguished.

17. Ὅτι, *since*) He proves, that the cup and the bread are the *communion*; for the bread by itself does not make them that eat it, become one body; but the bread does so, in so far as it is *communion*, etc.—εἷς ἄρτος (*one bread*), viz. *there is* [*and indeed it is such bread as is broken, and carries with it* (implies in the participation of it) *the communion of the body of Christ*.—V. g.]—οἱ πολλοί, *the many*) believers [Eng. Vers. is different, "We *being* many are one bread *and* one body"].—

ἐκ τοῦ ἑνὸς ἄρτου, *of the one bread*) and therefore also of the one cup.

18. Τοῦ θυσιαστηρίου, *of the altar*) and therefore, *of God.* He, to whom the offering is made, those things which are offered, the altar on which they are offered, have communion [a mutual tie in common], as is evident from the following verses, comp. Matt. xxiii. 20, 21.

19. Τί, *what*) In the Protasis, he has derived his argument from the sacred rites of the Christians and Jews; and now about to give the apodosis, he uses προθεραπεία, precaution in the way of anticipation, and sets down by implication the apodosis itself with pious caution, εὐλαβῶς, in ver. 20: he who eats things offered to idols, cultivates communion with demons. An idol[1] is a piece of wood, and nothing else; what is offered to an idol is a piece of flesh, and nothing else; but that cup and that bread, which have been spoken of at ver. 16, are not a mere cup and mere bread.

20. Ἀλλ᾽, *but*) viz. *I say.*—δαιμονίοις, *to demons*) rather than to idols.—κοινωνοὺς, *the associates*) Those who were present at the sacrifices of the Gentiles, which serve as an invitation to demons, opened the window to demons, to make an assault upon themselves.—Θεῷ, *to God*) in whose communion you ought to be: Deut. xxxii. 17,—ἔθυσαν δαιμονίοις, καὶ οὐ Θεῷ, *They sacrificed to devils and not to God;* comp. Baruch iv. 7.

21. Οὐ δύνασθε) *ye cannot,* without very great sin.—Κυρίου, *of the Lord*) Christ.—τραπέζης Κυρίου, *of the Lord's table*) The Lord's Supper is a feast, not a sacrifice; on a table, not on an altar.

22. Παραζηλοῦμεν) *do we provoke to jealousy?* namely, by idolatry, ver. 7; Ex. xx. 5. The kindred word is הלאות, ἀγῶνα παρέχειν, to cause one a conflict, to weary out, Is. vii. 13. So Deut. xxxii. 21,—αὐτοὶ παρεζήλωσάν με ἐπ᾽ οὐ θεῷ, *they have moved me to jealousy with that which is no god.*—ἰσχυρότεροι, *stronger*) so that we may flee from His jealousy when kindled? [The

---

[1] By inverting the order, the margin of both editions intimates, that εἰδωλόθυτον is to be placed first, and that εἴδωλον should be second in the order; but the Germ. Ver. follows the reading of the text.—E. B.

BC corrected later, D Vulg., *d* Memph., Theb. Versions, have the order εἰδωλόθυτον—εἴδωλον. A omits ἢ ὅτι εἴδωλόν τί ἐστιν.—ED.

weaker party *is provoked without danger ; but it is different* in the stronger.—V. g.]

23. Συμφέρει, *expedient*) ver. 33. The power, by which all things ἔξεστιν, *are lawful*, is given by *God* : συμφέρον, expediency, is a thing affecting *myself* : οἰκοδομή, edification, relates to *another*.

25. [1] Μηδὲν ἀνακρίνοντες, *asking no questions*) whether it has been offered to an idol or not. Curiosity is often more injurious, than simplicity.—διὰ τὴν συνείδησιν, *for the sake of the conscience*) of another, ver. 29, whose benefit is consulted by keeping silence, lest he should be disturbed.

26. Τοῦ Κυρίου, *of the Lord*) not *of idols*. Ps. xxiv. 1, τοῦ Κυρίου ἡ γῆ καὶ τὸ πλήρωμα αὐτῆς—*The earth is the Lord's and the fulness thereof.* Ps. l. (xlix.) 12, ἐμὴ γάρ ἐστιν ἡ οἰκουμένη καὶ τὸ πλήρωμα αὐτῆς—*The world is mine and its fulness.*—πλήρωμα, *fulness*) including all kinds of meats.

27. Θέλετε πορεύεσθαι, *you wish to go*) Paul does not much approve of this, nor does he forbid it.

28. Τὸν μηνύσαντα καὶ τὴν συνείδησιν, *for the sake of him that showed it, and for conscience' sake*) a *Hendiadys*. μηνύω denotes serious information given of a thing.

29. Τὴν ἑαυτοῦ, *thy own*) comp. the preceding verse; or rather, because he is there speaking in the plural, *my own;* comp. this with what immediately follows.—ἑτέρου, *of another*) of whom, ver. 28.—ἡ ἐλευθερία μου, *my liberty*) i.e. [Why am] *I, along with the liberty* of my conscience [judged]; so immediately after, *by the conscience of another,* i.e. by another along with his conscience which is encumbered with scruples.—κρίνεται, *is judged*) i.e., his weak conscience cannot deprive my conscience of its liberty.—ἄλλης, *another*) This word has greater force, than if it had been said, *of another* [*judged by* ANOTHER *conscience;* not as Engl. V. *another man's conscience*].

30. Ἐγώ, *I*) This expression has reference to his legitimate power [See ver. 23].—τί βλασφημοῦμαι, *why am I evil spoken of*) by him, who does not use his liberty, *i.e.* no man can *reprove* me (but βλασφημεῖν, *to speak calumniously of*, is even worse), as if *I were acting* contrary to my conscience.—ὑπὲρ οὗ, *for which*) *i.e.*

---

[1] πᾶν, *all*) As far as concerns the difference of meats, ver. 26.—V. g.

why am I assailed with reproaches for my thanksgiving?—εὐχα-ριστῶ, *I give thanks*) Thanksgiving sanctifies all meat; it denies the authority of idols, and asserts the authority of God.—1 Tim. iv. 3, 4; Rom. xiv. 6.

31. Εἴτε, *whether*) A great first principle, comp. Jer. xxii. 15, 16.—εἴτε τι ποιεῖτε) *or whatsoever ye do*, which is either more or even less common than eating or drinking. [*It is in the highest degree just to consider in all our words and actions, whether they tend to the glory of* GOD, 2 Cor. ix. 12; 1 Pet. iv. 11.—V. g.]—εἰς δόξαν Θεοῦ, *to the glory of God*) with thanksgiving and the edification of our neighbour.

32. Τῇ ἐκκλησίᾳ τοῦ Θεοῦ, *to the church of God*) the holy church called from among the Jews and Gentiles. The same name is found ch. xi. 16, 22.

33. Πάντα) κατα πάντα, *in all things.*—πᾶσιν, *all men*) Jews, Greeks, Christians.—ἀρέσκω, *I please*) with respect to their consciences.—ἵνα σωθῶσι, *that they may be saved*) By this standard we must determine what is *profitable*.

CHAPTER XI.

1. Μιμηταί μου, *imitators* [*followers*] *of me*) He adds this verse to the former to show, that we must look to Christ, not to him [the apostle], as our highest example.—Χριστοῦ, *of Christ*) who did not please Himself, Rom. xv. 3, but gave Himself at all costs for our salvation, Eph. v. 2.

2. Ἐπαινῶ, *I praise*) [*This verse is the proper commencement of the chapter.*—Not. Crit.] Nowhere else does Paul so directly praise any of those, to whom he writes. But here he resolves to write about anything, which does not properly fall under his παραγγελίαν, *admonition*, to them, ver. 17; in which, however, if they will follow the reasons, which he has set before them, and comply with the custom of the saints, ver. 16, which he finally lays down as somewhat stringent, he assures the Corinthians, that they will be worthy of *praise*, and declares, that *they will incur neither Peter's indignation, nor his.*—πάντα) κατὰ πάντα.—

μου, me) construed with *you remember*, or with *all things*, xvi. 14.
—παρέδωκα—παραδόσεις, *I delivered—traditions* [*ordinances*]) This is applied to doctrines, whether imparted to them by word of mouth, or by letters, whether they relate to mysteries, or ceremonies, ver. 23, xv. 3; 2 Thess. ii. 15: they have a greater relation however to ceremonies. In ver. 23, he says respecting the Lord's Supper, that he both received and delivered; but here, he says, that he delivered, he does not say that he had received.

3. Δὲ, *but*) On this subject Paul seems formerly to have given no commandment, but to have written now for the first time, when he understood that it was necessary. By the expression, *I would*, he openly professes his sentiments.—ὅτι, *that*) Even matters of ceremony should be settled according to the principles of morality, so that they may agree with those principles. It may be said, How does one and the same reason in relation to the head (*i.e.* of Christ, or of the man) require the man to uncover his head, and the woman to cover hers? *Ans.* Christ is not seen; the man is seen; so the covering of him, who is under Christ is not seen; of her, who is under the man, is seen.—ἀνδρὸς, γυναικὸς, *of the man, of the woman*) although they do not live in the state of marriage, ver. 8, and what follows.—ἡ κεφαλὴ, *the head*) This term alludes to the head properly so called, concerning the condition [the appropriate dress] of which he treats in the following verse. The common word, *Principal*,[1] is akin to this use of the term *head*. The article ἡ must be presently after twice supplied from this clause.—κεφαλὴ Χριστοῦ, *the head of Christ*) iii. 23, xv. 28; Luke iii. 23, 38; John xx. 17; Eph. iii. 9, where God is said to have created all things by Christ, therefore He is the head of Christ.—ὁ Θεὸς, *God*) ver. 12.

4. Προσευχόμενος ἢ προφητεύων, *praying or prophesying*) especially *in the church*, ver. 16, and *in the assembly* [the *coming together*], ver. 17.—κατὰ κεφαλῆς, [having a covering] *on his head*) The state of the head, the principal part, gives dignity to the whole body. [The face *is chiefly referred to, when he speaks of a covering.*—V. g.]—ἔχων) *having, i.e. if he has.* The men of Corinth used not to be covered, and in this respect, the women imitated the

---

[1] This word is given as it is in the original. In this form, it is not Latin, but it is probably the German substantive, which signifies *head*.—T.

men. In order to convince the women of their error, Paul speaks conditionally of the man.—τὴν κεφαλὴν αὐτοῦ, *his head*) properly so called, as just before in this verse; comp. note to ver. 6. Otherwise, the man praying with his head covered would sin more against Christ, than the woman against the man, with her head uncovered.

5. Πᾶσα δὲ γυνή, *but every woman*) δὲ, *but*, forms an epitasis [emphatic augmentation or addition]. In this whole passage the woman, especially the woman of Corinth, is principally admonished.—προσευχομένη ἢ προφητεύουσα, *praying or prophesying*) Therefore women are not altogether excluded from these duties; at least the Corinthian women did that, which, so far as it may be lawful, Paul at ch. xiv. [34, 35] puts off, namely, to some suitable occasion distinct from the more solemn assembly.—ἀκατακαλύπτῳ, *uncovered*) nature demands a covering, but how far the forehead with the face, and the hinder part of the head, should be covered, is a matter left to the customs of the people. It is probable, that Jesus and His disciples had their heads covered according to the customs of the Israelites; whence the rule is not universal, and not more ancient than Paul. And there was παράδοσις, an ordinance, not a rule strictly so called, but a custom [institutum] *eine Verordnung*. A question arises here, what is to be thought concerning *wigs*? First, they do not seem to be considered as περιβόλαιον, or covering for the head, for they are an imitation of the hair, and where that is too thin, they supply the defect, and in the present day are sometimes quite necessary for the sake of health, and they no more veil the face, than every man's own hair: and even if women were accustomed to wear wigs, they would not be considered as thereby sufficiently covered. Therefore the head of a man is scarcely more dishonoured by them, while he prays, than while he does not pray. The wig, however, especially one too long and bushy and having little resemblance to the natural hair, is in reality an adventitious thing, and originates in pride or at least in effeminacy either voluntary, or arising from a false necessity:—*it was not so from the beginning, and it will not be so always*. Paul, if we could now consult him, would, I believe, not compel those, who wear wigs to cast them off entirely; but he would teach those, at least, who have not begun to wear them, for ever to unlearn [avoid] them,

as a thing unbecoming men, especially men engaging in prayer.
—ἔστι, is) Such a woman does not differ from one, that has been shaved.

6. Κειράσθω, *let her be shorn*) As the hinder part of the head is by nature in the man and the woman respectively, so in general it is becoming the forehead to be in its mode of dressing: ver. 14. The imperative here is that of permission, but a permission, which has in it mimesis, or a deduction to something unsuitable.[1] So shaving is unbecoming in nuns.—αἰσχρὸν, *a shame*) So ver. 14. The opposite, *comely*, ver. 13 : *glory*, ver. 15.—τὸ κείρασθαι, ἢ ξυρᾶσθαι) the one is more than the other. Mic. i. 16, ξύρησαι καὶ κεῖραι. ξυρᾶται, the back part of the head ; κείρεται, the forehead. In Mic. already quoted, there follows a gradation in the *enlargement* of the baldness occasioned by shaving.

7–10. Οὐκ ὀφείλει, κ.τ.λ., *ought not*, etc.) The man has more freedom in regard to his head-dress, especially when he is not engaged in praying or prophesying, than the woman.—κατακαλύπτεσθαι, *to cover*) verses 7 and 10 have an exact antithesis. Observe, first, *he ought not*, and *she ought :* secondly, look at the diagram : The man *ought not* to be covered ; because the man is, A. the image of God, B. and the glory of God : but the woman *ought* to be covered : C. because she is the glory of the man, D. and on account of the angels. The man, he says, is the image of God ; supply, *and of Christ* from ver. 3 (see ver. 8 ; comp. ver. 12 ; ἐκ, *of*, concerning the man and concerning God ; but διὰ, *by*, concerning the woman): not only on account of his power over the woman itself, but also on account of the causes of that power, viz., because the woman is of the man ; but she is of the man, *for* (γὰρ, ver. 9) she was created for the man. But the man is, in a nearer relation, both of God and under God ; and so he represents God. Now because man is the image of God, he is at the same time the glory of God ; comp. *glory*, 2 Cor. viii. 23. *But the woman is the glory of the man ;* because the man is the head and lord of the woman. It is not said, *the image and glory of the man ;* but only *the glory of the*

[1] A woman would not wish κείρασθαι. But if she wishes to be *uncovered* in front, let her also be *uncovered* behind, i.e., κειράσθω. This allusion to the supposed words of the woman, whom he refutes, constitutes the mimesis. See Appendix.—ED.

man, as it were suspending the expression. But he proves, that she is the glory of the man, ver. 8, 9, as it were in a parenthesis; from which it may also be gathered, why the man is the *image and glory of God*. Now since the woman is the glory of the man, she might at the same time be called the image of the man; but Paul compensates for this by another expression, and says, *for this cause*, namely, because the woman is the glory of the man, she ought to be covered *because of the angels;* for in the diagram which we have just laid down, D is to A, as C to B. The meaning of this gnome-like sentiment[1] [*expressed entirely in the same way in the notes to the* Germ. Ver.] should be elicited from the very words that are added; let the woman *cover herself* because of the angels, *i.e.* because the angels are also covered. As the angels are to God, so the woman is to the man. The face of God is manifested: whereas the angels are covered, Isa. vi. The face of the man is manifested, [uncovered]; the woman is covered. Nor is the man on that account exalted above the angels; but he is merely considered so far as he represents God in regard to the woman, which cannot be said of the angels. But the woman ought to be covered especially in praying and prophesying; for it belongs to the man, in preference to the woman, to pray and prophesy; when therefore the woman takes upon her those functions, then some open avowal is most necessary on her part, that woman is still properly and willingly inferior to man. Both the outward dress of the body showing humility in the heart, which the angels cannot penetrate, and the external order delight the angels themselves, who also contemplate the order, and look at the conduct of men in the assembly of the Church, iv. 9; Eph. iii. 10; comp. Eccles. v. 6, where LXX. have πρὸ προσώπου Θεοῦ, *before the face of God*. The conclusion is drawn from angels to the uncreated Angel, as from the less to the greater. Add Ps. cxxxviii. 1. But if not covered, the woman offends the angels by what is unbecoming, Matt. xviii. 10, 31. Moreover the woman ought to be the more careful not to offend the angels on this account, that she requires their protection, somewhat more than the man. She needs it more, on account of her own weakness just as children [minors,

---

[1] See Appendix, under the title Noëma.

inferiors] do : comp. note on Greg. Thaum. Paneg. 160 ; as also *demons* lay more snares for the woman, 2 Pet. ii. 19. The sentence of the law against the man when seduced and overcome is in proportion to the seduction, and the victory gained over him; but the woman was first overcome; *or farther*, she is more assailed by those extremely limpure spirits, whom the Greeks, on account of their eagerness to obtain victims, call φιλούλους, *lovers of destruction*. Comp. Matt. viii. 31, xii. 43. This great superiority of the man over the woman is qualified in ver. 11, 12, by way of ἐπιθεραπεία [after-softening of a previous unwelcome truth. —Append.], lest the man should exalt himself, or the woman think herself despised. Jac. Faber Stapulensis says, "Man was immediately made by God, the image and likeness of God, for His glory : but the woman mediately through the man, who was as it were a veil placed between her and God; for the medium is viewed as an interposing object, and a veil. To mark this mystery, when a man turns himself to God, which he mostly does in praying or prophesying, he ought to do so with his head uncovered, having, so to speak, no veil between himself and God, offering thus to God the honour of his creation : but the woman with her head covered acknowledges her creation, and, as it becomes her, offers honour to God, in the second place and through the medium of the glory of the man, for the man is the first and immediate glory of God. The woman is mediate and second, and became immediately the glory of the man, and was made for the sake of the man himself." The same Stapulensis proceeds, "Both man and the angels were immediately created by God, and therefore man should have no covering, as a symbol of this event, when he is turned to God, any more than the angels ; but the woman ought to have it, not only on account of the man, but also on account of the angels; for it would be pride, if she made her creation equal to that of the angels, inasmuch as she has this power [the privilege of creation] by means of the man. For what else is this, that a woman has and ought to have power over her head, but that she has this privilege through the mediation of the man, *i.e.* through the mediation of her head, who is her husband ?" The discreet reader will skilfully qualify these remarks by those made by us above.

8. Οὐ γὰρ, *for not*) As his own wife stood in relation to the

first man, so is the whole race of women to the men.—ἐξ ἀνδρός, *from the man*) from the rib of the man.

10. Ὀφείλει, *ought*) This verb differs from δεῖ; it *is necessary* : ὀφείλει denotes obligation, δεῖ, necessity. The former is moral, the latter, as it were, physical necessity; as in the German, *wir sollen und müssen, we shall and must*.—ἐξουσίαν ἔχειν) *to have power over the head*. From that antithesis between ver. 7 and 10 [*ought—ought not*], it is evident that the *power* is the same as κάλυμμα, *a covering*: so Gen. xx. 16, כסות עינים. LXX, εἰς τιμὴν τοῦ προσώπου σου, *for a covering, i.e., for a testimony of undefiled matrimonial chastity*. On the contrary, the priest was commanded ἀποκαλύπτειν, to *uncover* the head of the woman, who had withdrawn from the *power* of her husband in consequence of adultery, or who was at least suspected of that crime. Num. v. 18. This passage agrees admirably with both quotations; only ἐξουσία, *power*, is a more suitable word here than τιμή, *honour*. Nor would it at all have been foreign to the purpose to compare Ps. lx. 9, *Ephraim is the strength of my head*. Paul uses ἐξουσίαν by an elegant metonymy of the sign for the thing signified; or even by a mild metonymy of the relative for the correlative, ὑποταγή, *subjection*, or the like; unless it be rather the sign, by which the woman avows and acknowledges that, although she prays and prophesies, still she is inferior to the man; in short, it is on this condition that the *power* of praying and prophesying falls to her share, and without that sign it must not be exercised. And this term is therefore more suitable, because it is closely connected with the δόξα, *glory*, ver. 15: and ἐξουσία, *power*, is also applied to the angels.

11. Ἐν Κυρίῳ, *in the Lord*) *in Christ*, by whom both the man and the woman have been created and redeemed. The difference between the man and the woman, Gal. iii. 28, begins now rather to disappear in respect of Christ in this ver., and in respect of God in the following verse, than in respect of the angels. Therefore ver. 9, 10, 11, 12, elegantly correspond with one another in their short clauses.

12. Ἡ γυνὴ ἐκ τοῦ) Only here, and at ver. 10, the articles are added. In ver. 10, the force of the relative is at ver. 9, and in ver. 12 at ver. 11.—ἐκ—διά, *from* [of]—*by*) The particles differ; presently afterwards ἐκ is also said of God.—πάντα, *all*

things) the man, the woman, and the mutual dependence of either upon the other.

13. Ἐν ὑμῖν αὐτοῖς, *in yourselves*) without a long explanation.—ἔστι, *is it?*) a direct interrogation, as vi. 5.—γυναῖκα—τῷ Θεῷ, *a woman—to God*) Paul describes the leap, which the woman uncovered takes, passing beyond both the *man* and *angels*. An excellent hypotyposis,[1] though short.

14. Οὐδὲ αὐτὴ) does *not even* nature *itself*, from which all learn very easily.—ἡ φύσις, *nature*) and its light concerning what is becoming.—ἐὰν κομᾷ) *if* he *has* long *hair*, like a *covering*; for he is not commanded to be altogether shorn.—ἀτιμία, *disgrace*) viz., if he do that without any reason; for sometimes even hair becomes men.—Num. vi. 5; 2 Sam. xiv. 26; Acts xviii. 18. The Nazarite, who had hair, however long, ought to retain it.

15. Ἀντὶ περιβολαίου, *for a covering*) Not but that an artificial *covering* ought to be added, but because her longer hair is a proof of covering the head as much as possible: the will ought to correspond to nature.—[2] δέδοται, *has been given*) by nature.

16. Εἰ δέ, *but if*) A curt [abrupt] hint,[3] as at xiv. 37. Paul perceives, that some exceptions may be taken, but he authoritatively represses them.—δοκεῖ φιλόνεικος, *seems contentious*) A disputer of this sort might think that he was contending rightly; but Paul calls him *contentious*. This is what he says: *If any one wishes to contend, and deems himself right in doing so*. In this passage it is rather intended to teach the Corinthians modesty, than to bind all: comp. 2 Cor. ii. 9. For he especially restrains their φυσίωσιν, *puffed up spirit*: comp. xiv. 34–38.—ἡμεῖς, *we*) your teachers, of the Hebrew nation.—συνήθειαν, *custom*) that a woman should not cover her head, especially when she prays.—αἱ ἐκκλησίαι τοῦ Θεοῦ, *the churches of God*) which ought not to be despised, xiv. 36.

---

[1] A vivid picture in words of some action. Appendix.

[2] The word αὐτή, the omission of which was thrust down by the marg. of 2d edition from the mark γ to the mark ε, is exhibited in the Germ. Ver.—E. B.

Αὐτῇ is read by Lachm. with AB*g* after δέδοται, and before it, in CH and later Syr. and Vulg. Tisch. omits it with D(Λ)G*fd*.—ED.

[3] The word in the original is præcisio, explained by Cicero to be a figure which rather gives a hint to the understanding, and leaves it to supply what is not expressed.—See De Or. iii. 53, Her. iv. 30.—T.

17. Τοῦτο) *this,* which follows.—παραγγέλλω, [Engl. Vers. *I declare*] *I command*) in the name of the Lord, ver. 23, xiv. 37. —οὐκ ἐπαινῶν, *not praising*) the opposite is, *I praise,* ver. 2. The two parts into which this chapter is divided, are closely connected by this antithesis; in the one the Corinthians were regarded as well-disposed, in the other, as committing sin.—εἰς τὸ κρεῖττον, *for the better*) An assembly of believers ought always to be progressing towards that, which is better.— εἰς τὸ ἧττον, *for the worse*) and therefore for *condemnation,* ver. 34. At first Paul speaks more gently. κρεῖττον, ἧττον, form a paranomasia.[1]

18. Πρῶτον, *first*) This word, when *secondly* does not follow, gives the discourse a degree of characteristic ἦθος or *feeling*.[2] Their assembly, even in the use of the gifts, might be held by the Corinthians for the better, xiv.—ἐν τῇ ἐκκλησίᾳ, *in the church*) *The church* here approaches to the signification of the place of meeting. ἐπὶ τὸ αὐτὸ, *into one place,* [*where it is right, that all things should be arranged with a view to harmony.*—V. g.]— σχίσματα) *divisions,* not only in your mental opinions, ch. i. 10, but also as to your outward meetings, ver. 21.—μέρος τι, *partly*) He excepts the innocent, and uses a mild term.—πιστεύω, *I believe*) while his love was unaffected by it, ch. xiii. 7.

19. Καὶ αἱρέσεις, *also heresies*) Schisms and heresies are here applied to one thing; nor is the *also* intended to make a distinction; but this is its meaning: not only many good things, not merely small stumbling-blocks, viii. 9, are found among you, but there must be also heresies, or different opinions and schisms, which generally arise out of them. Now there is at once both necessity for these and it is profitable to the godly, where *men less approved* are mixed up with them. A schism is a mutual separation; heresy is the separation of one party from the unity of the Church, in regard either to faith, or worship.—οἱ δόκιμοι, *those approved*) Therefore there were at least some such persons among them. A conciliatory (ἀστεῖος) mode of expression; for what he really meant to say, was, that those *less approved* should be openly manifested.

20. Συνερχομένων οὖν ὑμῶν, *when ye come together therefore*) The

[1] See App. The two words by the similiarity of sound forming the more striking contrast.—ED.

[2] Appendix on *moratus Sermo*.

therefore has the effect of resuming the discourse, ver. 18.—οὐκ ἔστι φαγεῖν) *there is not aught to eat, i.e. it does not fall to you to eat;* eating is prevented, viz. because the bread is withdrawn;[1] he therefore pointedly says, *to eat.* It is an indefinite expression. [*Man kommt nicht dazu, wegen Abgang des Brots und Weins,* " *we come not for that purpose, on account of the want of bread and wine.*"—Not. crit.] Sometimes they came in for the privilege of eating the Lord's Supper itself, ver. 26. Sometimes, they were excluded, some at least, who came too late, and had not been waited for, ver. 33. So ἐστί with the infinitive, Heb. ix. 5. So not merely on one occasion Chrysostom.—See 1. 2 de Sacerd., p. 388. There is a similar use of the verb γίνεται, Acts xx. 16. So לשמור אין, 2 Chron. v. 11; אין לבוא, Esth. iv. 2; οὐκ ἔστιν ἄραι, LXX., 1 Chron. xv. 2; οὐκ ἔστι πρός σε ἀντιστῆναι, 2 Chron. xx. 6, and decidedly Gen. vi. 21, καὶ ἔσται σοὶ καὶ ἐκείνοις φαγεῖν.—Κυριακὸν, *the Lord's*) An antithesis to *his own,* (ἴδιον) supper, next verse.

21. Ἕκαστος, *every one*) G. Raphelius says: " It was a custom at Athens, in the age of Socrates, for every one of those, who met at supper, to bring some meat for himself, which they did not set out for general use, but every one usually ate his own." Then, after he has referred to the testimony of Xenophon, he concludes, " That this very passage of the apostle, is a proof so far of the observance of this custom, even at that time, by the Corinthians, who had become Christians, that when they were about to celebrate the Lord's Supper, they brought at least bread and wine, if not other meats also, into the church, of which a part was afterwards taken and consecrated for the eucharist. For doubtless Paul calls the first *their own supper,* ver. 21, ἴδιον δεῖπνον, namely the meat, which every one had brought from home, and which they fell upon as their right, without waiting for others. Then, οἱ μὴ ἔχοντες, *those who have not,* ver. 22, can be understood to be no other than the poorer members, in whose presence, the richer, not without showing contempt for them, intemperately feasted, before the distribution of the elements in the Lord's Supper, which the poor were present (had come) to enjoy, while no other food besides was prepared for them."—

[1] Those who came first consumed it all, and left none for those who came late.—ED.

προλαμβάνει, *takes before*) when he ought to wait, ver. 33.—ἐν τῷ φαγεῖν, *in eating*) Language which relates to the feeding of the body, ver. 33, etc., from which the Lord's Supper very widely differs.—καὶ, *and*) *and one indeed* (inasmuch as he has not) *is hungry* (and thirsty) : but another (inasmuch as he has, is well filled and) *becomes drunken.* The one has more than is good for him, the other less.

22. Γὰρ, *for*) He presses upon them with questionings.—οἰκίας, *houses*) ver. 34.—τῆς ἐκκλησίας, *the Church*) of which the better part was the poor, James ii. 5.—τοῦ Θεοῦ, *of God*) This constitutes the honour of the Church.—καταφρονεῖτε, *do you despise*) when you do that apart in the church, which you might do *at home.*—μὴ ἔχοντας, *not having*) *Those, who have,* viz. the wealthy ; *those, who have not,* viz. the needy.—οὐκ ἐπαινῶ, *I praise you not*) Μείωσις [saying less than is intended], implying: You are very much to be blamed.

23. Ἐγὼ γὰρ παρέλαβον, *for I received*) by immediate revelation. "We ought therefore with great reverence to approach that most solemn mystery, which the Lord instituted, while He was yet upon the earth, as we are distinctly informed by Matthew, Mark, and Luke, and which He renewed, besides, when He ascended into heaven, by special revelation to the Apostle Paul."—Jac. Faber Stapulensis.—ἀπὸ τοῦ Κυρίου, *from the Lord*) Jesus Christ.—παρέδωκα, *I delivered*) in your presence.—ὁ Κύριος Ἰησοῦς, *The Lord Jesus*) This word *Jesus* is added with deliberate intention. He had just said *from the Lord.*—ἐν τῇ νυκτὶ, *on the night*) Hence it is called *the Supper.* Comp. Ex. xii. 6 ; although in regard to the paschal lamb, the time of the day was expressly appointed; not so in respect to the Eucharist.—ᾗ παρεδίδοτο, *on which He was betrayed*) This is thus brought forward with evident intention ; for His being betrayed broke off the conversation of Jesus with his disciples : comp. note at ver. 26.

24. Ἔκλασε, *broke*) The very mention of the breaking, involves the distribution, and refutes the Corinthian mode of making it every man *his own,* ver. 21.—τὸ ὑπὲρ ὑμῶν κλώμενον, *which is broken for you*) In the gospel by Luke the words are, *which is given for you.* In the Lord's Supper, with the bread *broken,* the body of Christ, which was given unto death for us, is taken and eaten, as real food ; although no one would be likely to affirm,

that the Lord would have used the *breaking* of bread, if it had not been the common practice at that period. The passion of Christ is [should be] naturally before the eucharist;[1] hence the institution of the Supper took place immediately before the death of Christ. Therefore the body of Christ is said to be *given* in respect of the passion considered in itself; to be *broken*, in respect of the passion fitting the Lord's body for being eaten: and the expression *for you* shows that the word *given* is at the same time indicated, so that it is an abbreviated phrase, with this meaning; *which* is given *for you* and *broken* to you. These remarks indeed refer to the common reading κλώμενον, from the verb ἔκλασε immediately preceding; but the Alexandrian reading had not the participle, as is evident from the fourth book of *Cyril* against Nestorius;[2] whence others have supplied διδόμενον from Luke. *My body, which for you,* is a nervous sentence, as John vi. 51, in the old copies, *my flesh for the life of the world.*[3]

25. Μετὰ τὸ δειπνῆσαι, *after supper*) Therefore you, Corinthians, ought to separate common meals from the Lord's Supper.—ὁσάκις, *as often as*) *As often as* is not a command, but it is implied that we should often eat and drink.—πίνητε, *you may drink*) this cup, ver. 26.—εἰς τὴν ἐμὴν ἀνάμνησιν, *in remembrance of me*) This is presupposed by Matthew and Mark. Luke uses it once, Paul twice, because it is very suitable to his purpose. The old sacrifices were useful *in bringing sins to remembrance*, Heb. x. 3; the sacrifice of the body of Christ, accomplished once for all, is revived *by the remembrance of forgiveness*.

26. Τὸν θάνατον τοῦ Κυρίου, *the death of the Lord*) the death, by which Christ was sacrificed for us [*and His blood was separated from His body. Hence he says separately*, This is my body; and

---

[1] Or rather, translate " Passio naturâ prior est quam eucharistia." The suffering is naturally prior to the thanksgiving.—Ed.

[2] Hence also the participle κλώμενον, and the preceding imperatives λάβετε, Φάγετε, are reckoned on the margin of Ed. 2, by a change of opinion, as weaker readings, and they are put doubtfully in the Germ. Ver.—E. B.

Τὸ ὑπ' ὑμῶν is the reading of ABC corrected later. G supports the κλώμενον added in Rec. Text. D corr. later *fg* add θρυπτόμενον. Memph. and Theb. favour διδόμενον. Vulg. Cypr. 107 have " Quod pro vobis tradetur."—Ed.

[3] BCDL Vulg., Theb., Orig., and Cypr. omit the ἣν ἐγὼ δώσω of the Rec. Text.—Ed.

separately, This is my blood.—V. g.] So also, He is mentioned in the Apocalypse as a *lamb, that had been slain.*—καταγγέλλετε, *ye announce* [*show*]) The Indicative, with the *for*, is to be referred to the, *I have delivered*, ver. 23. He convicts the Corinthians from their own practice, such as it was. New things *are announced* [*shown forth*], and the death of the Lord ought always to be new [fresh] in our memory; Ex. xiii. 8, καὶ ἀναγγελεῖς, and *thou shalt show* [announce]; referring to the passover; whence the paschal lesson is called הגדה, *the annunciation.* The Syriac version also has the indicative.—ἄχρις οὗ, *until*) Paul derives this from the particle ἕως, Matt. xxvi. 29, whatever seems to be lost to us by Christ's going away, is compensated by the Lord's Supper as by a kind of equivalent, so that from the time of the Lord's departure from the sight of believers to His visible and glorious coming, we still have Himself, whom for a time we do not see. *What was conspicuous in our Redeemer has passed into the sacraments;* Leo the Great, Serm. 2 on the ascension. On this account it is said *in remembrance of Me*: and of this mode of remembering there was no need, as long as He was in person with His disciples; consequently He did not institute the Supper sooner, but on that night, on which His being betrayed broke off the visible intercourse with Jesus upon the earth; but He instituted it then, lest He should also be forgotten, when no longer seen. It may be asked, why did He not institute the Supper, during the forty days that elapsed between His resurrection and ascension? *Ans.* 1. Because it chiefly relates to the remembrance of His *death.* 2. The Sacred Supper is a specimen as it were of communion at the same heavenly banquet with Christ in heaven, but after His resurrection, Christ did not eat and drink with His disciples, but merely ate with them, and only for the purpose of convincing them of His being truly raised from the dead and of His actual presence with them. This remembrance is of the closest and most vivid kind, such as is the remembrance of children towards their parents, of a wife towards her husband, of a brother towards a brother, united with faith, love, desire, hope, joy, obedience, and comprehending the whole of the Christian's present condition. This relation to Christ is in force from the close of His last feast with His disciples till His coming again,

Matt. xxvi. 29. This mystery joins the two closing periods of the two Dispensations, the Old and New.—ἄν) at whatever time His coming may take place.[1] Then it *will be drunk new*, Matt. xxvi. 29.—ἔλθῃ, *come*) in glory, iv. 5. It is not called *a return*; comp. Acts i. 11, note.

27. Ὥστε ὅς ἂν ἐσθίῃ τὸν ἄρτον τοῦτον ἢ πίνῃ τὸ ποτήριον τοῦ Κυρίου ἀναξίως) Some read ἢ formerly for καί, but καί[2] remains, as in what follows, *of the body* AND *blood of the Lord*. From the particle ἢ, Pamelius, writing to Cyprian concerning the Lapsed, impugns the necessity of communion in both kinds. The disjunctive particle, if any one thinks that Paul used it, does not, however, separate the bread and the cup; otherwise the cup might as well be taken without the bread, as the bread without the cup. Paul twice demands, both with the bread and with the cup, the *remembrance* of the Lord Jesus, according to His own words, ver. 24, 25; but in the manner, in which the Lord's Supper was celebrated among the Corinthians, a man might at the same time both eat this bread and drink the cup, and yet apart [separately] he might eat this bread unworthily *or* drink this cup unworthily, since the remembrance of the Lord was certainly profaned by any impropriety, though it were only in the case of *one* of the two elements, ver. 21. But if any one among the Corinthians even in that time of confusion took the bread without the cup, *or* the cup without the bread, on that very account he took it unworthily, and became guilty of the body and blood of the Lord.—ἀναξίως, *unworthily*) They do so, not only who are without repentance and faith, but who do not examine themselves. The unworthiness of him, who eats,

---

[1] Nay, but the margin of both editions, with consent of the Germ. Ver., implies rather that we should omit this particle ἄν, if we follow the copies.—E. B.

ABCD corrected later, G omit ἄν. Rec. Text has none of the oldest authorities on its side in reading ἄν.—ED.

[2] The margin of the second edition, with the Germ. Ver., confirms this, his more recent opinion, which is different from the decision of the first edition.—E. B.

BCDG*fg* Vulg., Cypr., read ἢ, which may seem to favour the Romish doctrine of communion in one kind being sufficient. A (and according to Lachm., which Tisch. contradicts, Λ or D) and translator of Orig. read καί.—ED.

is one thing, of eating, is another. "Some indeed say, that he excludes, not a person unworthy, but one receiving unworthily, from the sacred ordinance. If then even a worthy person approaching unworthily is kept back, how much more an unworthy person, who cannot worthily partake?"—Pelagius among the works of Jerome.

28. Δοκιμαζέτω, *let him prove* [*examine*]) by judging as to himself, and by judging as to [discerning, *i.e.* distinguishing from common food] the body of the Lord, ver. 29, 31.—ἄνθρωπος, *a man*) any one, iv. 1, even one that is in himself unworthy.—οὕτως) *so* at length.—ἐκ τοῦ) The preposition expresses circumspection of mind ; but τὸν ἄρτον, τὸ ποτήριον, *the bread, the cup*, ver. 27, forms a phrase showing that they had not been duly discerned, by the receivers at Corinth : see the preceding verse.

29. Κρίμα) [*without the article*, comp. v. 32.—Not. crit.] some *judgment*, a disease, or the death of the body ; see next verse ; so that those who do not discern the Lord's body have to atone for it in their bodies. He does not say τὸ κατάκριμα, *the condemnation*.—μὴ διακρίνων, *not judging as to* [*discerning*]) Comp. Heb. x. 29.—τὸ σῶμα, *the body*) supply, *and the blood*.—τοῦ Κυρίου, *of the Lord*) An Antonomasia [an appellative instead of the proper name], *i.e. Jesus*. The Church is not called *the body of Jesus*, or *the body of the Lord ;* but *the body of Christ :* The question here then is about the *proper body of the Lord Jesus*.

30. Διὰ τοῦτο, *for this cause*) The Corinthians had not observed this cause ; but in our day it is proper to attend to it.—ἀσθενεῖς καὶ ἄῤῥωστοι, *weak and sickly*) *weak* from slighter distempers ; *sickly* from more serious diseases ; comp. Rev. ii. 22.—κοιμῶνται, *sleep*) A word in a middle sense, [μέσον, midway between good and bad] as distinguished from the state after death. It does not denote here however a dreadful death.

31. Διακρίνομεν, *we would judge as to*) before the deed.—ἐκκρινόμεθα, *we should be judged*) after the deed. The simple verb and its compounds are elegantly used ; nor is it immediately added *by the Lord*. But Paul afterwards discloses it to us [who it is from whom the judgment comes], *wè are chastened by the Lord*, Rev. iii. 19.

32. Σὺν τῷ κόσμῳ, *with the world*) The world's *condemnation* is therefore certain, being without *chastisement*.

33. Ὥστε, *therefore*) The remedy and counsel suitably follow the reproof of vice, and the simpler the better.—Ἀδελφοί μου, *my brethren*) This appellation is suited to the conclusion.

34. Πεινᾷ, *is hungry*) that he may not wait. Anticipation.[1]— λοιπά, *the rest*) regarding the Lord's Supper; for presently after in this epistle he in like manner sets in order questions as to spiritual things.

CHAPTER XII.

1. Περὶ δὲ τῶν πνευματικῶν, *Now concerning spiritual gifts*) This is in the Neuter gender, ch. xiv. 1. Some may wonder, that there is no discussion in the other epistles also on the gifts, in which however other churches were not wanting, ch. xiv. 36; Gal. iii. 5; 1 Thess. i. 5, ii. 13. The abundance of gifts in the Greek churches was a powerful confutation of the learned but vain curiosity of the Greeks. The abuse of them afforded Paul an occasion of writing to the Corinthians; and here we may observe the mark of divine wisdom, inasmuch as every book of the Sacred Scripture, even of the New Testament, has discussed certain subjects peculiar to itself. The Corinthians abounded in *spiritual* gifts, and yet Paul had occasion to write to them, as well on other matters, as also on this topic, and that too without delay: comp. ch. xi. at the end. Now, there is set forth here; I. The unity of the body, verses 1–27. II. The variety of its members and functions, verses 27–30. III. The grand principle, on which the gifts may be rightly exercised, viz., by love, ver. 31, and in the whole of the following chapter. IV. The comparison of the gifts with one another, ch. xiv.—οὐ θέλω ὑμᾶς ἀγνοεῖν, *I would not have you ignorant*) This expression is repeated in ver. 3 in synonymous terms, as if after a parenthesis.—ἀγνοεῖν, to *be ignorant*) ch. xiv. 38.

2. Οἴδατε, *ye know*) nearly related to the verb *you remember*, which is found in Eph. ii. 11.—οἴδατε, ὅτι, ὅτε ἔθνη ἦτε, πρὸς τὰ

---

[1] See App. 'Occupatio.' It is the same as προκατάληψις. Anticipation of an objection which might be raised.—ED.

εἴδωλα τὰ ἄφωνα ὡς ἂν ἤγεσθε ἀπαγόμενοι) The analysis of these words will be easy, if we only keep hold of this thread of connection, ὅτι ἤγεσθε, *that you were led;* so that ἤγεσθε is not to be regarded as a mere accessory proposition [Syncategorema; see Append.], but the predicate itself; comp. Eph. ii. 12 ; where Gentiles and Gentilism are likewise distinguished in the enunciation. For, instead of ὅτι or ὡς, there is said conjointly ὡς ὅτι, Germ. *wie dass* (*as* or *how that*), and ὅτι ὡς, *that as* : and that too with another word interposed, as in Xiphilinus, in his Epitome of Dion, λεχθὲν αὐτῷ, ὅτι ἄρα ὡς Ἀλέξανδρος ἐλθὼν αὐτὸν διαδέξεται, *it being told to him, that* (ὅτι) *when* (ὡς) *Alexander comes, he will succeed him:* or even with a longer parenthesis, as in Xenophon, ἐνταῦθα γνόντες οἱ μάντινεῖς ὡς, εἰ μὴ ἀποκρούσονται αὐτοὺς, ὅτι., κ.τ.λ., *here the soothsayers knowing, unless they shall repel them, how that*, etc. : therefore *that* is doubled in Greek as ה אם in Hebrew, Gen. xvii. 17, supplying *I say*. Furthermore ἄν is joined with the verb ἤγεσθε, as we have also in Xenophon καιρὸς δὲ γράψαι ὡς ἄν ὀρθότατα ἑκατέρῳ χρῷτο, *I take the opportunity of stating how he should most suitably treat either of these* (the spirited or dull horse); where Devarius (who has suggested to us both of these quotations from Xenophon) shows that ἄν in the distribution of the construction is joined potentially to the verb χρῷτο. Therefore the principal meaning will remain, if ὡς ἄν be entirely put aside by itself (parenthetically) in the construction, as in 2 Cor. x. 9 [ἵνα μὴ δόξω ὡς ἂν ἐκφοβεῖν ὑμᾶς], where it signifies *as if;* and so it might be taken in this passage : nor even is ἄν easily construed with an indicative, such as ἤγεσθε is. Moreover in ἤγεσθε ἀπαγόμενοι, the passive is construed with the middle, the simple with the compound ; *you were led and led away*, you gave yourselves up to any guidance whatever. The Scholium of Chrysostom amounts almost to this [is much the same as this] : though that Scholium has been censured by later writers without a cause ; οἴδατε, ὅτε Ἕλληνες ἦτε, πῶς ἀπήγεσθε, ἑλκόμενοι τότε, *ye know, when ye were Greeks, how you were led, being at that time drawn away.* Add Castellio. ἄφωνα *dumb*, a proper epithet; comp. ver. 3, *you when blind* went to the *dumb;* you dumb [unable to *speak* as you ought, *by the Spirit of God*, ver. 3], to the blind.

3. Διὸ, *wherefore*) He infers this thesis, that *spiritual* things are with all Christians, and with [in the possession of] them

alone, *i.e.* with those who glorify Jesus; and that by means of those spiritual things faith in Jesus is proved; for idols bestow nothing *spiritual:* when the superstition of the Gentiles was overthrown, there was not the same need of miraculous gifts. This is the alternative, he who glorifies Jesus, has the Spirit of God; he who does not glorify Him, has not the Spirit of God, 1 John iv. 1, 2. Paul furnishes a test of truth against the Gentiles; John, against the false prophets.—γνωρίζω ὑμῖν, *I make known to you*) Divine operations of that sort had been formerly unknown to the Corinthians. Before receiving these letters of Paul, their knowledge had been less distinct, as they had been rescued not long before from heathenism.—ἐν πνεύματι Θεοῦ, *by the Spirit of God*) Immediately after he says, *by the Holy Ghost.* Godhead and sanctity[1] are synonymous especially when speaking of the Holy Trinity.—λαλῶν, *speaking*) This expression is of very wide application; for even those, who perform cures and possess miraculous powers, are accustomed to use words. The antithesis is to the *dumb* idols.—λέγει ἀνάθεμα, *calls Him accursed*) as the Gentiles did, but the Jews more so. There is a ταπείνωσις, or saying less than is intended. *He does not call Him accursed,* i.e. he in the highest degree *pronounces Him blessed. Accursed* and *Lord* are opposed. [*It is a proof of long-suffering patience, which surpasses all comprehension, that* Jesus *Christ, the Lord, at the right hand of the Father does not refuse to tolerate, for so long a period of time, such a mass of blasphemy from unbelievers, and especially from the Jews, in their wretched state of blindness. That consideration ought to suppress in the Christian any indignation felt by him on account of any reproach whatever, however little deserved.*—V. g.]—εἰπεῖν, *to say*) πνευματικῶς, *in a spiritual manner.*

4. Διαιρέσεις, *divisions*) The LXX. use this term to express the Hebrew word מחלקה, concerning the orders of the priests. Comp. *dividing,* ver. 11.—δὲ, *but*) an antithesis between the one fountain and the many streams.—χαρισμάτων, *of gifts*) Those endowments which in ver. 1 he had called *spiritual* things, now, after mentioning Jesus, he calls *gifts.*—πνεῦμα, *Spirit*) The Holy Spirit is spoken of in this verse; Christ in ver. 5; God the Father in ver. 6: and calling them gifts, ministrations, operations, agrees

---

[1] *Sanctitas,* Holy Majesty. See note, Rom. i. 4.—ED.

respectively with these names. The Spirit is treated of at ver. 7, etc.: the Lord at ver. 12, etc.: God at ver. 28, etc.—[Comp. Eph. iv. 4, 5, 6.]

5. Διακονιῶν, *of ministrations*) ver. 28.—ὁ δὲ αὐτὸς Κύριος, *but the same Lord*) The Son of God whom the Holy Ghost glorifies by those ministers.

6. Ἐνεργημάτων, *of operations*) ver. 10.—ὁ δὲ αὐτός [1]ἐστι Θεός, *but it is the same God*) by the working of His Spirit, ver. 11.—τὰ πάντα, *all things*) The working of God is seen somewhat more extensively than the offices of Christ, and the gifts of the Spirit. —ἐν πᾶσιν, *in all*) Masculine; comp. *to every man*, in the following verses.

7. Φανέρωσις, *manifestation*) various, by which the Spirit *manifests* Himself, as He is hidden in Himself.—πρὸς τὸ συμφέρον, *with a view to that which is profitable*) This is treated of at ver. 12, 13.

8–10. ᾧ· ἑτέρῳ· ἑτέρῳ, *to one, to another, to another*) Three Genera: comp. ch. xiii. 8, and among these the expression, *to another*, denotes many species, each one under its own genus. So also xv. 39, 40, 41. ἄλλος in turn is used for distinguishing the species; ἕτερος, the genera. By a change, ἄλλος is used to distinguish genera, ἕτερος, species: Heb. xi. 35. *Prophecy* is put here under the second genus, rather than under the first, because under the second such things are stated, as are more applicable to those, that are without, viz., to unbelievers, than to such as are stated under the first genus, viz., to believers.—διὰ, *by*) presently after follows κατὰ, *according to ;* ἐν, *in ;* which are severally used with great propriety. [The Engl. Vers. loses this nice distinction by translating the διὰ, κατὰ, and ἐν all alike '*by*'.] —λόγος, *the word*) Both wisdom and knowledge are set forth in the church by the word.—σοφίας—γνώσεως, *of wisdom, of knowledge*) Paul in various ways mentions *knowledge*, especially to the Corinthians, either by itself, 2 Cor. vi. 6, or with things closely connected with it; *in word* [utterance] *and knowledge*, 1 Cor. i. 5; comp. 2 Cor. xi. 6; *in faith and utterance and knowledge and in all diligence*, 2 Cor. viii. 7; *prophecy* (concerning mys-

---

[1] The word ἐστί should rather be rejected, as well by the margin of both editions as by the Germ. Ver.—E. B.

Rec. Text reads ἐστι Θεός with later Syr., Orig., and B, which puts ἐστι after ἐνεργῶν. But ACD(Λ)G*fg* Vulg. Iren. Hilar. omit ἐστι.—ED.

teries) and *knowledge, tongues* being added, 1 Cor. xiii. 2, 8; *either by revelation or by knowledge, or by prophesying, or by doctrine,* ch. xiv. 6 : and here of *wisdom* and *knowledge;* Col. ii. 3; Eph. i. 17, iii. 19. He speaks as of things, which are of daily occurrence among the Corinthians; at present we are in doubt as to the meaning and distinction of the words themselves. This is certain, that when they are ascribed to God, they differ only in their objects: see Rom. xi. 33, note; when they are attributed to believers, *wisdom* penetrates the length, the breadth, the depth and height, more than *knowledge*. *Knowledge* is, so to speak, sight; *wisdom* is sight coupled with taste.[1] *Knowledge* relates to things that are to be done; *wisdom,* to things eternal; hence also wisdom is not said to pass away; ch. xiii. 8, and knowledge is of more frequent occurrence; so Paul does not so much predicate the former as the latter concerning the Corinthians, ch. viii. 1, ii. 6. *Prophecy* belongs to the prophets *wisdom* to the wise; what is left, viz., *knowledge,* to the scribes, Matt. xxiii. 34; Luke xi. 52.—τὸ αὐτὸ) *the same,* by whom *the word of wisdom* is given.

9. Πίστις, *faith*) The *faith* here spoken of is not that, which is common to all the saints, but it is a peculiar gift, and distinguished too from the four species, which immediately follow; and yet it is joined more with them, than with that first and third genus of gifts, ver. 8, and ver. 10 at the end. This *faith* then is a very earnest and vividly-present apprehension of God, chiefly in regard to His will, as to the effects, that are particularly conspicuous either in the kingdom of nature or of grace; therefore it is connected with the *operation of the miraculous powers,* ch. xiii. 2 (of which the principal, because the most useful to others, was the power of *curing diseases*), and with *prophecy* (to which *the discerning of spirits* was closely related, ch. xiv. 37); Rom. xii. 6. And from this description, which we have now given, it is evident, how common or saving faith, and miraculous faith, which is a peculiar gift, may either agree or differ, how the one may, or may not be, without the other, and either of them may, or may not be, without love. Men even without righteousness and love may have an intelligent perception of the omnipotent will of God in Christ, Matt. vii. 22: but none but

[1] 'Sapor,' akin to *sapientia.*—ED.

holy men can apprehend the will of God reconciled to us in Christ: and in these things [as respects this apprehension] there is not one faith working miracles, another saving faith, but one and the same faith. In its first act it always has a miraculous power; for it is something entirely supernatural, Eph. i. 19, although not always in such a degree, or on such a particular occasion, as that it should exert itself conspicuously; see Note on Chrys. de Sacerd., § 416.—χαρίσματα ἰαμάτων, *gifts of healing*) "Not only miraculous cures are meant, Acts v. 15, xix. 12, xxviii. 8, but also the gracious blessing on the cure of the sick, by natural remedies; as it cannot be denied, that some physicians are more fortunate than others, which should be attributed not merely to their skill, but especially to Divine grace;" E. Schmidius. This remark may also be applied to other gifts; for as the king of Judah substituted shields of brass for those of gold, which had been lost; so after the Church lost what were purely gifts, grace still lends its aid more secretly beneath the guise of human efforts and instrumentalities, and that too the more abundantly, in proportion as the more opportunity is given to it.

10. Προφητεία, *prophecy*) See at Rom. xii. 6.—διακρίσεις πνευμάτων, *discerning of spirits*) so that he can show to others, what sort of a spirit each prophet possesses, ch. xiv. 29.—γένη γλωσσῶν—ἑρμηνεία, *kinds of tongues—interpretation*) ver. 30, xiv. 5, xiii. 26, 27.

11. Βούλεται, *wills*) the Spirit. So, *as God willed*, ver. 18, He gives the several gifts, or some gifts, in various measures, to the several individuals.

12. Οὕτω καὶ ὁ Χριστός, *so also Christ*) The whole Christ is the head and body. *The head is the only-begotten Son of God, and His body is the Church;* Augustine. This is in harmony with Ps. xviii. 51. *To His Anointed, to David and his seed:* for so the accent requires it to be.

13. Ἐν ἑνὶ πνεύματι, *by one Spirit*) The Holy Spirit is in baptism.—εἰς ἓν σῶμα, *into one body*) that we may be one body, truly animated by one Spirit.—εἴτε Ἰουδαῖοι, εἴτε Ἕλληνες, *whether Jews or Greeks*) who were *bodies* of men very different by nature.— εἴτε δοῦλοι εἴτε ἐλεύθεροι, *whether bond or free*) who were *bodies* of men very different by human institution.—πάντες ἓν πνεῦμα) *we*

1 CORINTHIANS XII. 14, 15.

all have been made to drink *one Spirit*. [*Omitting* εἰς, *we have the true reading*,[1] Not. crit.], John vii. 37, etc. Hence also the unity of the body is inferred. I do not think however, that there is any direct allusion here to the Lord's Supper, Mark x. 38, note.

14. Καὶ γὰρ, *for even*) This protasis concerning the body extends to ver. 26 : and is so adjusted, that the apodosis, ver. 27, is summarily added.

15. 'Εὰν, *if*) The more ignoble members ought not to be vilified by themselves, ver. 15, 16, nor can they be neglected by the more noble, ver. 21, 22.—πούς, *the foot*) The foot is elegantly introduced speaking of the hand, the ear, speaking of the eye, the part speaking of the part that most resembles itself. For so among men, every one usually compares himself with those, to whom in gifts he bears the greatest resemblance, rather than with those, who are far superior, or far inferior. Thomas Aquinas says : " Men devoted to active life are distinguished by the members, that serve the purposes of motion ; those who are devoted to a contemplative life are distinguished by the members that serve the purposes of the intellectual powers." He is therefore of opinion, that the *feet* are kept in subjection ; that the *hands* occupy a more dignified position ; that the *eyes* are the teachers ; that the *ears* are the learners.—οὐκ εἰμὶ ἐκ, *I am not of*) supply, *therefore*, from the following clause.

15, 16. Οὐ παρὰ τοῦτο οὐκ ἔστιν ἐκ τοῦ σώματος) Μὴ in interrogation expects a negative answer, as ver. 29, μὴ πάντες ἀπόστολοι ; [are all apostles, surely not ?] but οὐκ interrogative affirms, as ch. xiv. 23, οὐκ ἐροῦσιν ; [will they not say ?] Therefore the question, whereby some read [as Engl. Vers, etc.], οὐ παρὰ τοῦτο οὐκ ἔστιν ἐκ τοῦ σώματος ; is it not therefore of the body ? perverts the sense [Beng. reads it *without interrogation*]. Οὐ παρὰ τοῦτο οὐκ possesses a double, not a simple power of negation, as Acts iv. 20, οὐ δυνάμεθα μὴ λαλεῖν, 2 Thess. iii. 9, οὐχ ὅτι οὐκ ἔχομεν ἐξουσίαν [*not* that we have *not* power]. If the foot should say, *because I am not the hand, I am not of the body*: this saying of the foot is

---

[1] The εἰς is omitted by BCD corrected later, G ; " unum spiritum (*others*, uno spiritu) potati sumus" in the oldest MS. (Amiat.) of Vulg. *fg* Syr. Memph. Rec. Text has εἰς with later uncial MSS. A has ἐν σωμα ἐσμεν. —ED.

blandly contradicted: *Thou art not therefore not of the body,* thou dost not therefore cease to be of the body. The phraseology of Theophilus of Antioch is very like this: οὐ παρὰ τὸ μὴ βλέπειν τοὺς τυφλοὺς, ἤδη καὶ οὐκ ἔστι τὸ φῶς τοῦ ἡλίου φαῖνον, it does not follow, that, *because the blind do not see, now therefore also the light of the sun does not appear,* lib. ad Autol., c. 3; and in this passage παρὰ denotes *on account of,* as Deut. xxiii. 4. Origen, c. Cels., p. 385, οὐ διὰ τοῦτο οὐ μοιχεύουσι, *They do not for this cause cease to commit adultery.* Chrysostom, οὐ γὰρ δήπου ἐν τοῖς δυσχερέσι κοινωνοῦντες, ἐν τοῖς χρηστοτέροις οὐ κοινωνήσετε, *if you do not now partake of what is unpleasant, you will not partake of what is better,* on 2 Cor. i. 7.

16. Τὸ οὖς, *the ear*) a part less noble.—ὀφθαλμὸς, *the eye*) a most noble and most commanding (ἡγεμονικὴ) part of the body, comp. Num. x. 31. Sight excels hearing, ver. 17, 21.

17. Εἰ ὅλον ἀκοὴ, *if the whole were an ear*) It is not said, *and if,* for the *etc.* is supplied at the end of the verse, *or if the whole were smelling, where were the taste and the touch?*

18. Καθὼς ἠθέλησεν, *as it hath pleased Him*) We ought not to require other and deeper reasons for things, beyond the will of God: it is lawful to philosophize *in subjection to that* will; we may do so respecting the world in its best ideal, [in a state of optimism] as the apostle does here respecting the human body in its best ideal.

20. Ἐν δὲ σῶμα, *but one body*) From this unity there follows the mutual dependency of the members.

21. Χρείαν, *need*) To this refer the word *necessary,* ver. 22.— ἡ κεφαλὴ, *the head*) the highest part.

22. Ἀσθενέστερα, *more feeble*) the hand, compared with the eye.

23. Ἀτιμότερα, [less noble] *less honourable*) as the feet. The comparative is used to soften the expression; positively *dishonourable* [ignoble] was too severe. But he so calls those parts which are covered with garments.—ἀσχήμονα, *uncomely*) which stand in need of clothing.—τιμὴν—περιτίθεμεν) So the LXX., Esth. i. 20, περιθήσουσι τιμήν; likewise Prov. xii. 9.—ἔχει, *have*) from the attention which they receive from the other members.

24. Οὐ χρείαν ἔχει, *have no need*) Why then is it necessary to

adorn smooth cheeks with patches?[1]—συνεκέρασε) *hath tempered together.*—τιμήν, *honour*) comp. ver. 23, at the beginning.

25. Ὑπὲρ ἀλλήλων μεριμνῶσι, *care for one another*) This is explained in the following verse. The plural μεριμνῶσι, more expressly denotes the care of all the members, than if it were said in the Attic dialect, μεριμνᾷ.[2]

26. Συγχαίρει) *rejoice with it.* Both this expression and *suffer with* not only denote the affection, but also the effect.

27. Ἐκ μέρους, *in part* [*in particular*]) He adds this, because the Corinthians were not the sole constituents of the body of Christ and His members, ch. xiv. 36. Even Rome should hold it enough, if she be *a part* [*in particular*].

28. Ἐν, *in*) So, ἐν, *in* [the body], ver. 18, occurs with the same verb *set.*—πρῶτον, *first*) The apostles, not Peter apart from them, are in the first degree; the others follow them, according to the nature of their office, their time, their dignity, their usefulness.—προφήτας, *prophets*) Acts xiii. 1.—τρίτον διδασκάλους, *thirdly, teachers*) Teachers hold a high place, and are preferred to those very persons, who work *miracles.* Under prophets and teachers are included also evangelists and pastors; comp. Eph. iv. 11.—ἔπειτα, *then*) The other classes are not distinguished by members [*fourthly*, etc., as *first, secondarily*].—δυνάμεις, *powers*) The abstract for the concrete, and also in the following terms. —ἀντιλήψεις, κυβερνήσεις, *helps, governments* [κυβέρνησις properly is the *piloting* of a ship]) They hold governments, who take the lead [the helm] in managing the church. *Helps*, are those who, though they are not governors, yet exercise a certain power and influence, by which the others are supported; comp. xiii. 3. These two offices are not again taken up at ver. 30. Princes, as soon as they adopted the Christian faith, claimed for themselves the office of *helps* and *governments;* but at the beginning those who stood first in authority, prudence, and resources in the church, defended and governed it. *Government* is occupied with external things; therefore the Spirit reckons it as occupying an inferior place.—ἑρμηνείας γλωσσῶν, *interpretations of tongues*) The expression does not seem to be a gloss spuriously

---

[1] As was the custom, in Bengel's days, among fops.—ED
[2] Neut. plur. with verb sing.—ED.

introduced from ver. 10,[1] for ἑρμηνεία γλωσσῶν is there in the singular number, and it is repeated in ver. 30. The want of the connecting particle [the asyndeton] is equivalent to the closing formula, etc., or *et cetera*.

29. Μὴ πάντες, *are all?* [surely not]) *i.e.*, not very many are. —δυνάμεις, *powers*) viz., *are* all? For if Paul referred the *have all?* of ver. 30, to it, he would have expressed it here.

31. Ζηλοῦτε, *emulously desire*) The Spirit gives as He wills, ver. 11: but yet believers may freely follow out, and engage in, one thing in preference to another, ch. xiv. 26. God's operations are pleasant, not compulsory.—τὰ κρείττονα, *the better gifts*) according as each gift is more favourable to love. Theology is comparative: ch. xiv. 5, 19.—ἔτι) [*and yet*, Engl. Vers.] *nay even*: so ἔτι τε καὶ, *yea even also*, Luke xiv. 26. I not only exhort, but also show the method, and the way or plan [the true mode of viewing the subject].—καθ' ὑπερβολὴν) This expression attaches to the noun substantive the force of a superlative (Rom. vii. 13), as if he were to say, *the way most way-like* [*viam maximè vialem*].—ὁδὸν, *a way*) He does not add the article, keeping the Corinthians somewhat in suspense, while he explains the way: דרך, *the way* of love.—δείκνυμι, *I show*) The present. Paul is now waxing warm, and is carried on to love. When he has made this 'showing' of the way, he returns to the gifts, as the word *emulously desire* [ζηλοῦτε] repeated indicates, here and at ch. xiv. 1.

CHAPTER XIII.

1. Ἐὰν, *if*) All the gifts [*although they may be, in the highest degree, delightful, extensive, and useful.—*V. g.] ought to be estimated, exercised, and elevated, according to love and its standard. The apostle introduces into the discussion of the

---

[1] The margin of the second edition, with the Gnomon, is more favourable to the fuller reading, than the larger edition and the Germ. Ver.—E. B.

All the oldest MSS. and Versions read γένη γλωσσῶν only. Hilary 967 alone has " genera linguarum vel loquendi vel interpretandi."—ED.

gifts a more efficacious discussion respecting love. So in Disputations, we must always return to those points, which give a higher degree of grace.—ταῖς) all.—γλώσσαις, *tongues*) A gradation: with *the tongues*, ver. 1: *prophecy*, ver. 2: *faith*, ver. 2: *I shall have bestowed*, ver. 3.—λαλῶ, *I speak*) The tenor of love causes, that, whereas he just before used the expression, *to you*, he should now however speak in the first person singular. He does not except even himself in the condition supposed [viz., *Though* I speak, etc., and have not charity, etc.]—καὶ τῶν ἀγγέλων, *and of angels*) Angels excel men, and the tongue or tongues of the former excel those of the latter. Moreover, they use their tongues at least to address men: Luke i. and ii.— ἀγάπην, *love*) by which the salvation of our neighbour is sought. —μὴ ἔχω, *have not*) in the very use of the gifts, and in the rest of the life. Many indeed have prophecy and other gifts, without charity and its fruits, ver. 4; Matt. vii. 22, which are called *gifts*, not so much in respect of themselves, as of others.—γέγονα) *I have become*, for want of love. The language becomes severe [obtinet ἀποτομίαν].—χαλκὸς, *brass*) *Brass*, for example a piece of money of that metal requires less of the skill of the artist, than a cymbal, for instance, of silver. He may be compared to the one who speaks with the tongues of men without love; to the other, who speaks without love with the tongues of angels.—ἠχῶν—ἀλαλάζον, *sounding—tinkling*) with any sound whatever, mournful or joyful, without life and feeling. The language varies, *I am nothing; it profiteth me nothing*, ver. 2, 3. Without love, tongues are a *mere sound*: prophecy, knowledge, faith, *are not what they are* [seem to be]: Matt. vii. 22, 15; 1 Cor. viii. 1, 2; James ii. 14, 8; every such sacrifice [gift exercised without love] is *without* [the heavenly] *reward*,[1] however much such a man may please himself, and think that he is something, and promise to himself a great recompense. With love, the good things which are the antitheses to these defects, are understood.

2. Μυστήρια, *mysteries*) Rom. xi. 25, note. He does not add *wisdom*, which is nothing without *love*.—καὶ πᾶσαν τὴν γνῶσιν, *and all knowledge*) This is construed with εἰδῶ, *I understand*, as

---

[1] Comp. Matt. vi. 2.—ED.

being a word of kindred meaning and immediately preceding. Of those gifts, which are enumerated at ch. xii., Paul at ch. xiii. selected such as are more remarkable, and to which the peculiar prerogatives of love are fitly opposed. *Mysteries* relate to things concealed; *knowledge* comprehends things which are more ready at hand, and more necessary, as *Wissenschaften* is commonly said of natural things—πίστιν, *faith*) ch. xii. 9, note.

3. Καὶ ἐὰν, *and if*) This is the utmost that the *helps* and *governments* can do, ch. xii. 28.—ψωμίσω, *though I should distribute*) He puts in the highest place, what refers to the human will and seems to be the most closely connected with love, in regard to acting and suffering. He, who delivers up his *goods* and his *body*, has much love, 2 Cor. xii. 15; but he who delivers them up without *love*, keeps back his *soul* to himself:[1] for love is a faculty of the soul; therefore he speaks of *profit* (ὠφελοῦμαι) in the apodosis. On ψωμίζειν see Rom. xii. 20.—παραδῶ, *give up*) for others.—ἵνα) *even to such a degree as that I be burnt*, Dan. iii. 28; they gave up their bodies to the fire, παρέδωκαν τὰ σώματα αὐτῶν εἰς πῦρ.

4. Ἡ ἀγάπη, *love*) He points out the nature of love. He does not say, love speaks with tongues, prophesies, gives to the poor: but it is long-suffering. This is a metonymy for the man, who has love. But Paul chiefly mentions those fruits of love, necessary in the use of the gifts, which he requires from the Corinthians, and without which there may be prophecies, but there can be no profit. If we take 1 Cor. viii. 1, we may advantageously compare together the delineation of love which Paul adapted to the Corinthians, and the delineation of wisdom, which James in like manner adapted to [portrayed for] those to whom he wrote, Jam. iii. 17.—μακροθυμεῖ, *suffers long*) The twelve praises of love are enumerated by three classes, ver. 4–7—(if we reckon together one pair at the beginning, and two pairs at the end, as we show in the following notes). The first consists of two members, (1.) *it suffers long, is kind:* (2.) *envies not.* We have the same synthesis and antithesis, Gal. v. 22, 20. *Long-suffering* has respect to evil proceeding from others: *kind* has respect to the extending of good to others; on the other hand,

---

[1] He may give up his *body*, but he keeps back his *soul*.—ED.

1 CORINTHIANS XIII. 4, 5.

it does not grieve at another's good, nor rejoice at another's calamity. The conjunction is wanting to *is kind* [Asyndeton].

4, 5. Οὐ περπερεύεται, οὐ φυσιοῦται· οὐκ ἀσχημονεῖ, οὐ ζητεῖ τὰ ἑαυτῆς, *vaunteth not itself, is not puffed up, doth not behave itself unseemly, seeketh not its own*) The second class consists of four members : in the first and second, two things in excess, which are generally united, are taken away ; in the third and fourth two things in defect, which are likewise united, are also taken away : for ἀσχημονεῖν means the want of attention to that decency, and that civility, which propriety required to be observed : and ζητεῖν τὰ ἑαυτοῦ is connected with the neglect of others, when a man looks merely to himself and leaves others to themselves. Love avoids these two *defects*, and the third corresponds to the first, for both refer to the desire of approving one's self to others : the fourth is opposed to the second, for both refer to the necessity of avoiding party feeling. Οὐ περπερεύεται, *it does not act insolently*, with pride and ostentation ; again, οὐκ ἀσχημονεῖ, it is *not uncourteous*, unpolite, rude :[1] see what I have remarked on the verb περπερεύεται ad Gregorii Paneg., p. 141, etc. ; οὐ φυσιοῦται, *is not puffed up*, with too strong party-zeal for another ; comp. iv. 6 : again οὐ ζητεῖ τὰ ἑαυτῆς [*seeks not its own*], *does not show favour to itself*, and does not ask others to show it favour. In a way not dissimilar, twice two members have likewise respect to each other mutually (though they are occasionally placed in a different order by chiasmus direct or inverse) at ver. 7, and especially at xiv. 6.

5. Οὐ παροξύνεται—πάντα ὑπομένει, *is not provoked—beareth all things*) The third class, consisting of six members ; of which the third and fourth, and so the second and fifth, the first and sixth agree with one another. For there is a chiasmus, and that too retrograde, and quite agreeing with the double climax by steps negative and affirmative. And of all these our neighbour is the

---

[1] Where love flourishes, there also true modesty prevails, which is termed *civility* among people of the world (nor yet should *familiarity* be blamed as insolent): on the other hand, every degree of *elegance of manners*, even in its highest perfection, shows in men of the world something of an *insolent* character in it, on account of self-love. Let the world cease to boast of virtues; they apply only to true Christianity.—V. g.

personal object;—the real[1] object, as regards the future, is, *love is not provoked, it hopeth all things, it endureth all things;* as regards the past, the object of the thing is, *it thinketh no evil, it covereth* [Engl. Vers., *beareth*] *all things, believeth all things* : as regards the present, *it rejoiceth not at iniquity, but rejoiceth together with others in the truth;* now by thus transposing the members, the elegance of the order, which Paul has adopted, is the more clearly seen; which the following scheme thus represents, and its *evident* plan shows the thread and connection:

    1. *It is not provoked.*
    2. *It thinketh no evil.*
    3. *It rejoiceth not at iniquity.*
    4. *But rejoiceth at the truth.* Present.
    5. *Covereth all things, believeth all things,* past.
    6. *Hopeth all things, endureth all things,* future.

Thus the order is mutually consistent with itself; and the reason appears, why these last, *hopeth, endureth,* are put at the end, because in fact they are to be referred to the future.—οὐ παροξύνεται, *is not provoked*) although love glows with an eager desire for the Divine glory, yet it is not provoked; comp. Acts xv. 39. —οὐ λογίζεται τὸ κακὸν, [Engl. Vers. *thinketh no evil*]) *doth not meditate upon evil* inflicted by another, with a desire to avenge it. So the LXX. for חשב רעה often. [*It does not think thus, This or that man inflicts upon me this or that wrong; he has either done, or deserved this or that.*—V. g.]

6. Ἀδικίᾳ—ἀληθείᾳ, *in iniquity—in the truth*) On this antithesis see Rom. ii. 8.—συγχαίρει, *rejoiceth with*) congratulates, with joy. All truth cherishes *joy.*

7. Πάντα, *all things*) *all things* occurs four times, viz., those things, which are to be covered, or believed; and which are to be hoped for, and endured. These four steps beautifully follow one another.—στέγει, *covers*) conceals[2] in relation to itself and in relation to others στέγομεν, *we cover,* ch. ix. 12, note.—πιστεύει, *believes*) as he covers the *evil deeds* of his neighbour, which are apparent, so he believes the *good,* which is not apparent.—ἐλπίζει, *hopes*) See the ground of *hope* [viz., " *God* is able to make him

---

[1] The object of *the thing,* as contrasted with the object of *the person.* " reale objectum"—" objectum personale."—ED.

[2] Bears, without speaking of what it has to bear.—ED.

1 CORINTHIANS XIII. 8–10.

stand;" therefore, "*he shall be holden up*"], Rom. xiv. 4; σταθή-σεται; he likewise *hopes good* for the future, and endures *evils*.—ὑπομένει, *endures*) until hope at some time springs up, 2 Tim. ii. 25. Thus the praises of love describe as it were a kind of circle, in which the last and first mutually correspond to each other; *it is long-suffering, it is kind; it hopeth all things, it endureth all things;* and, that which is of far greater importance, *it never faileth*, pleasantly follows this fourth step.

8. Οὐδέποτε ἐκπίπτει, *never faileth*) is not destroyed, does not cease, it always holds its place; it is never moved from its position; comp. ἐκπίπτοντες, Mark xiii. 25, note.—εἴτε δὲ προφητεῖαι, *but whether prophecies*) viz., *there are*: so ch. xv. 11. Prophecies in the plural, because they are multifarious.—καταργηθήσονται, *they shall be done away with*) This is the expression in the case of prophecies and knowledge; but regarding tongues, παύσονται, *they shall cease*. Tongues are a most charming thing, but the least lasting; they were the first gift on the day of Pentecost, Acts ii., but they did not continue in the primitive church so long as the other miraculous gifts: nor have they anything analogous in a perfect state, as prophecy and knowledge have, to which they ought therefore to yield; whence presently after, respect is shown to those in preference to tongues, when he is speaking of "that which is perfect."—γλῶσσαι, *tongues*) These occupy a middle place, because they are the vehicle and appendage of prophecies; but prophecy and knowledge constitute two different genera, ver. 9, 12.

9. Ἐκ μέρους, *in part*) Not only does the apostle say this, This prophecy and this knowledge, which we have, are imperfect; for the same must be said even of love, *we love only in part* [not perfectly]; but such is the nature of prophecy itself, with the exception of the one prophet Jesus Christ, and such the nature of knowledge, that they ought to be reckoned among the things, which are *in part*, [not merely because they are now *imperfect*, but also] because we use them only in this imperfect life. On the phrase, comp. the note on Rom. xv. 15, *I have written more boldly*.

10. Ἔλθῃ, *is come*) in its own time, by degrees, not by a sudden bound. In spiritual things, those of weaker age ought not too eagerly to aim at what belongs to those, who have reached

VOL. III.   U

greater maturity. That, which is perfect, comes at death; 2 Cor. v. 7 : and at the last day.—τότε, *then*) not before. Therefore prophecy and knowledge never entirely pass away in this life.

11. Ὅτε, *when*) The progress from grace to glory, which awaits individual believers and the whole Church, is compared to the different stages of human life.—νήπιος, *a child*) Exemplifying the humility of Paul. The natural man does not willingly remember his childhood because he is proud; but the soul, pining away under adversity, confesses the early passages of its early growth, Job x. 10.—ἐλάλουν, *I spoke*) There is a reference to tongues.— ἐφρόνουν, *I understood* [*I had the sentiments*]) The reference is to prophecy; for it is something more simple.—ἐλογιζόμην, *I reasoned as a child*) The reference is to knowledge; for it is more complex.—ὅτε δὲ, *but when*) He does not say, *when I put away childish things, I became a man.* Winter does not bring spring; but spring drives away winter; so it is in the soul of man and in the Church.—κατήργηκα, *I put away*) of my own accord, willingly, without effort.—τὰ τοῦ νηπίου, *childish things*) childish speaking, childish understanding, childish counsel. τὰ, the Abstract. The humanity is not taken away, but manhood is assumed.

12. Βλέπομεν, *we see*) This corresponds in the LXX. to the Hebrew words ראה and חזה, 1 Sam. ix. 9 ; 1 Chron. xxix. 29, concerning the *Prophets ;* and this passage has a synecdoche of the nobler species for the whole genus ; and along with the verb, *we see*, supply, *and hear*, for the prophets both see and hear ; and it was usual generally to add words to visions. It will be of importance to read the Paneg. of *Gregory*, and the remarkable passage of Origen, which has been noticed by me in my observations on that book, pp. 104, 105, 217, 218, 219. But what a *mirror* is to the eye, that an *enigma* is to the ear, to which the *tongue* is subservient. On various grounds, we may compare with this Num. xii. 8. Moreover he says, *we see*, in the plural : *I know*, in the singular ; and to *see* and to *know* differ in the genus [classification] of spiritual things, as the external sense, and the internal perceptions differ in the genus [under the head] of natural things. Nor does he mention *God* in this whole verse ; but he speaks of Him, as He shall be *all in all.*—τότε, *then*) Paul

had a great relish for those things, that are future: 2 Cor. xii. 2, 3.—πρόσωπον πρὸς πρόσωπον, *face to face*) פָּנִים אֶל פָּנִים, with our face, we shall see the face of our Lord. That is more than פֶּה אֶל פֶּה, στόμα πρὸς στόμα, *mouth to mouth*. Vision is the most excellent means of enjoyment. The word βλέπομεν is elegantly used, and is adapted to both states, but under a different idea.—γινώσκω, ἐπιγνώσομαι) The compound signifies much more than the simple verb; *I know, I shall thoroughly know*. And so Eustathius interprets the Homeric word ἐπιόψομαι, ἀκριβέστατα ἐπιτηρήσω, *I shall observe most accurately*; and ἐπίσκοπος, *an overseer*, σκοπευτὴς ἀκριβής, *an accurate observer*; and adds the reason, ὅτι ἡ ἐπιπρόθεσις καὶ ἀκρίβειάν τινα σημαίνει καὶ ἐπίτασιν ἐνεργείας, that the ἐπὶ prefixed to the simple verb signifies a certain degree of accuracy and additional energy.—καθὼς καὶ ἐπεγνώσθην, *as also I am known*) This corresponds to the expression, *face to face*.

13. Νυνὶ δὲ μένει, *but now abideth*) This is not strictly said of duration; for these three things do not meet in it; since faith is terminated in *sight*, and hope in joy, 2 Cor. v. 7; Rom. viii. 24: love alone continues, ver. 8: but it refers to their value, in antithesis to prophecy, etc., in this sense: On calculating accounts [on weighing the relative values] these three things are necessary and sufficient; let only these three stand; these exist; these abide, nothing more. A man may be a Christian without prophecy, etc., but not without faith, hope, love. Comp. on the verb, μένω, *I abide*, Rom. ix. 11; 1 Cor. iii. 14; 2 Cor. iii. 11; Heb. xiii. 1. Faith is directed to God; hope is in our own behalf; love is towards our neighbour. Faith is properly connected with the economy of the Father; Hope with the economy of the Son; Love with the economy of the Holy Ghost, Col. ii. 12, i. 27, 8. And this too is the very reason of the order in which these three things are enumerated. *νυνὶ*, *now*, has the effect of an epitasis[1] [and *shows what are the especial duties* of us travellers on the way to the heavenly city.— V. g.]—τρία, *three*) only. Many are not necessary. Paul often refers to these three graces. Eph. i. 15, 18; Phil. i. 9, 10; Col. i. 4, 5, 22, note; 1 Thess. i. 3; v. 8; 2 Thess. i. 3, 4; Tit. i. 1, 2; Heb. vi. 10, etc. Sometimes he mentions both faith and

---

[1] An emphatic addition augmenting the force.—Append.

love, sometimes faith [by itself] denoting by synecdoche the whole of Christianity, 1 Thess. iii. 6, 5. In a wicked man we find infidelity, hatred, despair.—ταῦτα, *these*) Heb. הן, *i.e. are,* viz. greater than prophecies, etc.—μεῖζων, *greater*) the greatest, *of these,* of the three. He not only prefers love to prophecy, but even to such things as excel prophecy. Love is of more *advantage* to our neighbour, than faith and hope by themselves: comp. *greater,* xiv. 5. And God is not called *faith* or *hope* absolutely, whereas He is called *love.*

CHAPTER XIV.

1. Διώκετε, *follow after*) This word implies more than ζηλοῦτε, *emulously desire,* here, and in ver. 12, 39, xii. 31.—μᾶλλον, *rather*) in preference to tongues. Paul here does not now any longer speak expressly of *knowledge,* for it, in respect of the other gifts, coincides with *prophecy,* ver. 6.

2. Τῷ Θεῷ, *to God*) alone, who understands all tongues.— ἀκούει, *hears*) *i.e.* understands.—πνεύματι, *in spirit*) ver. 14.— μυστήρια, *mysteries*) which others may rather admire, than learn. The article is not added.

3. Οἰκοδομὴν, *edification*) Two principal species are added to this genus; παράκλησις, *exhortation,* takes away sluggishness; παραμυθία, *consolation* takes away sadness.

4. Ἑαυτὸν, *himself*) understanding the meaning of what the tongue speaks.—ἐκκλησίαν, *the church*) the whole congregation.

5. Γλώσσαις, *with tongues*) The Corinthians chiefly cultivated this gift; and Paul does not consider them as doing wrong, but he reduces it to order: see ver. 12.—μείζων, *greater*) more useful, ver. 6.—διερμηνεύει) διὰ elegantly expresses the position of the interpreter between him, who speaks in an unknown tongue, and the hearer. If the very same person, who speaks in an unknown tongue, also acts as interpreter, then the very same person in a manner comes in between himself and the hearer; according to the different point of view in which he is regarded.

—ἡ ἐκκλησία, *the Church*) *seeking* [ver. 12] edification; *may receive it in consonance with this* [viz. with *seeking*].

6. "Η ἐν ἀποκαλύψει, ἢ ἐν γνώσει, ἢ ἐν προφητείᾳ, ἢ ἐν διδαχῇ, *either in revelation, or in knowledge, or in prophecy, or in doctrine*) Here are four kinds of prophecy broadly so called; the two former refer to the person himself, who rejoices in the gift; the two latter at the same time show more of a leaning towards the hearers.[1] On the difference of *prophecy* (which corresponds to *revelation*) and of *knowledge* (with which *doctrine* agrees) see xii. 8, 10: and on the whole subject, below at ver. 26, etc. *Prophecy* has relation to particular points, formerly not well understood, to mysteries to be known finally [and only] by revelation. *Doctrine* and *knowledge* are brought from the common storehouse of believers, and refer to things obvious in the matter of salvation.

7. Αὐλὸς—κιθάρα, *a pipe—a harp*) Two of the chief musical instruments; not only the pipe, which is, as it were, animated by the breath of the piper, but also the harp.—τοῖς φθόγγοις, '*in the sounds*) The ablative case comp. *by*, ver. 9.—πῶς γνωσθήσεται, *how shall it be known*) how shall pipe be distinguished from pipe, and harp from harp? There is one and then another sound of one and the same instrument, when it is directed to different things.

8. Γὰρ, *for*) This serves the purpose of a gradation; for the higher confirms the lower step.—ἄδηλον, *uncertain*) One sound of a single trumpet summons soldiers to one class of duties, another sound to another class of duties.

9. Ὑμεῖς, *you*) who have life [opp. to *things without life*]; comp. ver. 7.—διὰ, *by*) *i.e.* then, when you speak in an unknown tongue.

10. Τοσαῦτα, εἰ τύχοι) εἰ τύχοι (the Latin, *verbi gratia*, for example; comp. xv. 37) makes τοσαῦτα have the force of a certain number. If men could ever have counted the number of voices, Paul would have set down the number here.—οὐδὲν ἄφωνον, *none without signification*) each one of them has its own power [*meaning*, ver. 11], δύναμιν.

11. Βάρβαρος, *a barbarian*) See Acts xxviii. 2, Note.

[1] What Ernesti approves in Moldenhauer evidently agrees with these views.—Bibl. Theol., T. viii., p. 673.—E. B.

12. Πνευμάτων, *of spirits*) [*of spiritual* gifts]. Plural as ver. 32, xii. 10. As there is one sea, and many seas, so there is one spirit, and many spirits; one *trumpet* gives many sounds.—προς τὴν οἰκοδομὴν, *to edification*) that the Church may be as much as possible edified.

13. Προσευχέσθω) *let him pray;* and he will do this with such fruit and effect, that the interpretation shall be added to the unknown tongue; see the following verse. It is implied that this will be obtained by prayers.

14. Τὸ πνεῦμα μου, ὁ δὲ νοῦς μου, *my spirit—but my understanding*) The *spirit* is a faculty of the soul, when it becomes the *passive object* of the Holy Spirit's delightful operations; but νοῦς, *the understanding*, is a faculty of soul, when it goes abroad, and *acts* with our neighbour :[1] as also when it attends to objects placed beyond itself, to other things and persons, although its reasonings may however be concealed, ἀπόκρυφος λογισμός (Ammonius); comp. ver. 20, note. So *understanding*, ver. 19; πνεῦμα, the inmost shrine of the understanding, τοῦ νοός, Eph. iv. 23; comp. Heb. iv. 12 : νοῦς from νέω, on account of its agitation or movement :[2] comp. Alexand. Aphrodit., 1. 2, περὶ ψυχῆς, f. 144, ed. Ald.—ἄκαρπος, *without fruit*) It has fruit, but does not bring it forth. Respecting this word, see Matt. xiii. 22.

15. Προσεύξομαι, *I will pray*) with the voice; the first person singular for the second person plural.—ψαλῶ, *I will sing*) with the voice, or play on an instrument.

16. Ἐπεὶ) if that be done with the spirit only.—εὐλογήσῃς, *thou shalt bless*) The most noble kind of prayer.—ὁ ἀναπληρῶν τὸν τόπον τοῦ ἰδιώτου, *he that filleth the place of the unlearned*) This expression is not a mere paraphrase of the word *unlearned*, but comprehends all, who, how much soever they may excel in gifts, did not at least understand the tongue, in which the person was speaking, any more than an unlearned man; and therefore Paul puts him more to shame, whom he here shows to be wrong. It is a common phrase among the Hebrews, *he fills the place of his fathers, i.e.,* he shows himself worthy of his ancestors.—πῶς ἐρεῖ τὸ ἀμήν, *how shall he say amen*) This was their usual practice even at that time; not only the unlearned, but all the hearers spoke,

---

[1] *i.e.* πνεῦμα is *passive*, when said of man : νοῦς, *active*.—Ed.
[2] Rather from the same root as γνῶναι, and *noscere*.—Ed.

1 CORINTHIANS XIV. 17–22.

giving their assent to *him who blessed*. And so also, those who could not speak much adopted the words of others, and declared, that they with their understanding assented to it.—Τί λέγεις, *what thou sayest*) Not only ought he to know, that thou hast said nothing evil, but also what good thou hast spoken.

18. Εὐχαριστῶ, *I give thanks*) Paul uses thanksgiving and προθεραπείαν,[1] anticipatory precaution against the charge of egotism, when he is to speak his own praises.—πάντων, *more than you all*) more than you individually or even collectively.—ὑμῶν, *than you*) Frequently, those, who are less accomplished are more proud and act with greater insolence.

19. Πέντε λόγους, *five words*) A definite for an indefinite number; the two thousandth part of *ten thousand*: comp. Lev. xxvi. 8.

20. Ἀδελφοί, *brethren*) The vocative put at the beginning has an agreeable force.—τῇ κακίᾳ· ταῖς φρεσί) Ammonius makes this seasonable observation: " νοῦς is covert reasoning, ἀπόκρυφος λογισμός; but φρένες implies GOOD thoughts," αἱ ΑΓΑΘΑΙ διάνοιαι. Nor does κακία denote *malice* [badness], but *vice*, or whatever is opposed to virtue.—νηπιάζετε, *be ye children*) νηπιάζω, similar to the forms ἀκμάζω, πυρράζω.—τέλειοι, *perfect*) and therefore determining the true value of every thing according to its use.

21. Νόμῳ, *in the law*) comprehending also the prophets.—ἐν ἑτερογλώσσοις καὶ ἐν χείλεσιν ἑτέροις) Is. xxviii. 11, LXX. διὰ φαυλισμὸν χειλέων διὰ γλώσσης ἑτέρας, ἑτερογλώσσοις ; masculine or neuter. The paraphrase accommodating the text of Isaiah to this passage of Paul may be as follows: *This people do not hear Me, though I speak to them in the language, to which they have been accustomed; I will therefore speak to them in other tongues, namely, of the enemies that are sent against them; but even then they will not listen to me*, comp. Jer. v. 15. Since God is said to speak in the tongues of enemies, the parity of reasoning holds good from them to the gift of tongues.—οὐδ᾽ οὕτως εἰσακούσονταί μου) Is. xxviii. 12, καὶ οὐκ ἠθέλησαν ἀκούειν, *And they would not hear*.

22. Εἰς σημεῖον) *for a sign*, by which unbelievers may be allured and *hear* [give ear to] the word; but οὐδ᾽ οὕτως, *not even*

---
[1] See Append.

thus do they hear [alluding to Isa. xxviii. 12, see last note].—εἰσὶν, *have their existence*) The accent has the effect of making the word emphatic.—ἡ δὲ προφητεία, *but prophecy*) namely, *is for a sign*, or simply *is*; comp. vi. 13.—τοῖς πιστεύουσιν, *to them that believe*) This must be taken as an instance of the figure Amplificatio;[1] inasmuch as prophecy makes believers of unbelievers; the speaking tongue leaves the unbeliever to himself [still an unbeliever]. The expression of Paul is indefinite. Unbelievers, generally, when tongues fall upon them, continue to be unbelievers, but prophecy makes believers of unbelievers, and gives spiritual nourishment to them, that believe.

23. Ὅλη ἐπὶ τὸ αὐτὸ, *the whole into one place*) That was a rare occurrence in so large a city.—εἰσέλθωσι δὲ, *and there come in*) as strangers or even from curiosity.—ἰδιῶται, *unlearned*) men who have some degree of faith, but do not abound in gifts. There follows by gradation, *or unbelievers*, who did not so readily come in, and yet were not debarred. In this verse Paul speaks in the plural, in the following in the singular. Many bad men, when together, prevent one another from believing by their bad conversation; individuals are more easily gained.—ὅτι μαίνεσθε, *that ye are mad*) For they will not be able to distinguish that earnestness from madness; hence they will speak to your prejudice; comp. Acts ii. 13.

24. Πάντες, *all*) one by one, ver. 31.—εἰσέλθῃ, *there come in*) We have an example of this at 1 Sam. xix. 20, 21.—ἄπιστος, *one that believeth not*) To this word we refer *is convinced*, comp. John xvi. 9.—ἰδιώτης, *an unlearned person*) to this word we refer *is judged:* comp. ii. 15. That *conviction* of *unbelief*, and that *judgment* of *unlearned* rudeness is accomplished by the power of this very prophecy, although this be done without application to individuals. And these are two successive steps; the third follows, *the secrets*, etc.

24, 25. Ἐλέγχεται ὑπὸ πάντων, ἀνακρίνεται ὑπὸ πάντων (καὶ οὕτω[2])

---

[1] See Append. The taking of the denomination of a thing, not so much from what it now is, as from what it is about to be. As here, "Prophecy is a sign to those who thereby are made believers." This seems Bengel's meaning.—ED.

[2] ABD corrected later, Gfg Vulg. omit καὶ οὕτω. The later Syr. and some later uncial MSS., support the words with Rec. Text.—ED.

τὰ κρυπτὰ τῆς καρδίας αὐτοῦ φανερὰ γίνεται· καὶ οὕτω πεσὼν ἐπὶ πρόσωπον προσκυνήσει τῷ Θεῷ, ἀπαγγέλλων ὅτι ὁ Θεὸς ὄντως ἐν ὑμῖν ἐστι) The first καὶ οὕτω is spurious; for the present of the verb γίνεται indicates that this clause, τὰ κρυπτὰ—γίνεται, is more closely connected with the preceding words, where the discourse runs in the present tense, than with the following, which have the future προσκυνήσει.—ὑπὸ πάντων, *by all*) partly speaking, partly assenting.

25. Τὰ κρυπτὰ τῆς καρδίας αὐτοῦ, *the secrets of his heart*) all the inmost thoughts of the heathen's heart, which has never experienced such feelings, and has now for the first time become acquainted with itself and makes confession concerning itself: for the *unbeliever* is here principally intended. The *unlearned* man is added by the way, on account of his case being not altogether dissimilar. Any one with the lowest degree of *faith* before entering an assembly of that kind knew, that God is truly in believers.—αὐτοῦ, *of him*) the unbelieving stranger.—φανερὰ γίνεται, *are made manifest*) Dan. ii. 30 at the end.—οὕτω) *so*, at last. —πεσὼν, *falling down*) a public declaration on the part of those, who feel and experience in themselves the power of the word, is generally made too sparingly in our times.—ἀπαγγέλλων, *declaring*) spontaneously, clearly, expressly announcing this fact either in the Church, or even out of it elsewhere: comp. on this word, Greg. Paneg. § 123 cum Annot.—ὅτι, *that*) comp. Dan. ii. 46, 47. A most conclusive argument for the truth of religion, from the operations of God on godly men.—ὄντως, *indeed*) He will confess, that you are not mad, but that God is truly in you, and that He is the true God, who is in you.

26. Ἕκαστος, *every one*) The public assembly was at that time more fruitful, than in the present day, wherein one individual, whatever may be the state of his mind, must fill up the time with a sermon.—ψαλμὸν ἔχει) *has a psalm*, in habit of mind or in actual fact, either a little before, or only now: comp. ver. 30. Extempory hymns were given to them by the Spirit. Individuals had a *psalm*, wherewith to praise God, or a *doctrine* to be imparted to his neighbour; or a *tongue*, by which they might speak every one to himself. The word ἔχει, *has*, repeated, elegantly expresses the abundance of the gifts, which had been divided.—ἀποκάλυψιν, *revelation*) by which God communicates something to man; Gal. ii. 2, prophetical *revelation*, ver. 30, 29.

—ἑρμηνείαν, *interpretation*) by which one man may interpret an unknown *tongue* to another.—οἰκοδομὴν, *edification*) the best rule.

27. Εἴτε, *If*) He now more particularly explains how all things may be done for edification.—τὶς, *any man*) Merely one person ought never to have spoken in an unknown tongue; but if one did speak, one or two should have followed to vindicate the abundance of the Spirit.—τρεῖς, *three*) *may speak.*—ἀνὰ μέρος) by a division of the times or even of the places of speaking.

28. Ἐὰν δὲ μὴ ᾖ, *but if there be not*) Either he himself, who spoke in an unknown tongue, might have interpreted, ver. 13; or another.—σιγάτω, *let him be silent*) who speaks in an unknown tongue.—ἑαυτῷ καὶ τῷ Θεῷ, *to himself and to God*) ver. 4, 2.—λαλείτω, *let him speak*) privately.

29. Προφῆται δὲ, *but let the prophets*) An Antithesis to *those who speak in an unknown tongue*. Prophecy, strictly so called, is opposed to *revelation*, ver. 6; *prophecy*, used in a wider sense, (as well as *revelation*) is opposed *to knowledge*: *ibid*. Again, comprehending *knowledge*, it is opposed to *tongues*, ver. 4.—λαλείτωσαν, *let them speak*) supply ἀνὰ μέρος, *one by one*, ver. 27.—οἱ ἄλλοι, *the rest*) viz., of the prophets.—διακρινέτωσαν, *decide* [*judge*]) even by word of mouth.

30. Καθημένῳ) *while he sits*, listening.—ὁ πρῶτος, *the first*) who formerly spoke.

31. Καθ' ἕνα, *one by one*) so that one person may always give way to another.—πάντες μανθάνωσι, *all may learn*) by conversing, inquiring, speaking, listening: *all*, being prophets. A man learns by teaching: he learns by speaking, and asking questions, ver. 34, 35. [*Many continue to be foolish and languid in spiritual things, because they almost never speak about such things.*—V. g.] —παρακαλῶνται, *may be comforted*) Sometimes the speaking of another produces in us more awakening effect, sometimes our own.

32. Καὶ) *and indeed*; so καὶ, 2 Cor. v. 15; 1 John iii. 4.—πνεύματα προφητῶν, *the spirits of the prophets*) The abstract for the concrete, the prophets, even while they are acted upon (under the Divine impulse).—προφήταις, *to the prophets*) He does not say, *to the spirits of the prophets.*—ὑποτάσσεται, *are subject*) not that a prophet would for the sake of another deny or cast away the truth of his prophecy; 1 Kings xiii. 17, etc.: for the word of prophecy is above the prophets, ver. 37; but that he should not

demand that he alone should be heard, but should do his endeavour to hear others also, while they are speaking, and should learn from them, what communications they have received [from God] in preference to himself: *subjection* is shown by keeping silence and learning,[1] ver. 34, 35, [1 Tim. ii. 12]. Every act of teaching involves a degree of absolute authority [authentiam]: *they are subject*, he says; not merely they *ought* to be subject. The Spirit of God teaches the prophets this.

33. Ὡς, *as*) This concluding clause is very like that of the next portion, ver. 36.[2]

34. Αἱ γυναῖκες, *the woman*) Paul uses the same expression, 1 Tim. ii. 11, 12, and yet it was expedient, that this should be written especially for the Corinthians; comp. note at xi. 16.—ὑμῶν ἐν ταῖς ἐκκλησίαις) *in your church assemblies;* when there are men present, that can speak.—ἐπιτέτραπται) *it is committed* [*permitted*, Engl. Vers.]—ὑποτάσσεσθαι, *to be subject*) so as to submit their own will to that of another, Gen. iii. 16. The application (desire) of the woman is to her husband מְשׁוּקָה, and that too as to her lord.—καί) *also;* comp. ix. 8, note.

35. Μαθεῖν, *to learn*) by speaking.—θέλουσιν, they *wish*) This is the figure[3] occupatio.—ἰδίους) *their own*, rather than others.—ἐπερωτάτωσαν) *let them ask*. It was the exclusive privilege of the men to put questions in the assembly.—ἐν ἐκκλησίᾳ) *in the assembly* either civil or sacred.—λαλεῖν, *to speak*) either in teaching or asking.

36. ἤ, ἤ) Latin *an—an?* [which is used in the second part of a disjunctive interrogation] You, Corinthians, (likewise you, Romans) are neither first nor alone. But women are also elsewhere silent.

37. Προφήτης, *a prophet*) The species; *spiritual*, the genus.

---

[1] This is the translation according to the printing of the London Ed., 1855; but according to the Tubingen Ed., 1773, and the Berlin Ed., 1855, which were afterwards consulted, the translation is as follows:—" But not to demand that he alone should be heard, but to endeavour to hear others also, while they are speaking, and to learn from them what they have received more than he himself, is the *subjection* of a man who is silent and is learning."—T.

[2] In both alike there is an appeal to the usage of other churches.—ED.

[3] See Append. Anticipating a reply or objection which might be made by a supposed opponent.—T.

The former endowed more than the latter with eloquence.—ἐπι-
γινωσκέτω, *let him perceive [acknowledge]*) Paul does not allow the
question now at last to be raised, whether he be writing correctly.
—τοῦ Κυρίου) *of the Lord*) Jesus.

38. Εἰ δέ τις ἀγνοεῖ, *But if any man be ignorant*) So that he has
not the capacity to *perceive [acknowledge]*. If any one knows
not, he says, or pretends not to know. This is an argument
which would have weight with the Corinthians, who were very
desirous of *knowledge*.—ἀγνοείτω, *let him be ignorant*) which means,
we cannot cast away all things for the sake of such a man; let
him keep it to himself. Those, who are thus left to themselves,
repent more readily, than if you were to teach them against
their will.

39. Ὥστε, *Therefore*) the summing up.—ζηλοῦτε, *emulously
desire*) This is more than, *forbid not*.

40. Εὐσχημόνως, *decently*) which applies to individuals.—κατὰ
τάξιν, *in order*) in turns, [after one another.]

CHAPTER XV.

1. Γνωρίζω, *I make known [I declare]*) construed with τίνι, *what*,
ver. 2: comp. Gal. i. 11. Paul had formerly made known the
gospel to the Corinthians, but he now informs them at greater
length, *in what way*, according to what method, on what foundation, and by what arguments he preached it to them. It had
been formerly *doctrine*, it now becomes *reproof*, which severely
stigmatizes ἀγνωσίαν, *their ignorance*, at ver. 34.—τὸ εὐαγγέλιον, *the
gospel*) concerning Christ, chiefly of His resurrection. A pleasing
appellation, by which he allures the Corinthians, and a conciliatory preface, by which he holds them as it were in suspense.—
παρελάβετε, *ye have received*) The preterite. [*This receiving involves an everlasting obligation.—V. g.*]—ἑστήκατε, *ye stand*) i.e.
ye have obtained a standing-place, [you have taken your stand.]
It is present, in sense.

2. Σώζεσθε, *ye are saved*) The future in sense, ver. 18, 19.—εἰ

1 CORINTHIANS XV. 3–5.

κατέχετε, *if ye keep*) *If* here implies a hope, as is evident from what follows, *unless*, etc.

13. Ἐν πρώτοις, *among the primary things*) The things, which are of greatest importance, ought to be taught *among the first things*. בראשונה, the LXX., ἐν πρώτοις, *i.e. in old time*; 2 Sam. xx. 18: but, *first*, in Deut. xiii. 9, and so here.—παρελάβον, *I received*) from Christ Himself, what I have spoken is no fiction, 2 Pet. i. 16.—ὅτι, *that*) Paul says that he had declared *among the first* points of faith, not only the resurrection of Christ, but also the resurrection of the dead, which flows from it; and the Corinthians believed in these doctrines, before they *were baptised* in the name of Christ, who was *crucified* for them, and so also died and rose again, i. 13: comp. Heb. vi. 2.—ὑπὲρ, *for*) a very effective expression, which means, *for* taking away *our sins*, Gal. i. 4; 1 Pet. ii. 24; 1 John iii. 5. So ὑπὲρ, Heb. v. 3; comp. Tit. ii. 14; Luke i. 71–74; 2 Cor. v. 15.—ἁμαρτιῶν, *sins*) on account of which we had deserved *death*, ver. 17.—γραφάς, *Scriptures*) *Many things* are said in Scripture respecting the death of Christ. Paul puts the testimony of Scripture before the testimony of those, who saw the Lord after His resurrection.

4. Ἐτάφη, *He was buried*) Matt. xii. 40. [*Here* the burial *of Christ is more closely connected with* His resurrection, *than with His death. Assuredly, about the very moment of His death, the power of His life incapable of dissolution exerted itself*, 1 Pet. iii. 18; Matt. xxvii. 52. *The grave was to Christ the Lord not the destined receptacle of corruption, but an apartment fitted for entering into life*, Acts ii. 26.—V. g.]—ἐγήγερται, *was raised again* [*rose again*]) This enlarging on the resurrection of Christ is the more suitable on this account, that the epistle was written about the time of the passover; ch. v. 7, note. We must urge the weight of the subject of *the resurrection*, inasmuch as it is one which is made light of in the present day under various pretexts.—κατὰ τὰς γραφάς, *according to the Scriptures*) which could not but be fulfilled.

5. Κηφᾷ, *of Cephas*) Luke xxiv. 34.—δώδεκα, *twelve*) Luke xxiv. 36. It is probable that Matthias was then also present. Photius in his Amphilochia and others read ἕνδεκα.[2]

[1] Εἰκῆ, *in vain*—a melancholy term, Gal. ii. 2, iii. 4, iv. 11.—Vg.
[2] D corrected later, *Gfg*. Vulg. and MSS., alluded to in Augustine,

6. Ἔπειτα, *after that*) advancing to a greater number.—ἐπάνω πεντακοσίοις, *more than five hundred*) A remarkable appearance. Paul puts himself behind all these.— οἱ πλείους, *the greater part*) About 300 at least; οἱ πλείους, *the majority* were providentially preserved in life so long for the very purpose of bearing testimony [*as they had obtained an authority akin to that of the apostles.*—V. g.]; comp. Jos. xxiv. 31.—μένουσιν, *remain*) in life. The opportunity of thoroughly sifting these witnesses remained unimpaired [undiminished.] Andronicus and Junius may be presumed to have been of that number, Rom. xvi. 7.—καί, *also*) It was not of less importance to bring forward these as witnesses. They had died in this belief.—ἐκοιμήθησαν, *have fallen asleep*) as those, who are to rise again.

¹7. Πᾶσιν, *by all*) More seem here to be called Apostles than the twelve, ver. 5; and yet the term is used in a stricter sense than at Rom. xvi. 7.

8. Ἔσχατον δὲ πάντων) *and last of all*, or rather, *after them all*, in order to exclude himself. Also after Stephen, Deut. xxxi. 27, 29.—ἔσχατον τοῦ θανάτου μου, κ.τ.λ., *after my death*. [*The appearances, that afterwards followed are not excluded by this expression*, Acts xxiii. 11.—V. g.]—ὡσπερεὶ τῷ ἐκτρώματι, *as by the abortion* [*one born out of due time*]) The LXX., ἔκτρωμα, Num. xii. 12. The article is emphatic. Paul applies to himself alone this denomination in reference to the circumstances of the appearance, and in reference to the present time of writing. What ἐκτρώμα, *an abortion*, is among children, he says, I am among the apostles; and by this one word he sinks himself lower than in any other way. As an abortion is not worthy of the name of man, so the apostle declares that he is not worthy of the name of apostle. The metaphor, is drawn from the same idea from which the term *regeneration* is used, 1 Pet. i, 3 [*Begotten again*—by the *resurrection* of Jesus, etc.]; εἰ in ὡσπερεὶ somewhat softens the phrase: *as if;* he shows that this ought not to be pressed too far.—κἀμοὶ, *by me also*) This word is elegantly placed at the end of the period.

9. Ἐλάχιστος) in Latin *Paulus, minimus*.—ὅς, *who*) The lan-

Photius, and Jerome, read ἕνδεκα. But AB Orig. 1, 434e read δώδεκα.—ED.

¹ Ἰακώβῳ, *James*) the Less.—V. g.

guage increases in strength.—ἐδίωξα, *I persecuted*) Believers even after repentance take guilt to themselves for the evil, which they have once perpetrated.

10. Χάριτι, *by grace*) alone.—ὅ εἰμι, *what I am*) i.e. an apostle, who saw Christ.—οὐ κενή, *not vain*) Paul proves the authority of the gospel and of his testimony to it by its effects.—αὐτῶν, *than they*) This word is referred to ver. 7.—πάντων, *all*) individually.—σὺν ἐμοί, *with me*) The particle *with* is suitable because he says, *I laboured*: comp. Mark xvi. 20.

11. Κηρύσσομεν, *we preach*) all the apostles with one mouth.—ἐπιστεύσατε, *ye believed*) Faith once received lays the foundation for subsequent faith: and its first firmness not only obliges [binds] those wavering, but also often retains them.

12. Εἰ) *if* [since], an affirmative particle.—πῶς, *how*) The connection between the resurrection of Christ from the dead and the resurrection of the dead was extremely manifest to Paul. Those, indeed, who held a resurrection in general as a thing impossible, could not believe even in the resurrection of Christ.—τινές) *some*, no doubt, of the Gentiles, Acts xvii. 32.

13. Εἰ δέ, *but if*) He now begins a retrospect, and enumerates all that he alleged at 3–11.

14. Κενόν—κενή, *vain—vain*) contrary to what you yourselves have acknowledged, ver. 11.—κενή, without reality, differs from ματαία, *vain*, ver. 17, without use.

15. Ψευδομάρτυρες, *false witnesses*) It is not lawful to declare concerning God what is not so; although it may seem to give glory to Him. False witnesses are, for instance, traders, who, for the sake of their gain, give fictitious accounts of earthquakes, inundations, and other great calamities, which have happened in distant countries, and lead souls otherwise not too credulous to thoughts and conversations concerning *divine* judgments, good in the proposition (thesis), but erroneous in the supposition (hypothesis) on which the proposition rests.

17. Ἁμαρτίαις, *in your sins*), even those of blind heathenism; ver. 34, [*deprived of the hope of life eternal.*—V. g.]

18. Ἀπώλοντο, *perished*) *they were, they are not.* Paul speaks conditionally: the heathen denying the resurrection might, if that supposition were true, regard the dead just the same as if they had never been. Nor was there here any necessity for

Paul distinctly to express, what it is for a man to be *in his sins*.

19. Εἰ, *if*) The statement of those topics which are discussed at ver. 20, etc., precedes this verse and ver. 18: and in this verse, there is a statement of those topics, which are treated of at ver. 29–34.—ἐν, *in*) ἐν, as *far as concerns, i.e.* if our hope in Christ revolves so as to be fixed wholly within the bounds of this present life, *only*, μόνον.—ζωῇ, *life*) Scripture does not readily call this life, *life*; oftener, it calls it αἰῶνα, *the age*: here it is spoken of after the manner of men, as Luke xvi. 25.—ἠλπικότες ἐσμὲν, *we have hoped*) *we have believed* with joyful anticipation of the future.—ἐλεεινότεροι, *more miserable*) the comparative degree is here in its strict sense: for if it had the force of the superlative, the article would have been put before it: *We are more miserable than all men*: the rest, viz. *all* other *men*, are not buoyed up with false hope, and freely enjoy the present life; we, if the dead rise not, are foolishly buoyed up with false hope, and through denying ourselves and renouncing the world, we lose the certain enjoyment of the present life, and are doubly miserable. Even now Christians are *happy*, but not in the things, by which the happiness of other men is maintained; and, if we take away the hope of another life, our present spiritual joy is diminished. Believers have immediate joy in God and therefore they are happy; but if there be no resurrection that joy is greatly weakened. This is the second weighty consideration; the first is, that the happiness of Christians is not placed in worldly things. By both of these weighty considerations, happiness from the hope of the resurrection is confirmed.

20. Νυνί, *now*) Paul declares, that his preaching is not in vain, that their faith is not worthless, that their sins are taken away, that the dead in Christ are not annihilated, that the hope of Christians does not terminate with this life.—ἀπαρχή, *the first fruit*) viz. οὖσα or ὤν *being*. The mention of *the first fruits* admirably agrees with the time of the passover, at which, as we have observed above, this epistle was written; nay more, with the very day of Christ's resurrection, which was likewise the day after the Sabbath, Lev. xxiii. 10, 11.

21. Καὶ) *also*. ἐπειδὴ γὰρ, *for since*, has here its apodosis.

22. Πάντες ἀποθνήσκουσιν, *all die*) he says, *die*, not in the prete-

rite, as for example, Rom. v. 17, 21, but in the present, in order that in the antithesis he may the more plainly speak of the resurrection, as even still future. And he says, *all*. Those who are in the highest degree wicked die in Adam; but Paul is here speaking of the godly, of whom *the first fruits*, ἀπαρχὴ, is Christ, and as these all die in Adam, so also shall they all be made alive in Christ. Scripture everywhere deals with believers, and treats primarily of their resurrection, 1 Thess. iv. 13, 14: and only incidentally of the resurrection of the ungodly.—ἐν τῷ Χριστῷ, *in Christ*) These are the emphatic words in this clause. The resurrection of Christ being once established, the quickening of all is also established.—ζωοποιηθήσονται, *they shall be made alive*) He had said; *they die*, not, they *are put to death;* whereas now, not, *they shall revive;* but they *shall be made alive, i.e.* implying that it is not by their own power.

23. "Εκαστος—ἀπαρχὴ—ἔπειτα) In this verse we must thrice supply ἐστί or εἰσί. In ver. 24 *is* must likewise be supplied.— τάγματι) *in order* divinely constituted. τάξις, however, is the abstract; τάγμα, the concrete. The conjugate, ὑπέταξεν, occurs in ver. 27.—ἀπαρχὴ, *first fruits*) The force of this word comprehends the force of the word ἀρχὴ *beginning*, to which *the end* corresponds as its opposite.—ἔπειτα—εἶτα) "Επειτα is more disjunctive; εἶτα more copulative, ver. 5, 6, 7. "Επειτα, *afterwards*, Latin, *posterius*, the comparative being opposed to *primum*, ' first,' ver. 46; of which *first* the force is contained in *first fruits*, in this passage: εἶτα, *afterwards*, is used in a more absolute sense. The disjunctive power of the ἔπειτα, and the copulative power of the εἶτα is clear in ver. 5, 6, 7. For the twelve are joined with Cephas by εἶτα; *The five hundred* are disjoined [from the Twelve and Cephas] and *James* from these; but the *Apostles* are coupled to the last named person by εἶτα. Therefore those, who are introduced by ἔπειτα, are put in between, as it were, by parenthesis. But here ver. 23 the matter seems to be ambiguous. If we make a twofold division, we may either insert Christ and those who are Christ's into the one member of the division, and τὸ τέλος, *the end*, into the other; or we may put Christ alone [by Himself] as the principal person, and join to the other side those who are Christ's, *and afterwards* τὸ τέλος *the end*. By the former method, Christians are the appendage

of their head; by the latter Christ everywhere retains His prerogative, and all the rest of persons and things are heaped together in one mass. By the former method, a comma is put in the text after χριστὸς,[1] by the latter also a colon; and so εἶτα retains a more absolute sense, and yet its copulative power more than the ἔπειτα. Paul describes the whole process of the resurrection, with those things that shall follow it, and therefore he renders the resurrection itself the more credible. For this resurrection is necessarily required to produce this result, that God may be all in all.—*οἱ τοῦ χριστοῦ, those who are Christ's*) A pleasant variety of cases, Polyptoton, Χριστὸς, Χριστοῦ. Christians are, so to speak, an appendage to τῆς ἀπαρχῆς, *the first fruits*. The ungodly shall rise at the same time; but they are not reckoned in this blessed number.—*ἐν τῇ παρουσίᾳ, at His coming*) then it shall be the *order* of Christians [their turn in the successive order of the resurrection]. They shall not rise one after another [but all believers at once] at that time. Paul does not call it the *judgment*, because he is speaking of and to believers.

24. Εἶτα, *afterwards*) after the resurrection of *those who are Christ's*; for He, as *King*, will consummate the judgment between the resurrection and the end.—τὸ τέλος) *The end*, viz., of the whole resurrection. This is the correlative to the *first fruits*. In this end all *orders* [referring to "every man in his own order"] will obtain their completion [consummated development]: 1 Pet. iv. 7; Rom. vi. 22. This noun contains the force of the verbs, *delivered up* [ver. 24] and *destroyed* [ver. 26]. See how great mysteries the apostle draws from the prophetic syllables עד and כל, Ps. cx. 1, viii. 6. Gr. *ἄχρις, until*, and *πάντα, all things*. Therefore even the words of Scripture are *inspired by God*, θεόπνευστα. For all Scripture words rest upon the same principles as these [The same reasoning is applicable to *all* Scripture *words*].—ὅταν—ὅταν) *when:*—namely, *when.* The former is explained by the latter; and the first part of the following verse is to be referred to the former; the second part, to the latter. So soon as the Son shall have delivered up the kingdom to the Father, the Father will destroy *all authority;*

---

[1] This is the punctuation of Lachmann and Tischendorf. The former, however, puts a comma between τέλος and ὅταν: the latter does not.—ED.

and the *deliverance of the* kingdom into His hands takes place, that *all authority* may be swept away.—παραδῷ τὴν βασιλείαν, *shall have delivered up the kingdom*) The Father will not then begin to reign without the Son; nor will the Son cease then to reign without the Father; for the divine kingdom both of the Father and of the Son is from eternity and will be to eternity. But the apostle is here speaking of the mediatorial kingdom of the Son, which will be delivered up, and of the immediate [*i.e.*, without mediation] kingdom of the Father, to which then it will give place. In the meantime, the Son manages the affairs, which the Father has put into His hands, for and by His own people, for the elect, by the instrumentality of angels also, and in the presence of the Father and against His enemies, so long as even an effort of these last continues. The Son will deliver up the kingdom to the Father, inasmuch as the Father gave it to the Son, John xiii. 3. The Father does not cease to reign, though He has appointed the Son to be king; nor does the Son cease to reign, when He delivers up the kingdom to the Father; and by the very circumstance, that it is said, not that it is to be *abolished*, but to be *delivered up to the Father*, it is signified, that it itself also is of infinite majesty. But the glory before the foundation of the world will remain, after the kingdom has been delivered up: John xvii. 5; Heb. i. 8: and He will not cease to be king according to His human nature, Luke i. 33.[1] If the citizens of the New Jerusalem shall reign for ever and ever, Rev. xxii. 5; how much more will God and Christ reign?—τῷ Θεῷ καὶ πατρί, *to God even the Father*) God is here regarded in a twofold point of view. He is considered, both as God and as the Father in respect to Christ, John xx. 17; even in His state of exaltation, Rev. iii. 12, 21: and in respect to believers, Col. iii. 17. He is considered as God, towards [in relation to] His enemies. καταργήσῃ [*shall have put down*] *shall have abolished*) viz., *God even the Father*, of whom it is also said (until) He *put* (θῇ, ver. 25) and He has *subjected* [ὑπέταξεν, ver. 27]. In a similar manner, the subject is changed to a different one [from God to Christ] in the third person, ver. 25 and 29 [the baptized

---

[1] S. R. D. Moldenhauer on this passage refers to it the passage in Luke; comp. Dan. vii. 14. He very often agrees with Bengel: for example, ver. 32, 49, etc.—E. B.

for the dead—the dead—*they*, *i.e.*, the former].—πᾶσαν ἀρχὴν καὶ πᾶσαν ἐξουσίαν καὶ δύναμιν, *all rule and all authority and power*) *Rule and authority* are also said of the powers of men, Tit. iii. 1 [*principalities* and *powers*] : but oftener of those of angels, Col. i. 16 : and that too in the concrete, to denote their very essence [substances] : here however they are in the abstract, as βασιλείαν, concerning the *kingdom* of the Son : for the essences of angels will not be destroyed. Ἀρχὴ denotes *rule*; subordinate to this are ἐξουσία, *authority*, magistracy, and δύναμις, *an army, forces.*—ἐξουσία and δύναμις are more closely connected as is seen by the fact that they have the one epithet, *all*, in common [The one πᾶσαν qualifies both ἐξουσίαν and δύναμιν; though ἀρχὴν has a separate πᾶσαν]. Here not only rule, authority, forces of enemies, are signified, ver. 25, such as is death, ver. 26 ; but the *all* intimates that the rule, authority, etc., even of good angels shall cease. For when the king lays down His arms, after His enemies have been subdued, the soldiers are discharged, and the word καταργεῖν, *to put down*, is not an inapplicable term even to these latter : xiii. 8 ; 2 Cor. iii. 7.

25. Δεῖ, *He must*) for it has been foretold.—αὐτὸν, *He*) Christ.— βασιλεύειν, *reign*) רדה, *reign Thou in the midst of Thy enemies*, Ps. cx. 2.—ἄχρις οὗ ἄν, *until*) There will be no further need of the mediatorial reign.—θῇ, *He hath put*) viz. the Father.—πάντας, *all*) Paul brings in this, to prepare for a transition to what follows.—τοὺς ἐχθροὺς, *enemies*) bodily and spiritual, supply *His*, from that expression, *His feet*, to wit, *the Son's* : but it is now elegantly elliptical ; since Christ has long ago *destroyed* these enemies, in so far as they were the enemies *of Christ;* He *will destroy* them [their destruction is still *future*], in so far as they are our enemies. The remaining part of His victory bears the same relation to His triumph already achieved, as any frontier or corner does to the whole extent of any human monarchy which has been subdued.

26. Ἔσχατος, *the last*) A pregnant announcement. *Death* is an enemy ; is an enemy, who is destroyed ; is the enemy, who is destroyed last of all ; last moreover, that is, after Satan, Heb. ii. 14 ; and after sin, ver. 56. For they acquired their strength in the same order ; and Satan brought in sin, sin produced death. Those enemies have been destroyed ; therefore

also death is destroyed. It may be said, *Does not the same principle hold good as to all the enemies alike? for in so far as all the others have been destroyed, death has been also destroyed,* 2 Tim. i. 10, *therefore inasmuch as death remains, the other enemies still remain, and therefore death is not destroyed last. Ans.* Christ, in so far as He formerly engaged with His enemies, first overcame Satan by His death; next sin, in His death; lastly death, in His resurrection; and in the same order, in which He destroys His enemies, He delivers believers from their power. Again, it may be said, *how is death destroyed last, if the resurrection of the dead precedes the destruction of* ALL RULE?" *Ans.* The resurrection is immediately followed by the judgment, with which the destruction of *all rule* is connected; and the destruction of death and hell immediately succeeds this. The order of destruction is described, Rev. xix. 20, xx. 10, 14. Moreover the expression ought to be taken in a reduplicative sense. The enemies will be destroyed, as enemies. For even after all this, Satan will still be Satan, hell will still be hell, the goats will still be accursed. They will indeed be first destroyed, before death, the last enemy; not that they may altogether cease to be, as death shall; not that they may cease to be what they are called, namely Satan, hell, accursed; but that they may be no longer enemies, resisting, and able to oppose, for they will be completely subdued, rendered powerless, taken captive, visited with punishment, put under the feet of our Lord. The destruction of ALL RULE ought not to be reckoned as the destruction [*i.e.* annihilation] of enemies; moreover the destruction of the power of our enemies according to Rev. xix. 20 is accomplished even before the destruction of death, which the destruction of ALL authority and of ALL rule straightway follows. The good angels are also then to obtain exemption from service. —ἐχθρὸς, *enemy*) Death, an enemy; therefore it was not at first natural to man. Those, who denied the resurrection, also denied the immortality of the soul. The defence of the former includes the defence of the latter.—καταργεῖται, *is destroyed*) The present for the future.—ὁ θάνατος, *death*) *Hell* is also included in the mention of death, so far as it is to be destroyed, ver. 55.

27. Πάντα γὰρ, *for all things*) not even excepting death. The Psalm [viii.] might seem by this syllable, כֹּל, *all things*, merely

to indicate animals and stars, which it expressly names; but the apostle teaches us, that it has a much more extended application. *Good things* are made subject to Him in a most joyous condition; *bad things* in a most sorrowful one: for these latter are *destroyed*, and are made His footstool.—ὑπέταξεν, *subjected*) viz. *God even the Father*; comp. at ὑποταγήν, Eph. i. 22; Phil. iii. 21; Heb. ii. 8; 1 Pet. iii. 22. He *will subject* all things, in His own time; He has already *subjected* them, because *He hath said it*.—ὑπὸ τοὺς πόδας αὐτοῦ) not only enemies, but also all other things are put *under His feet*, Eph. i. 22. This phrase is a synecdoche; *all things* are made subject to Him: and those things, which oppose themselves to Him, and do not wish to be subject, are altogether thrust down under His feet, as a footstool. There is a clear distinction between the expressions *being put under His feet* and *being given into His hands*. The former however need not be understood in so harsh a sense as the expression might seem to imply: otherwise, there would be no room for the *exception of Him, who subjected them*.—εἴπῃ, *saith*) viz. the prophet, Heb. ii. 6.—δῆλον, *manifest*) For the Father is not subject to the Son; *but* (δὲ, ver. 28) the Son is subject to the Father. The apostle with great power and wisdom points out the sum [the main issue] of all things, from the Psalm.

28. Ὑποταγῇ, *shall be subjected*) so that they shall remain for ever in subjection.—τότε) *then* finally. Previously, it is always necessary to contend with enemies.—καὶ, *also*)—αὐτὸς, *He himself*) spontaneously, so that it denotes the infinite excellence of the Son; and besides, as we often find, it signifies something *voluntary*; for the Son subordinates Himself to the Father; the Father glorifies the Son. The name, "God even the Father," and "the Son," is more glorious than the title 'King.' This latter name will be absorbed by the former, as it had previously been derived from the former.—ὁ υἱὸς, *the Son*) Christ, according to both natures, even including the divine; and this we may learn, not so much from the circumstance that He is *here* called the Son; comp. note on Mark xiii. 32, as that He is expressly considered in relation to the Father. Nor, however, is the Son here spoken of, in so far as the Father and the Son are one, which unity of essence is here presupposed; but in respect of the dispensation committed to Him, inasmuch as the Father

has rendered all things subordinate to Him.—ὑποταγήσεται, *shall be made subordinate*) for this word is both more proper and more becoming than *shall be subjected*. The word is one very well adapted for denoting things most widely different. For the subordination of the Son to the Father is manifestly one thing, of the creatures to God is another. The Son shall be made subordinate to the Father in such a way as He had not formerly been; for in the mediatorial kingdom, the brightness of the Son had been in a manner separated from the Father; but subsequently the Son shall be made quite subordinate to the Father; and that subordination of the Son will be entirely voluntary, an event desired by the Son Himself and glorious to Him; for He will not be subordinate as a *servant*, Heb. i. 14; comp. the foregoing verses; but as a Son. [So also *in human affairs there is not only the subordination* of subjects, *but also* of sons, Luc. ii. 51; Heb. xii. 9.—V. g.]—ὑποταγήσεται is therefore in the middle, not in the passive voice. *My goodness*, says He, Ps. xvi. 2, *is not independent of* THEE, O Jehovah [Engl. Vers., *extendeth not to Thee.*] Hesshusius remarks, *The subjection and obedience of the Son towards the Father, do not take away the equality of the power, nor produce diversity in the essence. The Son in all eternity, acknowledges with the deepest reverence that He was begotten from eternity by the Father; He also acknowledges that He has received the spiritual kingdom from the Father, and has been constituted Lord of the whole world by the same. He will show to the whole creation His most holy reverence, subjection, and filial love, so that all honour may be rendered to the eternal Father. But herein there is no derogation to the divine honour of the Son; since the Father Himself wills that all men should honour the Son, as they honour the Father.* John v., Exam. p. 10.—ἵνα ᾖ ὁ Θεὸς πάντα ἐν πᾶσι, *that God may be all in all*) Here something new is signified, but which is at the same time the consummation of all that has gone before, and everlasting. *All things* (and therefore all men) without any interruption, without any creature to invade His prerogative, or any enemy to disturb, will be made subordinate to the Son, and the Son to the Father. *All things* will say: *God is all to me.* This is τέλος, this is the *end* and consummation. Further than this, not even the apostle can go. As in Christ, there is neither

Greek nor Jew, circumcision nor uncircumcision, barbarian, Scythian, bond nor free, but Christ is all and in all, Col. iii. 11. So then there will be neither Greek nor Jew, etc., nor *principality* [rule: ver. 24], *power*, etc., but God will be all in all. God is esteemed as nothing in the world by ungodly men, Ps. x. 4, xiv. 1: and with the saints many things prevent Him from being alone all to them; but then He will be all in all.

29. Ἐπεὶ τί ποιήσουσιν οἱ βαπτιζόμενοι ὑπὲρ τῶν νεκρῶν; εἰ ὅλως νεκροὶ οὐκ ἐγείρονται, τί καὶ βαπτίζονται ὑπὲρ αὐτῶν; τί καὶ ἡμεῖς κινδυνεύομεν πᾶσαν ὥραν;) We shall first say something on the pointing of this verse.[1] Many rightly connect, and have long been in the habit of connecting this clause, εἰ ὅλως νεκροὶ οὐκ ἐγείρονται, with what follows; for the particle ἐπεὶ alone exhausts the force of the same clause in the first part of the verse. Εἰ begins the sentence, as in ver. 32, it does so twice; and often in ver. 12, and those that follow. Hence the pronoun αὐτῶν is to be referred to νεκροί.[2] Furthermore, *of the baptism for (over) the dead*, the variety of interpretations is so great, that he who would collect, I shall not say, those different opinions, but a catalogue of the different opinions, would have to write a dissertation. At that time, as yet, there were neither martyrdoms nor baptisms over sepulchres, etc., especially at Corinth; but baptism over sepulchres, and baptism for the advantage of the dead came into use from a wrong interpretation of this very passage; as fire was used among the Egyptians and Abyssinians in the case of the baptized, from Matt. iii. 11. Often, when the true interpretation is nearer and easier than we think, we fetch it from a distance. We must mark—I. The paraphrase: *Otherwise what will they do who are baptized for* (super) *the dead? If the dead rise not at all, why are they also baptized for the dead? and why also are we in danger every hour?* II. The sense of

---

[1] Lachm. and Tischend. punctuate as Bengel. Rec. Text puts the question not after νεκρῶν, but after ἐγείρονται; thus connecting this clause with what precedes, instead of with what follows.—ED.

[2] The Germ. Ver. repeats the noun τῶν νεκρῶν, instead of the pronoun at the end of the verse, and differs from the margin of both editions.—E. B.

Αὐτῶν is the reading of ABD corrected later, G*fg* Vulg. Memph., later Syr. Origen. Τῶν νεκρῶν of Rec. Text is only found in later Uncial MSS. and Syr. Version alone, of the oldest versions.—ED.

1 CORINTHIANS XV. 29.   329

the phrase, βαπτίζεσθαι ὑπὲρ τῶν νεκρῶν, *to be baptized for* (*over*) *the dead.* For they are baptized *for* (over) *the dead* [super mortuis], who receive baptism and profess Christianity at that time, when they have death set before their eyes, who are likely every moment to *be added to the general mass of the dead*, either on account of the decrepitude of age, or disease, or pestilence, or by martyrdom; in fact, those who, without almost any enjoyment of this life, *are going down* to the dead, and *are constantly*, as it were, *hanging over* the dead; they who might say קברים לי, *the graves are ready for me*, Job xvii. 1. III. The first part of the verse is of a milder character; but the last part which begins with *if after all*, has also an epitasis [an emphatic addition. Append.] expressed in its own protasis by *after all*, and in the apodosis by the *even* [τί καί]: and these two particles correspond to each other; and the same apodosis has an anaphora [the repetition of the same words in the beginnings of sections], joining its two parts by *why even.* IV. We must mark the connection of the subject under discussion. With the argument respecting the resurrection of Christ, from which our resurrection is derived, Paul connects the *statement* of two absurdities (indeed there are more than two, but the preceding absurdities are repeated, though they have been already sufficiently refuted by former reasonings) which would arise, if there be no resurrection of the dead, if Christ have not risen: and in the meantime, having disentangled the argument concerning Christ, ver. 20–28, he refutes those two absurdities by a *discussion* of somewhat greater length, which draws the sinews of its strength from the argument concerning Christ. The latter absurdity (for this has its relation to the argument more evident) regarding the misery of Christians in this life, he set forth at ver. 19, and now discusses at ver. 29 in the middle, and in the following verses; *if after all:* and in like manner he stated the former concerning the 'perishing' of the Christians that are dead, at ver. 18, and now discusses, or repeats, or explains it in the first part of ver. 29. V. The force of the apostle's argument, which in itself is both most clear and most urgent. VI. The propriety of the several words consistent with themselves. α) *What shall they do?* is future, in respect of eternal salvation, *i.e.*, such persons being baptized, will be disappointed, their efforts will be vain, if the dead sleep the eternal sleep. β) The term *baptism* continues to be used in its ordinary meaning; and indeed in this epistle Paul has made more mention of baptism than in any other, ch. i. 13–17, x. 2, xii. 13. γ) The preposition ὑπὲρ with the genitive might be thus also taken in various senses; of the object simply, as the Latins use *super, with respect to, about, so far as it concerns;* with this meaning, *that they may put the dead before them without consideration of the resurrection;* or the words may be used of paying as it were a price, viz., *that they should account the dead as nonentities;* or of obtaining as the price for their trouble, viz., *that they should be gathered to the dead for ever:* but we maintain the propriety with which ὑπὲρ denotes *nearness, hanging over* [such propinquity as that one hangs immediately over] *anything*, whence Theocritus speaks of ἀσφόδελον τὸν ὑπὲρ γᾶς, *the asphodel* (king's spear) *that grows on the ground*, Idyl. 26. Lexicographers give more examples, especially from Thucydides. So they are baptized *over* [*immediately upon*] the dead, who will be gathered to the dead immediately after baptism: and then *over the dead* is said here, as if it were said *over the sepulchre*, as Luke xxiv. 5, *with* [Engl. Vers., *among*] *the dead, i.e., in the sepulchre.* Nor is it incredible, that baptism was often administered at funerals. δ) The term *dead* is used in its ordinary sense of the dead generally, as the article also requires, taken in as wide a sense as the resurrection. ε) The adverb ὅλως, *after all*, is used by a Corinthian who is supposed to be led on by Paul, and who had rather peevishly opposed the resurrection, not reflecting on the loss of the advantages even in this life, which result in baptism: and εἰ ὅλως is employed in the same way as ἐπειδὴ ὅλως in Chrysost. homil. 5, c. Anomoeos: *Notwithstanding, though man differs little from an angel, since there is nevertheless* [after all] *some difference* (ἐπειδὴ ὅλως ἐστί τι μέσον), *we know not accurately what angels are.* ζ) καὶ is not redundant, but strengthens the force of the present tense, βαπτίζονται, *what do they do who are baptized?* in antithesis to the future, τί ποιήσουσι, *what shall they do?* Comp. καί, 2 Cor. i. 14, xi. 12; Phil. iii. 7, 8, iv. 10. Paul in fact places those who are baptized for the dead, as it were at the point of death, and shows that no reward awaits them either for the future, if they denied the resurrection, or for the past. Paul seems to confute those who denied both the resurrection of the body and the immortality of the soul. The vindication of the former is a sufficient and more than sufficient vindication of the latter. This is an example of the συγκατάβασις, *condescension* of Scripture, which, out of regard to the weak and simple, does not enter into that subtle controversy, but lays hold of the subject at that part of it, which is easier to be proved, and yet also carries along with it the proof of the more difficult part. η) The two clauses beginning with τί admirably cohere: with a gradation from those who could only for a little enjoy this life [*i.e.*, those baptized at the point of death] to (*us*) those who could enjoy it longer, if they had not had their hope fixed in Christ.—νεκροί, *dead*) Throughout this whole chapter, in the question, *whether* [dead men rise at all], Paul speaks of dead men, νεκρούς, without the article; afterwards, when this question has been cleared out of the way, in the question *how*, ver. 35, etc., he uses the article; but τῶν in this verse has the meaning of the relative [τῶν νεκρῶν, those *who* are dead already spoken of, ver. 12, 13, 16].

30. Ἡμεῖς, *we*) apostles, iv. 9.

31. Ἀποθνήσκω, *I die*) Not only by reason of the danger which was always set before him, 2 Cor. i. 8, 9, xi. 23, but also by a continual *dying* itself [mortification.] This agrees with the whole discourse.—νὴ τὴν ὑμετέραν καύχησιν,[1] ἣν ἔχω ἐν Χριστῷ Ἰησοῦ τῷ Κυρίῳ ἡμῶν, *by your glorying, which I have in Christ Jesus our Lord*) In swearing or making an asseveration, if a human being is appealed to, then that person is used, which is preferred as more worthy, and therefore sometimes the third, Gen. xlii. 15, 16.—νὴ τὴν ὑγίειαν Φαραώ, *by the health of Pharaoh*; sometimes the first, 2 Sam. iii. 35.—τάδε ποιήσαι μοι ὁ Θεὸς καὶ τάδε προσθείη, *God do so to me and more also*: comp. ibid. ver. 9., but generally the second, 1 Sam. i. 26, ζῇ ἡ ψυχή σου, *may thy soul live*: ibid. iii. 17, τάδε ποιήσαι σοι ὁ Θεὸς καὶ τάδε προσθείη, *God do so to thee, and more also*. So Paul here appeals to the very enjoyable condition of the Corinthians, even as to spiritual life, in opposition

---

[1] The vocative ἀδελφοί reckoned among the better readings in the margin of both Ed., and received by the Germ. Ver., is here thrown out.—E. B.
Lachm. reads ἀδελφοί, with AB Vulg. But Tisch. omits it with D (Δ) G*fg* Origen.—ED.

to his own death, which he bore for [in order to give them] their glorying [*rejoicing*, Engl.] comp. iv. 8; 2 Cor. iv. 12, 15; Phil. i. 26; Eph. iii. 13; and therefore he brings it forward to stir up the Corinthians themselves. They did not attend to this, who wrote ἡμετέραν for ὑμετέραν.[1] The first person indeed follows, ἣν ἔχω, but in the singular number; and ἣν is to be referred not to ὑμετέραν καύχησιν, but to καύχησιν; for so relatives are sometimes wont to be used, Gal. i. 6, 7; Eph. ii. 11; where *that which is called circumcision* is concrete, and there is added, however, *in the flesh made by hands*, which can only agree with the abstract, 1 Tim. vi. 20, 21; 2 Tim. i. 5. Paul shows that it is not without good cause that he dies daily, but that he is a partaker of the glorying of the Corinthians, 2 Cor. iv. 14.

32. Εἰ κατὰ ἄνθρωπον ἐθηριομάχησα ἐν Ἐφέσῳ, τί μοι τὸ ὄφελος; εἰ νεκροὶ οὐκ ἐγείρονται, φάγωμεν καὶ πίωμεν, αὔριον γὰρ ἀποθνήσκομεν, *if after the manner of men, I have fought with wild beasts at Ephesus, what advantageth it to me? if the dead rise not, let us eat and drink, for to-morrow we die*) This clause, *if the dead rise not*, is now for a long time properly connected with the words that follow; for in the foregoing, the formula, *after the manner of men*, is equivalent to it in force: that is, if, after human fashion, for a human consideration, with the mere hope of the present life, not in the hope of a resurrection to be expected on Divine authority, I have fought with beasts at Ephesus, etc.—ἐθηριομάχησα ἐν Ἐφέσῳ, *I have fought with wild beasts at Ephesus*) This one contest Paul expressly mentions, not only because it was a very great one, but also, because it was very recent. He was still at Ephesus; xvi. 8: and there, before this epistle was written, he had been exposed to extraordinary danger, which seems to be the same occasion as that described, Acts xix. 29, 30; 2 Cor. i. 8; wherefore he calls it *a fight with wild beasts*, in which his life was in jeopardy; comp. iv. 9: as Heraclitus of Ephesus had been in the habit of applying the term *wild beasts*, θηρία, to the Ephesians four hundred years before: comp. Tit. i. 12 concerning the Cretans and Epimenides.—φάγωμεν—ἀποθνήσκομεν, *let us eat—we die*) So the LXX., Isa. xxii. 13, that is, let us use the good things of the body and of the present life. This is a

---

[1] Ὑμετέραν is the reading BD (Λ) G*fg* Vulg. Ἡμετέραν is the reading of A, Orig. 2,710a.—ED.

Mimesis or the imitation of a supposed opponent's *wicked manner of speaking*.

33. Μὴ πλανᾶσθε) in the Middle voice.—φθείρουσιν) *they corrupt*. Its conjugate *corruption*, is found at ver. 42. He uses the well-known sentence of Menander in a sublimer sense, and opposes it to the Epicurean creed, ver. 32 ; presently after, at ver. 34, he was about to apply a more weighty stimulant. [*The multitude of wicked sayings and vicious* proverbs *in human life is indeed very great, by which a vast number repel things however sacred and salutary and endeavour to defend their own wantonness and hypocrisy. Scoffs of that kind were also common among the Israelites*, Ez. xi. 3, 15, xii. 22, xviii. 2.—V. g.]—ἤθη, *manners*) Good manners [principles] are those, with which a man passes from things that are fading to things that are eternal.—χρηστὰ) *good* or even *easy, light* [pliant dispositions]: see Scap. on this word, col. 1820. Comp. Rom. xvi. 18.—κακαὶ, *evil*) opposed to faith, hope, love. On the other hand, good communication [conversations] as for instance concerning the resurrection, puts an end to gluttony and depravity of manners.

34. Ἐκνήψατε) An exclamation full of apostolic majesty : *shake off lethargy* or *surfeiting*, ver. 32, so the LXX., ἐκνήψατε οἱ μεθύοντες, *Awake, ye drunkards*, Joel i. 5. He uses milder language, *watch ye*, in the conclusion, xvi. 13.—δικαίως, *to righteousness*) that righteousness, which is derived from the true knowledge of God. The antithesis is, *sinning* in this ver., and *corrupt manners*, ver. 33.—καὶ μὴ ἁμαρτάνετε) The Imperative after an imperative has the force of a future (John vii. 37, note) *and ye shall not sin*, either by an error of the understanding, or by evil communications [conversation] or by corrupt manners. Those, who place sin in the will alone, and not in the understanding, are in error, and therefore commit sin. Arguments calculated to rouse are added to those used as proofs, as Gal. iv. 12, note : for Scripture instructs the whole man.—ἀγνωσίαν, *ignorance*) ἀγνωσία is both *ignorance*, 1 Pet. ii. 15, and *forgetfulness*, 3 Macc. v. 24 : κατὰ πᾶν ἀγνωσίᾳ κεκρατημένος. *To have ignorance*, [To labour under ignorance] is a more significant phrase than *to be ignorant*,[1] and

---

[1] The former implies an *habitual* state of ignorance under which they labour. *To be ignorant*, may be but temporary, and restricted to one point. —ED.

includes in it the antithesis to *knowledge*, which in other respects was so agreeable to the Corinthians.— Θεοῦ, *of God*) and therefore also of the *power* and *works* of God, Matt. xxii. 29.—τινὲς, *some*) This word softens the reproof.—ἐντροπὴν, *shame*) The Corinthians claimed for themselves great *knowledge*. Ignorance and drowsiness are a disgrace, and from these they must awake. —ὑμῖν, *to you*) who are either ignorant, or have among you those that are ignorant. It is however at the same time the dative of advantage.—λέγω, *I speak*) boldly. He speaks more severely than at the beginning, when treating of another subject, iv. 14.

35. Τίς) *some one*, who dares deny the fact itself, because he is ignorant of the *manner*, in which it is accomplished, inasmuch as death has been so great a destruction, and it is asserted that the resurrection will be so glorious.—δὲ, *but then*) An Epitasis [Emphatic addition.]—ἔρχονται, *do they come?*) The living are said to *remain*, ver. vi. The dead *to have gone away*, ἀπελθόντες; Chrys. de Sacerd., p. 494: and *to return*, Ps. xc. 3; Eccl. xii. 7. But when they revive, they *come;* and they are said rather to *come*, than to *return*, on account of their complete newness [of their resurrection state and body]: see the verses following; comp. Acts i. 11, note. Paul, writing to the Corinthians who had doubts as to the question, *whether* [there is a future resurrection at all], so treats of the question *how* [it is to be], as to express the identity of the falling [dying] and the rising body somewhat more faintly, as it were, and more sparingly than he is wont to do on other occasions.

36. Ἄφρον, *Thou fool*) The apostle wonders, that any one could have any difficulty on this subject, he considered it as a thing so certain. This also appertains to the *shame* [which their *ignorance of God* reflected on them], ver. 34. To that man inquiring about the *way* [how are the dead raised?] of the resurrection, and the *quality* of the bodies rising [with what body do they come?] he answers first by a similitude, 36–42, at the middle; then, without a similitude, ver. 42, etc. In the similitude, the protasis and apodosis admirably correspond to each other: and the question is concerning the *way* of the resurrection in the protasis, ver 36; in the apodosis, ver. 42, *it is sown*, etc.: then concerning the *quality* of the bodies, in the protasis, ver. 37–41: in the apodosis,

ver. 43.—σὺ) *thou thyself*, silly fellow.—σπείρεις, *sowest*) in the field. A copious allegory follows.—οὐ ζωοποιεῖται, *is not quickened*) to a new sprout.—ἐὰν μὴ ἀποθάνῃ, *unless it die*) Paul completely retorts the objection [converts the very objection into an argument]: death does not prevent quickening, but goes before it, as the prelude and prognostication, as sowing precedes the harvest.

37. Οὐ τὸ σῶμα τὸ γενησόμενον, *not the body that shall be*) viz., the *body* that is beautiful, and no longer *bare* grain.

38. Ὁ δὲ Θεὸς, *but God*) Not thou, O man; not the grain itself. —αὐτῷ, *to it*) *to the grain*.—ἠθέλησε, *He hath willed*) The preterite in respect of creation, Gen. i. 11: or at least because *willing* is before *giving*,—ἑκάστῳ, *to every one*) not only to the seed of fruits, but also to that of animals. A gradation to the following verse. —ἴδιον, *its own*) suitable to the species, peculiar to the individual, produced from the substance of the seed. This *peculiarity* is further explained in the following verse.

39. Οὐ πᾶσα, *all not*) This is a universal negative. Every kind of flesh is different from the others. Paul shows, that terrestrial bodies differ from terrestrial, and celestial from celestial, ver. 41: but in such a way as to make each of these refer to the further illustration of the difference of the body from its seed, and of celestial bodies from those that are terrestrial; for in the apodosis he lays down nothing respecting the degrees of glory, but leaves it as it were in an enigma to be considered by wise men, while he accounts it sufficient to have openly asserted the glory of the resurrection bodies.—ἄλλη ἀνθρώπων, *one kind of flesh of men*) He elegantly omits the word *flesh*, when he places the flesh of brutes in opposition to that of *man*. κτήνη here is applied to all quadrupeds; for fishes and birds are opposed to them.—ἰχθύων, *of fishes*) Therefore those, who eat fishes, eat flesh, and that too the more sumptuously, as it is a delicate variety.

40. Ἐπουράνια, CELESTIAL *bodies*) The sun, moon, stars.— ἐπίγεια, *terrestrial bodies*) vegetables, animals.—ἑτέρα δὲ, *but is one*) Concerning the glory of terrestrial bodies, comp. Matt. vi. 28, 29; 1 Pet. i. 24.

41. Ἀστὴρ γὰρ, *for one star*) *For* intensive. Not only have the stars a glory differing from that of the sun and moon, but also, what is more to the point, one star often surpasses another star in brightness. There is no star, no glorious

body that has not some decided point of difference from another.

42. Οὕτω, *thus*) This word relates to the protasis already begun at ver. 36.—σπείρεται, *is sown*) a very delightful word instead of burial.—ἐν φθορᾷ, *in corruption*) The condition not only of the *dead* body but of the *mortal* body is denoted.

43. Ἐν ἀτιμίᾳ, *in dishonour*) in nakedness, ver. 37, to which is opposed *glory*, which is as it were a *garment put on*, ver. 53, 49. —σπείρεται ἐν ἀσθενείᾳ, *is sown in weakness*. The figure is continued ; but in the reality itself, a transition is made, that similitude being now finished, to a new part of the answer, of which this is the proposition [the statement to be elucidated] : *There is a natural and there is a spiritual body*. The expressions, *in power*, ver. 43, and *a spiritual* body, ver. 44, are akin to one another, Luke i. 17 : just as *incorruption and glory*, ver. 42, 43.

44. Ψυχικὸν, *animal* [*natural*] *body*) which, consisting of *flesh* and *blood*, ver. 50, is wholly moulded [given form and fashion to] by the animal soul.—πνευματικὸν, *spiritual*) which is wholly moulded by the spirit.—καὶ) *and so* consequently.

45. Γέγραπται, *it is written*) Gen. ii. 7, LXX., ἐγένετο ὁ ἄνθρωπος εἰς ψυχὴν ζῶσαν, *man became a living soul*. Paul adds other things in accordance with the nature of the contraries [the things antithetical to the former.]—πρῶτος) that is, *the* FIRST ; for *the last* is in antithesis to it ; but in ver. 47, πρῶτος means *the former* of the two ; for it is in antithesis to δεύτερος, *the second :* and each is there considered, as a model of the rest. ὁ ἔσχατος, *the last*, in like manner as ὁ δεύτερος, *the second*, points to Christ, not to the whole human race in its perfect consummation.—Ἀδὰμ) A proper name here ; but it is presently after repeated by antonomasia.[1]—ψυχὴν, *life—soul*) Hence ψυχικὸν *living, animal*, [*natural*] ver. 44.—ὁ ἔσχατος, *the last*) Job xix. 25. אחרן, the same as he who is called גאל, as is evident there from the parallelism of the double predicate. Christ is *last ;* the day of Christ is *the last day*, John vi. 39. [Christ is *a Spirit*, 2 Cor. iii. 17.—V. g.]— ζωοποιοῦν, *quickening*) He not only lives, but also makes alive.

---

[1] Append. The substitution of a proper name for a common name, or *vice versa*.

46. Οὐ πρῶτον,) *not the first.*—τὸ πνευματικὸν, *the spiritual*) body. This verse refers to ver. 44, ver. 45, making as it were a parenthesis, to which ver. 47 afterwards corresponds.—ἔπειτα, *afterward*) This should be carefully noticed by those, who so dispute about the origin of evil, as if all things should have been not only good at the beginning, as they were, but also such as they will be at their consummation.

47. Ὁ πρῶτος ἄνθρωπος, ἐκ γῆς, χοϊκός· ὁ δεύτερος, ὁ Κύριος ἐξ οὐρανοῦ, *the first man is of the earth, earthy; the second man is the Lord from heaven*) We have here an exact antithesis. The first man, ἐκ γῆς, viz. ὤν, *since he is of the earth*, is χοϊκὸς, *earthy*, affected in the same way as a heap of earth (χοῦς) χυτή, *accumulated*, and then scattered: the reason of this is, because he is sprung *from the earth*. This is the protasis; the apodosis follows, in which it would not have been appropriate to say, *the second man, from* [*of*] *heaven, heavenly;* for man owes to the earth his obligations for this, that he is *earthy;* but the Lord does not owe His glory to heaven, inasmuch as it was He Himself who made heaven what it is, and by descending from heaven, presented Himself to us as the Lord. Therefore the order of the words is now changed, *the Lord, from heaven* [*Lord* coming before *from heaven;* whereas *earthy*, the antithesis to *Lord*, comes after *of earth*]. The word *Lord* signifies the same thing in the concrete, as *glory* does in the abstract (Germ. *Herr, Herrlichkeit, Lord, Lordship*), whence it is properly opposed to *earthy*, ver. 43; Phil. iii. 20, etc.: and from this *glory* is derived the incorruptibility of Christ's flesh, Acts ii. 24, 31. In this way the received reading is defended, and the various readings, although ancient, which are mentioned in the *Apparatus*, are withdrawn.[1]

49. Καὶ καθὼς, *and even as*) From the former state Paul infers the latter.—ἐφορέσαμεν, *we have borne* [*worn*]) as a garment.—τὴν εἰκόνα, *the image*) This not only denotes the resemblance, but also the dependence.—φορέσωμεν καὶ τὴν εἰκόνα τοῦ ἐπουρανίου, *let us bear* [*wear*] *also the image of the heavenly*) Tertullian says: *Let us bear; not we shall bear, preceptively, not promissively.* Nay,

---

[1] BCD corr. later, G Vulg. *g* (these last three add οὐράνιος) *f* omit ὁ Κύριος. Rec. Text retains the words, with A (according to Tisch., but Lachm. quotes A against the words), Marcion (according to Tertullian) both Syr. Versions. Origen, 2,559*d* supports them. But in 4,302*d* he rejects them.—ED.

φορέσωμεν, *let us bear*, and yet in the way of promise.[1] The subjunctive renders the expression modal and conciliatory, by which Paul (comp. ver. 53, *must*) expresses the divine appointment and faith assenting to it. Comp. the subjunctive James iv. 13, 15, πορευσώμεθα, κ.τ.λ. Later copies have made it, φορέσομεν; and there is the same variety in the copies of Origen against Celsus, as Sam. Battier observes in Biblioth. Brem., Class vi., p. 102, etc., who approves of the reading φορέσωμεν out of Maximus, περὶ ἀγάπης.

50. Σὰρξ καὶ αἷμα, *flesh and blood*) An abstract phrase, [*meaning man, as far as the circulation of the blood quickens his flesh.—V. g.*] as φθορὰ, *corruption*. The one is applied to those, who live in the world, the other to the dead. Both of these must become altogether different from what they have been previously. The spirit extracted from the dregs of wine does not so much differ from them, as the glorified man from the mortal man.—βασιλείαν Θεοῦ, *the kingdom of God*) which is altogether spiritual, and in no respect merely animal [natural]. A great change *must* intervene, until man is made fit for that kingdom.—οὐ δύνανται, *cannot*) This is a Syllepsis[2] of number, for it denotes the multitude of those, who are flesh and blood.—οὐδὲ—κληρονομεῖ, *nor—obtains by inheritance*) It is not said, *cannot receive by inheritance*. *Flesh and blood* are farther distant [from the inheritance], than *corruption* itself; and it is evident from its very nature, that *corruption* cannot obtain this inheritance, although it is certainly the way to *incorruptibility*, ver. 36. The meaning of the present may be gathered from ver. 52 at the beginning.

51. Ὑμῖν, *you*) Do not suppose, that you know all things.—λέγω, *I say*) prophetically : xiii. 2 : 1 Thess. iv. 15.—πάντες μὲν οὐ κοιμηθησόμεθα, πάντες δὲ ἀλλαγησόμεθα, *we shall not all sleep, but we shall all be changed*) The Latins read with general consent; "Omnes quidem resurgemus, sed non omnes immutabimur,"

---

[1] Tisch. reads φορέσομεν with B (judging from silence) both Syr. Versions. But Lachm. as Beng., φορέσωμεν with ACD(Λ)G*fg* Vulg. Orig. 1,591*bc*, 2,26*b*, Iren. Cypr. Hilar.—ED.

[2] See App. The sing. subject had gone before. But the plural was *mentally intended*.—ED.

[3] So D(Λ) corrected later, *df* Hilary 91,315, and Latin MSS. in Jerome 1,810*c*, read παντες ἀναστησόμεθα, οὐ πάντες δὲ ἀλλαγησόμεθα.—ED.

We shall indeed all rise, but we shall not all be changed, and *Tertullian* and *Rufinus* and others besides follow this reading. And yet the Latin translator does not seem to have read the Greek different from our Greek copies, but to have expressed the sense, as he indeed understood it, rather than the words. For this is his common practice in this epistle, as when xii. 10 and 28, he translated γλωσσῶν, *words*, and on the other hand xiv. 10 φωνῶν, *tongues*, he seems therefore to have translated οὐ κοιμηθησόμεθα, as if it had been οὐ μενοῦμεν κοιμηθέντες, that is, *we shall rise again.* Hence it followed, that he presently after supplied *not*, for the sake of the antithesis, as he had suppressed *not*, chap. ix. 6: and here also Tertullian follows his footsteps. Moreover from the Latin the word ἀναβιώσομεν has been fabricated in the *Veles*. and ἀναστησόμεθα (a word which Paul does not use in this whole chapter) is a correction by the first interpolator of the *Clar.* MS. Some of the Greeks have πάντες μὲν οὖν κοιμηθησόμεθα, ἀλλ᾿ οὐ πάντες ἀλλαγησόμεθα; whence from μὲν οὐ, μὲν οὖν was easily produced. Indeed in this verse the apostle wished to deny nothing whatever concerning the change, but to affirm it, and to bring forward the mystery. The reading of the text remains, which is not unknown even to the Latin copies, quoted by Jerome from Didymus.[1] Moreover each of the two clauses is universal. *All indeed,* namely we, from whom the dead are presently after contradistinguished, *shall not sleep; but all,* even we the same persons, *shall be changed;* the subject of each of the two enunciations is the same: comp. πᾶς οὐκ, taken universally, xvi. 12; Rom. ix. 33; Eph. v. 5; Rev. xxii. 3; Acts xi. 8. The expression does not so much refer to the very persons, who were then alive, and were waiting for the consummation of the world, but to those, who are to be then alive in their place, ver. 52 at the end, 1 Thess. iv. 15, note.—ἀλλαγησόμεθα, *we shall be*

---

[1] Tisch. reads πάντες οὐ κοιμηθησόμεθα, πάντες δὲ ἀλλαγησομεθα, with B (from its silence), some Greek MSS. mentioned in Jerome 1,794c, 810c, also MSS. of Acacius and Didymus in Jerome 1,795e, 799b, both Syr. and Memph. Versions, Orig. 1,589f, and quoted in Jerome 1,804c. Lachm. reads πάντες [μὲν] κοιμηθησόμεθα, οὐ πάντες δὲ ἀλλαγησόμεθα, with CGg, Orig. 2,552bc, also Greek MSS. mentioned in Jerome 1,794c, 810c, also Didymus mentioned in Jerome 1,795d, and in 1,798b, Acacius, bishop of Cæsarea, who mentions it as the reading of very many MSS. A reads οἱ πάντες μὲν κοιμηθ. οἱ πάντες δὲ ἀλλαγ.—ED.

changed) While the soul remains in the body, the body from being animal [natural] will become spiritual.

52. Ἐν ἀτόμῳ, *in a moment*) Lest it should be considered hyperbolical, he adds a more popular phrase, *in the twinkling of an eye*. An extraordinary work of divine omnipotence! Who then can doubt, but that man even at death may be suddenly freed from sin?—σάλπιγγι, *at the trumpet*) The full description of the trumpets is reserved for the Apocalypse; yet some things may be gathered from Matt. xxiv. 31; 1 Thess. iv. 16, concerning the *last* trumpet; and this epithet is expressed here, as one that takes for granted the trumpets, that have preceded it; either because the Spirit has inspired Paul with an allusion, which anticipates the Apocalypse, or because Scripture long before teaches, that some trumpets, though not definitely enumerated, are before *the last*. Is. xxvii. 13; Jer. li. 27; Zech. ix. 14; Heb. xii. 19; 2 Esdr. v. 4: or especially in relation to the trumpet at the *ascension*, Ps. xlvii. 6, comp. Acts i. 11: for one may be called *the last*, where two only are referred to, ver. 45; not to say, where there is only one [sounding of a trumpet], without another following, Rev. x. 7.—σαλπίσει γὰρ) *for* the Lord [Engl. V. *the trumpet*] *shall sound* by His archangel, 1 Thess. iv. 16. The trumpet was formerly used on feast days for the purpose of assembling the people.—καὶ) *and* immediately.—ἄφθαρτοι, *incorruptible*) Strictly speaking, one would think, that they should have been called *immortal;* for *incorruptibility* will be put on by means of the *change*, ver. 53; but *incorruptibility* includes *immortality*.

53. Τοῦτο,) *this itself* our present *corruptible* state.—ἀφθαρσίαν, *incorruptibility*) by that transformation.

54. Ὅταν δὲ—ἀθανασίαν, *but when—immortality*) The frequent repetition of these words is very delightful.—τότε, *then*) not before. The Scripture is sure, therefore the resurrection is sure. —κατεπόθη ὁ θάνατος εἰς νῖκος, *death is swallowed up in victory*) Is. xxv. 8, LXX.—κατέπιεν ὁ θάνατος ἰσχύσας, *it was swallowed up at one instantaneous draught:* comp. Rev. xxi. 4.—εἰς νῖκος, Heb נצח, which the LXX. not here but elsewhere often translate εἰς νῖκος, *unto* or *in victory*.

55. Ποῦ σου, θάνατε, τὸ κέντρον; ποῦ σου, ᾅδη, τὸ νῖκος;) Hos. xiii. 14, LXX.—ποῦ ἡ δίκη (νίκη) σου, θάνατε; ποῦ τὸ κέντρον σου, ᾅδη; Heb.

אֱהִי דְבָרֶיךָ מָוֶת אֱהִי קָטָבְךָ שְׁאוֹל, *i.e., where are thy plagues, O death? where, O grave, is thy destruction?*—See by all means, Olearii diss. inaug. on Redemption from hell. In this hymn of victory, *where* signifies that death and hell were formerly very formidable: now circumstances are changed. Θάνατος, *death*, and ᾅδης, *hell* [the unseen world beneath], are frequently used promiscuously; but yet they differ, for the one can never be substituted for the other: *Hell* is in fact opposed to heaven; *death*, to life, and *death* precedes; *hell* is more profound; *death* receives the bodies without the souls, *hell* receives the souls, even without the bodies, not only of the wicked, but also of the godly, and that, before the death of Christ, Gen. xxxvii. 35; Luke xvi. 23. Therefore they are mentioned in connection with each other; and it is said in gradation, *death* and *hell*: comp. Rev. xx. 13, 14, vi. 8, i. 17: and in these passages it is evident, that the word *grave* cannot be substituted for *hell*. Furthermore, because the discussion here turns upon the resurrection of the body, therefore *hell* is only once named, death often, even in the following verse.— τὸ κέντρον, *the sting*) having a [*plague*-causing or] *pestilential* [Heb. "Where are thy *plagues* ?"] poison. Paul transposes the *victory* and the *sting*; which is more agreeable not only to the gradation of the Hebrew synomyms, but also makes a more convenient transition to the following verse, where *sting* and *strength* are kindred terms. A *stimulus* or *goad* is a larger κέντρον; comp. Acts xxvi. 14; *a sting* or *prick* [aculeus] is a less κέντρον; sometimes they may be used promiscuously, when we overlook the quantity [*i.e.*, a quantity of less *aculei* is tantamount to a *stimulus* or *stimuli*]; we may even kick against the *pricks* in thorns.—ᾅδη, *O hell*, [*grave*, Engl. V.]) It does not here denote the place of eternal punishment, but the receptacle of souls, which are again to be united with their bodies at the resurrection. There is nothing here said now any longer of the devil; comp. Heb. ii. 14: because the *victory* is snatched out of his hands, earlier than out of those of death, ver. 26.—νῖκος) LXX. δίκη or νίκη: Paul sweetly repeats νῖκος; comp. the preceding verse. The rarity of the word is well suited to *a song of victory*.

56. Ἡ ἁμαρτία, *sin*) If there were no sin, there could be no death; comp. Hos. xiii. 12. Against this *prick* no one could have *kicked* by his own strength; no one could have sung that song

of triumph, *where*, etc. The particle *but* indicates this fact.—
ὁ νόμος, *the law*) threatening death for sin; without the law sin is not perceived; under the law sin has dominion; Rom. vi. 14.

57. Τῷ δὲ Θεῷ χάρις, *but thanks be to God*) It had not been of our accomplishment [in our power to effect].—δὲ, *but*) Although both the law and sin, and death and hell, opposed us, yet we have overcome. This is the sentiment; but the mode or ἦθος, [expression of feeling] is added, *thanks be to God.*—τῷ διδόντι,[1] *who gives*) the present, to suit the state of believers.[2]—τὸ νῖκος, *the victory*) a repetition, suitable to the triumph: death and hell had aimed at the victory.—Χριστοῦ, *Christ*) in the faith of whom, we [being dead], dying to the law, have obtained life, ver. 3 and following verses.

58.[3] Ἀγαπητοί, *beloved*) The true consideration of the things, the last of all, kindles his love towards the brethren.—ἑδραῖοι, [steadfast] *stable*) do not ye yourselves turn aside from the faith of the resurrection.—ἀμετακίνητοι, *immoveable*) be not led away by others, ver. 12. So Col. i. 23.—ἐν τῷ ἔργῳ τοῦ Κυρίου, *in the work of the Lord*) Christ, Phil. ii. 30. It is called generally, *the work* which is carried on for the sake of *the Lord*. Its more particular definition depends on the circumstances of each particular text.—εἰδότες, *knowing*) He is now sure of the assent of the Corinthians. —οὐκ ἔστι κενὸς, *is not vain*) i.e., is most profitable. They were trying to make it *in vain*, who denied the resurrection. Paul mildly refutes these men even in the conclusion [as well as before].

---

[1] Διδόντι is read by ABCG*g*. But D (Λ) *f* Vulg. δόντι.—ED.

[2] Nevertheless both the margin of the 2d Ed. and the Germ. Ver., prefer the reading δόντι, and therefore the past tense.—E. B.

[3] Ὥστε, *therefore*) A grave error had to be refuted in this passage: and yet he does not neglect to subjoin the exhortation.—V. g.

CHAPTER XVI.

1. Λογίας, *collection*) A plain [not figurative] term well adapted to the commencement of this subject, ver. 2 : it is called *a blessing*,[1] 2 Cor. ix. 5.—εἰς τοὺς ἁγίους, *for the saints*) He would rather call them *the saints* than *the poor*; and he does so both because this appellation is suited to the importance of the object and fitted for obtaining it.—διέταξα, *I have given order*) by apostolic authority, which was familiar to the *Galatians*.—Γαλατίας, *of Galatia*) He proposes the Galatians as an example to the Corinthians, the Corinthians to the Macedonians, the Corinthians and Macedonians to the Romans : 2 Cor. ix. 2 ; Rom. xv. 26. There is great force in examples.

2. Κατὰ μίαν, *on the first day*) The Lord's day even already at that time was peculiarly observed. On the Sabbath the Jews and Christians met together; next day the latter engaged in the duties peculiar to themselves. *The Sabbath* is used by Synecdoche [see Append.] for *the week*; usually the form of expression is ἡ μία σαββάτων, the *one, i.e.*, the first day of *the week*; but here the article is not used, in order that κατὰ may retain its distributive meaning. The advice is easily put in practice. When men give once for all, not so much is given. If [when] a man every Lord's day *has laid by* something, more has been collected, than one would have given at once.—ἕκαστος, *every one*) even those not very rich.—παρ᾽ ἑαυτῷ, *by himself*) *apart*, that it may appear, what he himself lays by ; whether others lay by more sparingly or more liberally than he does. The Corinthians had not yet a common treasury in the Church.—τιθέτω, *let him lay by*) at the public meeting.—θησαυρίζων, *in store*) plentifully, a pleasant word, 1 Tim. vi. 19.—εὐοδῶται, *it may be convenient*)[2] according as one's mind is willing and one's means are easy. It is a matter of Christian prudence to put in practice, according as

---

[1] εὐλογία, a figurative term for *bounty*; whereas here the plain term λογία is used.—ED.

[2] So Vulg. " Quod ei placuerit." But Engl. Ver. "As God hath prospered him."

your circumstances enable you, what is inculcated at Eccl. ix. 10, 1 Sam. x. 7.—ἵνα μή, *that not*) This is by way of anticipation [occupatio[1]], that they may not think it necessary to have a collection also at that time, and in like manner there is boldness of speech, as much as to say, *I will certainly not pass you over.*—ὅταν ἔλθω, *when I come*) It would neither be pleasant for Paul nor for the Corinthians to do this in his presence. Now, says he, you will act the more generously; then, we shall attend to other matters. —λογίαι, *gatherings, collections*) This term, a less agreeable one, advises them not to delay.

3. Οὓς ἂν δοκιμάσητε) *whomsoever*, when I am present, *you shall approve,* as faithful.—δι᾽ ἐπιστολῶν τούτους πέμψω, *them will I send with letters*) in your name. The antithesis is, *Paul himself,* ver. 4: comp. διά, Rom. ii. 27 ; 2 Cor. ii. 4.—τὴν χάριν ὑμῶν, *your liberality*) a gracious term, and therefore frequently employed.— 2 Cor. viii. 4.

4. Ἄξιον, *worthy*) *meet, if it shall be worth while for me to carry it myself.* He invites them to be liberal.—κἀμέ, *that even I*) a just estimate of one's self is not pride, 2 Cor. i. 19. Paul mentions himself in the first place.—σὺν ἐμοί, *with me*) so that all suspicion may be obviated, 2 Cor. viii. 20, 21.

5. Ἐλεύσομαι δέ, *but I will come*) He had said ver. 2 *when I shall have come.*—ὅταν Μακεδονίαν) In this one passage an error in a single accent was discovered in the smaller edition, after a new preface had been written to it; and we are forced to mention this only on the ground, that the affirmation of that preface, in respect to our edition being correct even to the smallest point, may be consistent with itself.—διέρχομαι, *I pass*) we have here the figure Ploce,[2] of which the antithesis follows, *to pass through, to abide,* ver. 6. Wherefore we must not press the present tense. He was not yet in Macedonia, but he was thinking of it, ver. 8.

6. Τυχόν, *perhaps*) He speaks very familiarly.—οὗ ἐάν, *whithersoever*) For the sake of modesty he does not express how far he may be thinking to go, Acts xix. 21.

7. Ἄρτι, *now*) after so long delay heretofore.—ἐὰν ὁ Κύριος ἐπι-

---

[1] See App.

[2] See Append. The same word twice used, once in the sense of the word itself, and again used to express an attribute of it.

1 CORINTHIANS XVI. 8–12.

τρέπῃ,[1] *if the Lord permit*) a pious qualification. The destinations of the saints have some degree of liberty, which the divine goodness in various ways both precedes and follows.

8. Ἐν Ἐφέσῳ, *At Ephesus*) Paul was at Ephesus: comp. ver. 19, respecting *Asia*.

9. Θύρα, *a door*) It is the part of a wise man to watch opportunities.—ἀνέῳγε, *has been opened*) at Ephesus.—μεγάλη καὶ ἐνεργής, *great and effectual*) He was about to take advantage of so great an opportunity for some weeks; comp. ch. v. 7, note.—ἀντικείμενοι, *adversaries*) whom I must resist. Often good, and, its contrary, evil, flourish vigorously at one and the same time.

10. Δὲ, *now*) An antithesis between Paul himself and his substitute, Timothy.[2]—ἀφόβως, *without fear*) This will be the case, if no man shall have despised him. If some despised Paul, how much more readily would they depise the youthful native of Lystra.—Κυρίου, *of the Lord*) Christ.—ἐργάζεται, *worketh*) It is right that this work should be performed without fear. This constitutes the foundation of true respect to the ministers of the gospel.

11. Αὐτὸν, *him*) a young man, Ps. cxix. 141, νεώτερος ἐγώ εἰμι καὶ ΕΞΟΥΔΕΝΩΜΕΝΟΣ, *I am rather young and am* DESPISED. —ἀδελφῶν, *the brethren*) who likewise are looking for him; or else, who are likewise to come.

12. Πολλὰ παρεκάλεσα, *I strongly urged [greatly desired]*) Paul was not afraid of the Corinthians preferring Apollos, who was present with them, to himself. Apollos, when Paul sent this epistle, was not present, for he is not mentioned either at ver. 19 or at ch. i. 1.—μετὰ τῶν ἀδελφῶν, *with the brethren*) ver. 17. These are different from those at ver. 11.—οὐκ ἦν θέλημα, *the will was not*) An expression as it were impersonal; where the matter is considered, as to be or not to be the object of the wish [will], without expressing, whose will it is; wherein however the standard is the will of God; comp. Matt. xviii. 14. So also

---

[1] The Germ. Ver., after the margin of 2d Ed. has the reading ἐπιτρέψῃ. The Gnomon in this passage follows the former decision.—E. B.
Ἐπιτρέψῃ is the reading of ABC*fg* Vulg. Ἐπιτρέπῃ is that of D (Λ) G; so Rec. Text.

[2] Τιμόθεος, *Timothy*) was the bearer of this epistle.—V. g

the Greeks use the verb θέλω, Acts ii. 12.—ὅταν εὐκαιρήσῃ, *when he shall have convenient time*) The *convenience* indicated is not carnal convenience, but that which follows the will of God.

13. Γρηγορεῖτε, *watch*) The conclusion exhorting chiefly to *faith* and *love* [*This is the sum of all those things, which either Timothy or Apollos thought should be inculcated on the Corinthians.—*V. g.]—ἐν τῇ πίστει, *in the faith*, ch. xv. 2, 11, 14, 17.

14. Ἐν ἀγάπῃ, *in love*) viii. 1, xiii. 1.

15. Τοῖς ἁγίοις, *to the saints*) The Dative is governed by διακονίαν, *ministry*. To the saints of Israel, for they were the *first fruits* of Achaia.—ἑαυτοὺς, *themselves*) spontaneously [*These were the very persons, who had come from Corinth to Paul*, ver. 17.— V. g.] The more voluntary the service in difficult circumstances, the more agreeable and praiseworthy. 2 Cor. viii. 16, 17; Is. vi. 8.

16. Καὶ, *ye also*) in turn.—ὑποτάσσησθε, *ye submit yourselves*) corresponding to ἔταξαν, *they addicted themselves*.—συνεργοῦντι, [that helpeth with] *that worketh with*) others.—κοπιῶντι, *that laboureth*) by themselves.

17. Χαίρω, *I rejoice*) Paul in respect of God, *gives thanks*, when he might have said, *I rejoice;* ch. i. 14, but when he writes to men, he says, *I rejoice* or *I rejoiced*, instead of *I give thanks;* Phil. iv. 10; Philem. ver. 7: comp. Acts x. 33; 3 John v. 3. Now again the deputies of the Corinthians had departed; and yet he says in the present tense, *I rejoice;* for a pleasant remembrance of them remained, and the present is supposed to accord with the time of the reading of the epistle at Corinth.—Στεφανᾶ, *of Stephanas*) This person seems to have been the son of that Stephanas, whose house is mentioned, but not himself at ver. 15. —ὑστέρημα, [that which was lacking] *the deficiency*) So far as you had been awanting to me, and were not yourselves able to *refresh* me in my absence.

18. Ἀνέπαυσαν, *they have refreshed*) True brethren, although inferior, do not come or are present in vain. Such is *the refreshment* of the saints.—τὸ ἐμὸν πνεῦμα, *my spirit*) 2 Cor. vii. 13. —καὶ τὸ ὑμῶν, *and yours*) in regard to me : 2 Cor. vii. 3.—ἐπιγινώσκετε, *acknowledge*) The Antecedent [acknowledge] for the Consequent [Give them a kind reception], so εἰδέναι, *to know*, 1 Thess. v. 12. He who does not do so, is said to be ἀγνώμων

19. Πολλά, *much*) for especial affection, Acts xviii. 2, 1.—Ἀκύλας καὶ Πρίσκιλλα, *Aquila and Priscilla*) Elsewhere this woman is mentioned first. In the epistle to the Corinthians, she is put last; comp. xiv. 34.—κατ᾽ οἶκον, *in their house*) This couple afterwards set up a church *also in their house* at Rome; Rom. xvi. 5.

20. Ἐν φιλήματι ἁγίῳ, *with a holy kiss*) in which all dissensions might be swallowed up.

21. Τῇ ἐμῇ χειρί, *with mine own hand*) He therefore dictated all the rest of the epistle.

22. Εἴ τις οὐ, *if any man not*) Paul loves Jesus, do ye also all love Him.—φιλεῖ) *loves* with the heart : kisses virtually by his conduct : the corresponding word to φιλεῖ is φιλήματι, *with a kiss*, ver. 20; for φιλεῖν is used in the sense of *kissing*, Luke xxii. 47 ; and *to kiss* is used for *to love*, Ps. ii. 12.—τὸν Κυρίον, *the Lord*) He is to be preferred even before all the brethren, nay even before Paul and Apollos.—ἤτω ἀνάθεμα, μαρὰν ἀθά, *let him be anathema Maranatha*) So far from wishing him health [saluting him], I would rather bid him be accursed. The words Maranatha add weight to the anathema ; and this phrase, expressed in an idiom familiar to the Jews indicates, that he who loves not Jesus will partake with the Jews, who call Jesus anathema with bitter hatred, xii. 3, in that curse most righteously falling upon themselves, for he uses this language to soften the odiousness of the phrase [by Euphemism] instead of the expression, if any man hate Jesus. Μαρὰν ἀθά, *i.e. the Lord cometh;* μαρὰν in Syriac, *our Lord*, or simply *the Lord*. Hesychius says, μαραναθά, ὁ Κύριος ἦλθεν, κ.τ.λ. As in French *monseigneur* is the same as *seigneur.*, Μαρὰν ἀθά seems to have been a frequent symbol [watchword] with Paul, the meaning of which the Corinthians had either already known, or now, when they were to be seriously affected by it, might learn from others.

23. Ἡ χάρις, *grace*) This is the salutation set forth at ver. 21 : at ver. 22, the unworthy are excluded ; comp. 2 John v. 10, 11.

24. Ἡ ἀγάπη μου μετὰ πάντων ὑμῶν ἐν Χριστῷ Ἰησοῦ, *My love be with you all in Christ Jesus*) The Apostle embraces in Christ Jesus with love, which had been divinely kindled, not only those who had said they were of Paul, but all the Corinthians. In the Alexandrian copy alone, μου is omitted ; but this little word

evidently agrees with the beginning and end of this epistle.[1] There was afterwards added, ἐγράφη ἀπὸ Φιλίππων, *it was written from Philippi.* But it was written at Ephesus, as ver. 8 proves; perhaps, however, it was sent from Philippi, ver. 5, because the deputies of the Corinthians had accompanied Paul thither. At least, Aquila and Priscilla, who are spoken of at ver. 19, were at Ephesus (Acts xviii. 19); thence there was a road to Corinth above Philippi. I do not refuse a more convenient way of reconciling these two statements; comp. Ord. Temp., p. 282, lin. 4 and 9, and the end of the page 281.

[1] Μου is read in BCD (Λ) G*fg* Vulg. But A omits it.—ED

ANNOTATIONS

ON

PAUL'S SECOND EPISTLE TO THE CORINTHIANS.

CHAPTER I.

1. Παῦλος, *Paul*) While Paul repeats his admonitions, he shows his apostolic love and στοργή, *fatherly affection* to the Corinthians, who had been dutifully [devoutly] affected by the severity of his former epistle; and for the rest, as he had written therein about the affairs of the Corinthians, so he now writes about his own, but with a constant regard to the spiritual benefit of the Corinthians. But the thread and connection of the whole epistle is *historical;* other topics are introduced as digressions. See the leading points, at ver. 8, 15; ii. 1, 12, 13; vii. 5; viii. 1; x. 1; xiii. 1, concerning the *past, present,* and *future.* Whence we have this connected view [synopsis] of the epistle. There is in it—

I. THE INSCRIPTION, ch. i. 1, 2.

II. THE DISCUSSION [handling of his subject.]
  1. We were greatly pressed in ASIA:
    but God consoled us:
    for we act with sincerity of mind; even in this that I have not already come to you, who are in propriety bound to obey me, 3–ii. 11.

2. I hastened from TROAS to Macedonia, which is near you: keeping pace with the progress of the Gospel, whose glorious ministry we worthily perform, 12–vii. 1.
3. In MACEDONIA I received joyful tidings of you, 2–16.
4. In this journey I became acquainted with the liberality of the Macedonians. Wherefore it becomes you to follow that example, viii. 1–ix. 15.
5. I am on my way to you, armed with the power of Christ. Therefore obey, x. 1–xiii. 10.

III. THE CONCLUSION, 11–13.

Τιμόθεος ὁ ἀδελφὸς, *Timothy, our brother*) When Paul writes to Timothy himself, he calls him *son;* when writing of him to the Corinthians and others, he calls him *brother.*—τῇ ἐκκλησίᾳ τοῦ Θεοῦ, *to the Church of God*) This has the force of a synonym with the word *saints*, which follows.

3. Εὐλογητὸς, *blessed*) An elegant mode of introduction, and suited to the apostolic spirit, especially in adversity.—ὁ πατὴρ τῶν οἰκτιρμῶν καὶ Θεὸς πάσης παρακλήσεως, *the Father of mercies and God of all consolation*) *Mercies* are the fountain of *consolation*: comp. Rom. xii. 1: παρακαλεῖν is *zusprechen*, to console. The principle of exhortation and consolation is often the same; *consolation* is the proof [the evidence] of *mercies*. [*And Paul makes mention of mercies and help, before he mentions afflictions.*—V. g.] He exhibits his mercies in the very midst of calamity; and the calamity of the saints is neither contrary to the Divine mercy, nor does it beget suspicion against it in the minds of the saints: afterwards it even affords consolation; therefore πάσης, *of all*, is added.

4. Πάσῃ· πάσῃ, *in all, in all*) He who has experienced one kind of affliction is peculiarly qualified to console those in the same circumstances; he who has experienced all is able to console men under all kinds of affliction, Heb. iv. 15.—θλίψει, *in tribulation*) The antithetic words on the one side are παθήματα, *adversities* [the sufferings], and θλίψις, *distress* [straitness] *of mind;* of which the one is implied in the signification of the other—and on the other side, σωτηρία, *salvation;* and παράκλησις, *consolation;* of which the one is in like manner implied in the

signification of the other. The frequent occurrence of these words will be greatly relished, but only by the experienced. [*How great need is there of experience! how ill-qualified a guide is he, who is without it!*—V. g.] Adversity is treated of from ver. 8; consolation from ch. vii. 2, etc. Paul speaks generally of comfort at the beginning; he, however, refers especially to that, which he derived from the obedience of the Corinthians. —αὐτοί) *we ourselves*.

5. Τοῦ Χριστοῦ, εἰς ἡμᾶς· διὰ Χριστοῦ, ἡμῶν, *of Christ towards* (in) *us; ours by Christ*) The words and their order are sweetly interchanged.—παθήματα· παράκλησις, *adversities* (*sufferings*)*; consolation*) The former are numerous; the latter is but one, and yet exceeds the former.—οὕτως, *so*) There shines forth brightly from this very epistle, as compared with the former, a greater amount of consolation to the Corinthians, who had been deeply impressed with the first epistle, consolation being extremely well suited to their circumstances, after the distresses which had intervened; and so there shines forth brightly in it the newness of the whole inner man, increasing more and more day by day.

6. Εἴτε δὲ θλιβόμεθα, κ.τ.λ., and, *whether we be afflicted,* etc.) The meaning is this, εἴτε δὲ θλιβόμεθα (θλιβόμεθα) ὑπὲρ τῆς ὑμῶν παρακλήσεως καὶ σωτηρίας· εἴτε παρακαλούμεθα (παρακαλούμεθα) ὑπὲρ κτλ, *and whether we be afflicted* (*we are afflicted*) *for your consolation and salvation; or whether we be comforted* (*we are comforted*) *for your consolation, which operates in enabling you to endure the same adversities which we also endure, and our hope for you is stedfast; knowing that as you are partakers of the sufferings* (*adversities*)*, so also of the consolation.* As in Phil. i. 16, 19, θλίψις and σωτηρία are opposed to each other; so here θλίψις, *the affliction* of the ministers of the Gospel, and the *consolation and salvation* of the Corinthians, are opposed to each other, in the same way as the *death* of the former [the ministers] and the *life* of the latter [the Corinthians], iv. 12. Furthermore, as though *consolation* and *salvation* of the Corinthians depend on the *affliction* of the ministers of the Gospel; so the *consolation* of the Corinthians, and the *hope* of the ministers in their behalf, depend on the *consolation* of the ministers. The participle *knowing* depends on the verbs, *we are afflicted,* and *we are comforted,* understood. Thus the members of this period are con-

sistent with one another, of which the various transpositions are noticed in the *Apparatus*.[1] We shall now explain some of these words in particular.—εἴτε, *whether*) sometimes we are more sensible of adversities, sometimes of consolation.—ὑμῶν, *your*) The communion of saints, cultivated in the heart of Paul, Titus, the Corinthians, and other Churches, is admirably represented in this epistle, ii. 3, iv. 15, vi. 12, vii. 7, 13, ix. 12. These hearts were, so to speak, mirrors reflecting the likenesses of each other; comp. Phil, ii. 26, 27.—παρακλήσεως, *consolation*) in the soul. —σωτηρίας, *salvation*) in fact [in reality].—τῆς ἐνεργουμένης) in the Middle voice, iv. 12; Rom. vii. 5.—τῶν αὐτῶν) *the same*, in point of number. The *adversities* [sufferings] of Paul were the same as those of the Corinthians, who were in the heart of Paul: vi. 12; and the fruit of those sufferings redounded to their advantage, although they [the sufferings] had prevented him from coming to Corinth. A mutual participation [in sufferings and consolation] is declared.—πάσχομεν, καὶ ἡ ἐλπίς, *we suffer, and the hope*) Hope is usually joined with the mention of afflictions and patience, ver. 10; Rom. v. 3, 4, xv. 4.—βεβαία, *is stedfast*) It obtained stedfastness through adversity.

8. Ἐν τῇ Ἀσίᾳ, *in Asia*) 1 Cor. xv. 32, note. The Corinthians *were* not *ignorant* of that affliction, which had befallen him in Asia; but Paul now declares its magnitude and its advantageous result. [*The whole epistle presents a journal of his travels; but most excellent precepts are interwoven with the narrative of them.*—V. g.]—ὑπὲρ δύναμιν) *above* ordinary *strength*.—ἐξαπορηθῆναι, *that we despaired*) He affirms here, what he denies in another respect, iv. 8; for he is speaking here of human, there of Divine assistance.

9. Ἀλλὰ, *but*) i.e. nay; supply, *for this reason we ourselves*, etc.; *that not*, etc.—τὸ ἀπόκριμα) Hesychius says, ἀπόκριμα, κατάκριμα, ψῆφον. ἀποκρίνειν, *to pass sentence on one condemned*, to consider him as dead. The antithesis is *trusting*. Simonius takes a different view.—ἀλλ᾽ ἐπί, *but in*) illustrating the wonder-

---

[1] BD (Λ) G*fg* Syr. later, place εἴτε παρακαλούμεθα ὑπὲρ τῆς ὑμῶν παρακλήσεως καὶ σωτηρίας after ὑπὲρ ὑμῶν, and before εἰδότες. AC Vulg. Syr. Memph. omit καὶ σωτηρίας, (Many MSS. of Vulg. have the *et Salute*), and place the rest of the words before τῆς ἐνεργουμένης. Rec. Text without good authority, places the words before καὶ ἡ ἐλπίς.—ED.

ful nature of faith in the greatest difficulties, which seem to have no means of escape.—ἐγείροντι, *who raiseth*) 1 Cor. xv. He had written at great length on the resurrection of the dead; he now repeatedly touches on the same doctrine, and, taking for granted, that its truth is admitted by the Corinthians, urges its bearing upon their practice.

10. Ρύεται, *delivers*) The present, in respect of this *affliction, i.e. whilst* we are in a state of death, we are delivered.—ἠλπίκαμεν) *we have obtained hope* [*we have trusted*].—ῥύσεται, *He will deliver*) that I may be able to go to you.

11. Συνυπουργούντων, *you helping with*) ὑπουργεῖν is from ἔργον, a *work:* ἔργον, the *work* of effectual help, belongs to God; ὑπουργεῖν, *to help subordinately*, belongs to the apostles; συνυπουργεῖν, *to help subordinately along with*, belongs to the Corinthians.—καὶ) you *also*, not merely others.—[1]ἐκ πολλῶν προσώπων, *in many respects* [But Engl. Vers. "By the means of many *persons*"]) πρόσωπον, *face*, respect [point of view.] *In respect*, viz., of the past, present and future. *He has delivered, delivers, will deliver*. We do not translate it, *of many persons*, for that is included in the words, διὰ πολλῶν, *by many*.—τὸ εἰς ἡμᾶς χάρισμα) *the assistance, which is vouchsafed to us by grace*.—διὰ πολλῶν εὐχαριστηθῇ) *thanksgiving may be given by many*. χάρισμα and εὐχαριστία are correlatives; iv. 15.—ὑπὲρ ὑμῶν,[2] *for you*) Just now he had said, *for us*, in respect of prayers; now, he says, *for you*, in respect of thanksgiving. The fruit redounded to the Corinthians. Nor was it necessary, after εἰς ἡμᾶς, again to say, ὑπὲρ ἡμῶν.[3]

12. Γὰρ, *for*) The connection is: We do not seek in vain and we promise to ourselves the help of God and the prayers of godly men.—καύχησις, *glorying* [*rejoicing*]) even in adversity and against

---

[1] Τῇ δεήσει—εὐχαριστηθῇ, *that thanksgiving might be poured forth by prayer*). He who enjoys the communion of saints, will never want an opportunity for prayer; although he should have nothing remaining in relation to himself, for which he should feel any anxiety—[*i.e.* the concerns of his fellow-saints will always afford him ample subject for prayer and praise.]—V. g.

[2] Therefore the reading ἡμῶν, at the end of the verse, is disapproved by the margin of both Ed., and seems to have slipped inadvertently into the Germ. Ver.—E. B.

[3] All the oldest MSS. and Versions have ἡμῶν. Only a few MSS. of Vulg. have *vobis*.—Ed.

our adversaries.—*τῆς συνειδήσεως ἡμῶν*, *of our conscience*) whatever others may think of us.—*ἁπλότητι*, *in simplicity*) aiming at the one mark in the most direct way.—*εἰλικρινείᾳ*[1]) *in sincerity*, without the admixture of any foreign quality.—*οὐκ ἐν*, *not in*) The antithetic terms are, *fleshly wisdom*, and *the grace of God*, who wisely directs His own people, ver. 17, 18.—*ἐν τῷ κόσμῳ*) *in the world* which is wholly deceitful [as opposed to *godly sincerity and simplicity*.]—*περισσοτέρως*, *more abundantly*) ii. 4.

13. Ἄλλα) *other things*, contrary.—*γράφομεν*, *we write*) in this epistle. He appeals to a present thing.—*ἀναγινώσκετε*, *ye read*) in the former epistle.—*ἢ καί*, *or even*) *ἐπίγνωσις* is more than *ἀνάγνωσις*.—*ἕως τέλους*, *even unto the end*) of my course, comp. ver. 14, at the end, and 1 Cor. iv. 5: whence it is evident that regard to the day of the Lord is not excluded.

14. Ἀπὸ *μέρους*, *in part*) The antithesis, *even unto the end*, is in the preceding verse.

15. Ταύτῃ, *in this*) of which ver. 12 treats at the beginning. —*πρότερον*, *before*) We have frequent mention of this intention in the former epistle; it is construed with *I was minded*.—*δευτέραν χάριν*, *a second benefit*) They had had their first benefit [exhibited by Divine help; ver. 12] at the first visit of Paul: comp. *thy first love*, Rev. ii. 4. He designed a second benefit for them at his second visit. *Grace* is in itself one; but in *being had* [in the *having* of it], there is a first, second grace, etc.: comp. John i. 16. [Of His fulness have all we received, and *grace for grace*.]

16. Προπεμφθῆναι, *to be brought on my way*) to commit myself to you to be escorted [conducted] forward.

17. Τῇ ἐλαφρίᾳ, *lightness*) by promising more than I performed. —*ἤ*) *or*? [*an*? the second part of a disjunctive interrogation].— *κατὰ σάρκα*, *according to the flesh*) Paul gives them to understand that, if he were to consult according to [to listen to the sugges-

---

[1] The 2d Ed. prefers the reading *εἰλικρινείᾳ Θεοῦ*, which was left doubtful by the earlier Ed., and it is received without hesitation by the Germ. Ver. Ernesti interprets the *sincerity of* God to be, *such as* God *desires and approves*. Heumann, to be, *such as* God *Himself works and produces*.—See Bibl. th. T. II. p. 495.—E. B.

ABCD (Λ) have the *τοῦ* before *Θεοῦ*. Rec. Text, with G and Origen., omit *τοῦ*. Ἁγιότητι is the reading of ABC Memph. Origen. But *ἁπλότητι* of D (Λ) G*fg* Vulg.—Ed.

tions of] the flesh, he must rather have come, than not; for they who consult according to the flesh, endeavour by all means to make the *yea* of the promise, whatever may occur, to appear in the fulfilment, for the purpose of maintaining their consistency [*whether good or evil may result* from it.—V. g.] But the Apostle was neither inconsistent, nor carnally consistent: either of which might have been suspected by persons under the influence of prejudice against him. He had made a conditional promise, and afterwards he delayed his visit for an important reason, which had occurred to prevent it.—τὸ ναὶ καὶ τὸ οὔ) See App. Crit. Ed. ii. on this passage. Simple *yea and nay*[1] is quite approved of by Paul in the following verse, in which he denies the *yea and nay*, concerning the same things; but he affirms it, ver. 17, concerning different things. The word ἤ, *should be*, is emphatic; as it may be said, for example, of an unsteady [inconsistent] person. *You can never be sure of finding either his* " It is," *or his* " it is not," *to be as he says*—that is, no one can trust his word; or as if it were to be said of a consistent man, *His* " It is," *and his* " It is not," always hold good.

18. Πιστὸς, *faithful*) The categorical statement implied is this, " Our doctrine is sure." The mode [or *expression of feeling*, as opposed to a naked, categorical statement, see Append. on *modalis sermo*], however, is added: *God* is *faithful*, נאמן: comp. *amen*, ver. 20.—δὲ, *but*) The antithesis is between his intention of travelling to see them, and the doctrine itself. The external change of that intention for good reasons infers no inconsistency in the doctrine. In the mean time, Paul shows, that those who are light [fickle] in external matters are wont to be, and to appear to be, light also in things spiritual.—πρὸς) *with*, to; with (towards) *you*, is an antithesis to *with me*, ver. 17.—οὐκ ἐγένετο ναὶ καὶ οὔ, *was not made yea and nay*) Contradictories have no place in Theology.

---

[1] Although this reading is declared to be not quite so good in the margin of 2d Ed., yet, with the previous concurrence of the Gnomon, it is introduced into the Germ. Ver.—E. B.

All the old authorities, excepting the Vulgate, support the *double* ναὶ and οὔ; even the Fuld. MS. of the Vulg. as corrected by Victor of Capua, has " Est, est, non, non," and so agrees with the weightiest authorities (est, est = ναὶ, ναὶ; non, non = οὔ, οὔ.)—ED.

19. Ὁ γὰρ τοῦ Θεοῦ υἱὸς, Ἰησοῦς Χριστὸς, *for the Son of God, Jesus Christ*) who is the principal subject of our discourse. We should observe the joining together of the three appellations, thereby showing forth firmness;[1] as also their position in the natural order; for the first is evidently not the same as the third.—καὶ Σιλουανοῦ, *and Silvanus*) Luke calls him Silas; Acts xv. 22 note.—ἀλλὰ ναὶ) *but yea* pure and unmixed, on our part and yours.—ἐν αὐτῷ, *in Himself*) *Christ preached, i.e.* our preaching of Christ became *yea in* Christ *Himself*. So the reason assigned [aetiologia, see Append.] in the following verse is in consonance. All the promises in Christ are *yea*. Therefore truly also the testimony concerning Christ Himself is *yea* in Christ.

20. Ἐπαγγελίαι) *promises*, declarations.—τὸ ναὶ—τὸ ἀμὴν, *yea—amen*) The words *yea* and *amen* agreeing together, stand in pleasant antithesis to the words *yea* and *nay*, ver. 19, which are at variance with each other: *yea* by affirmation; *amen*, by an oath; or *yea* in respect of the Greeks; *amen* in respect of the Jews; comp. Gal. iv. 6 note; for *yea* is Greek, *amen* is Hebrew; or *yea*, in respect of God who promises, *amen* in respect of believers; comp. 1 John ii. 8; *yea* in respect of the apostles, *amen* in respect of their hearers.—τῷ Θεῷ πρὸς δόξαν [*to the glory of God*] to God for His glory) For the truth of God is glorified in all His promises, which are verified in Christ.—πρὸς δόξαν, *to the glory*) iv. 15.—δι' ἡμῶν, *by us*) construed with *there is*, again to be understood. *For whatever* may be the *number of* [as many soever as are] *the promises of God*, there is in Him the *Yea*, and in Him the *Amen* [every promise has its *yea* and *amen, i.e.* its fulfilment in Him]. *To the glory of God* (is that *Yea* and *Amen*) by us. The *yea* is re-echoed by us.

21. Ὁ δὲ βεβαιῶν, *now He who confirmeth* [*establisheth*]) The Son glorifies the Father, ver. 19: *whilst* [*autem, δὲ*] the Father in turn glorifies the Son.—βέβαιῶν, *confirming*) that we may be firm in the faith of Christ. The term *sealing* corresponds to this word; the one is from Christ and His anointing; the other from the Spirit, as an earnest. That *is sealed*, which is confirmed as the property of some one, whether it be a property

---

[1] For "union is strength."—ED.

purchased, or a letter, so that it may be certain, to whom it belongs; comp. 1 Cor. ix. 2. A trope[1] abstracts from the persons and things from which it is taken.—ἡμᾶς, *us*) apostles and teachers.—σὺν ὑμῖν, *with you*) He speaks modestly of himself.—εἰς Χριστὸν καὶ χρίσας, *in* [*into*] *Christ, and hath anointed*) Conjugate words. From the *oil* here, we derive *strength*, and a *good savour*, ii. 15. All things tend to the *yea;* εἰς Χριστὸν, in faith *in* [towards] *Christ*.

22. Ἀῤῥαβῶνα, *earnest*) ch. v. 5. ἀῤῥαβὼν, Gen. xxxviii. 17, 18, is used for a *pledge*, which is given up at the payment of a debt; but elsewhere for *earnest money*, which is given beforehand, that an assurance may be afforded as to the subsequent full performance of the bargain. Hesychius, ἀῤῥαβὼν, πρόδομα. *For the earnest*, says Isid. Hispal., *is to be completed* [*by paying the balance in full*] *not to be taken away: whence he who has an earnest does not restore it as a pledge, but requires the completion of the payment.* Such an *earnest* is the Spirit Himself, Eph. i. 14: whence also we are said to have *the first fruits of the Spirit*, Rom. viii. 23. See *Rittershusii*, lib. 7, sacr. lect. c. 19.

23. Ἐγὼ δὲ, *but I*) The particle *but* forms an antithesis: *I was minded to come, but I have not yet come.*—τὸν Θεὸν, *God*) the omniscient.—ἐπικαλοῦμαι, *I call upon*) The apostle makes oath. —ἐπὶ, *upon*) a weighty expression.—ψυχὴν, *soul*) in which I am conscious of all that passes within myself, and which I would not wish to be destroyed.—φειδόμενος, *sparing*) a term of large meaning; therefore it is presently after explained: He is able *to spare*, who has dominion; he also spares, who causes joy rather than sorrow. It confirms this force of the [in his] explanation, in that he says, *not for that*[2] *we have dominion:* not, *seeing that we have not* [*i.e.* because we have not] *dominion.*—εἰς Κόρινθον, *to Corinth*) This is elegantly used for *to you*, in using words showing his *power*. If face to face with them, he would have had to act with greater sternness:[3] for his presence would have been more severe. Comp. Exod. xxxiii. 3; Hos. xi. 9. Therefore the apostle had sent Titus before him.

24. Κυριεύομεν, *we have dominion*) It would have been a

---

[1] See Append., on *tropus*.   [2] On the ground that.   [3] 2 Cor. x. 10, 11.

serious matter for the apostle to have used even his lawful authority; and therefore he calls it *to have* [exercise] *dominion;* comp. 1 Cor. ix. 17, note, respecting such a mode of speaking.—τῆς πίστεως, *over the faith*) The faithful are free men.—συνεργοί, *fellow-workers*) not *lords.*—χαρᾶς, *of joy*) which flows from *faith,* Phil. i. 25. The antithesis *sorrow,* ii. 1, 2.—τῇ πίστει, *by faith*) Rom. xi. 20.—ἑστήκατε, *ye stand*) Ye have not fallen, although there was danger of it.

CHAPTER II.

1. Ἔκρινα δὲ ἐμαυτῷ, *But I determined for myself*) so far as I myself am concerned, for my own advantage. The antithesis is, *to you* in this ver.: comp. i. 23.—δὲ, *but*) This is an antithesis to *not as yet,* i. 23.—πάλιν, *again*) This is construed with *come;* not with, *come in heaviness (sorrow)*: he had formerly written *in heaviness,* he had not come.—ἐν λύπῃ, *in heaviness* (sorrow) twofold; for there follows, *for if I make you sorry,* and, *if any one have caused grief* [sorrow, ver. 5.] This repetition (anaphora[1]) forms two antithetic parts, the discussion of which elegantly corresponds to each respectively, *I wrote that you might know* [ver. 4]; *I wrote that I might know,* ver. 9; [the joy] *of you all;* [overcharge] *you all,* ver. 3. 5.

2. Λυπῶ, *I make you sorry*) either when present with you, or by letters.—καὶ τίς ἐστι, *and who is*) The *if* has an apodosis consisting of two numbers, *and who* [καὶ τίς], *and I wrote* [καὶ ἔγραψα]: *both, and,* i.e. as well, as also.—εὐφραίνων με, *that maketh me glad*) by the sorrow of repentance.—εἰ μὴ, *unless*) It affords me no pleasure to have struck with sorrow by my reproofs the man, who now gives me joy by his repentance. I would rather it had not been necessary.—ὁ λυπούμενος, *he, who is made sorry*) He indicates the Corinthians, but more especially him who had sinned.—ἐξ ἐμοῦ,

---

[1] See Append. The frequent repetition of the same word to mark the beginnings of sections.

by me) ἀφ' ὧν, *from whom*, in the following verse. These particles differ thus: ἀπὸ [coming *from*, or on the part of] applies to something more at large; ἐξ [*out of*, by means of], to something more within; comp. iii. 5; 1 Thess. ii. 6.

3. Καὶ ἔγραψα, *and I wrote*) He shows that he had this intention at the time, when he sent his first epistle, in which he had promised a visit, an intention which he explains at ver. 1.—ἀφ' ὧν, *from whom*) as from sons.—ὅτι, *that*) The joy of Paul itself is desirable not for his own sake, but for the sake of the Corinthians.

4. Ἐκ γὰρ, *for out of*) I wished to stir you up before I went to you, that afterwards it might not be necessary. *Anguish of heart* produced tears, *much anguish* produced *many tears*. The Corinthians might have seen the marks of tears on his letter, if he himself wrote it—a proof of anguish.—οὐ ἵνα), *not so much that*, etc. The fruit of sorrow is not sorrow, but the fruit of love is love.—λυπηθῆτε, *you should be grieved*) He is easily made sorry, who is admonished by a friend himself weeping.—τὴν ἀγάπην, *love*) The source of sincere reproof and of joy derived from it.— γνῶτε, *you might know*) according to my faithful admonition.— περισσοτέρως εἰς ὑμᾶς, *more abundantly to you*) who have been particularly commended to me by God, Acts xviii. 10.

5. Τίς, *any*) He now speaks mildly; *any one* and *any thing*, ver. 10. In both epistles Paul refrained from mentioning the name of him, of whom he is speaking.—οὐκ ἐμὲ λελύπηκεν, *he hath not grieved me*) *i.e.*, He has not made me lastingly grieved [I am not now so disposed towards him] ἀλλ' ἀπὸ μέρους, *only in part*) he has occasioned me sorrow.—ἐπιβαρῶ, *be heavy upon* [*overcharge*]) a weightier expression, than *I make sorry*, ver. 2.

6. Ἱκανὸν) Neuter, in place of a substantive; *it is sufficient for such a one*, so that no more can be demanded of him: ἱκανὸν, a forensic term. It is the part of Christian prudence to maintain moderation. A considerably long time intervened between the writing of the two epistles.—ἐπιτιμία, *reproof*) In antithesis to *forgive*, as also, to *comfort*, ver. 7.—τῶν πλειόνων, *by many*) not merely by those, who ruled [the bishops and ministers.] The Church at large bears the keys.

7. Χαρίσασθαι) This word has the meaning of an indicative,

whence he is rather forgiven; and the indicative is a very mild form of exhortation : xii. 9 ; Matt. xxvi. 18, note.

8. Κυρῶσαι, *to confirm*) the κῦρος is connected with love, not with sorrow. The majesty of the ecclesiastical government and discipline consists in love. It is this, which reigns. םק, LXX., κυροῦσθαι, Gen. xxiii. 20 ; Lev. xxv. 30.

9. Καὶ ἔγραψα) not only I write, but *I also did write.*—τὴν δοκιμὴν, *the proof*) whether you are genuine, loving, obedient sons.[1]—εἰς πάντα, *in all things*) in *reproof* [ver. 6], and in *love.*

10. Τὶ, *any thing*) He speaks very gently of the atrocious, but acknowledged sin.—χαρίζεσθε, *ye forgive*) He has no doubt, but that they will do what he wrote at ver. 7.—καὶ ἐγὼ, *I also*) He modestly subscribes assent to the act of the Corinthians, and regards himself, as it were in the same category with them.—εἴ τι κεχάρισμαι, *if I forgave any thing*) The matter is limited by *if any thing,* in order that Paul may show his willingness to follow up the forgiveness granted to the sinner by the Corinthians. From the present *I forgive,* the past immediately results, *I have forgiven,* while Paul is in the act of writing these things.—δι' ὑμᾶς, *for your sakes*) namely, *I forgave.*—ἐν προσώπῳ Χριστοῦ, *in the presence* [but Engl. Vers., *person*] *of Christ*) in the face of [before] Christ, 1 Cor. v. 4.—ἵνα μὴ πλεονεκτηθῶμεν, *lest we should be defrauded* [lest an advantage be gained over us.]) The loss of a single sinner is a common loss ; therefore he said *for your sakes.*—ὑπὸ τοῦ Σατανᾶ, *by Satan*) to whom Paul delivered or was about to deliver the sinner ; 1 Cor. v. 5. Satan not only *devised* to destroy the flesh, but the soul : and he seeks an opportunity of doing a very great injury by means of *sorrow.*

11. Οὐ γὰρ, *for not*) True ecclesiastical prudence. Those who have the *mind* [referring to νοῦς contained in νοήματα] of Christ are not ignorant of hostile *devices* and attempts. νοήματα and ἀγνοεῖν are conjugates.

12. Καὶ) *even* although [Engl. Ver., *and*]. Paul would have willingly abode at Troas.—θύρας, *a door*) Nevertheless Paul did not sin, in departing, inasmuch as it remained free to him to do so.—ἄνεσιν, *rest*) His spirit first began to feel the want of it, then

---
[1] See Tit. i. 4.

the flesh, vii. 5. He was desirous of knowing how the Corinthians had received his former epistle.—τῷ πνεύματι, *in spirit*) He perceived from this, that it was not imperatively necessary to avail himself of that *door*.—Τίτον, *Titus*) who was about to come from you.

13. Εἰς Μακεδονίαν, *to Macedonia*) where I would be nearer and might be sooner informed [*what was the fruit of my former epistle to you*.—V. g.]—These topics are continued at vii. 2, 5: and a most noble digression is here introduced in respect to events, which had in the meantime occurred and sufferings which had been endured by him elsewhere: the benefit of which he makes to flow even towards the Corinthians, whilst he hereby prepares the way for a defence against the false apostles.

14. Τῷ δὲ Θεῷ, *but* [*now*] *to God*) Although I have not come to Corinth, I did not remain at Troas; nevertheless there is no want of the victory of the Gospel even in other places: The modal expression is added [Append. on *Modus, i.e.* with expression of feeling, not a mere categorical proposition]; *Thanks be unto God*. —πάντοτε, *always*) The parallel follows, *in every place*.—θριαμβεύοντι ἡμᾶς) *who shows us in triumph*, not as conquered, but as the ministers of His victory; not only the victory, but the open 'showing' of the victory is denoted: for there follows, *Who maketh manifest*. The *triumph* forcibly strikes the eyes; the *savour*, the nostrils [sense of smell.]—τὴν ὀσμὴν, *the savour*) The metaphor is taken from all the senses to describe the power of the Gospel. Here *the sight* (of the triumph) and its *savour* occur. —αὐτοῦ, *of Him*) of Christ, ver. 15.—φανεροῦντι, *who maketh manifest*) a word, which often occurs in this epistle, and refutes the suspicions of the Corinthians [towards the apostle.] So 1 Cor. iv. 5.

15. Εὐωδία) *a sweet savour, i.e.*, powerful, grateful to the godly, offensive to the ungodly. The savour of Christ pervades us, as the odour of aromatics pervades garments.—ἐν) *in the case of*.— σωζομένοις· ἀπολλυμένοις, *in them, who are saved; in them, who perish*) To which class each may belong, is evident from the manner in which he receives the Gospel. Of the former class he treats, iii. 1–iv. 2; of the latter, iv. 3–6.—ἀπολλυμένοις, *in them that are perishing*) iv. 3.

16. Ὀσμὴ θανάτου, *the savour of death*) They reckon us [and

our Gospel message] as a thing dead; hence they meet with death as the natural and just consequence.—οἷς δὲ, *whilst to the former*) who are being saved. This verse, if we compare the antecedents and consequents, has a chiasmus.[1]—καὶ πρὸς ταῦτα τίς ἱκανός; *and who is sufficient for these things?*) Who? *i.e.* but few, viz., we. This sentiment [idea] is modestly hinted at, and is left to be perceived and acknowledged by the Corinthians; comp. the next verse. Paul asserts at considerable length both his own *sufficiency* (ἱκανότητα) and that of the few in the following chapter, and repeats this very word, ver. 5, 6, of that ch., so that his adversaries seem either expressly or in sense [virtually] to have denied, that Paul was *sufficient*.

17. Οἱ πολλοί, *the many*) so xi. 18. הָרַבִּים, 1 Kings xviii. 25. The article has force; *the many*, most men, ἄοσμοι, *void of savour:* comp. Phil. ii. 21.—καπηλεύοντες [cauponantes]) *corrupting* [adulterating for gain]; men who do not make it their aim to show forth as much virtue [as much of the power of the Gospel] as possible, but to make gain by it. These men speak of Christ, but not as "from [of] God," and "in the sight of God." κάπηλοι, [caupones], *vintners*, select their merchandise from different quarters; they adulterate it; they manage it with a view to profit. The apostles deal otherwise with the word of God; for they speak *as of God*, and *as of sincerity*, and so as to approve themselves unto God. δολοῦντες, *adulterating*, iv. 2 [Engl. Vers., *handling deceitfully*], is a synonymous expression, and also ἐμπορεύεσθαι, *to make merchandise of*, 2 Pet. ii. 3.—ἐξ εἰλικρινείας, *of sincerity*) We give our whole attention to [our whole aim is] the word of God by itself.—ἀλλ' ὡς ἐκ, *but as of*) a gradation [ascending climax], *but* being repeated; *as* is explanatory.[2]—κατενώπιον—λαλοῦμεν, *in the sight of God—we speak*) So decidedly, ch. xii. 19. We always think, that God, from [sent by] whom we speak, is present to the speakers; we do not care for men.—

---

[1] See App.
[2] The Germ. Ver., however, omits both the particle ὡς before ἐξ εἰλικρινείας and the particle ἀλλ' before ὡς ἐκ Θεοῦ, although the omission has by no means been approved of by the margins of both Ed.—E. B.

ABCD (Λ) read the ὡς after ἀλλ' (or ἀλλὰ in B), in the first ἀλλ' ὡς: G*fg* Vulg. Memph. Iren. omit it. In the second ἀλλ' ὡς, ABCD (Λ) support the ἀλλ'. G*fg* Vulg. (Fuld.), later Syr. Iren. omit it.—ED.

ἐν, *in*) Our discourse, which we hold *in* Christ, is given and directed from above.—λαλοῦμεν, *we speak*) We use the tongue the power belongs to God.

CHAPTER III.

1. Ἀρχόμεθα, *do we begin?*) A just reproof to *some* of those who *had so begun*.—πάλιν, *again*) as was formerly done in the first epistle; so, *again*, ch. v. 12.—συνιστάνειν, *to commend*) after the manner of men; xii. 19, by mentioning transactions that took place elsewhere.—εἰ μή) *unless*. A particle expressive of conciliation [*morata*]. Is it thus and thus only that we are equal to the task of commending ourselves [*i.e.*, by mentioning transactions that took place elsewhere], *if* we do *not* need [without needing] also letters? Some read ἤ.[1]—τινές, *some*) of many, ii. 17. In this respect also, he shows that he utterly differs from the false apostles. They *did need* letters of recommendation.—ἐξ ὑμῶν, *from you*) to others. This then was the practice at Corinth.

2. Ἐν ταῖς καρδίαις ἡμῶν, *in our hearts*) Your faith was written in our heart, in which we carry about it and yourselves—a faith everywhere to be known and read. It was reflected from the heart of the Corinthians to the heart of the apostle.—πάντων, *by all men*) by you and others. This is an argument for the truth of the Gospel, obvious to all, to be derived from believers themselves [iv. 2; 1 Cor. xiv. 25].

3. Φανερούμενοι, *manifested*) construed with ὑμεῖς, *ye*, ver. 2. The reason assigned [aetiologia, see Append.] why this epistle may be read.—Χριστοῦ—ὑφ' ἡμῶν, *of Christ—by us*) This explains the word *our*, ver. 2. Christ is the author of the epistle.—διακονηθεῖσα) The verb διακονέω, has often the accusative of the thing, viii. 19, 20; 2 Tim. i. 18; 1 Pet. i. 12, iv. 10. So Paeanius, τὴν μάχην διακονούμενος, *directing the battle*, b. 7, Metaphr.

---

[1] So CD(Λ)G*fg* Vulg. ("aut numquid"). But AB (judging from silence acc. to Tisch: But Lachm. quotes B for ἤ) read εἰ μή as Rec. Text.—ED.

Eutr. The apostles, *as ministers*, διηκόνουν, *presented* the epistle. Christ, by their instrumentality, brought spiritual light to bear on the tablets of the hearts of the Corinthians, as a scribe applies ink to paper. Not merely *ink*, but parchment or paper and a pen are necessary for writing a letter; but Paul mentions ink without paper and a pen, and it is therefore a synecdoche [*one* material of writing put for *all*. See Append.] Τὸ μέλαν does not exactly mean ink, but any black substance, for example, even charcoal, by which an inscription may be made upon stone. The mode of writing of every kind, which is done by ink and a pen, is the same as that of the Decalogue, which was engraved on tables of stone. Letters were engraved on stone, as a dark letter is written on paper. The hearts of the Corinthians are here intended; for Paul was as it were the style or pen.—οὐ μέλανι, *not with ink*) A synecdoche [ink for any means of writing]; for the tables in the hands of Moses, divinely inscribed without ink, were at least material substances.— ζῶντος, *of the living*) comp. ver. 6, 7.—λιθίναις, *of stone*) ver. 7.— πλαξὶ καρδίας σαρκίναις, *in fleshly tables of the heart*) Tables of the heart are a genus; *fleshly tables*, a species; for every heart is not of flesh.

4. Πεποίθησιν, *trust*) by which we both determine and profess to be such as are here described. The antithesis is, *to faint*, iv. 1.—διὰ τοῦ Χριστοῦ, *through Christ*) not through ourselves. This matter is discussed, ver. 14, at the end, and in the following verses.—πρὸς τὸν Θεὸν, *toward God*) This is discussed, ver. 6, and in the following verses.

5. [1] Λογίσασθαι, *to devise* [*to think*]) to obtain by thinking, much less to speak or perform. There seems to be here something of a mimesis [allusion to the words of the persons whom he refutes. Append.] For they do not think, whom God moves: *i.e.*, they frame or work out nothing by their own thinking, 2 Pet. i. 21.—τὶ) *anything*; even the least thing.

6. Καὶ, *also*) An emphatic addition [to the previous assertion. Epitasis. Append.] He has given *sufficiency* to us, even the *sufficiency* of ministers of the New Testament, which demands

---

[1] Ἐσμέν, *we are*) even yet at this very hour.—V g.

much more in order to realize it [than ordinary sufficiency].—
ἡμᾶς διακόνους, us ministers) Apposition.—καινῆς, new) An antithesis to old, ver. 14.—οὐ, not) of the New Testament, i.e., not of the letter, but of the spirit, see Rom. vii. 6, and the following verses, with the annot.—γράμματος, of the letter) Even while Paul *wrote* these things, he was the minister not of the letter, but of the *spirit*. Moses in that his peculiar office, even when he did not write, was yet employed about the letter.—πνεύματος, of the Spirit) whose *ministry* has both greater glory, and requires greater *ability* [sufficiency].—ἀποκτείνει, kills): the letter rouses the sinner to a sense of death; for if the sinner had life, before the letter came, there would have been no need of quickening by the Spirit. With this comp. the following verse, *of death*.

7. Ἡ διακονία, the ministry) which Moses performed.—ἐντετυπωμένη) LXX. κεκολαμμένη, Ex. xxxii. 10.—λίθοις, in stones) There were then two different tables, not of one stone. Ex. xxxiv. 1 : engraven in stones, is an explanation of this clause, in letters.[1]—ἐγενήθη ἐν δόξᾳ, obtained glory [was glorious]) γίνομαι, I become, and εἰμί, I am [ἔσται], ver. 8, are different.—μὴ δύνασθαι ἀτενίσαι) Ex. xxxiv. 30, ἐφοβήθησαν ἐγγίσαι αὐτῷ.—Μωϋσέως, of Moses) engaged in the duties of his office.

8. Ἔσται) shall be. He speaks as looking from the Old Testament point of view to the New. Add, hope, ver. 12 [which similarly looks from the Old Testament stand-point to the New].

9. Κατακρίσεως· δικαιοσύνης, of condemnation; of righteousness) The glory of God shines back more brightly by the latter, than by the former. The letter *condemns*; *condemnation* imposes death as the punishment. The Spirit, along with righteousness, brings life.—δόξα, glory) The abstract for the concrete, for the sake of brevity.

10. Οὐδὲ δεδόξασται, was not even glorified [had no glory]) The limitation immediately follows, in this respect. The greater

---

[1] ἐν γράμμασιν, in letters. Eng. Ver. written, etc., at the beginning of ver. 7.
So AC, and acc. to Lachm. G (but Tisch. makes G support γράμματι) *fg* Vulg. Orig. 1, 708*f* : 3, 498*c* : 4, 448*a*. But B and D(Λ) corrected later. γράμματι.—ED.

light obscures the less.—τὸ δεδοξασμένον, *that which was glorified*) So LXX., Ex. xxxiv. 29, 35, קָרַן, δεδόξασται.

11. Διὰ δόξης· ἐν δόξῃ, *marked by glory; in glory*) The particles are properly varied [the distinction is lost in Engl. Vers., *glorious* —*glorious*]. Supply *is*.—τὸ μένον, *that which remains*) The διακονία, *ministry*, itself, does not remain any more than whatever is *in part* [as for instance, *knowledge*], 1 Cor. xiii. 10; but the Spirit, righteousness, life remain; therefore the neuter gender is used.

12. Ἐλπίδα, *hope*) He spoke of *trust*, ver. 4; he now speaks of *hope*, as he glances at that *which remaineth*, ver. 11.— παρρησίᾳ) *a plain and open manner of dealing*.

13. Καὶ οὐ, *and not*) supply *we are*, or *we do*.—κάλυμμα, *a veil*) so LXX., Exod. xxxiv. 33.—πρὸς τὸ μὴ) πρὸς [*according as, because that*] denotes congruity. Comp. Matt. xix. 8: [πρὸς τὴν σκληροκαρδίαν, *by reason of, because of* the hardness of heart, by reason of the fact]: for τὸ μὴ ἀτενίσαι, *the not being able to look stedfastly*, took place before the veil was put on, but subsequent to the splendour of Moses ["the glory of his countenance"], ver. 7: wherefore, there, ὥστε is used [because their not being able to look stedfastly at him was subsequent to and *the consequence of* his glory.] What is affirmed of Moses is wholly denied by Paul respecting the ministers of the New Testament, namely, *the putting on of a veil, lest the Israelites should look upon them*. Often something is inserted in the protasis, which in the proper application is intended to belong to the apodosis. So in ver. 7 we have ὥστε μὴ δύνασθαι ἀτενίσαι; here, πρὸς τὸ μὴ ἀτενίσαι. Here to wit the act is denied, not the power. The power was wanting to all [the Israelites] in the case of Moses; to some [viz. to them that are lost, iv. 3] in the case of the apostles.—εἰς τὸ τέλος τοῦ καταργουμένου, *to the end of that which is abolished*) Paul turns the words to an allegory. *That, which is abolished*, has its end in Christ, ver. 14, at the end: Rom. x. 4, the law tends to and is terminated in Him, [Christ].

14. Ἀλλ' ἐπωρώθη, *but were hardened*) *but* is opposed to the phrase *to look stedfastly*.—τὸ αὐτὸ) *the same*, as in the time of Moses.—ἐπί, *upon*) i.e. *when they read*, and *although they read*.— ἀναγνώσει, *reading*) public, frequent, perpetual. Paul makes a

limitation. The veil is not now on the face of Moses, or on his writings; but on *the reading*, while they read Moses, and that too in such a way as not to admit Christ; it is also *upon their heart*, ver. 15.—μένει, μὴ ἀνακαλυπτόμενον) *remains* lying upon them, so that it is not indeed *taken away* [*so that* the veil *is not even lifted off*].—ὅτι, *because* it is not *done away*, save *in Christ*. [But Engl. Ver. "*which* veil is done away in Christ."]— This is a statement introductory to the things which follow.— καταργεῖται, *is abolished* [done away]) *the Old Testament;* comp. ver. 7, 11, 13. He does not say, *has been abolished,* but *is being abolished* in respect of those, that are about " to turn to the Lord."

15. 'Aλλ' ἕως, *but until*) *But* is opposed to the phrase *is not taken away*.—ἡνίκα) This is the only place, in which Paul uses this adverb. It seems to have readily occurred from his recent reading of the LXX., Ex. xxxiv. 33.—ἀναγινώσκεται Μωϋσῆς, *Moses is read*) and that too, studiously, without seeing Christ therein. The antithesis follows, *but when it shall have turned* to the Lord.

16. 'Ηνίκα δ' ἂν—περιαιρεῖται τὸ κάλυμμα, *but when the veil is taken away*) This is a paraphrase on Ex. xxxiv. 34, ἡνίκα δ'ἂν εἰσεπορεύετο Μωϋσῆς ἔναντι Κυρίου λαλεῖν αὐτῷ περιῃρεῖτο τὸ κάλυμμα. *But when Moses went in before the Lord to speak to Him, the veil was taken away.* Therefore ἡνίκα, meaning not *if*, but *when*, evidently affirms, as in the preceding verse, and frequently in the LXX., ἡνίκα ἐάν, ἡνίκα ἄν, Gen. xxiv. 41, xxvii. 40; Ex. i. 10, xxxiv. 24; Lev. vi. 4, x. 9; Deut. xxv. 19. ἡνίκα δ' ἄν, Ex. xxxiii. 8, 22, xl. 36.—ἐπιστρέψῃ, *shall be turned*) namely *their heart*. The truth is acknowledged by repentance, 2 Tim. ii. 25. The method, not of disputation, but of conversion, is to be applied to the Jews.—πρὸς Κυρίον, *to the Lord*) Christ, ver. 14. A distinguished appellation, iv. 5.—περιαιρεῖται) περιαιροῦμαι is passive, Acts xxvii. 20, and in the LXX., Lev. iv. 31, 35; but middle. very often in the LXX., and that too in the very passage to which Paul refers. The antithesis of ver. 15 and 16 shows, however, that here the signification is passive. *The veil lies* [κεῖται, ver. 15]; *the veil is taken away.* The present, *is* [that moment, and by that very fact] *taken away*, is emphatic [not as Engl. *shall be taken away.*]

17. Ὁ δὲ Κύριος τὸ πνεῦμά ἐστιν, *but the Lord is that Spirit*) *The Lord* is the subject. Christ is not the letter, but He is the Spirit and the *end of the law*. A sublime announcement: comp. Phil. i. 21; Gal. iii. 16. The particle *but*, or *now*, shows that the preceding is explained by this verse. The *turning* (conversion) takes place [is made] to the Lord, as the Spirit.— οὗ δὲ τὸ πνεῦμα Κυρίου, *and where the Spirit of the Lord is*) Where Christ is, there the Spirit of Christ is; where the Spirit of Christ is, there Christ is; Rom. viii. 9, 10. Where Christ and His Spirit are, there is liberty: John viii. 36; Gal. iv. 6, 7.— ἐκεῖ) *there*, and there only.—ἐλευθερία) *liberty*, opposed to the *veil*, the badge of slavery: *liberty*, without such fear in looking, as the children of Israel had, Ex. xxxiv. 30.

18. Ἡμεῖς δὲ πάντες, *but we all*) *we all*, the ministers of the New Testament, in antithesis to Moses, who was but one person.— ἀνακεκαλυμμένῳ προσώπῳ) our *face being unveiled* with regard to men; for in regard to God, not even Moses' face was veiled. The antithesis is *hid*, iv. 3.—τὴν δόξαν, *the glory*) divine majesty.— Κυρίου, *of the Lord*) Christ.—κατοπτριζόμενοι) The Lord *makes us mirrors*, κατοπτρίζει, puts the *brightness* of His face into our hearts *as into mirrors:* we receive and reflect that brightness. An elegant antithesis to ἐντετυπωμένη, engraved [ver. 7, *the ministration of death*—the law—*engraven on stones*] : for things which *are engraven* become so by a gradual process, the *images* which are *reflected* in a mirror are produced with the utmost celerity.— τὴν αὐτήν) *the same*, although we are many. The same expression [lively reproduction] of the glory of Christ in so many believers, is the characteristic mark of truth.—εἰκόνα, *the image*) *of the Lord*, which is all glorious.—μεταμορφούμεθα, *we are transformed*) The Lord *forms* by quick writing (ver. 3) His image in us; even as Moses reflected the glory of God. The passive retains the accusative; as in the phrase, διδάσκομαι υἱόν. —ἀπὸ δόξης εἰς δόξαν, *from glory to glory*) from the glory of the Lord to glory in us. The Israelites had not been transformed from the glory of Moses into a similar glory; for they were under the letter.—καθάπερ, *even as*) an adverb of likeness: comp. ver. 13. *As* the Lord impresses Himself on us, so He is expressed to the life by us. He Himself is the model; we are the copies [images].—ἀπὸ Κυρίου πνεύματος) *from* [by] *the*

Lord's (viz. Christ's, ver. 14) *Spirit*. This refers to ver. 17, but *where the Spirit of the Lord*, etc. If there were an apposition Paul would have said, ἀπὸ Κυρίου τοῦ πνεύματος. Elsewhere *the Spirit of the Lord* is the mode of expression; but here *the Lord's Spirit*, emphatically. Ἀπὸ is used as in i. 2, and often in other places.

CHAPTER IV.

1. Τὴν διακονίαν ταύτην, *this ministry*) of which iii. 6, etc.—καθὼς ἠλεήθημεν, *as we have received mercy*) The mercy of God, by which the *ministry* is received, makes men active and sincere. Even Moses *obtained mercy*, and hence he was permitted to approach so near, Exod. xxxiii. 19.—οὐκ—ἀλλ', *not—but*) A double proposition; the second part is immediately brought under our consideration by chiasmus;[1] the former from ver. 16. Wherefore οὐκ ἐκκακοῦμεν, *we faint not*, is there repeated; we admit of no serious falling off in speaking, in acting, in suffering.

2. Ἀπειπάμεθα) Hesychius: ἀπειπάμεθα, ἀπερριψάμεθα· ἀπείπαντο, παρητήσαντο, ἀπετάξαντο [bid farewell to], *we have renounced*, and wish them to be renounced.—τὰ κρυπτὰ τῆς αἰσχύνης, *the hidden things of shame* [*dishonesty*]) *shame*, having no regard to the glory of the Lord, acts in a *hidden* way: we bid farewell to such a mode of acting (to be discontinued), Rom. i. 16. The antithesis is *by manifestation*, which presently follows, and *we speak*, v. 13. —ἐν πανουργίᾳ, *in craftiness*) This is opposed to *sincerity; craftiness* seeks *hiding-places;* we do not practise it.—μηδὲ δολοῦντες, *not corrupting* [*not handling deceitfully*])—τῇ φανερώσει, *by manifestation*) comp. iii. 3.—τῆς ἀληθείας, *of the truth*) according to the Gospel.—ἑαυτοὺς, *ourselves*) as sincere.—πρὸς) *to*.—πᾶσαν) *all, every*, concerning all things.—συνείδησιν, *conscience*) ch. v. 11; not to carnal judgments; iii. 1, where the carnal *commendation of some* is by implication referred to and stigmatised.

3. Εἰ δὲ, *but if*) precisely the same as in the time of Moses.—καὶ ἔστι, *even is*) *even* strengthens the force of the present tense

[1] See App.

in *is.*—τὸ εὐαγγέλιον, *the Gospel*) which is quite plain in itself.—
ἐν, *in*) so far as it concerns *them*, that perish; so, ἐν ἐμοὶ βάρβαρος,
as far as I am concerned, a barbarian, 1 Cor. xiv. 11.—ἐν τοῖς,
in the case of them) not in itself.—ἀπολλυμένοις, *that perish*)
1 Cor. i. 18.

4. Ἐν οἷς, *as concerns whom*, [*in whom*])—ὁ θεὸς τοῦ αἰῶνος τούτου, *the god of this world*) A great, but awful description of
Satan [*corresponding to his great but awful work, mentioned here*.
—V. g.*]*, comp. Eph. ii. 2, respecting the fact itself: and Phil.
iii. 9, respecting the term. Who would otherwise think, that
he could in the case of men obstruct so great a light [as that
which the Gospel affords]? But there is somewhat of a mimesis;[1]
for those that perish, especially the Jews, think, that they have
God, and know Him. The ancients construed τοῦ αἰῶνος τούτου
with τῶν ἀπίστων, as if it were, *the unbelievers of this world*, in
order that they might give the greater opposition to the Mani-
cheans and the Marcionites.[2]—τοῦ αἰῶνος τούτου, *of this world*)
He says, *of this*, for the devil will not be able always to assail.—
ἐτύφλωσε, *blinded*) not merely *veiled* [ch. iii. 14, 15].—τῶν ἀπίστων,
of them who believe not) An epithet,[3] by supplying the relative
pronoun ἐκείνων, *of them;* for among those, that perish, are chiefly
those, who, though they have heard, do not believe. The *Gospel*
is received by *faith* unto *salvation*.—εἰς τὸ μὴ αὐγάσαι[4]) *lest should
shine*.—τὸν φωτισμὸν τοῦ εὐαγγελίου, κ.τ.λ., *the enlightening* [illumina-
tion] *of the Gospel,* etc.) He afterwards calls it *the enlightening of
the knowledge*, etc.—φωτισμὸς, *enlightening*, is the reflection or
propagation of rays from those, who are enlightened, for the purpose of enlightening more. The *Gospel* and *knowledge* are correlatives, as cause and effect.—τῆς δόξης, *of the glory*) iii. 18,
note.—εἰκὼν τοῦ Θεοῦ, *the image of God*) From this we may sufficiently understand how great is the glory of Christ, v. 6; 1 Tim.

[1] See Append. Allusion to an opponent's words or sentiments.
[2] Both which sects regarded matter as essentially evil and under the
power of the devil, which the rendering, *god of this world,* seemed to sanc-
tion.—ED.
[3] Beng. would make it thus, *The unbelieving lost*, spoken of above.
[4] The Germ. Ver. also exhibits the pronoun αὐτοῖς, which is more highly
esteemed in the margin of the 2d Ed. than in the larger Ed.—E. B.
ABCD corrected, G Vulg. *f* Orig. Iren. omit αὐτοῖς. Except one passage
of Origen there is none of the *oldest* authorities in support of it.—ED.

vi. 15. He, who sees the Son, sees the Father, *in the face* of Christ. The Son exactly represents and reflects the Father.

5. Οὐ, *not*) We do not *commend* ourselves, iii. 1; although they who perish think so.—γάρ, *for*) The fault of their blindness does not lie at our door.—Κυρίον, δούλους, *the Lord; servants*) An antithesis: we do not preach ourselves as masters; comp. i. 24. —δούλους ὑμῶν, *your servants*) Hence Paul is accustomed to prefer the Corinthians to himself, ver. 12, 13.—διὰ 'Ιησοῦν, *for Jesus' sake*) The majesty of Christians is derived from Him.

6. ῞Οτι, *because*) He proves, that they were true *servants*.— ὁ Θεὸς, *God*) *God—to shine*, constitutes the subject; then by supplying *is* (as in Acts iv. 24, 25) the predicate follows, [is He] *who hath shone.*—ὁ εἰπὼν, *He who spake the word*) who commanded by a word LXX., εἶπεν, Gen. i. 3.—ἐκ σκότους φῶς, *light out of darkness*) LXX., Job xxxvii. 15, φῶς ποιήσας ἐκ σκότους. A great work.—ἔλαμψεν, *hath shone*) Himself our Light; not only the author of light, but also its fountain, and Sun.—καρδίαις, *in our hearts*) in themselves dark.—ἐν προσώπῳ[1] 'Ιησοῦ Χριστοῦ, *in the face of Jesus Christ*) Who is the only begotten of the Father and His image, and *was manifested* in the flesh with His glory.

7. Τὸν θησαυρὸν τοῦτον, *this treasure*) described from [beginning with] ii. 14. He now shows, that affliction and death itself, so far from obstructing the ministry of the Spirit, even aid it, and sharpen ministers and increase their fruit.—ὀστρακίνοις, *earthen*) The ancients kept their treasure in *jars*, or *vessels*. There are earthen vessels, which yet may be clean; on the contrary a golden vessel may be filthy.—σκεύεσιν, *vessels*) It is thus he calls the *body*, or the *flesh*, which is subject to affliction and death; see the following verses.—ἡ ὑπερβολὴ τῆς δυνάμεως, *the excellency of the power*) which, consisting as it does in the treasure, exerts itself in us, while we are being saved, and in you, while you are being enriched; ver. 10, 11.—ᾖ, *may be*) may be acknowledged

---

[1] Both the margin of the 2d Ed. and the Germ. Ver. hint that the name 'Ιησοῦ is a doubtful reading; and the same may be said of the reading τοῦ Κυρίου, ver. 10.—E. B.

AB Orig. 1,632f omit 'Ιησοῦ. But C Orig. 4, 448c have it before Χριστοῦ; and D(Λ)Gfg Vulg. have it after Χριστοῦ. ABCDGfy Vulg. Orig. Iren. omit Κυρίου in ver. 10. It is supported only by some later uncial MSS. and later Syr., etc.—ED.

to be, with thanksgiving, ver. 15.—τοῦ Θεοῦ, *of God*) not merely *from God*. God not only bestows *power* once for all, but He is always maintaining it [making it good, ensuring it to His people].

8. Ἐν παντὶ θλιβόμενοι, *while we are troubled in every respect* [*on every side*]) So vii. 5, in *every*, namely, *thing*, and *place*; comp. *always* at ver. 10.—θλιβόμενοι, *while we are troubled*) The four participles in this verse refer to the feelings of the mind; the same number in the following ver. to outward occurrences, vii. 5, [*Without* were fightings; *within* were fears.] They are construed with ἔχομεν, *we have;* and in every member the first clause proves, that the *vessels are earthen*, the latter points out the *excellence of the power*.—οὐ στενοχωρούμενοι, *we are not* [*distressed*] *reduced to straits*) *a way of escape* is never wanting.—ἀπορούμενοι, *we are perplexed*) about the future; as, *we are troubled*, refers to the present.

9. Διωκόμενοι, *persecuted*) καταβαλλόμενοι, *cast down*, is something more [worse] than *persecution*, viz., where flight is not open to one.

10. Πάντοτε, *always*) ἀεὶ in the next verse differs from this word. πάντοτε, *throughout the whole time;* ἀεί, *any time whatever* [at every time]: comp. Mark xv. 8. The words, *bearing about, we are delivered*, in this ver. and in ver. 11 agree.—τὴν νέκρωσιν, *the dying*) This is as it were the act, *life* the habit.—τοῦ Κυρίου, *of the Lord*) This name must be thrice supplied in this and the following verse,[1] and advantageously softens in this first passage the mention of *dying*. It is called the *dying of the Lord*, and the genitive intimates communion, [*joint participation* of Christ and believers in mutual suffering] as i. 5.—Ἰησοῦ, *of Jesus*) Paul employs this name alone [without Χριστοῦ or Κυρίου accompanying it] more frequently in this whole passage, ver. 5, than is his wont elsewhere; therefore here he seems peculiarly to have felt its sweetness.—περιφέροντες, *carrying about*) in all lands.—ἵνα καὶ, *that also*) Consolation here takes an increase. Just before [ver. 8, 9], we had, *but*, four times.—ἐν τῷ σώματι ἡμῶν φανερωθῇ, *in our body might be made manifest*) might be made manifest in *our mortal* [dead] *flesh*, in the next verse. In the one passage

---

[1] Comp. marginal note on ver. 6.—E. B.

the noun, in the other the verb is put first, for the sake of emphasis. In ver. 10, glorification is referred to; in ver. 9, preservation in this life, and strengthening: the word, *our*, is added here [ἐν τῷ σώματι ἡμῶν], rather than at the beginning of the verse [ἐν τῷ σώματι without ἡμῶν.] The body is ours, not so much in death as in life. *May be made manifest* is explained, ver. 14, 17, 18.

11. Οἱ ζῶντες, *we who live*) An Oxymoron; comp. *they who live*, ch. v. 15. The apostle wonders, that he has escaped so many deaths, or even survived others, who have been already slain for the testimony of Christ, for example, Stephen and James. *We who live*, and *death; life*, and *mortal* are respectively antithetic.—παραδιδόμεθα, *we are delivered up*) He elegantly and modestly abstains from mentioning Him, *who delivers up*. Looking from without [extrinsically], the delivering up might seem to be done at random, [whereas it is all ordered by Providence.]

12. Θάνατος, *death*) of the body [*by the corruption* (decay) *of the outward man.*—V. g.]—ζωὴ, *life*) viz., that of the Spirit.

13. Τὸ αὐτὸ) *the same*, which both [*David had and you have*], comp. ver. 14.—κατὰ, *according to*) This word is construed with *we believe* and *we speak.*—ἐπίστευσα, διὸ ἐλάλησα) So LXX., Psa. cxvi. 10, Hebr. ἐπίστευσα, ὅτι λαλήσω. The one meaning is included [involved] in the other. Faith produced in the soul immediately speaks, and in consequence of speaking, it knows itself and increases itself.—λαλοῦμεν, *we speak*) without fear in the midst of affliction and death, ver. 17.

14 Εἰδότες, *knowing*) by great *faith*, ch. v. 1.—παραστήσει, *shall present*) This word places the matter as it were under our eyes [Hypotyposis; a vivid word-picture of some action, Append.]

15. Γὰρ, *for*) The reason, why he just now said, *with you.*—πάντα, *all things*) whether adverse or prosperous.—ἡ χάρις, *grace*) which preserves us, and confirms you in life.—πλεονάσασα·περισσεύσῃ) Πλεονάζω has the force of a positive; περισσεύω, of a comparative, Rom. v. 20. Therefore we must construe διὰ with περισσεύσῃ. πλέον, the same as πλῆρες, is not a comparative.—διὰ) *through* [on account of] the thanksgiving of many, for that grace. Thanksgiving invites more abundant grace, Psa. xviii. 3, 1. 23; 2 Chron. xx. 19, 21, 22.—εὐχαριστίαν *thanksgiving*) ours and yours, ch. i.

3, 4.—περισσεύσῃ,) *may abound to* [*be abundantly vouchsafed*] *us and you, this again tending to the glory of God*.
16. Διὸ οὐκ ἐκκακοῦμεν, *for which cause we faint not*) ver. 1, note.—ὁ ἔξω, *the outward* [*man*]) the body, the flesh.—διαφθείρεται, *be wasted away* [*perish*]) by affliction.—ἀνακαινοῦται, *is renewed*) by hope; see the following verses. This new condition shuts out all κακία, *infirmity* [such as is implied in ἐκκακοῦμεν, *faintness*.]
17. Παραυτίκα, [*but for a moment*]) *just now:* a brief present season is denoted, 1 Pet. i. 6 [ὀλίγον ἄρτι, *a brief season now*.] The antitheses are, *just now*, and *eternal; light*, and *weight: affliction*, and *glory; which is in excessive measure*, and *in an exceeding degree*.—καθ' ὑπερβολὴν, *in excessive measure*) Even that *affliction*, which is καθ' ὑπερβολὴν, *in excessive measure*, when compared with other less afflictions, i. 8, is yet light compared with the glory εἰς ὑπερβολὴν, *in an exceeding degree*. A noble Oxymoron.—κατεργάζεται) *works, procures,* accomplishes.
18. Σκοπούντων) *while we look*, etc. Every one follows that to which he *looks* as his aim [*scopus* from σκοπέω.]—μὴ βλεπόμενα, *things, which are not seen*) The term, ἀόρατα, *things invisible,* [*incapable* of being seen] has a different meaning; for many things, which are not seen [μὴ βλεπόμενα, things *not actually seen now*], will be *visible* [ὁρατά], when the journey of our faith is accomplished.—γὰρ, *for*) This furnishes the reason, why they look at those things, which are not seen.

CHAPTER V.

1. Γὰρ, *for*) A reason given [ætiologia] for this statement, *affliction* leads to *glory* [ch. iv. 17].—ἡ ἐπίγειος) *which is on the earth:* 1 Cor. xv. 47. The antithesis is, *in the heavens*.—ἡμῶν, *our*) The Antithesis is, *of* [*from*] *God*.—οἰκία τοῦ σκήνους, *the house of this tabernacle*) The Antithesis is, *a building, a house not made with hands.* A metaphor taken from his own trade might produce the greater interest in the mind of Paul, who was a *tent-maker* [Acts xviii. 3.]—καταλυθῇ, *were dissolved*) a mild expression. The Antithesis is, *eternal*.—ἔχομεν, *we have*) The present;

2 CORINTHIANS V. 2–6.

straightway from the time of the dissolution of the earthly house.—ἀχειροποίητον) *not made with the hands* of man.

2. Ἐν τούτῳ, *in this*) The same phrase occurs, ch. viii. 10, and elsewhere.—στενάζομεν, *we groan*) The epitasis[1] follows, *we do groan being burdened*, ver. 4.—οἰκητήριον, *a dwelling-place, a domicile*) οἰκία, *a house*, is somewhat more absolute; οἰκητήριον, *a domicile*, has reference to the inhabitant.—τὸ ἐξ οὐρανοῦ) *which is from heaven*: ἐξ here signifies *origin*, as, *of the earth*, John iii. 31. Therefore this domicile (abode) is not heaven itself.—ἐπενδύσασθαι, [to have the clothing put upon us] *to be clothed upon*) It is in the Middle voice: ἔνδυμα, the *clothing*, viz., the body: hence the expression, *being clothed* [ver. 3], refers to those living in the body; ἐπένδυμα, the *clothing upon*, refers to the heavenly and glorious habitation, in which even the body, *the clothing*, will be clothed. As the clothing of grass is its greenness and beauty, Matt. vi. 30, so the heavenly glory is the domicile and clothing of the whole man, when he enters into heaven.

3. Εἴγε καί, *if indeed even* [*if so be*]) That, which is wished for, ver. 2, has place [holds good] should the last day find us alive.—ἐνδυσάμενοι, *being clothed*) We are clothed with the body, ver. 4, in the beginning.—οὐ γυμνοί) *not naked*, in respect to [not stripped of] this body, *i.e.* dead.—εὑρεθησόμεθα, *we shall be found*) by the day of the Lord.

4. Καὶ γάρ, *for even*) The reason of the *earnest desire* [ver. 2.]—στενάζομεν βαρούμενοι, *we do groan being burdened*) An appropriate phrase. A burden wrings out sighing and groaning.—ἐκδύσασθαι) *to be unclothed, to strip off* the body. Faith does not acknowledge the philosophical contempt of the body, which was given by the Creator.

5. Κατεργασάμενος, *He that hath wrought* or *prepared* us) by faith.—εἰς αὐτὸ τοῦτο, *for this selfsame thing*) viz. that we should thus groan, Rom. viii. 23.—καί) *also; new proof* [*token to assure* us] of our coming blessedness.—τὸν ἀρραβῶνα, the *earnest*) ch. i. 22, note.—τοῦ πνεύματος, *of the Spirit*) who works in us that groaning.

6. Θαρροῦντες) The antithesis is between θαρροῦντες οὖν πάντοτε,

---

[1] See App. Strengthening of the words already used by something additional on their repetition.—ED.

and θαρροῦμεν δὲ καὶ εὐδοκοῦμεν μᾶλλον, κ.τ.λ. Its own explanation is subjoined to each of the two parts: *we are confident as well at all times* and during our whole life; as also *we are most of all confident* in the hope of a blessed departure.—καί) *and, even.*—ἐνδημοῦντες· ἐκδημοῦμεν) These two words here signify abiding [sojourning in a place]; but ver. 8, where they are interchanged, departure.—ἐκδημοῦμεν, *we live as pilgrims absent from the Lord*) In this word, there lies concealed the cause of *confidence*, for a pilgrim [though abroad yet] has a native country, whether he be about to reach it sooner or later, Heb. xi. 14.—ἀπὸ τοῦ Κυρίου, *from the Lord*) Christ, Phil. i. 23.

7. Διὰ πίστεως, *by faith*) Not to see, is nearly the same as being separated.—γάρ, *for*) This refers to ἀπὸ, *from* [ver. 6, absent *from* the Lord].—περιπατοῦμεν, *we walk*) in the world. So πορεύεσθαι, Luke xiii. 33.—οὐ διὰ εἴδους, *not by what appears to the eye* [Engl. V. *sight*]) The LXX. translate מראה, εἶδος, *vision, aspect, appearance.*[1] See especially Num. xii. 8: ἐν εἴδει, καὶ οὐ δι' αἰνιγμάτων, *apparently and not in dark speeches;* likewise Ex. xxiv. 17. Faith and sight are opposed to one another. Faith has its termination at death in this passage, therefore sight then begins.

8. Δέ, *indeed*) An epitasis [Repetition of a previous enunciation with some strengthening word added; Append.]; comp. ver. 6, note.—εὐδοκοῦμεν) *we have so determined* [we regard it as a fixed thing], *that it will be well-pleasing to us.*—ἐνδημῆσαι, *to go home*) ver. 6, note.—πρὸς τὸν Κυρίον, *to the Lord*) Phil. i. 23.

9. Διὸ καί, *wherefore also*) that we may obtain what we wish.—φιλοτιμούμεθα, *we [labour] strive*) This is the only φιλοτιμία, or lawful *ambition.*—εἴτε, *whether*) construed with *we may be [accepted] well-pleasing.*

[2] { ἐνδημοῦντες, *being at home*) in the body.
    { ἐκδημοῦντες *departing*), i.e. out of the body.

---

[1] Not the *act* or *power* of seeing (as 'sight' often means): but *the thing seen*, what presents itself to the eye, the appearance seen.—ED.

[2] Vulg. *g* and Syr. Versions, Origen Lucif. 151 read ἐκδημ. εἴτε ἐνδημ. But most MSS. and *f* have the order of Rec. Text.—ED.

The *margin* of both Ed. has *settled the reading* εἴτε ἐκδημοῦντες εἴτε ἐνδημοῦντες, *inverting the order, as equal to the received reading of the text*. But if the critical note (App. Ed. II. p. iv. nro. xiv. p. 896) *be compared, the*

2 CORINTHIANS V. 10. 377

—εὐάρεστοι, *well pleasing*) accepted especially in respect to the ministry.

10. Τοὺς γὰρ πάντας, *for all*) when treating of death, the resurrection, and eternal life, he also thinks appropriately, of the judgment. The motive is herein assigned for that holy *ambition*.—πάντας ἡμᾶς, *that we all*) even apostles, whether abiding as pilgrims here or departing.—φανερωθῆναι) not only to *appear* in the *body*, but to be *made manifest* along with [as well as] all our secrets, 1 Cor. iv. 5. Even the sins of believers, which have been long ago pardoned will then be laid open; for many of their good deeds, their repentance, their revenge directed against their sin, in order to be made known to the world, require the revelation of their sins. If a man has pardoned his brother an offence, the offence will also be exhibited, etc. But that will be done to them, with their will, without shame and grief; for they will be different from what they were. That revelation will be made indirectly, with a view to their greater praise [credit, honour]. Let us consider this subject more deeply.

§ 1. The words of sacred scripture respecting the remission of sins are extremely significant. Sins are covered: they will not be found: they are cast behind: sunk in the sea: scattered as a cloud and as mist: without being remembered. Therefore not even an atom of sin will cleave to any, who shall stand on the right hand in the judgment.

§ 2. On the other hand, the expressions concerning all the works of all men, which are to be brought forward in the judgment, are universal, Eccl. xii. 14; Rom. xiv. 10; 1 Cor. iii. 13, etc., iv. 5.

§ 3. The passage 2 Cor. v. 10 is consistent with these, where the apostle from the manifestation of all, whether of those going home or of those remaining as pilgrims, before the tribunal of Christ, infers the TERROR of the Lord and of the Judge, ver. 11, 12, and declares that terror to be the occasion of anxiety not only to the reprobate, but also to himself and to those like

Author seems afterwards to have changed both the order and the meaning *of the words,* such as the *Gnomon* shows. *For* the Crit. Not. has ἐνδημοῦντες, going home, *not* being at home; and the Germ. Ver. reads Wir mögen in der Fremde seyn, (*i.e.* ἐκδημοῦντες) oder heimgehen (*i.e.* ἐνδημοῦντες.)—E. B.

himself. Such fear would have no existence in the case of the saints if the opinion as to their sins not being about to be revealed were assumed to be true. Furthermore Paul says, that he, and such as he, would be manifested not only so far as they have acted well on the whole, but also so far as they have failed in any particular. There is wonderful variety of rewards among those, who are saved; and demerits [of saints] have effect, though not indeed in relation to punishment [which the saints wholly escape] but to loss,·as opposed to reward, 1 Cor. iii. 14, 15: comp. 2 Cor. i. 14; Phil. ii. 16, iv. 1. That phrase, *that every one may receive*, etc., shows, that the deficiencies in the case of the righteous will be also manifested. For thus and thus only will it be manifested, why each man receives neither more nor less than the reward, which he actually receives. The Lord will render to every one, AS his work shall be.

§ 4. Wherefore we ought not to press too far the words quoted in § 1. The sins of the elect, which are past, will not cease to be the objects of the Divine Omniscience for ever, although without any offence and upbraiding. And this one consideration is of more importance, than the manifestation of their sins before all creatures, though it were to continue for ever, much less as it is, in the day of judgment alone, when their sins will appear not as committed, but as retracted and blotted out in consequence of repentance.

§ 5. In the case of the elect themselves, their own sins will not cease to be the object of their remembrance, although without any uneasiness attending it. He, to whom much has been forgiven, loves much. The everlasting remembrance of a great debt, which has been forgiven, will be the fuel of the strongest love.

§ 6. So great is the efficacy of the Divine word with men in this life, that it separates the soul from the Spirit, Heb. iv. 12, and lays bare the secrets of the heart, 1 Cor. xiv. 25. Shame for what has been committed and remitted belongs to the *soul*, not the *spirit*. Men wallowing in gross sins often throw out their secrets; in despair they conceal nothing. But grace, much more powerful, renders those, who have received it, quite ingenuous. Men truly penitent proceed with the utmost readiness to the most open confessions of their secret wickedness,

Acts xix. 18. How much more in that day will they bear, that they be manifested, when the tenderness of the natural affections is entirely swallowed up? Comp. 1 Cor. vi. 9, 11. Such candour confers great peace and praise. If in the judgment there were room in the minds of the righteous, for example, for shame, I believe that those sins, which are now most covered, would cause less uneasiness, than those, of which they are less ashamed at the present time. We are most ashamed at present of the sins, which are contrary to modesty. But it is right, that we should be more ashamed of other sins, for example against the first table.

§ 7. That Adam was saved, we have no doubt, but his fall will be remembered for ever; for otherwise I do not understand, how the restitution made by Christ can be worthily celebrated in heaven. The conduct of David in the case of Uriah, the denial of Peter, the persecution of Saul, the sins of others, though they have been forgiven, have yet continued on record for so long a time in the Old and New Testament. If this fact presents no obstacle to the forgiveness long ago granted, the mention of sins will be no obstacle to their forgiveness even in the last judgment. It is not every manifestation of offences, which constitutes a part of punishment.

§ 8. Good and evil have so close a connection, as well as so inseparable a relation to each other, that the revelation of the good cannot be understood without the evil. But since certain sins of the saints shall be laid bare, it is fitting, that all the circumstances [all things] should be brought to light. This view tends to the glory of the Divine Omniscience and mercy; and in such a way as this the reasons for pronouncing a mild judgment on some, and a severe judgment on others, along with the accurate adjustment, $ἀκριβείᾳ$, of the retribution, will shine forth in all their brightness.

§ 9. I do not say, that all the sins of all the blessed will be actually and distinctly seen by all the creatures. Perhaps the accursed will not know them; the righteous will have no cause to fear each other. Their sins, when the light of that great day discloses all things, will not be *directly* manifested, as is done in the case of the guilty, who are punished, whence in Matt. xxv. no mention is made of them, but *indirectly*, so far as it will be proper; just as in a court of justice among men, it often occurs, that many things are wont to enter into the full *view* [aspect] *of the deed* incidentally. And in some such way as this also the good works of the reprobate will be made manifest. All things may be known in the light, but all do not know all things.

§ 10. This consideration ought to inspire us with fear for the future; for it had this effect on the apostles, as this passage 2 Cor. v. shows. But if more tender souls shrink back from that manifestation, on account of their sins past; when they have been duly instructed from what has been said, especially at § 6, they will acquiesce [acquire confidence in regard to the manifestation of all sins in the judgment]. Often does truth, which at first appeared bitter, become sweet after closer consideration. If I love any one as myself, he may, with my full acquiescence, know all things concerning me, which I know concerning myself. We shall judge of many things differently, we shall feel differently on many subjects, until we arrive at that point.

Κομίσηται, *may receive*) This word is used not only regarding the reward or punishment, but also regarding the *action*, which the reward or punishment follows, Eph. vi. 8; Col. iii. 25; Gal. vi. 7.—ἕκαστος, *every one*) separately.—τὰ διὰ τοῦ σώματος) Man [along] with his body acts well or ill; [therefore also] man [along] with his body receives the reward; comp. Tertull. de resurr. carnis, c. 43. τὰ—πρὸς ἅ, *those* inmost thoughts, *according to which* he *performed* outward *actions*. διὰ τοῦ σώματος, while he was in the body, ver. 6, 8–iv. 10, comp. διὰ Rom. ii. 27. —εἴτε ἀγαθὸν εἴτε κακὸν, *whether good or bad*) construed with *hath done*. No man can do both good and evil at the same time.

11. ¹Πείθομεν, *we persuade*) We bear ourselves so, by acting as well with vehemence, as also with sobriety ["Whether we be *beside ourselves*,—or whether we be *sober*"] ver. 13, that men, unless they be unwilling, may be able to give us their approbation. Comp. what he says on conscience presently after, and at iv. 2.—Πείθειν, ἀναγκάζειν are opposed; see at Chrysost. de

---

¹ Τὸν φόβον, *the terror*) Eccl. xii. 13.—V. g.—ἀνθρώπους, *men*). By many the things which God Himself does are not approved; and how can His *servants* be approved by any with regard to those things which they do? What is the counsel which His servants give [πείθομεν]? Thou hearest, reader, in this very passage.—V. g.

Sacer, p. 396, 392, 393.—πεφανερώμεθα, *we are made manifest*) we show and bear ourselves as persons manifest [to God and in your consciences]. Those, who have this character, may be *made manifest* without terror in the judgment, [φανερωθῆναι], ver. 10.—ἐλπίζω, *I hope*) To have been made manifest is past, whereas *hope* refers to a thing future. Paul either hopes for the fruit of the *manifestation*, which has been already made ; or else hopes, that the *manifestation* itself will still take place.—συνειδήσεσιν, *in your consciences*) The plural gives greater weight. [*It sometimes happens, that a man may be made manifest to the conscience even of such, as attempt to conceal the fact.*—V. g.]

12. Γὰρ, *for*) The reason assigned [aetiologia], why he leaves it to the conscience of the Corinthians to form their opinion.—διδόντες, *giving*) supply *we write*, or a similar general verb, the meaning of which is included in the particular expression, *we commend*. There is a participle of a similar kind, vii. 5–xi. 6. He says, we furnish you with arguments for glorying in our behalf.—καυχήματος, *glorying*) with regard to our sincerity ; so far am I from thinking, that there is after all need of any commendation of us.—ἔχητε, *you may have*) repeat, *occasion*.—ἐν προσώπῳ. καὶ οὐ καρδίᾳ, *in appearance; and not in heart*) The same antithesis is found at 1 Sam. xvi. 7, LXX., and in a different manner in 1 Thess. ii. 17.—καρδίᾳ, *in heart*) such was Paul's disposition [vein] of mind—truth shone from his heart to the consciences of the Corinthians.

13. Εἴτε ἐξέστημεν εἴτε σωφρονοῦμεν) The former is treated of ver. 15–21 :—the latter vi. 1–10. The force of the one word is evident from the other, to act *without* or *with moderation*. Paul might seem to be without moderation from the Symperasma,[1] which he gave in the preceding verse [*namely, adorning his office with so many encominiums.*—V. g.]—Θεῷ, it is to *God*) viz., *that we have acted without moderation*, although men do not understand us.—ὑμῖν, *it is to you*) Even godly men bear the moderation of their teachers with a more favourable feeling, than their ἔκστασις, *excessive enthusiasm;* but it is their duty to obey the Spirit.

---

[1] See App. A brief and summary conclusion from the previous premisses.—T.

14. Γάρ, *for*) The same sentiment is found at xi. 1, 2 ; but greatly augmented in force of expression; for he says here, *we have acted without moderation* [whether we be *beside ourselves*] and *the love* of Christ, etc., there, *in my folly* and *I am jealous*. —ἀγάπη) *love*, mutual : not only *fear* : ver. 11, the *love* of Christ, viz., toward us, in the highest degree, and consequently also our love towards Him [*That, which the apostle in this passage calls* love, *which may perhaps seem to go beyond bounds, he afterwards calls* jealousy, *which may be roused* by fear *even to* folly, xi. 1–3.—V. g.]—συνέχει, *constrains* ['distinct' *keeps us employed*]) that we may endeavour to approve ourselves both to God and you.

15. Κρίναντας, *judging*) with a most true judgment. Love and judgment are not opposed to each other in spiritual men.—ὑπὲρ πάντων, *for all*) for the dead and living.—ἄρα οἱ πάντες, *then these all*) Hence the full force of the ὑπὲρ, *for* and the utmost extent of the mystery is disclosed ; not only is it just the same as if all had died, but all are dead ; neither death, nor any other enemy, nor they themselves have power over themselves : they are entirely at the disposal and control of the Redeemer.—οἱ has a force relative to πάντων, *for all*. An apt universality. The teachers urge ; and the learners are urged, because Christ died for both.—ἀπέθανον, *are dead*) and so now no longer do they regard themselves. The generous lovers of the Redeemer apply that principally to themselves, which belongs to all. Their *death* was brought to pass in the death of Christ.—καὶ, *and*) this word also depends on ὅτι, *because*. First, the words, *one*, and, *for all*, correspond ; in the next place, *died*, and, that they should *live*.—οἱ ζῶντες, *they that live*) in the flesh.—ἀλλὰ, *but*) namely, *that they should live*, viz., in faith and a newly acquired vigour, Gal. ii. 20.—τῷ) he does not say, ὑπὲρ τοῦ. It is the dative of advantage, as they call it ; ὑπὲρ, denotes something more than this.—καὶ ἐγερθέντι, *and rose again*) Here we do not supply, *for them ;* for it is not consonant with the phraseology of the apostle ; but there is something analogous to be supplied, for example, ["that He might be Lord both of the dead and the living"] from Rom. xiv 9.

16. Ἀπὸ τοῦ νῦν, *henceforth*) From the time that the love of Christ has engaged [has pre-occupied] our minds. Even this

epistle differs in degree from the former.—οὐδένα, *no man*) neither ourselves, nor the other apostles, Gal. ii. 6 ; nor you, nor others. We do not fear the great, we do not consider the humble more humble than ourselves ; we do and suffer all things, and our anxiety is in every way to bring all to life. In this *enthusiasm* [ἔκστασις, being beside ourselves], ver. 13, nay in this *death*, ver. 15, we know none of them that survive,[1] even in connection with our ministry,—κατὰ σάρκα, *according to the flesh*) according to the old state, arising from nobility, riches, resources, wisdom, [so as *that from more natural considerations, we should either do or omit to do this or that.*—V. g.]—εἰ δὲ καὶ ἐγνώκαμεν) οἶδα and ἔγνωκα,[2] differ, 1 Cor. ii. 8, 11–viii. 1. Such knowledge was more tolerable, before the death of Christ : for that was the period of the days of the flesh.—κατὰ σάρκα, *according to the flesh*) construed with ἐγνώκαμεν, *we have known.*—Χριστόν, *Christ*) He does not say here *Jesus*. The name *Jesus* is in some measure *more spiritual* than the name *Christ;* and *they know Christ according to the flesh*, who acknowledge Him as the Saviour, not of the *world*, ver. 19, but only of *Israel*, ch. xi. 18, note : and who congratulate themselves on this account, that they belong to that nation from which Christ was descended, and who seek in His glory political splendour, and in their seeing Him when He formerly appeared, and in their hearing of His instructions of whatever kind, before His sufferings, some superiority over others, and in the knowledge of Him, the enjoyment of the mere natural senses : and who do not strive to attain that enjoyment which is here described, and which is derived from His death and resurrection, ver. 15, 17, 18 : comp. John xvi. 7 ; Rom. viii. 34 ; Phil. iii. 10 ; Luke viii. 21.

17. Εἴ τις ἐν Χριστῷ, *if any one be in Christ*) so as to live in Christ. If *any one* of those who now hear *us*, etc. Observe the mutual relation, *we in Christ* in this passage, and *God in Christ*, ver. 19 ; Christ, therefore, is the Mediator and Reconciler between us and God.—καινὴ κτίσις, *a new creature*) Not

---

[1] *i.e.* Those not yet dead with and in Christ, but *living in the flesh:* note on οἱ ζῶντες, ver. 15.—ED.

[2] οἶδα seems to be used as *scio* (of an *abstract* truth *well known*), or *novi* (of a *person*, with whom we are *well acquainted*). ἔγνωκα as *agnosco*, or *cognosco, come to the knowledge of*, I perceive, or *recognize.*—ED.

only is the Christian himself something new; but as he knows Christ Himself, not according to the flesh, but according to the power of His life and resurrection, so he contemplates and estimates himself and all things according to that new condition. Concerning this subject, see Gal. vi. 15; Eph. iv. 24; Col. iii. 10.—τὰ ἀρχαῖα, *old things*) This term implies some degree of contempt. See Gregor. Thaum. Paneg. cum annot., p. 122, 240.—παρῆλθεν, *are passed away*) Spontaneously, like snow in early spring.—ἰδοὺ, *behold*) used to point out something before us.

18. Τὰ δὲ πάντα, *and all these things*) which have been mentioned from ver. 14. Paul infers from the death of Christ his obligation to God, ver. 13.—ἡμᾶς, *us*) the world, and especially and expressly the apostles; comp. the following verse, where there is again subjoined [hath committed] *unto us*. That word *us*, especially comprehends the apostles; but not them alone; for at the beginning of ver. 18, the discourse is already widely extended [so as to apply to *all men*]. Thus the subject varies [is changed] often in the same discourse, and yet subsequently the mark of the subject being distinct from what it had been, is not expressly added.—ἡμῖν, *to us*) apostles.—τὴν διακονίαν, *the ministry*) the *word* [of reconciliation] in the following verse. The *ministry* dispenses the *word*.

19. Ὡς ὅτι) Explanatory particles.—ἦν καταλλάσσων) *was reconciling*, comp. ver. 17, note. The time implied by the verb ἦν is shown, ver. 21.[1]—ἐν Χριστῷ, ἐν ἡμῖν, *in Christ, in us*) These words correspond to one another.—κόσμον, *the world*) which had been formerly hostile.—καταλλάσσων· μὴ λογιζόμενος, *reconciling, not imputing*) The same thing is generally amplified by affirmative and negative words.—τὰ παραπτώματα) *offences* many and grave.—θέμενος, *having committed*) as it is committed to an interpreter what he ought to say.

20. Ὑπὲρ Χριστοῦ, *for Christ*) Christ the foundation of the *embassy* sent from God.—πρεσβεύομεν· δεόμεθα, *we are ambassadors, [we pray], we beseech*) two extremes, as it were, put in antithesis to each other, which relate to the words *we have acted without moderation* [whether we be *beside ourselves*, ver. 13]. In anti-

---

[1] viz. the time when God *made* Jesus to be *Sin for us*, etc.—ED.

thesis to these, the mean between those extremes is, *we exhort* [παρακαλοῦμεν, not as Engl. Vers., *We beseech*], ch. vi. 1, x. 1 which appertains to the σωφρονοῦμεν, *we act with moderation* [whether we *be sober*, ver. 13]. Therefore the discourse of the apostle generally παρακαλεῖ, *exhorts;* since the expression, πρεσβεύομεν, *we are ambassadors*, implies majesty, the expression δεόμεθα, *we beseech*, intimates a submission, which is not of daily occurrence; ch. x. 2, [comp. 1 Thess. ii. 6, 7]. In both expressions Paul indicates not so much what he is now doing, as what he is doing in the discharge of all the duties of his office. Ὑπὲρ Χριστοῦ, *for Christ*, is placed before the former verb [though *after* the latter verb], for the sake of emphasis; comp. the preceding verses. Presently after, the latter verb is placed first for the same reason.—καταλλάγητε, *be ye reconciled*).

21. Τὸν) *Him, who* knew no sin, who stood in no need of reconciliation;—a eulogium peculiar to Jesus. Mary was not one, ἡ μὴ γνοῦσα, *who knew no* sin.—ἁμαρτίαν ἐποίησε, *made Him to be sin*) He was made *sin* in the same way that we are made *righteousness*. Who would have dared to speak thus, if Paul had not led the way? comp. Gal. iii. 13. Therefore Christ was also abandoned on the cross.—ἡμεῖς) *we*, who knew no righteousness, who must have been destroyed, if the way of reconciliation had not been discovered.—ἐν αὐτῷ, *in Him*) in Christ. The antithesis is, *for us*.

CHAPTER VI.

1. Συνεργοῦντες, *workers together*) Not only as the *ambassadors of God*, or on the other hand, as *beseeching*, we deal with you; but also, as your friends, we *co-operate* with you for your salvation. [*This is the medium between the dignity of ambassadors and the humility of beseeching*, ch. v. 20. *That is, we try all means.*—Not. Crit.] For you ought to *work out* your own salvation, Phil. ii. 12. The *working together* with them is described, ver. 3, 4; the *exhortation*, ver. 2, 14, 15 [as far as ch. vii. 1.—

V. g.] He strongly dissuades them from Judaism, as an *am-* *bassador*, and by *beseeching;* as *working together* with them, he strongly dissuades them from heathenism. None but a *holy* [ch. vii. 1] minister of the Gospel can turn himself into all forms of this sort.—καὶ, *also*).—τὴν χάριν, *the grace*) of which ch. v. 18, 19 treats, [and ch. vi. 2, 17, 18.—V. g.]—δέξασθαι) This word is drawn from the δεκτῷ of ver. 2 [*receive*—For this is God's season of *receiving* sinners]. Divine grace offers itself: human faith and obedience avail themselves of the offer.

2. Λέγει, *He saith*) The Father to Messiah, Is. xlix. 8, embracing in Him all believers.—γὰρ, *for*) He is describing *grace*. —δεκτῷ, *accepted*) the acceptable time of the good pleasure of God. Hence Paul presently after infers its correlative, εὐπρόσδεκτος, *well-accepted*, that it may be also agreeable to us.[1]— ἐπήκουσά σου) *I have heard thee*, viz. praying.—ἐν ἡμέρᾳ, *in a day*) Luke xix. 42; Heb. iii. 7.—ἰδοὺ νῦν, *behold now*) The summing up of the *exhortation*, ver. 1; set before us in the way of a supposed dialogue.[2]

3. Ἐν μηδενί, *in nothing*) corresponds to ἐν παντί, *in every thing*, in the following verse.—διδόντες, *giving*) The participle depends on ver. 1.—προσκοπὴν, *offence*) which would be the case, if we were without 'patience' and the other qualifications, which are presently afterwards mentioned.—ἡ διακονία, *the ministry*) The Abstract. *The ministers of God*, the Concrete, ver. 4.

4. Διάκονοι, *ministers*) This word has greater force, than if it had been written διακόνους.—ὑπομονῇ, *in patience*) This is put first; ch. xii. 12: *chastity*, etc., follow in ver. 6. A remarkable gradation.—πολλῇ, *in much*) Three triplets of trials follow, which must be endured, and in which patience is exercised, *afflictions* [necessities, distresses]: *stripes* [imprisonments, tumults]: *labours* [watchings, fastings]: The first group of three includes the genera; the second, the species of adversities; the third, things voluntarily endured. And the variety of cases of the several classes of trial should be observed, expressed, as it is, by the employment of the plural number.—ἐν θλίψεσιν, ἐν ἀνάγκαις,

---

[1] The present time is δεκτός to God: let it be also εὐπρόσδεκτος to us. —ED.

[2] Or introduction of an imaginary speaker. See Append. on Sermocinatio.—ED.

2 CORINTHIANS VI. 5—8.

ἐν στενοχωρίαις, *in afflictions, in necessities, in distresses*) These words are in close relation, and are variously joined with one another and with the others, ch. xii. 10; 1 Thess. iii. 7; Rom. ii. 9, viii. 35; Luke xxi. 23. *In afflictions* [θλίψεσιν, the *pressure* of trials] many ways are open, but they are all difficult; in *necessities* [ἀνάγκαις], one way is open, though difficult; in *distresses* [*straits,* στενοχωρίαις], none is open.

5. Ἀκαταστασίαις, *in tumults*) either for, or against us.

6. Ἐν γνώσει) γνῶσις often means *leniency* [æquitas], which inclines to and admits of putting favourable constructions on things somewhat harsh; and this interpretation is consonant with the phrase, *in long-suffering*, which follows; comp. 2 Pet. i. 5; 1 Pet. iii. 7, note.—ἐν μακροθυμίᾳ, ἐν χρηστότητι, *in long-suffering, in kindness*) These words are also joined together in 1 Cor. xiii. 4 under the name of one virtue [*charity*].—ἐν πνεύματι ἁγίῳ, *in the Holy Spirit*) That we may always have the Holy Spirit present, that we may always be active, as also in the putting forth into exercise miraculous gifts, 1 Thess. i. 5. There immediately follows, *in love*, which is the principal fruit of *the Spirit*, and which regulates the use of *spiritual* gifts.

7. Δεξιῶν καὶ ἀριστερῶν) *by offensive* armour, when we are prospering; and *defensive*, when we are in difficulties. In the case of soldiers, κλίνειν, ἄγειν, ἐπιστρέφειν ἐπὶ δόρυ or ἐπὶ ξίφος signifies *towards the right hand;* the ἐπὶ ἀσπίδα, ἐφ' ἡνίαν or χαλινὸν, signifies, *towards the left hand*, just as the left hand is called by the French, the *bridle hand* (main de la bride), and the right hand is called the *lance hand* (main de la lance). Add the note to Chrysost. de Sacerd., p. 464. Paul has so placed these words, that they might at the same time form a transition; for he just now treated of the armour for the right hand, and he is forthwith about to treat of that for the left.

8. Δόξης, *glory*) δόξα and ἀτιμία, *glory* and *disgrace* are derived from those, who possess authority, and fall upon those, who are present; *evil report and good report* are in the hands of the multitude, and fall upon the absent. [*Furthermore,* glory proceeds from those, who recognise the character which the minister of God sustains; disgrace, from those, who do not recognise him as such, and therefore esteem more highly others, that in the affairs of this world perform any trifling work whatever. Infamy

or evil report *proceeds from the ignorant and malevolent;* good report *from the well-informed in like manner as also the well affected.* In proportion as a man has more or less of glory or good report, in the same proportion has he also more or less of either disgrace *or* infamy *respectively.*—V. g.] The contraries are elegantly mixed togother.—δυσφημίας, *evil report*) If not even the apostles escaped this evil report, who can ask to escape it?—ὡς πλάνοι, *as deceivers*) men of the deepest *infamy.*—ἀληθεῖς, *true*) in the opinion of believers, and in reality.

9. Ἀγνοούμενοι, *unknown*) [*so that we are either quite unknown and neglected, or we are considered altogether different from what we really are.*—V. g.]—Gal. i. 22; Col. ii. 1.—ἐπιγινωσκόμενοι) *well known.*—[1]ἰδοὺ, *behold*) suddenly and contrary to hope.

10. Ἀεί) *alway, at every time.* As often as we had been made sorrowful.—πλουτίζοντες, *making rich*) spiritually.—πάντα κατέχοντες [Engl. V. not so well, *possessing*], *holding fast all things*) lest they should be lost to others.

11. Τὸ στόμα, *the mouth*) A Symperasma,[2] by which Paul prepares a way for himself, in order that, from the praise of the gospel ministry, brought down from ii. 14 up to this point, he may derive an *exhortation* to the Corinthians.—ἀνέῳγε, *is opened*) hath opened itself. There is truly something very extraordinary in this epistle.—Κορίνθιοι, *O Corinthians*) a rare and very life-like address, expressive, as it were, of some privilege belonging to the Corinthians; comp. Phil. iv. 15, note.—ἡ καρδία, *the heart*) They ought to have concluded [drawn an inference] from the mouth to the heart [of the apostle]. To be *opened* and *enlarged*, are closely connected.—πεπλάτυνται, *has been enlarged*) *is diffused* [in a widely extended stream of love], 1 Kings iv. 29, רחב לב, *largeness of heart as the sand, that is by the seashore.*

12. Οὐ στενοχωρεῖσθε, *ye are not straitened*) The Indicative. The antithesis is, *be ye enlarged* [ver. 13].—ἐν ἡμῖν) *in us.* ἐν, in its strict sense, *in,* as at ch. vii. 3. Our heart has sufficient room to take you in. The *largeness* of Paul's heart is the same as that of the Corinthians, on account of their spiritual relation-

---

[1] Ἀποθνήσκοντες, *dying*) xi. 23.—V. g.

[2] See App. A conclusion or brief summary drawn from the previous premisses.

ship, of which ver. 13.—στενοχωρεῖσθε, *ye are straitened*) by the narrowness of your heart on account of your late offence.— ἐν τοῖς σπλάγχνοις ὑμῶν, *in your bowels*) which have been grieved on my account.

13. Τήν) supply κατὰ, *according to.*—αὐτήν) *the same;* that you may have the same feeling, as we.—ἀντιμισθίαν, *recompense*) which you owe to me as a father; comp. Gal. iv. 12.—ὡς τέκνοις λέγω, *I speak as to children*) He hints in this parenthesis, that he demands nothing severe or bitter.—πλατύνθητε, *be ye enlarged*) A double exhortation. Throw yourselves open before the Lord, and then before us; comp. viii. 5; *be enlarged*, that the Lord may dwell in you, ver. 14—ch. vii. 1, *receive us*, ch. vii. 2.

14. Μὴ γίνεσθε, *do not become*) a soft expression for *be not.*— ἑτεροζυγοῦντες, *yoked with an alien party* [one alien in spirit]) [*unequally yoked*], Lev. xix. 19, LXX. τὰ κτήνη σου οὐ κατοχεύσεις ἑτεροζύγῳ, *thou shalt not let thy cattle engender with a diverse kind.* The believer and the unbeliever are utterly heterogeneous. The notion of *slavery* approaches to that of a *yoke*. The word הנצמדים, Num. xxv. 5. The apostle strongly dissuades the Corinthians from marriages with unbelievers; comp. 1 Cor. vii. 39, *only in the Lord.* He however uses such reasons, as may deter them from too close intercourse with unbelievers even in other relations [besides marriage]: comp. v. 16; 1 Cor. viii. 10, x. 14. —ἀπίστοις, *to unbelievers*) heathens. He pulls up all the fibres of the foreign root [of foreign and alien connections].—τίς, *what?*) Five questions, of which the first three have the force of an argument; the fourth, *or what*, and the fifth, have at the same time also the force of a conclusion.—δικαιοσύνῃ κα᾽ ἀνομίᾳ, what fellowship is there between *righteousness and unrighteousness*) The state of believers and unbelievers is altogether different.

15. Βελιαρ, *Belial*) The LXX. always express in Greek words the Hebrew, בליעל; but here Paul uses the Hebrew word for the purpose of Euphemism [avoiding something unpleasant by the use of a term less strictly appropriate]. This word is an appellative, 1 Sam. xxv. 25, and occurs for the first time in Deut. xiii. 14. Hiller, Onom. S. p. 764. *Belijahal, without ascending;* *i.e.*, *of the meanest condition, of a very low and obscure rank.* Paul calls Satan Belial. Nevertheless Satan is usually put in

antithesis to God, Antichrist to *Christ*. Wherefore Belial as being opposed to Christ, seems here also to denote all manner of Antichristian uncleanness.

16. Συγκατάθεσις) LXX. Ex. xxiii. 1 : *οὐ συγκαταθήσῃ μετὰ τοῦ ἀδίκου, thou shalt not agree with the wicked.*—μετὰ εἰδώλων, *with idols*) He does not say, μετὰ ναοῦ εἰδώλων, *with the temple of idols* (although the Syriac version supplies *with the temple*), for idols do not dwell in their worshippers.—ὑμεῖς, *ye*) The promises, made to Israel, belong also to us.—ἐνοικήσω—λαὸς, *I will dwell in them—my people*) Lev. xxvi. 11, 12, LXX. Θήσω τὴν σκηνήν μου ἐν ὑμῖν —καὶ ἐμπεριπατήσω ἐν ὑμῖν, καὶ ἔσομαι ὑμῶν Θεὸς, καὶ ὑμεῖς ἔσεσθέ μοι λαός: *I will set my tabernacle among you—and I will walk among you, and I will be your God, and ye shall be my people.* Paul quotes a single verse, he wishes the whole paragraph to be considered as repeated.—ἐμπεριπατήσω, *I will walk among* [in]) *I will dwell* signifies the continuance of the Divine presence; *I will walk*, its operation. The subject of God's gracious dwelling in the soul and body of the saints may be explained from its contrary, viz., the subject of [the question concerning] spiritual and bodily [demoniacal] possession ; as every dispensation of evil and good may be compared together according to their opposite aspects [principles].—ἔσομαι, *I will be*) The sum of the Divine covenant, Ex. vi. 7; Heb. viii. 10.—Θεός· λαός, *their God : my people*) There is a gradation, [here Θεὸς ; but in ver. 18, εἰς πατέρα] *in the relation of a father ;* [again here λαός ; but εἰς υἱοὺς] *in the relation of sons*, ver. 18 ; Rev. xxi. 3, 7 ; Jer. xxxi. 1, 9.

17. Ἐξέλθετε—μὴ ἅπτεσθε) Is. lii. 11, ἀπόστητε, ἀπόστητε, ἐξέλθετε ἐκεῖθεν, καὶ ἀκαθάρτου μὴ ἅψησθε· ἐξέλθετε ἐκ μέσου αὐτῆς, ἀφορίσθητε, κ.τ.λ.—ἐκ μέσου αὐτῶν, *from the midst of them*) from the Gentiles. —λέγει Κύριος, *saith the Lord*) The additional epithet follows [in ver. 18, augmenting the force of the words by Epitasis (See Append.)], *the Lord* Almighty.—ἀκαθάρτου, *unclean*) The masculine, Is. lii. 11, 1 : comp. Is. lxv. 5. To this may be referred, *let us cleanse ourselves*, ch. vii. 1.—μὴ ἅπτεσθε, *touch not*) To see, when it is necessary, does not always defile : Acts xi. 6 ; to touch is more polluting.—εἰσδέξομαι, *I will receive you* [within] *to me*) as into a family or home [Comp. ch. v. 1-10.—V. g.] We are out of doors, but we are admitted within. The clause, *Come out from*, etc., corresponds to this. God is in the saints, ver. 16,

and the saints are in God. εἰσδέχομαι corresponds to the Hebrew word קבץ, Ezek. xx. 41; Zeph. iii. 19, 20.

18. Εἰς υἱοὺς καὶ θυγατέρας, *in the relation of sons and daughters*) Is. xliii. 6. The promise, given to Solomon, 1 Chron. xxviii. 6, is applied to all believers.—Κύριος παντοκράτωρ, *the Lord Almighty* [*the Universal Ruler*]. From this title we perceive the greatness of the promises. Now the word παντοκράτωρ, [*Universal Ruler*] *Almighty*, occurs nowhere else in the New Testament but in the Apocalypse; but here Paul uses it after the manner of the LXX. interpreters, because he quotes the passage from the Old Testament.

CHAPTER VII.

1. Καθαρίσωμεν, *let us cleanse*) This is the last part of the exhortation, set forth at vi. 1, and brought out *ib.* ver. 14. He concludes the exhortation in the first person. The antitheses are the *unclean thing*, vi. 17, and *filthiness* in this passage. The same duty is derived from a similar source, 1 John iii. 3, Rev. xxii. 11.—μολυσμοῦ, *filthiness*) *Filthiness of the flesh*, for example, fornication, and *filthiness of the spirit*, for example, idolatry, were closely connected among the Gentiles. Even Judaism, occupied, as it is, about the cleanness of the flesh, is now in some measure *filthiness of the spirit*. *Holiness* is opposed to the former; *the fear of God*, promoting holiness (comp. again 1 Cor. x. 22) to the latter.—πνεύματος, *of spirit*) Comp. Ps. xxxii. 2, lxxviii. 8. —ἐπιτελοῦντες, *perfecting*) even to the end. It is not enough to begin; it is the end that crowns the work. The antitheses are ἄρχομαι, ἐπιτελέω, *I begin, I finish*, ch. viii. 6, 10, 11; Gal. iii. 3; Phil i. 6.—ἁγιωσύνην, *holiness*) corresponds to *be ye separated*, ch. vi. 17.—ἐν, *in*) he does not say, *and* [perfecting] *the fear.* Fear is a holy affection, which is not *perfected* by our efforts, but is merely retained. [*The pure fear of* GOD *is conjoined with the consideration of the most magnificent promises*, ch. v. 11; Heb. iv. 1.—V. g.]

2. Χωρήσατε ἡμᾶς, *receive us*) The sum of what is stated in this

and in the tenth and following chapter.—ἡμᾶς) *us*, who love you and rejoice for your sake, receive also with favour our feelings, words, and actions.—οὐδένα ἠδικήσαμεν, οὐδένα ἐφθείραμεν, οὐδένα ἐπλεονεκτήσαμεν) He lays down three things by gradation, the first of which he treats from ver. 4, by repeating the very word ἀδικεῖν, at ver. 12; the second from ch. x. 1, by repeating the very word φθείρειν, at ch. xi. 3; the third from ch. xii. 13, by repeating the very word πλεονεκτεῖν, *ib.* ver. 17. I have marked however the beginning of the paragraph at ver. 11 of the chapter quoted. The point of transition [to the discussion of πλεονεκτεῖν] may be referred to what goes before or to what follows after ver. 11 [*i.e.*, may be fixed in the context before or after ver. 11]. The discussion of the clause itself, οὐδένα ἐπλεονεκτήσαμεν begins at ver. 13. This then is what he means to say: There is no reason, why you should not receive us [favourably: *capiatis*]: for we have injured no man, by our severity producing an absorbing grief [referring to ch. ii. 7, " lest such a one should be *swallowed up* with overmuch sorrow"]; nay, we have not even made a man worse by a too haughty mode of acting: nay, we have not even defrauded any man for gain; in everything we have consulted you and your interests: comp. ver. 9; and that too, without any reward. Whilst he declares, that he had been the occasion of no evil to the Corinthians, he intimates, that he had done them good, but very modestly keeps it as it were out of sight.

3. Οὐ πρὸς κατάκρισιν, *not* [*for condemnation*] *to condemn you*) He shows that he does not say, what he has said at ver. 2, because he supposes that the Corinthians dislike Paul and his colleagues, but that he speaks with a paternal spirit, ch. vi. 13: and in order to prove how far he is from entertaining that supposition, he calls it *a condemnation*, thus humbling himself anew.—προείρηκα, *I have said before*) ch. vi. 12.—γὰρ, *for*) The reason why he himself does not condemn them, and why they ought to receive the apostle and his associates [ver. 2 " Receive *us.*"]—ἐν καρδίαις, *in our hearts*) So Phil. i. 7.—εἰς τὸ συναποθανεῖν καὶ συζῆν, *to die and live with you*) ch. i. 6, iv. 12. The height of friendship.

4. Παρρησία, *boldness of speech*) ver. 16, ch. vi. 11.—ὑπὲρ ὑμῶν, *in behalf of you*) to others, the antithesis is πρὸς ὑμᾶς, *to* [*toward*] *you*.—παρακλήσει, *with comfort*) concerning which, see ver. 6, 7:

concerning *joy*, ver. 7, 8, 16 : concerning both, ver. 13 : *comfort relieves* ['refreshes,' ver. 13], *joy* entirely frees us from, sorrow.—ὑπερπερισσεύομαι, *I exceedingly* [*over* and *above*] *abound*) *above* [ὑπὲρ] all adversity.—θλίψει, *in* ['tribulation'] *affliction*) of which, ver. 5, θλιβόμενοι, ['troubled'] *afflicted*. To this belong all those trials which he has mentioned at ch. iv. 7, 8, vi. 4, 5.

5. Σάρξ, *flesh*) This is used in a large sense; weigh well the word φόβοι, *fears*.—θλιβόμενοι) [troubled] *afflicted*, viz., we were. —ἔξωθεν, *without*) on the part of the Gentiles.—ἔσωθεν, *within*) on the part of the brethren, comp. 1 Cor. v. 12, 2 Cor. iv. 16.

6. Τοὺς ταπεινοὺς, *the humble* [*them that are cast down*]) for those that are *exalted* and *puffed up*, do not receive [are not capable of] comfort.

7. Ἀναγγέλλων) *bringing back word* to us who were waiting for him. This is the meaning of the compound verb. The nominative [in its construction] depends on παρεκλήθη, *he was comforted*: the sense also refers to the words, ἐν τῇ παρουσίᾳ, *by his coming*.—τὴν ὑμῶν ἐπιπόθησιν, *your earnest desire*) towards me.— τὸν ὑμῶν ὀδυρμὸν, *your mourning*) concerning yourselves, because you had not immediately punished the sin.—τὸν ὑμῶν ζῆλον, *your zeal* [*fervent mind*]) for saving the soul [spirit] of the sinner. These three expressions occur again, ver. 11. A syntheton[1] is added to each of them: but here he deals with them more moderately, and for the sake of euphemism [see Append.] puts *earnest desire* in the first place, and uses the expression *mourning*, not *indignation*.—ὑπὲρ ἐμοῦ, *for my sake* [not as Engl. *toward me*]) Because the Corinthians showed a "fervent mind," Paul was relieved from the exercise of that fervour.—ὥστε με μᾶλλον, *so that I rather* ["the more"]) An imperceptible transition. I had not so much consolation, as joy : joy is *rather* to be desired than consolation, ver. 13 [μᾶλλον ἐχάρημεν].

8. Ἐν τῇ ἐπιστολῇ) *in the letter*, he does not add, *my* : presently after, he removes himself further from it, when he adds, ἐκείνη, *that* [same epistle.]—εἰ καὶ) *although* : Paul had wished to remove, if possible, sorrow from the repentance of the Corinthians. He uses this particle thrice in one verse ; also at ver. 12. Observe

---

[1] See the Append. The combination of two words which are frequently or emphatically joined together.

his paternal gentleness, he all but deprecates [his having caused them sorrow].—βλέπω, *I perceive*) from the fact itself.—*εἰ καὶ, although*) in this clause, ὅτι ἡ ἐπιστολὴ ἐκείνη εἰ καὶ πρὸς ὥραν ἐλύπησεν ὑμᾶς, the words εἰ καὶ should have a comma either before and after them, or else neither before nor after them. The apostle explains the reason, why he does not repent of having caused sorrow to the Corinthians. The letter, he says, has made you sad only for a time, or rather not even for a time. Whence also Chrysostom in his exposition repeats the words, ὅτι πρὸς ὥραν ἐλύπησεν ὑμᾶς, in such a way as to omit εἰ καὶ. The particle εἰ καὶ, put absolutely, expresses much feeling [Valde morata est. See Append.] Sextus πρὸς ἀστρολόγον, says, Μεθ᾽ ἡμέραν οὐδὲν τῶν προειρημένων δυνατόν ἐστι παρασημειοῦσθαι, μόνα δὲ, εἰ καὶ ἄρα, τὰς τοῦ ἡλίου κινήσεις. *By day none of the things previously mentioned can possibly be observed, but only the motions of the sun, if indeed even those;* wherein εἰ καὶ ἄρα, as Devarius properly remarks, *takes away the concession, that had been made*, namely, that the motions of the sun only can be observed; *if only*, says he, viz., even the motions of the sun can be observed. See Devar. on the Gr. particles, in the instance, εἰ καὶ, also in the case of ἀλλ᾽ εἴπερ and ἀλλ᾽ εἰ ἄρα, and Budaei Comm. L. Gr. f. 1390, ed. 1556, and, if you please, my notes on Gregor. Neocaes. Paneg., p. 174, on εἰ put absolutely. Luther very appropriately translates it *Vielleicht*. Others, without observing the force of the particle, have wondrously tortured this passage, which is most full of the characteristic ἦθος [See Append.] of the apostle. The οὐδὲ πρὸς ὥραν, Gal. ii. 5, is a kindred phraseology.

9. Νῦν χαίρω, *I now rejoice*) The *now* forms an epitasis;[1] not only do I *not repent*, that you had *brief sorrow, but I even rejoice*, because it has proved *salutary* to you.—εἰς μετάνοιαν, *unto repentance*) *Unto* here determines the kind of *sorrow*.—κατὰ Θεόν, [after a godly manner] *according to God*) *according to* here signifies the feeling of the mind, having regard to and following God. There is no sorrow with God; but the sorrow of penitents renders the mind conformable to God; comp. κατὰ, *according to*, Rom. xiv. 22; Col. ii. 8; 1 Pet. iv. 6. So in Philostr.

---

[1] *i.e.* He had already said, *I rejoiced*, in ver. 7: and here in ver. 9, *now*, added to the same word *I rejoice*, augments its force. See Append.—ED.

in Heroicis, p. 665, κατὰ θεὸν ἥκω, *I am come here under divine auspices.*—ἐν μηδενί, *in nothing*) This is consonant with that feeling, under which the apostle also speaks, xi. 9, ἐν παντί, *in everything.*—ζημιωθῆτε, *ye might suffer loss or damage*) All sorrow which is not *according to God*, is *damaging*, and deadly, ver. 10.

10. Μετάνοιαν—ἀμεταμέλητον, *repentance—not to be repented of*) From the meaning of the primitive word, μετάνοια belongs properly to the understanding; μεταμέλεια to the will; because the former expresses the change of sentiment, the latter, the change of care [solicitude], or rather of purpose. Whence *Thomas Gataker*, Advers. misc. posth., c. 29, where he treats very accurately of these words signifying repentance, closes a long dissertation with this recapitulation : *We have thus a series not completely, but exactly delineated, by which that feeling from its first origin, as it were by certain degrees and advances, is at length brought on, as Septimius would say, to its proper* maturity. In the first *place,* censure *or* punishment *is inflicted* [animadversio], a proceeding which is termed by the Hebrews שוב לב *for* שוב לב : *from this arises* acknowledgment of error, *and* μετάνοια, reformation [resipiscentia, *coming to a right state of mind*]. Δυσαρέστησις or λύπη, dissatisfaction with one's self and sorrow, *follow this* μετάνοια, *that which is explained by the Hebrew,* נחם, *penitence. The consequence of this, where it has become* efficacious, καὶ γνησία, genuine, *is* שוב, conversion, ἐπιστροφή, μεταμέλεια, *which finishes and crowns the work, since it brings in quite* a new mode of living, instead of the old." Such are his views. Furthermore, on account of the very close relationship between the understanding and the will, μεταμέλεια and μετάνοια occur together, and both the nouns and verbs are promiscuously used even by philosophers, and they correspond in the LXX. with the single Hebrew word נחם ; in both μετὰ signifies *after*. Whence Plato in the Gorgias, ταῦτα προνοήσασι μὲν, δυνατά· μετανοήσασι δὲ, ἀδύνατα. *These things are possible to them that think beforehand, but impossible to those that think afterwards.* Synesius, Ep. iv., τῷ ἐπιμηθεῖ, φασίν, τὸ μὲν μέλειν οὐκ ἦν, τὸ δὲ μεταμέλειν, ἐνῆν. *It is said, that Epimetheus had no care at the time, but that he afterwards had care.*[1] Both these

[1] *Epimetheus* was fabled, in contrast to *Prometheus,* to have had no *thought,* but to have had *after thought* when too late.—ED.

words are therefore applied to him, who repents of what he has done, and of the counsel which he has followed, whether his penitence be good or bad, whether it be on account of something evil or good, whether accompanied with a change of future conduct or not. If we consider their use however, μεταμέλεια is generally a term midway between good and bad [μέσον, indifferent[1]], and is chiefly referred to single actions; but μετάνοια, especially in the New Testament, is taken in a good sense, by which is denoted the repentance [regret on account] of the whole life, and, in some respects, [loathing] of ourselves,[2] or that whole blessed remembrance of the mind [the mind's review of the past, and of its own state heretofore] after error and sin, with all the affections entering into it, which suitable fruits follow. Hence it happens, that μετανοεῖν is often put in the imperative, μεταμελεῖσθαι never; but in other places, wherever μετάνοια is read, μεταμέλεια may be substituted; but not *vice versa*. Therefore, Paul distinctly uses both words in this passage, and applies to μετάνοιαν εἰς σωτηρίαν the term ἀμεταμέλητον, because neither he can regret, that he had occasioned this μετάνοιαν, *repentance*, to the Corinthians, nor they, that they had felt it.—εἰς σωτηρίαν, *to salvation*) all the impediments to which are thus removed.—κατεργάζεται, *worketh*) Therefore *sorrow* is not *repentance* itself, but it produces *repentance*; that is, *carefulness* (σπουδήν), ver. 11.—ἡ δὲ) *but* the mere sorrow of the world, etc., of which I was not a promoter among you.— τοῦ κόσμου) *of the world*, not merely, *according to the world* (answering to the epithet of λύπη, viz., ἡ κατὰ θεόν). [*Such was the sorrow of* Ahab *in the case of* Naboth. *Now and then the malignant powers of darkness also mingle themselves with it, as in the case of* Saul. *In such cases, even the innocent cheerfulness of children, or the singing of birds, or the frisking of calves sometimes move their indignation.* The sorrow *of the world, such as*

---

[1] Μεταμέλεια is often used of the *remorse* and *regret* of such a one as Judas. Μετάνοια of the true penitent.—ED.

[2] *Repentance of ourselves* is not English, and does not suggest any very clear idea. I think the author meant to apply it to our original depravity, which to believers is the subject of confession and lamentation before God. This may be considered as a species of repentance, and seems to agree with the qualifying phrase *in some respects*.—TR.

this, *is not less to be avoided than* the joy *of the world. The world experiences* joy *at their social feasts, for the rest of the time they are generally under the dominion of sorrow.*—V. g.]—θάνατον, *death*) chiefly of the soul, which is evident from the antithesis ['*salvation*'].

11. Ἰδού, *behold*) Paul proves this from their present experience.—ὑμῖν, *to you*) The Dative of advantage; comp. ver. 9, at the end.—σπουδήν, *carefulness*) Σπουδαῖον, is said of whatever of its kind is good, sound, and vigorous. A beautiful passage in the 2d book of Aristotle's Eth. Nicom. c. 5, furnishes an illustration, ἡ τοῦ ὀφθαλμοῦ ἀρετὴ τόν τε ὀφθαλμὸν σπουδαῖον ποιεῖ καὶ τὸ ἔργον αὐτοῦ· ὁμοίως ἡ τοῦ ἵππου ἀρετὴ, ἵππον τε σπουδαῖον ποιεῖ, καὶ ἀγαθὸν δραμεῖν, κ.τ.λ. "The vigour of the eye renders both the eye and its action excellent, in like manner the vigour of the horse renders the horse excellent and well fitted for running," etc.; so that τὸ σπουδαῖον is τὸ εὖ ἔχον, and is opposed to τῷ φαύλῳ, ib. c. 4. Therefore σπουδὴ signifies *activity, diligence;* and in the present case expresses the principal characteristic of repentance, when it seriously enters into the soul, a characteristic which καταφρονηταί, *despisers,* are devoid of, Acts xiii. 41. Six special characteristics presently follow this '*carefulness*;' and this one is again mentioned at ver. 12. The same word is also at ch. viii. 7, 8, 16, 17, 22.—ἀλλὰ ἀπολογίαν, κ.τ.λ., *but, clearing of yourselves*) *But* makes an emphatic addition [Epitasis]. Not only this, which I have said, *but* also, etc. Some of the Corinthians had behaved well, others not so well in that affair; or else even all in one respect had been blameless, in another, had been culpable; from which cause it was that various feelings arose. They had taken up the *clearing of themselves* [ἀπολογίαν, *self-defence*] and a feeling of *indignation,* in respect to themselves; they had *fear* and *vehement desire,* in respect to the apostle; *zeal* and *revenge,* in respect of him, who had been guilty of the sin. Comp. in this threefold respect ver. 7, note, and ver. 12, note.—ἀπολογίαν, *clearing of yourselves* [*self-defence*]) inasmuch as you did not approve of the deed.—ἀγανάκτησιν, *indignation*) inasmuch as you did not instantly restrain it.—ἀγανάκτησιν is used here with admirable propriety. It denotes the pain, of which a man has the cause in himself, for example in dentition; for E. Schmidius compares with this

passage that from Plato, κνῆσις καὶ ἀγανάκτησις περὶ τὰ οὖλα, *itching and pain about the gums*.—φόβον, *fear*) lest I should come with a rod.—ἐπιπόθησιν, *vehement desire*) to see me.—ζῆλον, *zeal*) for the *good* of the soul of him, who had sinned.—ἀλλ᾽ ἐκδίκησιν, *but revenge*) against the *evil*, which he had perpetrated, 1 Cor. v. 2, 3.—ἐν παντί) *in all* the respects, which I have stated.— συνεστήσατε ἑαυτοὺς, *you have approved yourselves to me*) you have given me satisfaction.— ἁγνοὺς εἶναι, *to be clear*) *To be* is a mild expression for *to have become;* for they had not been quite *clear*, 1 Cor. v. 6. A mutual amnesty is expressed in this and the following verse.—πράγματι, *in the matter*) He speaks indefinitely, as in the case of an odious occurrence.

13. Οὐχ ἕνεκεν τοῦ ἀδικήσαντος) Whatever I have written, I have written it, *not for the sake of him, who did the wrong*. He calls him τὸν ἀδικήσαντα, whom he calls, ch. ii. 5, τὸν λελυπηκότα. He now varies the term because the expression, *to make sorry*, he said concerning himself, ver. 8, 9; and he now dismisses this very *sorrow*. Inasmuch as you Corinthians have done what was just respecting him, who had committed the sin, by your *zeal* and *revenge*, I acquiesce.—οὐδὲ ἕνεκεν τοῦ ἀδικηθέντος, *nor for the sake of him, who suffered wrong*) The singular for the plural by euphemism. The Corinthians had *suffered wrong*, ch. ii. 5; and their *clearing of themselves*, and *indignation* put it now in Paul's power to acquiesce also on their account. Others explain it as referring to the offended parent, 1 Cor. v. 1.—τὴν σπουδὴν ἡμῶν, *our care*) Comp. ii. 4.—ἐνώπιον, *in the sight of*) Construed with φανερωθῆναι, that *it might be manifested*.

13. Ἐπὶ τῇ παρακλήσει ὑμῶν, *on account of your comfort*) which followed that very *sorrow*.—περισσοτέρως [1]μᾶλλον, *more abundantly rather* [*exceedingly the more*]) That feeling rather [μᾶλλον] takes the name of *joy* than *comfort;* and the *joy* was, περισσοτέρως, *more abundant*, than the *comfort*. So μᾶλλον with the superlative, xii. 9 : μᾶλλον for δὲ [2][autem], *yea and*, is put here with striking effect.

---

[1] Tischend. and Lachm. stop thus: διὰ τοῦτο παρακεκλήμεθα. ἐπὶ δὲ τῇ παρακλήσει, etc. The δὲ is put after περισσοτέρως by Rec. Text. But after ἐπὶ by BCD(Λ)Gfg Vulg.—ED.

[2] The omission, however, of the particle δὲ both in the margin of the 2d Ed. and in the Germ. Ver., is thought to be not quite so certain.—E. B.

14. Κεκαύχημαι, οὐ κατῃσχύνθην, *I have boasted, I am not ashamed*) ch. ix. 4, xii. 6.—πάντα, *all things*) He suitably refers to ch. i. 18.

16. Ἐν παντί, *in every thing*) This is applicable in the antecedent and consequent [in the context which precedes and that which follows]. He says, if I reprove you, you take it well; if I promise for you, you perform what is promised. So he prepares a way for himself with a view to what follows in viii. 1 and x. 1, where the very word θαρρῶ, *I have confidence*, is resumed.—ἐν ὑμῖν, *in you*) on your account.

CHAPTER VIII.

1. Γνωρίζομεν, *we make known*) This exhortation is inserted in this passage, which is extremely well suited to the purpose, and, after the preceding very sweet declaration of mutual love, with which it is connected by the mention of Titus; it is also set before them according to the order of Paul's journey, that the epistle may afterwards terminate in a graver admonition. Moreover the exhortation itself, even to the Corinthians, in respect to whom the apostle might have used the authority of a father, is even most especially liberal and evangelical.—τὴν χάριν, *the grace*) When anything is well done, there is *grace* to those, who do it, and also *grace* to those, to whom it is done. This word here is of frequent occurrence, ver. 4, 6, 7, 9, 19; ch. ix. 8, 14.

2. Θλίψεως, *of distress* (pressuræ) [*of affliction*]) joined to poverty, ver. 13, θλῖψις, *a burden of distress*.—περισσεία καὶ πτωχεία, *abundance and poverty*) An oxymoron and hendiadys pleasantly interwoven.—Κατὰ βάθους) Βάθους is the genitive, governed by κατὰ: comp. κατὰ, Matt. viii. 32: also E. Schmid., 2 John, ver. 3. He quotes his own syntax of Greek particles, an excellent book.—ἁπλότητος, *of* [liberality] *simplicity*) Simplicity renders men liberal, ch. ix. 11 [ἁπλότητα, which Engl. V. renders *bountifulness*].

3. Ὅτι, *because*) Anaphora with epitasis.[1]—μαρτυρῶ, *I bear witness*) This expression has respect to the words, κατὰ, *according to*, and παρὰ, *beyond*.—αὐθαίρετοι) *of their own accord;* not only not being besought, but they themselves beseeching us. See the following verse.

4. Δεόμενοι, *beseeching* [*praying*]) They had been affectionately admonished by Paul, not to do *beyond their power*. The Macedonians on the other hand besought [prayed], namely, that their gift might be received.—τὴν χάριν καὶ τὴν κοινωνίαν,[2] *grace and fellowship*[3]) a Hendiadys.

5. Ἔδωκαν, *they gave*) This word maintains the whole structure of the paragraph in the following sense: Not only have they given grace and a proof of fellowship, or δόμα, that gift, but they have altogether given their own selves. So Chrysostom, Homil. xvi. on 2 Cor.; comp. especially Homil. xvii., where he repeats ὑπὲρ δύναμιν ἔδωκαν. The nominatives αὐθαίρετοι, δεόμενοι are connected with the same verb ἔδωκαν; and the accusatives χάριν, κοινωνίαν, ἑαυτοὺς, depend upon it, in an easy and agreeable sense. The transcribers have thrust in δέξασθαι ἡμᾶς after ἁγίους; and those who consider these words as Paul's, give themselves great trouble, especially Beza. Different commentators have used different glosses, which are quite superfluous.—πρῶτον, *first*) their own selves, before [in preference and precedency to] their gift; comp. Rom. xv. 16.—τῷ Κυρίῳ, *to the Lord*) Christ.—καὶ ἡμῖν διὰ θελήματος Θεοῦ, *and to us by the will of God*) It is therefore called the *grace of God*, ver. 1. The Macedonians did not of themselves previously determine the amount of the gift, but left that to the disposal of the apostle.

6. Εἰς) Not the end, but the consequence is intended ["insomuch that"].—καθὼς προενήρξατο, *as he formerly began*) in regard to spiritual things, ch. vii. 15. To him, who has begun well, the things which are beyond turn out easy. He had gone to the Corinthians; he was going to the Corinthians.—ἐπιτελέσῃ, *he*

---

[1] See App. The same ὅτι, already used ver. 2, is again by Anaphora used here, to mark the beginnings of sections or sentences. The κατὰ δύναμιν makes an emphatic addition or epitasis.—ED.

[2] Rec. Text adds after ἁγίους the words δέξασθαι ἡμᾶς. But BCD(Λ)Gfg Vulg. omit them.—ED.

[3] = their free *gift of fellowship* to be ministered to.—ED.

would finish) *in this matter.* [*If you have attempted any good thing*, finish it.—V. g.]—εἰς ὑμᾶς, *in respect of you*) that you might imitate the Macedonians.

7. Ἀλλ' ὥσπερ, *but as*) He says, *but*. The things which Paul had formerly done with the Corinthians by means of Titus, had the force of an *injunction*, ἐπιταγὴ, vii. 15. Comp. 1 Cor. v. 7. He now acts differently: therefore the word *that* presently after depends on, *I speak*, in the following verse.—ὥσπερ, *as*) The Spirit leads to abundance in all respects.—γνώσει, *in knowledge*) This is mentioned appositely: comp. ch. vi. 6, note. Its conjugate γνώμην occurs presently at ver. 10: comp. 1 Cor. vii. 25, note.—καὶ πάσῃ σπουδῇ) *and in all diligence.* σπουδὴ here comprehends '*faith,*' and '*utterance*' (of the heart and of the mouth), '*knowledge,*' etc. And the genus or whole is often subjoined to the species or one or more parts, by introducing the connecting link, *and all;* ch. x. 5; Matt. iii. 5, xxiii. 27; Mark vii. 3; Luke xi. 42, xiii. 28, xxi. 29; Acts vii. 14, xv. 17, xxii. 5; Eph. i. 21, iv. 31, v. 3; Heb. xiii. 24, James iii. 16; Rev. vii. 16, xxi. 8, xxii. 15.—καὶ τῇ—ἀγάπῃ, *and in love*) He subjoins to the genus [σπουδὴ] the species [ἀγάπη] which is most connected with the matter in hand [viz. that they should contribute to their brethren in need].—ἐξ, *from*) He does not say, *in your love toward us*, but he says, *in love from you in us* [in the love which is on your part, and is treasured up in us], because the Corinthians were in the heart of Paul, ch. vii. 3. He pleads their love as an argument: he does not add, that they should give the more on account of Paul, who had preached to them the Gospel gratuitously.—ἵνα, *that*) This word depends on λέγω, *I speak*, elegantly subjoined [ver. 8].

8. Διὰ, *by*) Having mentioned to you in ver. 1, the diligence of others.—καὶ) *also.* This is more powerful than any *commandment.*—ἀγάπης, *of love*) nothing is *more forward* in zeal [referring to σπουδῆς] than love.—δοκιμάζων, *proving*) The participle depends on ver. 10.

9. Γινώσκετε γὰρ, *for ye know*) by that *knowledge*, which ought to include *love.*—χάριν, *the grace*) *love* most sincere, abundant, and free.—ἐπτώχευσε, *He became poor*) He bore the burden of poverty; and yet this is not demanded from you: ver. 14.—ἐκείνου, *of Him, His*) This intimates the previous greatness of

the Lord.—*πτωχείᾳ πλουτήσητε, through His poverty ye might be rich*) So through the instrumentality of all those things, which the Lord has suffered, the contrary benefits have been procured for us, 1 Pet. ii. 24, end of ver.

10. Καὶ, *and*)—*συμφέρει, is expedient*) An argument from *the useful,* moving them to give: So, ver. 16, ὑπέρ. A most pleasant paradox.—τὸ ποιῆσαι, *to do*) for the past year.—τὸ θέλειν, [to be forward] *to be willing*) for this year.

11. Τὸ ποιῆσαι, *the doing*) that you may do again.—ἐπιτελέσατε, *perform*) The beginning and especially the end of actions lays the foundation of praise or else blame, Gen. xi. 6; Josh. vi. 26; Jer. xliv. 25.—ὅπως, *that*) namely, *it may be.*—ἐκ τοῦ ἔχειν, *out of that which you have*) not more. The proposition [theme for discussion] in relation to what follows.

12. Πρόκειται, *if there be obvious* [if there be first]) So πονηρία πρόκειται ὑμῖν, *evil is before you,* Ex. x. 10.—εὐπρόσδεκτος, he is *well-acccepted* or *very acceptable*) to God, ch. ix. 7, with his gift. [Not as Engl. V. " it is accepted;" ix. 7 confirms this, " The Lord loveth a cheerful *giver.*"]—οὐ καθὸ οὐκ ἔχει, *not according to what a man has not*) For thus [were God's favour regulated by the amount of the gift, not by the willingness of the giver] a more humble person would be less acceptable.

13. Οὐ γὰρ) *for not,* viz. *the object aimed at is not.* The rule of exercising liberality.—ἄνεσις· θλίψις) The same antithesis is found, 2 Thess. i. 6, 7.—ἐξ ἰσότητος, *by an equality*) in carnal things. [*Love thy neighbour,* as thyself (not more).—V. g.]— ἐν τῷ νῦν καιρῷ, *at the present* [juncture] *time*) This limitation does not occur again in the following verse.—τὸ—περίσσευμα, *abundance*) in external resources [means]. The imperative γενέσθω is courteously omitted, for he does not *command,* ver. 8.

14. Καὶ τὸ—περίσσευμα, *that also their abundance*) in spiritual things.[1]—γένηται εἰς) We have the same expression at Gal. iii. 14.—τὸ ὑμῶν ὑστέρημα, *your* [spiritual] *want*) inasmuch as ye were Gentiles. Their [spiritual] abundance had already begun to supply the want of the Corinthians; he is therefore speaking

---

[1] As Jews. Eng. Ver. evidently takes it of *temporal* abundance, *i.e.,* that if *hereafter* ye be in want, their abundance may supply you, as you *now* supply them. But Beng. takes both "*your* abundance" (temporal) and *theirs* (spiritual) of the *present* time.—ED.

of continuation, increase, and reward [in spiritual things]. Nor yet would I venture to deny, that the *corporeal* abundance also of the Jews would sometimes supply the *corporeal* want of the Gentiles; for the limitation is omitted, ver. 13, note. Although [the view that the reference is to] the *spiritual* abundance of Israel is supported by the parallel passage, Rom. xv. 27.— ἰσότης, *equality*) in spiritual things.

15. Γέγραπται, *it is written*) Ex. xvi. 18, οὐκ ἐπλεόνασεν ὁ τὸ πολὺ, καὶ ὁ τὸ ἔλαττον, οὐκ ἠλαττόνησεν. The article τὸ adds to it the force of a superlative [τὸ πολὺ, *the most;* τὸ ἔλαττον, *the least*]. —ὁ τὸ πολὺ, *he who the most*) viz. συλλέξας, *gathered.* There is a similar expression, Num. xxxv. 8, ἀπὸ τῶν τὰ πολλὰ, πολλά.— οὐκ ἐπλεόνασε) *he had not more* than an homer.

16. Χάρις, *thanks*) There was earnest care in me [myself]: from which proceeded [to which was owing] the *exhortation* to Titus; but there was in Titus himself the same earnest care, divinely inspired; for which I return thanks to God. See how widely this duty of thanksgiving extends. Often in some particular case, one person has greater care than others, as was the case with Titus. This circumstance ought not to be blamed, but to be acknowledged as the *gift of God.*

17. Παράκλησιν, *the exhortation*) that which is given at ver. 6, namely, that he should go to you.—σπουδαιότερος, *more forward*) more active than to require exhortation, ver. 22.

18. Συνεπέμψαμεν, *we have sent along with him*) Timotheus and I. So ver. 1, etc. This word is repeated at ver. 22 by anaphora;[1] and in this passage, where it first occurs, is emphatic with μετά.—τὸν ἀδελφὸν, *the brother*) It was unnecessary to name this companion of Titus, and that 'brother,' who is spoken of at ver. 22. See ch. xii. 18. The ancients were of opinion, that Luke was intended; see the close of the epistle; comp. Philem. 24.—οὖ, *of whom*) He, who is faithful in the Gospel, will be faithful also in matters of inferior importance.

19. Χειροτονηθεὶς [*chosen*] *appointed*) This participle is not construed with, *he went unto you,* ver. 17: for that construction would interrupt the connection, ver. 18, 20, συνεπέμψαμεν—στελ-

---

[1] See Append. The repetition of the same word marking the beginnings of sections.

λόμενοι, *we sent along with—avoiding*. Therefore ὅς, *who*, is to be supplied, taken from οὗ, *of whom, whose*, in the preceding verse. The churches had given this companion to Paul, whithersoever he might go. Hence they are called the *apostles*, or *messengers of the churches*, ver. 23 : and Paul declares, that this office here also has respect to the present business. From this it is evident, that the rights of the churches are mutual [reciprocal].—συνέκδημος, *the companion of our travels*. Those, who read with Wolfius, συνέκδημος ὑμῶν, refer to it by mistake the various reading of the pronoun at the end of the verse.[1]—σὺν, *with*) construed with συνέκδημος, *the companion of our travels*. They carried along with them the gift of the Macedonians to Jerusalem.—πρὸς, *to*) construed with χειροτονηθείς, *chosen, appointed.*—αὐτοῦ τοῦ Κυρίου, *of the [same] Lord Himself*) viz. Christ, ver. 21.—καὶ προθυμίαν ἡμῶν, *our ready mind*) The proofs for reading ἡμῶν are by far the most numerous, and ὑμῶν has crept into a few copies, by an obvious exchange of the Greek pronoun, which was more readily made on account of the alliteration of the υ in ὑμῶν with προθυμίαν. The churches had charged the brother of whom he is here speaking, the companion of Paul, with their own gift, not with a view to the *readiness of the Corinthians*, which had less relation to the churches, but with a view to produce *readiness on the part of Paul* and of that brother, *i.e.* lest for fear of that *blame*, of which he afterwards speaks, their *willingness* to undertake and finish the business might be lessened.

20. Ἁδρότητι, *in this abundance*) This term does not permit the Corinthians to be restricted [niggardly] in their contribution.

21. Ἐνώπιον Κυρίου, *in the sight of the Lord*) in private, in truth : comp. Rom. xii. 17, note.

[2]22. Αὐτοῖς, *with them*) with Titus and the brother.—πεποιθηοει, *through the confidence*) construed with, *we have sent along with*, here and at ver. 18 : comp. v. 23.—εἰς ὑμᾶς, which we feel *towards [in] you*) concerning your liberality.

[1] Therefore both the margin of the 2d, as well as of the larger Ed. and the Germ. Ver., prefer the reading ἡμῶν.—E. B.
At the *end of the verse* ἡμῶν is the reading of all the best Uncial MSS., BCG, etc., Vulg., etc. Rec. Text has ὑμῶν with but slight authority.—ED.

[2] Ἐνώπιον ἀνθρώπων, *in the sight of men*) Men are depraved, and are therefore suspicious. Hence also it is just, that men of the highest integrity should avert all suspicion.—V. g.

23. Ὑπὲρ, [pro] *in behalf of, for*) This gives the motive of the confidence.[1]—Τίτου, κοινωνὸς, *in behalf of Titus, a partner*) These words are in apposition; comp. [ch. xi. 28] Luke xxii. 20 [διαθήκη ἐν τῷ αἵματί μου, τὸ ὑπὲρ ὑμῶν ἐκχυνόμενον], note.—ἀδελφοί, *brethren*) It might have been said *for*, or *in behalf of our brethren*, but the word κοινωνὸς, *partner*, coming in between as the nominative case, *brethren* is also put in the nominative, and the verb *are* is supplied, *i.e.*, whether they are and are regarded as our brethren for the sake of whom we are confident you will be liberal].—ἀπόστολοι) *deputies, messengers;* persons who on the public account execute a pious office. Again supply *are*.

24. Ἔνδειξιν ἐνδείξασθε) This expression is the same idiom as χαίρειν χαράν.[2]—εἰς αὐτοὺς, εἰς πρόσωπον τῶν ἐκκλησιῶν, *to them, in the face of the churches*) The knowledge of the matter was sure to spread by means of the messengers [deputies] among the churches.

CHAPTER IX.

1. Τὸ γράφειν, *to write*) For you will have witnesses present with you, and I know, that you are ready without writing letters to you.

2. Καυχῶμαι, *I boast*) The present tense. Paul was still in Macedonia.—[3] ὁ ἐξ ὑμῶν ζῆλος) *the zeal, which was propagated from you* to the Macedonians.—τοὺς πλείονας) *most* [not merely *very many*, as Engl. V.] of the Macedonians.

3. Ἔπεμψα, *I sent*) before me, ver. 5.—ἐν τῷ μέρει, *in this respect* [*behalf*]) He makes a limitation.—καθὼς ἔλεγον, *as I was saying*, ver. 2.

4. Ὑμεῖς, *ye*) much more so [you would feel still more ashamed than we].—ὑποστάσει, *stedfast confidence*) [concerning your liberality], ch. xi. 17.

---

[1] *i.e.* We feel confident you will be liberal *for the sake of* Titus.—ED.

[2] An accus. of a cognate signification to the verb, Manifest a manifestation.—ED.

[3] Ἀπὸ πέρυσι, *since last year*) owing to the former exhortation of Paul, 1 Cor. xvi. 1.—V. g.

5. Ἀναγκαῖον, *necessary*) not merely [suitable] *becoming*.—*προ-επηγγελμένην, promised before* [But Engl. V., *whereof ye had notice before*]) by me, among the Macedonians, concerning you [the liberality on your part, which I had vouched for to the Macedonians].—εὐλογίαν) as דבר is used for *word* and *deed*, so εὐλογία, *a blessing* and a *benefit* ['bounty'], a bountiful gift, LXX. Josh. xv. 19.—εἶναι) for τοῦ εἶναι, *that it may be*.—οὕτως, *so*) The Ploce is by this word [*so*] shown in regard to *bounty*.[1]—πλεονεξίαν, [covetousness] *avarice*) It is *avarice*, when men give niggardly, and receive [get] unjustly.

6. Φειδομένως) *sparingly*. [*The reaping corresponds to the manner and principles of the sowing. The very words lead to that inference.*—V. g.].—εὐλογίαις) The plural adds to the force.

7. Καθὼς προαιρεῖται) *according as he purposeth* [is disposed] *in his heart*, Gen. xxxiv. 8, חָשְׁקָה נַפְשׁוֹ, LXX.—προείλετο ψυχῇ. *He purposeth beforehand: grudgingly: from necessity: cheerful;* Four expressions, of which the first and third, the second and fourth are opposed to each other.—ἐξ ἀνάγκης, *from necessity*) on this account only, that he cannot refuse.—ἱλαρὸν, *cheerful*) like God, Prov. xxii. 9, LXX., ἄνδρα ἱλαρὸν καὶ δότην ἀγαπᾷ (Alex. εὐλογεῖ) ὁ Θεὸς, *God loves a cheerful man and a cheerful giver* (Alex. *blesses*, instead of *loves*).

8. Πᾶσαν χάριν, *all grace*) even in external goods.—περισσεῦσαι, *to render abundant*) even while you bestow.—ἵνα, *that*) What is given to us is so given and we have it, not that we may have, but that we may do well therewith. All things in this life, even rewards, are seeds to believers for the future harvest.—αὐτάρκειαν, *sufficiency*) that you may not require another's liberality. To this is to be referred the *bread*, ver. 10.—ἀγαθὸν, *good*) in regard to the needy. To this the *seed* is to be referred, ver. 10.

9. Ἐσκόρπισεν, *He hath dispersed*) a generous word; *to disperse* [scatter] with full hand, without anxious thought, in what direction every grain may fall. There is also a metonymy,[2] *hath dispersed* [scattered], i.e., he always has, what he may disperse [scatter]. Indeed in Ps. cxii. 9 it is a part of the promise.— ἡ δικαιοσύνη αὐτοῦ, *his righteousness*) righteousness, i.e., beneficence:

---

[1] Ploce, where a word is used, as εὐλογία here, first in the simple sense, then to express some attribute of it.—See Append.—ED.

[2] Here the substitution of the *consequent* for the *antecedent*.—ED.

see the next verse. The latter is marked in its strict sense. *Righteousness* is something more.—μένει, *remains*) unexhausted, uneffaced, unfailing.

10. 'Ο δὲ) God.—ἐπιχορηγῶν, *He that supplies, or ministereth*) There is [implied an] abundance, inasmuch as seed is given; bread, which is a necessary, is therefore given first. Paul hints, that, in the promise of the seed, which is denoted by the verb *he hath dispersed*, the promise of bread also is presupposed; but he adds more: for there is in the text a Chiasmus;[1] God, who presents *seed* to the sower, will supply and multiply *your seed*: God, who gives *bread* for food, will increase the *fruits* [produce] of your righteousness, which feeds the soul. Righteousness is the food of the soul, Matt. v. 6; vi. 31, 33.—ἐπιχορηγεῖν, *to supply*, or *administer*, is emphatic; but χορηγεῖν *to give or minister*, with the addition of πληθύνειν, *to multiply*, implies more.—Σπόρος, *the seed*, *i.e.*, resources [worldly means], so far as they are piously laid out: γεννήματα, the *fruits*, [the offshoots], *i.e.*, the growth of all spiritual improvement and corporeal blessing, springing from that *sowing*. This mode of pointing has been already noticed in the Apparatus, so that the comma should be placed after βρῶσιν, not after χορηγήσει.—καὶ ἄρτον, *and bread*) Is. lv. 10, ἕως ἂν δῷ (ὁ ὑετὸς) σπέρμα τῷ σπείροντι καὶ ἄρτον εἰς βρῶσιν, *until the rain give seed to the sower and bread for food*.—χορηγήσει, *will give*) The indicative.[2] The Corinthians will afford scope [opportunity for exercise] to the divine liberality, and it will evince itself towards them.—γεννήματα) so the LXX., γεννήματα δικαιοσύνης, Hos. x. 12.

11. Πλουτιζόμενοι, *being enriched*) This depends on, *that ye may abound*, ver. 8. The present here is used to imply; *having* more than a *sufficiency* [ver. 8].

12. Ἡ διακονία τῆς λειτουργίας ταύτης) *the administration of this service*, a becoming appellation. λειτουργία is the function itself, [service to be discharged,] διακονία, the *act*.—προσαναπληροῦσα, *still*

---

[1] See Append.
[2] Which is preferred both in the 2d Ed. and in the Germ. Vers. different from what had been the case in the first Ed.—E. B.

BCD(Λ) corrected later, *fg* Vulg. (but Fuld. MS. has præstavit—multiplicavit) Cypr. have χορηγήσει—πληθυνεῖ. G has χορηγήσαι—πληθύναι; and so Rec. Text. C has πληθύνῃ.—ED.

further supplies [supplies in addition]) a double compound. *Their wants were also supplied* from other quarters.—πολλῶν, *by many*) feminine [not " thanksgivings *of many*."]

13. Δοκιμῆς) [*the experiment*] *the proof afforded* by this ministration.—δοξάζοντες, *glorifying*) This depends on *thanksgivings*, ver. 12. Again the nominative case, on the same principle as viii. 23, note, [Τίτου, κοινωνὸς—ἀδελφοί.]—ἐπὶ τῇ ὑποταγῇ τῆς ὁμολογίας ὑμῶν, *for the subjection of your profession*) They were about to profess by their very acts, that they acknowledged the divine bounty shown to themselves in the Gospel, [*and had yielded* [victas dedisse sc. *manus*) *to the word of grace*.—V. g.]—καὶ εἰς πάντας, *and to all*) He, who benefits some of the saints, by that very act benefits all; for he shows, that he is favourable to all.

14. Δεήσει, *on account of their prayer*) [But Engl. Vers., "*by their prayer for you.*"] Construe, *glorifying* [δοξάζοντες, ver. 13] *for their prayer*; for we give thanks even for the prayers which have been given to us [which God has enabled us to offer], 2 Tim. i. 3 [*I thank God*, that without ceasing I have remembrance of thee in my *prayers*].—ἐπιποθούντων, *greatly desiring*) construe with αὐτῶν, *of them*.—διὰ, *on account of, for*) construe with *thanksgivings* [εὐχαριστιῶν, ver. 12].—ἐφ' ὑμῖν) which rests *upon you*, in such a degree as that it redounds to their advantage.

15. Χάρις, *thanks*) This is the meaning: God has given us τὴν δωρεὰν, the *gift*, abundance of good things both internal and external, which both is in itself *inexpressible*, and bears fruits of a corresponding description; comp. ver. 8, etc. (where there is an *expression* [an attempt to *express* the abundance of the gift], but its words are not adequate so as to satisfy Paul's mind), and ch. viii. 9, 1, and the *full expression* of these fruits, by reason of the copiousness of the topics, has rendered the language itself at the end of the preceding chapter somewhat perplexed. The modus[1] is added, *thanks be to God*.

---

[1] See Append. "Modalis Sermo." Here, the *modus* accompanying the simple naked proposition is thanksgiving.—ED.

CHAPTER X.

1. Αὐτὸς δὲ ἐγὼ Παῦλος, *now I Paul myself*) An expression very demonstrative and emphatic. *Myself* forms an antithesis, either to Titus and the two brethren, in reference to what Paul premised [viii. 18, 22, ix. 3] : or, to the Corinthians, who of themselves were bound to attend to their duty; or, even to Paul himself, who was about to use greater severity when in their presence [ver. 2, 11], so that αὐτὸς, *myself*, may signify, *of my own accord*.—παρακαλῶ) *exhort, advise*, for your sake ; when I might command and threaten. The antithesis is δέομαι δὲ, *but I beseech*, for my own sake, in the next verse [Engl. Vers. loses this antithesis by rendering both verbs, *I beseech*]. —διὰ, *by*) A motive equally applicable to Paul and the Corinthians.—πραότητος καὶ ἐπιεικείας, *the meekness and gentleness*) πραότης, *meekness*, a virtue more absolute: ἐπιείκεια, *leniency, gentleness*, is more in relation to others. Each of these is the true source of even his severest admonitions [and ought to be so in ours also].—τοῦ Χριστοῦ, *of Christ*[1]) This signifies, that he did not derive his meekness from nature. Or else, διὰ, *by*, is used as at Rom. xii. 1 [I beseech you *by the mercies of God*], so that the *meekness and gentleness* of Christ Himself seem to be understood ; but the objection to this view is, that ἐπιείκεια, *gentleness*, appears to be predicated of Christ Himself in no other passage, and this is a usual mode of speaking with Paul, to represent Christ as working and exerting His power in him and by him. Comp. the phrase, *the truth of Christ* [*is in me*], *i.e., the truth* in *Christ*, 2 Cor. xi. 10 ; and add Phil. i. 8, note.—ὃς, *who*) This is a pleasant mimesis or allusion to their usual mode of speaking, ver. 10, a figure which is also here repeated more than once in the verb λογίζομαι.[2]—ταπεινὸς) *humble* [lowly. Engl. Vers., *base*], timid.

---

[1] *i.e.* By the meekness and gentleness derived by me *from Christ*.—ED.

[2] Λογίζομαι, *I am thought*, Λογισμοὺς, ver. 5; λογιζέσθω, ver. 7 and 11, all refer to the λογισμοὶ of the Corinthians (ver. 2, λογιζομένους) by Mimesis.—ED.

2. Δέομαι, *I beseech*) *God;* as at xiii. 7, or here it is, *I beseech you.* Paul intimates, that, as he may beseech in his letters, so he can nevertheless act with severity in their presence.—λογίζομαι, *I am thought* [but Engl. Vers., *I think* to be bold]) Passive as in Rom. iv. 4, 5.—ἐπί τινας [*against*] *as to*, with respect to *some*) construe with *to be bold.*—τοὺς λογιζομένους, *thinking*) in the middle voice.—ὡς, *as if*) Connect it with *according to the flesh.* —κατὰ σάρκα, *according to the flesh*) as if they may despise us with impunity.

3. Ἐν σαρκί, *in the flesh*) with weakness. See the following verse.—[1] στρατευόμεθα, *we war*) By this word he opens the way for a transition to what follows; and the reason of *the boldness*, τοῦ θαρρῆσαι [ver. 2], is included.

4. Τὰ γὰρ ὅπλα, *for the arms* [*weapons*]) From the paternal *rod*, 1 Cor. iv. 21 [shall I come unto you with a rod?], he now proceeds to *arms*, with increasing severity; comp. presently ver. 6; also 1 Cor. v. 5, 13.—οὐ σαρκικὰ, ἀλλὰ δυνατὰ) *not carnal* and weak, *but* spiritual, and therefore *mighty.*—τῷ Θεῷ [Engl. Vers., "*through* God,"] *to God*) This is virtually an accusative case.[2] So ch. ii. 15, *to God.* In like manner, Acts. vii. 20; in the same way as the preposition ל is used as a prefix, Jonah iii. 3 [an exceeding great city, "lit. *a city of God*]. The power is not ours, but of God. The efficacy of the Christian religion is an argument of its truth.—ὀχυρωμάτων, *of strongholds*) A grand expression. [*The human understanding may here suspect inflated language; but it is no common force and power, to wit, the force and power of those things, which in the case of the soul are brought out on both sides* (both on the carnal and on the spiritual side).—V. g.]

5. Λογισμοὺς [*imaginations, reasonings*] *thoughts*) those very thoughts of which he speaks, ver. 2.[3]—καθαιροῦντες, *casting down*) This expression might be construed with ver. 3, but it rather depends on ver. 4, *the pulling down* [καθαίρεσιν]. Again, the

---

[1] Ἐν σαρκί—οὐ κατὰ σάρκα, *in the flesh—not according to the flesh*) There is a great difference.—V. g.

[2] As the Accus. is often used adverbially, forming an adverbial epithet. —ED.

[3] Λογισμοὺς alludes, by Mimesis, to the Corinthians, τοὺς λογιζομένους, etc., ver. 2.—ED.

nominative is used for an oblique case, as in ch. ix. 13, note.—παν ὕψωμα, *every high thing*) *Thoughts* is the species; *high thing*, the genus. He does not say, ὕψος; comp. Rom. viii. 39, note.[1]— ἐπαιρόμενον, *exalting itself*) like a wall and a rampart.—κατὰ τῆς γνώσεως τοῦ Θεοῦ, *against the knowledge of God*) True knowledge makes men humble [*attributing all power to* GOD *alone.*—V. g.] Where there is exaltation of self, there the knowledge of God is wanting.—αἰχμαλωτίζοντες πᾶν νόημα) Νόημα implies the *faculty of the mind*, νοός, of which λογισμοί, the *thoughts*, are the acts. The latter, hostile in [of] themselves, are *cast down*; the former *vanquished* and taken captive is wont to surrender itself, so that it necessarily and willingly tenders the obedience of faith to Christ the conqueror, having laid aside all its own authority, even as a slave entirely depends on the will of his master.

6. Ἐν ἑτοίμῳ ἔχοντες) viz., ἡμᾶς, he says, we are *ready* [having ourselves in readiness]. We have zeal already; and it will be brought forth into action at the proper time.—πᾶσαν, *all*) This has a more extensive meaning than ὑμῶν, *your*, presently after. —ὅταν, *when*) lest the weaker should be injured,[2] ver. 8. This is the principal point of pastoral prudence. [*Paul had already done something of this sort at Corinth*, Acts xviii. 7. *On a similar principle*, GOD *exercises so great long-suffering as He does, in regard to an immense multitude of wicked men, till those things which can be gained thereby, have been drawn forth.* See Exod. xxxii. 34.—V. g.]

7. Τὰ κατὰ πρόσωπον βλέπετε, *do you look on the things according to the face* [*outward appearance*]) The error of the Corinthians is noticed and refuted generally, ver. 7–9: then, having been specially detailed, it is specially refuted, ver. 10, 11. Therefore [ver. 7] *let him think this* [ver. 11], is repeated.— κατὰ πρόσωπον, *after the face* [*outward appearance*]) ver. 1. In antithesis to, *by letters*, ver. 9. He says, I can act with severity face to face [as well as *by letters*: πρόσωπον being opposed to ἐπιστολῶν].—εἴ τις) *if any one* of you.—πέποιθεν) πεποίθησις and πέποιθα, have been hitherto variously used by Paul in this epistle, ver. 2, etc.—ἀφ' ἑαυτοῦ, *of himself*) before he is in a more

---

[1] ὕψος the primitive, *height* absolutely: ὕψωμα a kind of verbal, not so much *high*, as a thing *made high*, elevated, elated.—ED.

[2] Were I prematurely before the time *to revenge disobedience.*—ED.

severe manner convinced of it by us. The Christian by his own feelings can measure his brother.—καθὼς, *even as*) The condescension of Paul, inasmuch as he merely demands an equal place with those, whom he had begotten by the Gospel; for he himself must previously have belonged to Christ, or been a Christian, by whom another was brought to belong to Christ. This was a cause [motive] for modesty [a modest feeling towards Paul] in the case of the Corinthians.—καὶ ἡμεῖς, *we also*) A fact which such a man [one that trusts he belongs to Christ] will be able to realize by experience.

8. Γὰρ, *for*) This word makes an emphatic addition to the previous enunciation [epitasis].—καὶ περισσότερον τι, *even somewhat more exceedingly* [excellently]) for they were not only Christians, but apostles, etc.—ἐξουσίας, *of the power*) ver. 6, xiii. 10.—ὁ Κύριος, *the Lord*) Christ.—οὐκ αἰσχυνθήσομαι, *I shall not be ashamed*) It will not be mere flashes of lightning from a basin;[1] I shall not shrink from exercising my authority.

9. Ἵνα μὴ) I say this, *lest*, etc.—ὡς ἄν) Apposite particles [*as though I would*].—ἐκφοβεῖν ὑμᾶς, *terrify you*) as if you were children, with vain terror.

10. Φησί) *saith he* [one], viz. he, who thus speaks: viz. he, who is mentioned at ver. 11. The concealed slanderer is intended, whom the Lord, or even Paul, by the Lord's pointing him out, saw. There was such a slanderer also among the Galatians; Gal. v. 10.—βαρεῖαι, *weighty*) the antithesis is *contemptible*.—ἰσχυραί, *powerful*) the antithesis is *weak*.—παρουσία, *his presence*) This was an instance of the same truth embodied in the saying of the present day: *One's presence diminishes one's fame*. The Anthologium of the Greek Church for the 29th day of June has a commemoration of Peter and Paul, with a representation of the form of both the apostles, and, so far as Paul is concerned, it agrees well enough with this passage.— ἀσθενής, *weak*) occasioning no fear to the spectators.

11. Τῷ λόγῳ, *in word*) In antithesis to τῷ ἔργῳ, *in deed*.

12. Οὐ γὰρ τολμῶμεν, *for we dare not*) Paul very fully vindicates his apostolic authority, under which the Corinthians are also placed: and he refutes the false apostles, who, [xi. 13, 14] assum-

[1] A figurative expression for, a man must not be ashamed to assert his authority, if he wishes to make it of avail to correcting abuses.—ED.

ing any specious form whatever, also obtruded themselves among them, and put the sickle into Paul's harvest. Reproving the *bold daring* of these drones, he says, *we dare not*; in which, while he tells what he himself does not do, he marks by implication, what they are doing. I, says he, claim nothing to myself from them [I own no connection with them]; let them in turn cease to join themselves to us [identify themselves with us], even at Corinth. He puts a hedge between himself and them.—ἐγκρῖναι ἢ συγκρῖναι) *to place* [*ourselves*] *on the same level*, as sharers of the same office; or *to compare* [ourselves] as partakers of the same labour; both, in respect to you: ἐγκρίνονται, *things are placed on the same level* with one another, which are of the same kind; συγκρίνονται, *things are compared*, which, though they differ in kind, are supposed to have at least the same relative aspect [rationem]. μετροῦντες presently after corresponds to ἐγκρῖναι, as συγκρίνοντες to συγκρῖναι.—τῶν) The Genitive. Of those, who commend themselves, the boldest ἐγκρίνουσι, *place themselves on the same level*, etc.—καὶ συγκρίνοντες, *and comparing*) This expression is put at the beginning of the clause for the sake of emphasis.—ἑαυτοῖς,[1] οὐχί, κ.τ.λ.) See App. Crit. on this passage. This phraseology does not indeed apply to the false apostles, who really attempted to measure themselves by others, and to obtrude themselves among them. Paul, on the contrary, says of himself and those like himself, *we measure ourselves by ourselves*, not by them, the false apostles; *we compare ourselves with ourselves*, not with them.[2]

13. Οὐχί, *not*) From ver. 13 to 16, both the ἔγκρισις and the σύγκρισις [alleged by the false apostles as subsisting] between the apostle and the false apostles are utterly set aside. This is the summary of his argument: οὐχὶ εἰς τὰ ἄμετρα καυχησόμεθα ἐν ἀλλοτρίοις κόποις. The first member, οὐχὶ εἰς τὰ ἄμετρα, is put in antithesis to the ἐν ἑαυτοῖς μετροῦντες, and is treated of ver. 13, 14, the word μέτρον being often repeated. The second, οὐχὶ ἐν ἀλλοτρίοις

---

[1] D(Λ)G*fg* Vulg. Lucif. omit οὐ συνιοῦσιν. But B reads the words (συνιᾶσιν, which Lachm. prefers): so also Memph. and both Syr. Versions.—ED.

[2] It is consistent with this, that the *Ger. Ver.*, although it expresses the words οὐ συνιοῦσιν ἡμεῖς δὲ, yet so arranges the agreement of the words, that the same sense comes out, which the *Gnomon* gives.—E. B.

κόποις, is put in antithesis to the ἑαυτοῖς συγκρίνοντες, and is treated of ver. 15, 16, the word ἀλλοτρίοις being repeated. Paul has a *measure;* they boast as to things that are *without measure* [*in immensa* gloriantur], and Paul will proceed to preach the Gospel among the *untutored* [rudes, *heretofore untaught*] Gentiles; they boast εἰς τὰ ἕτοιμα, *of things made ready* for them [ver. 16].—εἰς) *as to,* concerning; comp. ver. 15, note.—ἄμετρα, *things without measure*) an acute amphibology; ἄμετρον is that which either does not keep, or else has not a standard or measure. Paul keeps his measure; the false apostles have none at all.—ἀλλὰ) *but,* viz., we will act.—τὸ μέτρον τοῦ κανόνος, *the measure of the rule*) Μέτρον καὶ κανὼν is a phrase sometimes used as a combination of synonyms: here they differ. Μέτρον is said in respect of God who distributes the several functions, κανὼν, in respect of the apostle who labours in the discharge of his function. Therefore κανὼν is determined by μέτρον; for μέτρον with Eustathius is τάξις; and μέτρον and μερίζω are conjugates, because both are from μείρω, comp. Clavis Homerica, p. 222. Their respective provinces were apportioned to each of the apostles.—μέτρου, *a measure*) This word is repeated, so that the οὗ may be explicitly recognised as having relation to μέτρον.—τοῦ κανόνος is put absolutely. After the accusative μέτρον the genitive μέτρου is put, to mark *the part* [μέρος taken out of ἐμέρισεν, *i.e.* the province assigned to Paul] among the Corinthians.—ἐμέρισεν, *distributed*) By this verb the false apostles are openly excluded.—ἐφικέσθαι) *i.e.* τοῦ ἐφικέσθαι.—ἄχρι καὶ ὑμῶν) *even to you.* Meiosis.

14. Οὐ γὰρ ὑπερεκτείνομεν) *for we stretch not ourselves* beyond our measure.—ἄχρι γὰρ, *for as far as*) Paul proves from the effect, that the Corinthians were included in the rule marked out to him by God.—ἐν τῷ εὐαγγελίῳ, *in the office of* (preaching) *the Gospel*) comp. ii. 12, [ἐλθὼν—εἰς τὸ εὐαγγέλιον Χριστοῦ, *when I came to* (preach) *Christ's Gospel.*]

15. Οὐκ εἰς, *not in relation to*) This is the beginning of the second member [See beginning of note ver. 13], which, so far as the construction is concerned, is connected with the end of the first: comp. notes on Rom. viii. 1. *We* will *not* make an advance into any other man's province, saying: *These are*

---

[1] See App.

mine.—αὐξανομένης, *increasing*) The present [*as your faith is now increasing*. But Engl. V. *When your faith is increased*]. Paul wished neither to leave the Corinthians before the proper time, nor to put off [preaching to] others too long.—ἐν ὑμῖν, *in your case*, [*by you*]) Our altogether solid and complete success in your case will give us an important step towards still farther successes. —μεγαλυνθῆναι—εὐαγγελίσασθαι) to be truly *enlarged* by *preaching the Gospel* [lit. *So as to preach the Gospel*]. *To boast* is in antithesis to both verbs conjointly, but especially to *enlarged*.—εἰς περισσείαν) *abundantly*.

16. Εἰς, *to*) or in relation to. The antitheses are, *in the places beyond you*, and, *as to the things* (places) *that are ready to our hand*.—τὰ ὑπερέκεινα, *those places, which are beyond*) to which no person has yet come with the Gospel, towards the south and west; for he had come from Athens to Corinth, Acts xviii. 1.— οὐκ ἐν ἀλλοτρίῳ, *not in another man's*) The antithesis is, *according to our rule* [ver. 15].—εἰς) to intrude ourselves by boasting into [as to] those things (places) which are ready to our hand.—ἕτοιμα, *ready*. It denotes even more than ἡτοιμασμένα.[1]

17. Ὁ δὲ, *but he who*) He hereby in some measure sounds a retreat; and yet by this very clause of after-mitigation,[2] he again gives a blow to the false apostles.—ἐν Κυρίῳ, *in the Lord*) and therefore with the *approval* of the Lord [ver. 18].

CHAPTER XI.

1. Ὄφελον, *would that*) He step by step advances with a previous mitigation[3] and anticipation of blame to himself [προεπίπληξις] of a remarkable description, to which the after-extenuation [ἐπιθεραπεία] at xii. 11 corresponds.—μακρὸν, *a little*) The anti-

---

[1] *Made ready* for an occasion. But ἕτοιμα in a *state of* readiness, habitually ready.—ED.
[2] See App., under the tit. EPITHERAPIA.
[3] See App., under the tit. Προθεραπεία. Here, an anticipatory apology for what he is about to say, which might seem inconsistent with modesty on his part.

thesis is found at ver. 4, 20.—τῇ ἀφροσύνῃ, *in my folly*) He gives it this appellation, before that he explains it, and by that very circumstance gains over the Corinthians. This is a milder word than μωρία.[1]—ἀνέχεσθε, *bear with*) The imperative; comp. ver. 16.

2. Ζηλῶ γὰρ, *for I am jealous*) In this and the following verse the cause of his *folly* is set before us: for lovers seem to be out of their wits.[2] The cause of the forbearance due to Paul is explained ver. 4, comp. ver. 20.—Θεοῦ ζήλῳ, *with a godly jealousy*) a great and holy jealousy. [*If I am immoderate*, says he, *I am immoderate to God.*—V. g.]—ἡρμοσάμην, *I have espoused*) There is an apposition, *to one husband*, viz. *Christ*, and both are construed with, *that I may present you* [viz. *to one husband, Christ*]. Therefore *I espoused* is put absolutely. [But Engl. V. *I have espoused you to one husband.*] Moreover ἁρμόζομαι, *I espouse*, is usually applied to the bridegroom. But here Paul speaks of himself in the same feeling of mind as when he ascribes to himself 'jealousy,' which belongs properly to the husband; for all that he felt, and all that he did, was for the sake of Christ.—παρθένον ἁγνήν, *a chaste virgin*) not singly [the individual members], but conjointly [the whole body together]. He does not say, *chaste virgins*, παρθένους ἁγνάς.

3. Φοβοῦμαι, *I fear*) Such fear is not only not contrary to love, but it is a property of love, ch. xii. 20, 19. [*All jealousy doubtless arises from fear.*—V. g.]—δὲ, *but*) This is opposed to, *I have espoused.*—ὡς, *as*) a very apposite comparison.—Εὔαν, *Eve*) who was simple and unacquainted with evil.—πανουργίᾳ, *through subtilty*) which is most inimical to *simplicity.*—οὕτως, *so*) The saints, even though original sin were entirely quiescent, may be tempted.—φθαρῇ, *should be corrupted*) Having lost their virgin

---

[1] Ἄφρων, according to Tittmann (Syn. New Testament), is one who does not rightly use his mental powers. Paul, in ver. 16, calls himself ἄφρων, because after the manner of men he boasted ὡς ἄφρων. The fault of the ἄφρονες is ἀφροσύνη; that of the ἀνόητοι (those who follow false rules of thought and action) is μωρία, opposed to σοφία. 'Αφροσύνη, 'insipientia,' is applied to what is *senseless, imprudent*, ex. gr. *rashness in speaking*, Mark vii. 22. But Μωρία, 'stultitia,' *folly* of a perverse and often of a *wicked* kind, Matt. v. 22.—ED.

[2] The Latin words are, "*amantes* enim videntur *amentes*," which cannot be imitated in a translation.—T.

purity. Seducers threatened the Corinthians; see next verse. An abbreviated mode of expression for, *May be corrupted* and drawn from their *simplicity.*—ἁπλότητος, *the simplicity*) which is intent on *one* object, and most tender; which seeks not *another* [Jesus; ἄλλον] nor a *different* [Spirit: ἕτερον, *second* and *different*], ver. 4.

4. Εἰ, *if*) He lays down a condition, on the part of the real fact, which is impossible; he therefore says in the imperfect, *you might tolerate it* [but as the condition is impossible, you ought not tolerate it]; but as regards the attempt of the false apostles, not only is the condition laid down possible, but is actually realized and present. He therefore says in the present, *preacheth* [not Imperf. as, ἠνείχεσθε, *Ye might tolerate* it]; comp. Gal. i. 6, 7.—γὰρ) The reason of Paul's fear was the yielding character of the Corinthians.—ὁ ἐρχόμενος, *he that cometh*) any one; out of Judea, if you please; Gen. xlii. 5, ἦλθον μετὰ τῶν ἐρχομένων, *they came with those that came*. [*He already states, what the Corinthians were in duty bound to allow to be stated*, ver. 1.— V. g.]—ἄλλον· ἕτερον, *another—a different*) These words are different from each other. See Acts iv. 12, note. ἄλλον separates [from the true person] by a far less definite boundary here than ἕτερον.[1]—οὐκ ἐλάβετε, ye have not *received*.—οὐκ ἐδέξασθε, *ye have not accepted*) Distinct words, well suited to the respective subjects; the will of man does not concur in ' receiving' [λαμβάνετε—ἐλάβετε] the Spirit, as in ' accepting' [ἐδέξασθε] the Gospel.[2]—ἢ εὐαγγέλιον ἕτερον, *or another gospel*) The words, *if there be*, or, *if you receive*, are appropriately [for convenience' sake] left to be understood.—καλῶς ἠνείχεσθε, *you might well bear with*) This *forbearance*, as being likely to lead to *corruption* [ver. 3], is not approved, but the word, with καλῶς, is used as at Mark vii. 9. The fulness [saturitas, *fulness to satiety*] of the Corinthians is noticed, and their eagerness for

[1] Ἄλλος, according to Tittmann, denotes *another*, without regard to any diversity or difference, save that of number. Ἕτερος indicates not merely another, but also one different. Ἕτερος, according to Ammonius, is said ἐπὶ δυοῖν in the case of two; ἄλλος, ἐπὶ πλειόνων in the case of more than two.—ED.

[2] The Engl. V. has happily expressed the distinction by 'received,' ἐλάβετε, of a thing in receiving which we are passive, and which is not dependent on our will: 'accepted,' ἐδέξασθε of that, the receiving of which is at our own will; to receive to one's self, to accept, to welcome.—ED.

a more novel and splendid Christianity, if any such was to be found.

5. Γάρ, *for*) The particle connecting the discussion with the proposition [the subject he proposed to discuss]. The sum of Paul's *boasting* is here stated and repeated, ch. xii. 11.—τῶν ὑπερλίαν, *the very chiefest*) such as James, Kephas, John [*distinguished for their high privilege in being witnesses of the transfiguration of Jesus.*—V. g.], or even the other survivors of the twelve, Gal. ii. 2, not merely such as those, who are called apostles in a wider sense, *i.e.* I am as much an apostle as he who is most so. Peter has no title to any preference. [Acts xxvi. 13, 16; Gal. i. 16.]

6. Εἰ, *if*) He proves himself to be an apostle, 1. from his knowledge worthy of an apostle; 2. from his self-denial in refraining from asking them for maintenance, ver. 7, 8. He makes by anticipation a way to himself for stating both of these facts, so that the necessity of stating them may be clearly seen. —ἰδιώτης, *rude*) This word is opposed to *his apostolic eminence* [ver. 5]. His detractors spoke of Paul as 'rude' [untutored]. He declares that he was not rude in *knowledge*, which was the first gift of an apostle: and an extraordinary instance of it is found in the next chapter. That he was rude in speech, he neither very strongly denies, since that was not injurious to the apostleship, nay, it conduced to its advantage, 1 Cor. i. 17, etc.: nor does he confess it with greater prolixity [at greater length] than his power in speaking allowed; nor does he answer, that other apostles also may be considered rude in speech, but he leaves the matter undetermined, comp. ch. x. 10, 11, and to be decided by the Corinthians themselves; for he adds: *but we have been made manifest to you in all things*, etc. [*He therefore removes out of the way one after another of those things, which the Corinthians opposed to his prerogative as an apostle.*--V. g.]— ἀλλ' ἐν παντὶ φανερωθέντες ἐν πᾶσιν εἰς ὑμᾶς) The Vulgate has, *but we are manifested in all things to you*,[1] as if either ἐν παντὶ or ἐν πᾶσιν were superfluous. But the two expressions have a different meaning: ἐν παντί, *in every* thing, even in speech and know-

[1] *In omnibus autem manifestati sumus vobis.* So also the Ante-Hieronymic Lat. Versions *fg* and the uncial MS. G. But the weight of authorities support both ἐν παντὶ and ἐν πᾶσιν.—ED.

ledge; ἐν πᾶσιν, *in all* men, ch. i. 12, iii. 2, iv. 2. ἐν πᾶσι, is used in the Masc. gend., 1 Cor. viii. 7; Heb. xiii. 4, and in other places. At the same time it occurs in the Neut. gend., 1 Tim. iii. 11, iv. 15; 2 Tim. ii. 7, iv. 5; Tit. ii. 9, 10; Heb. xiii. 18. But ἐν παντί occurs only in the Neut. gend., and that too very often, ver. 9, ch. iv. 8, vi. 4, vii. 5, 11, 16, viii. 7, ix. 8, 11; Phil. iv. 6. Therefore in this passage ἐν πᾶσιν is masculine, ἐν παντί neut. So Phil. iv. 12, ἐν παντὶ καὶ ἐν πᾶσι μεμύημαι.—εἰς ὑμᾶς, *with respect to* [among] *you*) From the circumstance, that Paul was also engaged among others, the fruit redounded to the *hearts* of the *Corinthians*.

7. ἩΑΜΑΡΤΊΑΝ) *Or have I committed a sin?* So, an objection might be raised against that assertion of the apostle in last verse, ἐν παντί, *in everything*.—ταπεινῶν, *abasing myself*) in my mode of living. [*He had waived his* apostolic *right in this matter.*— V. g.]—ὑψωθῆτε, *ye might be exalted*) spiritually.—τὸ τοῦ Θεοῦ εὐαγγέλιον, *the Gospel of God*) *divine*, most precious.

8. Ἐσύλησα, *I robbed*) He imputes to himself the receiving of payment, to which he was most justly entitled, as *robbery*, and afterwards as *sloth* and a *burden*, comp. notes on 1 Cor. ix. 17. This word and *wages* are figurative expressions derived from military affairs.—λαβών, *taking wages*) for my journey, when I came to you. The antithesis is *present*, when I was with you [ver. 9].

9. Προσανεπλήρωσαν, [further] *supplied in addition*) A double compound. Paul *supplied* something by his own manual labour. —καὶ τηρήσω, *and I will keep*) so far is he from repenting.—See xii. 14.

10. Ἔστιν ἀλήθεια, *there is truth*) The verb is emphatically put first; *it stands* [fast as *the* (*a*) *truth* of Christ]. The expression refers to a special truth,[1] comp. Rom. ix. 1, note.—οὐ, *not*) a metonymy or substitution of the consequent for the antecedent: *my boasting will not be stopped*, *i.e.*, I will be in no way more burdensome to you hereafter than heretofore.

11. Ὅτι, *because*) *Love* is often offended even by refusing [favours].

12. Καὶ ποιήσω) *I will also still do*.—ἐκκόψω, *I may cut off*) It

---

[1] Not to the truth in general: therefore the article is omitted.—En

did not suit the false apostles to preach for nothing, ver. 20.—
τὴν ἀφορμήν, *the occasion*) in this matter, presently afterwards without the article, ἀφορμὴν, in any matter whatever.—ἐν ᾧ, *in which*) their boasting consisted *in* this, that they said: we are found to be, as Paul.

13. Οἱ γὰρ τοιοῦτοι, *for such*) The reason is herein given, [aetiologia] why he is unwilling, that they should be thought like him.—ψευδαπόστολοι, *false apostles*) This is now part of the predicate; the antithesis is at ver. 5. At length he calls a spade a spade. Δόλιοι, *deceitful*, presently afterwards, is in conformity with it. [*This is remarkable severity of language. Not a few have been of opinion:* Such men are of a disposition not altogether to be despised, and it was not proper, that they should be so invidiously covered with disgrace: viz., They saw Christ, and now give their daily testimony to Him; they therefore ought to hold some place among others. *But the cause of truth is most delicate; and the* Indifferentism, *which is so pleasant to many in the present day,* was not cultivated by *Paul.* (Er war kein so gefälliger Toleranz-Prediger. *He was no pleasant preacher of toleration.*) *There is this to be taken into account, that when his life was frequently in danger, the zeal of the apostle continued without showing any symptoms of weakness.*—V. g.]—εἰς ἀποστόλους Χριστοῦ, *as the apostles of Christ*) They did not altogether deny Christ, but they did not preach Him truly, ver. 23.

14. Οὐ θαυμαστὸν, *and no marvel*) *no great thing* in the following verse. It is more marvellous concerning [in the case of] Satan, inasmuch as he differs farther from an angel of light.—αὐτὸς) *he himself*, their author and master.—μετασχηματίζεται, *transforms himself*) Present, *i.e.* is accustomed to transform himself. He did that already in Paradise. The second Oration on the annunciation, ascribed to Gregory Thaumaturgus, in describing the character [Ethopoeia] of Mary, thus proceeds: μὴ πάλιν εἰς ἄγγελον φωτὸς μετασχηματισθεὶς ὁ ἀρχέκακος δαίμων, κ.τ.λ., *the devil the author of evil not being again transformed into an angel of light*, etc.—ἄγγελον φωτὸς, *an angel of light*) He does so, not only to injure us, but also to enjoy honour.—φωτὸς, *of light*) although Satan's power is still in darkness.

15. Οὐ μέγα, *no great thing*) no difficult matter.—αὐτοῦ, *his*) Satan's.—δικαιοσύνης, *of righteousness*) which is in Christ.—τὸ

τέλος, *the end*) Whatever may be the specious appearance, on which they now plume themselves, the *form* [alluding to their *transforming* themselves into "ministers of righteousness"] is at last stripped off from them. A most effectual criterion is derived from the future *end* of things, in the case of good and evil alike, Phil. iii. 19, 21.

16. Πάλιν λέγω, *I say again*) He begins this new subject of boasting with a prefatory repetition of the anticipatory mitigation [προθεραπείαν] from ver. 1, which certainly no man that is a *fool*, ἄφρων uses.—μὴ, *let not*) a particle of prohibition, *let no man think, that I am a fool.* This clause is not put in the way of parenthesis, but the meaning of the word λέγω, *I say*, falls upon this very clause.

17. Ὃ λαλῶ, οὐ λαλῶ κατὰ Κυρίον, *that which I speak, I speak it not after the Lord*) Therefore whatever Paul wrote without this express exception, was inspired and *spoken after the Lord;* nay even he wrote this passage, so as he has written it, and the exception peculiar to this passage, according to the rule of divine propriety, having received his instructions from the Lord; precisely as a literary man dictates to a boy a letter suited to a boy, though the boy could not have so written it of himself.

18. Πολλοί, *many*) What is allowed to many, is the more easily granted as an indulgence to one.—κατὰ σάρκα, *according to the flesh*) for example, that they are Hebrews, ver. 22.

19. Ἡδέως) [gladly] *willingly*.

20. Γὰρ, *for*) An intensive particle; ye suffer *fools;* for ye even suffer oppressors. Cleon in Thucydides, lib. iii.—πέφυκεν ὁ ἄνθρωπος τὸ μὲν θεραπεῦον ὑπερφρονεῖν· τὸ δὲ μὴ ὑπεῖκον θαυμάζειν, *the man was naturally disposed to treat with contempt flattering attentions, but to admire independence.*—εἴ τις, *if any one*) as the false apostles, who were given to much boasting.—καταδουλοῖ, *bring you into bondage*) The genus; two pairs of species follow.—κατεσθίει) So LXX., Ps. liii. 5.—λαμβάνει, *takes*) viz. from you; for ὑμᾶς, *you*, is not necessarily to be supplied, as appears if we compare the following clause.—ἐπαίρεται, *exalt himself* [*is exalted*]) under the pretext of the apostolic dignity.—εἰς πρόσωπον δέρει, *smite you on the face*) under the appearance of divine zeal. That may have happened to the Corinthians: comp. Is. lviii. 4; 1 Kings xxii. 24; Neh. xiii. 25; 1 Cor. iv. 11; 1 Tim. iii. 3

21. Κατὰ ἀτιμίαν, *in the way of ignominy* [*as concerning reproach*]) *as if I were already considered as one dishonoured* [*'despised'*]. See 1 Cor. iv. 10, and from the same passage we may also compare the term *weak* with this before us, and *wise*, φρόνιμοι, at ver. 19. Comp. with the use of κατὰ here, the καθ' ὑστέρησιν, *in respect of, in the way of, want*, Phil. iv. 11.—ὡς ὅτι ἡμεῖς ἠσθενήσαμεν) *as though we had been weak* in mind, having nothing, of which we might boast and in which we might show boldness. The antithesis follows : *but wherein soever any one is bold :* the *weak* and *dishonoured* [ἄτιμοι] cannot boast, but still I will be bold ; comp. ver. 30.—ἐν ἀφροσύνῃ, *foolishly*) So he terms it κατ' ἄνθρωπον, after the manner of men : comp. v. 16 ; and for the sake of modesty.

22. Ἑβραῖοι, *Hebrews*) He indicates the principal topics of boasting, of which the first and second are natural, the third and fourth are spiritual privileges : comp. Phil. iii. 5.—κἀγώ, *so am I*) a Hebrew (not a Hellenist) of the [sprung from] Hebrews.

23. Διάκονοι, *ministers*) outwardly.[1]—παραφρονῶν λαλῶ, *I speak as a fool*) Paul wrote these things, while he constantly laboured to deny himself.—ὑπὲρ) *above*, [I am] more than they. The more a man suffers, the more he *ministers*.—περισσοτέρως, *more abundantly*) The false apostles had also experienced *labours* and *imprisonments*, but in a less degree, the other hardships were peculiar to Paul.

24. Πεντάκις, *five times*) It is of advantage to the servants of God accurately to remember all that they have done and suffered with a view to relate them, according as it may be afterwards necessary. Comp. Gal. i.—τεσσαράκοντα παρὰ μίαν, *forty save one*) Thirteen strokes with a triple lash made thirty-nine. See Buxt. dedic. Abbrev.

25. Τρὶς ἐναυάγησα, *thrice I was shipwrecked*) before the shipwreck at Melita (Malta).—ἐν τῷ βυθῷ) ὁ βυθὸς denotes anything *deep :* but when it is used absolutely, *the sea*, especially here, as being connected with the mention of shipwrecks. The LXX. generally translate מצולה by βυθός.—ἐποίησα) *I have spent, swim-*

---

[1] And yet there was no need of this distinction, *if* the Critical Note on this passage be compared : "It is a question ; for he affirms, that they were not the ministers of Christ," ver. 15. The Germ. Ver. *agrees* with this.—E. B.

ming. Many persons, who have been shipwrecked, thus contend with the waters for many hours, so that they may at last escape.

26. Ὁδοιπορίαις, *in journeyings*) See Acts.—ἐν ψευδαδέλφοις, *among false brethren*) This danger is most distressing; being added to the others contrary to *expectation* [παρὰ προσδοκίαν], it has a pleasing effect. [*These men were bitter and pestiferous, although not destitute of the appearance of good.* Gal. ii. 4.—V. g.]

27. Ἐν, *in*) Five clauses; the second agrees with the first, the fourth with the third, in pleasant harmony.—ἐν λιμῷ, *in hunger*) Deut. xxviii. 48, ἐν λιμῷ καὶ ἐν δίψει, καὶ ἐν γυμνότητι, καὶ ἐν ἐκλείψει πάντων.

28. Χωρὶς, *beside*) The particle serves the purpose of connection.—τῶν παρεκτὸς) It is thus he terms *external* labours and troubles. Hitherto he describes his own; he now refers to those of others, that had been shared with him.—ἡ) The Apposition of the oblique and nominative case, such as that of Basil of Seleucia, ὦ φωνῆς, σωτηρίας πηγή : comp. note on Chrys. de Sacerd. p. 504.—ἐπισύστασίς μου, *that which cometh upon me*) The LXX. often use the verb ἐπισυνίστημι, and the verbal noun ἐπισύστασις, of the sedition of Korah and his associates : comp. Acts xxiv. 12. Here therefore we remark the disorderly conduct of those, who troubled Paul by the perverseness of their doctrine or life; for example, Gal. vi. 17.—καθ' ἡμέραν, *daily*) A large extent of time; and of place, in the words, *of all.*—πασῶν, *of all*) This is more modest than if he had said πάσης τῆς ἐκκλησίας, *of the whole church. Of all*, of those even, to whom I have not come, Col. ii. 1. Peter could not have alleged that of himself in an equal degree.[1]

29. Τίς, *who*) He not merely cares for the churches, but for the souls of individuals.—ἀσθενῶ, *I am weak*) not only through condescension, συγκατάβασις, 1 Cor. ix. 22, but through compassion.—σκανδαλίζεται, *is offended*) *To be weak* and *to be offended*, at least in this passage, differ, comp. Rom. xiv. 21, note. The former comes by itself; the latter, by means of others.—καὶ οὐκ ἐγὼ πυροῦμαι, *and I burn not*) He adds *I*, not in

---

[1] Since Peter was the apostle of the circumcision peculiarly. Whereas Paul was, of all the numerous churches of the uncircumcision.—ED.

the former [no ἐγὼ before ἀσθενῶ], but in this part of the verse, for there he suits himself to the weak man; here he confesses that he bears no resemblance to the party offending, as *he himself*, for the sake of the offended party, takes up the duties neglected by the offender. The duties, neglected by the person offending, are love, prudence, etc. Paul however at the same time takes upon himself the part of the offended person, or the inconvenience, which the offended person feels. All these things thus follow from the force of the relatives [the things mutually related]. Πυροῦσθαι τοῖς θυμοῖς is read more than once in 2 Macc. They think or speak badly, who, seeing a scandal or offence, say in the mother tongue [alluding to a German saying], *I have caused myself to offend.*

30. Εἰ) *if, i.e.* since.—τὰ τῆς ἀσθενείας μου καυχήσομαι, *I will glory of the things, which concern my infirmities*) an admirable oxymoron; xii. 5, 9, 10, for *infirmity* and *glorying* are antithetic terms.

31. Εὐλογητὸς, *blessed*) This increases the sacredness of the oath.—οἶδεν, *knoweth*) The persecution at Damascus was one of the first and greatest, and belonged particularly to this place; and Paul calls God to witness, for he could produce to the Corinthians no witness among men, concerning a matter which was known to few, and had happened long before: comp. Gal. i. 20. Luke afterwards recorded it, Acts ix. 25. This religious preface increases even the credit of the circumstances, related in the following chapter.

32. Ἐθνάρχης.) Thus Simon the high priest is called, 1 Mac. xiv. and xv.

CHAPTER XII.

1. Δὴ) *truly.*—οὐ συμφέρει μοι, *it is not expedient for me*) on account of the danger of becoming elated, and of the buffetings of Satan, and of hindering the exercise of Christ's power.— ἐλεύσομαι) *I will come*, he does not say, *I come*. He does not eagerly run at it; so, *I will glory*, not *I glory*, at the very con-

2 CORINTHIANS XII. 2.

clusion of ver. 5.—γὰρ, *for*) The cause, stated in the form of a short preface.—ὀπτασίας καὶ ἀποκαλύψεις, *visions and revelations*) *Visions*, in reference to seeing; *revelations*, to hearing, 1 Sam. ix. 15, LXX. Both in the plural number, because those *raptures* had two degrees [when he was *caught up* first " to the third heaven," ver. 2 ; then " into paradise," ver. 4], as he presently mentions. So *of revelations*, ver. 7. Paul had more visions and revelations, independently of these here.—Κυρίου, *of the Lord*) ver. 8, *i.e.*, of Christ, ver. 2.

2. Οἶδα· εἴτε· ἁρπαγέντα, *I knew : whether: caught up*) These things, repeated in the next verse, not only keep the reader in pleasant suspense, sharpen his mind, and add weight to well-considered [just] glorying (boasting) ; but also plainly express a double movement in this action. Clemens Alex. Strom. 1. v. ἕως τρίτου οὐρανοῦ, κἀκεῖθεν εἰς τὸν παράδεισον, f. 427. So also Irenaeus, l. 2, c. (56) 55 (where Grabius adds Justinus M., Methodius, and of more recent writers Jeremy Taylor), likewise l. 5, c. 36, where (comp. Matt. xiii. 23 ; John xiv. 2) he infers different habitations from the diversity among those who produce fruit [fruits of faith], and fixes a difference of abode, διαστολὴν οἰκήσεως, for those who have their joy in heaven, in paradise, in the splendour of the city. Athanasius in Apol., καὶ ἕως τρίτου οὐρανοῦ ἡρπάσθη καὶ εἰς τὸν παράδεισον ἀνηνέχθη, " and he was caught up into the third heaven, and was borne up into paradise." Orig. or his translator, on Rom. xvi., has these words, *into the third heaven, and thence into paradise*. Oecumenius, ἡρπάγη ἕως τρίτου οὐρανοῦ καὶ πάλιν ἐκεῖθεν εἰς τὸν παράδεισον, " he was caught up to the third heaven, and again thence into paradise." That different revelations are mentioned in this passage is acknowledged by Hilarius Diac. Primasius, Anselm, Pope Gregory in Estius, as well as Jerome on Ez. xxviii., Pelag. on this passage, Cassiodor. Haymo, Aquinas. The occurrence of the expression, *lest I should be exalted*, twice, corresponds to the fact, that he was twice caught up. Certainly *paradise*, coming last in the gradation with the emphatic article, denotes some inner recess in the third heaven, rather than *the third heaven* itself; an opinion which was very generally held by the ancients. See Gregor. Obs., c. 18 ; comp. Luke xxiii. 43, note, and Rev. ii. 7. Therefore the privilege was vouch-

safed to Paul only to *hear* the things of paradise; but he was permitted also *to see* the things of the third heaven; comp. the preceding verse; although even of the latter he speaks somewhat sparingly. The force of the verb οἶδα, *I know*, falls particularly upon the participle *caught*; comp. ὅτι, *how that*, ver. 4. —πρὸ ἐτῶν δεκατεσσάρων, *fourteen years ago*) construed with ἁρπαγέντα, *caught*. He recounts something that had occurred in former times: after a long period every one seems to have become different from himself (what he was before); so that he may the more freely relate the good and evil which he has experienced. [*Truly it was a long silence* (he had maintained as to the revelations to him), *and yet he had been engaged* (conversant) *among the Corinthians not for a short time, and was united to them in the closest bonds of intimacy.*—V. g.]—ἐν σώματι, *in the body*) This is without the article; then ἐκτὸς τοῦ σώματος, *out of the body*, with the article; and so consistently with this, the words are found in the next verse. Paul seems to *be of opinion*, that he was *out of* the body. Howsoever this may be, Claudianus Mamertus de Statu animae, c. 12, righty concludes from this, that the better part of man is incorporeal; and this, the soul itself, was the part caught up. Whatever existed, independently of the body of Paul, was without the body, or else within it.—οὐκ οἶδα, *I know not*. Ignorance of the mode does not take away the certain knowledge of the thing. The apostles were ignorant of many things.—ἁρπαγέντα, *caught up*) Comp. Acts viii. 39, note.—ἕως) *even to*, far *into* the third heaven; comp. εἰς, *into*, ver. 4. Is therefore paradise not included in the third heaven? Ans. ἕως, *even to*, is inclusive, as Luke ii. 15, etc.—τρίτου, *third*) The first heaven is that of the clouds; the second is that of the stars; the third is spiritual. The dual number in שׁמים denotes the two visible heavens. The nomenclature of *the third*, which eye hath not seen, has been reserved for the New Testament; comp. Eph. iv. 10, note.

3. Καί, *and*) The particle here is expressive of a new movement in this transaction. Suppose, that the *third heaven* and *paradise*, were quite synonymous; the force of Paul's language will be greatly diminished.—τὸν τοιοῦτον, *such a one*) τὸν ἐν Χριστῷ, *him who* was *in Christ*.—εἴτε, *whether*) This word is repeated, because, even if in the body he was caught up to the third

heaven, nevertheless, rising to a higher degree, he might have been caught up to paradise without the body.

4. Ἄῤῥητα) *unspeakable words*, not in themselves; otherwise Paul could not have heard them; but not to be spoken by *man*, as the word follows presently after, and therefore, by Paul himself. *Who* spoke those words? God, or Christ, or an angel or angels, or the spirits of the just? and to whom? Paul does not tell, if he knew. They were certainly words of great sublimity, for all heavenly words are not *unspeakable*, for example Ex. xxxiv. 6; Is. vi. 3, and yet these are very sublime. —οὐκ ἐξὸν, *it is not lawful*) ἐξὸν and δυνατὸν, *lawful* and *possible* are said of that which neither the thing itself, nor the law forbids. Therefore, *unspeakable words*, and *it is not lawful* mutually explain each other, and affirm either that man cannot speak these words, or that it is not lawful for him to do so. Others, who did not hear them, cannot; Paul, who did hear them, is not sufficiently able; and though he were able, yet it would not be lawful, it would not be proper in the state of mortality; because the inhabitants of the earth would not understand them, John iii. 12. Hearing has a wider range than speaking.— ἀνθρώπῳ, *for a man*) construed with *it is lawful*. The power of speaking is often narrower than that of knowledge.

5. Ὑπὲρ τοῦ τοιούτου, *in respect to such a one*) in the Masc. The antithesis is, *of myself*. We ought to remove the *I* from important matters. This verse has two parts, the one has the reason assigned [aetiologia] in the following verse; the other is explained, ver. 7, 8.—καυχήσομαι, *I will glory*) i.e. I might glory; comp. ver. 6 at the beginning.

6. Οὐκ ἔσομαι ἄφρων, *I shall not be a fool*) In the preceding chapter also he spake *the truth*, and yet he ascribes *folly* to himself; namely, because he gloried concerning things by no means glorious [viz. his sufferings], hence of things most glorious. —φείδομαι, *I forbear*) I treat of these things sparingly.—μή τις, *lest any one*) O how many are there even among theologians, who have no reverent dread in treating of such things! [*Not a few allow themselves to be thought of both at home and abroad more highly than is lawful; but how remarkably may they be considered as defrauding themselves in that way of a share in the honour which is in the power of* GOD. *If indeed you rejoice in*

the privileges of the sons of God, *see that this your light may shine, but remember to use* with caution and moderation *extraordinary circumstances.*—V. g.]—βλέπει· ἀκούει, sees, hears) in common life, while I am unable to prevent it.

7. Ἵνα μὴ ὑπεραίρωμαι, *lest I should be exalted*) In all the things, which Paul did, and which rendered him great, beloved, and admired among men, he might be less worthy of praise [elated] than in those, of which he was alone conscious to himself. The mind is vain and weak, which applauds itself on account of the applause of men. The better things [the preferable objects of desire] are within. [*How dangerous must* the exaltation of one's self be, *when* the apostle *required so much restraint.*—V. g.]— σκόλοψ) Hesychius : σκόλοπες, ὀξέα ξύλα ὀρθὰ, σταυροί, a sharp pointed stake is denoted; comp. the LXX., Num. xxxiii. 55; Ez. xxviii. 24. This general word is presently explained in a particular manner by those *buffetings :* and this double explanation does not require a third, variously attempted by those, who give a wrong meaning to the *buffetings.*—τῇ σαρκί, *in the flesh*) The ablative case, *in the flesh*, for the purpose of macerating the flesh. The same case occurs, 1 Pet. iii. 18, iv. 1, 6. This weakness was greater than all those, which had been enumerated in the preceding chapter, and that he might give an account of this weakness, he considered it necessary to mention revelations.—Ἄγγελος Σατᾶν, *the messenger of Satan*) Paul, after having had some experience of the *state* of the blessed *angels*, begins now to discover an *angel* of a different description. The word Σατᾶν only occurs in the LXX. twice or thrice, and that too as indeclinable; but Σατανᾶς is declined in thirty-four places in the New Testament, and among these, nine times by Paul; and in this single passage it is used as an indeclinable noun, by a well-weighed apocope [the loss of a syllable at the end], certainly not without good reason. Ἄγγελος Σατᾶν then does not seem in this passage to be in apposition, as if it were said *the angel Satan* for the devil, for the devil is nowhere called an angel, but he himself has his angels. Therefore Satan is either a proper name in the genitive or an adjective in the nominative, so that there is denoted either *an angel sent by Satan* or a *very destructive angel,* an angel like Satan himself or the devil, as distinguished from the fact of his being sent by Satan. The ambiguity seems to

intimate, that the apostle himself, with a view to his greater humiliation, must have been ignorant of what was the character of this angel. He had a revelation from heaven, a chastisement from hell. Job and Paul were harassed by an enemy: the angel of the Lord struck Herod.—ἵνα με, *that me*) Therefore Paul is not the angel himself (comp. however Num. as above quoted [wherein the Israelites are represented as making the inhabitants of the land whom they drive not out *thorns* in their sides]), but what is stated is, that the angel harassed Paul with blows: ἵνα, *that* is again elegantly placed in the middle of the clause, that the antithesis may twice precede the particle, twice follow it. For the *excellence of the revelations* and *the angel of Satan* are in antithesis, and likewise *to be exalted* and *to be buffeted.*—κολαφίζῃ, *buffet*) *With blows* (μεγάλαις ἀφαῖς; for this is considered the original root, by Eustathius). Slaves were beaten, 1 Pet. ii. 20, nor is there any obstacle to its being taken here in its proper acceptation, Job ii. 6, 7. For if the apostles and the Lord Himself received blows and other troubles from men, ch. xi. 24, 25; 1 Cor. iv. 11; Matt. xxvi. 67, comp. iv. 5; why should not Paul receive such from Satan or his angel, either visibly or invisibly. Such evils also befel Antony, as Athanasius mentions in his life. Opposition of every kind came in the way of the apostle, ver. 10, which he did not deprecate, but here he mentions something in particular, which harassed him with *infirmities* and met [counteracted] his exaltation with pain and disgrace, even more so or at least not less than the rage of lust, which has been excited in the members of the body (with which how wonderfully very holy souls may be tormented, may be learned by reading the writings of Ephraim Syrus, of Estius on this passage, of Joh. a Cruce and P. M. Petruccius), or the most violent headaches. Paul had become as it were of late afraid of the recurring attacks of these blows, inasmuch as he restrains himself in the time of boasting with such frequency as a reader in his natural state would despise and of which he would be weary. Chrysostom remarks, that Paul says κολαφίζῃ, that it *may buffet*, not κολαφίσῃ, that it *might buffet*, as concerning the present. The *sight* and *hearing* of Paul had been directed to the most magnificent objects: The *touch* [for the thorn was *in the flesh*] had been most severely tormented.

8. Τούτου, *for this*) Demonstrative. He had forgotten his exaltation.—τρίς) *thrice*, as the Lord Himself did on the Mount of Olives. Paul presented his three requests, I know not at what intervals. Then he patiently endured the thorn, when he saw, that it must be borne; he does not seem to have been without the thorn, even then when he wrote these things and so long as he was liable to exalt himself: comp. what follows.— τὸν Κυρίον, *the Lord*) Christ; see the next verse. Satan is not to be asked to spare us.

9. Εἴρηκέ μοι, *He said to me*) when I prayed for the third time. —ἀρκεῖ σοι ἡ χάρις μου, *My grace is sufficient for thee*) A very gracious refusal, expressed in the indicative mood. The Lord as it were put these words into Paul's mouth, that following them up he might say: O Lord, Thy grace is sufficient for me. There may be grace, even where there is the greatest sense of pain.— ἡ γὰρ δύναμις ἐν ἀσθενείᾳ τελειοῦται, *for* [power] *strength is perfected in weakness*) For δύναμις several have written δυναμίς μου, from the alliteration with χάρις μου. If Paul had written δυναμίς μου, I believe he would have subjoined ἐν ἀσθενείᾳ[1] σου. It is however here intimated, that, as *is the grace of Christ*, so *is the power of Christ*: γὰρ, *for*, here as often elsewhere, is a discriminative particle, by which a distinction is made between *grace* and *strength. Grace is sufficient:* do not ask sensible *strength; for strength* [is made perfect in weakness]. So in short the particle, *for*, obtains the meaning of causing, not immediately, but mediately by the distinction between *grace* and *strength.*—ἐν ἀσθενείᾳ, *in weakness*) From the fact of its being the language of the Lord, Paul often repeats this word; ch. xi. xii. xiii.—τελειοῦται, *is perfected*) It [ἡ δύναμις] performs, it perfects all that belongs to it;

---

[1] *This* decision *of the Gnomon, however, does not obscurely differ from* the margin of both Ed. *and* from the Germ. Ver. *Therefore* it is not quite right to blame Bengel *on this account that he wished* μου *to be omitted after* δύναμις (as Ernesti *has it, Bibl. th.* T. iv. p. 705); *nay, indeed, in this very passage, he would have had occasion to free Bengel from the blame* of critical pertinacity. *Any one may easily suspect from* Bibl. th. l. c. *that Bengel wished to strike out the particle* μᾶλλον *after* ἥδιστα, *but they who use their eyes will find the contrary*.—E. B.

The σου is omitted in AD later corrected, G (and acc. to Lachm. but not Tischend. B) *fg* Vulg Iren. Cypr. But A and Orig. 3,200*d* add μου, and so Rec. Text.—ED.

therefore we ought not under the pretext of false self-sufficiency to cast away the power [strength] of Christ.—μᾶλλον καυχήσομαι, *I will rather glory*) in my infirmities, than in revelations, for if I glory in these, I shall prevent the exercise of the power of Christ. He adds the pronoun to the former, not to the latter.— ἐπισκηνώσῃ ἐπ᾽ ἐμὲ, *may cover me over*) as a tent.—σκῆνος, *a tent*, the body ["our earthly house of this tabernacle," ch. v. 1].—τὸ ἐπισκηνοῦν, *covering over*, something external; he does not say, that it may *dwell in me*; for he would thus [had he said that] diminish the sense of his infirmities.—ἡ δύναμις τοῦ Χριστοῦ, *the power of Christ*) that is Christ with His *power*. We ought *most gladly* to receive whatever promotes this object.

10. Εὐδοκῶ, *I am well contented* [Engl. V. too strongly, *I take pleasure*]) He does not say here, *I rejoice*, which would denote more than he meant.—ἐν ἀσθενείαις, *in infirmities*) This is the genus; hence we have immediately after, *I am weak*; two pairs of species follow.—ἐν ὕβρεσιν, ἐν ἀνάγκαις, *in reproaches, in necessities*) which also the messenger of Satan occasions.—ἐν διωγμοῖς, ἐν στενοχωρίαις, *in persecutions, in distresses*) which were caused by men.—ὑπὲρ, *for the sake of*) construed with εὐδοκῶ, *I am well contented*.—τότε) *then*, in particular [then and then only].— δυνατός, *strong*) *in the power* of Christ.

11. Γέγονα, *I am become*) He sounds a retreat.—ὤφειλον, *I ought*) An interchange of persons, *i.e.*, *you ought to have commended me* [instead of my having to commend myself].—ὑφ᾽ ὑμῶν) *by you*, among you.—οὐδέν εἰμι, though *I am nothing*) of myself.

12. Μὲν, *indeed* [*truly*]) This particle is as it were a crumb that feeds modesty.—σημεῖα, *signs*) The proofs of the facts are at hand.—τοῦ ἀποστόλου, *of the apostle*) The article has this force; [the signs] *of one who is an apostle.*—σημείοις) So *Al. Lat.* (in Cod. Reutl.) *Hilarius*. A reading standing midway between the extremes:[1] whence most copies have ἐν σημείοις; καὶ σημείοις is the reading of *Chrys. Boern. Lat.* in the MSS.: σημείοις τε is the reading of *Lin.* also *Syr.*[2] On σημείοις and τέρασι, see Matt.

[1] 'Media,' so as to form a kind of common starting point from which the various other erroneous readings took their rise.—ED.

[2] Σημείοις is read by AD corrected later ƒ Vulg. Breads σημείοις τε. Gg Syr. read καὶ σημείοις. Rec. Text reads ἐν σημείοις.—EN

xxiv. 24. Δυνάμεις are most palpable works of divine *omnipotence*.

13. Τί, *what*) This word refers both to the antecedents and the consequents.—λοιπὰς, *other churches*) planted either by me or by the other apostles.—εἰ μὴ—ταύτην, *unless—this*) a striking Asteismus [instance of refined pleasantry].—αὐτὸς, *I myself*) The antithesis follows, *nor by others*, ver. 16, 17. I did not burden you *myself*, nor make a gain of you *by those others* whom I sent, Titus, etc.—ἀδικίαν, *wrong*) The apostle might *rightly* [as opposed to ἀδικίαν] have accepted his maintenance from the Corinthians, and when he did *not* avail himself of this *right*, he imputes it to himself, as a *wrong*; and he gives it this name, not in the way of irony, with which the language of the apostle is inconsistent, but in the way of amphibology, for he uses ἀδικίαν in this passage, in a very unusual sense, which may be expressed in Latin by *non-jus*, and it has *a* in the privative sense, as ἄνομος, ἀνόμως, are sometimes used [*without law; not contrary to law*], Rom. ii. 12; 1 Cor. ix. 21: so ἀνυπότακτον [*not subjected*, instead of *insubordinate*], Heb. ii. 8: and yet it admits at the same time the idea of *injustice, deprecating* thereby all suspicion of want of love to the Corinthians [in his not accepting maintenance from them]; *forgive me*, comp. xi. 11.

14. Τὰ ὑμῶν, *yours*) Phil. iv. 17.—ὑμᾶς, *you*) that I may gain you. Matt. xviii. 15. He heaps up spiritual treasures for the *souls* of the Corinthians, ver. 15 [ὑπὲρ τῶν ψυχῶν ὑμῶν].

15. Ἐγὼ δὲ, *but I*) The δὲ makes an Epitasis [emphatic addition to the enunciation already made].—δαπανήσω) *I will spend* what belongs to me.—ἐκδαπανηθήσομαι, I myself *will be spent*)—ἧττον, *less*) Love rather descends, than ascends. [*It is unworthy to repay the most devoted love with a scanty measure of love.*—V. g.]

16. Ἀλλ' ὑπάρχων, *but inasmuch as I was*) an objection which the Corinthians [*moved by suspicion*, V. g.] might frame.[1] The answer is in the following verse.—ἔλαβον, *I caught*) that you might not escape the net, that was set with a view to my gain.

17. Μή τινα ὧν—δι' αὐτοῦ) for μὴ διά τινος τούτων, οὓς ἀπέσταλκα.

[1] *i.e.*, You may object and say that though I did not burden you, I yet, as being crafty, caught you by guile.—ED.

[*The good faith of his associates wonderfully assisted Paul.*
—V. g.]

18. Παρεκάλεσα, *I exhorted*) to go to you.—τὸν ἀδελφὸν, *the brother*) he seems to have been a Corinthian.—πνεύματι, *in spirit*) inwardly.—ἴχνεσι, *steps*) outwardly.

19. Πάλιν δοκεῖτε) Some read πάλαι δοκεῖτε :[1] a reading indeed, which would imply a more determined aversion of mind from Paul on the part of the Corinthians; comp. ch. iii. 1 ; for πάλαι, with a verb in the present tense, denotes long-continued perseverance. Plato in Gorgias, ἀλλ' ἔγωγε καὶ πάλαι λέγω, *but as I said long before, so I still say*. The more approved reading is πάλιν δοκεῖτε; comp. again ch. iii. 1.—ὑμῖν, *to you*) as if it were necessary for our own sake in this way to retain your favour.—ὑπὲρ τῆς ὑμῶν οἰκοδομῆς, *for your edification*) that you may rather see, than experience with sorrow, how much I am an apostle.

20. Οὐχ οἵους, *you not such as I would*) This is treated of to the end of the chapter. Then, the clause, *such as ye would not*, is treated of from ch. xiii. 1 and onwards. Such as is the hearer, so is the pastor to him.—ἔρεις, ζῆλοι, θυμοί, ἐριθεῖαι) Gal. v. 20.

21. Μὴ πάλιν, *lest again*) There is here an Anaphora,[2] *lest haply, lest haply, lest* [μή πως—μή πως—μή]. And indeed in this verse he speaks with greater severity.—ταπεινώσῃ, *will humble*) A Metonymy [Substitution] of the consequent [for the antecedent].—ὁ Θεός μου, *my God*) He by this expression gives the reason, why he considers acts committed against God, as appertaining to himself.—τῶν προημαρτηκότων) *who have sinned before my last coming*.—ἀκαθαρσίᾳ) *the uncleanness*; for example, of married persons : 1 Thess. iv. 7.—πορνείᾳ, *fornication*) among the unmarried, ἀσελγείᾳ, *lasciviousness*) sins contrary to nature.

---

[1] ABGƒ Vulg. read πάλαι. Only D (Λ) *g* of the oldest authorities support the πάλιν of the Rec. Text.—ED.

[2] See App. The frequent repetition of the same word in beginnings.

CHAPTER XIII.

1. Τρίτον) The decisive number, *the third time.* So the LXX. τρίτον τοῦτο, Num. xxii. 28.—ἔρχομαι, *I am coming*) I am now in readiness to come.—μαρτύρων, *of witnesses*) Therefore in this matter the apostle thought of depending not on an immediate revelation, but on the testimony of men; and he does not command the culprits to be cast out of the Church before his arrival.

2. Προείρηκα καὶ προλέγω, *I told you before and I tell you beforehand*) Refer to the former the words, *as if I were present the second time;* to the latter, the words, *being now absent.* He seriously forewarns them. There is in the text, which excludes the word γράφω as an inferior reading,[1] an uninterrupted chiasmus throughout the three members of the sentence, in the following order:

I told before,

as if I were present the second time
(viz. no doubt when he had come to
the neighbourhood towards Corinth,
and had already determined to go
thither himself also, although he
afterwards forbore),

to those who have heretofore sinned,
namely before this second visit.

and

and

and

and I tell beforehand,

being absent now

to all others, who
afterwards sinned,
after my second
coming, and yet
before my third.

—οὐ φείσομαι, *I will not spare*) He had formerly spared, i. 23.

---

[1] ABD (Λ) corrected later, G*fg* Vulg. reject γράφω. Rec. Text supports it without any of the oldest authorities for it.—ED.

3. Δοκιμὴν ζητεῖτε, *ye seek a proof*) A metonymy for, you provoke me; you tempt me; you desire to find out what I am; see ver. 5 [ἑαυτοὺς δοκιμάζετε, *prove* your own selves].—δοκιμή has its conjugates in ver. 5, 6 · [ἀδόκιμοι].—τοῦ Χριστοῦ) *i.e.*, *whether Christ is speaking in me.* The Corinthians had doubts; he presently proves that they ought not to doubt.—εἰς ὑμᾶς, ἐν ὑμῖν, *to you-ward, in you*) The particles differ; see ch. x. i.— οὐκ ἀσθενεῖ, *is not weak*) by me and this very epistle.[1]—δυνατεῖ) The ardour of his mind produced this new word by a paraphrase in respect to ἀσθενεῖ.

4. Εἰ, *if* [though]) a concessive particle.—ἐσταυρώθη, *was crucified*) *The cross*, the utmost weakness; it includes death, for *life*, is put in antithesis to it.—ἐξ ἀσθενείας, *owing to* [through] *weakness*) It is the part of weakness to be crucified. This is the force of the particle.—ἀσθενοῦμεν ἐν αὐτῷ, *we are weak in Him*) Presently after, the particle is varied, σύν, *with* Him, being employed instead of the ἐν here; *we are weak*, we do not exercise δύναμιν, *power*, and therefore we ourselves are less sensible of it, inasmuch as the sense of tribulation prevails.

5. Ἑαυτοὺς, *your own selves*) not Paul. If you examine yourselves, you will perceive what we are. Where there are true teachers and true learners, we may judge from the feeling of the one party concerning the other, what is the character of that other.—ἐν τῇ πίστει, *in the faith*) and therefore in Christ.— δοκιμάζετε, *prove*) The milder admonition [δοκιμάζετε, *prove*] is subjoined to the severer word [πειράζετε, lit. *tempt, make trial of*] *test* [Engl. Vers., *examine* yourselves]: *if you are in the faith, prove yourselves to be so*;[2] εἰ, *if*, is used as presently after in εἰ μήτι.—ἤ) *an*, the second part of a disjunctive interrogation; *i.e.*, you can truly prove yourselves: for Jesus Christ is in you, and you know Him to be in you. [*In fact, any one may test himself, whether he be in the faith or not; no man can prove himself and search out his own true character unless he be a believer.* —V. g.]—ἐπιγινώσκετε, *do you perceive?*) an emphatic compound.—ὅτι, *how that*) the grounds upon which.—Ἰησοῦς, *Jesus*)

[1] [Christ, who] is not weak towards you, as far as I and this very epistle can effect.—ED.
[2] Engl. V. and Tischend. and Lachm. connect εἰ ἐστὲ ἐν τῇ πίστει with πειράσ?ετε, " Examine yourselves whether ye be in the faith."—ED.

not only a sense [perception] of Christ, but Jesus Christ Himself, [*as is evident from the addition of the proper name,* Jesus ; comp. 2 Tim. iv. 22.—V. g.]—εἰ μήτι, *unless somewhat*) So εἰ μὴ, ch. iii. 1 ; τί, *somewhat*, softens the language.—ἀδόκιμοι, *reprobate*) in a passive and active sense ; for the conjugate δοκιμάζετε is considered to be in a reciprocal sense.

6. Γνώσεσθε, *you shall know*) by the *proving* of yourselves, without any experimental proof of my power, ver. 10.

7. Εὔχομαι) The same verb occurs with the accusative and infinitive, Acts xxvi. 29.—μὴ ποιῆσαι ὑμᾶς κακὸν μηδὲν, *that ye do no evil*) The Vulgate has thus correctly translated it. For there follows, *that you may do good.* Grotius interprets it, *that I may not be forced to inflict evil,* punishment, *on any one.* But in this way the antithesis just noticed is lost. ποιεῖν has the accusative of the person, but Paul says, ποιεῖν πρός τινα, εἰς τινα.—οὐχ ἵνα, *not that*) δόκιμοι, *approved*) by restraining you when you do evil.—ὡς ἀδόκιμοι, *as reprobate*) no cause being given to us for exercising authority : ὡς, *as if*, softens the expression.

8. Δυνάμεθα, *we are able*) comp. *the power* which he claims, ver. 10.—ἀληθείας, *truth*) Truth here denotes the exact authority to be exercised over the Corinthians.

9. Ἀσθενῶμεν, *we are weak*) in body and with our authority unemployed.—δυνατοί, *strong*) in faith.—καὶ εὐχόμεθα, *we also wish*) Weakness is welcome, not wished for ; κατάρτισις, is even (καὶ) wished for.—κατάρτισιν) *perfect union, perfection,* ver. 11 ; 1 Cor. i. 10 ["perfectly joined together"] : that there may be no need to use *severity* in *cutting off*[1] any one from the body.

10. Μοι, *to me*) Paul, in treating of his peculiar apostolic power, returns from the plural to the singular.

11. Λοιπὸν, *finally*) The conclusion. Paul had written somewhat severely in discussing this matter ; now more gently, without however dismissing the subject itself, comp. ch. xii. 20.—χαίρετε) *rejoice.* He returns to that with which he first set out, i. 24 ; but the word χαίρετε here is appropriately used, as by it men are accustomed to bid *farewell.*—παρακαλεῖσθε, *be of good comfort,* ch. i. 6.

---

[1] ἀποτόμως ver. 10, Th. ἀποτέμνειν, *to cut off.*—ED.

13. ʽH) This prayer corresponds in both epistles. The first epistle, indeed, has also its own conclusion and prayer; but yet because the first epistle is taken up and renewed in many important particulars by the second, this prayer is also suitable to it, and in the very universality of the prayer, the apostle seems also to have had reference to the first epistle.— χάρις, *grace*) This is mentioned in the first place, for by the grace of Christ we come to the love of the Father. [*An admirable testimony to the Holy Trinity.*—V. g.]—ἡ ἀγάπη τοῦ Θεοῦ, *the love of God*) ver. 11.—ἡ κοινωνία, *the communion*) which has also come to you Gentiles, and which produces harmony.

ADDENDUM TO NOTES.

Rom. x. 11, "Duplex voluntas divina," viz. "voluntas beneplaciti et voluntas signi." A scholastic distinction introduced by Thomas Aquinas, who, in the *Summa Theologiæ*, par. i. qu. 19, art. 11, writes, "Ideo in Deo distinguitur voluntas propriè et metaphoricè dicta. Voluntas enim propriè dicta (*used in the plain and literal sense*) vocatur *voluntas beneplaciti.* Voluntas autem metaphoricè dicta (*used in the figurative sense*) est *voluntas signi*, eò quod ipsum signum voluntatis voluntas dicitur ;" *i.e.* God uses language which would seem among men to indicate will : but this is only a *metaphorical* or *ostensible* will, "voluntas signi," not His will in the same strict sense in which His secret purpose, "voluntas beneplaciti," is His will.—ED.

END OF VOL III.

www.ingramcontent.com/pod-product-compliance
Lightning Source LLC
Chambersburg PA
CBHW060911300426
44112CB00011B/1422